Windows® XP Professional Network Administration

Robert Elsenpeter with Toby J. Velte

McGraw-Hill/Osborne

New York Chicago San Francisco
Lisbon London Madrid Mexico City Milan
New Delhi San Juan Seoul Singapore Sydney Toronto

McGraw-Hill/Osborne
2600 Tenth Street
Berkeley, California 94710
U.S.A.

To arrange bulk purchase discounts for sales promotions, premiums, or fund-raisers, please contact **McGraw-Hill**/Osborne at the above address. For information on translations or book distributors outside the U.S.A., please see the International Contact Information page immediately following the index of this book.

Windows® XP Professional Network Administration

Copyright © 2002 by The McGraw-Hill Companies. All rights reserved. Printed in the United States of America. Except as permitted under the Copyright Act of 1976, no part of this publication may be reproduced or distributed in any form or by any means, or stored in a database or retrieval system, without the prior written permission of publisher, with the exception that the program listings may be entered, stored, and executed in a computer system, but they may not be reproduced for publication.

1234567890 FGR FGR 0198765432

ISBN 0-07-222504-1

Publisher
  Brandon A. Nordin
Vice President & Associate Publisher
  Scott Rogers
Acquisitions Editor
  Francis Kelly
Project Editors
  Madhu Prasher, Carolyn Welch
Acquisitions Coordinators
  Emma Acker, Martin Przybyla
Technical Editor
  James Kelly
Copy Editor
  Ami Knox

Proofreader
  Leslie Tilley
Indexer
  Valerie Robbins
Computer Designers
  Michelle Galicia, Elizabeth Jang
Illustrators
  Michael Mueller, Lyssa Wald
Series Design
  Lyssa Wald, Peter F. Hancik
Cover Series Design
  Jeff Weeks

This book was composed with Corel VENTURA™ Publisher.

Information has been obtained by **McGraw-Hill**/Osborne from sources believed to be reliable. However, because of the possibility of human or mechanical error by our sources, **McGraw-Hill**/Osborne, or others, **McGraw-Hill**/Osborne does not guarantee the accuracy, adequacy, or completeness of any information and is not responsible for any errors or omissions or the results obtained from the use of such information.

For Jeni, Rick, and Maddy

ABOUT THE AUTHORS

Robert C. Elsenpeter is an author, web content writer, and award-winning journalist. He is coauthor of *eBusiness: A Beginner's Guide* and *Optical Networking: A Beginner's Guide*.

Toby J. Velte, Ph.D., MCSE+I, CCNA, CCDA, has started four high-tech companies and is the coauthor of the best-selling *Cisco®: A Beginner's Guide*.

ABOUT THE TECHNICAL REVIEWER

James Kelly is co-owner of Those Computer People, Inc. He graduated with an English degree from The University of West Florida and an Industrial Engineering degree from Florida State University. He has over 9 years experience in the IT field and currently calls Houston, TX, home.

CONTENTS

Acknowledgments xiii
Introduction. xv

Part I   Windows XP Networking

❖ 1   Networking Fundamentals 3
Bits and Bytes 4
    Data—From the Computer's Perspective 4
    Network Devices 8
OSI Reference Model 12
    The Seven-Layer Stack 13
    OSI Implementation by Layer 15
Network Technologies 16
    Ethernet 18
    Token Ring 21
    ATM 22
    Wireless 23
WAN Technologies 24
    Dial-in Technologies 26
    WAN Trunk Technologies 30

❖ 2   Introduction to Windows XP Professional Networking 33
What's New in Windows XP Professional 34
    Networking Features 34
    Other Features 40

Windows XP Professional Networking Features 42
    File Systems 43
    Internet Connection Sharing 44
    Security 46
Upgrading from Windows NT/9X/2000 49
    System Requirements 49
    Upgrading from Another Flavor of Windows 55
    Migration Preparation 56
    Servers 61
    Making the Move 66
    Activation 68

❖ 3 TCP/IP and Other Protocols 71

TCP/IP 72
    Understanding TCP/IP 73
    IP Addressing 77
    IP Addresses, Subnet Masks, and Default Gateways 83
TCP/IP Addressing in Windows XP Professional 92
    Upgrading 92
    Assigning an IP Address 93
    Configuring a TCP/IP Connection 94
    Managing TCP/IP Addresses 96
Setting Up Addresses in Windows XP Professional 97
    TCP/IP Autoaddressing (APIPA and DHCP) 97
    Static IP Addressing 100
    Alternate IP Configuration 103
    Name Resolution 104
    Other Protocols 110

Part II Internetworking

❖ 4 Creating Network Connections 115

Hardware 116
    Hardware Connection Overview 116
    Analog Modems 120
    ISDN Hardware 125
    DSL Hardware 127
    Cable Hardware 129
    Solving Hardware Problems 130
Creating Internet Connections 134
    Meet the New Connection Wizard 134
    Using the New Connection Wizard 137

Contents **vii**

Managing Connections	139
Configuring Dialing Locations	139
Area Code Rules	141
Using Calling Cards	144

❖ 5 Workgroup Connections — 149

Connecting Clients to the Workgroup	150
Network Setup Wizard	150
Manual Configuration	154
Using Internet Connection Sharing	159
ICS Features	160
Setting Up ICS	161
ICS VPN Model	165
ICS Troubleshooting	166
ICF on a Workgroup	167
ICF Overview	167
Using ICF	167
ICF Incompatibilities	168
Logging	169
Configuring ICF	169
Wireless Connections	170
WPAN	170
WLAN	171
Setting Up Wireless Connections	176
Configuration	177

❖ 6 Domain Connectivity — 183

Windows Domains 101	184
What Is a Domain?	184
How Domains Work	185
How Windows XP Fits into the Domain Model	186
Domain Connectivity	187
Joining a Domain	187
Troubleshooting Domain Connection Problems	190
Accessing Domain Resources	194
Security	194
Network Neighborhood/My Network Places	194
Universal Naming Convention	195
Active Directory	198
IntelliMirror	199
Organizational Units	200
Global Catalog	202
Groups	202
Administrative Tools	203

❖ 7 Internet Information Services 207
What Is IIS? 208
    IIS 5.1 Features 208
    FrontPage 214
    Intranet Content Management 217
Installing IIS 217
    Placement Considerations 217
    Hardware and Networking Components 218
    Software Components 219
    Installation Steps 219
Configuring IIS 221
    IIS Management 221
    HTTP IIS Manager 221
    Configuring Web Services 222
    Configuring an FTP Server 226
Using IIS 227
    Setting Default Pages 227
    Managing Security 228
    Managing Content 232

❖ 8 Connectivity Problem-Solving Tools and Techniques 237
Troubleshooting Windows XP 238
    Startup Modes 238
    Boot Floppy Disk 241
    Installation Repair 241
    Hung Programs 242
    Stopping Startup Programs 245
    MMC 246
    Event Viewer 247
    Status Menu Command 249
    Network Support Help 251
    Network Diagnostics 252
    Repairing a Connection 253
    System Restore 255
    Dr. Watson 258
Problem Solving 259
    LAN Problems 260
    Remote Access Problems 264
Helpful Network Tools and Scenarios 265
    ping 265
    arp 267
    Ipconfig 267
    tracert 268
    nbtstat 270
    pathping 271

Part III Network Resources

❖ 9 Network Security 277
Windows XP Professional Security Features 278
    What's New in Windows XP Professional 278
    Local Security Policy 279
    ICF Security Logging 281
    Security Templates 284
    Auditing Security 287
    Security Configuration and Analysis Snap-In 291
Securing Servers 294
    IPSec 294
    Logon 299
    Protocols 302
    Authentication 304
    Access Control Lists 311
    Group Policy 313

❖ 10 NTFS Security Options 317
NTFS Features 318
    4.0 vs. 5.0 318
    Compression 319
    Disk Quotas 323
    EFS 327
    NTFS Optimization 330
    Sparse Files 331
NTFS Permissions 332
    Individual User Permissions 332
    Folder and Volume Permissions 334
Converting/Formatting Drives with NTFS 337
    Issues 338
    Converting 340

❖ 11 Network Shares 343
Understanding Shares 344
    Folder and Drive Sharing 344
    Drive Mapping 347
    Printer Sharing 349
    Application Sharing 352
Controlling Shared Access 356
    Security 356
    Using the Computer Management Snap-In 361

❖ 12 Offline Files and Folders 367

Using Offline Files and Folders 368
    Enabling 369
    Making Files and Folders Available Offline 369
    Downloading Files for Offline Use 372
    Deleting Offline Files 374
    Security 376
    Printing in Offline Mode 380
Synchronization 382
    Synchronizing Offline Files and Folders 382
    Laptop Synchronization Options 386
Windows Briefcase 388
    Using the Briefcase 389
    Moving Files to the Briefcase 390
    Copying the Briefcase to a Laptop 391
    Using Briefcase Files 391
    Briefcase Synchronization 392
Troubleshooting Offline Files 394
    Inability to Make a Folder an Offline Folder 394
    Files Available Online Are Not Available Offline 395
    Fast User Switching Enabled 395
    Resolve File Conflicts Message Appears 396
    Inability to Synchronize Offline Files 396

Part IV Advanced Networking

❖ 13 Remote Desktop and Remote Assistance 401

Understanding Remote Desktop 402
    Features 403
    Remote Desktop Protocol 404
    Security Issues 404
Using Remote Desktop 407
    Configuring a Server for Remote Desktop 407
    Configuring a Client for Remote Desktop 410
    Establishing Remote Desktop Connections 412
    Remote Desktop Function 415
    Other Remote Desktop Settings 417
Understanding Remote Assistance 417
    Features 419
    Security Issues 420
Using Remote Assistance 420
    Configuring Remote Assistance 420
    Sending Invitations 420
    Accepting an Invitation 426

Contents   xi

❖ 14   Remote Access and Virtual Private Networks   429
     Remote Access   430
         Understanding Remote Access   430
         Configuring a Computer to Accept Remote Access Calls . .   431
         Laptop ("Road Warrior") Connections   435
     VPN Connections   440
         Understanding Virtual Private Networks   441
         Creating a VPN Connection   444
         Receiving a VPN Connection   446
         Troubleshooting VPN Connections   448

❖ 15   Quality of Service   453
     What Is QoS?   454
         Raw Bandwidth Is Not Enough   454
         QoS Concepts   456
         RSVP   458
         DiffServ   460
     QoS in Windows XP   461
         Windows XP Usability   461
         Setup Steps   462
         Management   464
         Monitoring QoS   469

❖ 16   Interconnectivity with Other Systems   473
     NetWare Connections   474
         Client Service for NetWare   474
         Gateway Service for NetWare   477
         Accessing NetWare Resources   480
         Printing   482
     Linux/UNIX Connections   483
         Services for UNIX 3.0   484
         SAMBA   488
         NFS Servers   490

❖ 17   Monitoring XP Network Performance   493
     Network Performance Overview   494
         Concepts   494
         Network Construction   496
         Network Segmentation   497
     System Monitor   501
         Basics   501
         Views   502
         What to Monitor   512

Capacity Planning 515
    Network Simulation 515
    Network Simulation Tools 519
Third-Party Tools 521
    Lucent VitalSuite 521
    Concord eHealth 522
    HP OpenView 522
    Compuware NetworkVantage 523

❖ **A Windows .NET Administration Tools** **525**

Active Directory Domains and Trusts 527
Active Directory Sites and Services 528
Active Directory Users and Computers 529
Certification Authority 530
Cluster Administrator 531
Component Services 532
Computer Management 533
Connection Manager Administration Kit 534
Data Sources (ODBC) 534
DHCP 536
Distributed File System 537
DNS 538
Event Viewer 539
Local Security Policy 540
.NET Framework Configuration 540
.NET Wizards 542
Network Load Balancing Manager 542
Performance 544
Remote Desktops 544
Remote Storage 545
Routing and Remote Access 546
Server Extensions Administrator 547
Services 548
Telephony 549
Terminal Services Manager and Terminal Server Licensing 550
WINS 552

❖ **Index** **553**

ACKNOWLEDGMENTS

The folks at Osborne/McGraw-Hill were fantastic to work with. Acquisitions editor Francis Kelly got the ball rolling on this project. Acquisitions coordinators Emma Acker and Martin Przybyla, along with project editors Madhu Prasher and Carolyn Welch, kept the information flowing in and out of the publishing house. Jim Kelly did a great job ensuring the technical accuracy of this project, while Ami Knox made sure our i's were aptly dotted and t's were suitably crossed.

INTRODUCTION

Keeping up with the different versions and flavors of Microsoft Windows can be as confusing as trying to keep track of the Baldwin brothers. It seems as though every year Microsoft comes out with a new version of its flagship product. The latest version of Windows—Windows XP—comes in versions for both homes and businesses. Windows XP Home is geared for the consumer and includes a number of excellent improvements over its predecessors, Windows Me and Windows 9X. Windows XP Professional is aimed at the business market and is meant as the operating system for client computers. Our focus here is on Windows XP Professional, which includes a number of tools and features significant for business, but not present in the home version.

Windows XP Professional is built on Windows NT and 2000 architectures, which, among other improvements, ensures a high level of stability. This book will show you how you can use Windows XP Professional for your organization's workstations and how you can squeeze every ounce of functionality possible out of it.

WINDOWS XP AND THE NETWORK

Windows XP Professional includes a number of useful tools for your organization, no matter what its size. Smaller businesses will benefit from such features as Internet Connection Sharing (ICS) and Internet Connection Firewall(ICF). ICS allows computers to connect to the Internet through a single connection, like a dial-up modem or digital subscriber line (DSL). ICF is a firewall, included with Windows XP Professional, that provides basic firewall functions to keep your network safe and secure.

On the other end of the spectrum, Windows XP Professional can be deployed in large environments. Rather than the workgroup network configurations that a small business might employ, Windows XP Professional takes full advantage of Active Directory domains, which are the basic architecture of modern Windows 2000 networks. Active Directory domains allow even the largest organizations to share its resources with all its members.

Networks are moving targets. A number of years ago, networks were simply used to connect computers in the organization's local environment. We can all remember when the Internet started to become more and more prevalent, and organizations started including Internet access as part of their networks. Now, however, networks have evolved even further. The Internet has become an integral part of many organizations. For instance, virtual private networks (VPNs) allow your organization to connect two offices via the Internet. A VPN provides a secure tunnel through the Internet. In the past, you'd have to pay extra for a dedicated wide area connection between your two offices. Now, however, the public Internet provides a way for you to connect those offices without having to pay additional costs.

Peeking into the near future, Microsoft is continuing its efforts to develop its .NET initiative, which takes business/Internet integration to new levels. .NET uses the Internet to share information among an organization's various resources. Windows XP Professional is a solid operating system that will make fine use of this new initiative.

Earlier, we noted Microsoft's Active Directory environments. Though Windows XP Professional was designed to work with Windows 2000 and .NET Servers, it is also capable of working with Windows NT environments. This is an important consideration if you are considering upgrading your clients (perhaps buying new workstations, or updating the operating system) but aren't keen on renovating your servers.

WHO SHOULD READ THIS BOOK

Windows XP Professional Network Administration was written for the network architect, administrator, or anyone with an "intermediate" knowledge of Microsoft Windows and networking. If you are in the position to decide how Windows should be deployed in your organization, then this book is for you. Furthermore, there are a number of chapters that will explain how to use the various features of Windows XP Professional, from ICS to the varied wizards that can help make Windows XP Professional computing much easier.

What this book does not cover in any great depth is networking. It is explained as needed and the first chapter is meant as a quick-and-dirty primer on networking. However, this chapter is only meant for reference and as a way to get a general understanding of the world of Windows networking.

WHAT THIS BOOK COVERS

Windows XP Professional Network Administration is structured around four parts, each one explaining a facet of Windows XP Professional network development and use. The first section is "Windows XP Networking." In this part, networking components of Windows XP Professional are explored. Basic network configuration is covered as well as implementing Windows XP Professional workstations.

- **Chapter 1:** *Networking Fundamentals*   This chapter provides a back-of-the-envelope sketch of networking. It contains a very simple introduction to some of the networking terms and concepts used later in the book.

- **Chapter 2:** *Introduction to Windows XP Professional Networking*   An overview of Windows XP Professional, its features, its functions, and how it can be used in a network environment are presented here.

- **Chapter 3:** *TCP/IP and Other Protocols*   The TCP/IP protocol suite is the standard for Internet and private networking in today's networks. This chapter focuses on TCP/IP configuration, but also explores additional protocols supported by Windows XP Professional.

The second section is called "Internetworking" and covers not only issues of local area network (LAN) connectivity, but also networking that takes place across the Internet.

- **Chapter 4:** *Creating Network Connections*   In this chapter, we explore the ins and outs of Internet connections with Windows XP Professional. This chapter covers configuring modem and broadband hardware, how to create connections, and then how to manage and troubleshoot connections to the Internet.

- **Chapter 5:** *Workgroup Connections*   Windows XP Professional is designed to function in both large and small networks. In this chapter, workgroup configuration and connectivity issues are explored.

- **Chapter 6:** *Domain Connectivity*   The previous chapter addressed small networks called workgroups. Windows XP Professional has all the tools and functionality to provide high-level networking features in a Windows 2000/.NET domain. In this chapter, domain connectivity is explored.

- **Chapter 7:** *Internet Information Services*   Windows XP Professional provides Internet Information Services (IIS), the web-hosting software used on Microsoft servers. Using Windows XP Professional, you can perform limited web hosting tasks, which are explored in this chapter.

- **Chapter 8:** *Connectivity Problem-Solving Tools and Techniques*   Network connectivity can be a difficult troubleshooting issue and a frequent one as well. In this chapter, we explore a number of problem solving techniques, scenarios, and troubleshooting tools that can help resolve network connection problems.

The primary reason for networking computers together is to access resources. In the third part, called "Network Resources," we explore the features and configuration of shared network resources and the management of shared resources.

- **Chapter 9:** *Network Security*   A secure network is important to any organization. However, there are details germane to network security that are governed based on network design and implementation. This chapter describes how networks (whether native Windows XP or a mixed environment) can be built to ensure security.

- **Chapter 10:** *NTFS Security Options*   Windows XP Professional is designed to work with the NTFS file system, which provides advanced data management and security features. This chapter explores the features and usage of NTFS.

- **Chapter 11:** *Network Shares*   With Windows XP Professional, you can share just about anything you like so that users on the network can access the resource. This chapter explores shares and share configuration.

- **Chapter 12:** *Offline Files and Folders*   Windows XP Professional supports offline files and folders, which allows users to store files and folders on the local hard drive, and then synchronize those files and folders with the network's original version.

Windows XP Professional provides a number of advanced networking features and functions. In the final section, "Advanced Networking," we examine Remote Desktop, Remote Assistance, VPNs, network monitoring, and interconnectivity with other systems.

- **Chapter 13:** *Remote Desktop and Remote Assistance*   Windows XP Professional includes two new features, known as Remote Desktop and Remote Assistance. In this chapter, we explain the features of these remote networking tools and how to use them.

- **Chapter 14:** *Remote Access and Virtual Private Networks*   Windows XP Professional supports remote access and VPN connections. This chapter examines the remote access (essentially, the ability to dial into a Windows XP Professional computer) and VPN functionality of Windows XP Professional.

- **Chapter 15:** *Quality of Service*   As network applications and the users on them consume more and more bandwidth, it can be expensive to continually upgrade network hardware and infrastructure. Windows XP Professional includes a software solution to deliver Quality of Service (QoS). This chapter explains how to set up and manage XP QoS.

- **Chapter 16:** *Interconnectivity with Other Systems*   Windows XP Professional works best in a Windows network, but Windows XP can connect with other computer systems. In this chapter, interconnectivity with other systems is explored.

- **Chapter 17:** *Monitoring XP Network Performance*   Network performance is an important issue for any network. In this chapter, we explain how to examine your Windows XP Professional computers and network, exploring potential network performance problems and developing a plan to resolve them.
- **Appendix:** *Windows .NET Administration Tools*   While Windows XP Professional is used for client workstations, the servers in the Windows XP Professional network are likely to be Windows 2000 or .NET. Microsoft has a set of tools that allows your .NET Server to be managed from a Windows XP Professional client. This appendix talks about the various features of the Windows .NET Administration Tools.

HOW TO READ THIS BOOK

Books like this one can be a little challenging, organizationally speaking. Once we cover "the basics," you might have different needs and different interests that won't necessarily follow the chapters in any sort of linear fashion. As such, the book has been written so you can pick it up, flip to any chapter, and find the information you need. For example, if you want to know how Windows XP Professional can be used to manage NTFS security, flip ahead to Chapter 10. If you prefer, you can sit down and read the whole thing cover-to-cover.

In the beginning of this book, we give a brief overview of networking. Although the book is meant for an intermediate audience, it doesn't hurt to make sure everyone's on the same page. If you are up to speed on networking basics, feel free to skip Chapter 1—our feelings won't be hurt.

PART I

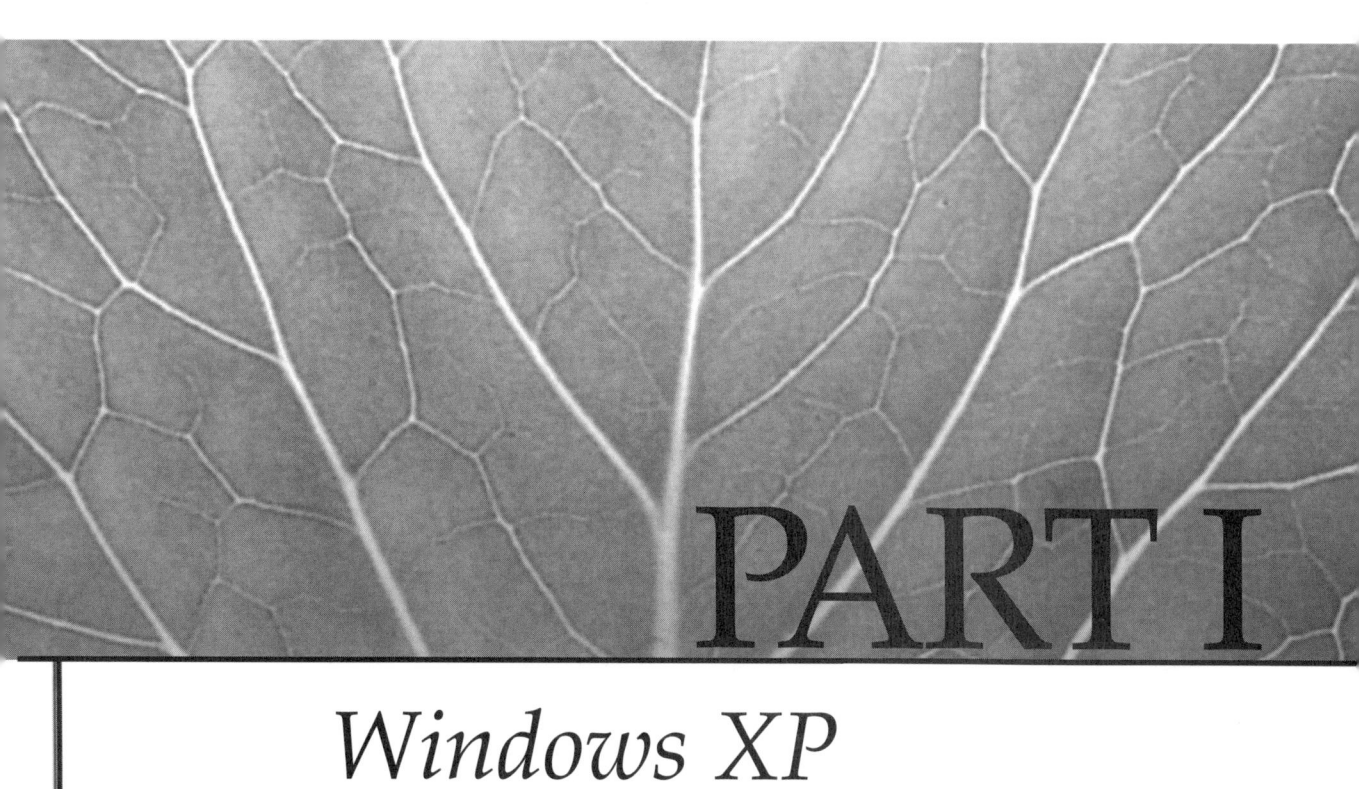

Windows XP Networking

CHAPTER 1

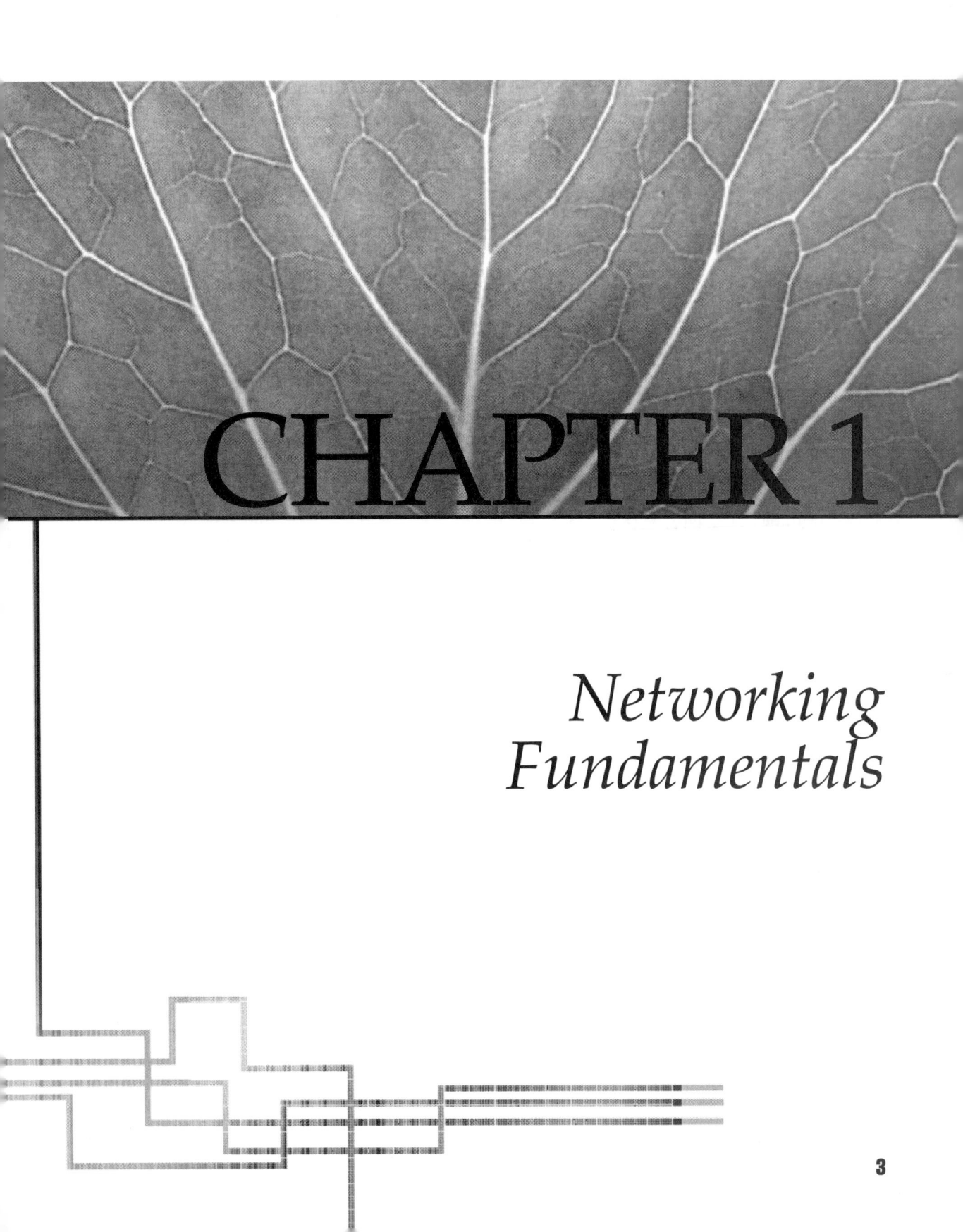

Networking Fundamentals

Before we leap into the details of Windows XP Professional, let's start with a quick overview of networking concepts and terminology. This ensures you have a firm understanding of some important basics before tackling more complex issues.

In this chapter, we give an overview of networking concepts, including a primer on how computers understand data and how that is germane to networking. In addition, we cover the seven-layer Open Systems Interconnect (OSI) reference model and the networking protocols you are likely to come in contact with when working with Windows XP Professional, in Ethernet, Gigabit Ethernet, and wireless environments. We'll round things out with a discussion of wide area network (WAN) technologies. First, however, let's talk about some computer fundamentals.

If you already have a good understanding of networking, feel free to skip this chapter. We'll pick up with Windows XP Professional specifics in Chapter 2.

BITS AND BYTES

Before exploring networks and networking, you need to know how computer technology actually works. This is important because how the computer processes information is directly applicable to network functioning. In this section, we'll give a back-of-the-envelope sketch about how computers share data.

Data—From the Computer's Perspective

For most computer users, what goes on in the server room or that corner of the office where the server and hub sit is a mystery. In fact, some are befuddled enough by how their computer works that they don't even want to know what the server does or what the "computer guys" do to it. In reality, however, the servers—like other networking devices—are just computers. The biggest difference between the users' PCs, the server, and a router is a matter of configuration.

Networking devices are essentially the same as PCs, except they tend not to have monitors or disk drives. This is because these devices have a sole mission—to move traffic. They don't care about storing or displaying information. Networking devices are similar to PCs in that they have CPUs, memory, and operating systems.

Bits Compose Binary Messages

For networked computers to share data, they must send electrical signals among themselves, via several hardware devices (we'll expand on such devices as routers, switches, and hubs later in this chapter). These signals course through a maze of transistors and microscopic wires within the computers. From there, they travel to other network devices through whatever cabling has been put in place.

Network Interface Cards

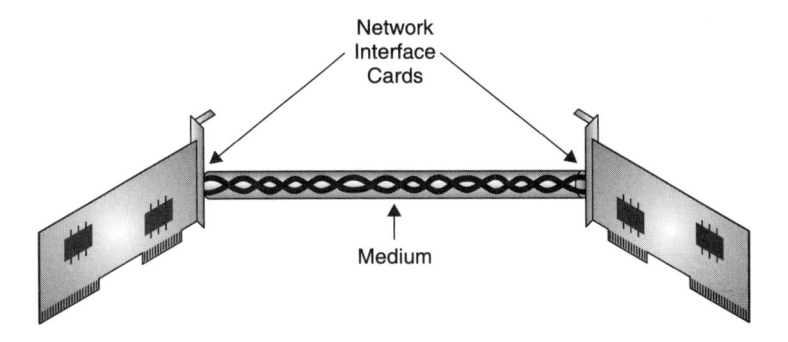

Medium

As signals pass from one device to another, they are first received at network interface cards (NICs). These cards keep track of the electrical pulse waveforms and decode those signals into data the computer can understand. A NIC interprets each wave pulse as one of two signals: on or off. This is known as a *binary* transmission—a system in which two states are recognized: when the signal is *on* the NIC translates the signal into the number 1. When the signal is *off*, the NIC translates the signal into the number 0. Once those binary signals enter the computer, they are understood in machine language as *bits*. When all the bits come together in a single computer file, they are known as a *binary file*.

NOTE In optical networking, flashes of light (again representing on or off) are used for binary transmission.

Fluctuations in the voltage of the electrical pulses (think of them as high-tech Morse code) are sensed as a binary transmission. As you might imagine, these fluctuations occur quite quickly, during very short periods of time. The period of time between pulses is known as a *cycle* or *hertz* (Hz). For example, the processor in a 100 megabits per second (Mbps) NIC can generate 100 million cycles per second. This means that the NIC can process 100 million pulses per second.

Taking a Byte Out of Computing

Earlier, we said that bits were the building blocks of computing. Although that's certainly true, it is a complicated matter for the computer to deal with data one bit at a time. Think of it this way: if you're building a backyard barbecue pit, you don't go to the local Home Depot and buy one brick, bring it home, cement it in place, and then go back to the store and repeat the process until it's time to roast up a pig. Rather, you buy as many bricks as you'll need and make one trip, and then build your barbecue pit all at once.

This is more or less how computers process bits. Rather than process 1 bit at a time, they clump 8 of them together into a *byte*. A byte is perceived as a single unit. For instance, a byte represents a single character on your keyboard. The "k" in "keyboard" is a single byte, or 8 bits. The entire word "keyboard" is 8 bytes, or 64 bits, long.

```
        Bit
         ↑
      01101001
      ⎵⎵⎵⎵⎵⎵⎵⎵
        Byte
```

Grouping bits into bytes is a logical way to make computing more efficient. This results in a system that is not only faster, but also immensely easier to program and debug. Specifying individual bit locations is a task left up to the computer.

Computer Words

Though applications (and by extension the human users and programmers of those applications) use bytes, computers must still process each individual bit. It would take too much time to perform a bit-to-byte translation inside a CPU. To facilitate this, computers have what's known as a *word size*. Bytes are to words what bits are to bytes. Words are the number of bytes a CPU is designed to handle in each cycle.

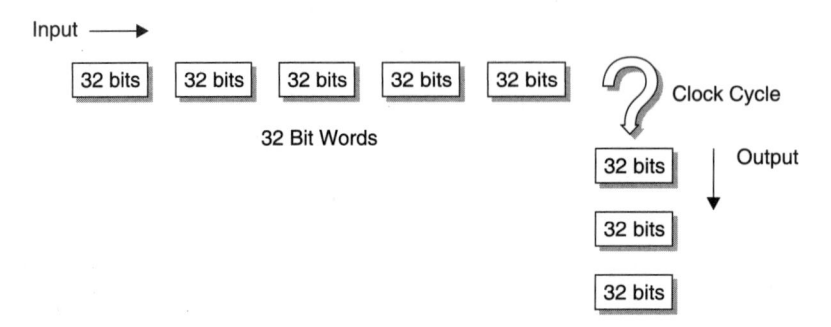

For instance, a computer containing a CPU such as the Intel Pentium III is a 32-bit machine. This means it processes 32 bits (or 4 bytes) per clock cycle. However, as technology tends to do, processor speeds have matured. As a result, 32-bit processors have been supplanted by 64-bit processors, such as Intel and Hewlett-Packard's joint venture, the Itanium processor. This means that the processor handles 8-byte words in each clock cycle.

Computing Architectures

A *computing architecture* is a blueprint of the components that make up a system. When published, computing architectures are rather detailed and can be thousands of pages in length. Despite their size, there are parts that remain abstract. This leaves the exact implementation of those specific portions of the architecture up to the designer.

Function
Functionality
Arrangement
Look and Feel
Abstract Interface
Dependencies
Extensions
Products
Implementation

The separation of architecture from a product specification is implemented through *abstract layering*. A so-called abstraction layer is a fixed interface between two system components. This layer oversees the relationship between each side's function and implementation.

The abstraction layer proves useful when something changes on one side, because it does not require the other side to change. These layers help guarantee compatibility in two environments:

- Between sundry components within the system
- Between the various products that implement the architecture

Abstraction sounds like a pain in the neck, but it solves a lot of problems. For instance, it enables different development teams to work on projects that will have a common outcome. An example of this is DVD drives. The published interface between the layers allows scores of DVD drive manufacturers to develop their own products that are compatible with DVD specifications.

There are a number of computing architectures, each with varying levels of openness. For instance, the Microsoft/Intel 80×86 architecture is probably the best known. Other architectures include Java, RAID (short for Redundant Array of Inexpensive Disks), and scores more. The most important computing architecture is the OSI reference model, which allows the Internet to exist and provides communication between different computing platforms.

NOTE We'll talk about the specifics of the OSI later in this chapter, in the section "OSI Reference Model."

Network Devices

At first blush, it might seem that two computers should just be able to plug into each other and share data with no problems. Unfortunately, the task tends to be more complicated than simply plugging in a cable or two.

Network devices are used for different reasons and in different locations within a network. In a small office, computers might be joined via a hub or a small switch connected to a server. As an organization grows, the switch might be replaced with several switches feeding off a number of servers. Once the Internet gets involved, routers need to be added to the mix. Let's take a closer look at these devices by examining what they do and where they are located in a network.

> **NOTE** If you're not familiar with hubs and switches, you'll have a chance to learn about them later in this chapter.

A couple of decades ago, the acronym LAN, which stands for local area network, was applied liberally to describe networks of most any size. Whether a couple of devices or 4,000 computers at a corporation, everyone connected to the same network. Then, because networks were getting so big, they started to be subdivided into smaller and smaller networks.

> **NOTE** It's because of LAN segmentation that we have the router—the foundation of the Internet. The router was invented by a man at Stanford (whose workstation was located on one LAN) who wanted to talk to his wife (whose workstation was located on another LAN). These two started a little company you might have heard of, called Cisco.

Routers

Without routers, there could be no Internet. In a nutshell, routers do exactly what their name says: they route data from one LAN to another router, and then another router, and so on, until data arrives at its destination. Routers also act as traffic cops, allowing only authorized machines to transmit data into the local network so that private information can remain secure. In addition to supporting these dial-in and leased connections, routers also handle errors, keep network usage statistics, and deal with security issues.

Because the Internet provides a data link between two or more computers, designers realized there needed to be a tool that would facilitate that link. For the most part, the Internet uses existing telecommunications lines. In order for Computer A in the United States to communicate with Computer B in Holland, two things must happen:

1. The ideal route along the telecommunications system must be plotted.
2. Packets, which are small data units sent across the Internet, must be transmitted along that path.

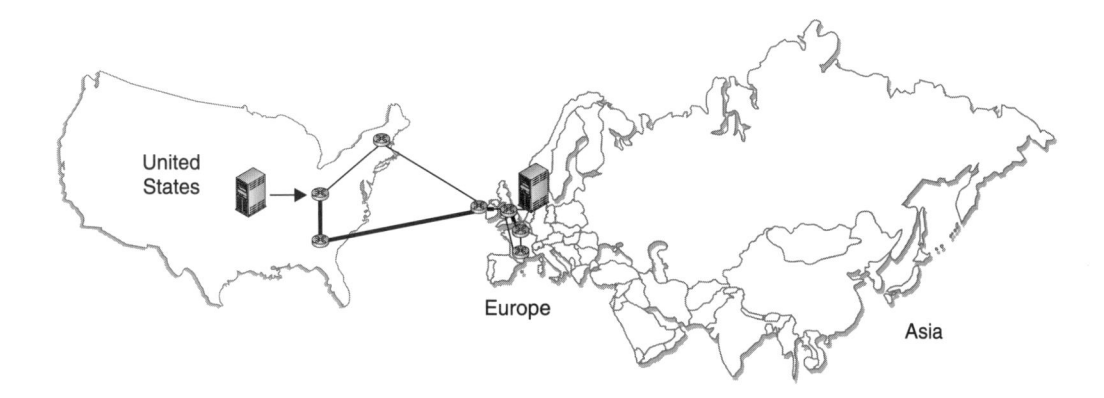

Routers accomplish these two tasks, and they do it one packet at a time.

NOTE A packet is similar to a word in that it is an equal-sized grouping of bytes. However, rather than being processed within the computer, packets are sent out across the telecommunications system, where they are converted back into usable data by the receiving device.

Routers have a unique function in internetworking and serve several important roles:

- Routers concurrently support different protocols (such as Ethernet, Token Ring, ISDN, and others), effectively making virtually all computers compatible.
- They flawlessly connect LANs to WANs, making it feasible to build large-scale internetworks with minimum centralized planning.
- Routers filter out unwanted traffic by isolating areas in which messages can be "broadcast" to all users in a network.
- They act as security gates by checking traffic against access permission lists.
- Routers ensure reliability by providing multiple paths through internetworks.
- They automatically learn about new paths and select the best ones, eliminating artificial constraints on expanding and improving internetworks.

Routers are like the Star Trek universal translators of the networking world. A router's most important feature is its ability to simultaneously support a variety of networking protocols. It is because of this function that otherwise incompatible computers can communicate with one another, regardless of architecture, operating system, data format, or any one of a dozen incompatibilities.

Furthermore, the router's ability to filter out unwanted traffic is also important to internetworking. The Internet is sometimes perceived as a lawless land where anyone can do anything. The truth of the matter is that network administrators can keep out undesired traffic by properly configuring their routers. This ability makes online productivity possible, while alleviating the feeling that there's someone out there looking at your sensitive documents and files.

Servers

The servers are the machines on your network that control various mission-critical operations. From the point of view of a LAN, servers feed client computers and in large networks govern such functions as file and printing services.

But servers' functions can become extremely specialized, depending on the needs of your organization and the deployment of your network. Also, depending on the size of your network, you may have several servers—some performing unique functions, others duplicating functions because of the sheer magnitude of the work demanded of them.

The number and placement of servers is dependent on several factors. Small organizations might need just one server to connect their client computers. In larger settings, servers have very specialized functions. As Figure 1-1 shows, Acme Consolidated Consumer Products uses a number of servers for different functions:

- **Web server** Where web site information (such as the web page design and online catalog) is stored
- **File server** Where the company's files are centrally stored
- **Print server** The server that serves as a custodian of jobs for the printer
- **Application server** The server on which web site visitors or employees run applications (such as databases, for instance)
- **E-mail server** The server that controls e-mail

It is also important to note that each of these can be separate devices, but they don't have to be. A single device can logically house a number of specific servers, so long as they are configured properly.

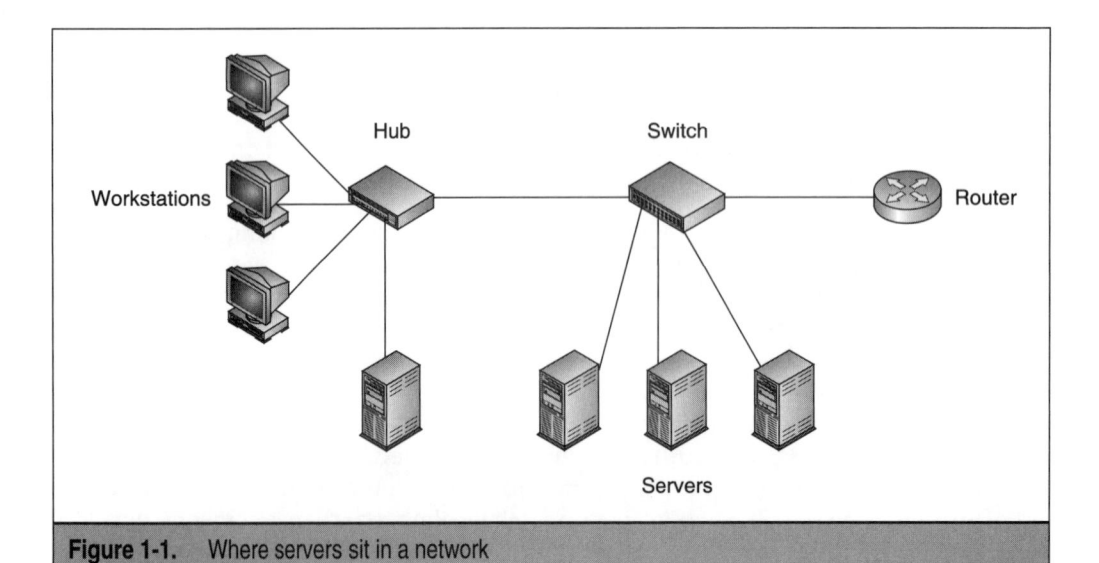

Figure 1-1. Where servers sit in a network

Hubs and Switches

Hubs and switches are probably the items that most users get frightened by when they poke their heads into the server room. These are the pieces of hardware with patch panels of connector ports that are tethered to their PCs with a length of Category 5 cabling. Hubs and switches have the task of connecting multiple devices (for instance, PCs, printers, and even more hubs and switches) to servers.

Hubs   Hubs are used to connect a number of PCs to a single server. An easy way to think about a hub is by likening it to a power strip. Rather than connect all the components of your entertainment center into a single power outlet (which is impossible), you use a power strip. This provides a half-dozen or so outlets so you can connect your TV, stereo, gaming console, DVD player, and satellite dish without running extension cords across your house. Similarly, in order for the server to be able to share data between its clients, it needs a hub to split the connection.

Since the hub repeats the signal to all its output ports, all the data is shared with every other device in the hub-based LAN. But what keeps your PC from picking up the packets that are meant for the guy in the next cubicle? Even though the packets meant for individual computers are sent to every device, each computer filters out packets that aren't intended for it.

Switches   Switches are much like hubs, but with an important functional difference. Both devices contain banks of phone jack–like connection ports into which twisted-pair cables are plugged. Both hubs and switches compose a LAN domain, and both can be used to direct messages into network backbones.

> **NOTE**   The technical name for a switch is a "switched hub." In common usage, the term has been shortened to simply "switch."

What differentiates a switch from a hub is the capability to create a private connection between devices on a network. In our power strip example, electricity is split between all the devices in the entertainment center. But the analogy doesn't hold true for switches, because switches are selective. The most appropriate comparison is to the switching system used by your local phone company. When you ring up your mother across town, your call is sent to a switch that isolates a circuit so that you and mom can have a private discussion about your loopy Aunt Julie. Conversely, if the connection were made with a hub, then the communication would be broadcast to every telephone connected to that hub. Figure 1-2 contrasts hub and switch functionality.

Switches are useful because they split bandwidth. Instead of all the devices on the LAN duking it out for bandwidth in the hub's shared medium, devices in a switch-based LAN are allowed full access to the medium's bandwidth for the split second it takes to complete the transmission.

Put simply, a hub takes frames received from one attached host and retransmits them to all hosts connected to it. A switch looks at the frames coming into its ports and immediately transfers them to one or more other switch ports. Because the process is

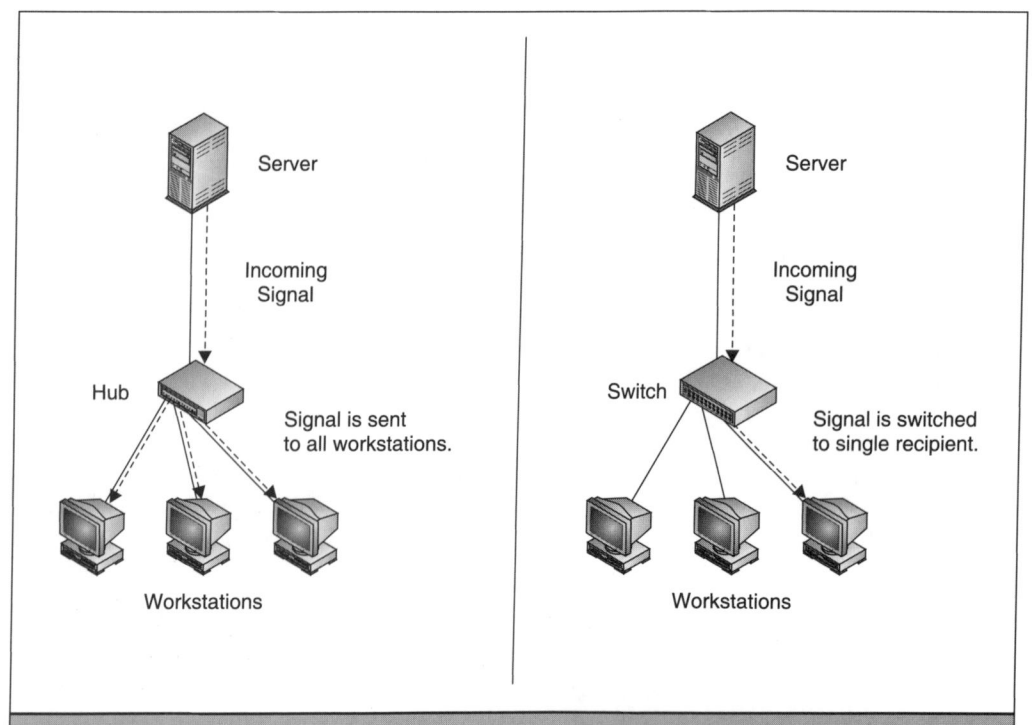

Figure 1-2. A hub repeats a signal; a switch delivers it to a specific port.

so fast, switches allow multiple data streams to pass simultaneously. This is how switches are able to support dozens of hosts funneled into a single switch port. Only one frame is actually being switched between ports at any given instant. But the process is so fast that it's transparent to the hosts involved.

OSI REFERENCE MODEL

In order for network devices to communicate, they must speak a common language. However, because there are so many companies developing their own proprietary devices and operating systems, who's to say which system is the best? Who's to say what language these devices will use to share information?

The answer comes from the International Standards Organization (ISO), an international engineering organization based in Paris. In 1978, the ISO published what is called the Open Systems Interconnection (OSI) reference model. This model comprises seven layers and has become the standard for developing communications interfaces among devices. It served as the basis of the popular Internet Protocol (IP).

The raison d'être of the seven-layer OSI reference model is to provide a foundation for interoperability. That means a computer system developed by one vendor would be able to exchange data with the computer system from another vendor. It's easy to understand the inherent problems of getting two different systems to talk to each other if you think about computer systems as being people from different countries. If you try to get someone from Germany to converse with someone from Argentina, there will be a communications breakdown if neither person speaks the other's language. It's even worse for computers, because they can't wave their arms around and gesticulate to get their point across. Without the OSI reference model, it would be impossible for a Macintosh to access a PC-based business-to-business server or a Microsoft PC to exchange information with a Novell server.

The Seven-Layer Stack

The OSI model divides networks into seven functional layers. Another term for the OSI reference model is the *seven-layer stack*. Each layer in the stack defines a function or set of functions that are performed as data traverses the network. Because the seven-layer stack is a *standard*, it doesn't matter which protocols are attempting to communicate with each other. If the protocols stay within the seven-layer stack, the same rules are applied at each stratum, providing interprotocol connectivity.

As shown in Figure 1-3, each layer contains its own protocol for communications between linked devices. To forge that link of standardized communication, each layer speaks to its counterpart to manage a particular portion of the network connection. Even though different protocols are trying to form a link, a fixed interface setting sits

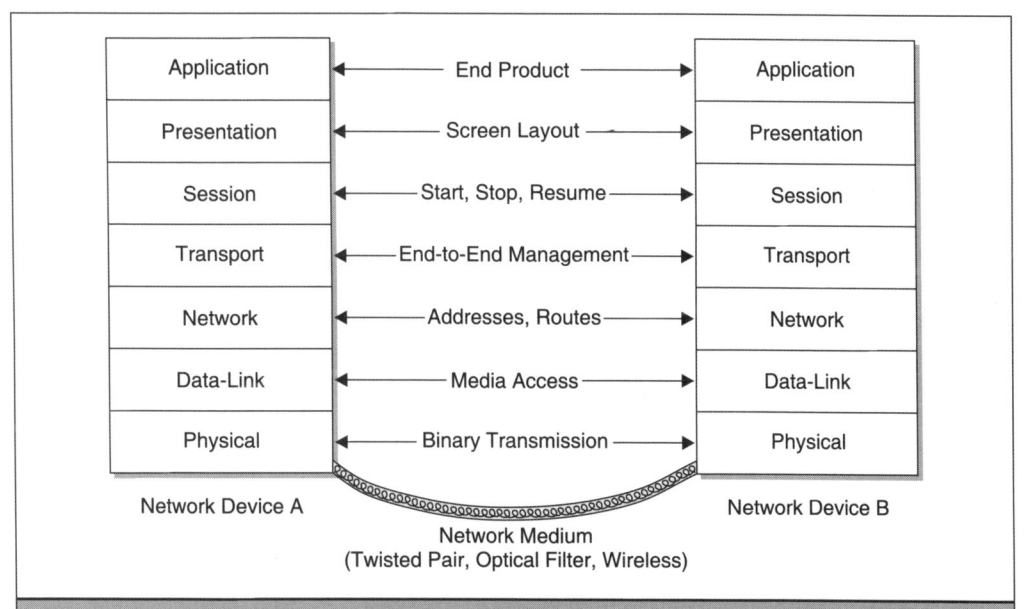

Network Device A		Network Device B
Application	← End Product →	Application
Presentation	← Screen Layout →	Presentation
Session	← Start, Stop, Resume →	Session
Transport	← End-to-End Management →	Transport
Network	← Addresses, Routes →	Network
Data-Link	← Media Access →	Data-Link
Physical	← Binary Transmission →	Physical

Network Medium
(Twisted Pair, Optical Filter, Wireless)

Figure 1-3. Each OSI layer runs a protocol to manage connections between devices.

between each layer. The result is that abstract layering reduces the seemingly impossible task of forming connections. The further up the stack we go, the closer we get to the user. We start at a very basic level—with pulses of electricity on the medium connecting the computers, ultimately working to the actual content of the data being transferred. The seven layers are described here:

- **Layer 1—the physical layer**   At the first layer, the two devices standardize the transport medium. At this level, the electrical and mechanical characteristics of the signal are established. Examples are twisted-pair cabling, fiber-optic cabling, coaxial cabling, and the NIC.
- **Layer 2—the data-link layer**   The next layer of the stack controls access to the network and makes sure that frames can be transferred across the network. The most popular data-link specification is Ethernet's Carrier Sense Multiple Access with Collision Detection (CSMA/CD).
- **Layer 3—the network layer**   At the third layer, the movement of data between different networks is managed. At this layer, protocols are responsible for finding the device for which data is destined. Examples of network layer protocols include IP, Internetwork Packet Exchange (IPX), and AppleTalk.
- **Layer 4—the transport layer**   The midpoint of the seven-layer stack ensures that data makes it to its destination in one piece and in the proper order. The Transmission Control Protocol (TCP) and User Datagram Protocol (UDP) operate at this layer.

NOTE   We'll discuss TCP and UDP in Chapter 3.

- **Layer 5—the session layer**   The fifth layer in the stack sets up and tears down connections and arranges sessions between two devices. Session layer protocols include Lightweight Directory Access Protocol (LDAP) and Remote Procedure Call (RPC).
- **Layer 6—the presentation layer**   This layer formats data display on a monitor or for printing. At this layer, protocols include Lightweight Presentation Protocol (LPP) and NetBIOS.
- **Layer 7—the application layer**   At the top of the stack are the protocols used to perform tasks over a network. Some examples of protocols at this layer include Simple Mail Transfer Protocol (SMTP) for e-mail, the Hypertext Transfer Protocol (HTTP) for web browsers and servers, Telnet for remote terminal sessions, and countless others.

NOTE   Don't be confused by the name "application layer." This layer runs *network* applications, not applications software like word processors or spreadsheet programs. Network applications include e-mail, web browsing (HTTP), and FTP (file transfer protocol) programs, among others.

OSI Implementation by Layer

Understanding how the OSI reference model works might be helpful if we turned things on their side, so to speak. Even though we tend to think of the OSI reference model as a vertical thing (after all, we refer to it as a *stack*), it might be helpful for you to think of it in horizontal terms—meaning we'll tip the stack onto its side. Here, we'll throw a monkey wrench in the works and talk about the stack in reverse. That is, in the last section, we started at layer 1 and worked up to layer 7. This time, we'll start at layer 7 (which is the layer closest to the user) and work our way down the stack toward the physical layer. Even though this might sound confusing, it will help you make sense of how the different layers of the stack interact.

At the heart of a message is the payload. The size and contents of a message's payload vary depending on the software application. It is important to realize that a single message does not normally contain all the payload data in a transmission. Rather, the payload is broken up into small chunks and then message-handling protocols are added on top of the payload data. Payload data differs based on what application is running. For instance, if you are running a Telnet session with a library, only a small amount of data (keystrokes and number selections, for instance) will be transferred. On the other hand, if you are transferring a file from an FTP site, then the size of the payload will be much larger, spreading millions of bytes across thousands of packets.

On top of the payload are all the message-handling protocols. The first three layers in this model handle the network application in use (application layer), in what format the data is represented (presentation layer), and details of the connection (session layer). For instance, port number 25 identifies an SMTP e-mail application.

NOTE Ports are not physical entities, as the name suggests. Rather, they are the logical "locations" within the computer where it expects to receive specific types of information.

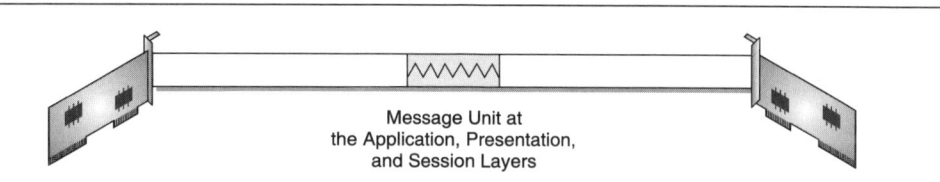

Message Unit at
the Application, Presentation,
and Session Layers

At the next layer, the transport layer, the message gets a bit larger. Here, tasks include ensuring that the receiving computer knows that a message is coming and ensuring that the receiver won't be drowned in packets. Also, this layer ensures that the receiver got all the packets that were sent, retransmitting any that were dropped.

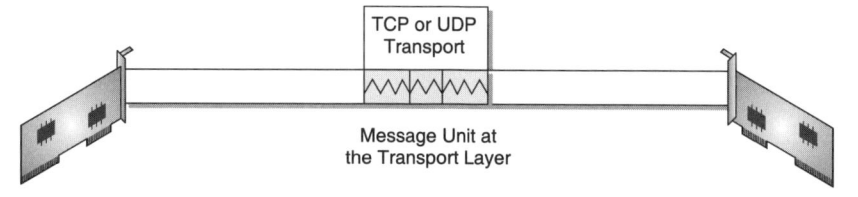

TCP or UDP
Transport

Message Unit at
the Transport Layer

The next layer added to the message is the network layer. At this point, the message actually becomes a *packet* or a *datagram*. Each packet's header contains a logical network address that is used to walk the message through the internetwork. Network protocols include IP, among others.

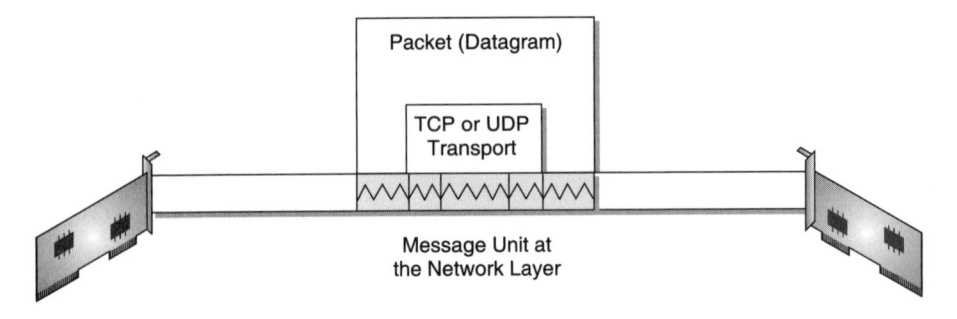

Packet (Datagram)

TCP or UDP Transport

Message Unit at the Network Layer

The second to last layer is the data-link layer. It is at this layer that binary information is read and added to a format called a *frame*. The frame's format is established by the NIC's network protocol (for instance, Ethernet or ATM). Each frame header contains a media access control (MAC) address for the networking device. MACs are unique identifiers for each device.

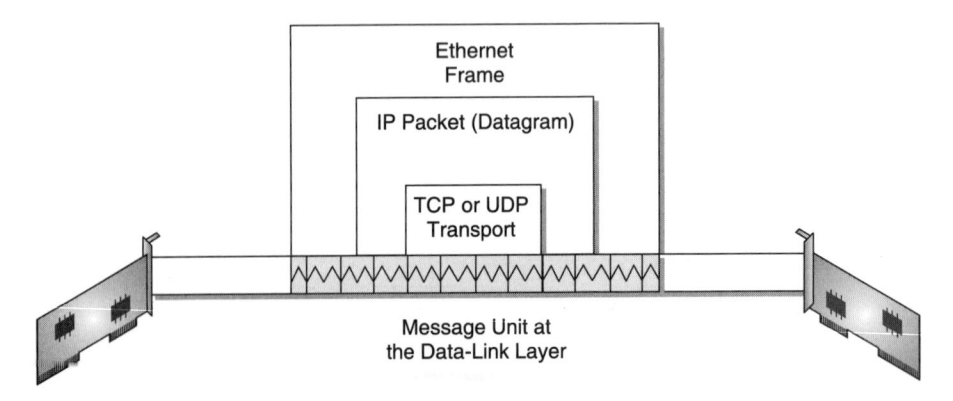

Ethernet Frame

IP Packet (Datagram)

TCP or UDP Transport

Message Unit at the Data-Link Layer

Finally, we reach the physical level. Remember that this is the level at which the message has been converted into a series of pulses, transmitting data in a binary code. Whether these pulses are electrical impulses in a conventional network or a series of flashing lights in an optical network, this is the last layer of the stack. The pulses are processed by the NIC, not by software in the networking device.

NETWORK TECHNOLOGIES

Now that you understand how bits and bytes move among computers in a network, it's necessary to talk about the technologies that actually carry data packets. Network technologies run LAN segments (you might also hear these technologies referred to as

LAN technologies or *network specifications*, which are somewhat interchangeable). The most popular network technology is one you've probably heard of before—Ethernet. Though Ethernet is the most prevalent LAN technology, you might find other technologies more appropriate for your networking needs.

In this section, we'll discuss Ethernet and its more robust siblings, Gigabit Ethernet and 10 Gigabit Ethernet. Additionally, we'll talk about Token Ring and Asynchronous Transfer Mode (ATM). We'll round out the section with a discussion of wireless networking technology.

You might remember from the last section that network technologies are implemented at the data-link layer (layer 2) of the OSI reference model. In practical terms, this means that network technologies are characterized both by the physical media they share and how they control access to those media. Put another way, networking is about connectivity. But for connectivity to really occur, order must be maintained among the connected devices. For that reason, the data-link layer is also known as the *media access control layer*, or *MAC layer* for short. At this level, the messages are called the *data frame* or frame.

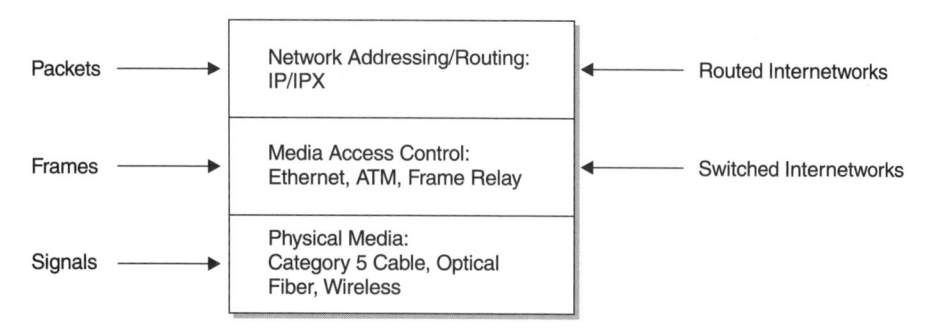

```
Packets  ───▶  ┌─────────────────────────────┐  ◀───  Routed Internetworks
               │ Network Addressing/Routing: │
               │ IP/IPX                      │
               ├─────────────────────────────┤
Frames   ───▶  │ Media Access Control:       │  ◀───  Switched Internetworks
               │ Ethernet, ATM, Frame Relay  │
               ├─────────────────────────────┤
Signals  ───▶  │ Physical Media:             │
               │ Category 5 Cable, Optical   │
               │ Fiber, Wireless             │
               └─────────────────────────────┘
```

Because order must be maintained in a network connection, network technologies can only deal with MAC addresses. These are the serial number–like identifiers that were mentioned in the last section. In order to route messages outside of the LAN, a network layer protocol (IP, for instance) is needed. Network technologies by themselves can only function in switched internetwork environments. That means they are only good for LANs or simple paths across long distances where a lot of direction isn't needed.

Network technologies operate at two different levels:

- **Access LANs** At this level, network technologies connect to cabling from devices, join workgroups, and share resources, such as printers and servers. These LANs are formed by hubs or access switches and provide users and devices connectivity to the network at a local level. For instance, in a large office, an access LAN would be located on a single floor.
- **Backbone LANs** At this level, network technologies connect access LANs and share more robust devices such as database servers and mail servers. Backbone LANs are composed of routers or LAN switches. Backbones connect access LANs, normally within a building or a campus. Figure 1-4 illustrates the differences between access and backbone LANs.

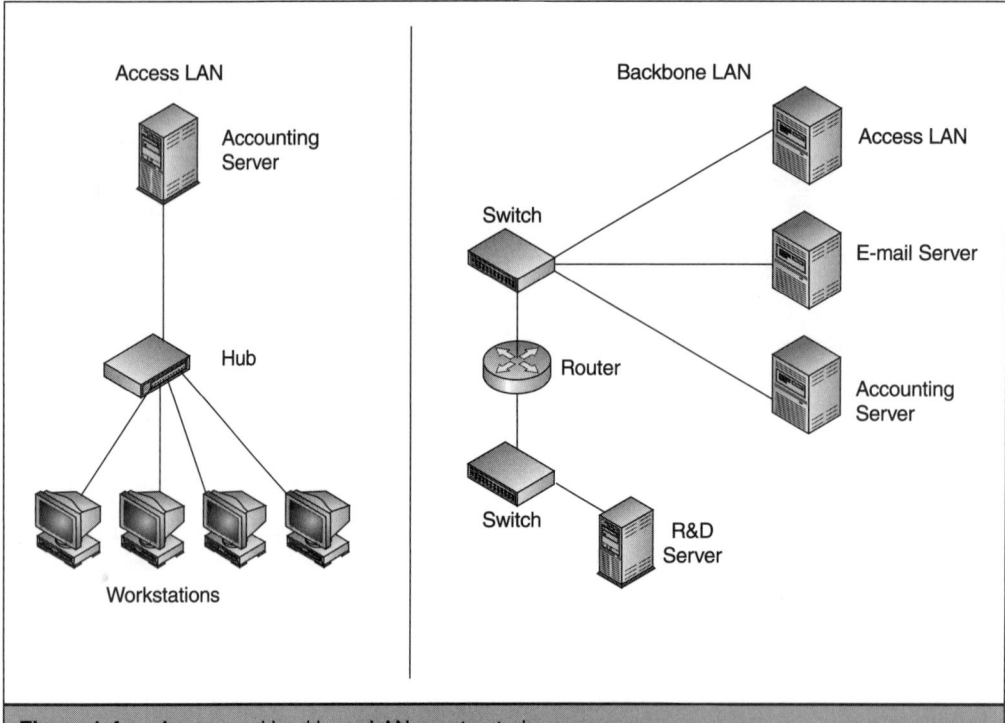

Figure 1-4. Access and backbone LANs contrasted

    Thus far in this chapter we've discussed the fact that different computers talk to each other in unique and proprietary ways. But it isn't just the computers that are doing the talking. Individual companies have developed their own means of bridging the networking gap—whether on a local scale or worldwide.

Ethernet

    In 1970, the Xerox Corporation developed version 1 of Ethernet. Over the course of the decade, Xerox joined forces with Intel and Digital Equipment Corporation (which later became Compaq) to release version 2 in 1982. In the past 20 years Ethernet has grown to become the most predominant network technology. Probably the chief reason that Ethernet has become so popular is that it is inexpensive. Add to that the fact that many IT professionals have cut their teeth on Ethernet and know of its proven track record. Ethernet is so popular that a networking card can be bought for less than US$10 and computer manufacturers are even integrating Ethernet NICs into their motherboards.
    Furthermore, Ethernet has grown in power, in addition to popularity. Technically speaking, "Ethernet" is used to describe the 10 Mbps flavor of the technology. Fast Ethernet (introduced in 1995) increased networking speeds to 100 Mbps. In 1996, Gigabit Ethernet kicked the transfer rates up another notch to 1 Gbps. Slated for standardization

in 2002 is 10 Gigabit Ethernet, which will boost Ethernet out of the realm of LANs and into the world of WANs. Ethernet is implemented as the IEEE 802.3 specification.

> **NOTE** The Institute for Electrical and Electronics Engineers (IEEE) has been around since the 19th century and establishes standards for layers 1 and 2 of the OSI reference model. The work of the Internet Engineering Task Force (IETF) picks up at layer 3 and above.

Ethernet Architecture

In some regards, it is surprising that Ethernet is so popular. It is not an inherently efficient technology. In fact, at times only 37 percent of the bandwidth is truly available by virtue of the way it operates. Ethernet operates by *contention*, which means that devices connected to an Ethernet LAN segment listen to the wire and wait to send a message until the medium is clear. If two devices transmit at the same time and their packets collide, then both transmissions are aborted and the stations back off, waiting a random amount of time before they attempt another transmission.

Ethernet uses the CSMA/CD algorithm to listen to the wire, sense collisions, and abort transmissions. Basically, CSMA/CD is Ethernet's traffic signal, controlling what would otherwise be a chaotically busy intersection. Figure 1-5 illustrates how CSMA/CD operates.

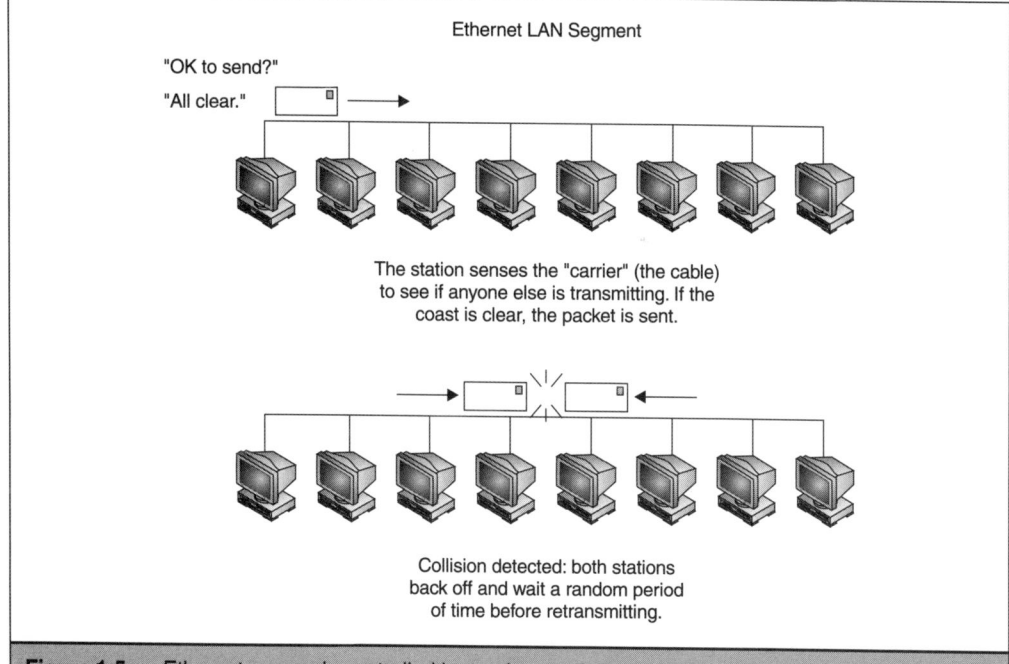

Figure 1-5. Ethernet access is controlled by carrier sensing and frame collisions.

Because Ethernet uses a shared medium, each device on an Ethernet LAN receives every message, and then checks to see whether the destination address matches its own address. If it does, then the message is accepted and works its way up the seven-layer stack. If the address isn't a match, the packets are dropped.

Employing a switched Ethernet architecture is advantageous because the links between the switch and device get maximum bandwidth usage. This is because the packets are not being broadcast to every device on the network—rather, they are being sent back and forth between the switch and the intended device.

Gigabit Ethernet

Gigabit Ethernet is the 1000 Mbps extension of the Ethernet standard. The push for Gigabit Ethernet is largely motivated by its inherent compatibility with other Ethernet specifications (the original 10 Mbps Ethernet and 100 Mbps Fast Ethernet).

Gigabit Ethernet is ATM's main competition as the backbone of choice. (We'll talk about ATM shortly.) Given that Ethernet is the most popular network technology, Gigabit Ethernet's greatest advantage over ATM is familiarity. Although originally designed and deployed as a LAN technology, when speeds get up to 1 Gbps, then Gigabit Ethernet can handle WAN deployments.

As good as gigabit-per-second rates sound, Ethernet is not the most perfect solution for WANs. Ethernet uses variable-sized frames—ranging from 64 bytes to 1400 bytes per frame. As such, it does not enjoy the Quality of Service (QoS) characteristics of ATM.

NOTE Quality of Service is a means of ensuring that packets are sent and received in the most expeditious manner. We'll go into more details about QoS in general and Windows XP's implementation of QoS in particular in Chapter 15.

Of course, there is a lot to be said about an organization's particular needs and deployment options. For instance, if an organization isn't too concerned with QoS and has a solid knowledge base in Ethernet, Gigabit Ethernet might be a perfect fit for the needs of that organization. A popular way to configure Gigabit Ethernet is with Fast Ethernet–configured access LANs interconnected through a Gigabit Ethernet backbone LAN.

10 Gigabit Ethernet

The next rung of the Ethernet ladder is 10 Gigabit Ethernet. At 10 and 100 Mbps speeds, Ethernet is used as an access technology. Gigabit Ethernet makes Ethernet a WAN contender. However, as 10 Gigabit Ethernet enters the scene, Ethernet can settle in as a true WAN technology.

Like other Ethernet technologies, 10 Gigabit Ethernet uses the IEEE 802.3 Ethernet MAC protocol, the IEEE 802.3 Ethernet frame format, and the IEEE 802.3 frame size. Variable frame sizing can still be an issue; however, it is easy to aggregate many smaller signals into a large 10 Gigabit Ethernet trunk. Again, the pros and cons must be weighed for each situation and organization.

Token Ring

Even though the world seems connected by Ethernet, that isn't the only LAN standard out there. Token Ring is Ethernet's main contender in the fight for LAN supremacy. At least, it used to be. Token Ring is different from Ethernet in its architectural approach and is incompatible with Ethernet in terms of NICs, cable connectors, and software.

> **NOTE** Whereas Ethernet is defined by the IEEE in specification 802.3, Token Ring is defined in specification 802.5.

Token Ring is so called because it arranges hosts into a logical ring. Token Ring LAN segments behave like a ring in that they pass signals round-robin style from one host to the next as if the cable were actually one giant ring. In practice, hosts need not be connected in an actual ring—rather they can be configured in the more common hub-and-spoke topology known as a *star topology*, which is illustrated in Figure 1-6. Note that instead of a hub or a switch at the center of the star, there is a device called a *media access unit (MAU)*.

Whereas Ethernet uses contention to decide which host would broadcast, Token Ring takes a more orderly approach: a *token-passing* protocol controls traffic flow by passing a frame called the *token* from host to host, around the ring. Only the host with the token in its possession is allowed to transmit, thus eliminating packet collisions. In essence, Token Ring trades wait times for collisions, because each host waits until

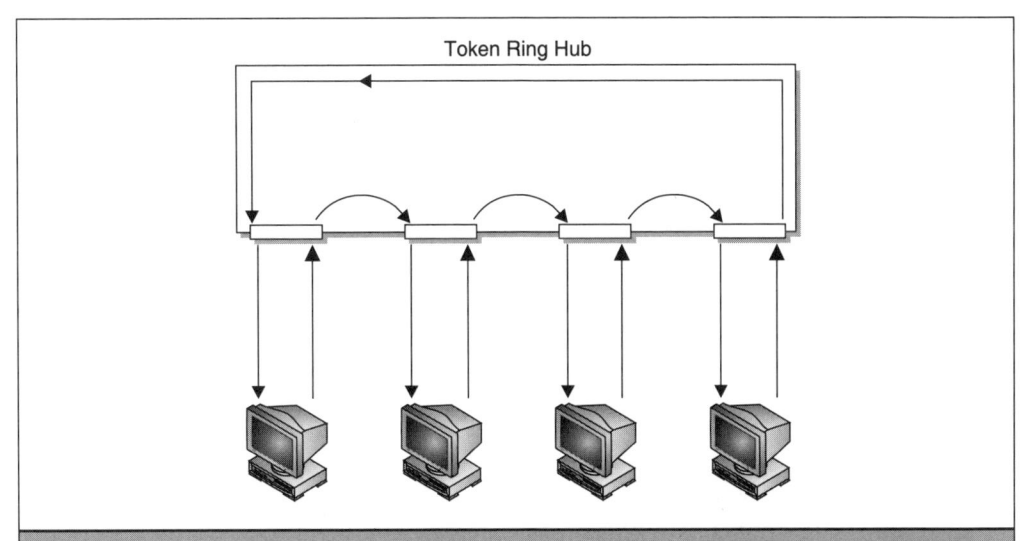

Figure 1-6. Token Ring LANs are logical rings, not actual physical loops.

its turn to transmit. This trade-off isn't an even swap, however. Eliminating packet collisions vastly improves Token Ring's utilization of raw bandwidth. Token Ring can use up to 75 percent of raw bandwidth, compared to Ethernet's theoretical maximum of about 37 percent. When first introduced, Token Ring ran at 4 Mbps. Since then, most Token Ring LANs have kicked their speed up to 16 Mbps. Though this seems slow compared to Fast Ethernet's 100 Mbps rates, as we noted earlier, Token Ring is much more efficient than Ethernet.

Never let it be said that money doesn't matter, however. Token Ring hasn't caught on as the predominant standard because it only pays off above certain traffic volumes.

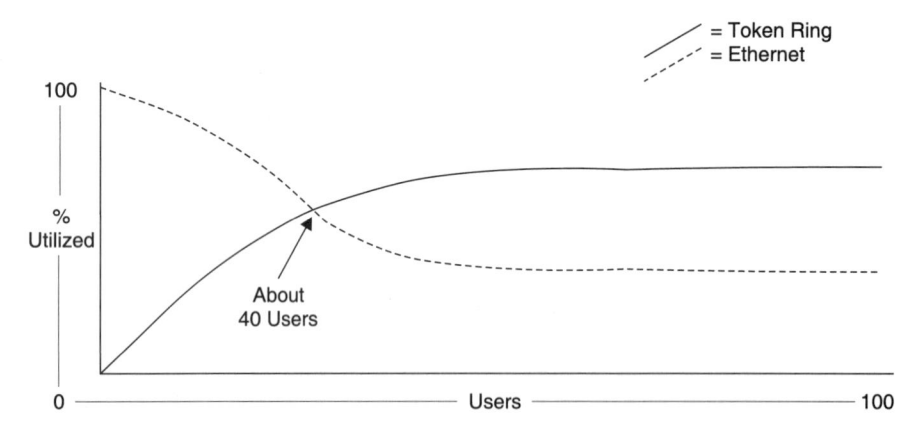

Furthermore, Token Ring NICs are expensive to produce because of the technology's intricate token-passing mechanisms. Compared to Ethernet, it's much more expensive to produce a NIC that transmits packets in an orderly fashion than a NIC that uses brute force to get a spot on the wire.

ATM

Asynchronous Transfer Mode is different from other networking technologies in that each ATM transmission is composed of 53-byte cells instead of packets. *Cells* are a fixed-length message unit, and like packets they represent pieces of a message. The fixed-length format results in unique characteristics:

- **Virtual circuit orientation**   Networks that use cells run better in point-to-point mode—that is, the receiving station is active and ready to receive and process the cells.

- **Speed**   Because of the uniform size of cells, ATM hardware knows precisely where the header ends and the data begins in each and every cell. This speeds up the processing operations and allows ATM networks to run at speeds up to 622 Mbps.

- **Quality of Service (QoS)**   Predictable throughput rates and virtual circuits enable cell-based networks to better guarantee service levels to priority traffic.

Another difference between ATM and Ethernet and Token Ring is that ATM is a switching technology in which a so-called *virtual circuit* is established before the transmission starts. By contrast, Ethernet and Token Ring don't set up a circuit before transmitting. Rather, they send a message to the host without prior notification, leaving it to the routers to determine the best path for the message to follow.

Furthermore, ATM cells are small (53 bytes) when compared to Ethernet packets, which range from 64 to 1500 bytes. Because ATM cells are about 25 times smaller per message unit, they are much more granular, quicker to process, and easier to control.

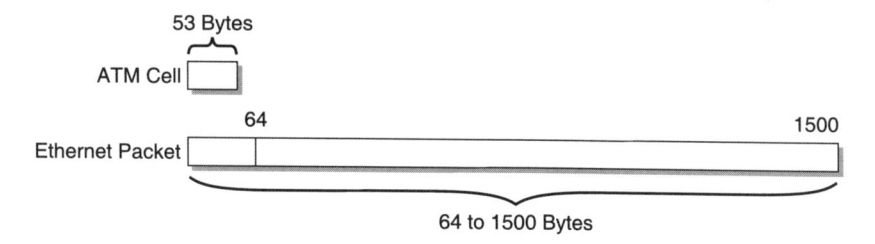

```
                53 Bytes
                  ⌢
    ATM Cell   [  ]
                  64                                          1500
Ethernet Packet [  |                                           ]
                   ⌣
                           64 to 1500 Bytes
```

Yet another difference between ATM and other networking technologies is that ATM is designed to run over fiber-optic cable operating the Synchronous Optical Network (SONET) specification. SONET is an ANSI standard that specifies the physical interfaces that connect to fiber-optic cable.

Like Token Ring, ATM's design yields high bandwidth from the raw wire speed. ATM is so efficient that it exceeds Token Ring's 75 percent. Most ATM backbone LANs run at OC-3 (155 Mbps) or OC-12 (622 Mbps). Most intercity links run at OC-12 with OC-48 (2.488 Gbps) speeds on the heavier trunks.

> **NOTE** OC stands for optical carrier and is a measure of optical transmission speed.

Wireless

The preceding network technologies offered very different functionality from one another. Some are more popular than others; some are more expensive than others; some are more efficient than others. However, even though Ethernet, ATM, and frame relay are all unique in their functionality, they share one common trait—they require a physical connection between hosts. Whether that means twisted-pair copper cable or fiber optics, these devices are tethered together. Wireless LANs (WLANs) are cutting those tethers and allowing devices to roam free while remaining connected to the network.

The core technology that allows WLANs to communicate is the IEEE 802.11 standard. This standard was established in the early 1990s and operates in the unlicensed 2.4 GHz frequency band. The first incarnations of 802.11 supported 1 to 2 Mbps. A later refinement of the standard, namely 802.11b, brought speeds up to 5.5 Mbps and 11 Mbps. This is accomplished by using direct sequence spread spectrum (DSSS), a different modulation scheme than the one used in 802.11.

An up and coming version is the 802.11a protocol. This standard boasts speeds of 54 Mbps but hasn't quite caught on as popularly as 802.11b. Furthermore, where 802.11 and 802.11b use 2.4 GHz, 802.11a will use 5.8 GHz. Also, instead of relying on DSSS, 802.11a will use Orthogonal Frequency Division Multiplexing (OFDM).

The 802.11 standard was developed with three goals in mind:

- To serve as a MAC and physical layer specification for wireless connectivity
- To provide wireless connectivity to automatic machinery, equipment, or stations that require fast connectivity
- To represent a standard that could be used and applied globally

NOTE It's the third requirement that led the IEEE to embrace 2.4 GHz as the preferred operating frequency. This is an unlicensed band that is reserved for industrial, scientific, and medical use on a global basis.

802.11 WLANs are based on an architecture that is very similar to that of cellular telephone networks. By using a comparable network design, as described in the following list, wireless networks can reap the same roaming benefits of cellular, while providing high data rates.

- **Cells and sets** Like a cellular telephone network, an 802.11 WLAN is subdivided into cells. Each cell is governed by an *access point (AP)*. APs are the devices that communicate with wireless NICs. However, since a single AP may not be capable of satisfying the network's wireless needs, it is possible to connect multiple APs to a common backbone. When several APs are used together, they constitute what is known as a *distribution system*. No matter how large or small the network, no matter how many nodes are connected, the grouping of wireless equipment is viewed as a single IEEE 802.11 network to upper layers of the OSI reference model.
- **The physical layer** The 802.11 protocol covers the physical and MAC layers. But rather than a single media type, 802.11 embraces three kinds of wireless "media": frequency hopping spread spectrum, direct sequence spread spectrum, and infrared. A single MAC layer supports all three physical layers.

Using a cellular telephone architecture allows wireless devices to join, leave, or roam from cell to cell. For more information about wireless networking with Windows XP Professional, check out Chapter 5.

WAN TECHNOLOGIES

Networks aren't simply limited by the reach of Category 5 cabling or the range of an 802.11 device. Many organizations connect their assets across great distances using

WAN technologies. Furthermore, these are the technologies that allow networking devices around the world connect to the global mesh known as the Internet.

There are two basic kinds of WANs that allow remote users and offices to connect to an organization's network:

- **Dial-ins** A *dial-in* connection is what allows a home user to connect to his or her Internet service provider, or a worker in a small office to connect to the network via a telephone line. A dial-in connection establishes a point-to-point connection between a central location and one or a few users. Once the connection is no longer needed for that session, the telephone circuit is disconnected. Because the connection handles reasonably few users and small amounts of data, a dial-in connection is ideal.

- **Trunks** On the other end of the spectrum is a *trunk*. Trunks are high-capacity point-to-point links that connect offices. Normally, a trunk will connect several remote users to a central site. Most trunks run over T1 (1.5 Mbps) or T3 (45 Mbps) telephone lines, although technologies such as fiber optics are pushing those speeds ever higher.

Regardless of the WAN connection employed, the public telephone system is used to carry data between users and offices. The difference in the utilization of the telephone system lies in which lines are used:

- Between the home or office and the switching station
- Between two switching stations

NOTE The zone between the home or office and the switching station is traditionally known as the *last mile*. This is the site of most bottlenecks to WAN networking speed, largely because the infrastructure in this zone is not meant to handle large amounts of data.

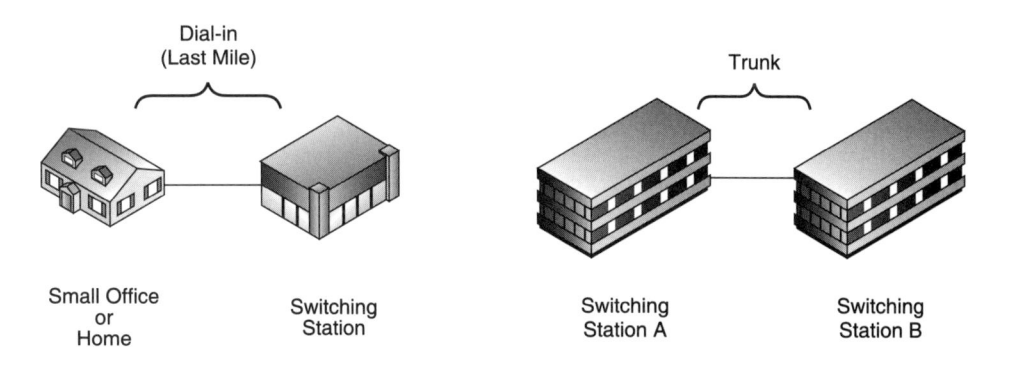

You might have heard the term "last mile" thrown around in the last few years. This is because as the Internet becomes increasingly popular and important, customers are tiring of slow dial-in connections from their homes and small offices. It isn't just kids downloading MP3s who are demanding more bandwidth—it's also telecommuters and small business owners who need speedy connections.

In this section, we take a closer look at the technologies that have popped up to reduce the last mile problem. Digital subscriber lines (DSL) and Integrated Services Digital Network (ISDN) are two digital telephony technologies that have made a dent in the last mile problem. Additionally, cable television operators and satellite companies have joined the fray, managing to avoid the telephone grid entirely. Finally, we'll examine the trunk technologies that aggregate bandwidth, sending billions of packets per second on their way.

Dial-in Technologies

One of the big differences between dial-in and trunk technologies is that dial-in connections are temporary. That is, when a computer user is done with a particular session, the circuit is terminated by hanging up the telephone. The majority of telephone lines connecting homes are *analog*. That means sound traverses the phone system as an audio wave. In order for computers to communicate across the telephone system, they must use *modems* (modem being short for modulator/demodulator). Modems convert binary signals into sound, and then back into binary signals. This is why, when dialing into an ISP or sending a fax, you hear that electronic screeching from your modem or fax machine.

Analog circuits wouldn't be so disagreeable if they weren't so slow. They are poky because the acoustic signals use a small portion of the raw bandwidth available in copper telephone system cables. If you think about it, this makes sense—the telephone network was designed for voice, not data. This is why even the fastest modem signal travels at 56 kilobits per second (Kbps). This is a turtle's pace compared to the hare of Fast Ethernet, traveling at 100 Mbps. Figure 1-7 compares the throughput of each representative speed and technology. Think of the wires as "pipes" that allow ever increasing numbers of packets to speed through.

The two high-speed dial-in technologies that rely on the existing telephone infrastructure are ISDN and DSL. ISDN was introduced in the late 1980s, but it had problems taking off because local telephone carriers didn't go out of their way to make it available. DSL is the newest technology and offers even faster rates than ISDN. Unfortunately, even though there's high demand for DSL, local carriers aren't deploying it or supporting it as quickly as the public would like.

ISDN

ISDN was the first digital service to the home. Because this technology is digital, special equipment is needed in the customer's home or small office to use it. Unfortunately, depending on the customer's location in relation to the telephone company's central office, ISDN isn't always available.

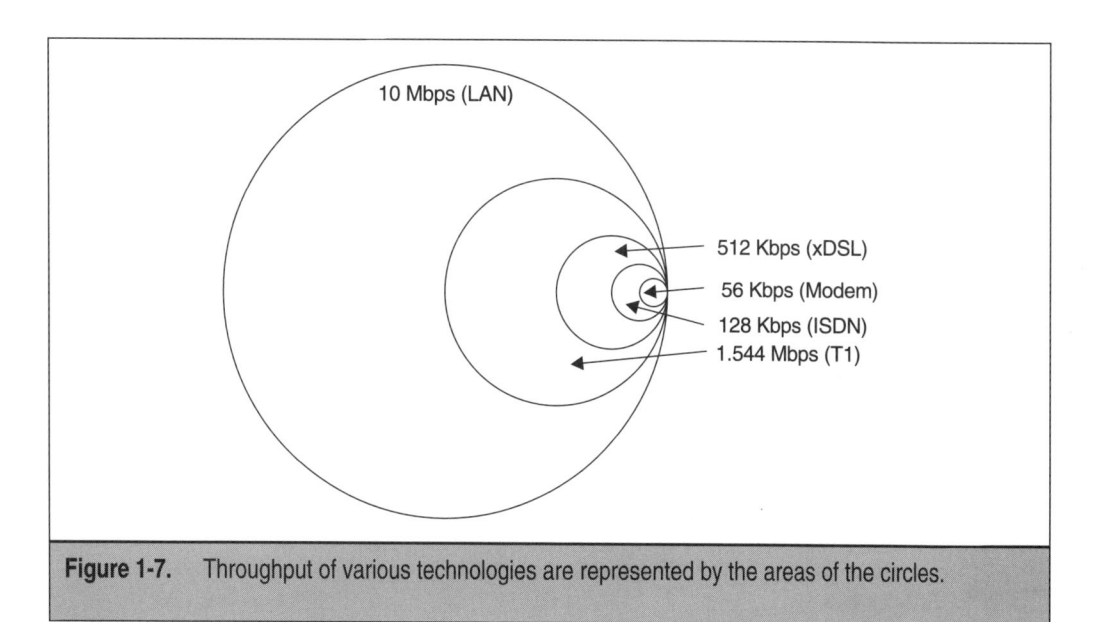

Figure 1-7. Throughput of various technologies are represented by the areas of the circles.

BRI ISDN creates multiple channels over a single connection. A *channel* is a data path that is multiplexed across the telephone line, along with other channels. The basic ISDN circuit is a Basic Rate Interface (BRI) circuit with two *B-channels*, or bearer channels, for payload data. Figure 1-8 compares an analog/modem circuit with an ISDN BRI circuit.

NOTE *Multiplexed* means that multiple signals are combined over a single line.

Each B-channel runs at about 64 Kbps, for a total bandwidth of 128 Kbps. You might be wondering why ISDN subdivides the line into two channels. Why not have a single channel with a higher bandwidth? The answer is that separate B-channels enhance throughput for symmetrical connections, which are connections that both send and receive traffic. A third channel called the *D-channel* (or delta channel) carries 16 Kbps. This channel doesn't carry payload data as do the B-channels. Rather, the D-channel carries network control information. This separation of payload from control data improves ISDN's performance and reliability.

PRI There is a second kind of ISDN circuit called a Primary Rate Interface (PRI). Functionally, PRI is the same as BRI. However, PRI is much beefier in that it carries up to 23 B-channels and one 64 Kbps D-channel for a total bandwidth of 1.544 Mbps. This is often referred to as a T1. PRI is appealing for small businesses that need to connect multiple users.

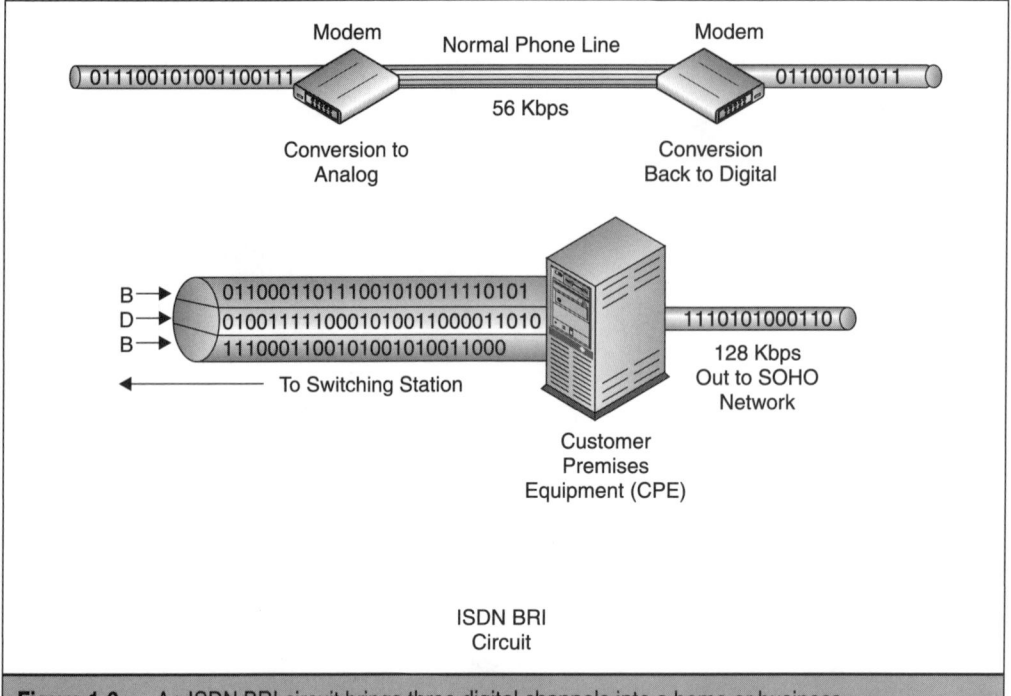

Figure 1-8. An ISDN BRI circuit brings three digital channels into a home or business.

DSL

Like ISDN, DSL is a digital technology that runs on the public telephone network. DSL uses sophisticated algorithms to modulate signals so that more bandwidth is milked from the last mile infrastructure.

Whereas ISDN is symmetric, DSL is asymmetric. This means data can be moved downstream much faster than it can be sent upstream. For home users, this is fine because they tend to receive more data then they send. There are several types of DSL, but the two most important flavors are as follows:

- **aDSL** Asymmetrical DSL, a two-way circuit that can handle about 640 Kbps upstream and up to 6 Mbps downstream.
- **DSL Lite** Also called G.Lite, a slower, less expensive technology that can carry data at rates between about 1.5 Mbps and 6 Mbps downstream, and from 128 Kbps to 384 Kbps upstream. The exact speeds will depend on what deal you make with the telephone carrier and what hardware you use.

Like ISDN, special equipment is needed for DSL connections. DSL modems split signals into upstream and downstream channels. The distinction with DSL Lite is that the splitting is done at the telephone switching station, not the home or small office. This is shown in Figure 1-9. Luckily, DSL modems are inexpensive. In fact, most telephone carriers offer promotions in which they will give you a free modem if you sign up for their service.

DSL provides significant cost savings over ISDN because the DSL hardware is less expensive than ISDN, and DSL splits the signal in the home. DSL isn't a panacea, however. As we noted earlier, DSL is not available everywhere. You must be within about five miles of a telephone switching station to get DSL.

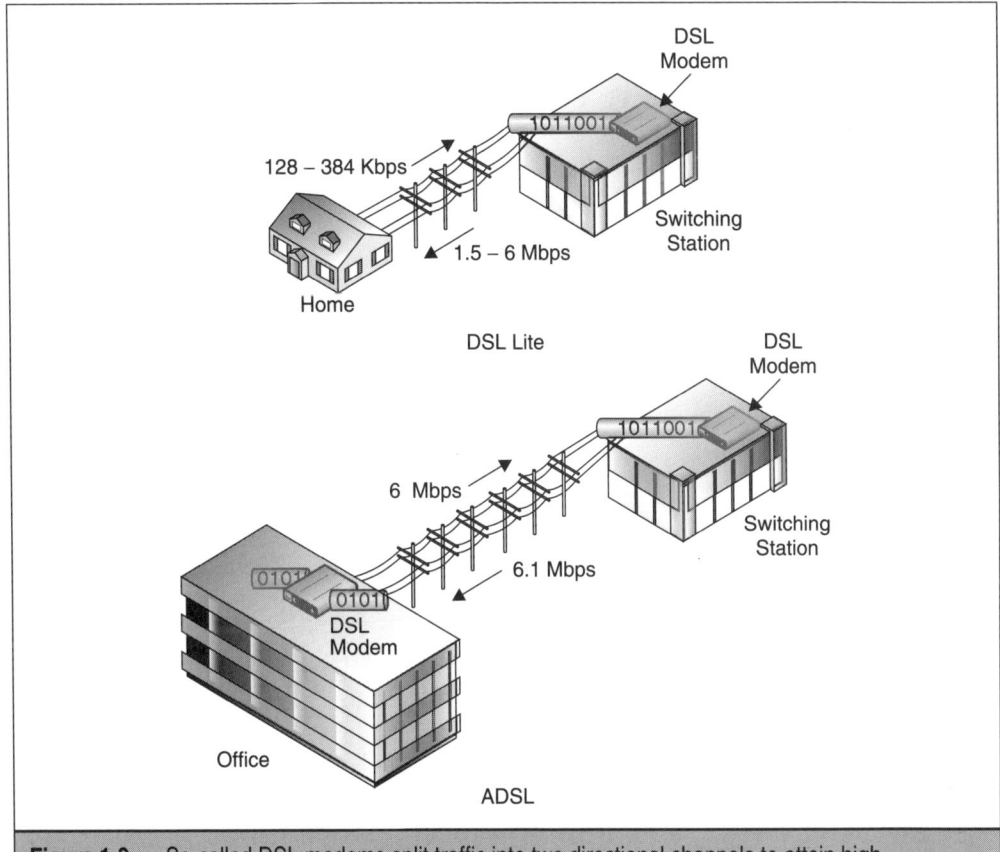

Figure 1-9. So-called DSL modems split traffic into two directional channels to attain high bandwidth.

Cable Modems and Satellite Connections

If the thought of relying on the telephone company to carry your high-speed data is just too much to bear, then there are two more ways you can bridge the last mile. Cable modems and satellite connections are gaining popularity as ways to access the Internet at high speeds.

Cable Modem   A cable modem uses the coaxial cable coming from your cable television circuit as a transport medium. The cable modem connects to the cable television feed, then into an Ethernet NIC in the computer.

Depending on what the cable company offers in terms of packages, you can expect to get anywhere from 384 Kbps to several million bps downstream. The downside of cable modems is that they share bandwidth within a neighborhood. This is great if you're the only one on the block with a cable modem. However, if other people have cable modems, the speed will drop off sharply every time someone else logs on.

Satellite Connection   Major limiting factors in your last mile solutions are the availability of DSL from the phone company or cable from the cable company. However, even if you're in a remote cabin on the North Shore of Lake Superior, you can still ameliorate the last mile problem.

You've probably seen those 18-inch satellite dishes that are bolted on the sides and roofs of millions of homes around the country. In the past, they used to offer simple television programming and movies. Now, however, companies like Hughes Network Systems offer satellite delivery of Internet content over those satellite signals.

In the past, satellite connectivity was a one-way street—high-speed data could only be downloaded from the satellite. However, in recent months, this functionality has been expanded to allow two-way high-speed transfers.

WAN Trunk Technologies

Earlier in this section, we said that a trunk is a high-capacity point-to-point data link. Trunks don't have to exist just between cities and across town. They can be within buildings and on campuses. That having been said, they are still best known as WAN links connecting cities, countries, and continents.

The last portion of this chapter examines T1, T3, and frame relay connections.

T1 and T3 Leased Lines

T1 and T3 lines are the most popular leased-line technologies in North America and Japan today. *Leased lines* are circuits (or part of a circuit) that are reserved for the organization that rents it. The organization pays a flat rate, no matter how much—or how little—of it is used.

NOTE   In Europe, rough equivalents of T1 and T3 are E1 and E3, respectively.

Of the two lines, T1 is the most popular digital line technology. It uses a telecommunications scheme called *time-division multiplexing (TDM)* to squeeze 1.5 Mbps out of the line. TDM aggregates each stream of data into the line by assigning each stream a different time slot. T1 lines use copper wire, and you can lease one from your local telephone company. If 1.5 Mbps is too much throughput for your needs, you can also rent a portion of a T1 line called a *fractionalized T1*.

T3 lines are more robust versions of T1s. But whereas a T1 offers 1.5 Mbps, T3s offer 45 Mbps of data. T3 lines are typically used by Tier 1 ISPs. These are the big ISPs (such as Sprint) that connect smaller ISPs to the Internet. Like T1 lines, T3 lines can be fractionalized. This is a good thing, because the bandwidth and expense of a T3 line would be too much for most organizations to handle.

Frame Relay

The last WAN technology we'll discuss is frame relay. Frame relay switches packets across a network owned by a carrier, such as a regional telephone company, like AT&T. As Figure 1-10 shows, frame relay uses phone circuits to connect remote locations. The long distance hauls are carried over a telecommunications network owned by the frame relay provider and shared by a number of customers.

Frame relay is an appealing solution because it is cost efficient. Frame relay is so called because it converts data into variable-sized messages called *frames*. Network speed and performance are enhanced because session management and error correction are delegated to nodes located throughout the network.

Frame relay customers tend to rent permanent virtual circuits (PVCs). A PVC allows the customer a continuous, dedicated WAN link without having to pay for a leased line, as with a T1. As you recall, T1 and T3 are leased connections and you pay for the circuit, no matter how much of it you use. Conversely, frame relay customers are

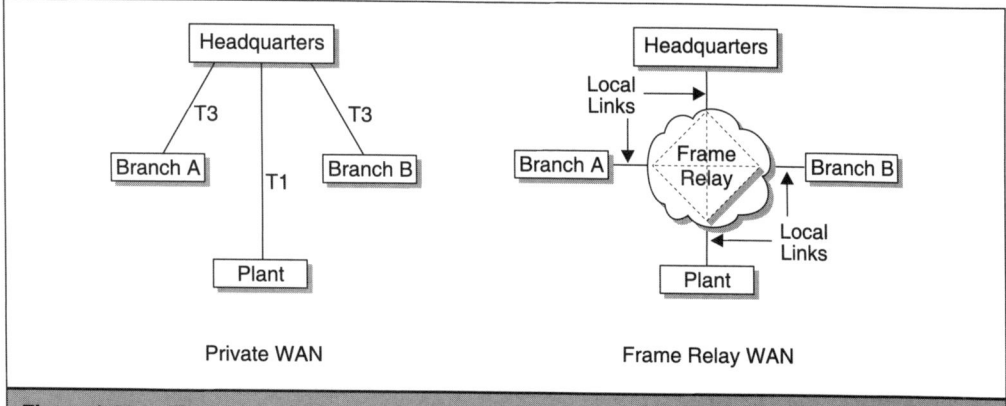

Figure 1-10. Frame relay is a more efficient WAN link for intermittent traffic.

only charged for the amount of the circuit they use. They can also establish a set level of service where QoS is determined based on the customer's service contract.

Frame relay networks reside on T1 or T3 trunks operated by the frame relay network operator. Use of frame relay makes economic sense when traffic isn't heavy enough to require a dedicated T1 or T3 connection.

Networking is a broad and expansive topic. To be sure, entire books can (and have) been written just on basic network functions. Our goal here was to discuss some of the basics of networking and internetworking. This will provide a foundation for our discussion of Windows XP Professional networking.

CHAPTER 2

Introduction to Windows XP Professional Networking

The first chapter was dedicated to understanding the basics of networking and computer data transfer. In this chapter, we turn our attention to Windows XP Professional—specifically what Windows XP Professional offers over earlier incarnations of Windows and how Windows XP Professional is used for networking. After covering those topics, we'll talk about making your transition to Windows XP Professional—be it from an earlier version of Windows or as a clean installation.

WHAT'S NEW IN WINDOWS XP PROFESSIONAL

If you even walked by a television set during the weeks surrounding Windows XP Professional's release, you were inundated with commercials touting its ease of use, improved graphics, and ability to handle digital photos and MP3s. This is all nice and good for the home user, but is there really anything new for networks and the enterprise user? The answer is, "Yes."

This section covers the new features found in Windows XP Professional—in terms of both overt network functionality and some built-in features that will only enhance your network's robustness and dependability.

Networking Features

Even though Windows XP includes prettier graphical user interfaces and slick multimedia capabilities, that doesn't mean it's lacking important tools for enterprises.

NOTE Technically, Microsoft refers to the Windows XP Professional desktop and working environment as an *Intelligent User Interface (IUI)*. You can decide for yourself if that's a good moniker or the result of a brainstorming session of Microsoft's overactive marketing department.

Some of the best improvements over earlier versions of Windows include wireless networking capabilities, remote access, and improved virtual private network (VPN) support.

Wireless

One of Windows XP Professional's major improvements over previous editions of Windows is its inclusion of wireless networking capabilities—specifically Wireless Ethernet, also known as Wi-Fi or 802.11b. In recent years, wireless networking has gained in popularity. First, the functionality can't be beat. Wireless networking doesn't require a Category 5 tether and delivers speeds at 11 megabits per second (Mbps). Even better, the price of wireless networking adapters has come down to less than US$100, and wireless networking access points (APs) are popping up in major metropolitan areas and airports.

We'll talk about the specifics of setting up a Wi-Fi connection in Chapter 5, but in this discussion, let's cover what Windows XP Professional brings to the wireless party. Windows XP Professional supports a number of wireless network adapters right out of the box, without the need to install third-party drivers. Because of this functionality, you can have a wireless network set up and running in just a few minutes. Figure 2-1 shows a wireless networking setup dialog box.

However, just because the network is easy to initially set up doesn't mean it's all smooth sailing. Even though Wi-Fi provides wireless networking, it is also a security hole through which you could drive a Sherman tank. Once you set up a wireless network in Windows XP Professional, it's a good idea to take the time to configure the appropriate security measures to keep unauthorized people out of your network. Remember, all it takes is someone with a laptop and a wireless adapter sitting in the parking lot, and your network can be compromised. Furthermore, someone in the same building could get into an unsecured wireless network with little more than a computer and a wireless adapter.

For more information about Windows XP Professional wireless networking, see Chapter 5.

Remote Features

Windows XP Professional also features two new remote access programs. To some degree, Remote Desktop and Remote Assistance complement each other. However, they are each distinct features with unique functionality. Let's take a closer look at these tools and explain what they do and how they can help, after which a discussion of Windows XP Professional's VPN capabilities is in order.

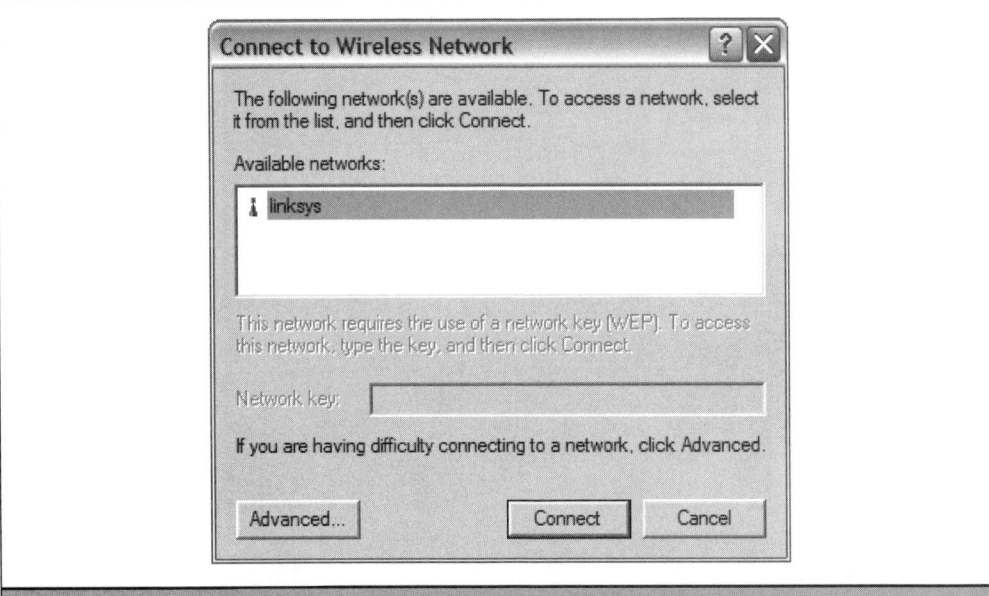

Figure 2-1. Setting up a wireless network is easier than ever with Windows XP Professional.

Remote Desktop   Windows XP Professional can act as a host that can be controlled from other Windows computers, whether they are running Windows XP Professional or an earlier version of Windows. This application provides some of the same remote control features found in longtime third-party desktop remote control applications PCAnywhere, Carbon Copy, and others. Figure 2-2 shows the Remote Desktop tool.

You need to be aware of a couple issues when working with Remote Desktop:

- As a security feature, Remote Desktop does not come enabled with the default installation. It must first be activated from the System Control Panel.
- Remote Desktop uses the standard Windows user access controls and security, actually logging into the host machine. But unlike third-party remote control applications, the remote control session completely takes over the host computer. This means anyone sitting at the host computer will see a mostly blank screen when Remote Desktop is enabled. Third-party remote control software generally lets a user sitting at the host machine see what's going on across the remote link.

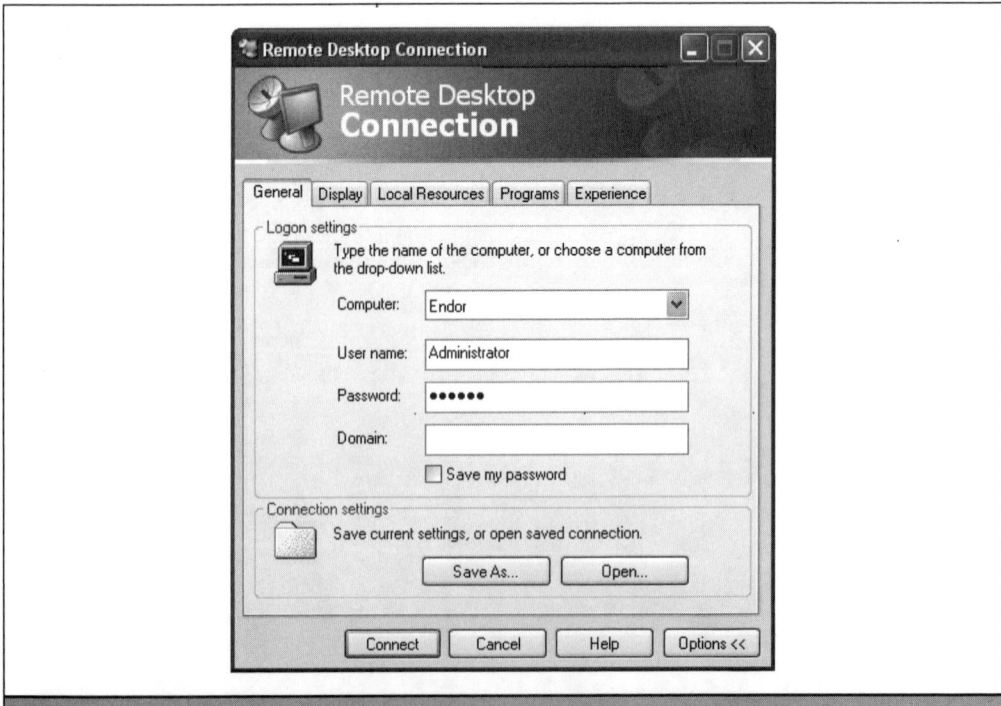

Figure 2-2.   The Remote Desktop tool allows a computer to be accessed remotely.

If a host user is accessing the host machine when a remote user wants to connect, the host user will be logged off. This is beneficial because if someone from an organization's support services department needs to troubleshoot problems with a PC, he or she can see what the host user was doing before the remote session was initiated, as long as the remote user enters the same logon information as the host user. The Internet Connection Firewall, or ICF (which is discussed in Chapter 5), must be disabled in order for Remote Desktop to operate properly.

NOTE Only one user can access a host computer remotely at one time.

Remote Desktop is also useful in environments where a user needs to log on to his or her machine from a remote location—be it a telecommuter synchronizing files or a road warrior accessing client files on his or her desktop PC.

Remote Assistance The second remote feature that comes with Windows XP Professional is called Remote Assistance. One of the advantages of Remote Assistance over Remote Desktop is that a remote machine can be controlled and both parties can review screen activity simultaneously.

NOTE This feature is only available when both machines are using Windows XP Professional. It does not work with earlier versions of Windows or with Windows XP Home Edition.

Remote Assistance enables IT departments and the local help desk staff to assist users troubleshoot a problem or demonstrate new applications. Remote Assistance sessions can be initiated via Windows Messenger or via e-mail. Be aware, however, that the latter can pose a security risk if not used properly. For e-mail invitations, a password must be sent (this need not be included in the e-mail, but can be communicated in a telephone call). You can also limit the amount of time that an invitation to control your desktop is extended.

There are three basic steps to using Remote Assistance:

1. The user requests assistance, either via messenger or e-mail. The e-mail will contain a specially encoded "ticket" as an attachment. This step is shown in Figure 2-3.
2. The expert answering needs to click the ticket or the request in Windows Messenger.
3. Both parties agree to initiate a Remote Assistance session.

Additionally, the expert can initiate an offer to help the user. Once connected, the expert and user can send text messages between themselves. Unfortunately, there are some hurdles to smooth Remote Assistance sessions. First, if the user and the expert are not on the same LAN, then Remote Assistance might not work. If one of the computers

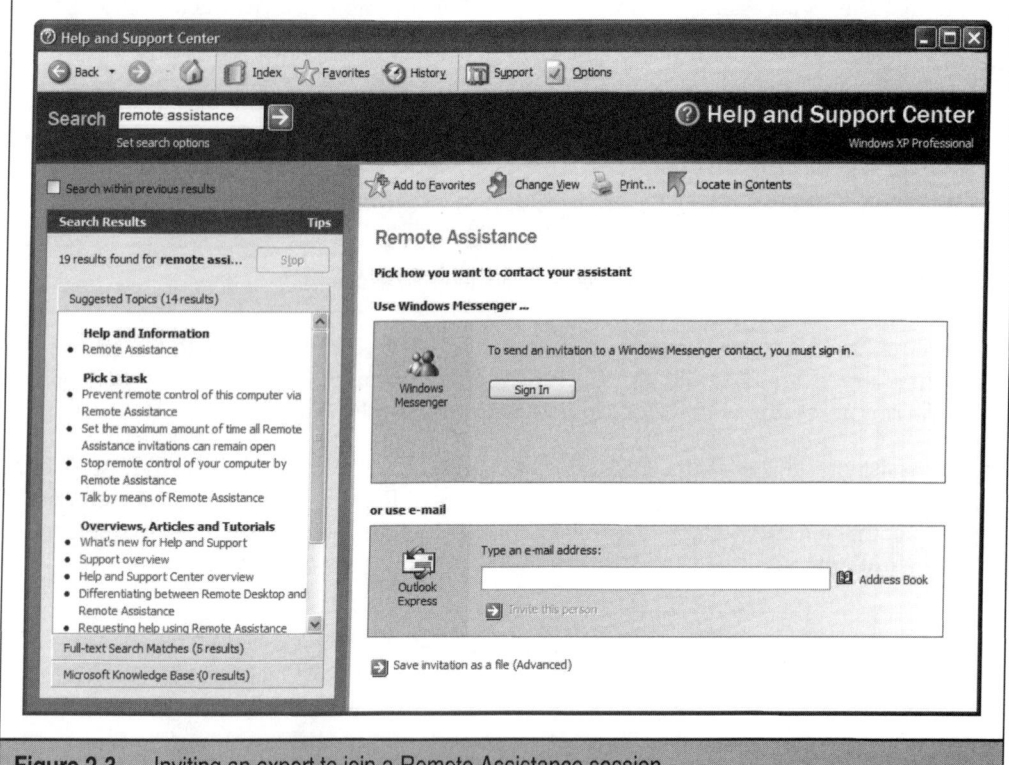

Figure 2-3. Inviting an expert to join a Remote Assistance session

is sitting behind a firewall and blocking port 3389, or is using Network Address Translation (NAT), the session might not work.

If an organization is worried about security, then Remote Assistance can be restricted via Group Policy. A number of permissions can be established, such as limiting Remote Assistance to devices within the organization's firewall or between computers on the same LAN.

VPNs To hear the evening news tell it, the Internet is a wanton place full of perverts and criminals. Whether you subscribe to this belief or not, some red flags should pop up in your mind when pondering the notion of transmitting your organization's sensitive data across this lawless etherworld. But even though there are a number of dangers, an organization can still protect itself against harm if it takes the appropriate steps.

Data sent across the Internet is not normally protected from evildoers. However, you can protect your organization's data by securing your communications and extending your private network across the Internet via a technology known as a virtual private network.

VPNs use a technique called *tunneling* to transfer private data across public networks (like the Internet) to a remote access server on your workplace network. A VPN saves you money, because you use the Internet, rather than employ a private WAN or make long-distance phone calls to connect to your network. The connection, made through Microsoft's Point-to-Point Tunneling Protocol (PPTP), is encrypted and secure. Authentication and encryption protocols are enforced by the remote access server.

Figure 2-4 shows a sample dialog box for creating a VPN connection.

There are two ways to create a VPN connection:

- **Dialing into an ISP**   If you dial into an ISP, your ISP makes another call to the private network's remote access server to establish the PPTP or Layer 2 Tunneling Protocol (L2TP) tunnel. Once authenticated, you can access the private network.
- **Connecting to the Internet**   If you are already connected to the Internet (whether on a LAN, cable modem, or DSL connection), you can create a tunnel through the Internet and connect directly to the remote server. Once the connection is authenticated, you can access the private network.

NOTE   We'll talk about setting up a Windows XP Professional VPN in more detail in Chapter 14.

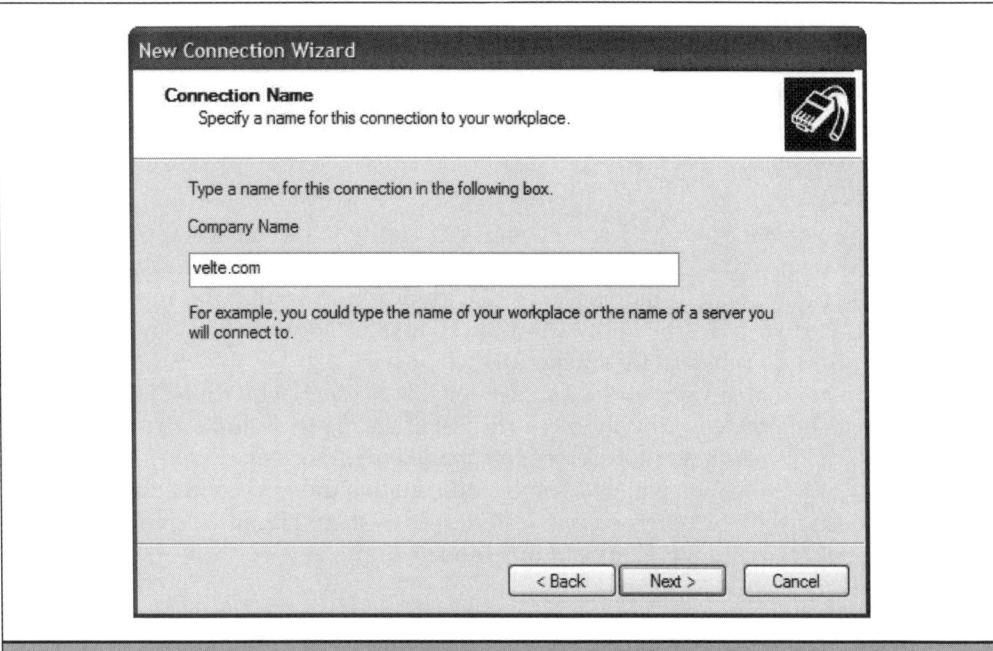

Figure 2-4.   Creating a VPN connection

Other Features

Because we're covering network administration in this book, we started with some of the topics that were most germane to the subject of networks and internetworks. However, there are several other features—new to Windows XP Professional—that will help build stable, secure networks.

Such features as stability, compatibility, and system restoration don't necessarily fit into the category of networking. However, thanks to these improvements, your networks will be better off.

Stability

One of the aspects of Windows XP Professional that Microsoft is heralding as an achievement is the operating system's reliability and stability. Though each incarnation of Windows has been proclaimed by Microsoft as more stable and more reliable than the one before, Windows XP Professional demonstrates a marked improvement over previous versions.

Windows XP Professional achieves this level of reliability and stability because it is not built on Windows 98 (as was XP's predecessor, Windows Me). Rather, XP is built on Windows NT and Windows 2000, which have proven themselves to be far more stable operating systems than Windows 9X. The reason that Windows 2000 and NT are more stable is that applications run in their own memory spaces. This prevents applications from becoming ensnarled in each other and causing problems.

Furthermore, Windows XP Professional also throws up a red flag to notify you if it thinks a driver may cause problems, because the source is unverified. In fact, Windows XP Professional includes a mechanism called *Driver Protection*, which blocks third-party drivers known to pose stability problems.

Compatibility

Another feature of Windows XP Professional is its ability to run legacy applications that weren't designed to run on Windows XP Professional. By using the *Compatibility Mode*, the user can emulate Windows 95 or NT, for example, so that the application will run properly. Furthermore, the application can be associated with the Compatibility Mode so that future problems are ameliorated.

One might ask that, if Windows XP Professional is so great, why isn't it inherently compatible with other flavors of Windows? The fact of the matter is that each successive version of Windows was never 100 percent compatible with the versions before it. At least Windows XP Professional allows some modicum of backward compatibility so that applications need not be tossed out with the old system. Figure 2-5 shows the setup dialog box for Windows Compatibility Mode.

System Restore

Still, Windows XP Professional is not 100 percent bulletproof. In the event there is a crash and the computer will not start except in Safe Mode, the operating system (OS)

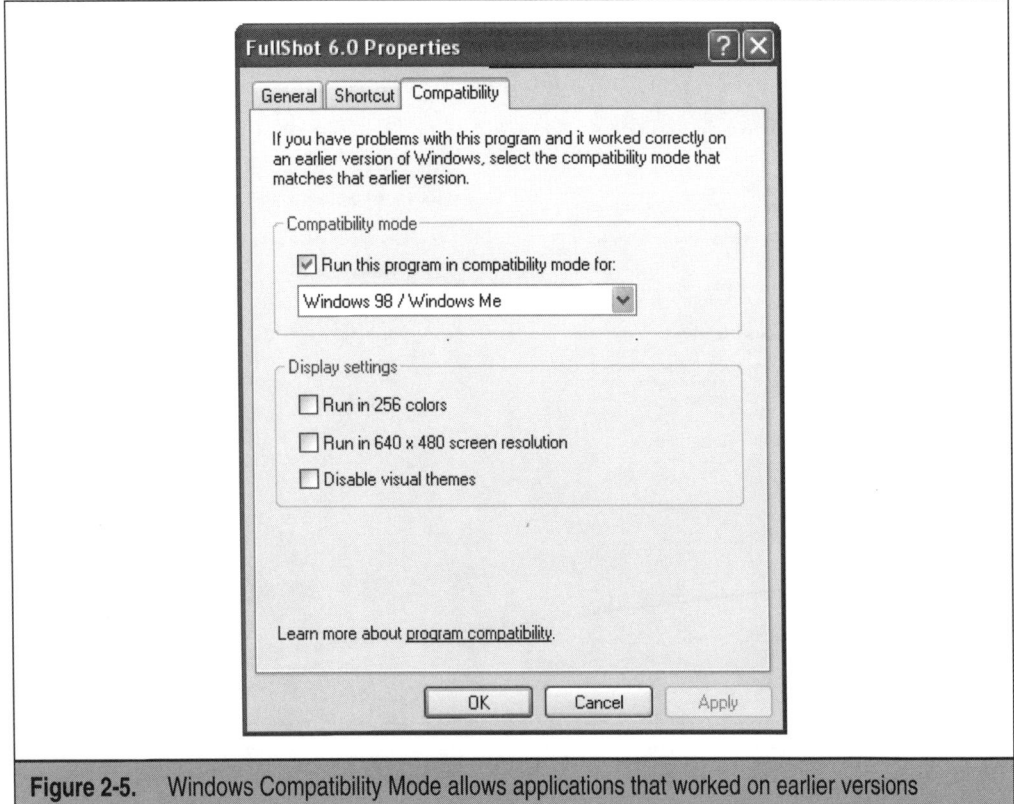

Figure 2-5. Windows Compatibility Mode allows applications that worked on earlier versions of Windows to remain functional.

offers a rollback feature called *System Restore*. This allows the user to roll back the machine settings to a time prior to any incident. So-called *restore points* can be established by the user anytime he or she desires. Also, the OS establishes its own restore points periodically and whenever new software is installed. By rolling back the computer to a restore point, the OS grabs its settings from a time when the OS was known to have worked properly. Figure 2-6 shows the setup screen for System Restore.

A feature that debuted with Windows 98 is still present in Windows XP Professional—automatic update. This allows the OS user to visit Microsoft's web site and download, free of charge, updates to Windows XP Professional.

Backing Up and Getting Help

Backing up and restoring computer files is easier with Windows XP Professional as well. Built into the OS is the ability to use any type of media that you choose for backup purposes. In the past, Windows required you to make a backup file, and then it was

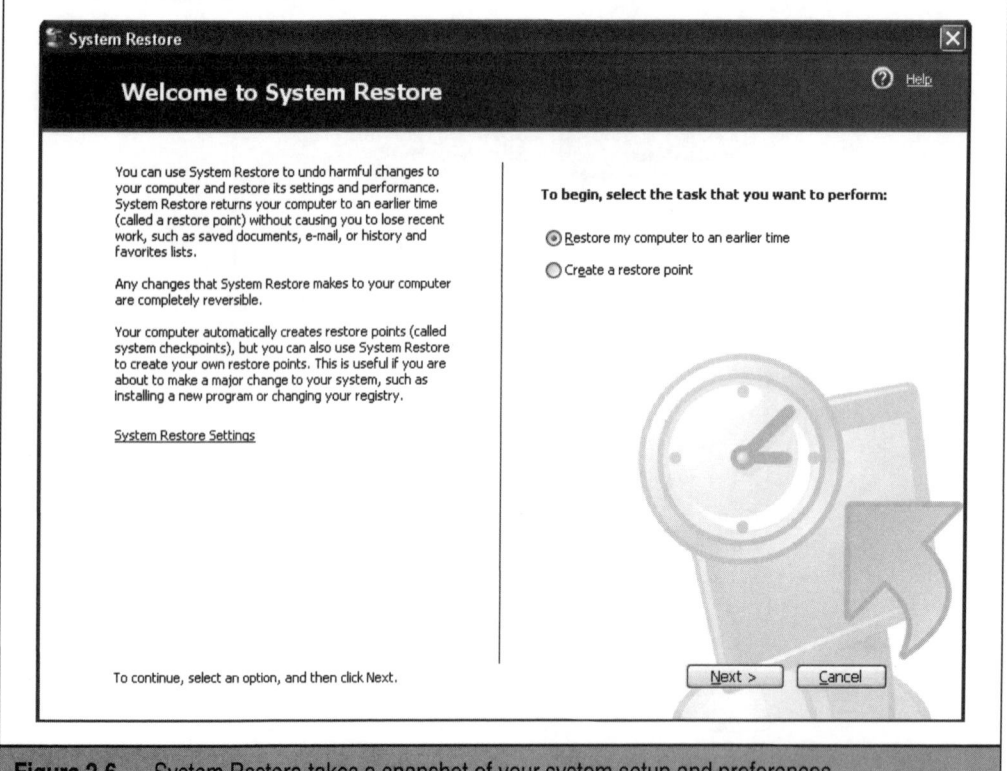

Figure 2-6. System Restore takes a snapshot of your system setup and preferences.

up to you to use a third-party application and burn it onto a CD-ROM or send it to a tape drive. In Windows XP Professional, there is built-in support for backing up to CD-ROMs, tape drives, and other media.

Finally, the help system in Windows XP Professional has been entirely revamped. New in Windows XP Professional is the *Help and Support Center,* which integrates content from developers and other third parties. While accessing the Help and Support Center, a user can get online help from Microsoft or from a friend using the Remote Assistance feature.

WINDOWS XP PROFESSIONAL NETWORKING FEATURES

As the world becomes more dependent on computer networks and the Internet, so must the pace of making networking powerful and easy increase. This section examines what Windows XP Professional offers, specifically, to networking. Topics covered include file systems, Internet Connection Sharing (ICS), and security.

File Systems

One of the first steps in a Windows XP Professional migration is to decide whether you will use FAT32 (FAT being short for file allocation table) or NTFS (which stands for New Technology File System). In fact, XP will prompt you to designate the file system on the partition where XP will be installed. The preferred file system is NTFS, although FAT32 works just as well. The only difference is that NTFS offers many more features (especially security features) that you might prefer to use.

Table 2-1 lists some of the differences between FAT and NTFS.

NTFS Is Robust

One look at Table 2-1 reveals a number of differences between FAT and NTFS. But as you look through the table, you'll notice that the differences go beyond naming conventions and multiple extensions. NTFS is a more robust file system for file servers because it is recoverable and offers hot fixing. NTFS is *recoverable* because it logs all directory and file updates.

If for any reason the system fails, NTFS will automatically complete the process begun during the interruption. This ensures that all changes to the file system will be completed, even in the event of an interruption. Another reliability feature of NTFS drives is called *hot fixing*. Hot fixing senses bad sectors on a disk drive, transfers all the data from the bad sector over to a good sector, and then flags the sector as "bad." This all occurs without the application even knowing that there was a problem.

Furthermore, NTFS has built-in compression for user data. You can designate which directories or drives are to be compressed. Then, when a file is moved to one of those locations, it is compressed. This process is invisible to both the user and the application. The amount of compression you can expect depends on the file type.

FAT32	NTFS
8 characters in filenames.	Up to 255 characters in filenames.
3-character extensions.	Multiple extensions with many "." (dots).
Not case sensitive, case not preserved.	Not case sensitive, case preserved.
4 gigabytes (GB) maximum file size.	16 terabytes (TB) minus 64 kilobytes (KB) maximum file size.
Volumes from 512 megabytes (MB) to 2TB. Windows XP Professional allows volumes to be just 32GB.	Recommended minimum volume size is 10MB. Recommended practical maximum is 2TB (although much larger sizes are possible).
4,177,920 maximum files per volume.	4,294,967,295 maximum files per volume.

Table 2-1. Key Differences Between the FAT System and NTFS

NTFS Is More Secure

A major design goal for NTFS was to make the file system more secure—moving it from its DOS roots and toward a UNIX model. NTFS accomplishes this by assigning a security descriptor to each file, storing it as part of the file. This descriptor outlines the following:

- Who created the file
- What users and groups may access it and at what level

Before an application is allowed to open the file, NTFS checks to see if the user or process has the permissions to access the file. In a small office or home setting, this might not seem important, but in a large network, it is crucial.

FAT has taken its knocks over the last page or so, but that's not to suggest it's bad. FAT has less overhead and is ideal for small hard drives. NTFS uses such large overhead that floppies cannot use NTFS formatting because the overhead is so great that it would overwrite the entire floppy. Furthermore, FAT is all you really need for DOS and Windows 95 systems or if you need access to drives from these OSs and XP. Finally, you can always convert your hard drive from FAT to NTFS. The reverse is not true, however. Once you go to NTFS, you can't go back.

You can either elect to convert to NTFS when Windows XP Professional is being installed, or you can do it at a later date by using the CONVERT utility at the command line:

```
convert <drive:> /fs:ntfs
```

where *<drive:>* is the letter of the drive you want to convert. If CONVERT can't get exclusive access to the drive, you will have to reboot so the conversion can take place on startup.

Internet Connection Sharing

Internet Connection Sharing enables a Windows computer to share its Internet connection with other computers on the LAN. This is a great feature for small offices or home LANs that might have a lone connection to the Internet. ICS isn't new to Windows XP Professional. In fact, it's been around since Windows 98 SE. Happily, in Windows XP Professional, it's gotten better. ICS in Windows XP Professional offers the following advantages over earlier versions:

- ICS is easier to set up. There is no additional software to install, and it doesn't add any network components or protocols.
- It's more reliable and less likely to cause network problems.
- You can create a network bridge by connecting two or more LANs and sharing the Internet connection with all the computers on them. This is useful if your Windows XP Professional computers are connected to both conventional and wireless networks.

Figure 2-7 shows the ICS tool.

Figure 2-7. The Windows XP Professional ICS tool

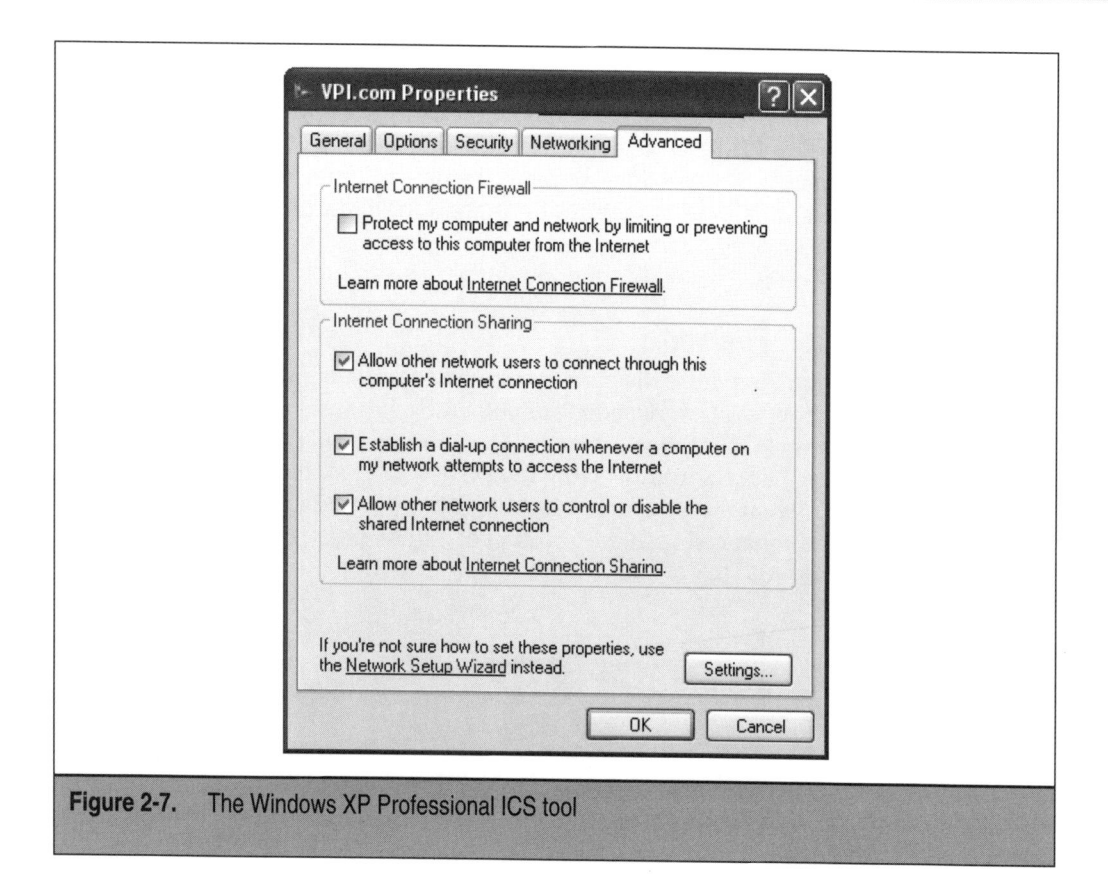

However, ICS under Windows XP Professional is missing some good features from its earlier incarnations. You can't disable the DHCP server, change the server computer's IP address, or change the range of addresses allocated by the DHCP server. As such, there are some things to be aware of when using Windows XP Professional ICS:

- When you enable ICS, the network adapter connected to the LAN is assigned a static IP address of 192.168.0.1. The client computers are assigned other IP addresses in the 192.168.0.2–254 range. These addresses may not be compatible with an existing network.

- Don't enable ICS if any computer in your network is configured as a domain controller (DC), DHCP server, or DNS server. Don't enable it if another computer is running ICS or NAT.

- If you establish a VPN connection while sharing a different connection, the client computers won't be able to access the Internet until the VPN connection is ended.

With these caveats in mind, ICS is a great tool to use to get multiple computers on the Internet via a lone connection.

Security

Like so many of Windows XP Professional's other features, security tools that were once only available from third-party vendors as add-ons are part of Windows XP Professional's functionality. This section examines the new Internet Connection Firewall, thwarting virus attacks, and security features from previous editions of Windows that worked so well, Microsoft brought them back for more action. That's not to mean that XP is bulletproof, however. We'll also talk about potential security breaches.

Internet Connection Firewall

The Internet Connection Firewall is ideal for users who access the Internet via cable or DSL connection. These types of connections are vulnerable because of their "always on" functionality. The Internet Connection Firewall causes the computer to be "invisible" on the Internet, preventing hackers from viewing the PC as a target. The firewall, however, has been described by researchers from the Gartner Group as "rudimentary." For best results, security will be enhanced with the addition of a third-party firewall. Figure 2-8 shows the ICF tool.

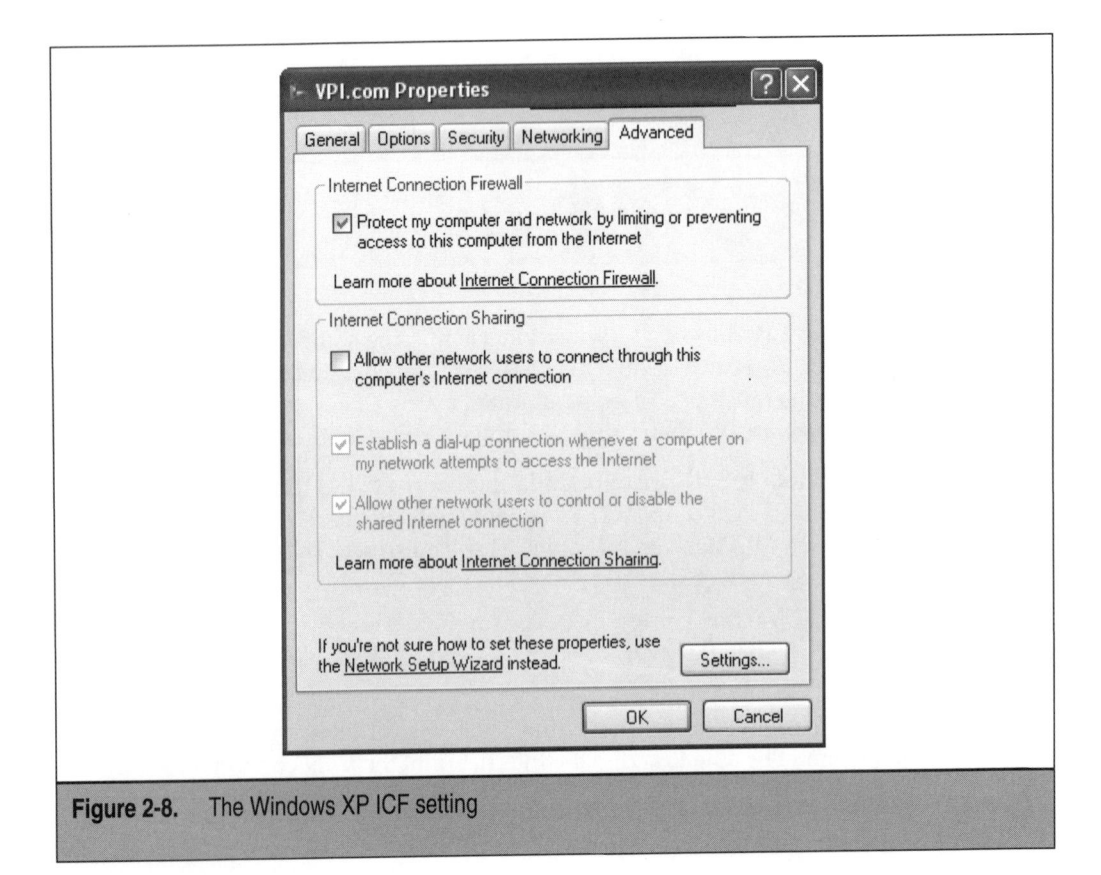

Figure 2-8. The Windows XP ICF setting

Virus Blocking

Virus attacks are dealt with via a new software restriction policy. This policy allows administrators to block executable code that could delete files or cause other damage when an unwitting user opens a malicious file. In conjunction with this tool, McAfee, a company that specializes in virus protection, has optimized its VirusScan Online antivirus software specifically for Windows XP Professional. This software is automatically updated via the Internet when new viruses are added to McAfee's database.

If It Works, It Works

The fundamental code of Windows XP Professional has been solidified over earlier versions of Windows. As previously noted, Windows XP Professional is based on Windows NT code, and as such is inherently more difficult for a hacker to attack than Windows 98 or Me, for instance.

Other NT-esque additions to Windows XP Professional include the Windows NT file system, which allows users to establish user IDs and access controls on files within the computer. This is useful when more than one person is using the same computer (be it at home or in the workplace). A file created by one user cannot be accessed by another user.

Potential Security Holes

Unfortunately, Windows XP Professional is not without its weaknesses. Several features in Windows XP Professional can be used by hackers to gain access to the system.

For example, Windows XP Professional automatically sends information between the PC and Microsoft about product registration, bugs, and software updates. Furthermore, the remote control feature allows an organization's help desk or administrator to manage the computer from his or her own PC. These are both points of attack for intruders.

Windows XP Professional is yet another step in Microsoft's journey away from the desktop and toward Web services. Microsoft's .NET program stores applications and information on servers connected to the Internet and accessible from any location. Although this might be useful within the framework of the .NET initiative, it also poses a point of attack that a hacker might be able to exploit.

While Windows XP Professional is largely more secure than earlier versions of Windows, it is not perfect—there are many places where an attacker can probe the network. Still, Windows XP Professional incorporates virus protection, firewall protection, and overall user security.

Kerberos

A security feature implemented in Windows 2000—and carried over to Windows XP Professional—is Kerberos version 5. The Kerberos protocol provides a means for mutual authentication between a client (whether a user, computer, or service) and a server.

Kerberos provides a very effective and efficient way to furnish authentication, even in very large networks. The protocol operates under the assumption that initial transactions between clients and servers take place on an unsecured network. As such, an unauthorized user can pose as either client or server and intercept or tamper with authentication communications.

Kerberos uses secret key encryption to protect logon credentials as they traverse the network. The same key can then be used to decrypt these credentials at the receiving station. The decryption and subsequent logon tasks are performed by the domain controller's Kerberos Key Distribution Center (KDC).

NOTE Domain controllers are explained in more detail in Chapter 6.

NOTE Kerberos is named for the two-headed dog that guards Hades. Who knew it needed guarding?

An *authenticator* is a piece of information (such as a time stamp, for instance) that is different each time it is generated. The authenticator is used with each encrypted logon to ensure that previous logon credentials are not being reused.

If the initial logon credentials are accepted, then the KDC issues a ticket-granting ticket (TGT) that is used by the Local Security Authority (LSA) to get service tickets. These service tickets can be used to access network resources without having to reauthenticate the client—as long as the service ticket remains valid. The tickets contain encrypted data that confirms the user's identity to the requested service. With the exception of entering a password or smart-card credentials, the process is transparent to the user.

Figure 2-9 illustrates the Kerberos logon procedure.

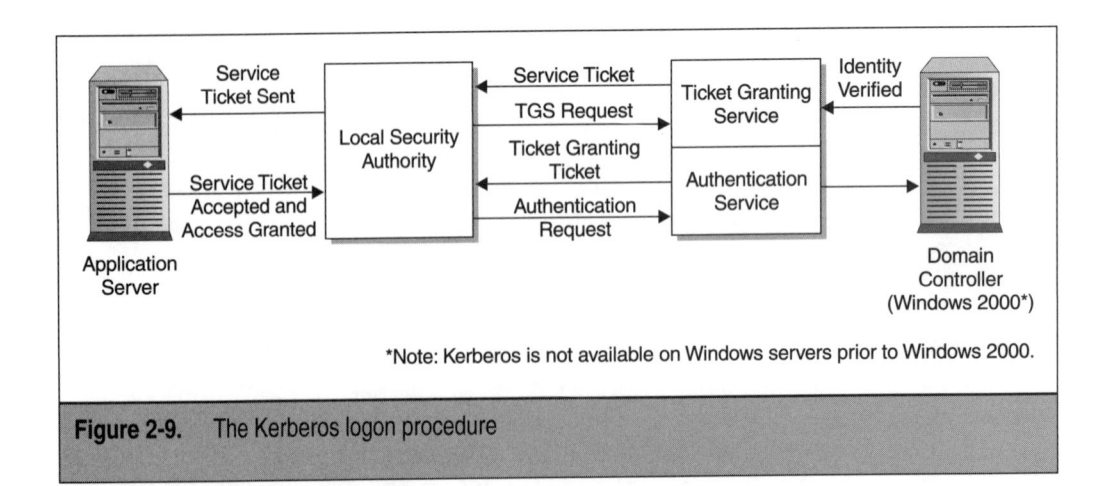

*Note: Kerberos is not available on Windows servers prior to Windows 2000.

Figure 2-9. The Kerberos logon procedure

UPGRADING FROM WINDOWS NT/9X/2000

The last section of this chapter gets into the meat and potatoes of your own network. All the talk about Windows XP Professional's enhancements over earlier versions of Windows is nice, but how can you make the move from your existing system to a Windows XP Professional system? We'll talk about upgrading from an earlier version of Windows and actually making the move.

System Requirements

Checking your system requirements is a lot like checking the gas pump to ensure that you're using unleaded. Unless you are using a computer with enough juice, Windows XP Professional installation will be an exercise in futility and aggravation.

This section examines the system minimums for Windows XP Professional (along with a quick talk about the 64-bit version of Windows XP Professional) and explores some tools for checking your system to ensure compatibility.

Windows XP Professional

With each new version of Windows, the system minimums continue to grow. It should come as no surprise that Windows XP Professional isn't going to work on your old 25 MHz, 2MB RAM machine. Forget that it doesn't have a CD-ROM drive and possibly the last 5.25-inch floppy drive on the face of the Earth—it just doesn't have enough juice.

In order to get Windows XP Professional to work, your computer must meet the following minimum requirements:

- 300 MHz or higher processor (recommended); 233 MHz minimum; Intel Pentium/Celeron family, or AMD K6/Athlon/Duron family, or compatible processor recommended.
- 128MB of RAM or higher recommended (64MB minimum is supported, but may limit performance and some features).
- 1.5GB of available hard disk space.
- Super VGA (800×600) or higher-resolution video adapter and monitor.
- CD-ROM or DVD drive.
- Keyboard and mouse or compatible pointing device.

It can't be stressed often enough: this just represents the bare minimum to install Windows XP Professional. If you want it to work faster and more efficiently, you'll need more power in any, if not all, of the aforementioned areas.

Windows XP Professional 64-Bit Edition

Even though we aren't specifically discussing Windows XP Professional 64-Bit Edition in this book, you might find that it better suits your organization's needs. Let's take a moment to look at what the 64-bit version offers and what its requirements are.

Windows XP Professional and Windows XP Professional 64-Bit Edition differ in both performance and capacity. As such, setup, disk space, and device driver requirements also differ. Likewise, so does some software installation and running some applications, such as the Microsoft Management Console (MMC).

System Requirements   Table 2-2 outlines the differences between Windows XP Professional and Windows XP Professional 64-Bit Edition.

Device Drivers   Because Windows XP Professional 64-Bit Edition is a 64-bit environment, it requires 64-bit drivers. Some device drivers allow the installation of both the 32- and 64-bit drivers from the same .inf file. The extension .ia64 is used within the .inf file of these drivers to identify the installation files that can be installed on a 64-bit system. Earlier incarnations of Windows won't recognize the .ia64 extension.

> **NOTE**   Be aware of the verbiage on device packaging. Even though a package says it is compatible with Windows XP Professional doesn't mean the device is compatible with Windows XP Professional 64-Bit Edition.

MMC   Starting with Windows 2000, Microsoft began including the Microsoft Management Console (MMC) with its operating systems. This is a central management application into which snap-ins are plugged, allowing customized management environments. The use of the snap-ins allows administrators to monitor and manage a plethora of data from a single location, without having extraneous data to sift through. The MMC can be used to manage Group Policy and network details. Furthermore, the use of snap-ins allows third-party software designers to generate their own snap-ins. Figure 2-10 shows the MMC.

In the 64-Bit Edition, both the 64- and 32-bit versions of the MMC are included. By default, the 64-bit version is activated; however, the 32-bit version can be selected if needed. Snap-ins are not interchangeable between versions of the MMC. Windows XP Professional looks at the number of snap-ins available on your system, and activates the version based on an algorithm's analysis of the snap-ins available.

Component	Windows XP Professional	Windows XP Professional 64-Bit Edition
CPU (minimum)	233 MHz	733 MHz
CPU (recommended)	300 MHz	N/A
RAM (minimum)	64MB	1GB
RAM (recommended)	128MB	N/A
Hard drive space	1.5GB	1.5GB

Table 2-2.   Windows XP Professional and Windows XP Professional 64-Bit Edition System Requirements

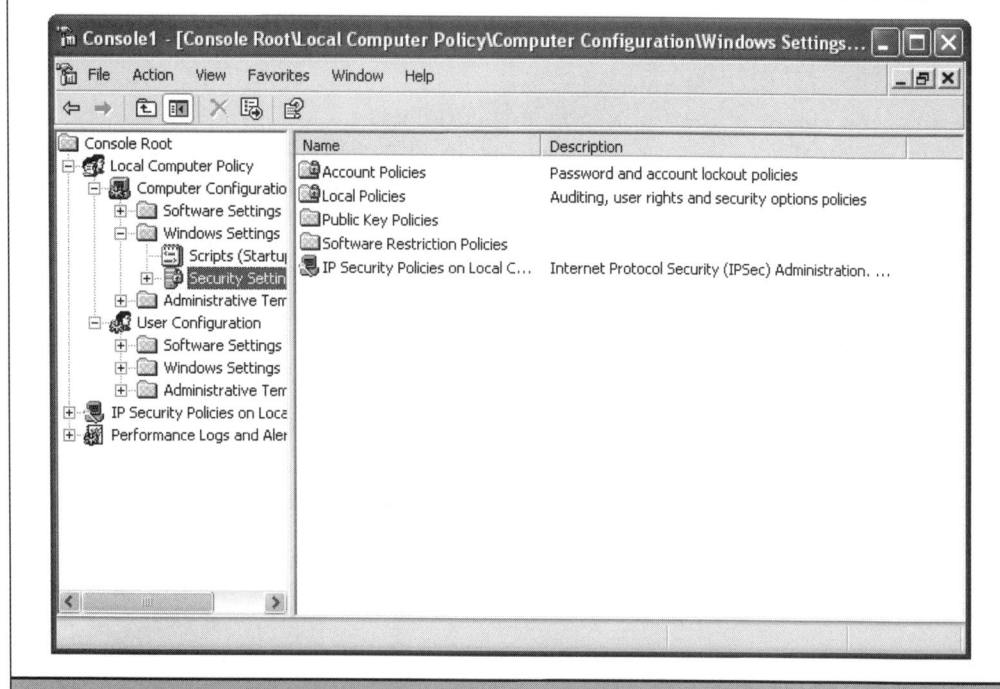

Figure 2-10. The MMC in Windows XP Professional

Dual-Boot Installations

If you already have Windows NT, Windows 2000, or Windows 98 installed on your computer, you have the option of upgrading the existing OS or installing a new copy of Windows XP Professional alongside it. For instance, if you choose to install a new copy in tandem with NT, you will have at least two OSs into which you can boot your machine. This is called a *dual-boot system*.

If you choose to have DOS or Windows 9X as an alternate OS on your dual-boot system, you must have at least one partition formatted as a FAT partition. For best results and the least errors, this OS should be installed prior to the Windows XP Professional installation. It is highly recommend that you locate Windows XP Professional on its own partition. Although the OS resides in its own directory, if you install multiple copies of Windows on the same partition, they will write to the same Program Files directory that is used by the other Windows OSs. XP may write over some files there or change the permissions on some important files that might disable a boot into the alternate OS. Furthermore, if you have selected NTFS for your XP file system, it is impossible to keep NTFS files on a drive formatted for FAT.

Compatibility

To help you ensure your computer, hardware, and software are compatible with Windows XP Professional, Microsoft has provided a product compatibility checking page at its web site (http://www.microsoft.com/windowsxp/pro/howtobuy/upgrading/compat.asp). Because the page is so lengthy, Microsoft has streamlined the compatibility check process. Users can input their computer and hardware model or software version and the site will do the rest. Figure 2-11 shows what this web page looks like.

If you are unsure about a specific model, the Product Compatibility site allows you to enter a type of hardware, plus the vendor name. Figure 2-12 shows the result of a search for Hewlett-Packard LaserJet printers. With no specific model selected, the search generated a list of all compatible Hewlett-Packard LaserJets.

Even if you don't check the Product Compatibility list before you install Windows 2000, during installation the program will take you to the Product Compatibility web page and you can check your hardware and software. However, it's a good idea to determine your computer's readiness before you start the installation.

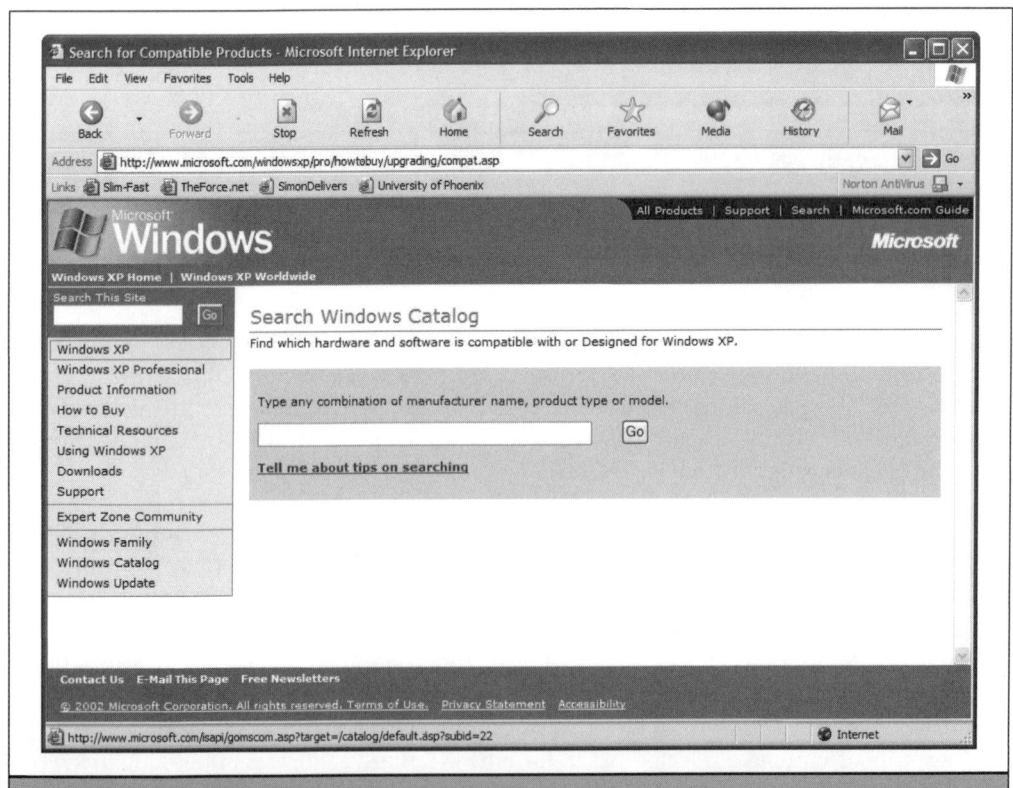

Figure 2-11. Specific brands and models of computers, hardware, and software can be checked against Microsoft's Product Compatibility list.

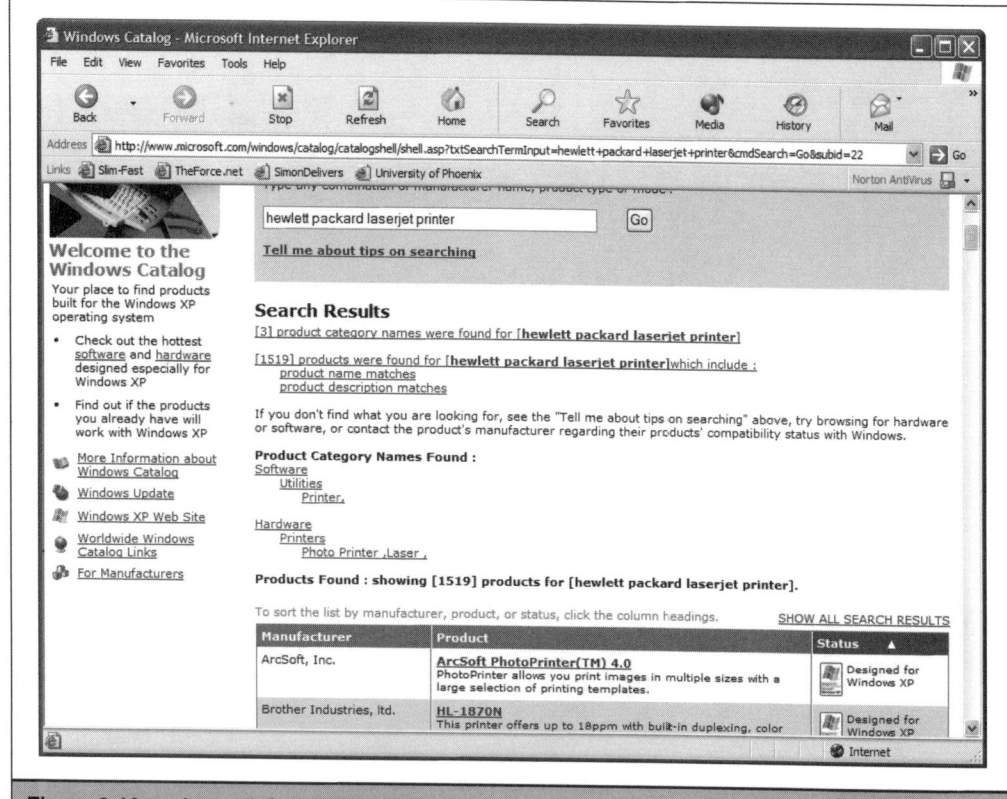

Figure 2-12. A search for Hewlett-Packard LaserJet printers produces many matches.

If the thought of sifting through pages of devices is too much for you to stomach, there is an alternative, an application Microsoft has developed and made available for download (http://www.microsoft.com/windowsxp/pro/howtobuy/upgrading/advisor.asp). The Windows XP Professional Upgrade Advisor (shown in Figure 2-13) checks your system, generating a list of compatible and incompatible devices.

NOTE The upgrade advisor is a little more than 8MB, so depending on your Internet connection, it might take a while to download.

Advanced Hardware

Certainly, the systems you build should exceed the minimum requirements outlined in the last section. How much hardware you add to your system depends heavily on the designated role for the computer and your budget. The major areas of upgrade include RAM, hard drives, and processors. We will consider each of these areas briefly.

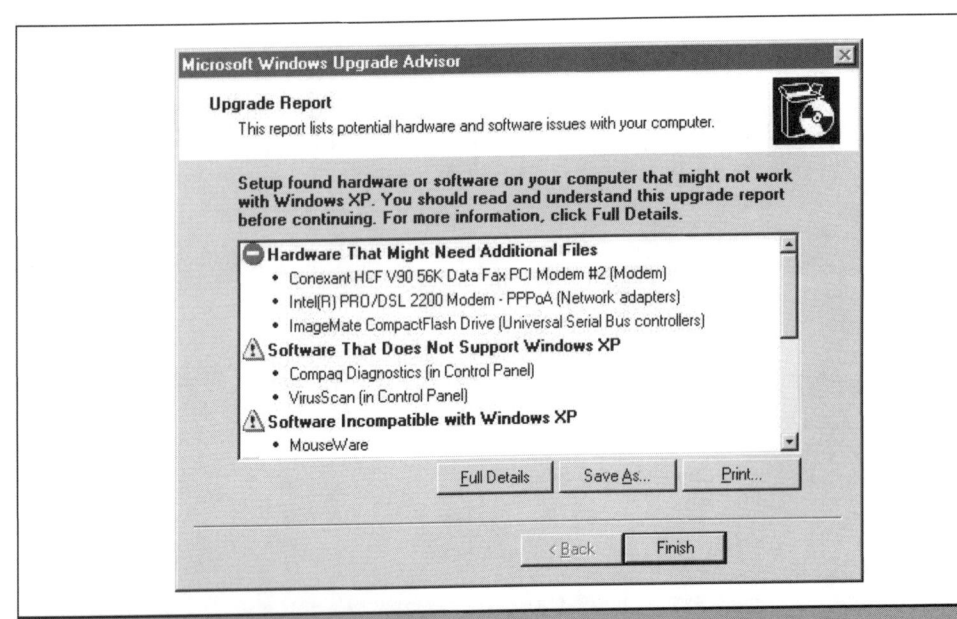

Figure 2-13. The Windows XP Professional Upgrade Advisor checks your system for any potential incompatibilities with Windows XP Professional.

RAM XP loves RAM. A few years ago, RAM was expensive. So expensive, in fact, it was seen as a major impediment for users to migrate to a Windows environment. Happily, now that RAM prices have taken a sharp nosedive, it doesn't cost as much as the computer itself to boost the RAM up to 256MB. Five years ago, if you had mentioned a workstation with 256MB RAM, people would roll their eyes, guffaw, and fidget nervously with their wallets. Now, however, 256MB is a good starting point for memory. Even so, for some specialized workstations (like those used for CAD or graphic design) 256MB might not be enough. It's not uncommon to see these machines with 512MB or even 1GB. The best bet is to start with 256MB for workstations and 512MB on servers and work your way up from there.

NOTE For the sake of simplicity in upgrading, make sure you use the largest capacity SIMMs you can, right from the start. For instance, if you have 8 slots, don't fill them all with 64MB SIMMs. It's best to buy two sticks of 128MB, leaving you with two slots to use for future upgrades.

Hard Drives When Microsoft recommends 1.5GB of free hard drive space for an XP installation, they are referring only to the OS and nothing else. If you install Windows XP Professional on a system with only 1.5GB, you'll be disappointed to learn that it is enough to install the system, but not enough to actually *run* the system. It's more than a little likely that you'll be adding an application or two on top of the OS, which is sure to absorb even more hard drive space. Furthermore, you'll need room for XP's swapfile on at least one drive. This is the file that the OS uses when the RAM employed actually exceeds the amount of physical memory present in the machine. It uses the swapfile as *virtual memory*. This file can be upwards of 50MB or more even before it is used.

Fortunately, if you try to buy a hard drive in today's market, you're not too likely to find one with just 2GB of space. It's important to be aware of the space limitations in case you're trying to install XP on an existing system or cobbling one together from spare parts in a closet.

Multiprocessor Systems If you have an especially demanding application or are expecting many users to use a particular server, you should consider getting a computer with symmetric multiprocessors (SMP). XP Professional ships with support for two processors. SMP systems may seem too good to be true, and indeed there are some caveats. You shouldn't expect to double your performance by doubling your processors. In fact, there have been some cases where adding a processor caused the system to actually run slower. When adding an extra processor, there is some OS overhead involved. Furthermore, code must be written specifically to take advantage of multiprocessor machines.

Upgrading from Another Flavor of Windows

Since the Windows OS is the big dog on the block, it is fair to assume that you already have some flavor of Windows installed on your network. Depending on which version of Windows you're upgrading from, you might discover that you have a fair amount of work to perform.

Regrettably, the Windows XP Professional upgrade path will not work with any machine running Windows 95 or Windows 3.X. If you are a license holder, you can purchase an upgrade, but you'll still have to perform the installation on a clean system.

NOTE If you are still running machines with Windows 95 or 3.X, it isn't just the OS code that is incompatible; it's likely that much of your system's hardware is outdated as well. Earlier in this chapter we listed the hardware minimums for Windows XP Professional. It's a safe bet any computer with Windows 95 or 3.X isn't going to cut the mustard for Windows XP Professional system minimums.

Your best bet, if you have machines with Windows 95 or 3.X, is to bite the bullet and buy new machines. Chances are, if the last time you bought workstations was in 1995 or earlier, you're more than due for an upgrade. Even better, if you buy new machines, they'll come with Windows XP Professional preinstalled.

Upgrading from Windows 98 or Me might require some additional planning on your part. The main issue is the Registry structure and the setup process. If you do choose to upgrade your machines, some things aren't going to work with Windows XP Professional and might have to be uninstalled before any upgrade takes place. Such Windows 98 system tools as ScanDisk, PCAnywhere, and DriveSpace cannot be upgraded to Windows XP Professional.

The easiest upgrade path is from Windows NT and Windows 2000, because these versions have the most features in common with Windows XP Professional.

Migration Preparation

There are things you can do now to ensure an easy migration later and reduce the disruption of service common to new deployments. First, we'll discuss how to organize your new network. Then, we'll look at how you can prepare for a Windows XP Professional migration, including hardware and software considerations.

Migrating to XP

As with any migration to a new OS, the process is anything but a simple matter of inserting the installation CD-ROM into the CD-ROM drive and letting the computer do all the work. The process requires careful planning, meticulous testing, and a well-designed rollout.

The easiest way to migrate to Windows XP Professional is to buy workstations that have it preinstalled. This avoids any configuration problems with the machines, causing fewer headaches. However, since you're likely to be operating on some sort of budget, this might not be the most feasible plan.

If you decide to migrate from an existing Windows platform, Microsoft recommends a four-stage deployment plan, shown in Table 2-3.

These steps are explained in greater detail below.

NOTE Obviously, for one or two PCs, this is overkill. These steps are meant for large organizations with PCs that have a standard configuration.

Logical Design The logical design stage involves picking the preferred features and configuration options of your "ideal" Windows XP Professional system configuration for both desktop and mobile users. This is the stage at which you should consider network parameters and protocols as well as your file system structure and applications that will be used on the system. For instance, if you will be using a certain word processor, will it

Design Stage	Purpose
Logical design	To determine the fundamental features and framework of the preferred Windows XP Professional configuration
Lab test	To build, configure, and test your design in a controlled environment
Implementation design	To evaluate and select Windows XP Professional automated installation methods
Pilot design	To approve the pilot Windows XP Professional configuration and implementation process

Table 2-3. Design Stages for Migration to Windows XP Professional

be compatible with Windows XP Professional? It's best to check with the Microsoft web site to make sure everything will run properly.

Additionally, now's the time to think about file system structure. Windows XP Professional supports FAT16, FAT32, and NTFS. As we pointed out earlier, NTFS offers the most advantages, including support for encrypted files and larger disk volumes, along with better security features and reliability.

Test System The next stage is to build a test system. At this stage, you will take your "ideal" system and install it on a few computers in an isolated lab. Don't connect this test lab to your production network. You want to test your system to ensure that it operates properly and that you have all the necessary device drivers.

> **NOTE** Windows XP Professional is compatible with a slew of device drivers, right out of the box. However, in the event a peripheral or two is not supported by Windows XP Professional, it is a good idea to go to your peripheral manufacturer's web site and check for updated device drivers.

Implementation Design Once you've tweaked and fine-tuned your Windows XP Professional system in an isolated lab, you should decide how you will deliver the new OS to your system. Again, this method should be tested in your lab to ferret out any problems that might arise.

You could run around from computer to computer with an installation disk and a list of product keys, but with Windows XP Professional, you can install the OS automatically from your administration PC. One of the chief determiners in what rollout method you choose will be dependent on whether or not you use Active Directory, which is included with versions of Windows 2000 Server. If you do, you'll have access to several Group Policy tools and more deployment choices.

Pilot Design In the last phase, you should roll out Windows XP Professional to a few users and perform some last minute checks before making the final rollout. Finally, you conduct your rollout using any one of a half-dozen different installation options, which are explained in the following section.

Installation Options

When you're ready to install Windows XP Professional on your client workstations, it is possible to perform the upgrades in several ways. The installation path you choose should be based on a number of factors. What method you opt for will be dependent on how you answer these questions:

- Are you upgrading from an existing OS or performing a clean installation?
- How many computers are in the deployment?
- Are you willing to let the users install the OS themselves, or do you want to perform unattended installations?
- How much customization is necessary for the installations?

- What hardware is available and how do they differ?
- Are you using Active Directory?

By answering the preceding questions, and reading the following paragraphs on installation paths, you should be able to decide which method is best for your organization.

Unattended Installation   Unattended installation allows installation to occur—big shock—unattended. Using this method, scripts answer questions during setup. You can use Setup Manager 3.0 to guide you through the process of setting up unattended scripts. To start an unattended installation, run WINNT32.EXE from the command prompt on a computer with Windows NT 4.0, 98, or 2000 installed, then choose the appropriate command options to run the scripts.

Advantages of unattended installation include the following:

- Scripts save time and money by cutting down on manpower costs.
- The OS can be simultaneously deployed on numerous computers.
- Scripts can be written so that users can provide varying levels of input during the installation, thus allowing more flexibility for the administrator and the installer.

The disadvantage of unattended installation is that only OS upgrades can be performed. Clean installations cannot be done automatically.

NOTE   Actually, clean installations can be performed automatically, but they require the use of third-party software. However, when using only the tools available from Microsoft, automatically performing a clean installation is not possible.

SysPrep   The System Preparation tool (SYSPREP.EXE) allows you to take a "snapshot" of a configured client, and then send that image to multiple clients using a third-party tool, such as Symantec Ghost Corporate Edition 7.5. This process is also called *cloning*, *disk-image copying*, or *ghost imaging*.

The advantages of cloning include the following:

- Sharp reduction in deployment time, as every component (OS, applications, settings, and so forth) is configured once, and then deployed to client machines without user interaction.
- The image can be burned onto a CD-ROM (see the next section, "Bootable CD-ROM") and distributed to clients without network access.
- Using a clone allows standardized desktops, administrative policies, and restrictions.
- SysPrep does not perform full plug-and-play enumeration, which reduces this portion of the setup from 30 minutes to a few minutes for each computer.

This method does have some disadvantages:

- SysPrep cannot upgrade earlier versions of the OS.
- Backup data and user settings must be arranged prior to the installation, and then data and individual user settings restored after installation.

Bootable CD-ROM   Once an image has been created with SysPrep, it can be copied onto a CD-ROM. This disk can be provided to any user who does not have a network connection or in cases where the users are going to upgrade their systems individually. As with the SysPrep installation, users can enter pertinent data themselves, or a script can be generated and provided to the user on a floppy disk that is run at the same time as the CD-ROM during setup.

Bootable CD-ROMs have the following advantages:

- They are, functionally speaking, the fastest option. They save time because they do not download system files from the network.
- OS deployment is simplified for computers that do not have high-speed connectivity.
- Clients can be fully configured for the network, even if they are not connected to the network (such as on road warrior machines).

The disadvantages include the following:

- They require manual installation at each computer.
- They are not suitable for large images (over 650MB, the limit of a CD-ROM's storage capabilities).

Remote Installation Services   Where unattended installation only allows OS upgrades, Remote Installation Services (RIS) allows for a clean installation of Windows XP Professional on supported computers throughout an organization. RIS works by allowing the client to boot from a network interface card. Administrators can use RIS to create, and then store images of Windows XP Professional on a server running RIS. Once a client boots from the NIC, the RIS image is downloaded over a network connection. Installation is flexible. The RIS image can be completely automatic, or the user can be required to enter specific information, such as a password or computer name.

A client computer must support the Pre-Boot Execution Environment (PXE) for RIS to occur. Furthermore, RIS can be used only if Active Directory has been configured. For computers that do not contain PXE-based remote ROM, RIS includes a tool called Remote Boot Floppy (RBFG.EXE) to create a boot disk to use in conjunction with RIS.

Here are some of the advantages of RIS:

- It provides an easy way to replace a computer's OS.
- It enables standardization of Windows XP Professional installations.

- It enables customization and control of the end-user installation. This is done using a setup wizard with choices that can be controlled using Group Policy.
- Physical media does not need to be distributed, and the image size is not constrained by the capacity of any physical media.

Disadvantages include the following:

- RIS can be used only on clients that are connected to a network running any current version of Windows Server with Active Directory configured.
- It can be used only on clients equipped with PCI network adapters that are enabled for PXE.
- RIS only works with images that have been created from the C: drive and will not use images from other hard disk partitions
- RIS is not usable for client OS upgrades, only clean installations.

Systems Management Server   The Systems Management Server (SMS) is an integrated set of tools for managing Windows networks composed of thousands of computers. SMS includes desktop management and software distribution tools, making the task of upgrading much easier on huge networks. SMS can only be used for upgrades, not clean installations. The benefit of upgrading via SMS is that the administrator can control the upgrade from a centralized location. Administrators can decide when the upgrade will take place, which computers will be upgraded, and how to apply specific policies.

The advantages of SMS are as follows:

- Computer upgrades can be performed in locked-down or low-rights environments.
- After-hours upgrades can occur without the user being signed on.
- SMS allows the usage of deployment policies: deployment can be "optional," "absolutely mandatory," or "delayed mandatory."
- Automatic load balancing between distribution points accommodates large numbers of simultaneous upgrades.

The disadvantage of SMS is that you must already be using SMS within your network. Furthermore, there is a pretty steep learning curve when using SMS.

Quick Comparison   The preceding sections threw a lot of information at you about the various installation and upgrade paths available with Windows XP Professional. In case it all blurred together into one large, gray mass, Table 2-4 compares and contrasts the specifics of each method.

Requirements	Unattended Installation	SysPrep	Bootable CD-ROM	Remote Installation Services	Systems Management Server
Clean Installation or Upgrade	Either	Clean installation	Either	Clean installation	Upgrade
Hardware Requirements	Network boot disk if using a remote distribution share	Similar hardware configurations for all clients	CD-ROM drive	PXE-enabled desktop computers or computers with NICs supported by the Remote Boot Floppy tool	A fast connection to the SMS site
Server Requirements	None	None	None	Active Directory on a server running Windows 2000 Server or later	Windows-based server with SMS running an SMS site
User Interaction Requirement	Nominal	Nominal (if using SysPrep.inf)	Nominal for upgrades, more involved for clean installations	Nominal	Nominal

Table 2-4. Comparison of Different Methods for Windows XP Professional Installation over a Network

Required Input

Depending on how you decide to proceed with your setup and what features are already installed on your computer, you will have to respond to a few questions as Windows XP Professional is installed. Table 2-5 lists the items on which you are likely to be prompted for a decision.

Taking some time up front to anticipate the answers to some of these questions will save valuable time during installation. This is especially important if you will be installing Windows XP Professional on a number of computers and using a script.

Servers

Previous incarnations of Windows business OSs (namely NT and 2000) included a version to be installed on workstations and a version to be installed on servers. However, Windows XP Professional is only meant for workstations—as of this writing, there is no Windows XP Professional Server.

> **NOTE** There won't actually be a Windows XP Professional Server. Rather, the next server product will be called Microsoft .NET Server and will fit in with Microsoft's .NET vision (you can learn more about this vision at http://www.microsoft.com/net). At this time, .NET Server is still in the beta testing phase, but it is slated to be released in mid 2002.

Issue	Explanation
Licensing agreement	Select "I accept" to agree with Microsoft's terms. If you do not agree, Windows XP Professional will not install.
Special options	The Windows XP Professional installation can be customized for specific language and accessibility settings.
File system	Windows XP Professional can automatically convert your hard drive or portions of your hard drive to NTFS.
Regional settings	Change the system and user locale settings for different regions and languages.
Personalize your OS	Enter the full name of the person who will be using this copy of Windows XP Professional.
Computer name and administrator password	Enter a unique computer name that differs from others on your network. The wizard will suggest a name, but you can certainly change it. During installation, the wizard automatically creates an administrator account. Whoever uses this account will have full rights over the computer's settings and can create user accounts on the computer. It's a good idea to establish an administrator password (rather than just hit ENTER) and keep it somewhere safe.
Date and time settings	Verify the time for your region and set the appropriate time zone. This allows XP to automatically adjust your computer for daylight savings time.
Network settings	In a "normal" installation, it is best simply to select the "Typical" settings option for network configuration. However, to manually configure network clients, services, and protocols, select the "Custom" settings option.
Workgroup or computer domain	At this point, you select which workgroup or domain you will join.
Network Identification Wizard	If this device is connected to a network, this wizard asks you to identify the users who will use the computer. If there is only one user, he or she will be assigned administrator rights.

Table 2-5. Input Requested During Windows XP Professional Installation

You can install XP on workstations via NT servers, but your best bet is to use Windows 2000 Servers. Not only is this the more robust version of Windows Server, but it also allows a network to enjoy the benefits of Active Directory.

NOTE Active Directory is a database that can search for objects within your entire network. This is effective because, for instance, an administrator can apply policies for an entire group of people across many domains with a couple of clicks of a mouse button. As powerful a tool as Active Directory is, however, it has only been implemented on about 15 percent of the systems that have migrated to Windows 2000.

Organization

If you decide to transition your servers from Windows NT to Windows 2000, you'll need to do more than just install some software and maybe add a few sticks of RAM. One of the cornerstones of Windows 2000 is an entirely new philosophy on network organization.

The point of this section is not to veer away from Windows XP Professional into Windows 2000, but for the sake of building the best possible deployment, it is necessary to talk about setting up your organization's servers with Windows 2000. If you already have Windows 2000 Servers, you can skip this section.

At the focal point of any Windows 2000 domain are the domain controllers. Windows 2000 differs from Windows NT because administrators are no longer forced to decide whether a server was going to act as a domain controller or not. Under Windows NT, promoting a member server to domain controller status required a new installation. Under Windows 2000, normal server systems can be promoted to act as domain controllers by using a simple utility (DCPROMO.EXE).

Preparation

Before you make any changes to your servers, you should have a good idea of how your network operates, and how it will work when transitioned to Windows 2000. In any migration, the majority of the work involves determining the current status of your network, where you expect your network to go, and how the new system will get you there.

This is also the stage at which you should get anyone else who is involved in the migration up to speed on Windows 2000. They should understand the key features of Windows 2000 (like Active Directory) and how it will be used in conjunction with your Windows XP Professional workstations.

Make an Inventory

Next, you should develop an inventory of your network. Depending on the size of your network, this might seem to be a daunting task. However, getting an inventory of what you have will certainly help you understand the big picture of your network.

In addition to listing the hardware and software on your network, you should also document the network topology, the domain model, the servers and their roles (how many primary domain controllers [PDCs] and backup domain controllers [BDCs] there are), and where your Domain Name System (DNS) and Dynamic Host Configuration Protocol (DHCP) servers are located. How many clients are there? How many laptops are there? What OS are they all running? Will they all be migrated to Windows XP Professional? Which devices have which trusts bonding them?

> **NOTE** Trusts are relationships established between two computers. They allow the user of one computer to access information on another computer.

Active Directory

One of the chief reasons to upgrade to Windows 2000 is to take advantage of Active Directory. Not only is Active Directory a powerful component of Windows 2000, but it is also a very useful feature in Windows XP Professional.

By using Active Directory, you can establish and regulate such variables as the following:

- **Roaming user profiles** This feature allows a user's personal settings to be downloaded to the server when he or she logs off. When the user logs in again, the settings are transferred to the computer. This is useful if a user moves from computer to computer within the network or logs in remotely.

- **Offline files and folders** Users who are not in constant contact with the network (for instance, mobile and remote users) can still have access to network files. Administrators can make network files available when the local computer is disconnected from the server. Once the user reconnects to the network, the file can be synchronized with the network copy.

- **Folder redirection** Administrators can redirect folders—such as My Documents—from the user's desktop to a server.

- **Internet Explorer maintenance** Administrators can use Internet Explorer Maintenance to manage and customize Internet Explorer on Windows XP Professional. The Internet Explorer Administration Kit allows administrators to standardize versions of Explorer across the network, centrally distribute and manage browser installations, and configure automatic connection profiles for users' machines.

- **Group Policy and administrative templates and scripts** Administrators can use these tools to configure and govern the behavior of services, applications, and OS components. Scripts can be assigned to run when a computer is started, shut down, or when users log on or off their machines.

- **Security settings** A security configuration can be assigned within a Group Policy Object. A security configuration is a series of security settings applied to one or more security areas within Windows XP Professional.

The state of your organization's network topology is a key determiner of whether a transition to Windows 2000 will be smooth sailing or rough water. If you have a single-domain model, migration won't be too difficult. However, if you use a multidomain model, you're going to have to do a little work.

> **NOTE** Single- and multiple-domain models are just what their names describe—domains with either a single PDC or multiple PDCs. Furthermore, they apply to Windows NT Server environments, not Windows 2000 Server environments.

The challenge is a holdover from Windows NT. Because of limitations in the NT domain architecture, multidomain models were a necessity. Quite often the IT staff would be located at the top of a domain model. This was fine for the IT department, but it didn't bode well in those organizations whose administrators felt they should be at the top of the domain. Using Windows 2000, however, organizations can change their network's hierarchy with little or no problems.

To adopt Active Directory, it is a good idea to flatten out your domains. Consolidating and reducing the size of multidomain structures will make the transition much smoother.

As nice as domain flattening may be, it just might not be the right thing for your organization—for instance, if you choose to keep your organization's subdivisions separate until the actual migration.

Put It on Paper

The next stage involves designing how your new Active Directory will be structured. In your sketch, be sure to include the Windows 2000 Servers that will play key roles in the network. Even though Windows 2000 uses the more flexible DCs instead of PDCs and BDCs, there are still servers that perform such important roles. These DCs are known as Operation Masters (in Windows NT they are known as Flexible Single Master Operations). Some of these servers are limited to a single domain and don't extend to the entire network.

The last step is to decide how Active Directory's Organizational Units (OUs) will be structured.

> **NOTE** An OU is the basic building block of an Active Directory domain. It contains users, files, and devices.

You should decide which users, folders, and computers will compose each OU, then group them together accordingly.

Standardize Networking Protocols

The next step is to ensure that you have common networking protocols extending across your network. The de facto standard is Transmission Control Protocol/Internet Protocol (TCP/IP). It has become popular because it provides a uniform protocol,

	Hard Drive	Processor	Memory
Servers	At least 2GB, but use a SCSI-based disk subsystem to reduce processor usage	Pentium II	128MB
Domain Controllers	At least 2GB, but use a SCSI-based disk subsystem to reduce processor usage	Pentium II	256MB

Table 2-6. Hardware Minimums for Windows 2000 Server Systems

supporting many OSs. If you haven't already moved your devices to the same protocol, it is a good idea to do so now.

NOTE We'll talk about TCP/IP and how it is used in Windows XP Professional networks in Chapter 3.

Upgrade Your Equipment

Earlier in this chapter we talked about the equipment demands of Windows XP Professional. Now, let's cover what you need for a Windows 2000 Server. The same caveats as before apply: these are just the bare minimums—for best results, use more powerful machines with more memory.

Table 2-6 above outlines what you should have for each server on your network.

Again, this represents the bare minimum recommended sizes and speeds for Windows 2000 Servers. Testing Windows 2000 in your laboratory will help you determine your organization's needs and can help you better understand future budgeting.

Making the Move

After over a dozen pages about migration, now's the time when we'll actually show you how to do it. We'll start by covering how to upgrade the servers to Windows 2000, promote servers to domain controllers (if you want to continue using Windows NT as the foundation of your network, you can skip this section), and finally migrate workstations to Windows XP Professional.

Upgrading Servers

As if transferring your workstations to Windows XP Professional wasn't enough of a chore, migrating servers is another kind of headache. The migration requires a tremendous amount of planning and testing. However, once you're confident that everything has been planned out and tested, you can start the process of migration.

There are three steps involved in domain upgrades:

1. Upgrade a primary domain controller to a Windows 2000 Domain Controller.
2. Create or upgrade other domain controllers to Windows 2000 Domain Controllers.
3. Once all the servers have been switched over to Windows 2000, convert the domain into all Active Directory mode to take advantage of Windows 2000's features.

Ultimately, this all leads to enhanced Windows XP Professional functionality, first in terms of installation and then in everyday use.

Step 1—Upgrading the First PDC   The first step is upgrading the PDC in the NT domain. This is because the domain can join a tree (if one exists) and administrators can create Active Directory objects (like OUs). Furthermore, when other members of the domain are upgraded, they will have a domain to join.

> **NOTE**   In Active Directory parlance, *trees* are collections of domains. *Forests* are collections of trees.

If for some reason you decide not to convert all the servers in your domain to Windows 2000 Servers, the PDC will still be able to function with NT BDCs, clients, and other NT Servers.

A good way to perform the upgrade is to take the PDC offline and upgrade that machine in your lab. You can test it there without having to worry about problems with the rest of the network. If everything checks out, then you can bring it back to the production network. In the event something goes awry, you can always promote an NT BDC. Once you have a stable Windows 2000 DC, you can move on to the next step.

> **TIP**   The migration process almost always should occur from the top down, simply because Windows 2000 can then join a forest, domain, or tree immediately.

Step 2—Creating More Domain Controllers   The second stage is to add more domain controllers for the sake of Active Directory redundancy. During the migration process, it's a good idea to keep an NT BDC just in case something goes awry with the Windows 2000 DCs. If anything does go wrong, you can always promote the BDC to the PDC and go back to an NT domain.

The DC that was formerly the PDC for the NT domain is still considered as such for the NT system. It uses the old protocol for replication with BDCs, but it also uses the Windows 2000 protocol for replicating Active Directory with its Windows 2000 DC partners.

Step 3—Going Native As soon as all the BDCs have been converted to Windows 2000 DCs, you can take the final step toward converting your servers to Windows 2000 and Active Directory. You change the DCs from *mixed mode* to *native mode*. Mixed mode allows NT Servers to cohabitate with Windows 2000 Servers. Unfortunately, mixed mode does not allow you to take advantage of Active Directory—and isn't that the whole point here?

> **CAUTION** Once you go native, you can't go back. If you work in a mixed mode environment, you can always switch to native mode. However, it's a one-way trip. Make sure you won't ever want to add another NT domain controller to your network—because you can't.

Furthermore, the switch to native mode allows clients to benefit from transitive trusts. This means that the resources of all the devices are shared amongst themselves. What's available on one device is available on another.

Migrating Workstations

Once your servers have been migrated and promoted, you can begin the task of migrating workstations. This is the stage at which you will move your workstation model from the testing or pilot phases and into wide-scale deployment. If you're using Windows 2000 Server, you'll have a much easier time deploying Windows XP Professional to your workstations and establishing user policies. However, as we noted earlier, which deployment method you choose to use will be based on a number of variables unique to your organization.

> **NOTE** The task of migrating your servers to Windows 2000 is more involved than space permits us to discuss here. We recommend that you pick up a copy of *Windows 2000 Enterprise Networking* for a more in-depth look at Windows 2000 and its ins and outs.

Activation

One of the most talked about features of Windows XP Professional has nothing to do with user interfaces or networking abilities. Rather, it has to do with Microsoft's latest stab at thwarting piracy—it's called *activation*.

Windows Product Activation (WPA) is a technology used to enable or activate a copy of Windows XP Professional for a specific PC. Under the Microsoft End User License Agreement (EULA), users are allowed to install Windows XP Professional on a single machine.

> **NOTE** Naturally, when you're buying Windows XP Professional for multiple computers, you'll buy multiple licenses from Microsoft.

When you activate Windows XP Professional, it examines key components of your computer and creates an internal value that is combined with your 25-digit product ID code. This produces a 50-digit number called the *Installation ID*. This number is transmitted to Microsoft in exchange for a 42-digit *Activation ID*, which disables the activation lock. If an attempt is made to activate the same copy of Windows XP Professional from another machine, the folks at Microsoft will deny your Activation ID.

The problem with activation is that it takes a snapshot of your system settings and shoots them back to Redmond, Washington. Privacy advocates contend that Microsoft doesn't need to know that much about you. Furthermore, if you decide to change your system hardware, your Activation ID will no longer work. Microsoft will allow some wiggle room for extra memory and so forth, but when it comes down to adding or changing hard drives, for instance, Microsoft's grip begins to tighten. Microsoft says if you add hard drives or make serious changes to your hardware, you can call them and they'll issue a new Activation ID.

In the event you choose not to activate your system, you'll only be able to use Windows XP Professional for 30 days before the system locks down, allowing you to do nothing but activate it. Periodically, within that 30-day time frame, Windows XP Professional will give you reminders to activate the system. Figure 2-14 shows the tool used for activation.

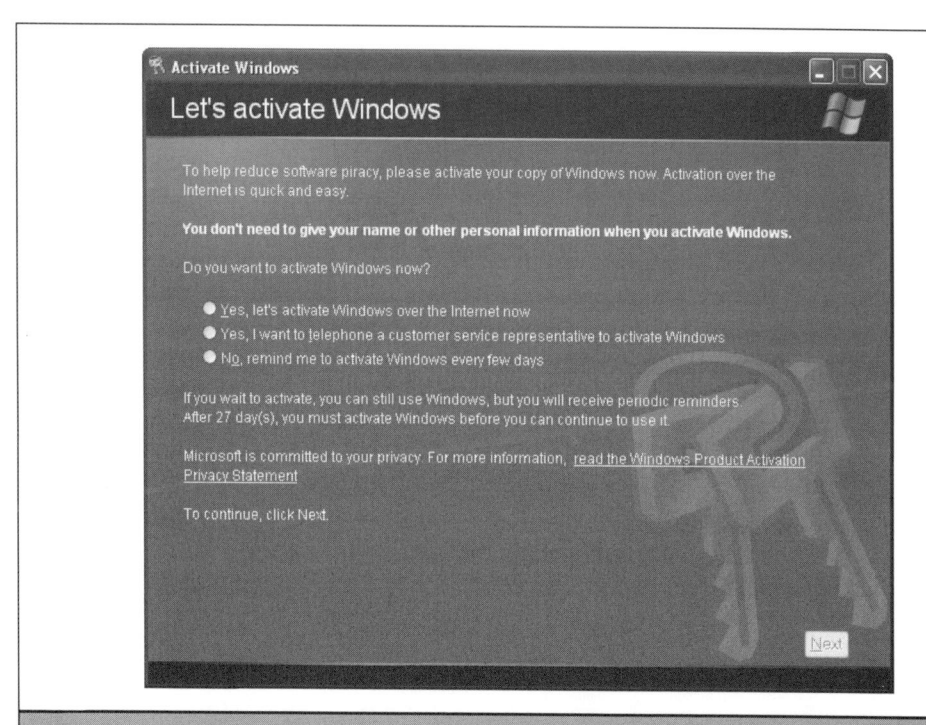

Figure 2-14. Windows XP Professional allows you to activate it at any time during the 30-day trial period.

As much as Microsoft has been demonized for implementing activation in Windows XP Professional, activation isn't new. Other companies like Novell, Adobe, and Symantec have required registration and activation to use their products.

Migrating to a new OS can be a troublesome chore. It can be especially tough if you must also upgrade servers. However, taking the time to understand what's involved in the migration process can make the whole chore much easier to manage.

CHAPTER 3

TCP/IP and Other Protocols

Transmission Control Protocol/Internet Protocol (TCP/IP) was, and continues to be, the protocol suite that makes the Internet run. And, while the Internet still relies on TCP/IP, the protocol suite has evolved into protocols that are used in networks of all shapes and sizes. This chapter examines the TCP/IP protocol suite and discusses how you can use it to connect your Windows XP Professional network.

TCP/IP

The beauty of the TCP/IP suite is its ability to allow computers with different operating systems to communicate amongst themselves. For instance, a Novell NetWare product can speak TCP/IP, as can Windows XP Professional.

TCP/IP was developed by the Defense Advanced Research Projects Agency (DARPA) in the 1970s. The goal of its development was to allow dissimilar computers to freely exchange data, regardless of location. Initially, the TCP/IP suite was developed on UNIX computers, which helped fuel the protocol's popularity as vendors included TCP/IP software inside each UNIX computer. TCP/IP maps to the OSI reference model, as illustrated in Figure 3-1.

As Figure 3-1 shows, TCP/IP resides on layers 3 and 4 of the OSI reference model. The theory behind this is to leave networking technologies up to the LAN vendors. TCP/IP's goal is to move messages through any LAN product and establish a connection using any network application.

What allows TCP/IP to function is that it links to the OSI model at its two lowest levels—the data-link and physical layers. This allows TCP/IP to speak with just about any networking technology and, as a result, any computer platform. TCP/IP contains four abstract layers, listed here:

- **Network interface** Allows TCP/IP to interact with all modern network technologies by complying with the OSI model
- **Internet** Defines how IP directs messages to move through routers over internetworks, such as the Internet
- **Transport** Defines the mechanics of how messages are exchanged between computers
- **Application** Defines network applications to perform tasks such as file transfer, e-mail, and other useful functions

Because of TCP/IP's popularity, it has become the Internet's de facto standard. A computer that implements an OSI-compliant layer network technology (such as Ethernet or Token Ring) will be able to connect with other devices. In Chapter 1, we discussed layers 1 and 2 in our coverage of LAN technologies. Now, we'll move up the OSI stack and consider how computers can be connected over either the Internet or a private network. This section examines the TCP/IP protocol suite and how it is configured.

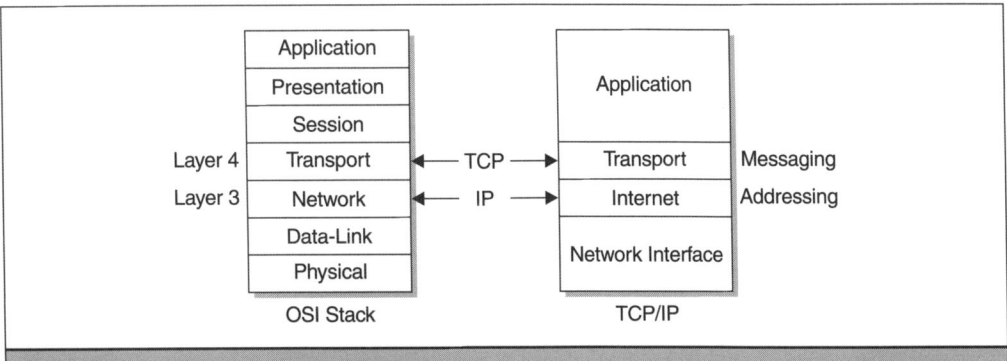

Figure 3-1. The TCP/IP stack is compliant with the OSI seven-layer reference model.

Understanding TCP/IP

If you think about it, the fact that computers can even communicate at all is a small miracle. There are computers from different manufacturers, running different OSs, running different protocols. Without some sort of common ground, these devices wouldn't be able to share information amongst themselves. When data traverses a network, it must be in a format that both the sending and receiving devices understand.

TCP/IP accommodates this with its Internet layer. This layer maps directly to the OSI model's network layer and is based on a fixed message format called the *IP datagram*. The datagram can be thought of as a basket that holds all the information comprising the message. For instance, when you download a web page into your browser, what you see on your screen was delivered piece by piece—inside datagrams.

It's easy to confuse datagrams with packets. A datagram is a unit of data, whereas a packet is the physical message entity (created at levels 3 and up) that actually passes through a network. Although the terms are used interchangeably by some, the distinction really is only important in certain contexts—certainly not here. What's important to understand is that messages are broken into pieces, shot across the network, and reassembled at the receiving end.

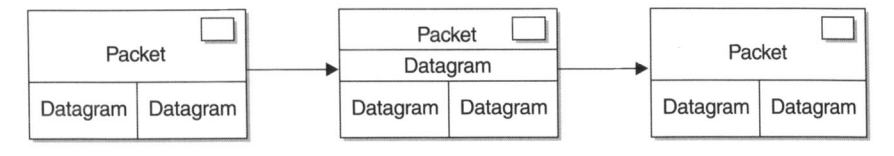

An advantage of this approach is that if a single packet is corrupted during transmission, then only that packet needs to be re-sent, not the entire message. Another benefit is that no single host must wait an inordinate amount of time for another's transmission to complete before being able to send its own message.

TCP vs. UDP

When an IP message travels across a network, it does so using one of two transport protocols: TCP or UDP. TCP stands for Transmission Control Protocol and is the first half of the TCP/IP acronym. UDP stands for User Datagram Protocol and is used in place of TCP for less critical messages. Either protocol serves to transport messages as needed though TCP/IP networks. There is a major difference between the functionality of TCP and UDP messages:

- TCP is called a *reliable* protocol, because it checks with the receiver to ensure that the packet was received.
- UDP is called an *unreliable* protocol, because no effort is made to check with the receiver and verify delivery.

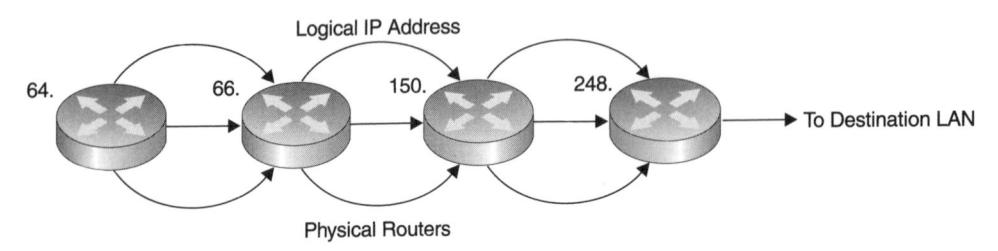

The important thing to remember is that only one transport protocol can be used to manage a message. For instance, if you download a web page, the packets are managed by TCP with no involvement from UDP. On the other hand, a Trivial File Transfer Protocol (TFTP) upload or download is overseen by the UDP protocol.

The transport used depends on the application, such as e-mail, HTTP, network management applications, and so forth. Network software designers use UDP whenever possible because it cuts down on overhead traffic. On the other hand, TCP makes more efforts to ensure delivery and transmits many more packets than UDP. Figure 3-2 shows a brief list of network applications, illustrating which applications use TCP and which applications use UDP. For example, FTP and TFTP do basically the same thing. However, TFTP is generally used to download and back up network device software. TFTP can use UDP because if a message fails, it is tolerable since the message isn't meant for the end user, but rather network administrators who have a much lower priority. Another example is a voice/video session, which can utilize ports for both TCP and UDP sessions. For instance, a TCP session will be initiated to share information while setting up the call, whereas the actual call will be sent via UDP. This is because of the speed involved with streaming voice and video. In the event a packet is dropped, then it makes no sense to resend it, as it will no longer fit in with the data stream.

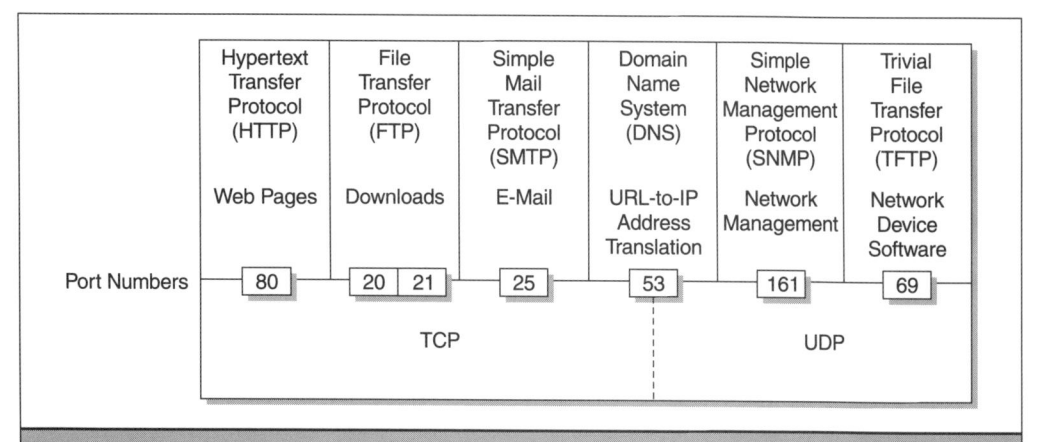

Figure 3-2. TCP and UDP handle different network applications (port numbers).

The IP Datagram Format

IP packets can be broken down into datagrams. The datagram's format provides fields for both the payload and message handling data. Figure 3-3 illustrates a datagram's layout.

NOTE Don't be thrown by the size of the data field in the datagram. The datagram is not top heavy with overhead. The data field is actually the largest field in the datagram.

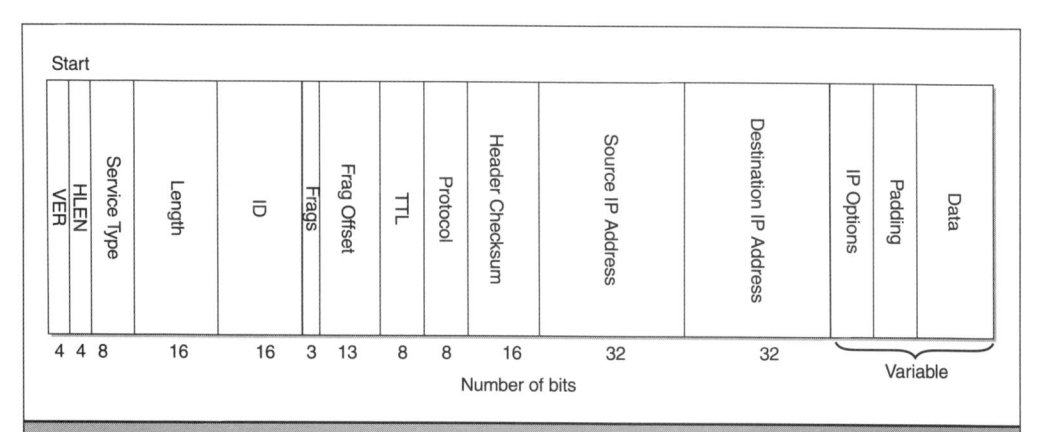

Figure 3-3. The IP datagram format is variable in length.

An important bit of information to remember about IP packets is that they are variable in length. As you might remember from Chapter 1, IP packets traversing an Ethernet network can be anywhere from 64 to 1400 bytes long. In a Token Ring network, they might be 4000 bytes. In an ATM network, they will all be 53 bytes.

> **NOTE** The use of bytes in datagrams might be confusing because we tend to think of data transmission in terms of megabits and gigabits per second. However, because computers prefer to handle data in bytes, datagrams are referred to in such terms.

If you take another look at the datagram format from Figure 3-3, you'll notice that the leftmost fields are a consistent size. That is because the CPU handling the packets must know where each field starts. Without some standardization in these fields, the resulting bits would be an undecipherable mess of zeros and ones. To the right of the datagram are the variable-length packets. This is what the various datagram fields do:

- **VER** The version of IP being used by the station that originated the message. The current version is IP version 4. This field lets different versions coexist in an internetwork.
- **HLEN** For *header length*, this tells the receiver how long the header will be so the CPU knows where the data field begins.
- **Service type** A code to tell the router how the packet should be handled in terms of level of service (reliability, precedence, delay, and so on).
- **Length** The total number of bytes in the entire packet, including all header fields and the data field.
- **ID, frags, and frags offset** These fields identify to the router how to handle packet fragmentation and reassembly, and how to offset for different frame sizes that might be encountered as the packet travels through different LAN segments using different networking technologies (Ethernet, FDDI, and so on).
- **TTL** Short for Time to Live, a number that is decremented by one each time the packet is forwarded. When the counter reaches zero, the packet is dropped. TTL prevents router loops and lost packets from endlessly wandering internetworks.
- **Protocol** The transport protocol that should be used to handle the packet. This field almost always identifies TCP as the transport protocol to use, but certain other transports can be used to handle IP packets.
- **Header checksum** A *checksum* is a numerical value used to help ensure message integrity. If the checksums in all the message's packets don't add up to the right value, the station knows that the message was garbled.
- **Source IP address** The 32-bit address of the host that originated the message (usually a PC or a server).

- **Destination IP address** The 32-bit address of the host to which the message is being sent (usually a PC or a server).
- **IP options** Used for network testing and other specialized purposes.
- **Padding** Fills in any unused bit positions so that the CPU can correctly identify the first bit position of the data field.
- **Data** The payload being sent. For example, a packet's data field might contain some of the text making up an e-mail.

As we mentioned earlier, the packet has two basic components: the message handling data contained in the header and the data. The data portion is where the payload is kept. Think of it as the cargo bay of a space shuttle. The header can be thought of as all the onboard computers in the shuttle's cockpit. It handles all the information needed by the sundry routers and computers that will send the packet on its way and will be used to maintain order when it's time to bring this packet together with its siblings to form the message.

IP Addressing

In order to find a web site on the Internet, you must enter a Uniform Resource Locator (URL) into your web browser. A series of unique domain names can be combined with an organization category to form a URL (such as http://www.whitehouse.gov, http://www.velte.com, or http://www.harvard.edu).

But URLs only exist to make life easier for us dumb humans; they aren't true IP addresses. In order for computers to connect with other computers across the Internet, they rely on 32-bit addresses (called *IP addresses*), which act much like telephone numbers. For a URL to be used to connect to a web site, the URL must be converted into the IP address. For instance, if you enter the URL http://www.velte.com into a web browser, a request is sent to the nearest domain name system (DNS) server, which looks up the URL and converts it to an IP address. This is shown in Figure 3-4.

It's necessary to make this conversion because routers and switches can't tell what a domain name is. In fact, in order to even communicate with your DNS server, an IP address must be entered to make the query. Figure 3-5 shows the DNS server entry in Windows XP Professional.

Every address on the Internet is an IP address. However, there are two organizations involved with the issuance of IP addresses and domain names. The Internet Assigned Numbers Authority (IANA) is responsible for IP addresses; the Internet Corporation for Assigned Names and Numbers (ICANN) is responsible for domain names. For instance, velte.com was issued by InterNIC (the organization that preceded ICANN in 1999) and an IP address of 64.66.150.248 was given to this address by its ISP, which was handed down from the IANA.

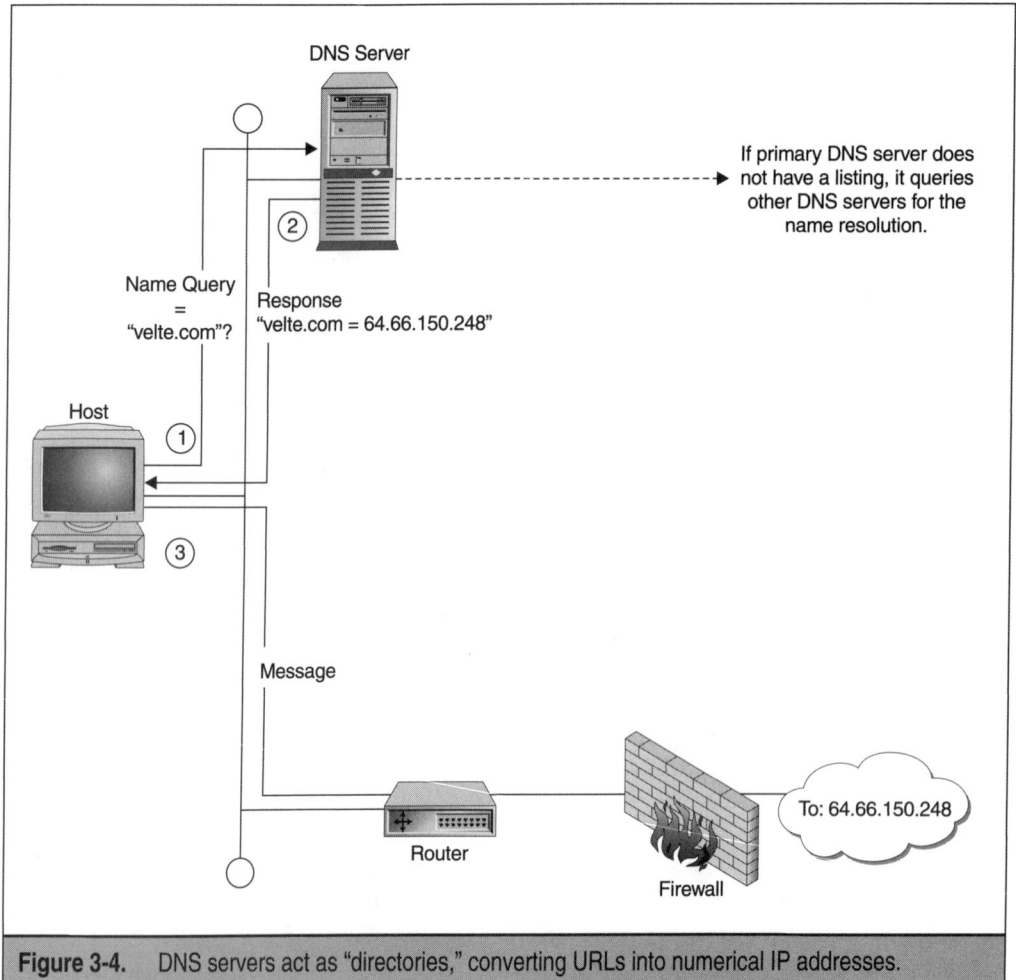

Figure 3-4. DNS servers act as "directories," converting URLs into numerical IP addresses.

The IP Address Format

Consider the IP address to be a sort of super telephone number. It uses a format that crosses continents and is large enough to allow millions of devices to be connected. This includes host devices, as well as networks. No matter what device or network, if they are connected to the Internet, they must use IP addresses. Even devices that are connected to a LAN with their own addressing system (such as AppleTalk, for instance) must translate to IP addresses if they are to connect with the Internet.

IP addresses are unique to each device on the Internet. Unlike telephone numbers, which are different lengths and use different country codes around the world, IP

Figure 3-5. This is where you enter the location of your DNS server.

addresses have the same format the world over. IP addresses are 32 bits long and divided into four sections, each 8 bits long, called *octets*.

Routers rely on IP addresses to forward messages from one internetwork to another. As a packet moves from router to router, it works its way from left to right across the IP address until it reaches the router of the destination address.

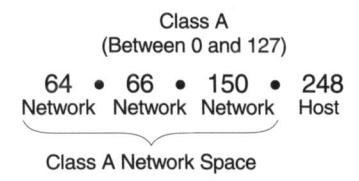

```
                    Class A
              (Between 0 and 127)
         64  •  66  •  150  •  248
        Network Network Network  Host
              Class A Network Space
```

A message might have to accomplish several router hops before moving closer to its final destination. More often, however, messages can skip over entire octets and move to the destination LAN segment in just one or two hops.

From Bits to Dotted-Decimal Format

As we pointed out in Chapter 1, computers only understand data in binary format. This is also true for IP addresses. However, again thinking of the telephone number example, the dotted-decimal format was invented so people could read binary IP addresses. Looking at a North American telephone number, as shown in Figure 3-6, the area code is used to find the specific region of the country to which the telephone number refers. Next, the prefix is examined and the telephone call moves into the desired neighborhood. The final four digits send the phone call to the selected telephone subscriber.

This is more or less how the dotted-decimal format works. *Dotted-decimal* takes its name from the fact that it converts the bits into decimal numbers for each octet, separated by periods. Figure 3-7 shows how an IP address is converted to dotted-decimal format.

IP Address Classes

The IETF, the organization that oversees the Internet, divides IP addresses into three generalized classes. Each class differs in the way the octets are designated for addressing networks as opposed to hosts. Figure 3-8 shows the first octet number ranges. The shaded octets show how much of the IP address space is reserved for addressing networks. As the shaded portion proceeds to the right, there are more possible networks, but fewer possible hosts.

> **NOTE** The IETF also divides IP addresses into two specialized addresses, one for multicasting and one for research, which we don't discuss here.

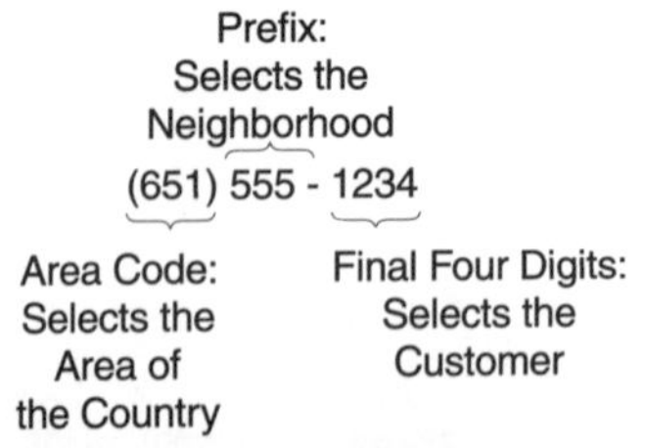

Figure 3-6. IP addresses are similar to telephone numbers.

First Octet in Binary

128	64	32	16	8	4	2	1
1	1	0	1	1	1	0	0

128 + 64 + 0 + 16 + 8 + 4 + 0 + 0 = 220

Second Octet in Binary

128	64	32	16	8	4	2	1
1	0	0	1	0	1	1	1

128 + 0 + 0 + 16 + 0 + 4 + 2 + 1 = 151

Third Octet in Binary

128	64	32	16	8	4	2	1
0	1	1	0	0	1	1	0

0 + 64 + 32 + 0 + 0 + 4 + 2 + 0 = 102

Fourth Octet in Binary

128	64	32	16	8	4	2	1
0	0	0	1	1	0	0	1

0 + 0 + 0 + 16 + 8 + 0 + 0 + 1 = 25

Broadcast Octet

128	64	32	16	8	4	2	1
1	1	1	1	1	1	1	1

128 + 64 + 32 + 16 + 8 + 4 + 2 + 1 = 255

Network Octet

128	64	32	16	8	4	2	1
0	0	0	0	0	0	0	0

= 0

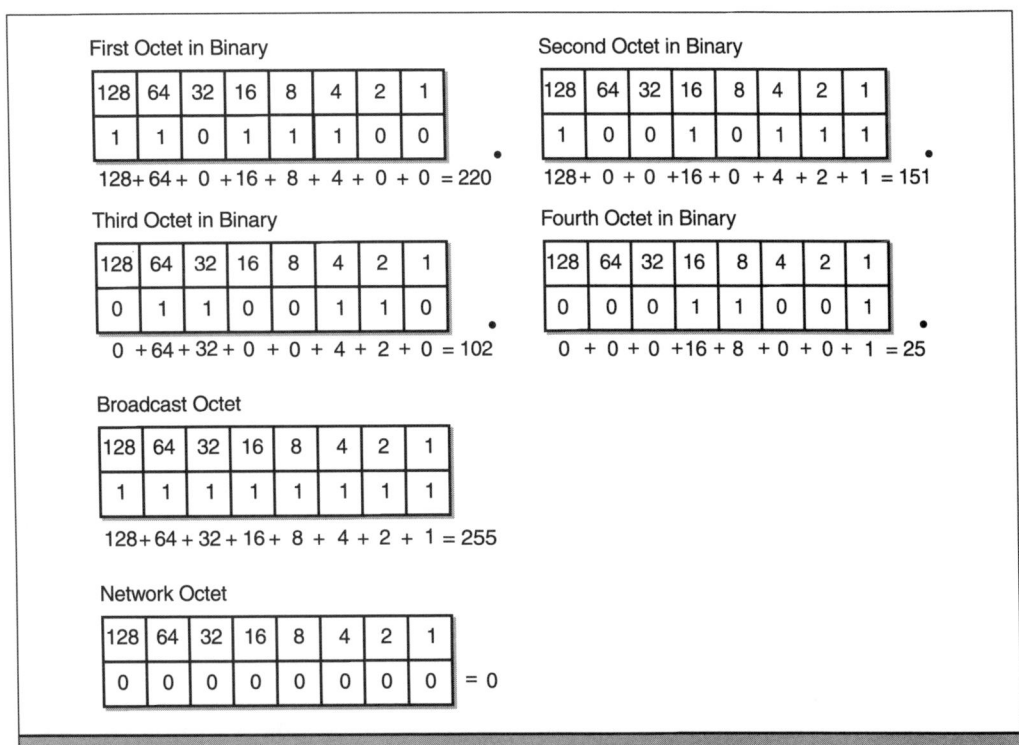

Figure 3-7. 32 bits define the IP addresses you see in dotted-decimal format.

This division of ranges is known as the *first octet rule*. Any router in the world can read the first octet of an IP address and be able to interpret the bits as network addresses versus host addresses. Most networks are numbered using either Class B or Class C IP addresses. The octet ranges are as follows:

- **0 to 127** Class A, range of network numbers is 0.0.0.0 to 127.0.0.0 for 128 networks. However, the network must not consist of only zeros, and 127.0.0.0 is reserved for loopback. Remaining are 126 networks—1 to 126. There are 16,777,214 possible host addresses (16,777,216 minus 2).

- **128 to 191** Class B, range of network numbers is 128.0.0.0 to 191.255.0.0 for 16,384 networks. There are 65,534 possible host addresses (65,536 minus 2).

- **192 to 223**   Class C, range of network numbers is 192.0.0.0 to 223.255.255.0 for 2,097,152 networks. There are 254 possible host addresses (256 minus 2).

NOTE   In order to perform host calculations, two reserved addresses must be removed from the pool: 0 for "this network" and 255 for broadcast. Addresses 1 through 254 can be assigned to hosts.

Looking at the preceding list, you might surmise that only a few very large organizations can have Class A addresses—only 126 or them, to be exact. Most users use Class B and Class C IP addresses when they connect to the Internet.

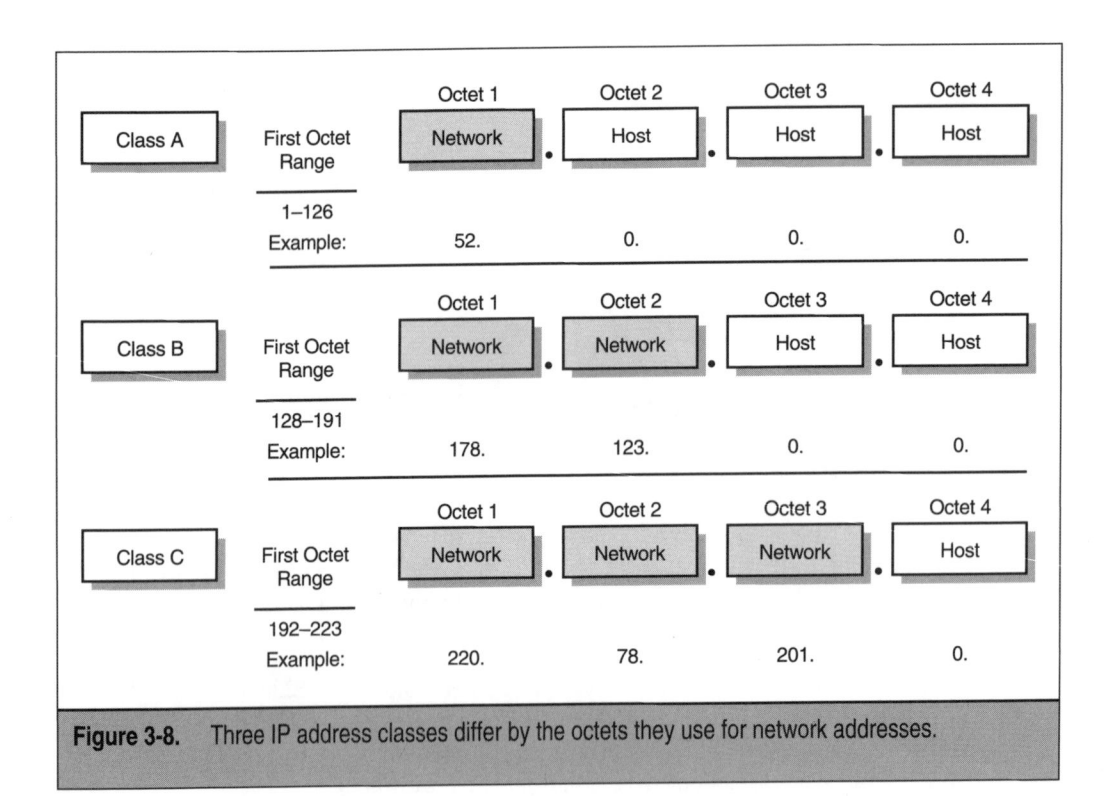

Class	First Octet Range	Octet 1	Octet 2	Octet 3	Octet 4
Class A	1–126	Network	Host	Host	Host
	Example:	52.	0.	0.	0.
Class B	128–191	Network	Network	Host	Host
	Example:	178.	123.	0.	0.
Class C	192–223	Network	Network	Network	Host
	Example:	220.	78.	201.	0.

Figure 3-8.   Three IP address classes differ by the octets they use for network addresses.

IP Addresses, Subnet Masks, and Default Gateways

When setting up a Windows XP Professional network, you'll need three important pieces of information:

- IP addresses
- Subnet masks
- Default gateways

These are important addresses that allow your computer to see and be seen on a network. Additionally, they provide a means to squeeze more room out of an IP address and make it possible for computers on one subnet to talk to computers on another subnet.

Before we talk about how to implement this information in Windows XP Professional, let's take a look at what these three addresses do and why you need them.

Public IP Addresses

The first group of IP addresses are known as *public addresses*, sometimes called *globally routable addresses.* These are the addresses that anyone with a computer connected to the Internet can use to access a web site.

The IANA assigns ranges of public IP addresses to organizations that can then assign those addresses to individual computers. This prevents multiple organizations from using the same public IP address.

In Windows XP Professional, an IP address can be assigned through a Dynamic Host Configuration Protocol (DHCP) server available at your organization, or configured manually by an ISP through a dial-up connection.

> **NOTE** The current version of IP, IP version 4, defines a 32-bit address, which means that there are only 2^{32} (4,294,967,296) addresses available worldwide. As the Internet has gained in popularity over the past few years, the number of available IP addresses on the Internet has started to run out. Consequently, a new generation of IP addresses (IP version 6) is in the works. The current IP system will not become obsolete overnight, however, as the two systems will coexist for some time after the new version has been implemented.

Subnet Masks

There might be instances when you simply need to squeeze even more network addresses out of a given IP address. If you can't find enough IP addresses, *subnetting* can help you out. IP address classes define which bits by default will address networks versus hosts. *By default* means that upon reading the first octet in an IP address, a router can tell which bits should be treated as network bits. For example, when looking at a Class C address, the router will by default see the first three octets as network bits and the final octet as host bits.

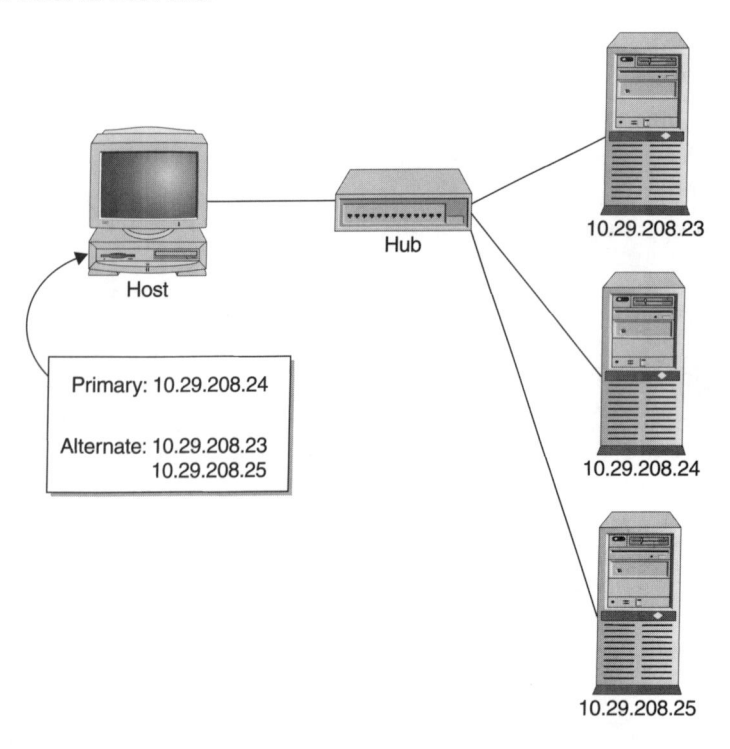

Even though there might seem to be an abundance of IP addresses out there, the truth of the matter is most organizations need more network address space than what their ISP assigns them. It's easy enough to get around this limitation by claiming some of the default host bits for use in addressing networks. This is accomplished by inserting a third zone between the default network and host address space. Figure 3-9 shows two IP addresses: one a subnetted Class B, the other a Class C.

An IP address class is important because subnets start at the leftmost bit and move to the right. In other words, only the bit positions in the shaded portion of Figure 3-9 may be used for subnet addressing.

Most organizations are assigned Class C addresses. This means that they have at most only about 8 bits with which to work. Most networks are assigned only a range of host addresses, for example, 222.198.25.0–15.

Whole Octet Subnet Example   Subnetting allows public IP addresses to be used more efficiently without changing them. Consider the example in Figure 3-10. This organization issues a Class B public IP address (151.22.0.0) and subnets the entire third octet.

Chapter 3: TCP/IP and Other Protocols 85

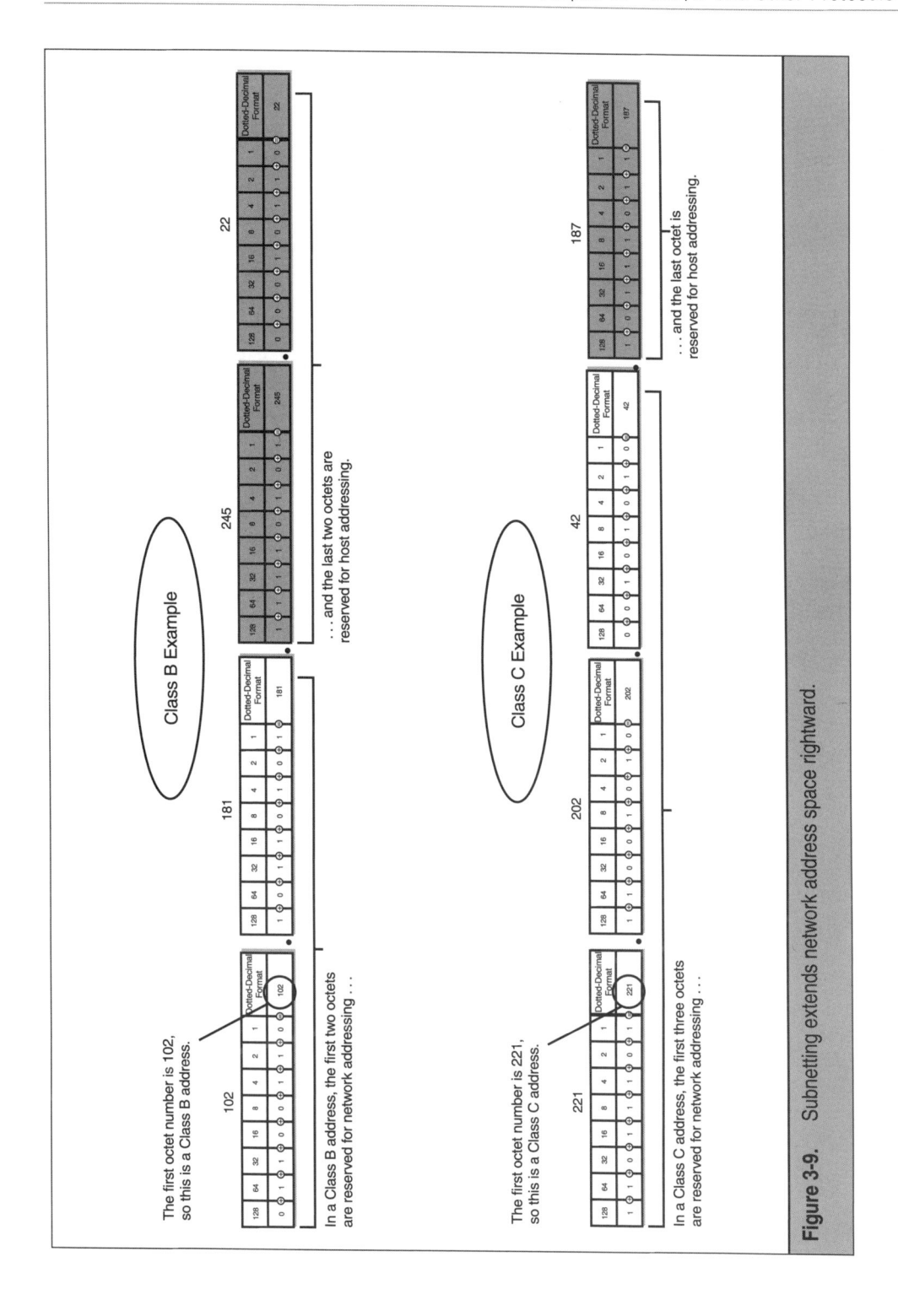

Figure 3-9. Subnetting extends network address space rightward.

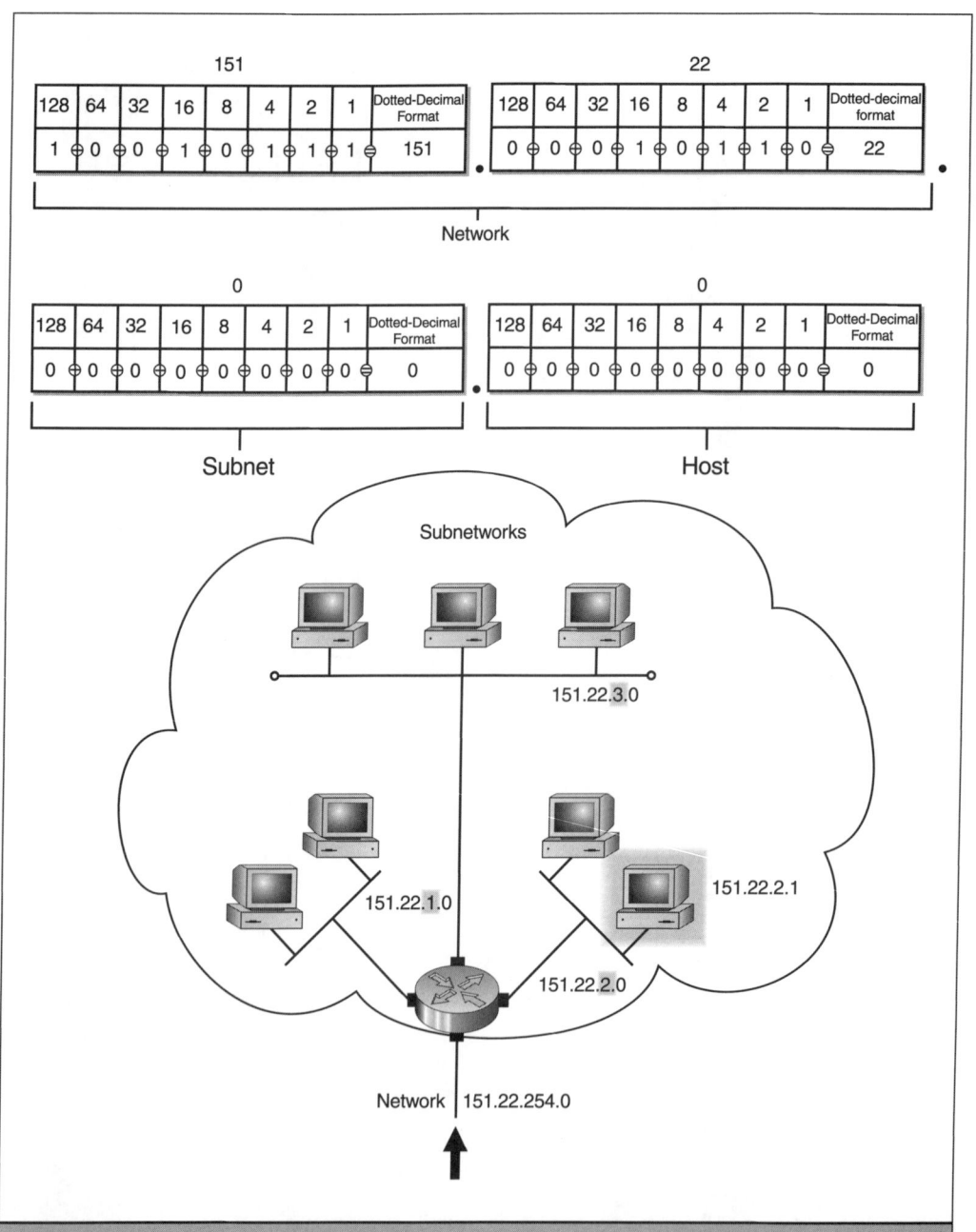

Figure 3-10. Subnetting makes efficient use of address space. This Class B example has room for 254 subnets.

As you examine Figure 3-10, you can see that there is now address space for 254 subnetworks, with room for 254 hosts per subnetwork. The shaded host at the bottom right shows a complete subnet address. In this example, host number 1 is connected to subnet number 2 within IP address 151.22.0.2.

When someone wants to connect to these devices, remote routers will work their way, from left to right, through the subnetted addresses. As they move through the address, the packets will automatically move to the correct interface of the edge router at the bottom of the cloud.

What They Look Like and Where They Exist   At this point, you might be confused about what subnets are. They are not actual IP addresses. Rather, they are 32-bit-long overlays that define how an IP address is to be used. They differ from IP addresses in two important ways:

- **Form**   A subnet mask is represented as a string of 1s in binary, or 255 in dotted-decimal format.
- **Location**   A subnet is applied to a specific network interface within the configuration file of the router to which the subnetwork is attached.

Put another way, a subnet mask is the contiguous string of 1 bits extending from the end of the network address space into the host portion. Where exactly that point is depends on the address class. In Figure 3-10, we used a Class B address. To implement a subnet mask, it is entered into the router's config file.

Partial Octet Subnetting   Subnetting might seem to be a simple matter, but in practice it can be quite challenging. This is because most organizations are issued Class C IP addresses. Only the fourth octet is reserved by default as host address space in Class C IP addresses. As such, the subnet mask extends partway into the host address space and is represented by a dotted-decimal number less than 255.

The shaded portion of Figure 3-11 shows the bits that are claimed for subnetting from the fourth octet. In this example, you'll notice that only half of the bits were claimed—not all eight. This is known as the *.240 mask*, which permits up to 14 subnets. Each subnet has enough address space for 14 hosts, or 196 total hosts.

You can choose from a number of subnet masks, as Table 3-1 shows. The important thing to remember is that the farther right a mask extends into the host address space, the fewer the number of possible hosts. The mask you use will depend on the network application. For instance, if a network router is connected to a point-to-point connection with a remote office, there are only two host addresses required—one for each end. This example requires the .252 mask, which only uses two host addresses.

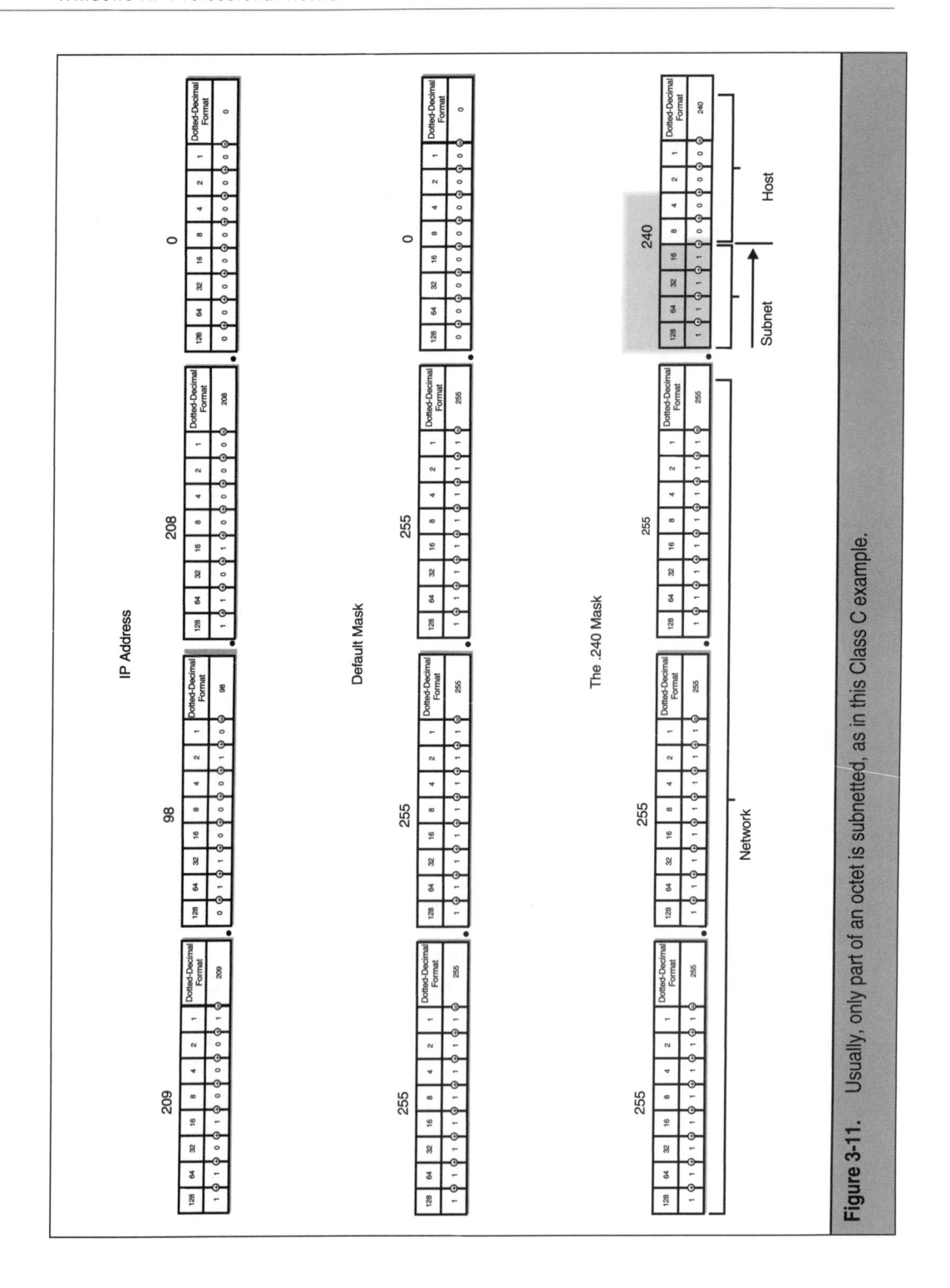

Figure 3-11. Usually, only part of an octet is subnetted, as in this Class C example.

Subnet Mask	Network ID Bits	Host ID Bits	Example Notation	Number of Subnets	Number of Hosts per Subnet
.192	26	6	209.98.208.34/26	2	62
.224	27	5	209.98.208.34/27	6	30
.240	28	4	209.98.208.34/28	14	14
.248	29	3	209.98.208.34/29	30	6
.252	30	2	209.98.208.34/30	62	2

Table 3-1. Subnet Masks Listed by Number of Network ID Bits

Private Addresses

If you connect a Windows XP Professional device to your LAN, it will have to be assigned an IP address. However, if the Internet uses IP addresses to connect, what prevents some weirdo from typing in your IP address and getting at your personal files? Among other reasons, the use of private addressing allows different LANs to employ the same IP addresses. This is because these addresses are only used within the confines of your LAN.

The IANA reserves three blocks of IP addresses for private usage. This keeps the world from running out of IP addresses (because more than one organization can reuse the same IP addresses for devices it doesn't want on the Internet anyway). The three blocks of reserved private addresses are as follows:

- **10.0.0.0 through 10.255.255.255**   The *10 block* is a single Class A network number.
- **172.16.0.0 through 172.31.255.255**   The *172 block* is 16 contiguous Class B network numbers.
- **192.168.0.0 through 192.168.255.255**   The *192 block* is 256 contiguous Class C network numbers.

There are no official rules for when to use a particular private network IP address block of the ones just listed. The IP address police won't come and arrest you for using the 172 block when you should be using the 192 block. Generally speaking, the one with the most suitable size is used. For obvious reasons, there is no need to use 10.x.x.x if it is unthinkable that your LAN will ever grow to more than 254 hosts. However, when using private addresses, the network administrator can be liberal on the usage of the addresses when assigning them to the different parts of a network, as the strict rules that govern public IP address assignment do not apply.

Once the network uses a device that is a boundary to the Internet (a so-called *edge device*), then a public IP address must be assigned. The use of private IP addresses is meant only to link hosts that make the bulk of their connections from within the private network.

So if you have a private IP address on your workstation, how is it that you can connect to the Internet? After all, isn't the point of private addressing to keep your connection confidential? That is true, but only to a certain degree. There are two IP address translation services that temporarily assign a valid public Internet IP address to hosts that use permanent private IP addresses:

- Network Address Translation (NAT)
- Port Address Translation (PAT)

The functionality of these two services is shown in Figure 3-12.

Normally, address translation is performed by your firewall. Bear in mind that these public-to-private translations are only temporary and go back into a pool of IP addresses when you disconnect from the Internet.

The greatest advantage to using private addressing is to have nearly unlimited address space for numbering internal networks and devices. If a firewall is properly configured to perform NAT or PAT address translation, then the respective devices

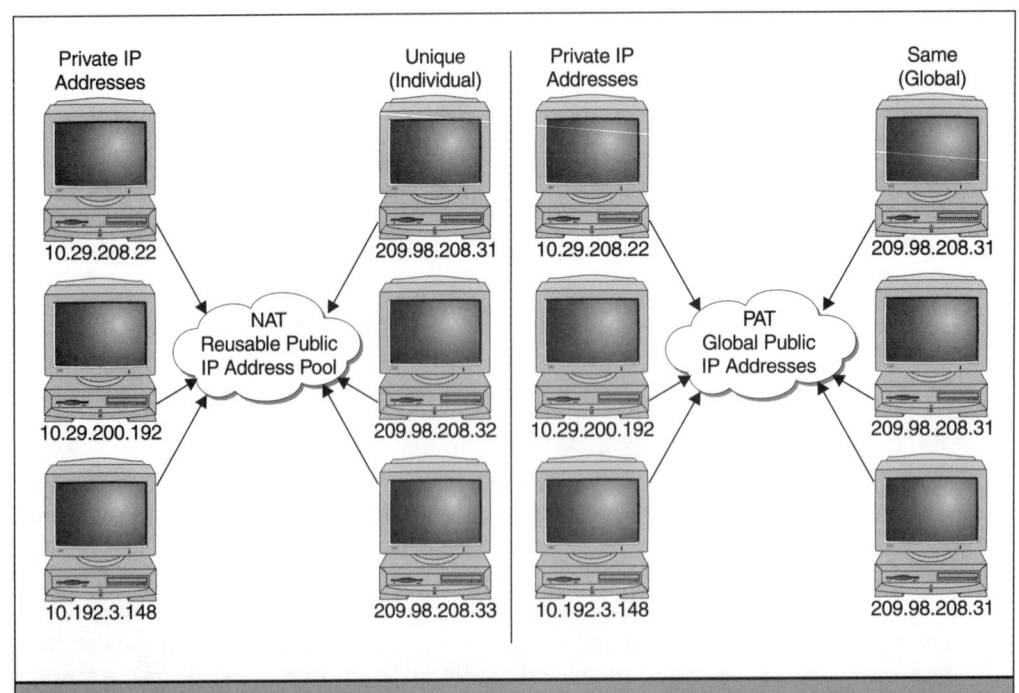

Figure 3-12. NAT temporarily assigns unique reusable public IP addresses; PAT assigns a global IP address.

are allowed access to the Internet. On a security level, because the actual addresses of network devices are "spoofed" by a temporarily assigned address from the pool, hackers can't get any idea of the private network's topology.

Private IP addresses can be assigned in two ways:

- **Authorized private IP addressing**   If a user wants to connect multiple Windows XP Professional computers, he or she can use the Automatic Private IP Addressing (APIPA) feature in Windows XP Professional. This allows each computer to automatically assign itself a private IP address. The user need not configure an IP address for each computer, and a DHCP server is not necessary. Computers with authorized private IP addressing can connect to the Internet by using another computer having proxy or Network Address Translation (NAT) capabilities.

NOTE   Windows XP's Internet Connection Sharing (ICS) feature provides NAT services to clients on a private network.

- **Unauthorized private IP addressing**   If he or she is so inclined, a user can manually configure a private IP address. This is only recommended if there is a relative certainty that the devices will never go on the Internet. In the event these computers do connect to the Internet, you might have to run around and change the IP addresses of each host.

Default Gateways

Earlier, we talked about the slick way network engineers are able to get around the limitations on the number of IP addresses available by implementing subnets. However, as nice as this is, subnetting raises another problem—the inability to get from one subnet to another (for instance, a computer in accounting might not be able to access a server in administration). To ameliorate this problem, routers, or *gateways*, are placed between LAN segments. If a device wishes to contact another device on the same segment, it transmits to that station directly using a simple discovery technique. If the destination station does not exist on the same segment as the source station, then the source can't figure out how to get to the destination.

To get from one subnet to another, one of the configuration parameters transmitted to each network device is its *default gateway*. This is the router's IP address, configured by the network administrator, and it tells each client or other network device where to send data if the destination station does not exist on the same subnet.

NOTE   An easy way to tell if your default gateway is incorrectly configured is if you are able to communicate with other devices on the same subnet (normally in the same building or same floor), but cannot access devices outside your subnet.

When making your TCP/IP connections, DHCP will provide the default gateway address. However, if you are configuring your network manually, you'll need to track down your router's IP address.

TCP/IP ADDRESSING IN WINDOWS XP PROFESSIONAL

In Windows XP Professional, TCP/IP addressing is the most common way to connect devices. Not only is it widely used for LANs, but it is also necessary for Internet connectivity. In this section, we show you how to set up and manage your TCP/IP addresses.

Upgrading

Windows XP Professional installs the TCP/IP protocol by default. However, if you are upgrading to Windows XP Professional from another flavor of Windows, Windows XP Professional studies which protocols you already have in place, and then automatically installs the protocols you're using.

If you are using a third-party TCP/IP protocol stack, Windows XP Professional removes it and replaces it with its own version. In the event the third-party protocol stack offers functionality beyond what Windows XP Professional provides, you must reinstall the third-party TCP/IP stack from your vendor installation tool.

If you need to install the TCP/IP protocol, you must follow these steps:

1. In the Control Panel, select Network and Internet Connections.

2. In Network and Internet Connections, select Network Connections.

3. In Network Connections, right-click the LAN you wish to change.

4. Select Properties, click the General tab, which is shown in Figure 3-13, and then click Install.

5. In the Select Network Component Type box, choose Protocol, and then click Add.

6. In the Select Network Protocol box, you'll be able to choose from a list of protocols Windows XP Professional has on hand. Alternatively, if you wish to install a third-party protocol, you can click the Have Disk button.

7. Click OK to finish the installation.

8. Windows XP Professional will have to reboot for the protocol to complete the installation.

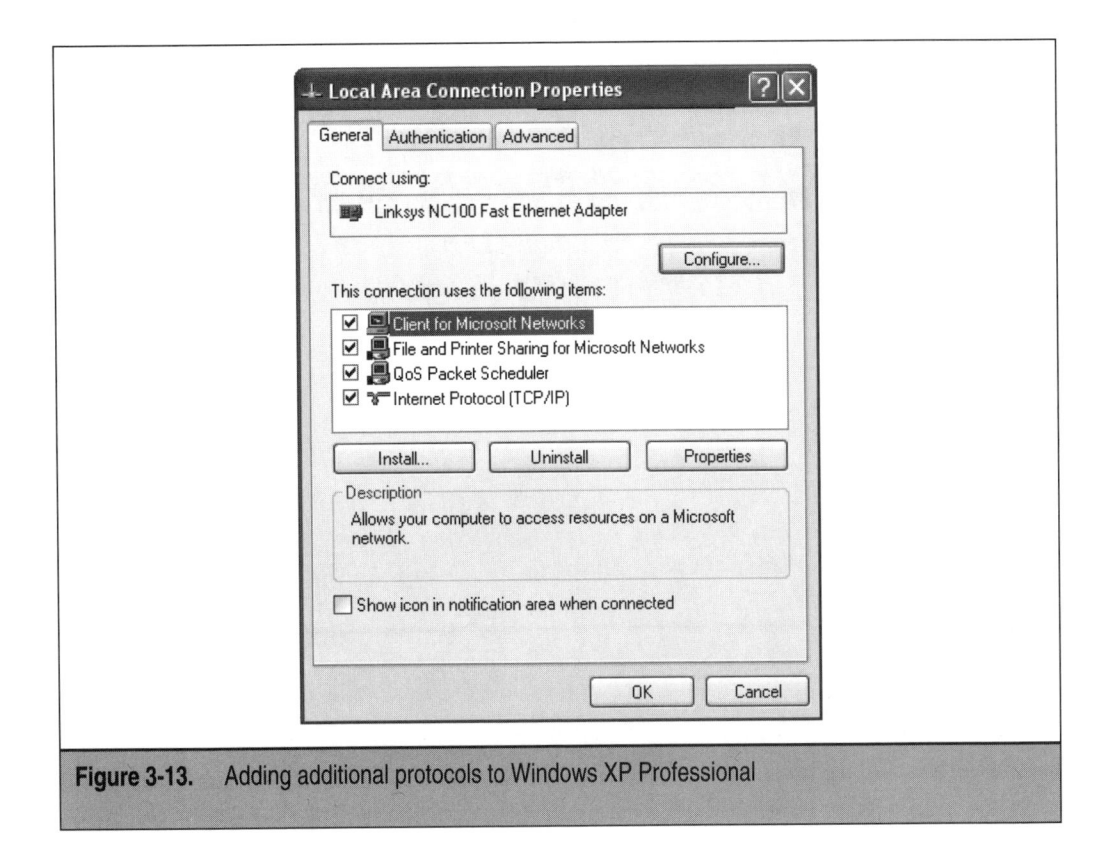

Figure 3-13. Adding additional protocols to Windows XP Professional

Assigning an IP Address

When it comes time to set up IP addresses, there are four ways in which the task can be completed by Windows XP Professional:

- **Dynamic Host Configuration Protocol**   The most popular method of assigning IP addresses (and the default of Windows XP Professional), DHCP provides automatic IP address assignment for clients on networks with one or more DHCP servers.
- **Automatic Private IP Addressing**   This method automatically assigns IP addresses to clients in single-subnet environments where no DHCP server is

present. When clients are communicating with other clients within their subnet, computers using APIPA-assigned IP addresses can only communicate with other clients assigned IP addresses by APIPA.

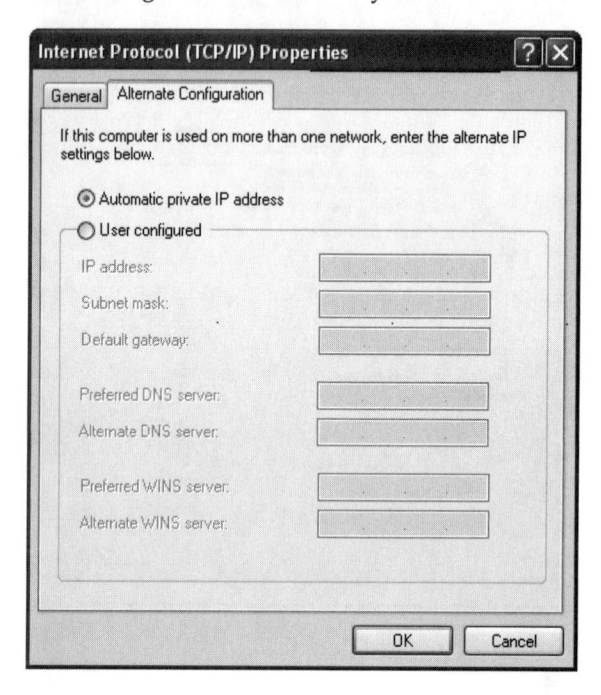

- **Static IP addressing** This method allows you to manually configure the IP address. You would use this method if both DHCP and APIPA were unavailable (for instance, when ICS is used). The downside to this method is that it is prone to error and can present a giant headache, especially in a large organization.

- **Alternate IP addressing** New to Windows XP Professional, this allows a single interface to make use of two IP addresses, so long as only one is used at a time. This is useful in situations where an IP address (either configured manually or automatically) might not be available and a backup is needed. Alternate IP addressing is also useful for laptop clients who connect to an office LAN and an ISP at home.

Configuring a TCP/IP Connection

When connecting either to the Internet or a LAN, chances are you'll also need to configure the TCP/IP protocol. We'll give you a quick overview of the process first, and then drill down into some of the subtleties later in this chapter.

To access the tool that allows you to configure this connection, follow these steps:

1. In the Control Panel, select Network and Internet Connections.
2. In Network and Internet Connections, select Network Connections.
3. In Network Connections, right-click the LAN you wish to change and select Properties.
4. Next, click the Networking tab and select Internet Protocol (TCP/IP).
5. Click Properties.

The result is shown in Figure 3-14.

When the Properties dialog box appears, make the following entries:

- **IP address**   This is the space in which you will enter your IP address. The IP address, as we mentioned earlier, must be unique to each machine on your network. No two devices can have the same IP address. If you try to access

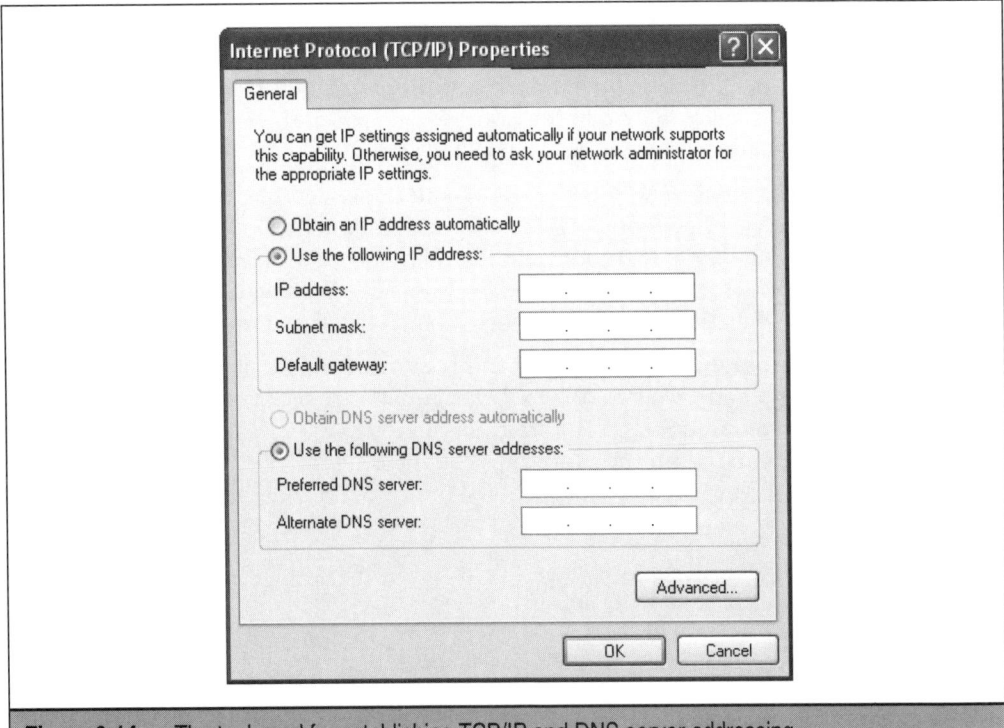

Figure 3-14.   The tool used for establishing TCP/IP and DNS server addressing

the Internet through an ISP, you should select the option Obtain IP address automatically, because unless you've decided to pay for a static IP address from your ISP, you'll probably have your IP address assigned dynamically.

- **DNS server address**   This box allows you to select the location of your DNS server. It shows a location to enter preferred and alternate addresses. Like the IP address selection, which choice you pick will depend largely on your network. If your LAN or ISP uses DHCP, then it can automatically tell Windows XP Professional the DNS address when you connect. As such, you need only select the Obtain DNS server address automatically option. If the address must be assigned manually, select the Use the following DNS server address option and enter the primary and secondary DNS addresses.

Managing TCP/IP Addresses

When connecting to a LAN or the Internet, your computer must have a unique IP address—no two machines can share the same address. However, a computer can (and most often will) have more than one IP address if connected to both the LAN and Internet.

There are three ways to display the IP address of your Internet connection:

- **Dial-up connection icon**   Dial-up connections can be examined by clicking the dial-up connection icon in the notification area of the taskbar. Go to the status dialog box, and then click the Details tab.

- **View Status of This Connection**   No matter how you're connecting to the Internet, you can view your IP address by displaying the Network Connections window, clicking the connection, and then clicking View Status of This Connection in the Network Tasks section of the Task pane. Users using dial-up connections should click the Details tab; LAN users should click the Support tab.

- **IPCONFIG program**   The IPCONFIG utility shows information about your TCP/IP connection. To run this tool, you must open a command prompt window by selecting Start | All Programs | Accessories | Command Prompt. When the command prompt appears, type **ipconfig /all** and press ENTER. The following listing gives an example of the information generated and displayed by Windows.

```
Microsoft Windows XP [Version 5.1.2600]
(C) Copyright 1985-2001 Microsoft Corp.

C:\Documents and Settings\Administrator>ipconfig /all

Windows IP Configuration

        Host Name . . . . . . . . . . . . : geonosis
        Primary Dns Suffix  . . . . . . . :
```

```
        Node Type . . . . . . . . . . . . . : Unknown
        IP Routing Enabled. . . . . . . . . : No
        WINS Proxy Enabled. . . . . . . . . : No

Ethernet adapter Local Area Connection:

        Connection-specific DNS Suffix  . :
        Description . . . . . . . . . . . : Linksys NC100 Fast Ethernet Adapter
        Physical Address. . . . . . . . . : 00-04-5A-69-CC-60
        Dhcp Enabled. . . . . . . . . . . : Yes
        Autoconfiguration Enabled . . . . : Yes
        IP Address. . . . . . . . . . . . : 192.168.1.100
        Subnet Mask . . . . . . . . . . . : 255.255.255.0
        Default Gateway . . . . . . . . . : 192.168.1.1
        DHCP Server . . . . . . . . . . . : 192.168.1.1
        DNS Servers . . . . . . . . . . . : 192.168.1.1
        Lease Obtained. . . . . . . . . . : Thursday, March 28, 2002 4:35:50 PM
        Lease Expires . . . . . . . . . . : Thursday, March 28, 2002 4:40:50 PM

C:\Documents and Settings\Administrator>
```

In this example, the details of our LAN configuration are shown. As you can see, the computer has an IP address of 192.168.1.100. If we were connected to the Internet, another block of data would list the IP address, subnet mask, and default gateway of our Internet connection.

SETTING UP ADDRESSES IN WINDOWS XP PROFESSIONAL

Windows XP Professional offers several ways in which IP addresses can be established, managed, or altered. In this section, we examine each of these tools and explain how and why you would use one method over another. Then we discuss the different means of name resolution in Windows XP Professional. Finally, we round out the chapter with a quick overview of some other networking protocols that you might find useful.

TCP/IP Autoaddressing (APIPA and DHCP)

Earlier, we gave a very quick overview of the IP address configuration process in Windows XP Professional. However, different network designs and implementations will call for different IP address configuration options. This section explains how to configure your IP addresses automatically.

DHCP

As mentioned earlier, DHCP allows the automatic assignment of public IP addresses. A configured DHCP server provides a database of available IP addresses and can also be set up with configuration options for clients, including the addresses of DNS servers, gateway addresses, and other information. DHCP servers are typically used in large organizations and ISPs because it is simple to assign and reuse IP addresses.

When a Windows XP Professional DHCP client starts up, it requests setup information from the DHCP server. This allows the IP address to be automatically assigned, along with subnet masking and other information. The IP address is assigned to each client for a limited amount of time. This is known as a *lease*. Leases can be renewed from time to time to provide an interruption-free session. Leases are renewed about halfway through the lease duration. If the renewal is successful, then the IP address remains assigned to the client. If it is unsuccessful, the IP address is returned to the pool for another client.

When the TCP/IP protocol suite is installed on Windows XP Professional, you are automatically afforded an opportunity to obtain an IP address from a DHCP server. This option can be disabled if your network does not use DHCP servers or if you choose to manually enter an IP address. The IP Configuration tool (IPCONFIG.EXE) allows users and administrators to review the current IP address configuration assigned to the computer.

> **NOTE** To receive a complete list of IPCONFIG.EXE'S commands, enter **ipconfig /?** for instructions.

APIPA

Whereas DHCP is useful in large organizations with numerous clients, APIPA is helpful in small networks where only one subnet is used. With APIPA, the Windows XP Professional client takes on the role of establishing IP addresses if no DHCP server is present.

> **NOTE** In the event an APIPA address has been assigned and a DHCP server becomes available, the client will change its address to one the DHCP server hands out.

APIPA assigns a Windows XP Professional client an IP address from a preset range with a subnet mask of 255.255.0.0. A computer configured with an APIPA IP address cannot communicate with other hosts outside its subnet, including Internet hosts. APIPA is best used for single subnet networks, like a home or small office.

> **NOTE** If no DHCP server is found on the network, Windows XP Professional automatically uses APIPA.

You can determine if APIPA is already enabled by entering the following at the command prompt:

```
ipconfig /all
```

The resulting statistics show, among other things, your IP address and lease renewal times (as shown in Figure 3-15). Check the line that reads "Autoconfiguration Enabled." If the setting reads "Yes" and the IP address is between 169.254.0.1 and 169.254.255.254, then APIPA is enabled.

If you care to disable APIPA, it can be done one of two ways:

- Set up a static IP address. This disables both APIPA and DHCP.
- Disable APIPA through the Registry.

This is accomplished using the regedit.exe tool. Simply edit the Registry entry IPAutoconfigureEnabled with a value of 0. This is located in the subkey HKEY_LOCAL_MACHINE\SYSTEM\CurrentControlSet\Services\Tcpip\Parameters\Interfaces*interface-name* (where *interface-name* is the name of the network interface).

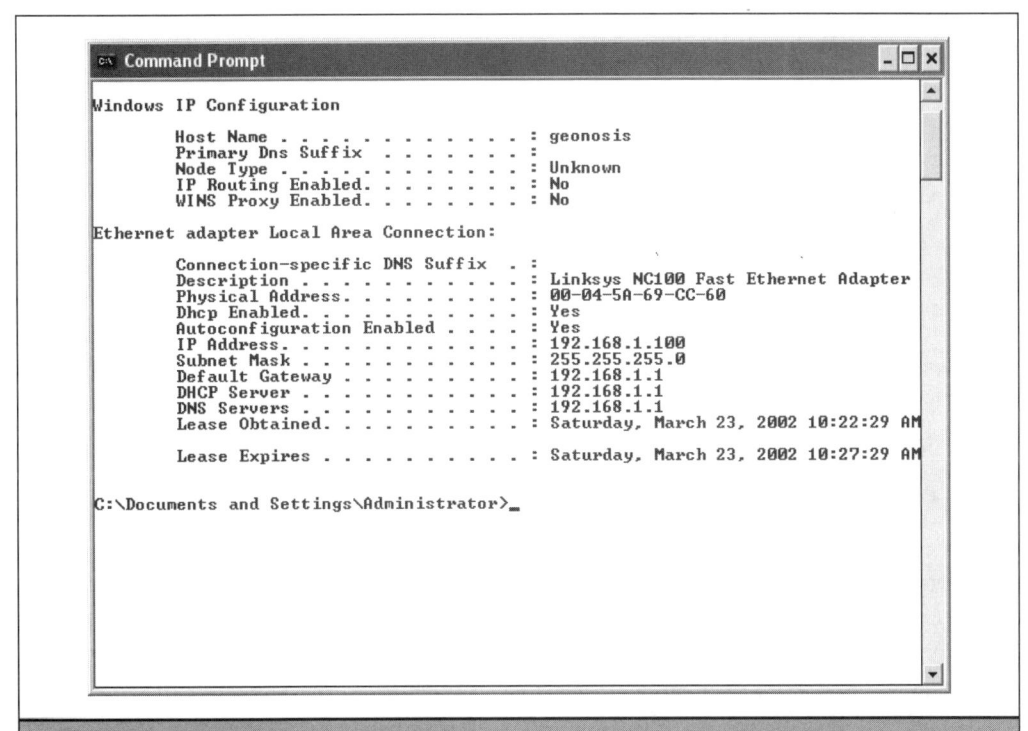

Figure 3-15. The ipconfig.exe tool can be used to check IP address assignment.

> **CAUTION** It's best not to fiddle with the Registry unless you know what you're doing. Mistyping a line can cause your computer not to boot or other catastrophes.

If you need to disable APIPA for multiple adapters using the Registry, set the value of IPAutoconfigurationEnabled to 0x0 in the following subkey: HKEY_LOCAL_MACHINE\SYSTEM\CurrentControlSet\Services\Tcpip\Parameters.

Static IP Addressing

Static IP addressing is a way to manually configure your IP address. This is probably the method you would use if neither DHCP or APIPA were available to you (for instance, if no DHCP server was present and there was more than one subnet). In addition to the IP address, you must also configure the subnet gateway. As we mentioned before, this is not the ideal way to configure an IP address, especially if you intend to connect to the Internet.

Configuring on a Single Network

To configure your IP address statically, you'll need the IP address for each network adapter installed on your computer and the subnet mask for each local network. Next, follow these steps to configure the IP address manually. The result is shown in Figure 3-16.

1. In the Control Panel, select Network and Internet Connections.
2. In Network and Internet Connections, select Network Connections.
3. In Network Connections, right-click the LAN you wish to change.
4. Select Properties, and then click the General tab.
5. Select Internet Protocol (TCP/IP) from the list, and then click Properties.
6. On the General tab, select the option Use the following IP address.
7. Enter the IP address, subnet mask, and default gateway.
8. Click OK to exit the Internet Protocol (TCP/IP) Properties window, and click OK to exit the Local Area Connection Properties window.

Multihoming

In the last example, we set up a connection using a single NIC. However, there might be instances where a computer has more than one network adapter installed. This is called *multihoming*. Furthermore, Windows XP Professional also supports *logical multihoming*, which allows multihoming on devices with a lone network adapter. To configure multihoming, follow these steps:

1. Select Control Panel, and choose Network and Internet Connections.
2. Select Network Connections.

Figure 3-16. Setting an IP address manually

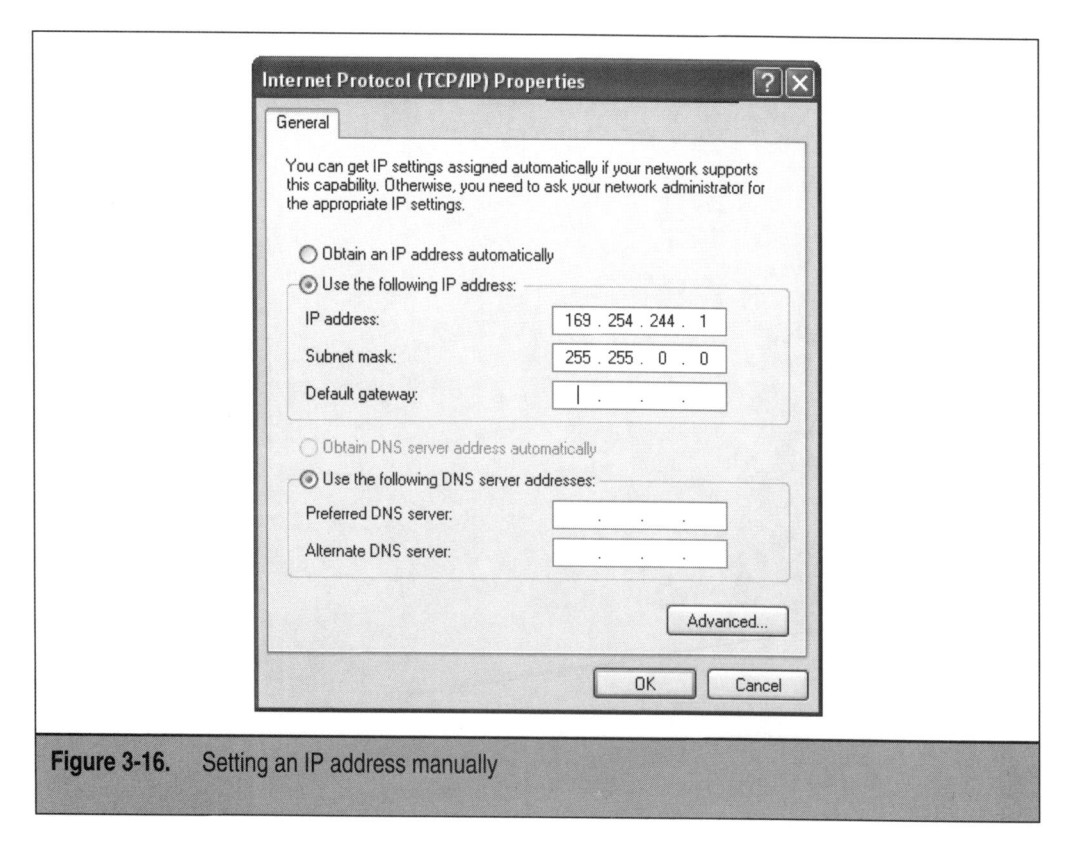

3. Right-click the LAN you wish to modify and select Properties.
4. Select General, and then select Internet Protocol (TCP/IP) from the list. Click Properties.
5. In the Internet Protocol (TCP/IP) sheet, select the General tab, and then select the option Use the following IP address.
6. Enter the TCP/IP configuration information for the first IP address, and then click Advanced.
7. Under IP address (shown in Figure 3-17), click Add to assign additional IP addresses to the same NIC.
8. In the TCP/IP Address box, shown in Figure 3-18, enter the IP address and subnet mask to assign an additional address to the same NIC. To repeat the process, click Add.
9. In the Advanced TCP/IP Settings page, click Default Gateways, and click Add to assign additional default gateways to the same NIC.
10. Select the TCP/IP Gateway Address box, and then enter an IP address for an additional default gateway for the same NIC.

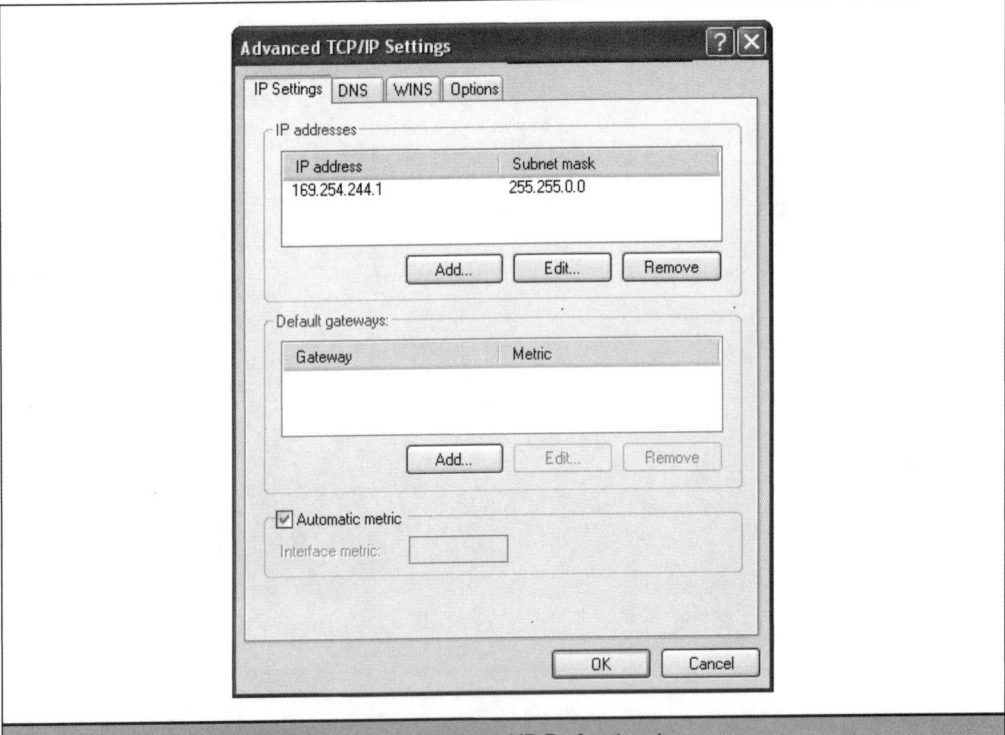

Figure 3-17. Setting up multihoming on Windows XP Professional

11. Click the check box to assign the gateway's metric automatically. If it is not to be assigned automatically, enter it in the appropriate box. When you're finished, click Add and repeat the process for additional gateway addresses.
12. Exit out of the message windows by clicking OK.

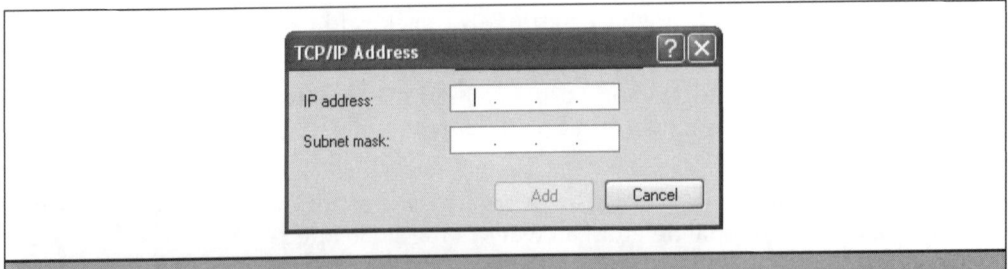

Figure 3-18. Enter additional IP addresses one by one in this dialog box.

> **NOTE** A metric determines how many router hops will be needed to get to the destination.

Alternate IP Configuration

Alternate IP Configuration allows you to configure your network interface with more than one IP address. This is useful if you need to connect to more than one network (for instance if you are a road warrior and must connect your laptop to two different networks). Furthermore, Alternate IP Configuration is useful if one network uses DHCP to assign IP addresses (at the office, for instance) and your other network uses a static IP address (a broadband connection to your home ISP, for instance).

Alternate IP Configuration allows your computer to try connecting to the first network, and if it is unavailable, it will automatically attempt a connection to the second.

Configuring a Dynamically Assigned Alternate IP Address

The following steps should be followed when configuring Windows XP Professional for dynamically assigned alternate IP addresses:

1. Select Control Panel, choose Network and Internet Connections, and then select Network Connections.
2. Right-click Local Area Connections, and then select Properties.
3. Click the General tab, and pick Internet Protocol (TCP/IP) | Properties from the list.
4. On the Alternate Configuration tab, select Automatic private IP address to choose a dynamically assigned private address as your alternate, as shown in Figure 3-19.
5. Click OK.

Configuring a Static Alternate IP Address

The window shown in Figure 3-19 can also be used to select alternate IP addresses statically. If your alternate address must be selected statically, follow these steps:

1. Select Control Panel, choose Network and Internet Connections, and then select Network Connections.
2. Right-click Local Area Connections, and then select Properties.
3. Click the General tab, and pick Internet Protocol (TCP/IP) | Properties from the list.
4. On the Alternate Configuration tab, select the option User configured.
5. Enter the alternate IP address, subnet mask, and default gateway.
6. Enter the preferred and alternate DNS server address.
7. Enter the preferred and alternate WINS server address.
8. Click OK.

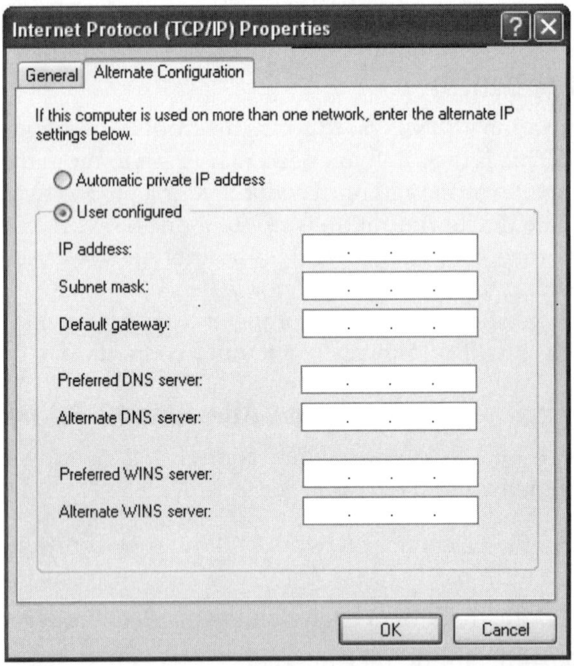

Figure 3-19. You can set up alternate IP addresses either statically or automatically.

Name Resolution

In addition to setting the TCP/IP address, you must also set up name resolution services. As we noted earlier, computers and devices use IP addresses to identify one another, but humans rely on computer names for identification. Windows XP Professional allows four methods to resolve names to IP addresses:

- **Domain Name System (DNS)** This is used for applications and services requiring hostname–to–IP address resolution. An example is Active Directory.

- **Windows Internet Name Service (WINS)** This is Microsoft's proprietary name resolution service and isn't used, by default, in Windows 2000 or beyond. However, for the sake of backward compatibility, it is included in Windows XP Professional. WINS offers compatibility with services and applications that require NetBIOS–to–IP address resolution.

- **Hosts and Lmhosts files** These provide hostname–to–IP address resolution and NetBIOS name–to–IP address resolution using locally maintained files.

- **Subnet Broadcasts** These can be used for NetBIOS name resolution within the local subnet.

> **NOTE** NetBIOS (short for Network Basic Input/Output System) is a program allowing applications on different computers to communicate within a LAN. It was created by IBM for its early PC network, was then adopted by Microsoft, and has since become a de facto industry standard.

To resolve a name to an IP address, the Windows XP Professional resolver follows these steps:

1. First, it submits the name query to DNS.
2. If the DNS query fails, then the resolver checks the length of the name. If it is longer than 15 characters, it fails.
3. If the name is 15 characters or shorter, then the resolver checks to see if NetBIOS is running.
4. If NetBIOS is not running, the resolver fails.
5. If NetBIOS is running, then the resolver tries NetBIOS name resolution.

Choosing a Name Resolution Method

Depending on your network components, you will need to determine whether your Windows XP Professional clients need to be configured to use DNS, WINS, or a combination of both. You should use DNS if the following conditions are present:

- The Windows XP Professional client is a member of an Active Directory domain.
- The client is connected to a network that uses a DNS server.
- The client connects to the Internet.

Other means of name resolution should be used as follows:

- WINS is only used for the sake of backward compatibility. If your network has a WINS server, then configure your name resolution service for WINS.
- If a WINS server is unavailable, then configure your Windows XP Professional clients to use Lmhosts for NetBIOS name resolution. If this option is not available, then name resolution must be performed by broadcasts. Unfortunately, this does not work outside the local subnet.

The good news is that if you use a DHCP server, then your name resolution method will be configured automatically. However, if you do not use a DHCP server, then all this information must be configured manually.

Setting and Changing the DNS Hostname

If you've upgraded from an earlier version of Windows, Windows XP Professional saves you some trouble and automatically rolls over the old DNS name into the new OS. For new installations, the Setup tool will ask you to enter the DNS name for this client. With

DNS the hostname can be up to 63 characters long and is used in conjunction with the primary domain name to supply the *fully qualified domain name (FQDN)*.

For instance, if a client computer is named "gilligan" and is part of the domain castaways.com, then the FQDN is gilligan.castaways.com.

The NetBIOS name is only 15 characters long, and when Windows XP Professional needs to assign a NetBIOS name, it takes the DNS name and shortens it to 15 characters.

For example, as *Star Wars* fans will probably note, the computer shown in Figure 3-20 would most accurately be referred to as "The Forest Moon of Endor," rather than simply "Endor." However, because NetBIOS only allows 15 characters, this was originally concatenated to "The_Forest_Moon." This cramped our style a bit, so we changed it to "Endor."

After installation, you can change your DNS hostname (which in turn will change your NetBIOS name) by following these steps:

1. Select Control Panel, choose Performance and Maintenance, and then select System.
2. Select the Computer Name tab (as shown in Figure 3-20).
3. Click Change.

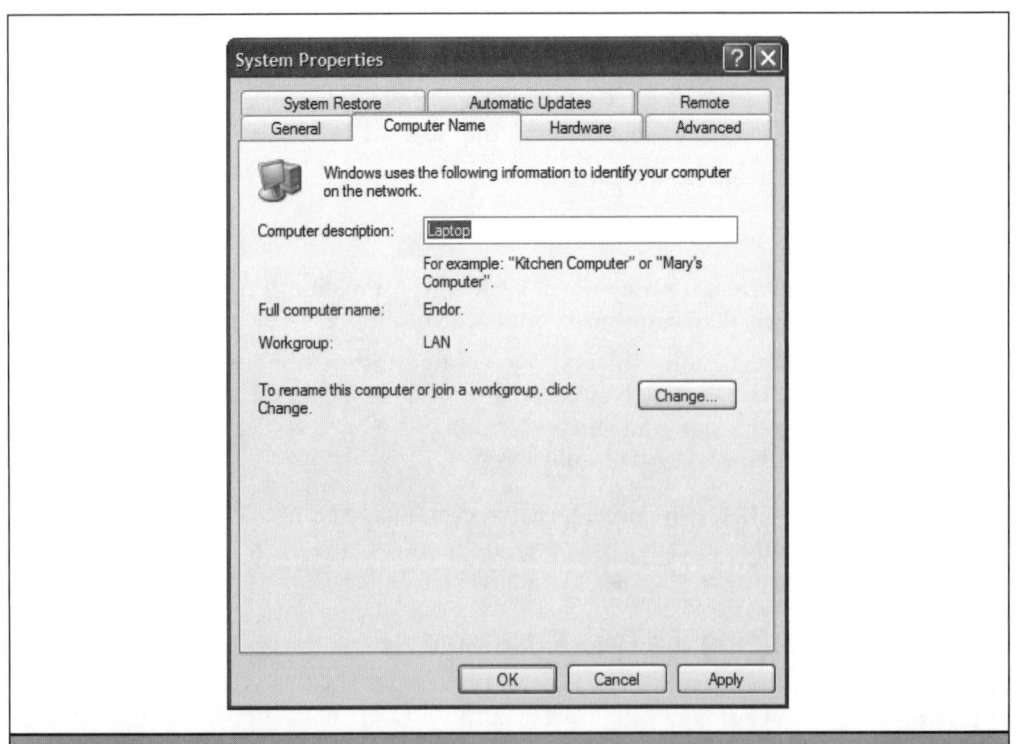

Figure 3-20. The name for this host is Endor.

4. Enter the new hostname and click OK.
5. You will have to restart the computer for the name change to be finalized. Click Yes to restart.

NOTE You can only use the characters a–z, A–Z, 0–9 and -. If any other characters are present in your name, Windows XP Professional will issue a kind warning message.

Changing the Primary DNS Suffix

The primary DNS suffix is the name of the DNS domain to which the client is attached. If you are using Active Directory domains, then the Windows XP Professional client's domain name is automatically set to the Active Directory DNS name. However, if the client is a member of a Windows NT domain, a DNS suffix is not automatically selected. The primary DNS suffix can be changed as follows:

1. Select Control Panel, choose Performance and Maintenance, and then select System.
2. Select the Computer Name tab.
3. Click Change, and then click More.
4. In the text box, enter the primary DNS suffix.
5. Click OK.

In the event you are connecting your Windows XP Professional clients to a Windows NT domain but plan on migrating to Windows 2000 or .NET servers in the future, then the client can automatically change its DNS suffix when you migrate. Simply ensure that the Change DNS domain name when domain membership changes box is checked. (This is the default setting.)

Connection-Specific Domain Names

Windows XP Professional allows you to name your computer differently, depending on which network you're connecting to. This is known as a *connection-specific domain name*. For example, if your organization's suffix is castaways.com and your computer is named "gilligan", then your FQDN is gilligan.castaways.com. However, when you connect to your ISP (dobiegillis.net), you can set your DNS name to "maynardgkrebs", which would give you the FQDN of maynardgkrebs.dobiegillis.net.

Connection-specific domain names for each NIC can be assigned either automatically or manually. The following steps illustrate the manual setup process:

1. Select Control Panel, and click Network and Internet Connections.
2. Next, choose Network Connections, right-click your selected network connection, and choose Properties.

3. On the General tab, select Internet Protocol (TCP/IP) from the list, and then click Properties.
4. Click Advanced, and then select the DNS tab.
5. In the DNS suffix for this connection box, enter the domain name for the connection.
6. Click OK to exit the three dialog boxes.

Preferred and Alternate DNS Servers

Depending on your network, you may have one DNS server, a dozen, or even more. Windows XP Professional allows you to pick which DNS server you will primarily access for name resolution. Additionally, you can also set an unlimited number of alternates, in case you are unable to query the preferred DNS server.

To specify a preferred and alternate DNS server, do the following:

1. Select Control Panel, choose Network and Internet Connections, and then select Network Connections.
2. Right-click the LAN you wish to modify and select Properties.
3. On the General Tab, select Internet Protocol (TCP/IP) from the list, and then click Properties.
4. In the Internet Protocol (TCP/IP) sheet, select the General tab, and choose the method you will use to access the DNS servers:
    a. Select Obtain DNS server address automatically if a DHCP server is available for automatic IP addressing.
    b. Select Use the following DNS server addresses if you wish to manually configure the DNS server, and then enter the appropriate IP address of your DNS server.
5. Click OK to exit the dialog boxes.

Specify additional alternate servers by following these steps:

1. Select Control Panel, choose Network and Internet Connections, and then select Network Connections.
2. Click the General tab, and then click Advanced.
3. Click the DNS tab.
4. Under DNS server addresses, in order of use, click Add.
5. Enter the IP address of your alternate DNS server.
6. Click Add.

You can remove a DNS server from the list by selecting it, and then clicking Remove. If you want to establish the DNS server search order, do the following:

1. Select Control Panel, choose Network and Internet Connections, and then select Network Connections.
2. Right-click the LAN you wish to modify and select Properties.
3. On the General tab, pick Internet Protocol (TCP/IP) from the list, and then click Properties.
4. Click Advanced.
5. Select the DNS tab.
6. In the DNS server addresses, in order of use, highlight the IP address of the DNS server you wish to change, and then click the up- or down-arrow buttons to change its position in the list.
7. Click OK.

WINS

WINS is a name resolution service for NetBIOS name–to–IP address mappings. It can be used either on its own or in conjunction with DNS. WINS is useful in reducing the number of local name resolution broadcasts and allows users to locate computers on remote networks. Additionally, DHCP can be used for autoconfiguration if a DHCP server is available on the network.

Configuration The following steps are used to configure a Windows XP Professional client to employ WINS for name resolution:

1. Select Control Panel, choose Network and Internet Connections, and then select Network Connections.
2. Right-click the LAN you wish to modify and select Properties.
3. On the General tab, pick Internet Protocol (TCP/IP) from the list, and then click Properties.
4. If a DHCP server is operational, select Obtain an IP address automatically.
5. If a DHCP server is neither available nor operational, follow this path:
    a. Select Advanced.
    b. Under the WINS tab, click Add.
    c. Enter the address of the WINS server and click Add.
6. Click OK to exit the dialog boxes

Search Order   Like DNS servers, you can have more than one WINS server on your network. If that is the case, perform the following steps:

1. Select Control Panel, choose Network and Internet Connections, and then select Network Connections.
2. Right-click the LAN you wish to modify and select Properties.
3. On the General tab, pick Internet Protocol (TCP/IP) from the list, and then click Properties.
4. Click Advanced, and then select the WINS tab.
5. Under the WINS addresses, in the order of use box, select the IP address of the WINS server you wish to move around.
6. Use the up- and down-arrow buttons to change the order of the WINS servers.

Other Protocols

TCP/IP isn't the be-all and end-all of networking protocols. In fact, you might encounter quite a few other protocols in your networking endeavors that might be more useful than TCP/IP. Even though TCP/IP has found its niche, there are a number of other protocols that you might want to implement either instead of or in conjunction with TCP/IP.

Let's take a look at two main issues—security and interconnectivity—and then we'll provide a quick overview of some other protocols that you can install on Windows XP Professional.

Security

We're all worried about security these days, and the truth of the matter is that even though the Internet is *mostly* secure, it isn't bulletproof. Realistically, if you want to move your sensitive data across the public Internet, you need a way to do it that won't compromise your organization or your bank account. As such, TCP/IP simply isn't good enough. You need something beefier, more robust.

This is where such protocols as Layer 2 Tunneling Protocol (L2TP) and Point-to-Point Tunneling Protocol (PPTP) come into play. When used in conjunction with VPNs (which we discuss in Chapter 14), these protocols can ensure that your data is sent in a secure fashion.

Interconnectivity

As much as TCP/IP has become a worldwide standard, there are still some computers and devices out there that will not connect with it. Or, more accurately, you won't be able to maximize your computers' connection using TCP/IP.

PPP

The *Point-to-Point Protocol (PPP)* is a set of framing and authentication protocols included with Windows remote access. This protocol ensures interoperability with third-party remote access software.

A variation of PPP is PPP over Ethernet (PPPoE). This allows the user to connect a series of hosts over a simple bridging device to a remote access concentrator. Each host uses its own PPP connection. In order to establish the PPP connection over Ethernet, each PPP session must know the Ethernet address of the remote peer and establish a unique session identifier. PPPoE includes a discovery protocol that enables the session identifier.

PPTP

Point-to-Point Tunneling Protocol (PPTP) was developed by Microsoft (and others) and is an open standard, used for virtual private networks (VPNs). PPTP allows the tunneling of PPP frames. *Tunneling* allows frames to move across the public Internet in a safe, secure manner. PPP frames can include IP and other networking protocols. There are two other protocols (namely L2TP and IPSec) that make VPNs more secure; however, PPTP is much easier to set up. PPTP uses PPP authentication, compression, and encryption.

NetBEUI

The NetBIOS Extended User Interface (NetBEUI) is a Microsoft protocol used by its networking products. It is an extremely simple protocol to use, requiring very little configuration. However, that simplicity comes at a price. NetBEUI is nonroutable, which means that it only works on very simple networks that do not use routing devices to connect multiple LAN segments.

NetBEUI can only be used on LANs with 200 or fewer clients, relying on Token Ring source routing as its only method or routing.

Protocols provide a language of sorts, which enables computers to speak to one another. The most popular protocol is TCP/IP, which is used for Internet connectivity and is the most prevalent standard in organizational networks. Windows XP Professional allows TCP/IP to be installed, configured, and managed in a straightforward, easy way.

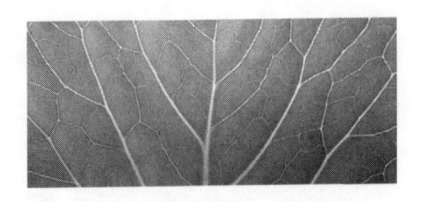

PART II

Internetworking

CHAPTER 4

Creating Network Connections

There are a number of ways in which Windows XP Professional computers can connect remotely to networks—whether a corporate local area network (LAN), an Internet service provider (ISP), or a single computer set up to receive dial-in traffic. The technologies that support these types of connections include analog modems, integrated services digital networks (ISDNs), digital subscriber lines (DSLs), and cable modems, or plain old Ethernet.

In this chapter we look specifically at the steps you would take to connect to the Internet or to a LAN from a remote location using these technologies. First, we examine ways in which Windows XP Professional forms connections with these devices. Next, we talk about modem installation and configuration and provide some troubleshooting tips. Finally, we cover the Add New Hardware Wizard, which is the heart of Windows XP Professional's device installation process.

HARDWARE

This section looks at the different types of hardware connections that can be made by Windows XP Professional—whether via an analog dial-in modem, DSL, ISDN, or cable connection. Additionally, Windows XP Professional provides a couple of tools that can help you determine if your peripheral devices are installed properly and, if not, how to correct them.

Before getting into the nuts and bolts of making a network connection, it's prudent to cover the applications that Windows XP Professional uses to bridge the gap between the operating system (OS) and the device.

Hardware Connection Overview

The hardware you use to connect to the Internet (or your WAN) will depend largely on your networking needs, budget, and organizational politics.

NOTE For a review of the different types of network connection hardware, flip back to Chapter 1.

Windows XP Professional contains a number of tools that will help you connect, manage, and troubleshoot network connections—be they LAN, WAN, or otherwise. The weapons in Windows XP Professional's device connection and management arsenal include the following:

- Device Manager
- Plug and Play
- Device drivers

An examination of these tools can help you forge strong connections between your Windows XP Professional client and the device to which you are connecting.

Device Manager

You can see a list of the devices connected to your computer by using the *Device Manager*. The Device Manager is a great tool for seeing what devices you've got attached and to examine their settings and properties. The Device Manager (the window of which is shown in Figure 4-1) lists all the devices that make up your computer and allows you to modify their configuration. If the Add New Hardware Wizard detects a device conflict, then the Device Manager starts automatically.

To examine the contents of the Device Manager, follow these steps:

1. Select Start | Control Panel.
2. Select Performance and Maintenance.
3. Click the System icon and select the Hardware tab.
4. Click the Device Manager button.

Device Manager allows you to view devices by *type* or *connection*. Type view appears when the hardware itself has a problem, with the troublesome device expanded. Connection view is best used for device driver debugging.

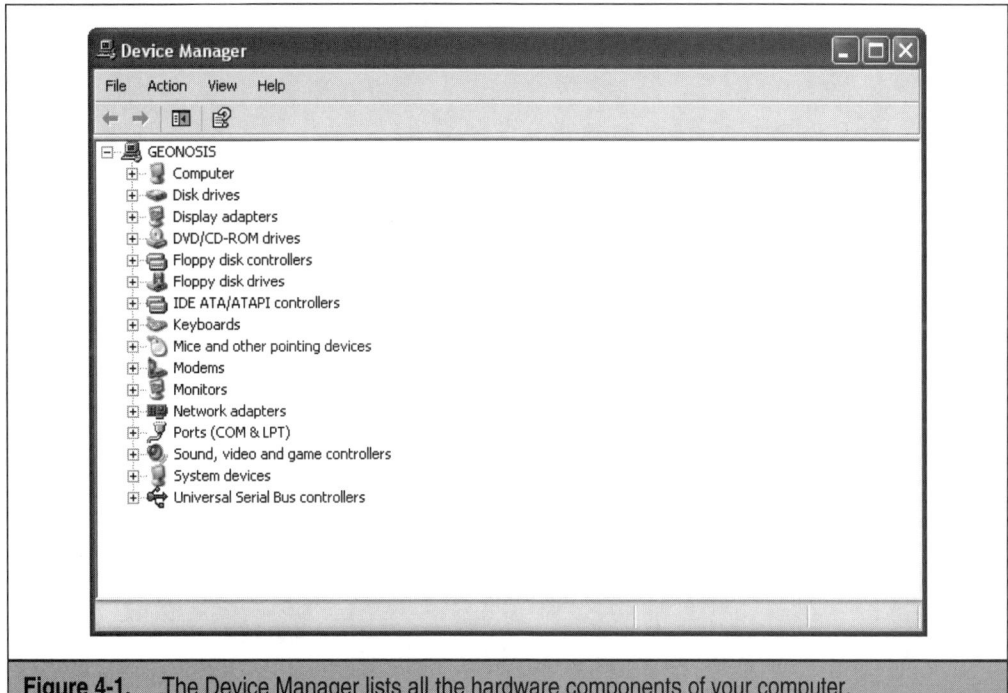

Figure 4-1. The Device Manager lists all the hardware components of your computer.

NOTE You can also start the Device Manager with the Microsoft Management Console (MMC). Click Start, right-click My Computer, select Manage from the menu to see the MMC, and select Device Manager in the left pane of the window. This view is shown in Figure 4-2.

Plug and Play Devices

A few years ago, if you wanted to install a printer, a modem, a monitor, a joystick, or virtually any other peripheral in Windows, you had the arduous task of installing device drivers. Worse yet, there were even some devices that required you to specify interrupt request (IRQ) and direct memory access (DMA) settings. This was all fine and good if you were a gearhead, but if you didn't have the technical juice, installing a peripheral to Windows could be a huge irritant.

When Windows 95 and NT came along, things got a little simpler; it was possible to install the device, and then add a simple device driver. Things got better still with Windows 98 and Windows 2000 when Plug and Play was introduced.

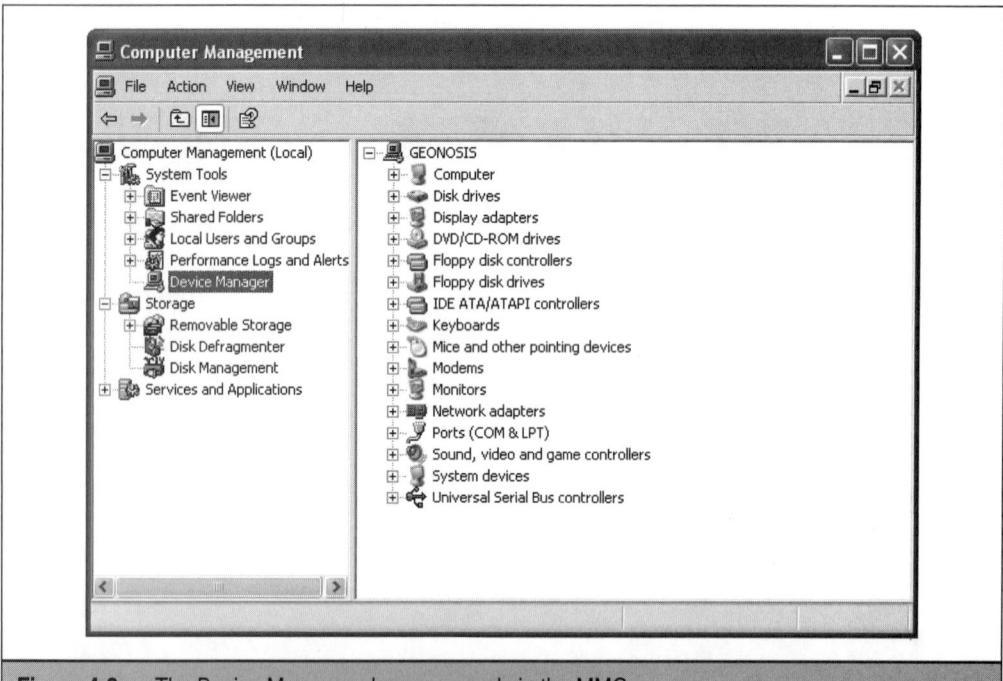

Figure 4-2. The Device Manager when accessed via the MMC

> **NOTE** Plug and Play wasn't perfect, however. Some spotty functionality brought on the moniker "Plug-n-Pray." Whether or not Windows XP Professional smoothes out these issues remains to be seen.

Plug and Play does exactly what it implies—when a Plug and Play–compatible device is connected, Windows reads the device information and sets everything up automatically. Windows might request that the user provide a device driver disk, but for the most part, everything installs smoothly and efficiently.

Under Windows XP Professional, Plug and Play offers the following services:

- Detection of a Plug and Play device, determining its hardware resources needs and device identification number
- Allocation of hardware resources
- Automatic loading and initializing of drivers
- Notification to other devices and drivers when a new device is present

Some buses, such as Peripheral Computer Interface (PCI) and Universal Serial Bus (USB) offer full support for Plug and Play. Older buses, such as Industry Standard Architecture (ISA), don't offer the same support for Plug and Play and need more user interaction for the correct installation of device drivers.

If your client computers are *x*86-based systems, the way BIOS code interacts with Plug and Play devices might vary. This will depend on whether the system BIOS or the operating system takes on the task of configuring hardware. Your BIOS settings (if available on your computer) can determine whether or not Plug and Play is enabled.

Table 4-1 lists system conditions and recommended BIOS settings.

System	BIOS Setting
ACPI system (ACPI BIOS present; ACPI hardware abstraction layer installed)	Either Yes/Enabled or No/Disabled
Noncompliant ACPI system (ACPI BIOS present, ACPI HAL not installed)	No/Disabled
Non-ACPI systems	No/Disabled
Dual-boot Windows XP Professional with Windows 9X, Me	No/Disabled

Table 4-1. *x86-Based Computer BIOS Settings for Plug and Play Devices*

Device Drivers

Because there are so many thousands of peripherals made by hundreds of different vendors, it would be impossible for Microsoft to keep track of all the devices and form connections between them and the OS. To ameliorate this problem, Windows uses *device drivers*. These are small programs that are created by the device vendor to allow functionality with Windows XP Professional.

Windows XP Professional comes with number of standard drivers for a wide variety of monitors, printers, game controllers, modems, and so forth. When you buy a peripheral (a modem, for instance), you normally receive a CD-ROM containing the driver for that device developed by software engineers at that company. The CD-ROM will contain drivers for most flavors of Windows.

NOTE If you already have a device that you need to connect with Windows XP Professional, you should always check the vendor's web site—they might have an updated device driver.

If you want to see information about a specific device driver, open the Device Manager window, right-click the device name, and select Properties. If there is a Driver tab, click it. Most driver tabs will contain the following buttons:

- **Driver Details** A list of files that compose the driver
- **Update Driver** Used for installing a new driver
- **Roll Back Driver** Used for reinstalling an earlier version of a driver
- **Uninstall** Used for uninstalling the driver

NOTE When installing a new device, you might get a pop-up window telling you that Microsoft has not approved the driver. Microsoft uses this as a safety measure to keep bad drivers from corrupting Windows XP. Unfortunately, there are more than a couple of vendors who don't want to pay the money to get their devices vetted and approved by Microsoft. Just go ahead and click through this window and install the driver. If it doesn't work, you can always uninstall it.

Since Windows XP Professional is built on Windows 2000, if you are given a choice of OSs, and XP isn't one of them, then try Windows 2000.

Analog Modems

Depending on your client's remote access needs, it will probably be necessary to install and configure a modem. For the past few years, it's been almost impossible to buy a computer that doesn't already come with a modem installed. However, you might find yourself swapping the modem out for a different one. On the other hand, if you have a cubicle farm full of client PCs, you were probably able to save a few dollars by buying them without the modems installed. Whatever the case, if you find yourself needing to install a modem, just follow the instructions in the next section.

Installation

If you're installing an internal modem, the steps are very common for each vendor's device. In essence, you must power down your computer, remove the cover, locate an open PCI slot, and plug in the modem. You then replace the cover, plug the modem into the wall outlet, plug a telephone into the modem, and power on the computer.

This is the end of the physical work involved in modem installation. Next, Windows XP Professional takes over. Once you power up your computer, Plug and Play will indicate that a new modem has been installed and will activate the Install New Modem Wizard.

NOTE This wizard can also be activated by selecting the Modems icon in the Control Panel.

At this point, the wizard will ask you if you're installing a PCMCIA modem (for laptops) or an internal or external modem. The wizard will look for a driver from its files. If it fails to find a driver, it will ask you to insert a device driver disk. (Alternatively, you can go to your modem manufacturer's web site, download the driver, and simply tell Windows XP Professional where the driver file is located on your hard drive.)

After Windows has installed your modem's driver, it will ask you for some information:

- The country in which you are located and corresponding code
- Any digits needed to dial an outside line
- Whether your phone is pulse or tone

All this information is maintained in your default Dialing Location. (We'll explain what Dialing Locations are and how they can be used later in this chapter in the section "Configuring Dialing Locations.")

Configuration

Once your modem has been installed, you must configure it so that Windows XP Professional can use it properly. You can examine or change your modem configuration settings by choosing Start | Control Panel, clicking Printers and Other Hardware, and then clicking Phone and Modem Options. Figure 4-3 shows the resulting window.

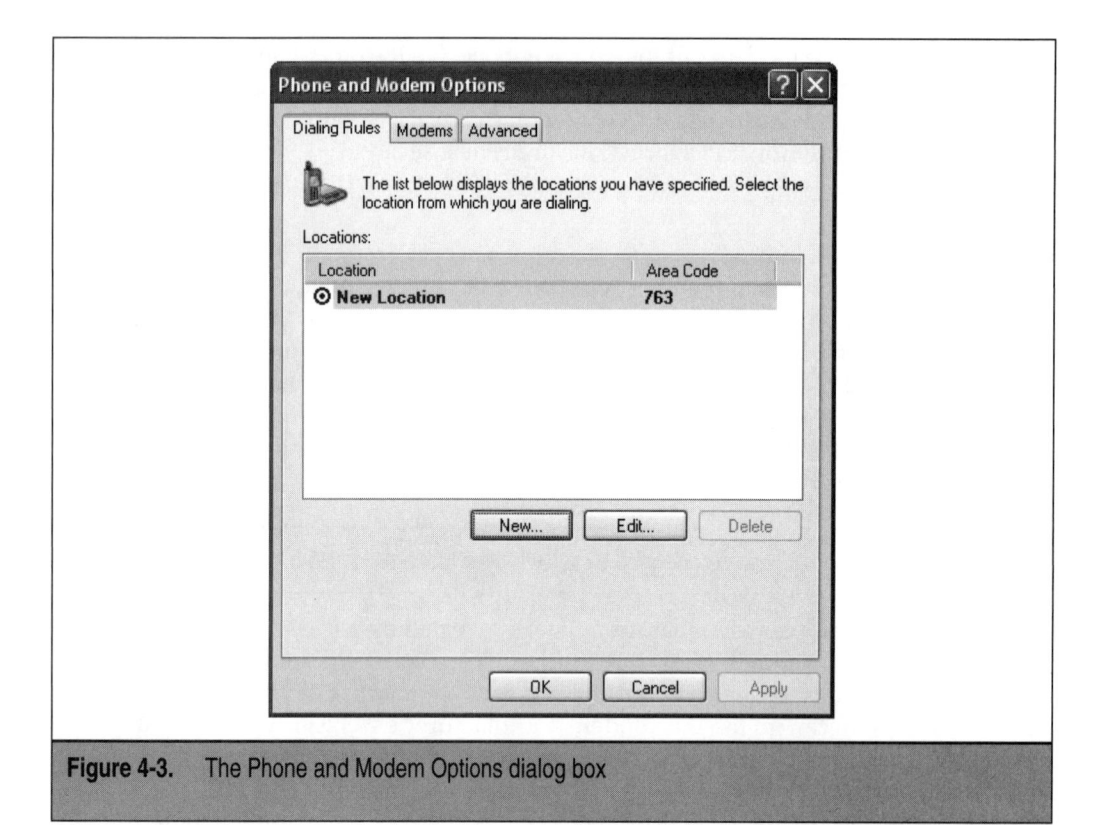

Figure 4-3. The Phone and Modem Options dialog box

Once this box appears, click the Modems tab to see a list of the modems installed on your system. Select your modem and click Properties. Your modem's Properties box appears, as shown in Figure 4-4.

NOTE If you have more than one modem driver installed, click the Driver tab in the modem's Properties dialog box.

Table 4-2 lists the various properties that can be adjusted on your modem.

Back in your modem's Properties dialog box, you can select the Change Default Preferences button for a list of default modem settings. These settings and their descriptions are listed in Table 4-3.

For the most part, these settings never need to be changed; however, it's nice to know what they're for and how you can adjust them if necessary.

Chapter 4: Creating Network Connections **123**

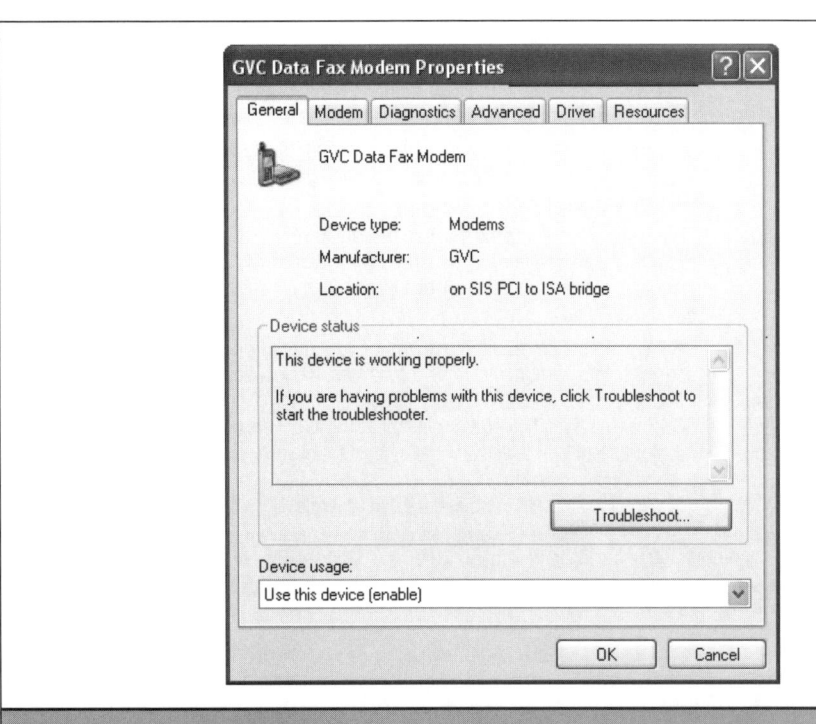

Figure 4-4. The Properties box for the selected modem

Tab	Property	Description
General	Device Usage	Enables or disables your modem. For instance, if your internal modem fails, you can disable it while you use another modem.
Modem	Port	Specifies on which port your modem is installed: COM1, COM2, COM3, COM4, or LPT. If your modem is a USB or FireWire port, it will be listed here.
Modem	Speaker Volume	Sets the volume of your modem's speaker. Don't like that whining and whistling when you connect? Turn it all the way off.
Modem	Maximum Port Speed	Establishes how fast your modem can communicate with the computer. Typically, this is set to 115,200 bits per second. Note: This is not how fast your modem will exchange information with other computers over the telephone line.
Modem	Dial Control	Specifies whether the modem needs to wait and hear a dial tone before attempting a connection. This is useful if you have voicemail from your telephone company. When you have voicemail, the stuttering dial tone can be misinterpreted by modems as a lack of dial tone.

Table 4-2. Settings Within the Modem Properties Dialog Box

Tab	Property	Description
Diagnostics	Modem Information	Displays information about your modem, such as its serial number. Clicking Query Modem will generate a list of responses to the information noted here.
Diagnostics	Logging	Indicates whether information sent to and from the modem will be stored in a log file. This log is useful for troubleshooting purposes. To see the contents of the log, click View Log.
Advanced	Extra Settings	Lists additional commands that can be sent to your modem after Windows XP Professional sends its own, standard initialization commands. Your modem's manual or the manufacturer's web site should have a list of the commands that are unique to your modem.
Driver	Driver Provider, Driver Date, Driver Version, Digital Signer	Contain information about the driver for your modem. Click Driver Details for additional information, including the names and locations of driver files. Clicking Update will install a new driver. Clicking Roll Back Driver will reinstall a previous version of the driver. This is a new feature of Windows XP Professional that allows you to reinstall the previous driver version. Clicking Uninstall will remove the driver entirely.

Table 4-2. Settings Within the Modem Properties Dialog Box *(continued)*

Tab	Property	Description
General	Disconnect a call if idle for more than *xx* min	Indicates how long a call should remain connected if data is not being transmitted.
General	Cancel the call if not connected within *xx* sec.	If no connection occurs during dialup, this specifies how long the timeout should last.
General	Port Speed	Same as Maximum Port Speed in Table 4-2.
General	Data Protocol	Indicates which type of error correction to use. If no error correction is selected, connections will still be made, but they will be less reliable.
General	Compression	Indicates whether data will be compressed before transmitting. This is normally selected, but it will depend on whether your modem supports compression.
General	Flow Control	Indicates whether flow control will be used to control the flow of data between your modem and computer. There are two choices: Xon/Xoff and Hardware.
Advanced	Data Bits	Indicates how many bits will be contained in each byte. This must be set to 8.
Advanced	Parity	Indicates if the modem will send an error-detection bit (usually the eighth bit) of each byte. Normally, this is set to None.
Advanced	Stop Bits	Indicates how many extra stop bits are sent after each byte. This should be set to 1.
Advanced	Modulation	Indicates how your modem converts digital signals to analog waves for transmission over the public telephone system.

Table 4-3. Modem Properties on the Advanced Tab of the Modem Options Dialog Box

Troubleshooting

If you experience problems getting your modem to connect, the following are some good places to look for trouble:

- **Double-check your modem driver**   Examine the Modems tab on the Phone and Modems Options dialog box. Do you have the correct driver installed? If you have more than one modem listed, remove extra modems and drivers. Is your modem driver enabled? Go to the Device Manager, choose View | Devices By Type, and then click the + (plus) sign next to the Modems entry. If your modem has an X or ! next to it (or if your modem isn't even listed), then you've got a problem. Select the modem, and then right-click Properties. Under the General tab, make sure that Device Usage is set to Use This Device.

- **Is your modem connected to the right port?**   Look at the Properties dialog box, and then on the Modem or General tab, make sure that the port to which your modem is physically connected jibes with this setting.

- **Slow down!**   On the Modem tab in the Properties dialog box, double-check your Maximum Port Speed setting. Dropping it down a notch might solve your problems.

> **NOTE**   Windows XP Professional also includes a Modem Troubleshooter to help ferret out problems. The Troubleshooter can be started by clicking the General tab in the modem's Properties box and then clicking Troubleshoot.

ISDN Hardware

Like previous versions of Windows, Windows XP Professional provides ISDN support, right out of the box. But, unlike installing a dial-up modem, there are a number of prerequisites that must be in place before installing and configuring an ISDN connection.

First, you must have ISDN services available on your telephone line. Without these services in place, both at the location you're dialing from and the location to which you will be connecting, your hardware will not work. For example, if you are using the ISDN connection to link a remote office to a central office, then both locations must have the ISDN service activated. If you are connecting to your ISP via ISDN, you must sign up for its ISDN service and ensure the service has been activated at the ISP before continuing with your configuration.

> **NOTE**   Before proceeding with any ISDN connection, you should call your ISP and make sure that it offers ISDN connections and that you understand its policies for ISDN links.

Once service has been set up on both ends of the connection, you need to have the necessary hardware—be it an internal or an external ISDN adapter. Furthermore, for purposes of configuration, there are some bits of information that Windows XP

Professional will ask you when setting up your ISDN adapter. This information is listed in Table 4-4 and should be acquired from your telephone carrier before you configure your ISDN adapter.

Installation

Windows XP Professional will recognize that you've installed an ISDN adapter and automatically install the device driver if it supports Plug and Play. If it does not support Plug and Play, the following steps will walk you through the manual installation process:

1. In the Control Panel, select Printers and Other Hardware.
2. Select Add New Hardware.
3. Once the Add Hardware Wizard begins, select Next. (At this point, Windows XP Professional will automatically check your computer for newly installed devices.)
4. If the wizard cannot find the ISDN adapter, a dialog box will pop up and ask if the hardware has been connected yet. If it has, click Yes. If not, click No. (If you click No, Windows XP Professional will tell you to connect the device, and then try again.)
5. Click Next.
6. If your ISDN adapter still is not automatically detected, select Add a new hardware device, and then click Next.
7. To allow Windows XP Professional to find the ISDN adapter automatically, click Search For and Install The Hardware Automatically. If you'd rather manually select the ISDN adapter, select Install The Hardware That I Will Manually Select From A List, and then follow the resulting directions.
8. Click Show All Devices.
9. Select your modem manufacturer from the left pane, and the model from the right pane, and click Next. If your manufacturer and model are not listed, insert the device driver CD-ROM and click Have Disk.

NOTE You can also download the driver from your device manufacturer's web site, click Have Disk, and direct Windows XP Professional to that location, either on your hard drive or on a network share.

Once the ISDN adapter has been installed, Windows XP Professional prompts you to configure it. We'll show you how in the next section.

Configuration

To configure your ISDN adapter, Windows XP Professional asks you for various bits of information about the adapter. Table 4-4 lists the information that Windows XP

Setting	Description
Switch Type	Your ISDN adapter needs to know what type of switch it will connect to at the telephone company. The switch types Windows XP Professional lists are: • ESS5 (AT&T) • National ISDN1 • Northern Telecom DMS 1000
Service Profile Identifier (SPID)	The SPID is the telephone number, along with some extra digits tacked on to the beginning and the end. The SPID is used by the switch to help understand details of the ISDN connection.
Telephone number	Depending on your ISDN line, each B-channel might have its own telephone number, or they might all use the same number.

Table 4-4. ISDN Configuration Information You'll Be Asked by Windows XP Professional

Professional needs to configure your adapter. You'll need to get this information from your telephone company.

If you need to change these settings at any time, you can do so by following these steps:

1. Under Control Panel select Performance and Maintenance then select System and click Hardware.
2. Select the Device Manager.
3. Right-click the ISDN adapter you wish to change and choose Properties.
4. Select the ISDN tab.

To make changes to this information, you can select the switch type from the list. The SPID and telephone numbers are changed by clicking Configure.

DSL Hardware

Digital Subscriber Lines are, in some ways, easier to set up than dial-up analog modems. In other ways, they are more difficult.

Like ISDN, you cannot simply buy a DSL modem, plug it in, and take off. You must sign up for DSL service from your telephone company. However, you may or may not be eligible for DSL service, depending on your location's proximity to the so-called central office (CO). Also, given the different flavors of DSL out there, you should make sure that the modem you buy will work with the DSL line.

The process can be simplified, however, by calling your ISP and having it set up the DSL service. Most times, your ISP can call your phone company and get you the correct modem. As a cost savings, you can sometimes get the DSL modem free, depending on whether your telephone company is running a promotion.

Setting up and buying the modem are the hard parts. The easy part to enabling a DSL connection is actually configuring the device. First, let's take a look at what's involved in DSL modem installation.

Installation

Installing a DSL modem is largely an easy process. There are three types of DSL modems, each with a slightly different method of connection:

- **Using a NIC**   An external DSL modem simply uses a length of Category 5 cabling to connect to your computer's NIC.

  NOTE   Depending on the DSL modem manufacturer's design, you might have to use a crossover cable.

- **Using a USB port**   The DSL modem plugs into one of your computer's USB ports. The action of plugging in the USB cable will activate the New Hardware Wizard. Simply follow the onscreen commands to install the requisite driver, if Windows XP Professional doesn't already have one listed.

  NOTE   It should go without saying that you need to have a NIC installed on a computer that will be using an external DSL modem. We talk about NIC installation and setup in Chapter 5.

- **Internal connection**   Installing an internal DSL modem is a matter of removing your computer's case, locating an open PCI slot, and installing the modem. When you reconnect power and start up your computer, if your DSL modem supports Plug and Play, it will install a driver. If it does not support Plug and Play, you will have to install the driver manually, by using the Add New Hardware Wizard.

  NOTE   Be sure to check your manufacturer's instructions for installation. They should supersede any other instructions.

Configuration

In order to see your DSL configuration, follow these steps:

1. Select Start | My Network Places, and then click View Network Connections.
2. Right-click your DSL connection.
3. Choose Properties.
4. Click the Networking tab.
5. Click Internet Protocol (TCP/IP) and click the Properties button.

Your configuration settings will most likely come from your ISP with your welcome package. This is normally a sheet of paper that tells you your IP addresses and DNS server addresses. It's a good idea to keep this sheet of paper in a safe place in case you need to reinstall your device or adjust your settings for any reason.

Cable Hardware

Connecting to a cable modem involves plugging into a cable television line. Depending on the manufacturer and the model, like DSL, the modem can either plug into your NIC or a USB port, or it can be an internal device.

Installation

Installing a cable modem is generally very straightforward. There are three types of cable modems, each with a slightly different means of installation. In all cases, the modem itself will not only plug into your computer, but also to the coaxial cable supplying cable television to your home.

- **Using a NIC**   The external cable modem simply uses a length of Category 5 cabling to connect to your computer's NIC.

NOTE   Depending on the cable modem manufacturer's design, you might have to use a crossover cable.

- **Using a USB port**   The cable modem plugs into one of your computer's USB ports. The action of plugging in the cable will activate the New Hardware Wizard. Simply follow the onscreen commands to install the requisite driver, if Windows XP Professional doesn't already have one listed.

- **Internal connection**   Installing an internal cable modem is a matter of removing your computer's case (don't forget to disconnect the power, or you will be able to pick up 197 channels on the back of your eyelids), locating an open peripheral component interconnect (PCI) slot, and installing the adapter. When you reconnect power and start up your computer, if your cable modem supports Plug and Play, it will install a driver. If it does not support Plug and Play, you will have to install the driver manually, by using the Add New Hardware Wizard.

Depending on your cable company's Internet options, you might also have to plug your cable adapter into a telephone jack. This is because some cable systems only allow one-way transfer of data on the coaxial cable. If you want to send information, you may have to do it across a conventional telephone line.

Configuration

Configuring a cable adapter is much less involved than setting up a modem or an ISDN connection. Basically, because Windows XP Professional communicates with the cable modem using the TCP/IP networking protocol, all you need to do is configure your TCP/IP settings and you'll be set.

To configure the TCP/IP protocol, first you'll need to get the necessary IP and DNS server addresses and other information from your cable company. It's more than likely this information came on a sheet of paper when you signed up for the service. To configure your TCP/IP settings, do the following:

1. Select Start | My Network Places, and then click View Network Connections.
2. Right-click your cable Internet connection.
3. Select Properties and click the Networking tab.
4. Click Internet Protocol (TCP/IP) and click the Properties button.

This will give you a listing of your TCP/IP settings for the cable adapter. Again, you should only enter the values that came from your cable company.

Solving Hardware Problems

For all the nice and easy wizards that Microsoft provides, for all the reassuring advertising telling you this is the smoothest version of Windows ever, installing a device can still present its fair share of issues. Tracking them down and resolving them can take just a couple of minutes, or it can take much longer. The following steps can help streamline the troubleshooting process.

Windows XP Installation Glitch

When you try to install a device, sometimes Windows attempts to install files from *cabinet files*, also known as *CAB* files (so named because they end with the extension .cab). These files are located on your Windows XP Professional CD-ROM.

> **NOTE** If your OS was preinstalled by your computer manufacturer, then the cabinet files are likely located in your C:/I386 directory.

From time to time, Windows XP Professional is unable to locate the cabinet file and needs you to help it along. To locate the missing file, click the Details button in the dialog box that appears when Windows XP Professional asks for the location of this file. Next, you should select Start | Search and enter the name of the file that Windows is looking for. Then select your hard drive (or the Windows XP Professional CD-ROM) to locate the misplaced cabinet file. Switch back to the dialog box to tell Windows XP Professional where it should look for the cabinet file.

Safe Mode

Every so often the installation of a device driver simply causes Windows XP Professional to crash (thus Microsoft's device driver approval program). If you've fallen victim to this, you can use Windows XP Professional's Safe Mode. Safe Mode uses default settings (VGA monitor, mouse driver, no network connections, and a minimum set of device drivers) to at least start the computer. If a problem does not reappear when you are in Safe Mode, you can assume default settings and minimum device drivers are not the problem (see Figure 4-5).

Windows XP Professional has a more robust Safe Mode than earlier versions of Windows and will help track down setup and installation problems more effectively. Safe Mode can be entered by pressing F8 during bootup. The Windows XP Professional Safe Mode options are listed here:

- **Safe Mode** Starts Windows XP Professional with minimal drivers (mouse, monitor, keyboard, mass storage, and default system services) and in VGA Mode.
- **Safe Mode With Networking** Starts Windows XP Professional in Safe Mode, but allows network connectivity.
- **Safe Mode With Command Prompt** Starts in Safe Mode, but instead of a traditional desktop, a command prompt is displayed.

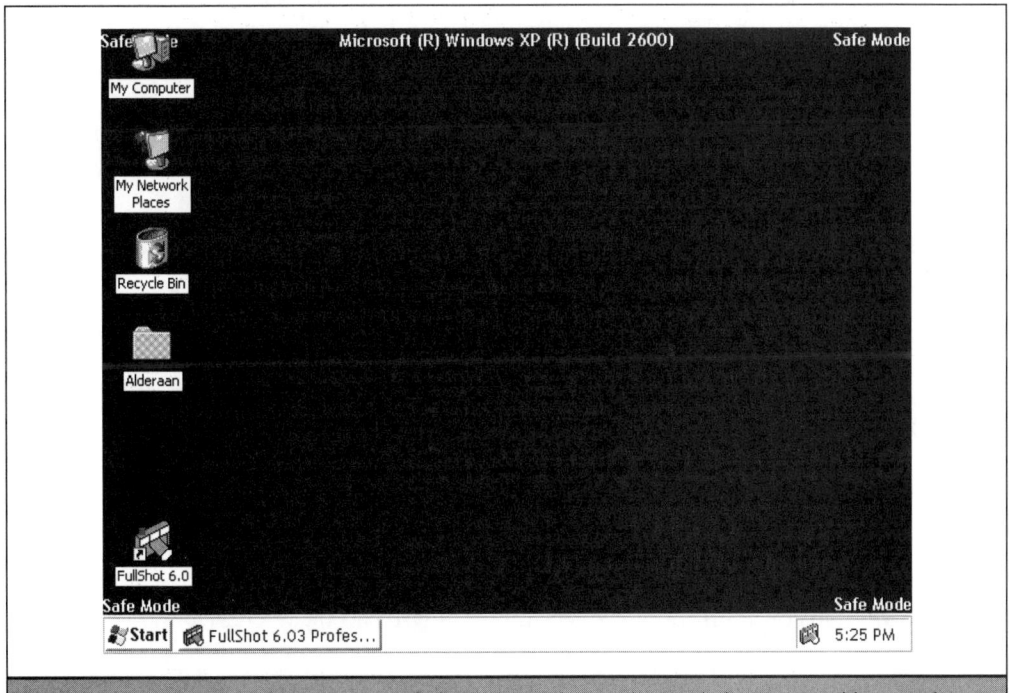

Figure 4-5. Windows XP Professional Safe Mode can be used to track down errant drivers and misconfigured settings.

- **Enable Boot Logging** Starts Windows XP Professional and logs all drivers and services that were or were not loaded. The list is saved in a file called ntblog.txt and is located in the C:\Windows directory.
- **Enable VGA Mode** Starts Windows XP Professional with a basic VGA driver. This option allows users to repair their system if they install a video driver improperly.
- **Last Known Good Configuration** Starts Windows XP Professional using the Registry information from the last time that the system loaded properly. This mode does not repair anything, and changes made since it was last loaded will be lost.
- **Debugging Mode** Starts Windows 2000 while sending debugging information via serial cable to another computer.
- **Selective Startup** This mode isn't shown on the Windows startup menu that appears when you press F8; rather, it is enabled by running the System Configuration Utility.
- **Normal Mode** This starts Windows normally.

We'll talk about Safe Mode in more detail in Chapter 8. However, for the sake of this discussion, it's important to know how it can be used to resolve driver problems.

Using the Device Manager

We mentioned the Device Manager earlier in this chapter, but let's take a closer look at it to understand how it can be used to isolate and troubleshoot device installation problems. To work out configuration issues, open the Device Manager by following these steps:

1. Select Start | Control Panel then click Performance and Maintenance.
2. Open the System icon and select the Hardware tab.
3. Click the Device Manager button to bring up the Device Manager (which is shown in Figure 4-1, earlier in this chapter).

If a device is having a problem, its icon will have a yellow exclamation point next to it or a red X over it. You can examine a particular device by right-clicking the icon and selecting Properties from the pop-up menu. You can examine the various tabs for more information about the conflict—most likely what you're looking for will be found in the General or Resources tabs. In the event a device has a conflict, then it will appear as shown in Figure 4-6.

There are two common sources of conflict that you can try to change to resolve the problem:

- **A problem with the driver** If there is a problem with the device's driver, you can right-click the device and select Update Driver from the resulting menu.

This activates the Hardware Update Wizard and takes you by the hand through the process of updating the driver for your device. If your device came with a CD-ROM or a floppy disk (most likely it did), choose Install From a List Or Check Specific Location and put the disk into your drive. Make sure to check your device manufacturer's web site and remember that drivers that worked with Windows 98 or Me might not work with Windows XP Professional.

- **IRQ conflict**   If two separate devices have Xs over their icons, they might be trying to use the same interrupt (IRQ) settings. In this case, click the Resources tab on each device's Properties box to see which IRQ the device is using. To see a list of IRQ settings and which device is using which one, select View | Resources By Type in the Device Manager window. Select the + (plus) box by the Interrupt Request (IRQ) item and change the IRQ for one of the devices. Be careful, however, that you don't select an IRQ for another device. An IRQ conflict might not always occur, however, because now there is a technology called *IRQ Sharing*. This allows multiple devices to share a single IRQ setting. If IRQ Sharing is present, you need not worry about an IRQ conflict occurring.

The Device Manager can be a handy tool for tracking down hardware problems. Checking the information in this window is an excellent place to start to determine the problem you're experiencing.

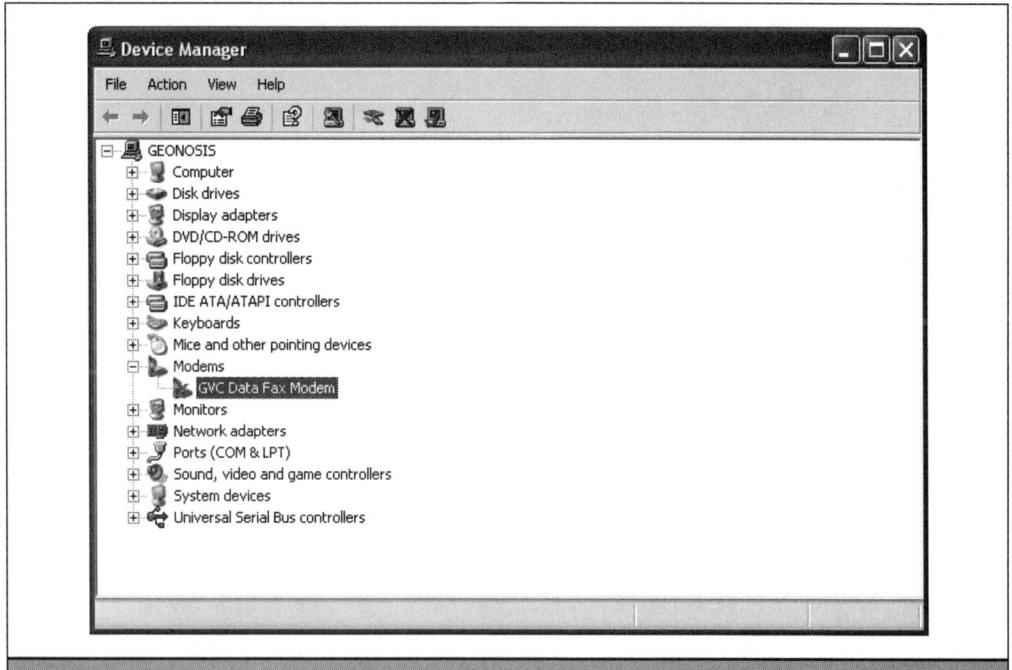

Figure 4-6.   A modem's device driver with a conflict

CREATING INTERNET CONNECTIONS

Chances are your Windows XP Professional client will need a connection to the Internet. Happily, Windows facilitates this with a very helpful wizard—the New Connection Wizard.

This tool allows you to tell Windows XP Professional what type of connection you're using and how to configure that connection. It can automatically establish and configure analog, DSL, ISDN, or cable modem connections. The following section outlines how to use this wizard and what information it will need.

Meet the New Connection Wizard

The New Connection Wizard makes the process of establishing a new connection easier than it was in previous incarnations of Windows. This wizard can be activated by performing the following steps:

1. Select Start | Control Panel then click Network and Network Connections.
2. Click Create a New Connection in the upper-left pane.

The New Connection Wizard is shown in Figure 4-7.

Figure 4-7. The New Connection Wizard

When you start the New Connection Wizard, it allows you to build one of three types of network connections:

- An Internet connection
- A LAN connection
- An advanced connection

These connections are explored in more depth in the following sections.

Connecting to the Internet

The Connect to the Internet selection invokes the Internet Connection Wizard, helping you build your connection for Internet access. When the wizard starts, one of the default options is to disable file and printer sharing for Microsoft networks. This adds a measure of security to keep your assets out of the vile clutches of scuzzwads on the Internet.

The next window that appears asks if you'd like to choose from a list of ISPs, set up the connection manually, or use a CD you received from an ISP. We'll follow the manual connection, which is the most common connection type.

By selecting Connect to the Internet, you can specify one of the connection types, broadband (DSL or cable modem, for instance) or dial-up.

Specifying a Broadband Connection   When you select the Broadband connection option, you are setting up your Windows XP Professional computer to access the Internet over an ever-present, high-speed technology, such as DSL, T1, or cable. You can tell Windows XP Professional what type of technology you'll be using for your broadband connection, but if you do not, it will automatically search your system and configure the connection automatically, assuming that the device is already in place on your computer.

Before following this connection path, you should call your ISP and get such information as

- Your IP address (or at least find out whether the IP address is assigned dynamically or statically)
- Domain Name System (DNS) addresses and domain names
- Other relevant information from your ISP

Specifying a Dial-up Connection   A dial-up connection is a connection that uses a telephone line for a limited amount of time, namely those made through conventional analog modems or ISDN. By selecting this access route, you should have details of your connection (ISP telephone numbers and so forth) on hand. If you don't have an ISP selected, the Internet Connection Wizard can automatically connect you to the Microsoft Referral Service, giving you the chance to pick one of the ISPs that are on Microsoft's list.

You will be connected to the Microsoft Referral Service if you pick one of the following choices:

- I want to sign up for a new Internet account. (My telephone line is connected to my modem.)
- I want to transfer my existing Internet account to this computer. (My telephone line is connected to my modem.)

There are a few pieces of information you should have on hand before starting this wizard:

- Domain Name System (DNS) addresses and domain names
- Other relevant information that the ISP might offer

Connecting to a Network

The Connect to the network at my workplace selection allows you to connect to a LAN from home, the field, or any other location. When you select this option, two more subcategories are presented.

Making a Direct Connection   A direct connection is one in which you will connect to the LAN via a dial-up or broadband connection. Rather than going through an ISP, you'd connect directly to the LAN if you choose the Direct connection option, assuming there was another computer set up to accept incoming calls (see "Setting Up an Advanced Connection").

Making an Internet Connection   If you choose to connect via an Internet connection, you will access your LAN by creating a secure virtual private network (VPN) connection.

> **NOTE**   We talk about VPN connections in more detail in Chapter 14.

Setting Up an Advanced Connection

When you select the Set up an advanced connection option, you are presented with two more selections, as described in the text that follows.

Accepting Incoming Connections   The Accept incoming connections selection allows you to configure a Windows XP Professional client to act as a remote access server. The computer will take incoming calls from computers attempting dial-up connections.

Connecting Directly to Another Computer   Selecting the Connect directly to another computer option allows you to connect your Windows XP Professional client directly to another computer, via parallel, serial, or infrared connection. When you select this option, you must configure your computer to act as the *host* or as the *guest* computer. The host is the computer that will be sharing data; the guest is the computer accessing that data.

Using the New Connection Wizard

Microsoft makes establishing a connection an almost painless process with its New Connection Wizard. The New Connection Wizard allows you to pick from three types of connections:

- Connect using a dial-up modem
- Connect using a broadband connection that requires a user name and password
- Connect using a broadband connection that is always on

Using a Dial-in Connection

When you invoke the New Connection Wizard, it will ask you a number of questions that will be used to create the connection. Table 4-5 lists the information the Wizard will ask you for and describes the input you should give.

Information Requested	Setting
Network Connection Type	Select Connect to the Internet.
Getting Ready	Select Set up my connection manually.
Internet Connection	Select the phone line type you will use (dial-in or broadband).
ISP Name	Enter what you want this connection to be called on the associated icon. It need not be the actual ISP name.
Phone Number	Enter the telephone number your ISP issued you.
Internet Account Information	Enter your username and password.
Use this account name and password when anyone connects to the Internet from this computer	If all accounts will use this connection, check this box. Otherwise, leave it unchecked.
Make this the default Internet connection	If you intend to use this connection whenever you need to use an Internet application but you're not online, leave this check box enabled.
Turn on Internet connection firewall for this connection	Decide if you wish to use ICF with this connection. Unless you're going to use applications that don't work well with ICF (like online games, for instance), it's best just to leave this box checked.
Add a shortcut to this connection on my desktop	If you want this connection placed on your desktop, select this option.

Table 4-5. Information Requested by the New Connection Wizard

Broadband

If you establish a broadband connection, Windows XP Professional automatically sets up the connection in your Network Connections folder (select Start | Connect To | Show All Connections). Once the connection icon appears in your folder, you must right-click it, select the Networking tab, click Internet Protocol (TCP/IP), click Properties, and then enter the TCP/IP properties.

ISDN

The New Connection Wizard using ISDN is a hybrid of both dial-in and broadband connections. However, about halfway through setup, it offers different options, as Table 4-6 enumerates.

The New Connection Wizard makes the ISDN connection, but you must still configure it. To do so, follow these steps:

1. Right-click the dial-up connection icon in the Network Connections window.
2. Choose Properties.
3. On the General Tab, select the ISDN channel you wish to configure.
4. Choose Configure.
5. In the ISDN Configuration dialog box, specify the line type, negotiate line type, and other settings. This information will come from your ISP or telephone company.

The next step is to configure *bundling* if you have a multilinked ISDN connection, which means combining both ISDN channels. Click the Options tab of the dial-up connection's Properties dialog box, and then select the bundling settings, as shown in Table 4-7.

Information Requested	Setting
Network Connection Type	Select Connect to the Internet.
Getting Ready	Select Set up my connection manually.
Internet Connection	Select Connect using a dial-up modem.
All Available ISDN Lines Multi-Linked (enabled by default)	Keep this check box selection enabled if you wish to bundle both channels of your ISDN connection. Alternatively, if you clear it, then you can select just one of the channels from the device list that shows the individual ISDN lines, if you want to connect with a single 64 Kbps channel.

Table 4-6. ISDN Connection Information Requested by the New Connection Wizard

Behavior	Setting
Dial only first available device	Allows you to send and receive telephone calls by using the first free ISDN channel only.
Dial all devices	Enables both channels for a 128 Kbps connection.
Dial devices only as needed	Uses one channel. If all its resources are used, then second channel will be invoked.

Table 4-7. Bundling Settings for ISDN Connections

MANAGING CONNECTIONS

Once you've configured the device you wish to use to access the Internet or a LAN, Windows XP Professional allows you to streamline the process by establishing a number of dialing rules. These rules encompass such issues as Dialing Locations, area codes, and calling card management.

This section will examine these issues and explain how you can make Windows XP Professional more user friendly, especially when your computer needs to make a connection from different locations.

You might want to check your connections—either to the LAN or the Internet—from time to time to see if you're connected or to check the quality of the connection. To monitor network connections, open Network Connection, right-click the connection, and select Status. You can automatically enable the status monitor each time the connection is active. Simply right-click the connection, select Properties, and then select the Show icon in notification area when connected check box.

If you've enabled this check box, then you have a quick way to check the network connection by floating your mouse pointer over the appropriate icon in the notification area (located in the lower-right portion of the taskbar). If there is no connection, the icon will appear with a red X over it, along with a little window explaining what the connection is supposed to be. If a connection is present, there will be no red X on the icon, and the pop-up window will list the connection, its speed, and other data, depending on the device and the manufacturer.

Configuring Dialing Locations

If your Windows XP Professional client is located on a laptop computer, problems can occur if you travel or if you need to dial-in from several locations. For instance, say your dial-in connection is established to your ISP, which is located in the same area code when you are at home. If you have to dial into that ISP from work, the dial-up connection will run into trouble, because the area code and dialing rules will be different. Likewise, if you take your laptop on the road often, the dialing behavior will change depending on the city and state in which you find yourself. To ameliorate this problem, Windows XP Professional allows you to establish a number of Dialing Locations.

Dialing Locations define which locations you'll be dialing from. The information a Dialing Location stores includes the following:

- Telephone number
- Area code
- Call waiting settings
- Tone or pulse dialing
- When to dial 1 before a phone number
- Calling card options
- PIN numbers for calling cards

These are all details that could vary, depending on your location.

What Is Your Dialing Location?

Your default Dialing Location is established when you run the New Connection Wizard and indicate your dial-up settings. You can look at and change your Dialing Location by doing the following:

1. Select Start | Control Panel.
2. Select Printers and Other Hardware, and then select Phone and Modem Options.
3. In the resulting dialog box, select the Dialing Rules tab (shown in Figure 4-8, which is an expansion of Figure 4-3).

You can examine, edit, or delete these locations by pressing the New, Edit, or Delete buttons at the bottom of the dialog box.

Setting the Windows XP Professional Dialing Location

If you want to add a Dialing Location to your list, follow these steps:

1. Press the New button in the Phone and Modem Options dialog box (the resulting screen is shown in Figure 4-9), and make sure the General tab is selected.
2. Enter a name for the new Dialing Location in the Location name box.
3. Choose a country from the list and enter the area code.
4. In the Dialing rules area, enter the following information:
    a. The digits you need to press to access an outside line for local calls
    b. The digits you need to press to access an outside line for long-distance calls
    c. The carrier codes you need to make long distance and international calls
5. If you want to disable call waiting, make sure the check box under the frame is selected and the correct code to disable the service is entered (#78 or something similar).
6. Select tone or pulse dialing, depending on your location.

Figure 4-8. Dialing Locations stored in Windows XP Professional

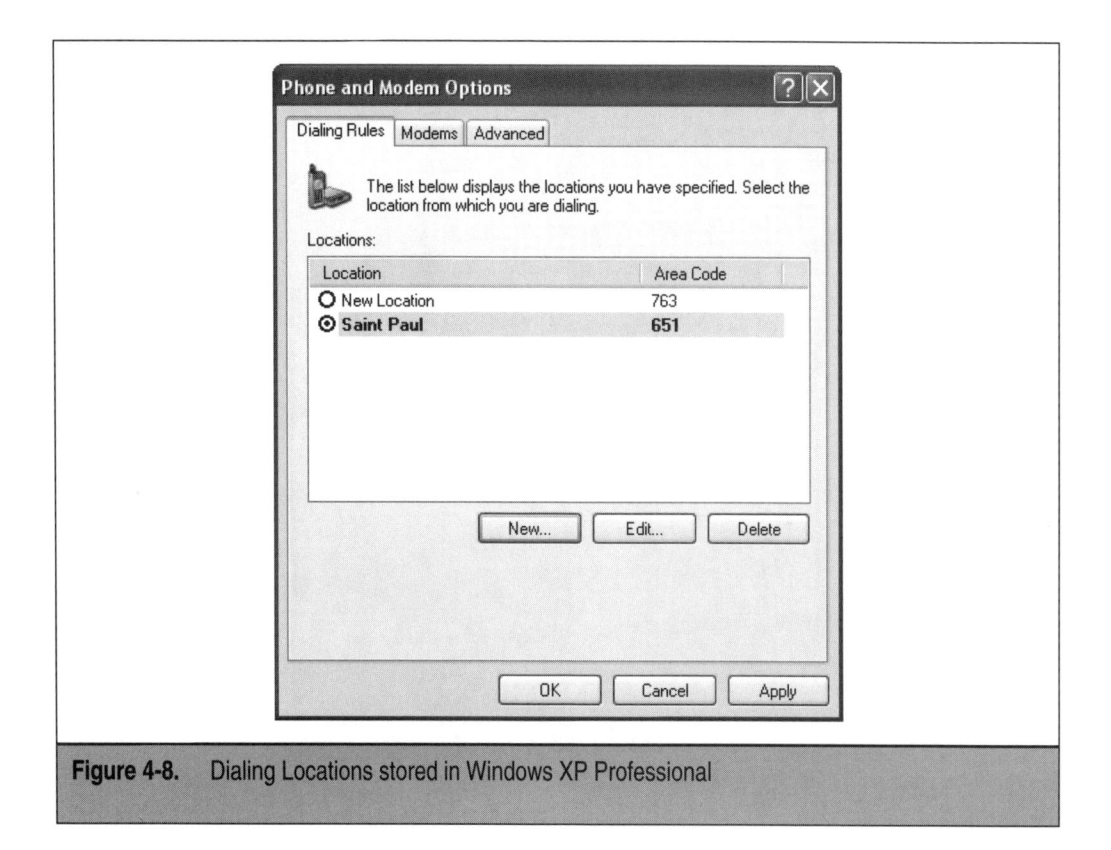

NOTE When you're done creating a new Dialing Location, click Apply, and choose a default location by selecting one of the radio buttons to the left of the Dialing Location names.

The Dialing Locations are useful not only for dialing into your ISP or workplace, but also for sending faxes through the Windows Fax Console. To change your location, in the Send Fax Wizard, select the Use Dialing Rules check box, and then choose a dialing location. For more information on so-called road warrior functions, see Chapter 14.

Area Code Rules

Since cellular telephones and pagers have been introduced to the world, telephone numbers have been exponentially gobbled up. This means that more area codes are needed (especially in metropolitan areas), as well as more complex dialing rules. For instance, if you have to call home from your workplace, you might have to use a different area code, and you might even have to dial 1 before entering that

Figure 4-9. Entering a new Dialing Location

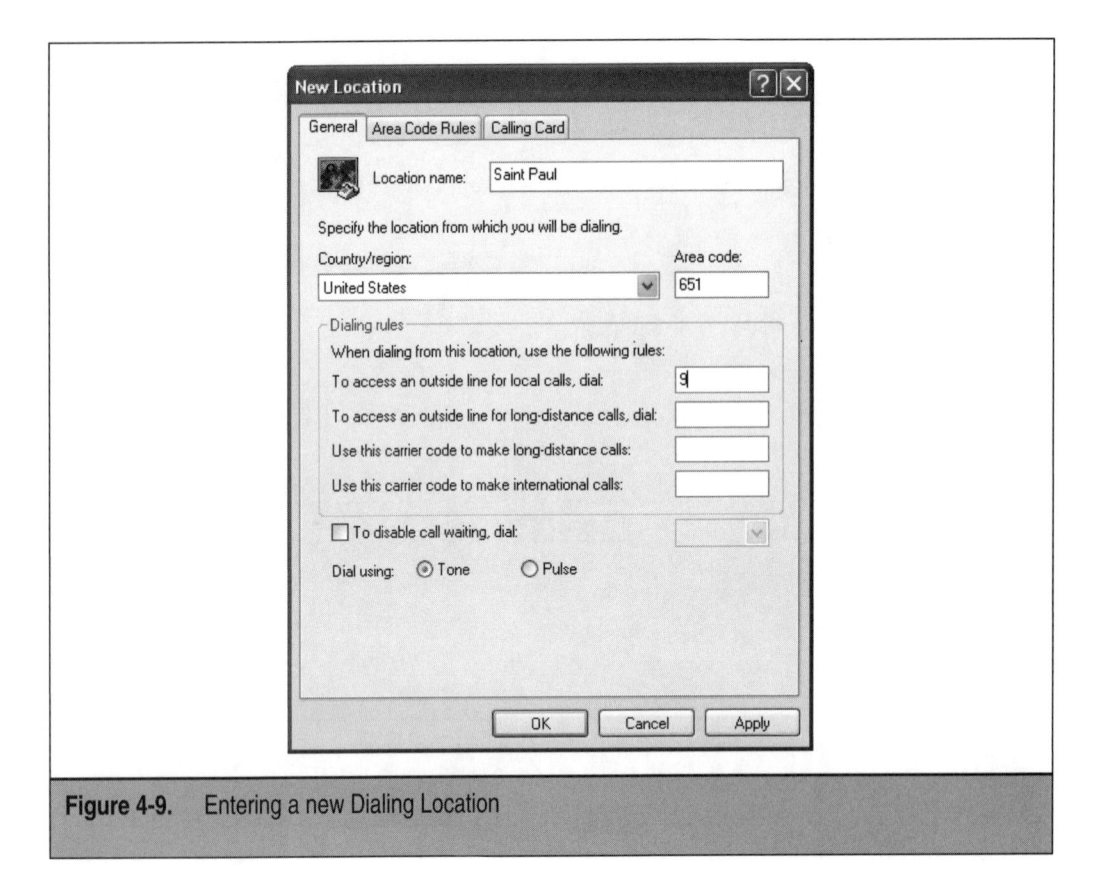

phone number. Windows XP Professional allows you to manage these rules for your Dialing Locations, as follows:

1. Select Start | Control Panel.
2. Select Printers and Other Hardware, and then select Phone and Modem Options.
3. In the resulting dialog box, select the Dialing Rules tab, specify the Dialing Location you wish to change, and click Edit.
4. Click the Area Code Rules tab (which is shown in Figure 4-10), and then click New.

NOTE Area code rules can also be established when entering a new Dialing Location. Click the Area Code Rules tab when you're finished entering the basic Dialing Location information.

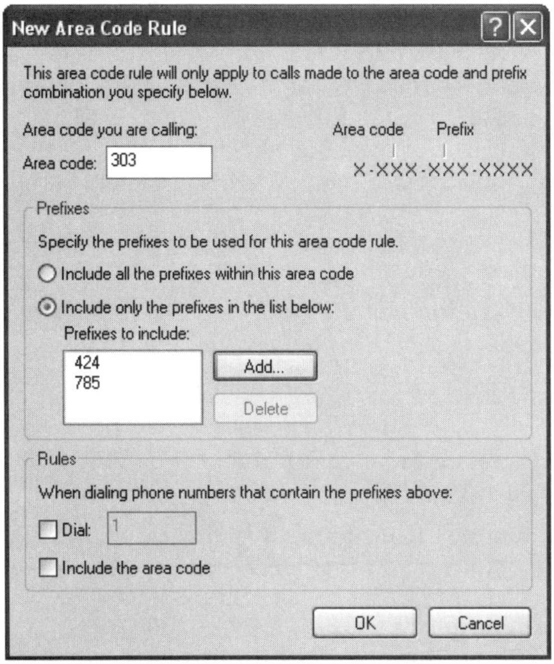

Figure 4-10. The New Area Code Rule dialog box

5. Enter the area code that will be affected by this rule (Windows XP Professional can use this information for all calls to this area code from the Dialing Location).

6. In the Prefixes frame, establish whether the rule will apply to all exchanges (the three digits that come after the area code in a phone number) in this area code, or just selected prefixes.

7. If you must dial 1 or any other digits to access these telephone numbers, click the Dial box and enter the numbers.

NOTE The number 1 appears there by default.

8. If you must dial the area code for these numbers, make sure the appropriate check box is selected.

9. Click OK to complete the entry of this information.

Using Calling Cards

Naturally, when you have to call into a different area code, the question of paying for that call arises. If you're on the road, you could just let the call be charged to your hotel room, or you could save $147 per minute by using a calling card. Windows XP Professional allows you to store calling card information and automatically enter it when needed.

In order to use your calling card, Windows XP Professional needs some information about it:

- **Account number**   Your calling card account
- **Personal Identification Number**   The secret number you use to verify your identity
- **Long-distance access number**   The number you dial to connect to your calling card company before the destination telephone number is entered
- **International access number**   The number you dial when you want to place an international call
- **Local access number**   The number you dial to connect to your calling card number when you want to place a local call

Entering a Calling Card

To establish calling card rules, follow these steps:

1. Select Start | Control Panel.
2. Select Printers and Other Hardware, and then select Phone and Modem Options.
3. In the resulting dialog box, select the Dialing Rules tab, select the Dialing Location you wish to change, and click Edit.
4. Click the Calling Card tab (which is shown in Figure 4-11).

NOTE   The calling card rules can also be established when entering a new Dialing Location. Click the Calling Card tab when you're finished entering the basic Dialing Location information.

5. You'll see a list of calling card types—Windows XP Professional comes preloaded with most calling card types. Choose the calling card you'll be using.
6. Windows XP Professional will display a list of properties for that card. All you should need to enter are your account and PIN numbers.

NOTE   Double-check the access numbers for your calling card, just to make sure Microsoft didn't get them wrong or your company didn't change its access numbers.

7. Click OK to complete the setup.

Figure 4-11. Entering calling card information

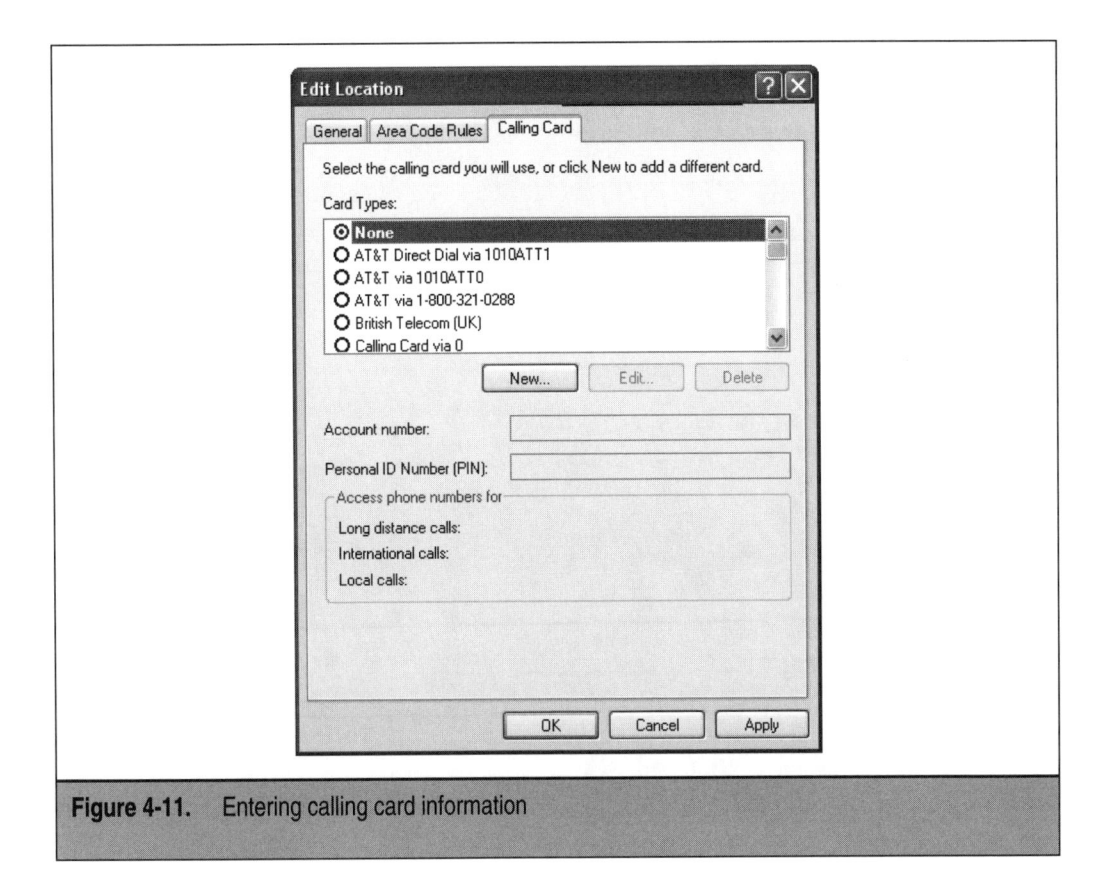

Entering a New Calling Card

It is quite conceivable that your calling card isn't on the list provided by Windows XP Professional. You aren't limited to this list. You can add a new one by following these steps:

1. Open the Edit Location dialog box and select the Calling Card tab (shown in Figure 4-11).
2. Click the New button. The resulting dialog box is shown in Figure 4-12.
3. Enter the name of the calling card, your account number, and your PIN.
4. Click the Long Distance tab.
5. Enter the access number used for long distance calls.
6. Using the buttons shown in Figure 4-13, enter the behavior that your calling card must display in order to make the connection. You'll end up writing a

Figure 4-12. Entering a new calling card

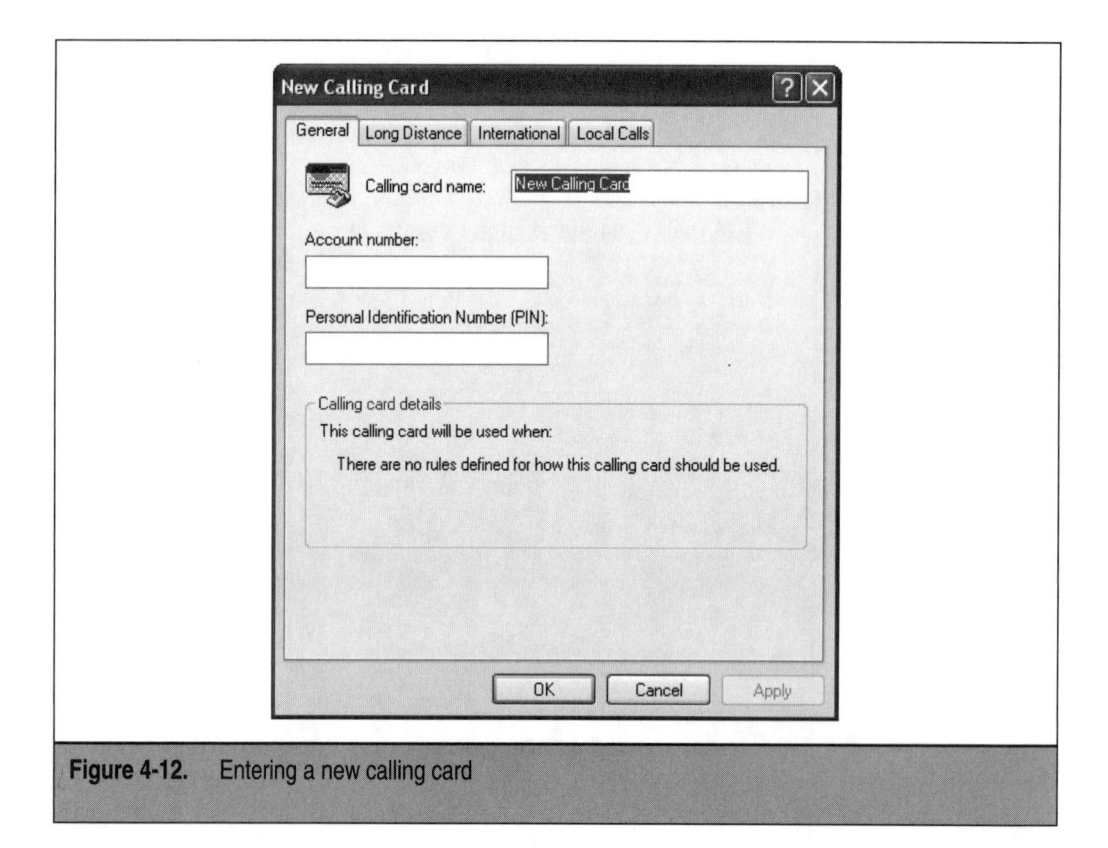

script of sorts to tell Windows XP Professional how to access your calling card. For example, click Access Number to enter your calling card's access number, click Account Number to enter your account number, and click Destination Number to enter the phone number you'll be calling. Also, you can use the Wait for Prompt button to specify a predetermined amount of time to wait before entering an access number, PIN, or other information.

7. You can move up or down through the steps using the buttons on the right side of the Calling Card Steps pane. You can also delete steps with the appropriate button.

NOTE It will help to make a test call and document the series of numbers and lengths of pauses are needed to make a call.

---

8. Repeat Steps 4 and 5 to establish rules for international calls and local calls.

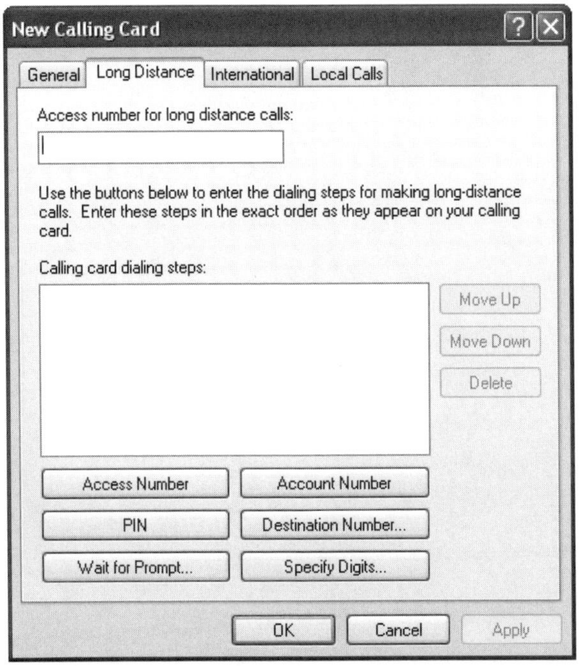

Figure 4-13. Calling card details

To use the calling card, when placing a call via a dial-up connection, in the Properties box for the connection click the Dialing Rules button, and then select a Dialing Location. Next, click Edit, click the Calling Card tab, and choose the calling card to use.

If you want to send a fax using your calling card, in the Send Fax Wizard, choose the Use Dialing Rules check box, pick a dialing location, and then click the Dialing Rules button to see the calling card.

Installing, configuring, and managing connection hardware is much more simplified and powerful in Windows XP Professional. By taking advantage of the tools at your disposal, you can provide your clients with much more robust and feature-filled connections.

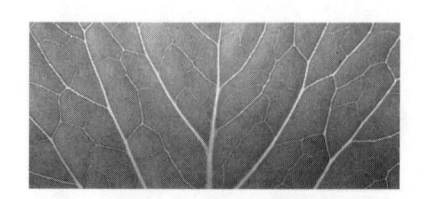

CHAPTER 5

Workgroup Connections

Chapter 4 highlighted the different ways in which you can connect a client computer to the Internet. This chapter turns its focus to the functionality of the Windows XP Professional on the local area network (LAN). Windows XP Professional has a number of tools useful for constructing a network for a Fortune 500 company or building a very small network for a mom-and-pop shop.

Not only is configuration and setup fairly straightforward, but Windows XP Professional also includes several tools that can help maximize your workgroup's needs. In this chapter, we discuss the different ways you can use Windows XP Professional to both build and enhance your networking. First we talk about connecting your clients to the LAN, including coverage of the Network Setup Wizard, which streamlines the whole affair. Next, we cover Internet Connection Sharing (ICS), which is an excellent way for a small office or home office with more than one computer (but only one Internet account) to connect all their devices to the Internet. We also show you Microsoft's Internet Connection Firewall (ICF), a tool to keep your data safe while on the Internet. Finally, we explore Windows XP Professional's new level of support for wireless networking connections.

CONNECTING CLIENTS TO THE WORKGROUP

There are two ways that you can connect your Windows XP Professional clients to the LAN: automatic and manual. Automatic is probably the most preferred method, because it is reasonably foolproof and speedy. However, situations might arise in which you need to manually install a client or enable a particular protocol or service.

The first section of this chapter is devoted to your client's interaction with the LAN—that is, how you connect them and how you tweak their functionality.

Network Setup Wizard

The first step in configuring your Windows XP Professional client for connection to a LAN is to install your NIC and connect it to the network. If you have an Internet connection, make sure you are connected, and then turn on all printers. This allows the wizard to see them. To invoke the Network Setup Wizard, follow these steps:

1. Select Start | All Programs | Accessories | Communications | Network Setup Wizard, or select Start | Control Panel, and then click Network and Internet Connections. Select Network Connections and click Set up or change a home or small office network.

2. Click Next.

3. The wizard will display a series of steps you should follow. They include the following:

    - Install network cards, modems, and cables.
    - Turn on all computers, printers, and external modems.
    - Connect to the Internet.

4. Click Next to move to the next screen.
5. You'll be asked how you will connect to the Internet (if at all)—that is, whether this computer will connect directly to the Internet or whether it will connect to the Internet over the LAN.
6. The next screen (shown in Figure 5-1) is where you provide the computer description and computer name. Enter that information, and then click Next. The following window asks for your workgroup name.
7. The Network Setup Wizard will finish by asking if you would like to create a Network Setup Disk that you can run on Windows Me, 2000, 9X, and NT. If you choose to do so, you'll need a blank floppy disk. If you are setting up a new network with different versions of Windows, it's a good idea to create the setup disk.

So what, exactly, does the wizard do? It installs these items:

- Client for Microsoft Network
- TCP/IP protocol suite
- Printer Sharing service

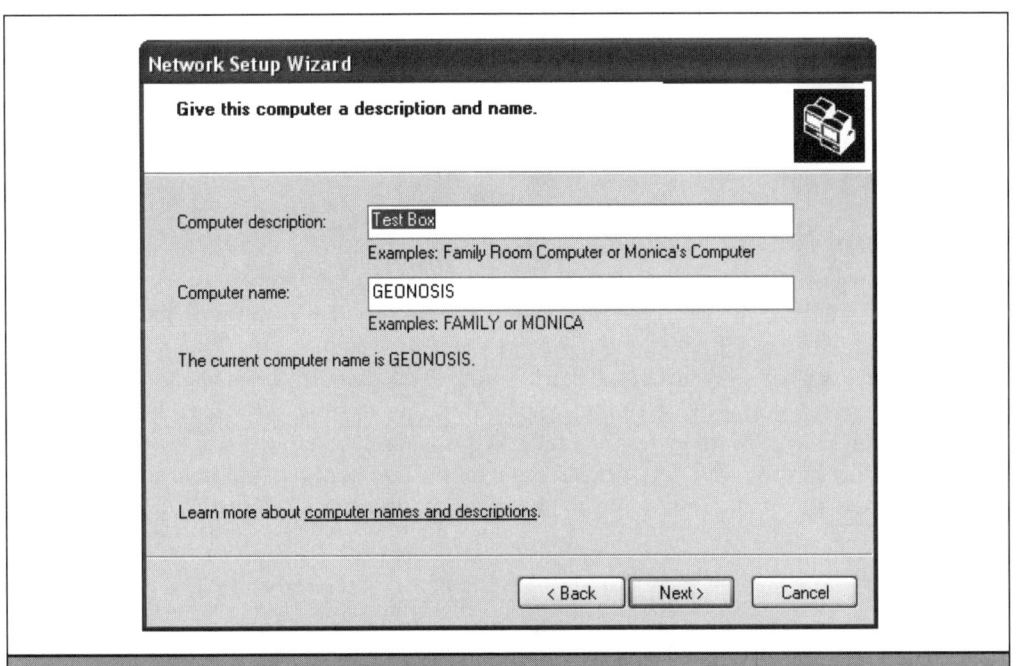

Figure 5-1. The Network Setup Wizard asks for your computer's description (optional) and its unique name.

These services and protocols could be installed manually, if you like, but why bother if the wizard will do it for you?

> **NOTE** If you intend to use ICS, you can save some time and let the wizard install ICS during network setup. We talk about ICS in more detail later in this chapter.

Using the Setup Disk

If you've opted to create a network configuration setup disk for use in other versions of Windows, installation is a reasonably simple process. After creating the disk, you put the disk in the floppy-disk drives of your other Windows computers. Select Start | Run, type in **a:setup** (where *a:* is the letter of your floppy-disk drive), and click OK. The wizard completes the installation on your Windows clients and might necessitate a reboot.

You need not use a floppy disk for client installation. If you prefer, you can simply use the Windows XP Professional CD-ROM. The steps are as follows:

1. Place the Windows XP Professional CD-ROM in the client's CD- or DVD-ROM drive. The CD-ROM should start automatically. If it does, skip ahead to Step 5. If not, go to Step 2.
2. Select Start | Run.
3. Type in **d:setup** (where *d:* is the letter of your CD- or DVD-ROM drive). Click OK.
4. Select Perform additional tasks.
5. Select Set up a home or small office network.
6. The Network Setup Wizard will present you with a series of instructions you should follow.

Viewing Your Network

When the Network Setup Wizard has completed its tasks, the My Network Places icon will show up on the right side of the Start menu. The icon will also show up in applications' Open dialog boxes, making it easier to access shared folders.

If the icon does not show up in the Start menu, it's likely that Windows XP Professional has not recognized your NIC. Use the Device Manager to see if your card is working properly. (The Device Manager is covered in Chapter 4.)

Double-clicking the My Network Places icon will present a list of shared folders on your LAN. (Chapter 11 covers network shares in greater detail.) Figure 5-2 gives an example of this folder.

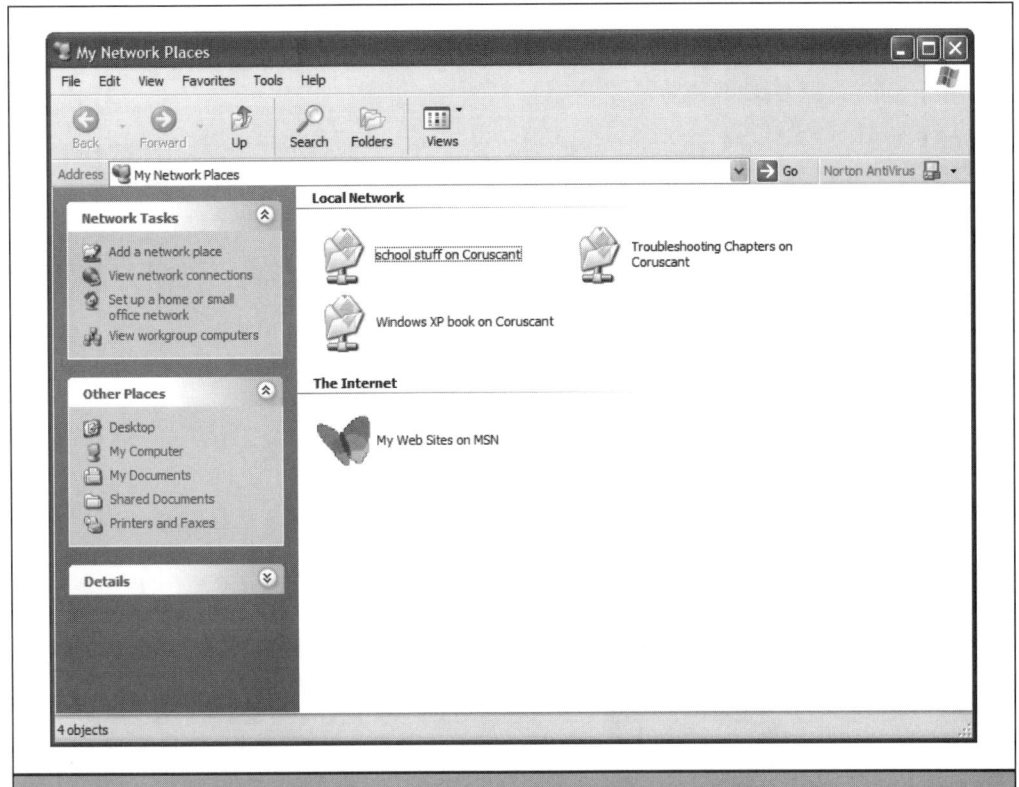

Figure 5-2. My Network Places displays a list of shared folders on the LAN.

Viewing Network Connections

Windows XP Professional provides an excellent way to show the various connections that your computer can accommodate. By opening the Network Connections window, you can see various LAN (wireless and hardwired) and Internet (dial-up and broadband) connections.

There are two ways you can access the Network Connections window:

- Click Start, right-click My Network Places, and then choose Properties.
- If Connect To is on your Start menu, select Start | Connect To | Show All Connections.

Figure 5-3 shows an example of the Network Connections window.

Figure 5-3. The Network Connections window

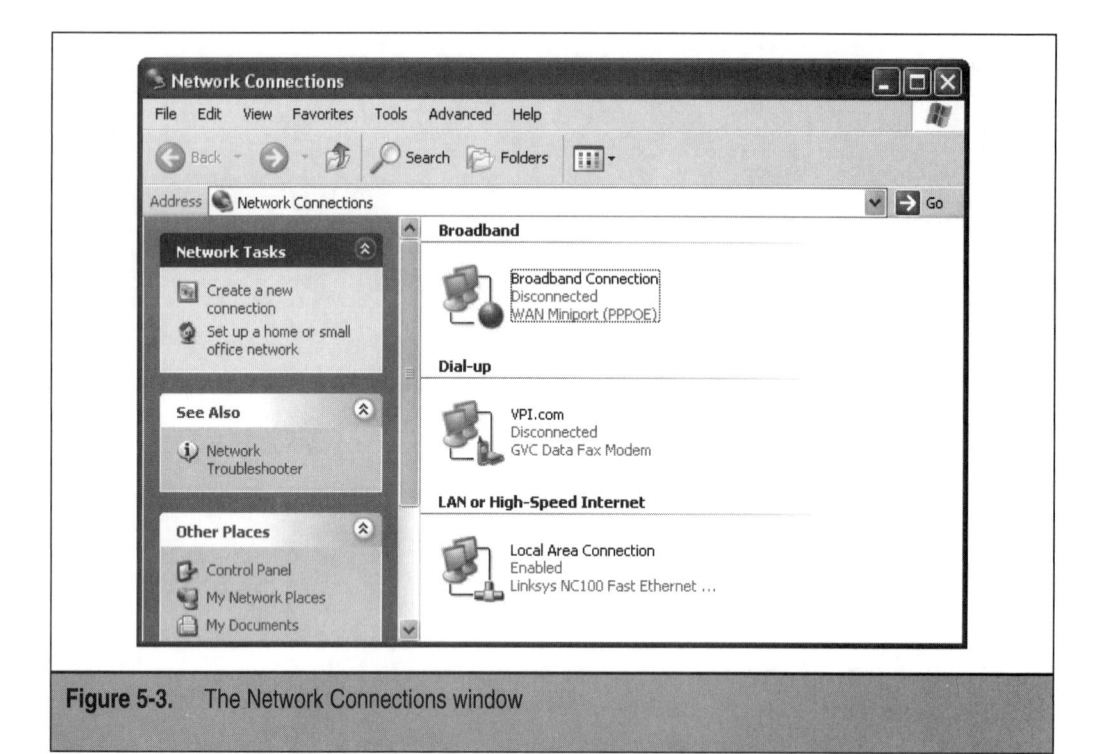

Manual Configuration

For the most part, it is a simple matter to run the Network Setup Wizard to form your LAN connections: It's automatic, and it's painless. There might be times when you'll need to do more than run the wizard to form a connection, however. Some connections might require the installation or removal of network components such as clients, protocols, or services.

Within each network connection listed in the Network Connection window are certain properties that can be examined, configured, or adjusted by right-clicking the connection and selecting Properties. Figure 5-4 shows an example of a network connection's properties.

As Figure 5-4 shows, the connection's NIC is listed, along with the clients, protocols, and services that it uses. In a conventional TCP/IP-based LAN, there are four components that should be installed:

- **Client for Microsoft Networks** The client that enables the computer to exchange data with other Microsoft computers
- **File And Printer Sharing For Microsoft Networks** The service that allows Microsoft computers to share files and printers

- **QoS Packet Scheduler** The service that establishes when packets are to be sent, based on Quality of Service (QoS) standards
- **Internet Protocol (TCP/IP)** The TCP/IP protocol suite

Before installing, configuring, or uninstalling any client, service, or protocol, you must first install and configure your adapter. The adapter is the device driver used by Windows XP Professional to communicate with the NIC. When you install your NIC, Plug and Play should detect it. If it is not Plug and Play compatible, then you will have to install the device driver manually. Start the Add New Hardware Wizard to begin the driver installation.

NOTE Of course, if you migrated from another flavor of Windows and already have a NIC, Windows XP Professional should have automatically upgraded your network connection settings.

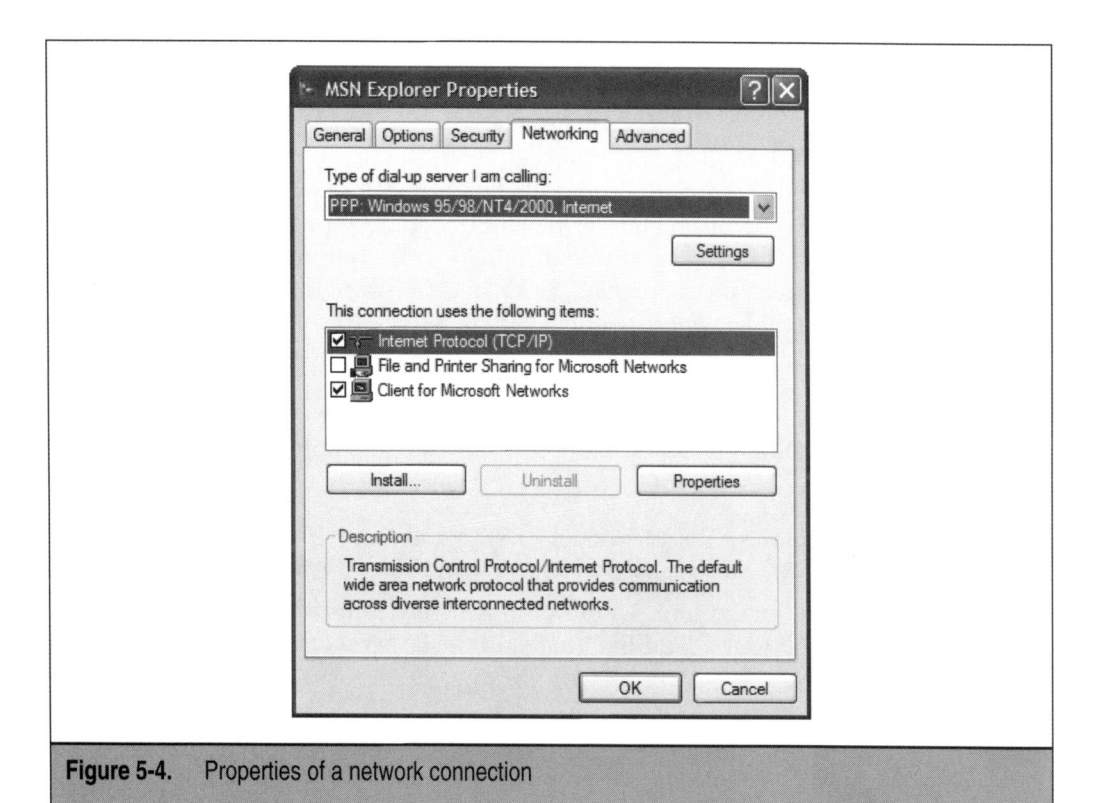

Figure 5-4. Properties of a network connection

Installing a Client

Next, you should install the client component of your network connections. This identifies on which type of network you'll be connecting. By default, Windows XP Professional installs the Client For Microsoft Networks. To see which clients are installed on your computer, examine the area underneath This connection uses the following items, as shown in Figure 5-4.

If you need to install another type of client, do the following:

1. Select Start and right-click My Network Places. Select Properties, right-click the desired Local Area Connection, and choose Properties.
2. Click the Install button. This will call up the Select Network Component Type dialog box.
3. Select the Client network component, and then click Add.
4. The Select Network Component Type dialog box will pop up. Choose the network client you wish to install. If you are installing the client from a floppy disk or CD-ROM, then insert the disk and click Have Disk.
5. Click OK. You might be prompted to insert the Windows XP Professional CD-ROM for final installation chores.
6. Click OK.

Installing a Protocol

By default, the TCP/IP protocol suite is installed on your Windows XP Professional client. This makes sense, because it has become the standard for networking. However, there might be other protocols you wish to install. One example is NetBEUI.

Microsoft is no longer supporting NetBEUI with Windows XP Professional. If your small network uses NetBEUI, you can still install the protocol from your Windows XP Professional CD-ROM; however, it's a better idea to simply upgrade your network to TCP/IP.

If you want to install NetBEUI, you first need to copy the files from the Windows XP Professional CD-ROM. Follow these steps to copy the files onto your hard drive or network share:

1. Insert the Windows XP Professional CD-ROM. When the welcome screen pops up, select Perform Additional Tasks, and then choose Browse This CD.
2. Next, you'll see an Explorer window showing the contents of the Windows XP Professional CD-ROM. Find the Valueadd\msft\net\netbeui folder.
3. Within that folder, copy the Nbf.sys file into your C:\Windows\System32\Drivers folder.
4. Copy Netnbf.ini to the C:\Windows\inf folder.

Installation Once the files have been copied, you must install them. To install a protocol (NetBEUI or any other protocol for that matter), do the following:

1. Select Start and right-click My Network Places. Select Properties. Then right-click the desired Local Area Connection, and choose Properties.
2. Click the General tab.
3. Click the Install button.
4. Select Protocol, and then click Add.
5. Select the protocol you wish to install. If you are installing a third-party protocol, insert the disk containing the protocol and click the Have Disk button. Click OK.
6. You might be prompted to reinsert the Windows XP Professional CD-ROM for additional files.
7. Click OK to complete the protocol installation.

Binding When a protocol has been installed, Windows XP Professional automatically *binds* the protocol to all the services and clients that are installed. Simply put, a binding tells Windows XP Professional to use a specific protocol with a specific client or service. If you choose not to use a specific protocol with a specific service or client, you can also unbind it.

However, as nice as this automatic configuration is, you might not want your new protocol bound to every service or client. You can manage which protocols are bound to which clients and services by doing the following:

1. Select Start | Control Panel, and then click Network and Internet Connections.
2. Click Network Connections.
3. In the menu bar, choose Advanced | Advanced Settings (the resulting dialog box is shown in Figure 5-5).
4. Click the Adapters and Bindings tab.
5. In the Connections box, select Local Area Connection.
6. The Bindings for Local Area Connection frame lists all the clients and services for that connection. The installed protocols are listed underneath each client or service.
7. Using the check boxes next to each protocol, check or clear the box, depending on whether you wish that protocol to be bound to the client or service.
8. You can change the order in which the protocols are used (moving the most common protocol up the list and the least used protocol to the end) by selecting one, and clicking the up or down arrow on the right side of the dialog box.

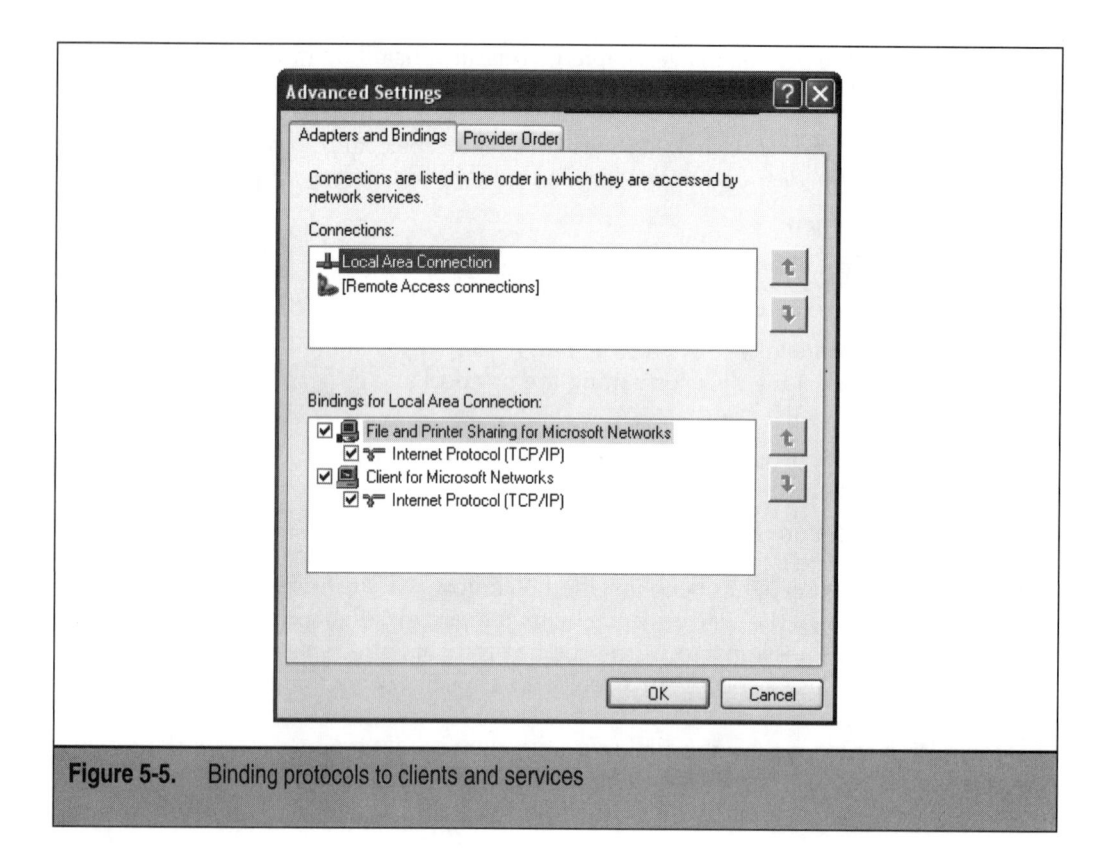

Figure 5-5. Binding protocols to clients and services

Setting the order in which protocols are used is a good idea if you plan to employ one protocol more often than another for a certain connection.

9. When you're finished, click OK.

Installing a Service

The last type of network component you will add is a service. Services are the mechanisms that allow you to share a computer's resources on the network. Unlike protocols and clients, services are optional. That is, you don't need a service installed to make a connection. However, without a service installed, it would be impossible to share printers, files, and so forth.

To install a service, follow these steps:

1. Select Start, and right-click My Network Places. Select Properties, right-click the desired Local Area Connection, and choose Properties.
2. Click the General tab.

3. Click the Install button.
4. Click Service, and then click Add.
5. Select the service you wish to install, and then click Add (the resulting dialog box is shown in Figure 5-6).
6. Choose the service you wish to install (if you have a third-party service on a floppy disk or CD-ROM, insert the disk, and click the Have Disk button).
7. Click OK. You may be prompted to reinsert the Windows XP Professional CD-ROM.
8. Click OK to complete the setup.

USING INTERNET CONNECTION SHARING

It's almost trite to say that your client computers need to connect to the Internet, because it's something that has been said over and over—and to a certain degree Internet connectivity is taken for granted. Big organizations don't seem to have any problems getting their users online. However, smaller organizations or home offices (collectively known as SOHOs) might run into problems getting their users onto the Internet.

The problem is that SOHOs tend to have a single connection to the Internet. They don't have enough need to buy a large line—like a T1—to connect dozens of devices. As such, there might be a lone computer that is able to access the Internet. Think of a

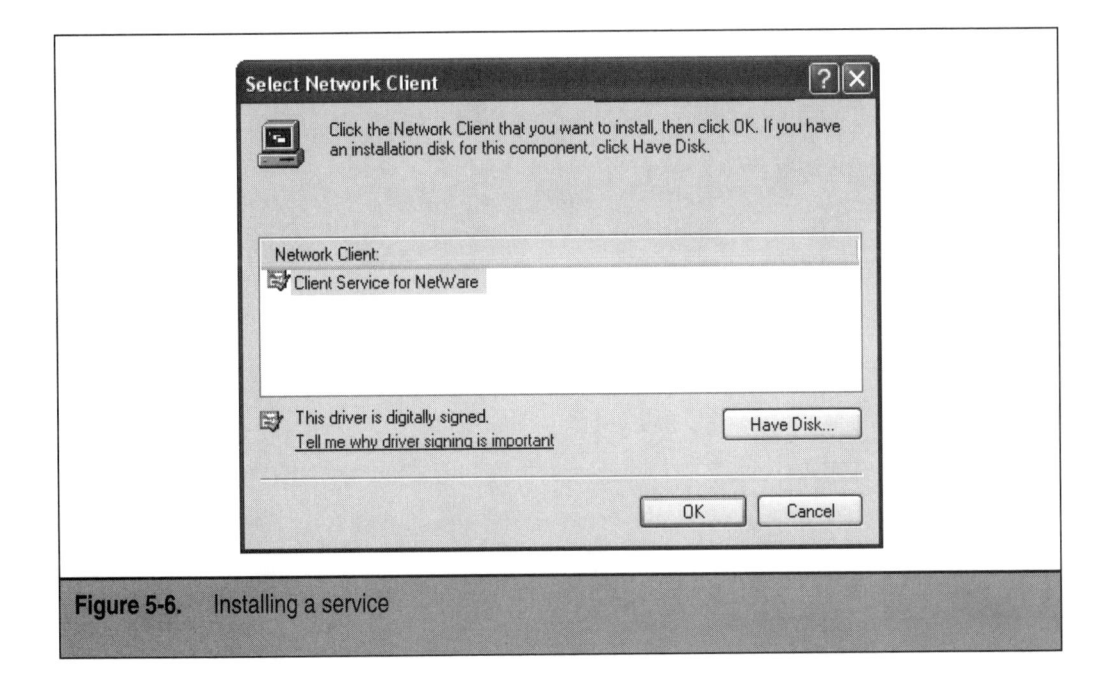

Figure 5-6. Installing a service

small office with five client computers. If more than one person wants to get onto the Internet at the same time, then there are likely to be some conflicts. If one user is downloading a large file from the Internet, then that file must be transferred to the appropriate client computer once the download is completed. Furthermore, think of the privacy issues that arise when one computer is used for all e-mail.

To work around this problem, Microsoft introduced Internet Connection Sharing (ICS) with Windows 98 and fine-tuned it with Windows XP Professional.

ICS Features

ICS is a Network Address Translation program that, as Figure 5-7 shows, allows the client computer with Internet access to share that computer with other clients on the LAN.

The computer with Internet access is known as the *ICS server*. The other computers are known as the *ICS clients*. The ICS clients can be Windows XP Professional, Windows XP Home, Windows 2000, or Me, or even other operating systems (such as the Mac OS), just as long as they support TCP/IP.

ICS uses IP addresses in the 192 block (specifically, 192.168.0.xxx). ICS includes a Dynamic Host Configuration Protocol (DHCP) server on the ICS server, doling out IP addresses to the ICS clients. In Figure 5-7 you can see that the DHCP server assigns the IP address of 192.168.0.1 to itself, and then incrementally assigns addresses to other clients (192.168.0.2, 192.168.0.3, and so forth). However, as you remember from our

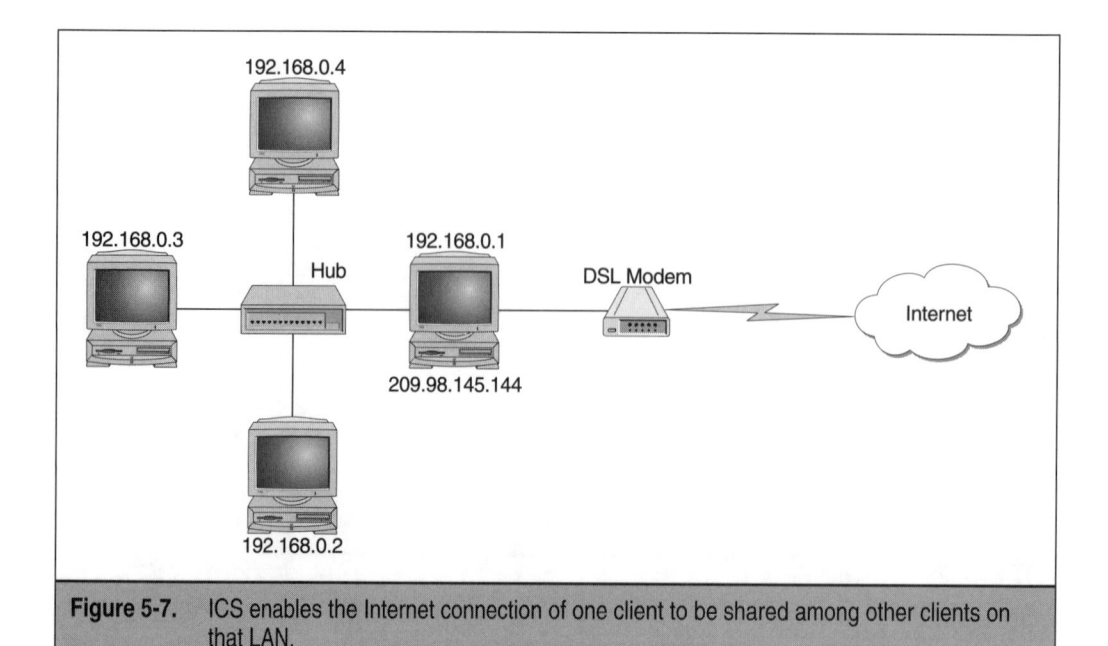

Figure 5-7. ICS enables the Internet connection of one client to be shared among other clients on that LAN.

discussion of TCP/IP in Chapter 3, the ICS server has two IP addresses—the one that the Internet service provider assigns (in this case 209.98.145.144) and the one appropriate to the LAN (192.168.0.1).

> **NOTE** ICS allows up to 254 devices to be shared on a single connection with addresses in the range of 192.168.9.1 to 192.168.9.254.

ICS contains three components:

- **DHCP Allocator**   Responsible for assigning IP addresses to the ICS clients
- **NAT**   On packets, replaces an ICS client's IP address with the ICS server's ISP-assigned IP address
- **DNS Proxy**   Provides translation services between IP addresses and host names via the ISP's DNS server

Setting Up ICS

Now that you understand the overall functioning of ICS, let's go through the setup and configuration process. As with most Windows XP Professional tools, this one also uses a wizard to make the setup process straightforward and simple. However, if you're in a situation where manual configuration is best, we've got that covered as well.

The first step is to configure the ICS server, which is the device that connects to the Internet. From there, you configure your ICS clients.

Configuring the ICS Server

The best, easiest way to set up ICS is to use the Network Setup Wizard in Windows XP Professional. Once the wizard runs on your ICS server, it will create an installation disk that you can use to configure Windows Me, 9X, 2000, and NT clients on your network.

To invoke the Network Setup Wizard, on the computer that will be the ICS server (remember, this is the computer that connects to the Internet), select Start | All Programs | Accessories | Communications | Network Setup Wizard.

When the wizard starts (you'll have to click through a couple of informational dialog boxes), you will be asked to make the choices shown in Table 5-1.

Connecting Others to This Device

As mentioned in the preceding section, connecting the ICS clients is a simple matter of either using the installation disk prepared by the Network Setup Wizard (in Windows 9X, Me, 2000, NT 4, or XP), or running the Network Setup Wizard on the client (Windows XP Professional only).

> **NOTE** You could also transfer the installation disk files to a network share for diskless installation.

Setting	Description
Select a Connection Method	Choose This Computer Connects Directly To The Internet. Note: Make sure you already have an Internet connection configured. Flip back to Chapter 4 for more information on making this connection
Select Your Internet Connection	Next, you'll be shown a list of both LAN and Internet connections that are available on your computer. Choose the connection to the Internet.
Give This Computer a Description and Name	At this point, you'll be asked to give your computer a name so that it can be identified by other devices on your LAN. In all likelihood, if you're already on a LAN, this information is filled in automatically.
Name Your Network	Give your workgroup a name.
You're Almost Done	Finally, you must make sure all your clients are set up to work with the settings you've just established (see Figure 5-8). That means you need to configure your ICS clients to use the ICS server as their DHCP server. You can do this by either running the Network Setup Wizard on the ICS clients (assuming they're running Windows XP Professional) or creating a startup disk that can be distributed to the ICS clients.

Table 5-1. Settings for ICS in the Network Setup Wizard

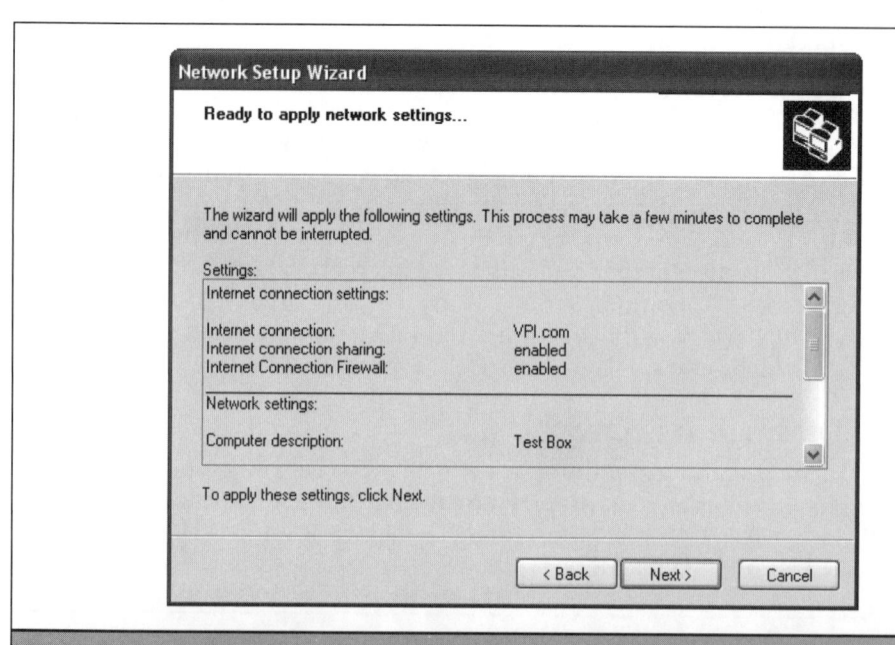

Figure 5-8. The final step in configuring the ICS server with the Network Setup Wizard

The configuration process installs TCP/IP as a network protocol (if it's not already installed) and tells the computer to get its IP address from the DHCP server—in this case, the ICS server.

To configure your ICS client with a floppy disk, simply put the disk in your drive and then follow these steps:

1. Select Start | Run.
2. Type **a:setup**.
3. Click Open.

To configure your clients (assuming they are running Windows XP Professional), select Start | All Programs | Accessories | Communications | Network Setup Wizard.

You'll then be asked to make settings shown in Table 5-2. At this point, it is a good idea to test the ICS to make sure that everything has been set up properly.

Manual ICS Configuration

Although the Network Setup Wizard provides a smooth, relatively painless process for setting up the ICS, there is an even faster way to do so. Manual configuration assumes that your LAN and Internet connections already work.

On the ICS server, perform the following steps:

1. Select Start | Control Panel. Click Networks and Internet Connections, then select Network Connections.
2. Click the Internet connection you'll use.
3. Click Change Settings Of This Connection in the Network Tasks. This spawns a Properties box (shown in Figure 5-9).

Setting	Description
Select a Connection Method	Choose This Computer Connects To The Internet Through Another Computer On My Network Or Through A Residential Gateway.
Give This Computer a Description and Name	Enter a unique name for your computer and enter a description.
Name Your Network	Enter the same workgroup name you entered for the Name Your Network setting in Table 5-1. Clicking Next produces a screen similar to the one shown in Figure 5-8, allowing you to verify your settings.
You're Almost Done	You'll be asked if you would like to create a Network Setup Disk. This is useful if you have more clients to set up that do not have Windows XP Professional installed.

Table 5-2. Settings for ICS Clients

Figure 5-9. Manually configuring ICS

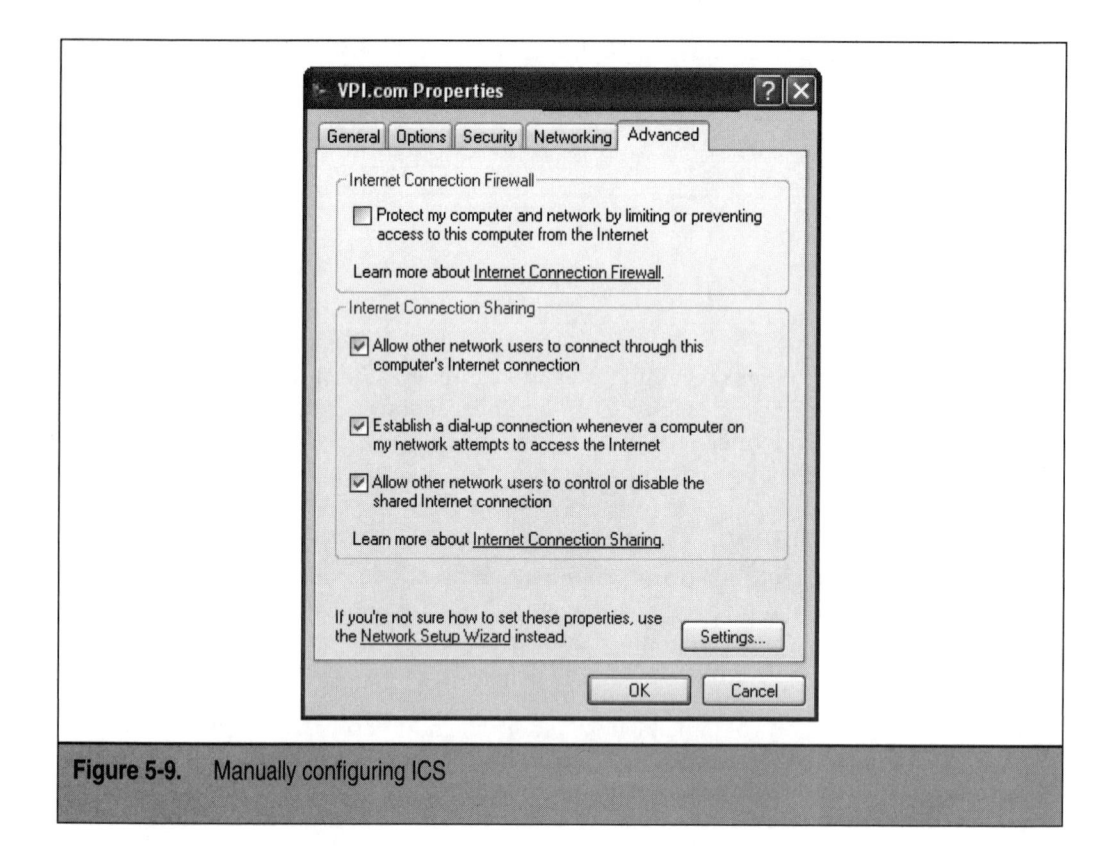

4. Select the Advanced tab. You'll see a number of settings for both ICS and the ICF. Set them according to Table 5-3.
5. Click OK.

You should be aware of these other issues when manually configuring the ICS server:

- Make sure your Internet connection works. That is, if you've just established the connection, test it and make sure you can get on, check out web sites, and send and receive e-mail.
- Make sure your Internet connection is configured as the default connection.
- Make sure you have the username and password entered.
- Make sure the ICS server is configured to automatically connect to the Internet if one of the clients wishes to connect.

Setting	Description
Protect my computer and network by limiting or preventing access to this computer from the network	This is a long-winded way of saying, "Turn on the ICF." It is recommended that you select this check box for the layer of security it provides. We'll talk about the ICF later in this chapter.
Allow other network users to connect through this computer's Internet connection	Click the check box to turn ICS on, clear the check box to turn ICS off.
Establish a dial-up connection whenever a computer on my network attempts to access the Internet	This prevents users from having problems trying to log onto the Internet if the ICS server is disconnected from the Internet. Depending on your access needs, you can either enable this function or disable it.
Allow other network users to control or disable the shared Internet connection	ICS clients can be given a modicum of control over the Internet connection by being able to connect or disconnect the ICS server. Note: They can only enable a connection to the ISP if the previous check box is enabled.

Table 5-3. Manual ICS settings

ICS VPN Model

If you want to really make some alphabet soup of networking acronyms, try setting up a VPN across an ICS using PPTP. In English, this means a virtual private network using the Point-to-Point Tunneling Protocol is established across the ICS.

NOTE Layer Two Tunneling Protocol (L2TP) connections cannot be established using ICS.

Consider the network shown in Figure 5-10. In this scenario, a client on the SOHO network needs to make a VPN tunnel to the corporate headquarters. It could be the manager sending payroll or weekend sales data or any other sensitive information requiring a secure channel.

When a VPN connection is made between the ICS client and the corporate network, the client sees only the resources available to it on the corporate network—it is shut off from the Internet for the duration of the VPN connection. However, this does not mean that the ICS client can't get back on the Internet. The ICS client can access the Internet through the corporate network's Internet connection.

When enabling this connection, it is important not to establish the VPN tunnel from the ICS server. Using the ICS server will, by default, send all traffic from the ICS server across the VPN tunnel to the corporate network. This would prevent Internet resources from being reachable by the ICS clients (as their connection will only see and be seen by the corporate network).

Figure 5-10. VPNs across ICS

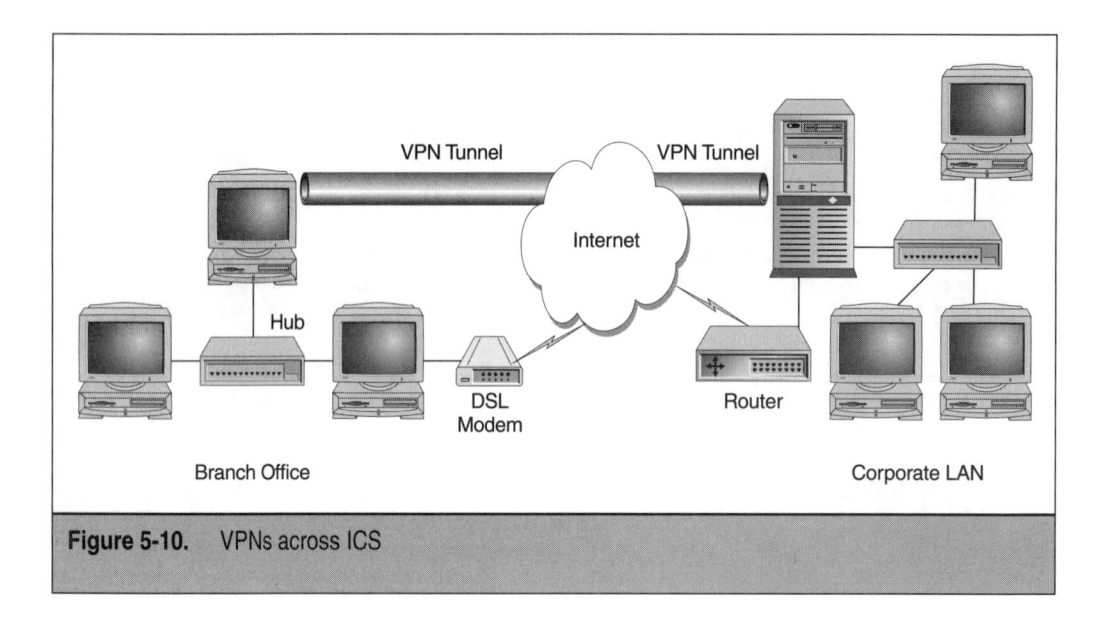

> **NOTE** Chapter 14 contains more information about VPNs in Windows XP Professional.

ICS Troubleshooting

If you run into trouble with ICS, there are several things you should check, including the following:

- Give the ICS server some time to log onto the Internet, especially if you're using a dial-up connection. The ICS client might time out before the ICS server makes its Internet connection.
- Windows XP Professional offers the Internet Connection Sharing Troubleshooter. Run this program on both the ICS server and at least one ICS client. You can invoke the ICS Troubleshooter by following these steps:
    1. Select Start | Help And Support.
    2. In the Help and Support Center window, select Fixing A Problem.
    3. Click Networking Problems.
    4. Click Internet Connection Sharing Troubleshooter.
- If you've restarted your ICS server, go ahead and restart the ICS clients, too.
- Make sure that your ICS server can actually connect to the Internet. If it isn't able to connect, you'll have to double-check that connection.

The easiest tool to use is the Internet Connection Sharing Troubleshooter. It can help you ameliorate your ICS problems by walking you step by step through a number of issues. Though some might seem elementary (such as whether your ICS client is turned on), sometimes it is the simple issues that cause the problem.

ICF ON A WORKGROUP

Most organizations keep their networks safe and secure by placing a firewall between their network and the Internet proper. Normally, these are devices that sit in a rack in the server room, quietly filtering out probes, attacks, and other unsolicited packets. Windows XP Professional includes its own firewall. Not as robust as a stand-alone device, Internet Connection Firewall (ICF) is a software tool that places restrictions on what information is communicated between your device and the Internet.

ICF is especially functional if you use ICS. By utilizing ICF on your ICS server, you prevent the ICS clients from coming under attack. Even though the ICF is key in ICS deployments, it is also quite useful for single computers connected to the Internet.

ICF Overview

ICF is a *stateful* firewall, meaning that it monitors all aspects of the communications link, inspecting source and destination address information of all packets. In order to keep unwanted traffic from entering your network from the Internet, ICF maintains a table of all communications that have originated from the source computer. Incoming traffic is compared against the data maintained in the table. Unless there is a matching entry in the table, the packets are blocked. This stops hacking attempts, such as port scanning. ICF doesn't bother the user with a pop-up message each time an unsolicited message is received. Rather, the ICF activity is maintained in a security log.

NOTE Internet Connection Sharing and Internet Connection Firewall are not available on Windows XP 64-Bit Edition.

Not all unsolicited traffic is inherently evil, however. As such, ICF can be configured to let traffic through and channel it to the appropriate device. For instance, if you have a web server, ICF can funnel those packets to the web server.

Using ICF

The ICF should not be enabled on any connection that is not connected to the Internet. For instance, if ICF is enabled on an ICS client (rather than the ICF server), it will disrupt communications between that computer and all others on the network. It is for this very reason that the Network Setup Wizard does not enable the ICF on the private connection between ICS server and ICS clients. If it were enabled at this point, communications between the ICS server and ICS clients would be blocked.

NOTE If you already have a firewall or proxy server in place, ICF is not necessary.

Refer to the network in Figure 5-11. In this configuration, there are two places at which an ICF should be used. First, the connection between the ICF Server and the ISP should have ICF enabled. Second, one of the ICS clients has its own connection to the Internet. By enabling the ICF on the Internet connection (but not on the private link between ICS server and ICS client), unsolicited packets are filtered out. Without ICF on both locations, your network is vulnerable to attack.

ICF Incompatibilities

At first blush, ICF might seem like a very useful means to keep attackers out of your network. And, to a point, it is. However, because ICF blocks every unsolicited packet coming into your network, some applications (like various e-mail and online chat programs) might have problems with ICF. This is because some e-mail programs such as Outlook Express wait a preset amount of time before polling the e-mail server. This is fine, because ICF will note in its table that the e-mail program sent a packet to the e-mail server. When the data comes back from the e-mail server, ICF will have a record in its table and will allow the return message through.

On the other hand, a program such as Outlook connects to the Microsoft Exchange Server. Using a remote procedure call (RPC), the server sends out a message to its clients that a new e-mail has arrived. Because ICF won't have a listing in its table that the client initiated the contact, it will block the RPC notification. This does not mean

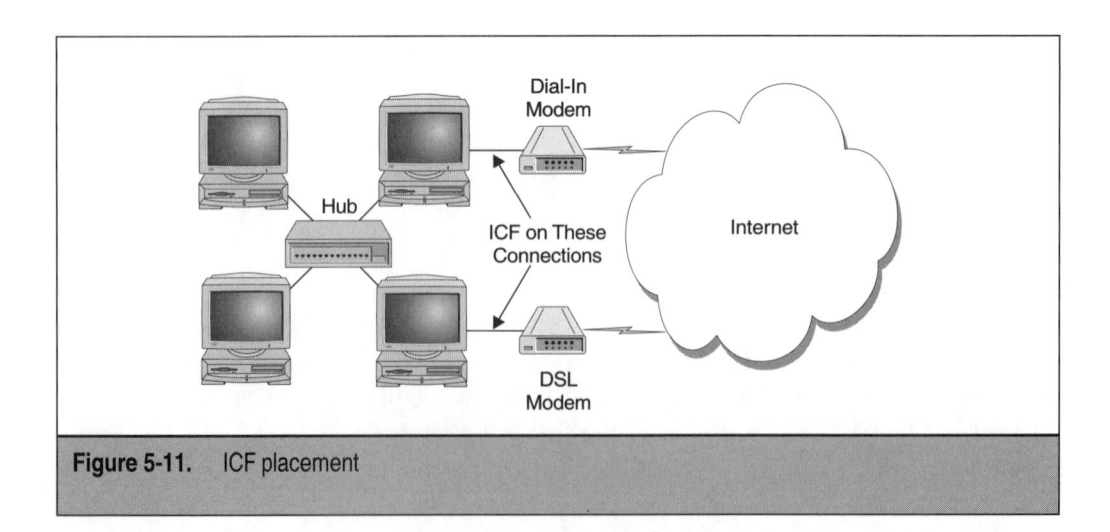

Figure 5-11. ICF placement

that the e-mail is lost. It will still be kept on the Exchange Server; however, the clients must check for e-mail manually.

Logging

To inspect a listing of the unsolicited packets that ICF has dropped, you can check the ICF security log. This log can be viewed by following these steps:

1. Select Start | Control Panel. Click Networks and Internet Connections, then select Network Connections.
2. Click the connection for which ICF is enabled.
3. Under Network Tasks, click Change settings of this connection.
4. On the Advanced tab, click Settings.
5. On the Security Logging tab, in the Log file options area under Name, select Browse.
6. Locate pfirewall.log. Right-click it, and then select Open.

The log can be set up to keep track of both permitted and rejected traffic. If the Internet Control Message Protocol (ICMP) Allow incoming echo request option is not enabled, then the incoming packet will be dropped and a note made in the log.

There are a number of ICMP options that can be enabled (located under the ICMP tab of the Advanced Settings dialog box, which you accessed by following Steps 1 through 4 to reach the security log). These ICMP options allow you to adjust your ICF's functionality. ICMP options include the following:

- Allow redirect
- Allow incoming timestamp request
- Allow incoming router request

You can manage the size of the security log to keep it from filling up and overflowing, caused by a barrage of denial-of-service (DoS) attacks. Furthermore, by clicking the Services tab, you can establish which services you will be using on your Windows XP Professional device.

Configuring ICF

Enabling or disabling ICF is a very simple matter. Follow these steps:

1. Select Start | Control Panel and double-click Network Connections.
2. Click the Internet connection you wish to protect with ICF.
3. Under Network Tasks, click Change settings of this connection.

On the Advanced tab, you can either enable or disable ICF by checking or clearing the box next to Protect my computer and network by limiting or preventing access to this computer from the Internet.

WIRELESS CONNECTIONS

The alphabet soup of acronyms surrounding the world of networks and networking seems to get thicker and thicker with each new technology or methodology. Two of the more useful acronyms you might encounter are WPAN, which stands for Wireless Personal Area Network, and WLAN, which stands for Wireless Local Area Network. As you have no doubt surmised, WPANs and WLANs are built when wireless connectivity is added to a personal computer.

Don't confuse WPANs and WLANs. Whereas a WLAN occurs in a 100-meter area, WPANs are much smaller—about 10 meters. Furthermore, WPANs and WLANs use different technologies.

WPAN

There is more to a WPAN that simple proximity. The technology upon which WPANs are built for Windows XP Professional is called *Infrared Data Association* (IrDA). IrDA is a technology allowing users with infrared devices on their computers to transfer data between themselves, forming dial-up network connections and access LANs.

IrDA

IrDA defines a data protocol for computers, printers, personal digital assistants, and many other peripherals to transmit and receive data across short distances using infrared light. Unlike visible light, infrared light does not propagate very well. As such, two devices on a WPAN must have a clear line of sight (much like your television's remote control).

> **NOTE** Infrared light is light in the spectrum between 850 and 900 nanometers. This light is invisible to the human eye because the wavelengths are slightly longer than visible light.

There are a number of pros and cons to using infrared light, as Table 5-4 enumerates.

IrDA operates in three different modes, each with a different maximum data transfer rate:

- **Serial IR (SIR)**   Maximum data rate of 115.2 kilobits per second (Kbps)
- **Fast IR (FIR)**   Maximum data rate of 4 megabits per second (Mbps)
- **Very Fast IR (VFIR)**   Maximum data rate of 16 Mbps

Pros	Cons
Large bandwidth	Can be inconvenient to point two devices at each other
Is not regulated by the Federal Communications Commission	Short range
Does not interfere with radio frequency (RF) wireless networks	Cannot penetrate walls or other obstacles
Difficult to eavesdrop on an infrared transmission	

Table 5-4. Pros and Cons of IrDA

Using IrDA with Windows XP Professional

Windows XP Professional supports IrDA with five different user profiles:

- **File Transfer (IrOBEX)**   File transfers between IrDA devices is simplified.
- **Printing (IrLPT)**   This makes it possible to print from one IrDA device to an IrDA printer.
- **Dial-up Networking (IrCOMM)**   Internet access is possible through an IrDA-enabled cellular telephone.
- **Imaging (IrTran-P)**   Allows transfer of digital camera files between an IrDA-enabled camera and computer.
- **LAN Access/Peer-to-Peer Networking (IrNET)**   LAN and P2P connections are enabled on IrDA-enabled computers.

WLAN

On the other end of the spectrum (so to speak) is the 802.11x standard, which is the more popular means of sharing data wirelessly.

Besides the "gee whiz, this is cool" aspect of a computer network that operates without wires, a number of important factors make wireless networking a useful, productive technology:

- **Mobility**   With WLANs, users can get real-time access to their LAN from virtually anywhere. This ability comes without having to be hardwired into the network.
- **Reduced cost of ownership**   Even though startup costs for WLAN hardware are more expensive than the cost of a traditional LAN, when the complete lifecycle expenses are considered, WLAN expenses can be considerably lower. The greatest long-term cost benefits are seen in dynamic environments where there are frequent moves and changes.

- **Scalability** WLANs can be easily configured in a number of networking topologies to meet the needs of specific applications and installations. Configurations are highly flexible, can easily be changed, and range from simple peer-to-peer networks that are ideal for a few users to full infrastructure networks of thousands of users that enable roaming across a broad area.

- **High-speed data rates** WLAN transmission speeds are comparable to wired networks. Users can access information at 11 Mbps, which is on par with conventional wire speeds. Though not yet touching the 100 Mbps and 1 Gbps speeds that are possible in wired networks, wireless has a respectable functional speed.

- **Interoperability** Manufacturers who build their products using the 802.11 standard ensure functionality with other compliant equipment or brands within the network.

- **Encryption for high-speed LAN security** By incorporating wireless equivalent privacy (WEP), network security can be ensured. WEP serves 11 Mbps access points, PC cards, ISA cards, and PCI adapters.

- **Installation speed and simplicity** Before wireless technology, connecting computers to a LAN required stringing and plugging in a mess of wires. The task could be further complicated if the wiring needed to be strung through walls or between different floors. Wireless technology simplifies and speeds up the installation process.

- **Installation flexibility** Because WLANs aren't restricted by the physical barriers that constrain wired LANs, wireless networks can provide network access to those users and workstations where connecting to a LAN is simply impossible.

Like cordless telephones, WLANs use electromagnetic radio waves to communicate information from one location (your laptop, for instance) to another (an access point), without having to use any physical medium to transfer the message. Figure 5-12 illustrates this.

In a WLAN, the device that physically connects to the wired LAN is a transceiver (a combination of a transmitter and receiver), commonly called an *access point*. The access point receives, buffers, and transmits data between the WLAN and the wired network. As shown in Figure 5-13, another way to think about an access point is to consider it as a wireless hub—a single access point can serve hundreds of clients. Depending on the range of the access point, clients can be located within a few feet or up to 1,500 feet away from the access point. Optimally, the antenna for the access point would be situated high above the floor. However, an antenna can be located anywhere space permits.

To connect to the access point, client computers use WLAN adapters, which are small PC cards for notebook and palmtop computers and cards in desktop computers.

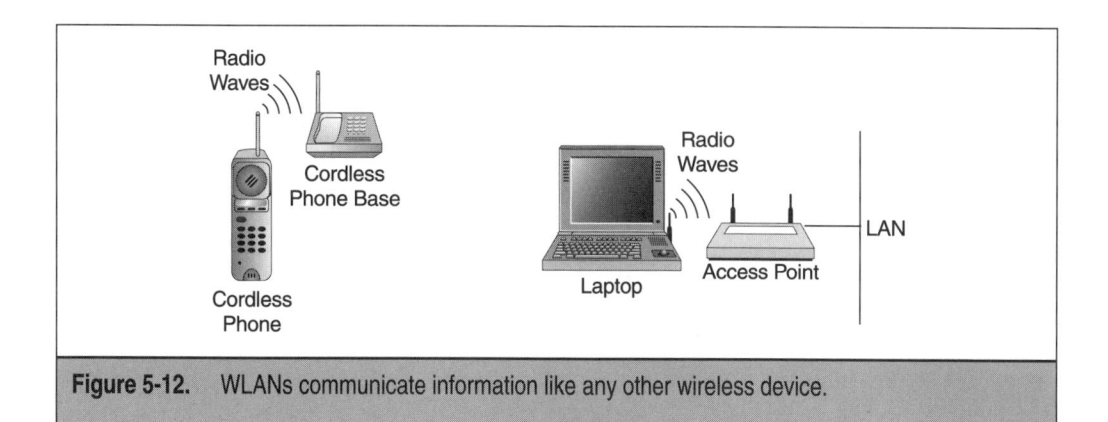

Figure 5-12. WLANs communicate information like any other wireless device.

They can also be integrated within handheld computers. These cards have built-in antennas and transceiver components.

WLANs can be as small as two people, sitting at a table sharing data over lunch, or as big as hundreds of people sharing multiple access points.

Let's take a look at the two basic ways you can build your Windows XP Professional wireless networks.

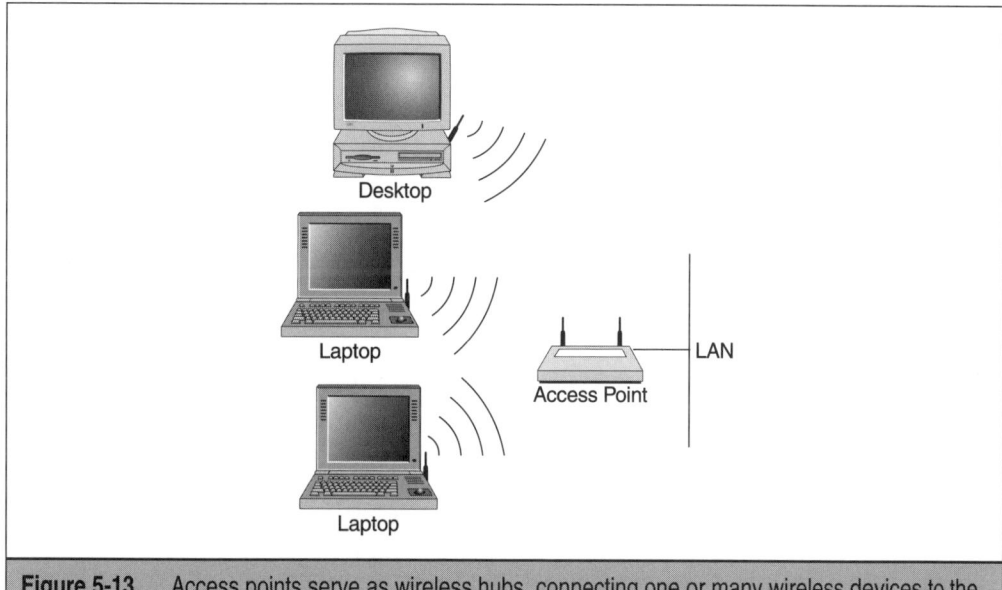

Figure 5-13. Access points serve as wireless hubs, connecting one or many wireless devices to the wired LAN.

Peer-to-Peer Network

The simplest, most basic wireless network consists of two PCs, equipped with wireless adapter cards. As shown in Figure 5-14, no access point is needed, and whenever these two computers get within range of each other, they form their own independent network. This is called a *peer-to-peer network*. On-demand networks like this are extremely simple to set up and operate. They require no administration or preconfiguration. And, in this case, each computer would only have access to the resources of the other computer, but not to a central server or the Internet. As we noted earlier, this is the same type of network afforded by a WPAN.

This type of network is ideal for home networking or small businesses or spontaneous networking.

In-Building Network

Much like a conventionally wired network, in-building WLAN equipment consists of a PC card, PCI and ISA client adapters, as well as access points.

Like wired LANs for small or temporary networks, a WLAN can be constructed with just two computers in a peer-to-peer design or on-the-fly topology using only client adapters. To extend the range of your WLAN, as shown in Figure 5-15, or to increase functionality, access points can be used in the network's topology and will also function as a bridge to an Ethernet network.

By applying WLAN technology to desktop systems, an organization is afforded flexibility that is simply impossible with a conventional LAN. Clients can be deployed in places where running cable is simply impossible. Furthermore, clients can be redeployed anywhere at any time. This makes wireless ideal for temporary workgroups or fast-growing organizations.

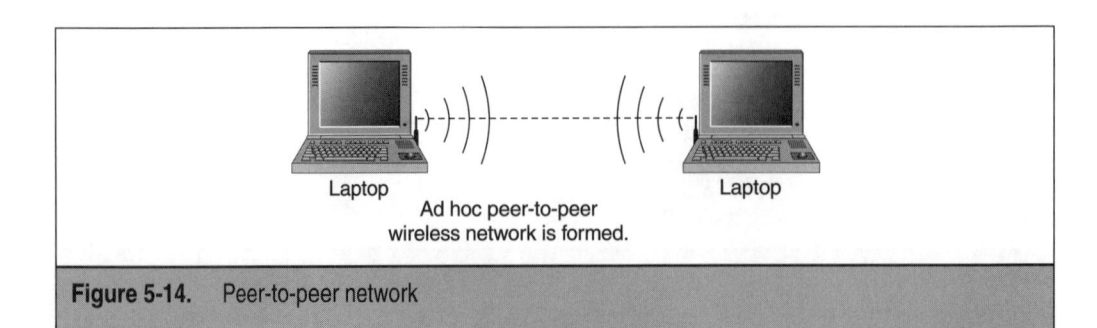

Figure 5-14. Peer-to-peer network

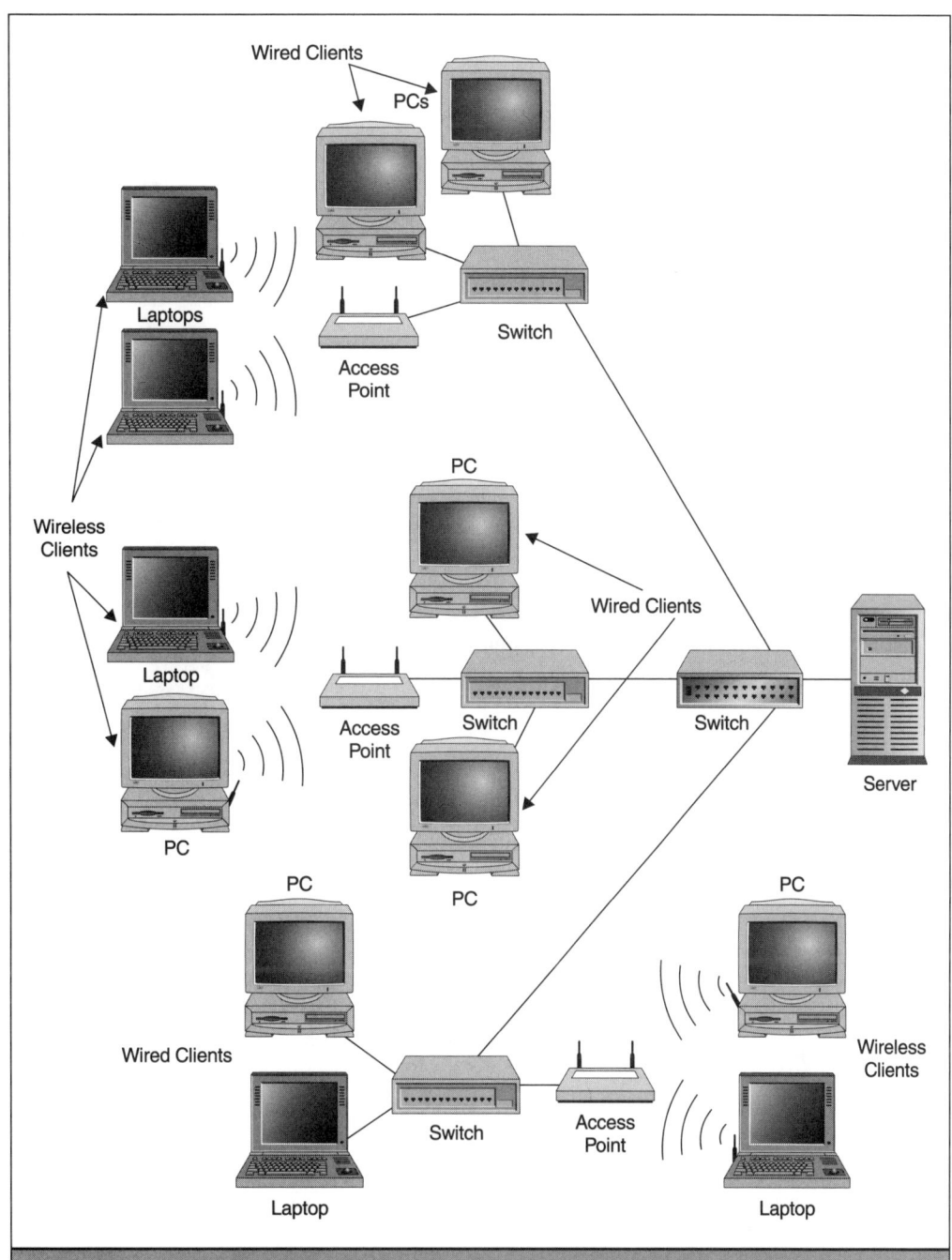

Figure 5-15. Using several access points, availability of the WLAN can be increased.

The Mechanics

The 802.11 LAN is based on architecture that is very similar to the design of cellular telephone networks. By using a comparable network design, wireless networks can reap the same benefits of cellular, while providing high data rates.

- **Cells and sets** An 802.11 LAN is subdivided into cells, and each cell is referred to as a *basic service set (BSS)*. Each BSS is controlled by an access point. But because a single access point may not be capable of fulfilling the network's wireless needs, several access points can be connected to a common backbone. When a configuration of several access points is used, this is called a *distribution system*. No matter how large or small the network, no matter how many nodes are connected, the grouping of wireless equipment is viewed as a single IEEE 802.11 network to upper layers of the OSI Reference Model. In 802.11 terminology, the upper layers of the OSI Reference Model are referred to as an *extended service set*.

- **The physical layer** The 802.11 protocol covers the physical and media access control. But instead of a single type of media, 802.11 supports three kinds of media: frequency-hopping spread spectrum, direct-sequence spread spectrum, and infrared. A single MAC layer supports all three physical layers. Additionally, the MAC layer provides a link to the upper-layer protocols. These functions include fragmentation, packet retransmission, and acknowledgments.

By basing wireless networking on cellular architecture, wireless devices can join, leave, or roam from cell to cell much like cellular telephones do.

Setting Up Wireless Connections

Setting up a WPAN or WLAN using a Microsoft operating system has never been easier than it is with Windows XP Professional. Microsoft has incorporated a number of tools to smooth out not only the installation, but also day-to-day use of wireless networks.

Roaming

One of the chief improvements over earlier versions of Windows for wireless networking is enhanced roaming capabilities. Like cellular telephone technology, WLANs utilize so-called roaming features. This allows devices to detect if they are entering (or leaving) an area served by an access point. Windows XP Professional improves on Windows 2000's roaming features by sensing when a device has moved to a new access point, requiring reauthentication to ensure the correct levels of network accessibility. This is also known as *media sense*. Furthermore, media sense also allows the detection of changes to the IP subnet so that the ideal IP address can be assigned, ensuring best use of resources.

Windows XP Professional allows for multiple IP address configurations and for the best address to be assigned automatically. When the IP address must change, Windows XP Professional also allows reconfiguration to occur.

When a device moves from the auspices of one access point to another, information about that device must be moved along with it (like the location of the device, so that messages can be properly delivered). This information can be passed from one access point to another. A number of wireless vendors have worked together on a protocol to facilitate this data transfer. The protocol is called Interaccess Point Protocol (IAPP). It is not yet a standard, but it is a good sign that vendors are putting aside proprietary protocols to the benefit of the end user.

Zero Client Configuration

A nice feature of wireless networking in Windows XP Professional is the ability to move between wireless LANs without having to reconfigure your device or the connection. For instance, if you have a WLAN at the office, and one at home, you can use the same configuration on your Windows XP Professional device. This is called *zero configuration*.

Zero configuration uses the Windows XP Professional user interface when trying to form a connection between wireless devices.

Configuration

Because Windows XP Professional supports the 802.11x standard for wireless networking, there is precious little configuration that needs to take place. If automatic configuration is enabled on your device, you can roam freely between different WLANs without having to reconfigure your Windows XP Professional client.

When you move from one WLAN to the next, Windows XP Professional scans for a new WLAN and automatically configures your network adapter card to work in the new environment. If you happen to be in an area where several WLANs are available, then you can create a list of preferred WLANs, and set up the order in which you'd like to connect.

Automatic Wireless Configuration

The process of setting up an automatic wireless configuration is very straightforward. Follow these steps:

1. Select Start | Connect To | Show All Connections.
2. Right-click the connection you wish to associate with your wireless NIC, and then select Properties.
3. On the Wireless Networking tab (as shown in Figure 5-16), do one of the following:
    - Select the Use Windows to configure my wireless network settings option to automatically enable wireless network configuration.
    - Clear the Use Windows to configure my wireless network settings option to disable automatic wireless network configuration.

Figure 5-16. Wireless connection properties

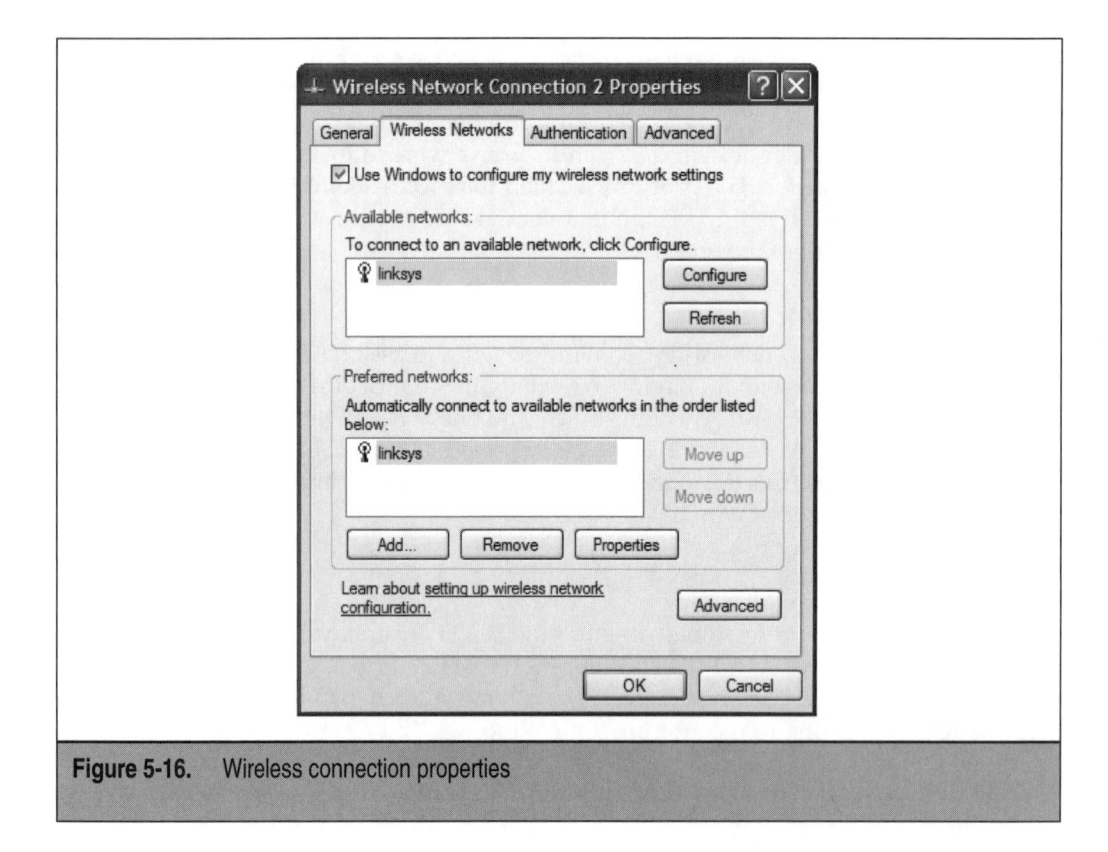

4. The list of available WLANs is detected and appears under Available networks. You can alter this list and its settings by making the following adjustments:
   - To add an available WLAN to your preferred list, under Available networks, select the network you wish to add, and then click Configure.
   - To add a new wireless network to your Preferred networks list, under Preferred networks, click Add. In Wireless Network properties, enter the network name (its SSID), wireless network key, and if the network is an ad hoc network.
   - To change the order in which WLANs are listed in the Preferred networks list, click the WLAN you wish to move, and then click Move up or Move down.
   - To delete a WLAN, simply click the WLAN, and then click Remove.
5. Finally, you can set which type of wireless network you'll be accessing by clicking the Advanced button, and then selecting the network you wish to manage. Next, you can tell Windows XP Professional if this connection will be ad hoc or infrastructure.

> **NOTE** Ad hoc networks are those created by two wireless devices for a temporary network—for instance, two coworkers sharing data around a conference table. Infrastructure, on the other hand, is a wireless network in which wireless devices access the organization's LAN through an access point.

Authentication

Naturally, if you have one or more WLANs, the process of connecting your computers to that network is very easy. However, it is also very easy for someone who shouldn't have access to your network to sit in a nearby parking lot and start checking out your files. As such, you should make sure that your WLAN(s) are set up for 802.1x authentication.

Be careful not to confuse authentication with a WEP key. Authentication is a means for a computer to verify its identity. A WEP key provides an encryption key for the established connection. In other words, once a device authenticates itself, then it uses WEP to keep a third party from sniffing around and reading the data being shared.

The following steps outline how 802.1x authentication is enabled:

1. Select Start | Connect To | Show All Connections.
2. Right-click the network connection for which you want to enable or disable 802.1x authentication.
3. On the Authentication tab, you can enable 802.1x authentication by selecting the Network access control using IEEE 802.1x check box. Alternatively, to disable this feature, clear the check box. (This window is shown in Figure 5-17.)
4. In EAP type, select the Extensible Authentication Protocol type this connection will use.
5. If you have selected Smart Card or other Certificate in the EAP type section, you can configure additional settings. To do so, click Properties, and then do the following:
    - Select the Use my smart card option to use the certificate contained on your smart card for authentication.
    - Select the Use a certificate on this computer option to use the certificate stored on your computer. You can check the validity of the certificate on your computer by selecting the Validate server certificate check box. You must also establish whether to connect only if the certificate is valid with a particular domain, and then specify the trusted root certification authority.
    - Select the Authenticate as guest when user or computer information is unavailable option to try logging on as a guest if user or computer information is unavailable.
6. To tell Windows XP Professional whether or not to attempt authorization to the network if the user is not logged on or if the user information is not available, select either the Authenticate as computer when computer information is available check box or Authenticate as guest when user or computer information is unavailable check box.

Figure 5-17. 802.1x authentication properties

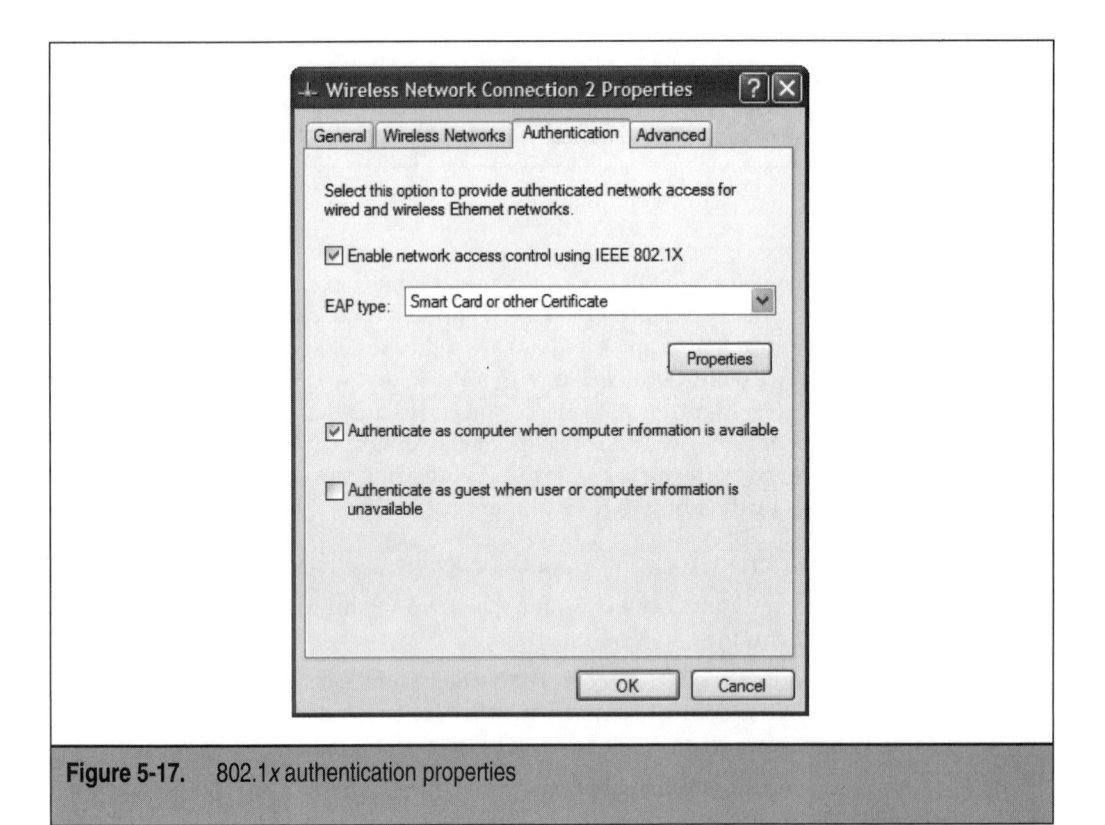

Connecting

Finally, you get to connect your wireless device to the WLAN. Mercifully, Windows XP Professional makes it simple to do. Just follow these steps:

1. Select Start | Connect To | *your wireless connection.*
2. Right-click the network connection icon, and then click View Available Wireless Networks.
3. Under Connect to Wireless Network, click the wireless network to which you wish to connect. (This is shown in Figure 5-18.)
4. If a WEP key is needed, do one of the following:
    - If the WEP key is stored in the computer's wireless NIC, leave Network Key blank.
    - If the WEP key is not automatically entered, type it in.
5. Click Connect.

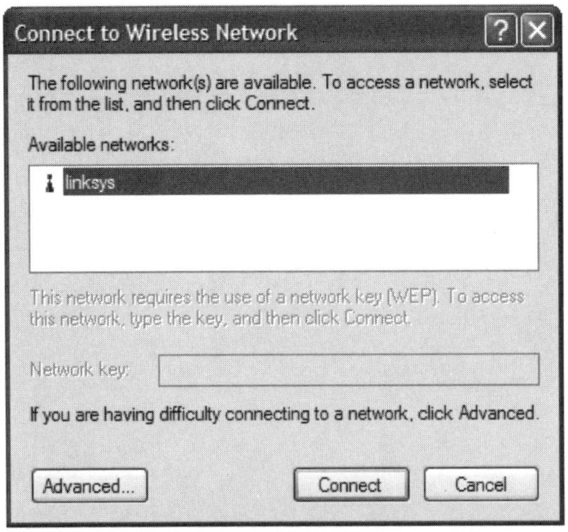

Figure 5-18. Connecting your wireless device to a WLAN.

Setting up your clients to work in Windows XP Professional workgroups is a largely simplified affair over previous versions of Windows. For the most part, setup is easy, thanks in part to the number of wizards that can be employed. Also, Windows XP Professional workgroups can take advantage of wireless connectivity, whether as part of a WLAN or a WPAN. Finally, even the smallest networks can take advantage of Windows XP Professional's enhanced workgroup functionality, by having the ability to share one connection to the Internet, and use a built-in firewall to keep out evildoers.

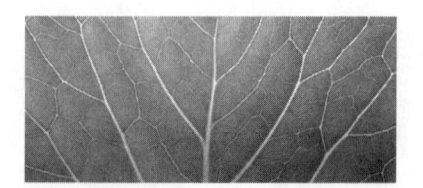

CHAPTER 6

Domain Connectivity

In the world of Microsoft networking, there are two types of logical networks that a client can be part of: a workgroup or a domain. Chapter 5 talked about the specifics of workgroups, which are ideal in peer-to-peer connections or for small environments. This chapter discusses domains, which are typically used for large networks.

But a discussion of domains isn't limited to the size of a network. Rather, domains contain specialized functions (such as acting as a unified security boundary for all devices within the domain). In this chapter, we talk about domains and how Windows XP Professional can be part of a domain. Finally, we round out the chapter with a discussion of a compelling tool that makes domains even more robust and powerful—Active Directory (AD).

WINDOWS DOMAINS 101

If you use Windows 2000, then you probably already use domains. However, if your network is running on a pre–Windows 2000 version of the OS (or does not even run a version of Windows, for that matter), then it's a good idea to get a primer on what exactly domains are and how they are used.

This section gives a quick look at domains—what they are, why they're useful, and how Windows XP Professional fits into the larger domain picture.

What Is a Domain?

The last chapter focused on workgroup connections. As you remember, workgroups are small units or networks that are made up solely of Windows XP Professional computers. Workgroups are fine for smaller networks or peer-to-peer environments. However, larger organizations will likely share their computational resources on a *domain*.

A domain is a grouping of accounts and network resources that are organized under a single domain name (NASA.gov, for example). These devices and accounts also fall within the security boundary that the domain affords. That is, if the head of NASA is trying to log into the NASA.gov domain, he'll be required—just once—to give the appropriate passwords to access the domain's resources.

Domains provide ease of use for the user because he or she need not know multiple passwords for various devices, as one would have to in a workgroup. In a domain, however, passwords and permissions are managed centrally, along with other network and account details. When the head of NASA wants to access the domain through either his office computer or even another workstation, his information is automatically sent to the computer he's currently using from one of the domain controllers.

NOTE In Windows NT, Microsoft used primary domain controllers (PDCs) and backup domain controllers (BDCs). In Windows 2000 and .NET environments, domain controllers (DCs) replace PDCs and BDCs.

Microsoft advises using domains as much as possible (sure, they can sell more server products that way). But domains have some features that are not present in workgroups. A major part of domain functionality is via Microsoft's Active Directory system. We'll talk about Active Directory and Windows XP Professional's role in AD later in this chapter.

How Domains Work

As we noted in the previous section, domains are a grouping of network resources, controlled by a central authority. In Windows NT, PDCs and BDCs were used. It was useful to employ a primary device to control the network, with backup devices ready in the event of problems. However, Microsoft made the system even slicker in Windows 2000 by including domain controllers. With DCs, all the functions are replicated on each DC, as shown in Figure 6-1, whereas in Windows NT, only certain responsibilities were given to each PDC and BDC.

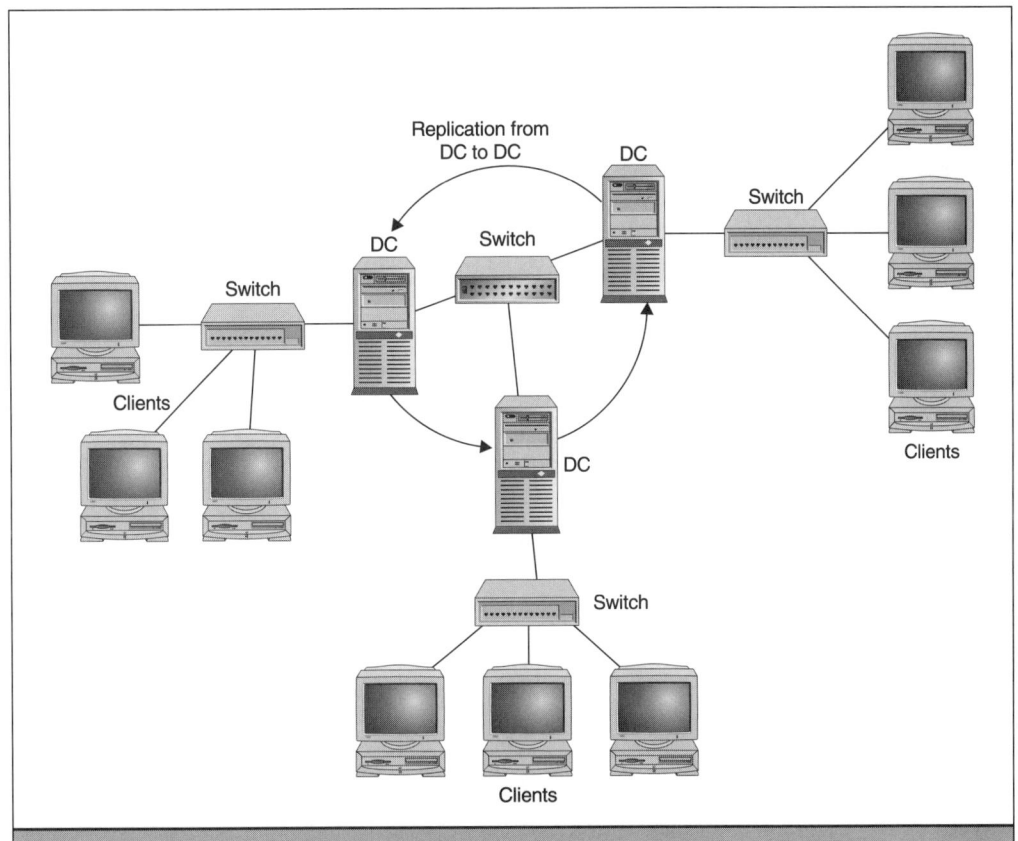

Figure 6-1. Domain controllers share the network administration workload evenly

> **NOTE** For simplicity's sake, we'll refer to a domain as being controlled by a Windows 2000 Server. However, the functionality will still be present with a .NET Server.

For a domain to function properly, the contents of Active Directory must be updated to all DCs in a timely fashion. To do this, Windows 2000 uses multimaster replication to keep information amongst its DCs current. Rather than using a line database for the domain that is replicated to subordinate DCs (as is done in Windows NT), all Windows 2000 DCs are treated as peers. As such, a change made on one DC will be replicated to all DCs.

By default, replications are called every 5 minutes within the same site. To ensure smooth replication, the Knowledge Consistency Checker (KCC), a software component that runs on DCs, creates a logical ring topology of all DCs within a site and automatically creates connections to achieve this topology. The replication proceeds around the ring until it reaches the starting DC.

How Windows XP Fits into the Domain Model

With so many different versions of Windows in the marketplace (and more seemingly on their way), it's a good idea to understand how these versions fit together within a domain. Each version of Windows has its own place in the domain model, and for best results they will be organized accordingly. Figure 6-2 shows where the various flavors of Windows exist in a domain.

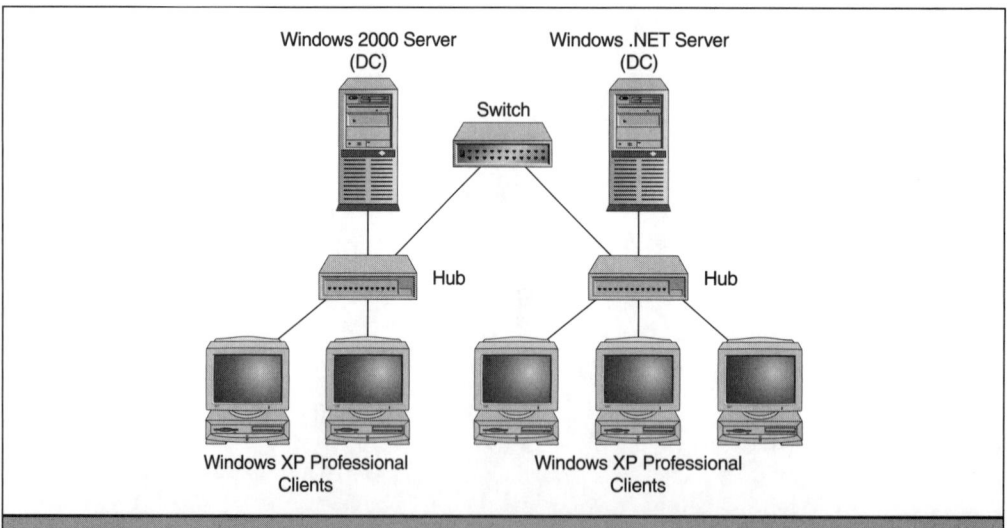

Figure 6-2. Where various Windows products reside in a domain

Windows 2000 Server

As we've already noted, the core of a Windows domain is Windows 2000 Server (or the beefier Advanced Server or Datacenter). Windows 2000 Server is the device on which Active Directory is maintained. Since Windows XP Professional doesn't have a specific version for server use, you would be better off using Windows 2000 in server roles than trying to get Windows XP Professional to fill the role. Additionally, these are the devices that will act as DCs.

Windows XP Clients

As you have probably surmised, Windows XP Professional serves as the client computer in a Windows domain. Windows XP Professional can integrate with the Windows 2000 Servers to provide the interface for the end users.

Although Windows 2000 is best suited for server roles, in some instances Windows XP Professional can be used as a server. However, these are specialized cases involving peer-to-peer connections—for instance, when using Internet Connection Sharing (ICS) (which we talked about in Chapter 5), or when using Internet Information Server (IIS) (which we'll cover in Chapter 7). However, for this discussion (with a conventional domain model) Windows XP Professional will serve as the client component.

.NET

The next iteration of Windows servers will be the .NET Server. This will be used in place of (or in conjunction with) Windows 2000 Servers. .NET is Microsoft's vision for a new environment in which information, people, services, and devices are connected. The goal is to seamlessly connect applications through the use of Extensible Markup Language (XML) Web services. These are small applications that connect together over the Internet.

NOTE For more information about Microsoft's .NET initiative, visit their web site at http://www.microsoft.com/net.

DOMAIN CONNECTIVITY

Now that you understand how domains work and how individual operating systems function within the confines of the domain, let's talk about making the connection to a domain. Additionally, there are some troubleshooting tools and techniques that can be helpful if you encounter problems making that domain connection.

Joining a Domain

The last chapter considered how to join Windows XP Professional-based networks: that is, clients connecting in a peer-to-peer fashion are said to be part of a *workgroup*. These types of networks are fine for smaller environments. However, in large organizations we move from workgroups to domains. Your Windows XP Professional client can be manually configured to join a Windows domain.

Using the Network Identification Wizard

An easy way to join a domain is to use one of the many wizards that Windows XP Professional supplies. In this case, you would use the Network Identification Wizard. This wizard provides a means to connect Windows XP Professional clients to Windows NT– or Windows 2000–based domains.

> **NOTE** The Network Identification Wizard can also be used to connect your Windows XP Professional client to a workgroup.

To start the Network Identification Wizard, follow these steps:

1. Right-click My Computer, and then select Properties.
2. On the Computer Name tab, click Network ID, and then click Next.
3. Pick This Computer is part of a business network and I use it to connect to other computers at work, and then click Next.
4. The wizard will give you instructions to gather certain information that will be needed to complete the wizard. The information includes
    - Username
    - Password
    - User account domain
    - Computer name
    - Computer domain

Figure 6-3 shows the Network Identification Wizard, seeking the username, password, and domain.

Joining Manually

You can join a domain manually, if you'd rather not invoke the Network Identification Wizard, or you have another reason to do so. To join a Windows domain manually, perform the following steps:

1. Select Start | Control Panel, and then click Performance and Maintenance.
2. Select System.
3. Under System Properties, select the Computer Name tab (this is shown in Figure 6-4).
4. Click Change.
5. If the computer account has been created and is on the domain controller, enter your user name, password, and domain name. Click Next, and skip to step 7.

Figure 6-3. Entering username, password, and domain name in the Network Identification Wizard

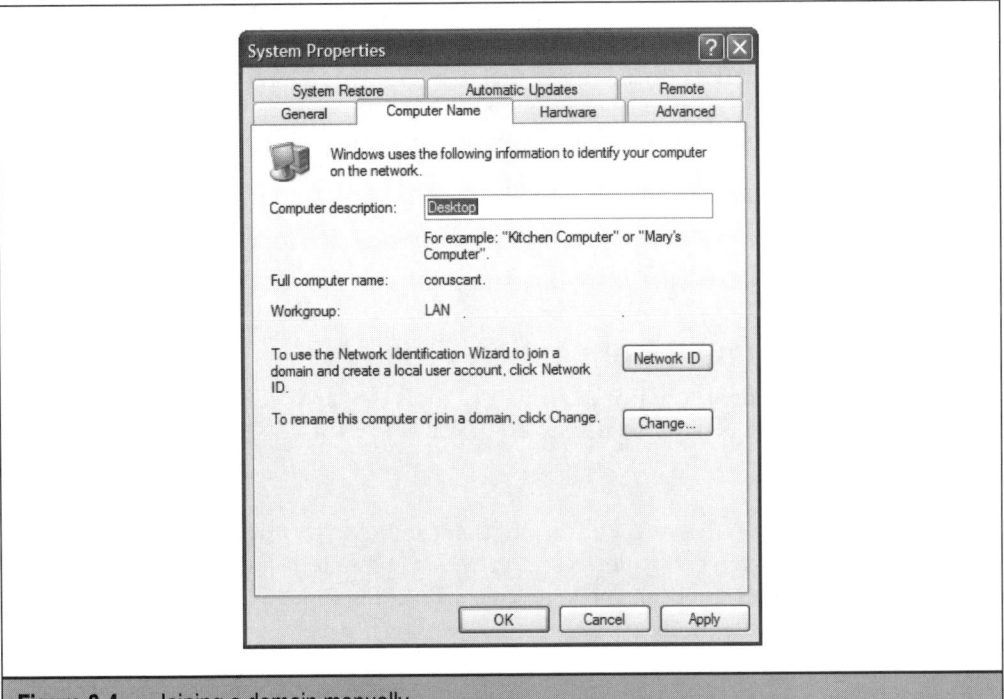

Figure 6-4. Joining a domain manually

6. If the computer account has not been created at the domain controller, then do the following:
   a. Type in the username, password and domain name, and then click Next.
   b. When prompted, enter the username and password of an administrator account, and then click OK.
7. Click OK three times.
8. You will be prompted to restart the computer. Click Yes.

Once you have completed these steps, it's a good idea to verify your membership to the domain. This is accomplished by restarting the computer and then pressing CTRL-ALT-DEL. This will call up the Log On To Windows dialog box. To the right of the logon box is an arrow. Click that arrow to review a list of domains. The list should contain the domain you just joined, along with any other trusted domains. The domain account can be tested by logging into the domain or one of its trusted domains.

> **NOTE** A *trusted domain* is a domain that shares a relationship with another domain. For instance, say you were logging onto the domain corporate.jeep.com. Assuming there was a trust relationship in place (and assuming you had the requisite permissions), you would also be able to access information stored at the company that makes its steering wheels—www.steeringwheelworld.com.

If you are able to log onto the domain using the logon credentials at the domain controller, then the account is functional. If you get a message that says you have connected using credentials stored in the cache, then the domain controller could not be contacted during the authentication process.

A few items to check in case the verification process fails:

- Are the network adapter and cables plugged in?
- Is the transport protocol set up to allow access to the domain controller?
- Is the domain controller up and running?

Troubleshooting Domain Connection Problems

Windows XP Professional contains a number of tools that are useful in troubleshooting domain controller connections, as discussed next.

Nltest.exe

Windows XP Professional comes with a tool that can help you check your logical connection to the domain controller. NLTEST.EXE is a command-line tool that is included with Windows Support Tools on the Windows XP Professional CD-ROM. This tool is used in NT- or 2000-based networks.

> **NOTE** NLTEST.EXE is located in the cabinet file support.cab in the tools\support folder on your Windows XP Professional CD-ROM.

By using NLTEST.EXE, you can find out if a domain controller can authenticate a client. NLTEST.EXE is also useful in deciding which domain controller performed the authentication and gives a list of trusted domains.

A *secure channel* is the logical connection between the Windows XP Professional client and the domain controller. The secure channel is used to authenticate computer accounts between Windows XP Professional, Windows 2000, Windows .NET, and Windows NT. Furthermore, a secure channel is used when a remote user connects to a network resource. The NLTEST.EXE tool can be used to test secure channels and reset them, if necessary.

Let's say that you've got a Windows 2000 domain (called Domain1.com). Your account is called User1 on the Windows XP Professional computer, Client1. The syntax for this command is

```
nltest [/OPTIONS]
```

To identify the DCs of the domain1.com domain, enter the following:

```
nltest /dclist:domain1
```

You can determine if a known DC (which can be found using NLTEST.EXE if you don't already know the name) will authenticate a user. To do so, at the command prompt enter

```
nltest /whowill:domain1 User1
```

You can check to see if Client1 has a secure connection with the DC by entering

```
nltest /server:Client1 /sc_query:domain1
```

For a complete listing of the NLTEST.EXE commands, enter the following at the command line prompt:

```
nltest /?
```

Unable to Join Domain

If you are attempting to connect a Windows XP Professional client to a Windows 2000 or Windows NT domain, you might encounter the following message:

```
Unable to connect to the domain controller for this domain.
Either the user name or password entered is incorrect.
```

For Windows XP Professional to join a Windows NT or 2000 domain, an account name must be entered that is part of the domain's Admins group. Furthermore, the user must have permission to add clients to a domain.

Unable to Find Domain Controller

If during your attempt to add a Windows XP Professional client to a Windows 2000 or Windows NT domain you encounter this message:

```
The specified domain does not exist or could not be contacted.
```

you need to do the following:

1. Your first course of action is to ensure that the proper domain name is entered in the Workgroup and Domain fields on the Computer Name tab of the System Properties dialog box.

2. The next place to check is the TCP/IP protocol suite, which might be misconfigured. To check the TCP/IP configuration, log on with an administrator account, and then do the following:

   - Ping the domain controller by using its NetBIOS name or its fully qualified DNS domain name. If this doesn't work, try the ping using the domain controller's IP address.

   NOTE If you're unfamiliar with the PING command, we talk about it more in Chapter 8.

   - If the ping attempt is unsuccessful and your domain uses DNS or WINS, double-check the IP addresses of the name servers. Try pinging the domain controller again.

   - If you're still unsuccessful, and your Windows XP Professional client is on the same subnet as the domain controller, double-check the client's IP address to ensure that it is correct.

   - If your Windows XP Professional client is on a different subnet than the domain controller, make sure the default gateway address is correct.

3. If a domain controller has an Internet Protocol Security (IPSec) policy set at Secure Server, then IP packets to clients are denied if they do not also have IPSec enabled by the local or domain-based security policies. Your best bet is to contact the domain administrator and talk about revising the IPSec policy. (For more information about IPSec, flip ahead to Chapter 9.)

4. If Routing Information Protocol (RIP)–enabled routers are used in this domain, install RIP support.

Unable to Rename Computer

You might run into trouble if you try to rename a client with a name that is similar to the domain controller. As such, you might see the following message:

```
The new computer name may not be the same as the Workgroup (Domain) name.
```

Even if your computer name is similar—but not exactly the same—as the domain controller, you might see this message. For instance, if your domain name is crazyearlsstereoshop.com and your client name is crazyearlsstereomanager, then you will receive the aforementioned message. The reason? If NetBIOS is enabled on all clients and servers, then the first 15 characters of the name of the Windows XP Professional client (in this case, crazyearlsstere) cannot be the same as the domain controller, server, client, or any other device.

Unable to Log onto a Domain

If you are unable to log onto a domain, you might get the following message:

```
The system cannot log you on due to the following error:
There is a time difference between the Client and Server.
Please try again or consult your system administrator.
```

This error occurs because the Kerberos security protocol inspects the timestamp of the authentication request of a logged on client. If the difference between the client and the server is more than 5 minutes, then authentication fails. This can be remedied by checking with a coworker who is logged onto the domain and making sure your computer's clock is set to the correct time. Also, it's a good idea to check your time zone and make sure that it is set appropriately. This is because Kerberos automatically converts all times to Greenwich mean time for an apples-to-apples time comparison.

Other logon errors that can keep a client from getting onto the domain include

- Username incorrectly entered
- Password incorrectly entered
- CAPS LOCK on while trying to enter username or password
- No common protocol between DC and client

In the event that there is a problem with the protocol between the DC and client, look for the following details, which can cause incompatibilities:

- Mistyped IP addresses or subnet masks
- Dynamic Host Configuration Protocol (DHCP) enabled when no DHCP server is used
- Incorrect addresses for DNS and WINS servers

ACCESSING DOMAIN RESOURCES

Once you've joined a domain, then what? The whole point of becoming part of a domain is to take advantage of the resources available to you. This means that you'll be part of the domain's security structure, and you'll be able to access data and other computers within that domain.

Security

In addition to the organizational issues that domains resolve, they also allow centralized security functions. Information about domain accounts is stored by Active Directory running on Windows NT, 2000, or .NET Server. Once a user logs into a domain, the Windows XP Professional client fetches settings and permissions information from AD. Domain accounts are used on large networks where maintaining accounts on individual computers would be impractical. For instance, domain accounts can use *roaming user profiles*. These profiles allow users to move from computer to computer with their permissions, settings, and even desktop layouts following them.

> **NOTE** As a security measure, Windows XP Professional password-protects files in your My Documents folder, so that others using that client cannot read them.

Network Neighborhood/My Network Places

Anyone who's been through a few updates to Windows will come to understand Microsoft's penchant for taking an existing application or tool, giving it a different icon, and renaming it. Microsoft strikes again with My Network Places, which replaces the familiar Network Neighborhood. Although the GUI is "XP-ized," My Network Places is where you go to check out your network.

Viewing Connections

To view a connection on your network, simply open the My Network Places icon.

> **NOTE** My Network Places is commonly found by clicking the Start button. However, you might find it infinitely more useful to place this icon on your desktop. This is done by clicking Start, right-clicking My Network Places, and selecting Show on Desktop.

Consider the screen shown in Figure 6-5. The resources on this network are displayed according to each computer. This is accomplished in the My Network Places screen by selecting View, and then selecting Computer under Arrange Icons By. You will notice that there are two computers shown: Coruscant and Endor.

The window displays the computers and the folders that are shared on each.

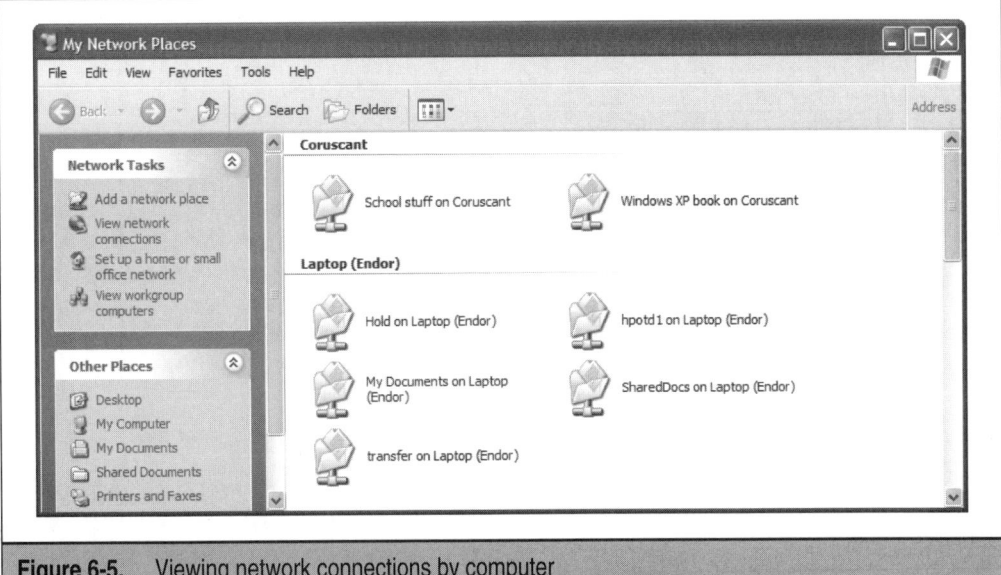

Figure 6-5. Viewing network connections by computer

Viewing Network Resources

Networks aren't only made up of other computers and file folders (although they largely are). In addition to these devices, there are other resources that many people will share. For instance, My Network Places also lets you check your network resources, such as printers, as shown in Figure 6-6.

In this case, the Brother printer is connected to the computer Coruscant. However, the computer need not be connected to any computer—it could just easily be a network printer that is connected to its own print server.

Universal Naming Convention

Because Windows provides a graphical way to interact with your computer and your network, it's easy to forget that everything in computers and networking used to be controlled via a command-line interface. A Windows GUI certainly makes the day-to-day use of a computer much easier, but there are still times when it is helpful to be able to enter a simple command and get Windows to do what you want.

In a network, the Universal Naming Convention (UNC) is a way to identify a shared file or share in a computer without having to know which storage device it is on. UNC is not unique to Windows systems. As the name suggests, UNC is universal. UNC can be used on Novell NetWare, Linux, and other operating systems.

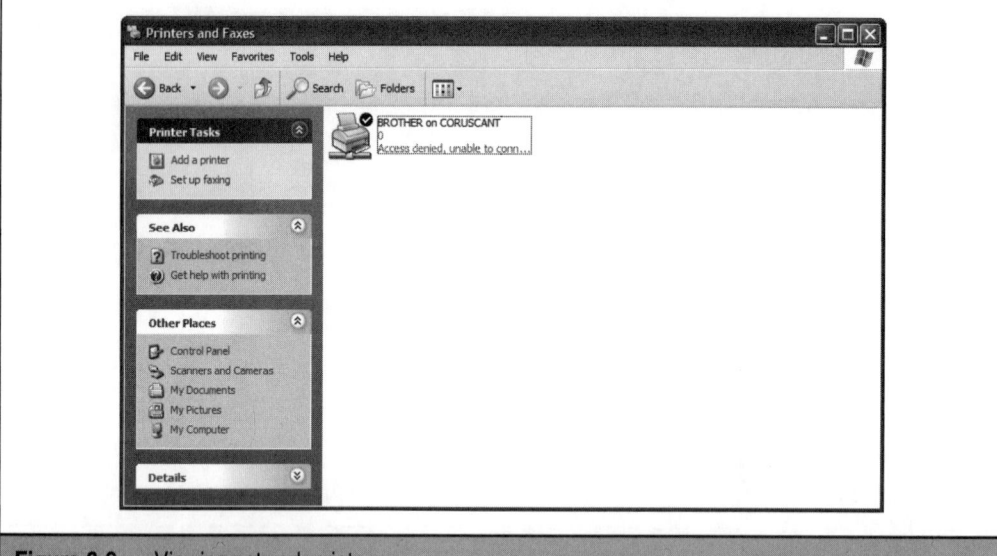

Figure 6-6. Viewing network printers

In Windows operating systems, the UNC name format is

`\\servername\sharename\filename`

The UNC breaks down as follows:

- **Servername** The name of the computer storing the file
- **Sharename** The name used to identify the shared resource on the server
- **Filename** The name of the desired file

For instance, consider the following UNC:

`\\ENDOR\webfiles\html\osborne.html`

This UNC specifies the server (ENDOR) that is maintaining a shared file (osborne.html), which is kept with other HTML files in a part of the server dedicated to World Wide Web files. However, if the HTML folder is a shared resource, the sharename and path data can be left out.

`\\ENDOR\HTML`

will get you to the shared folder, and

`\\ENDOR\HTML\osborne.html`

will get you directly to the desired file.

Usage in Windows XP

Whether to use UNC in Windows XP Professional is largely a matter of personal preference. Perhaps you prefer clicking through icons to get where you want to go. On the other hand, you might find that you use the same resource over and over, and it is easier simply to type in the UNC.

Windows XP Professional allows you some flexibility in the ability to see the UNC of various network resources. If you care to know what a particular object's UNC is, you should make sure that the capability to see the UNC is enabled. This is accomplished by doing the following:

1. Select Start | Control Panel. Click Appearance and Themes, and then select Folder Options.
2. Click the View tab (which is shown in Figure 6-7).
3. Under Files and Folders, ensure that either the Display full path in the address bar option or the Display full address in the title bar option is checked.

Whether or not you enable Windows XP Professional to show you UNC information, you can still use the UNC to move to a specific network folder. For instance, Figure 6-8, shows the result of simply typing in the UNC of a desired network share: Windows XP Professional takes you directly to that folder. The UNC is a useful tool because you needn't click through all those icons if you know the path to the folder you're searching for.

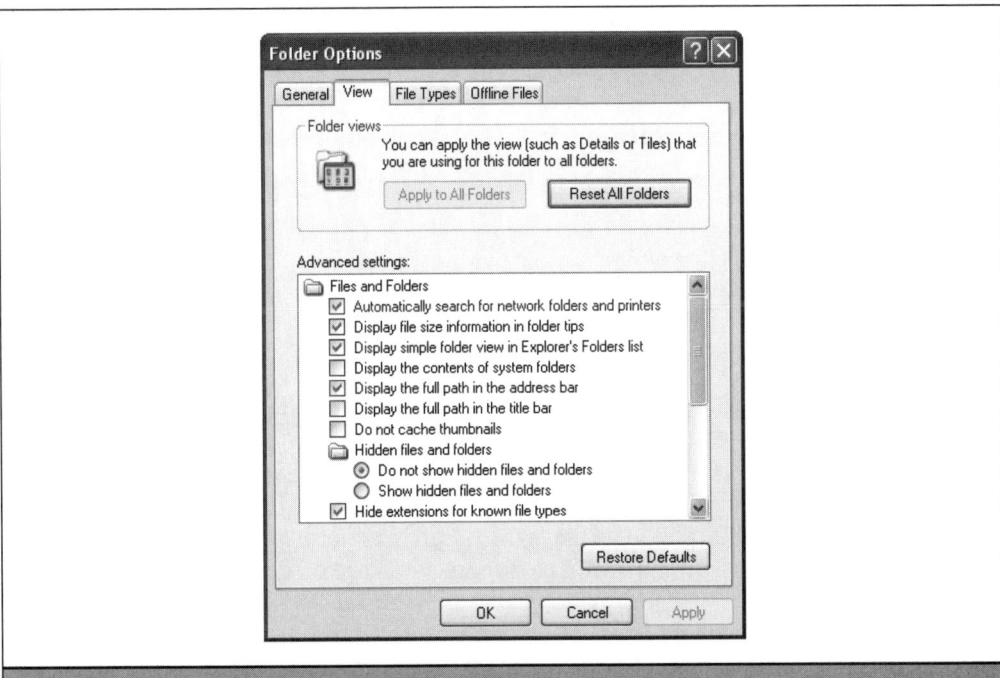

Figure 6-7. Showing UNC details in Windows XP Professional

Figure 6-8. Using UNC in Windows XP

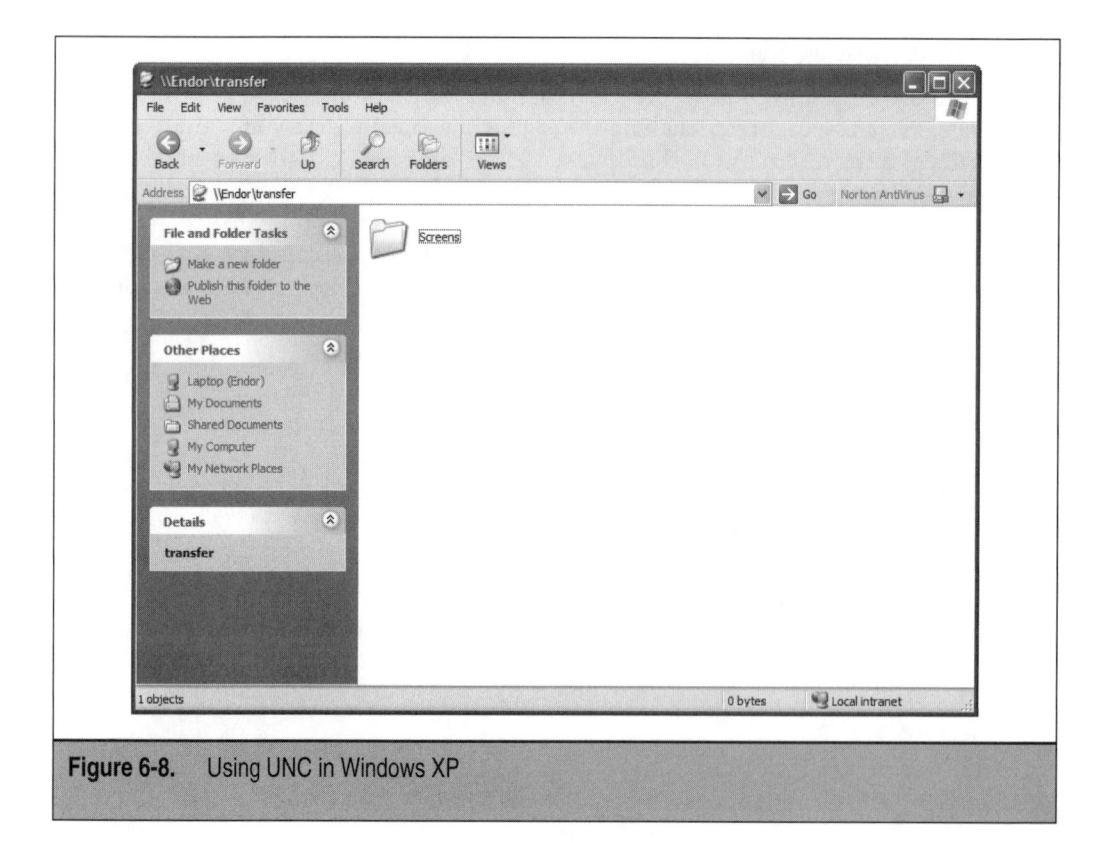

UNC can be used in a number of applications to get to the desired network share and file. For instance, if you have a web browser open, you can simply enter the appropriate UNC into the address bar, and you will be directed to that folder or file.

ACTIVE DIRECTORY

The heart of Windows domain functionality is a tool called Active Directory. Simply put, Active Directory is a database of your entire domain. It maintains lists of data about the different attributes of objects in your system including users, permissions, computer appearance settings, peripherals, and so forth.

Like any database, AD contains fields of information. We can compare AD to a car repair shop's parts database. The fields of information (light bulbs, steering wheels, and distributor caps in the parts database) are similar to fields AD holds. In the case of AD, however, it isn't recording moving parts and crankcase oil grades being maintained, rather AD is holding bits of information (like names and descriptive information) about objects in your domain.

> **NOTE** AD objects include (but are not limited to) such things as printers, user permissions, and computers.

Active Directory's logical, hierarchical structure allows the database to be sorted from the largest element down to the smallest. Using the car shop database example, it would start with the broadest category (distributor cap manufacturers) down through smaller fields (four-cylinder vehicles, six-cylinder vehicles, and so forth).

But what if the repair shop wants to add different kinds of information to its database? What if it wanted to add a field like "Windshield Wiper Blades"? In AD, that's not a problem, because AD is extensible. *Extensible* means that it allows you to customize the database by adding extra fields to track information.

IntelliMirror

The fact that AD allows such a robust networking environment is all well and good, but what really is the payoff for Windows XP Professional users? Why do they care about AD, domains, and so forth? One key is in AD's IntelliMirror.

IntelliMirror is not a single product or application, but rather a set of features that are provided by Windows 2000 Servers. IntelliMirror is the manifestation of how AD is useful for Windows XP Professional clients. For instance, IntelliMirror provides tools that promise ease of use and administration by allowing users to have their settings, documents, and applications available to them no matter where they log on within the domain. There are three ways that IntelliMirror enables a user to take his or her applications and data wherever logon within the domain may occur.

Applications Follow Users

In this case, when a user logs on, the system detects that the user's desired software is not available on the current client computer. To ameliorate this, it goes ahead and begins installation of that software package. The system knows which applications to install because when the user logs on, the computer-based software installation Group Policy is checked. If the policy requires an application that is not present, the application is downloaded to that client.

Settings Follow Users

Featured in Windows NT and called the *roaming profile*, this tool allows individual computer settings to follow the user from computer to computer. Within AD, however, the job is taken over by Group Policy. This policy dictates how the desktop, menu items, and other application properties are presented to the user no matter where he or she logs on. Users like this because it means their environment is always familiar. Administrators like this because it means they can lock down certain parts of the OS that users might meddle with.

Data Follow Users

Settings and applications are nice to have when a user hops from computer to computer. However, if you can't access the spreadsheet you've been working on, or your Word document is on another computer, then having the right desktop theme and icons is sort of useless. AD allows special folders to be established on a DC, replicating a network drive.

While you are working on the fourth quarter payroll spreadsheet, for example, in the My Documents folder, it can be replicated to a secure network location. When you log off your computer and log onto another machine, the system checks with the special folder, ensuring the files are the most recent, and retrieves your documents.

Organizational Units

The manner in which Active Directory is structured is important. Earlier in this book we talked about such objects as Organizational Units (OUs), domains, forests, and trees. These are the building blocks of Active Directory. Just to refresh your memory (and as Figure 6-9 shows):

- OUs are groups of people, computers, files, printers or other resources that need to be combined into one unit for organization and management purposes.
- Domains are collections of OUs.
- Trees are collections of domains.
- Forests are collections of trees.

In a Windows 2000 or Windows .NET environment, OUs are the basic unit of delegation. By comparison, NT's basic unit was the domain. Because OUs allow more granular organization of resources, this network hierarchy enables much more precise control over your network and its attributes. For instance, if you have specific attributes that you'd like to assign to two users in a branch office, they can be designated as an OU. By comparison, in NT you would have to assign those traits to the entire domain.

Another key part of Active Directory is its *schema*, which is the database's internal structure. The schema (which is part of the NTDS.dit file) defines relationships between classes of objects. For instance, using the repair shop database example, you may have a class called "Hubcaps," which has the attribute "Number of Spokes." This

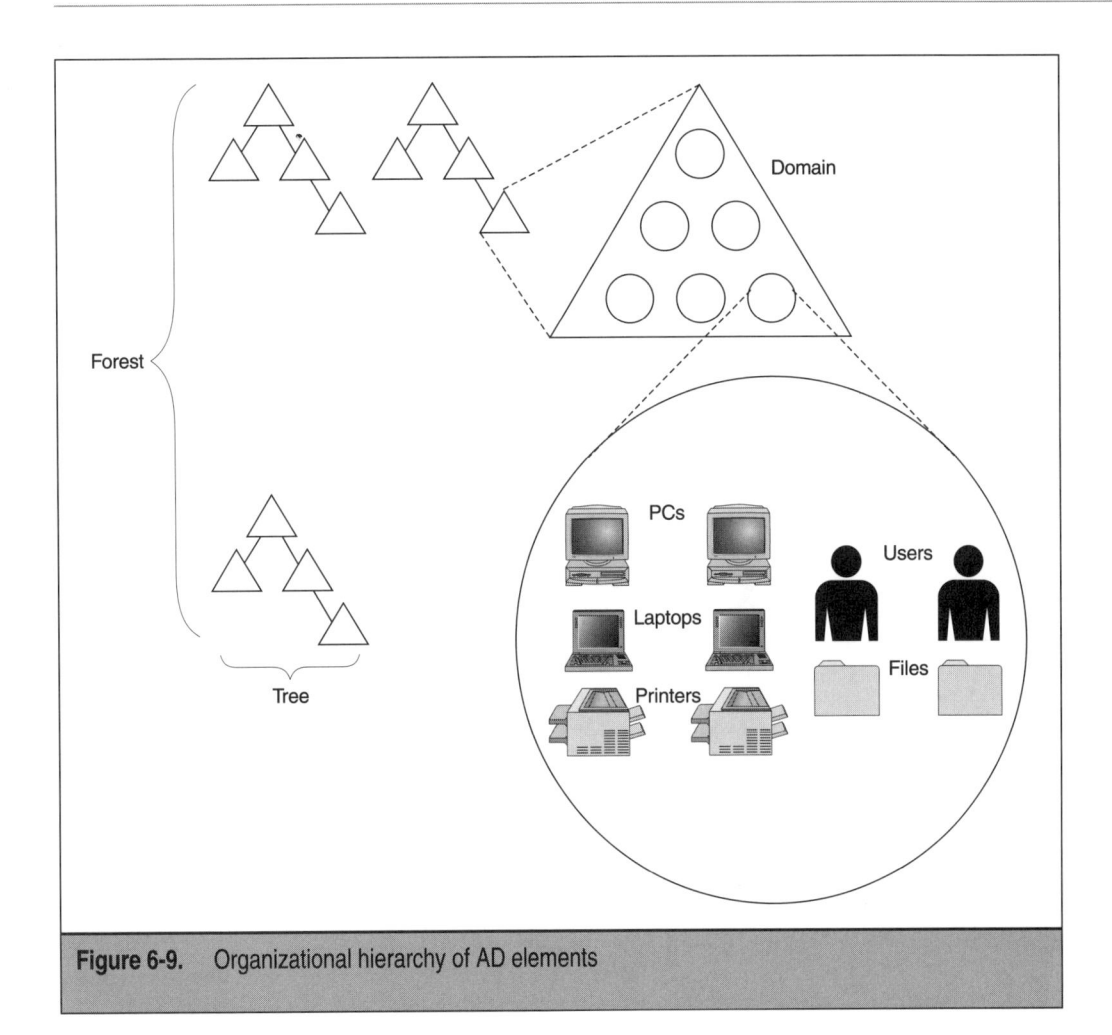

Figure 6-9. Organizational hierarchy of AD elements

specifies that objects in the Hubcaps class must contain information about the number of spokes in each hubcap. Classes can inherit from other classes, forming a hierarchy of classes. Figure 6-10 shows a class and subclass hierarchy, using the auto parts database example.

Figure 6-10. Subclasses exist under classes.

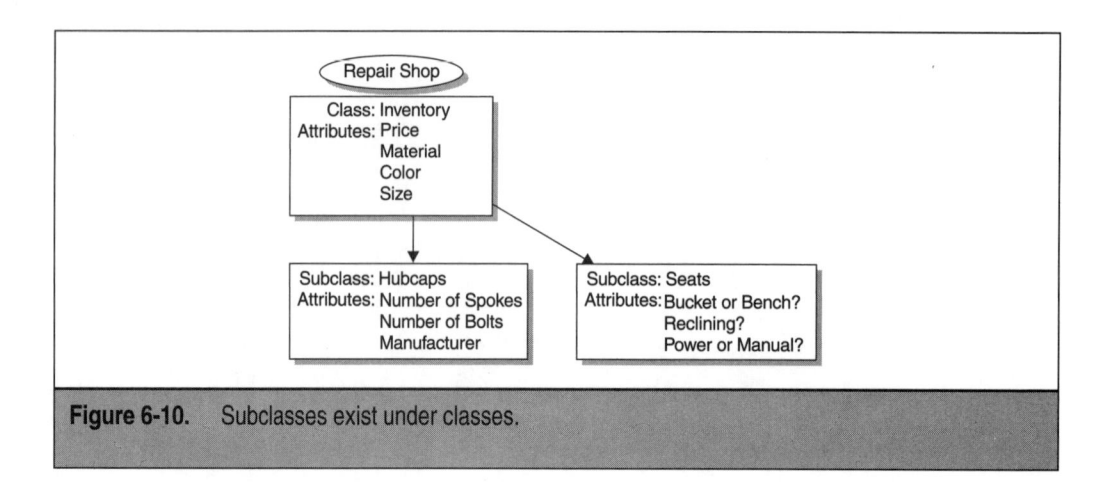

Global Catalog

The Global Catalog is a separate database of AD objects. This index contains all the objects in the main database, but only a subset of those objects' attributes. The Global Catalog lets users quickly find objects across a forest. The Global Catalog is especially helpful if you have many domains and domain trees spread across a large network.

NOTE An easy way to think of the Global Catalog is as an index of your domain's resources.

The Global Catalog, by default, is established on the first domain controller in your tree. Later, if you choose, you can use the MMC snap-in Active Directory Sites to manually select other Global Catalog domains.

As you deploy your Windows 2000 or .NET network, make sure you locate your Global Catalogs carefully. Each Windows XP Professional client computer needs easy access to Global Catalog to optimize search functions.

Groups

Windows NT had two user groups: *global* and *local*. These groups existed to assign security attributes and only contained user objects. Active Directory adds a third group called a *universal group*. These groups differ as follows:

- **Local groups**   Are used only within their local domain. They grant permissions to resources within the domain, and administrators can only view them from within their domain.
- **Global groups**   Grant permissions to trusted domains. You can view them anywhere within a particular tree. You can also nest global groups in other global groups.

- **Universal groups**   Can be viewed across all domains in a forest. Universal groups are used to contain global groups. For instance, an administrator can create two separate global groups (like employees from two different departments), and then combine them into a universal group. Now, the administrator need only deal with one universal group, rather than two (or more) global groups.

Table 6-1 provides an easy reference to the specifics of local, global, and universal groups.

Administrative Tools

Although Active Directory is maintained and administered from Windows 2000 or .NET servers, it can still be managed remotely from a Windows XP Professional client. This is accomplished via the Windows .NET Administrative Tools, which is a suite of snap-ins that can be added to your Windows XP Professional client's MMC.

> **NOTE**   It is important to remember that the Windows XP Professional client you are using must be part of the Windows 2000 domain that you are trying to administer. *Remotely* does not mean that you can manage a domain across the Internet.

As we mentioned earlier, the MMC is a useful tool in that it allows you to create a customized environment for network and computer management. This is accomplished via snap-ins. You can add as many or as few snap-ins as you like, so you can manage just the things you wish to manage.

Windows .NET Server Administration Tools Pack (adminpak.msi) provides server management tools that allow administrators to remotely manage Windows 2000 Servers from Windows XP Professional machines.

To install Windows .NET Administration Tools Pack on a local computer, you can download it from Microsoft at this URL: http://www.microsoft.com/downloads/release.asp?ReleaseID=34032&area=search&ordinal=1.

The Windows 2000 flavor of adminpak.msi was included on the Windows 2000 installation disk. However, the XP version is not contained on the Windows XP Professional installation CD-ROM, although adminpak.msi is included on the .NET installation disks.

Group Scope	Visibility	Contains
Local	Local domain	Users, global, or universal groups
Global	Throughout forest	Users or global groups
Universal	Throughout forest	Users, global, or universal groups

Table 6-1.   Group Types and Scopes

NOTE As of this writing, the Windows XP Administration Tools Pack is in its beta 3 version. The file is 10.4MB, so be aware of this file size if downloading via a slow connection.

The Windows .NET Server Administration Tools Pack provides a number of commonly used tools for administering network servers and services remotely. The administration tools pack are provided as snap-ins to the MMC. It can be used for any of the Windows .NET Server operating systems and Windows XP Professional computers.

NOTE The administration tool pack will not run on Windows XP Home Edition or 64-bit versions.

Adminpak.msi includes the following applications:

- Active Directory Domains and Trusts
- Active Directory Sites and Services
- Active Directory Users and Computers
- Certification Authority
- Cluster Administrator
- Component Services
- Computer Management
- Connection Manager Administration Kit
- Data Sources (ODBC)
- DHCP
- Distributed File System
- DNS
- Event Viewer
- Local Security Policy
- .NET Framework Configuration
- .NET Wizards
- Network Load Balancing Manager
- Performance
- Remote Desktops
- Remote Storage
- Routing and Remote Access
- Server Extensions Administrator
- Services

- Telephony
- Terminal Server Licensing
- Terminal Services Manager
- WINS

An example of the Network Load Balancing Manager application is shown in Figure 6-11. We cover the specific functions of each of Windows .NET Administration Tools in the appendix.

Domains are an important part of the Microsoft networking solution. They are not only the mechanisms used for larger networks, but are also important in the functionality of Active Directory and as a security boundary. Beyond its use on client machines, Windows XP Professional isn't part of the meat and potatoes of a domain, but it can be used to manage domain resources.

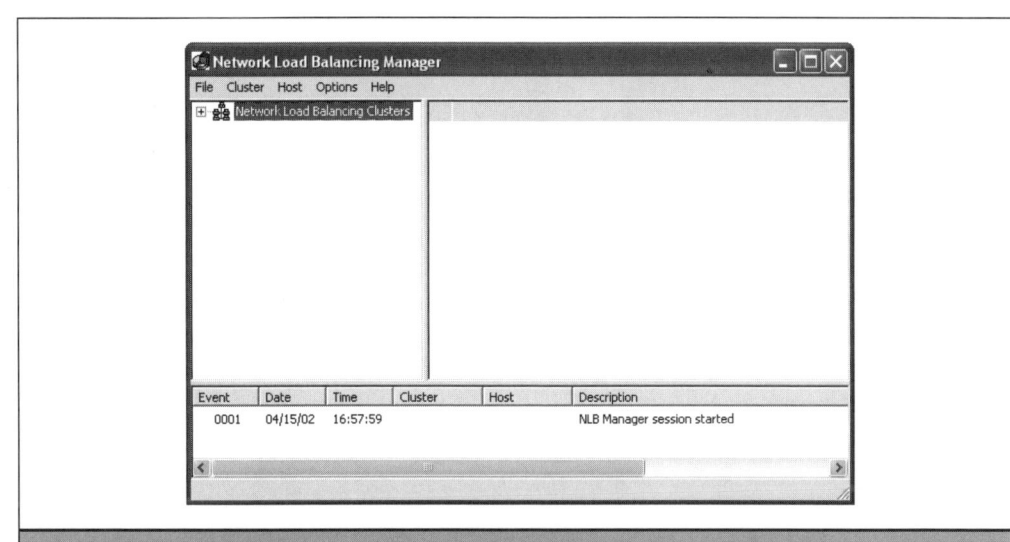

Figure 6-11. The Network Load Balancing Manager is part of the Windows .NET Administration Tools package.

CHAPTER 7

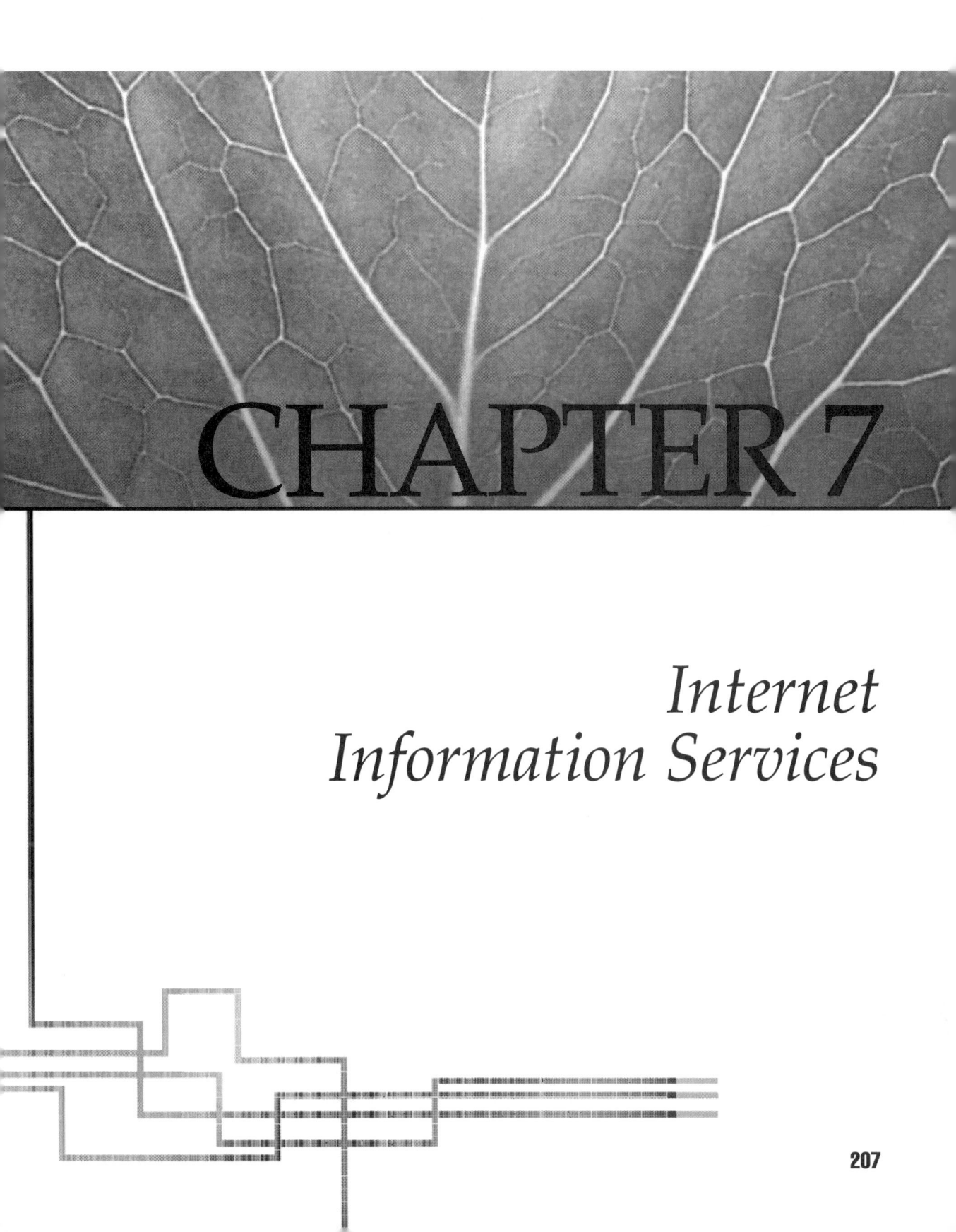

Internet Information Services

Even though Windows XP Professional boasts new tools for enhanced Internet use, one of the most powerful is a tool that has been around since Windows NT. The Internet Information Server (IIS) provides integrated Hypertext Transport Protocol (HTTP) and File Transfer Protocol (FTP) services. IIS also includes add-on components and third-party applications that extend its capabilities beyond basic Internet services. Some of these include e-mail, security, and site management tools.

This chapter takes a look at Microsoft's premier Web service tool and how it can be used with Windows XP Professional. First, we talk about what IIS is and how you can use it. Next, we'll discuss installation steps on Windows XP Professional. Finally, we'll round everything out with some tips for IIS usage.

WHAT IS IIS?

IIS is a group of Internet servers, including a web server and an FTP server. IIS includes applications for building and administering web sites, a search engine, and support for writing web-based applications that access databases.

Microsoft developed IIS to build web services using the architecture provided by the domain or Active Directory organization of user accounts. This makes it possible to use existing user databases, rather than build new ones. The benefit of this feature is clear when the needs of large organizations with huge user databases are considered. Furthermore, the ability to tightly integrate a new service with the domain makes the whole affair much more efficient.

Another good feature of IIS is that it is integrated into Windows XP Professional and Windows 2000, along with NTFS. It works in tandem with standard server tools, such as Event Viewer, Performance Monitor, Simple Network Management Protocol (SNMP), and Systems Management Server (SMS), allowing enhanced troubleshooting and management.

IIS also supports the Internet Server Application Programming Interface (ISAPI). With ISAPI, it is possible to create programs that manipulate data coming into the server or data being sent back to the client. ISAPI is used to create connections to other servers like database servers via the Open Database Connectivity (ODBC) service. This section talks about IIS 5.1, and is included with Windows XP Professional.

IIS 5.1 Features

IIS version 5.1 is the latest version of Microsoft's Internet services application. IIS 5.1 builds off of earlier versions for Windows NT and Windows 2000, providing many tools that ease administration and web development.

As we noted earlier, many of IIS's improvements align with the inner workings of Windows XP Professional. This provides a solid base of both functionality and reliability. For the end user, such benefits as improved security and administration are immediately accessible. IIS 5.1 features improvements and enhancements in four particular areas: reliability, security, management, and application environment.

Reliability

The first area in which IIS 5.1 shows improvements over earlier versions is in its reliability and stability. For example, it is much easier and faster to restart IIS in the event of a crash. In earlier versions, if there was a problem and IIS stopped, an administrator had to restart four different services. With version 5.1, IIS can be restarted by right-clicking an item in the Microsoft Management Console (MMC) or by using a command-line application.

The protocol responsible for data sharing across the Internet, Hypertext Transport Protocol, also enjoys some beefed-up features in IIS. Web site administrators can generate their own customized error messages. IIS also includes HTTP Compression, which can be used to pack both static and dynamic web pages for zippier transmission. Although dynamic pages must be compressed individually, static pages can be kept in a cache, which further speeds up transmissions for future data requests.

Finally, IIS employs application protection. This allows web applications to run in a pooled process separate from other core IIS processes. In the event one of the applications crashes, it won't take IIS down with it.

Logging and Throttling   The process of logging is enhanced in IIS 5.1. Administrators have more options for keeping track of what's going on with their Web services. Not only can IIS generate hourly logs, it can be configured to maintain *process accounting data logs*. These logs track such information as user and kernel time, page faults, and terminated processes. These enhanced logs allow administrators to determine where system resources are being used, how they might need to change those resources, and what might have run afoul.

If after reviewing the logs an administrator decides he or she needs to take some sort of action, then there is another tool that can be used: throttling. Two types of throttling are available for managing web server resources:

- **Process throttling**   Allows administrators to govern the use of the CPU by *out-of-process* applications. Out-of-process applications run in a separate memory space from the core IIS processes. This feature also enhances IIS's reliability. If an out-of-process application becomes unstable, it will not affect the core processes of the application.

- **Per web site bandwidth throttling**   Used to limit bandwidth if your web server contains other services, such as e-mail or FTP. This throttling feature allows administrators to regulate the amount of server bandwidth used by each site.

WebDAV   The World Wide Web is an excellent place to publish content so that many people can access it. However, as handy as it is for viewing content, it's not so handy when collaborating on a project. Microsoft's solution to this problem is its Web Distributed Authoring and Versioning (WebDAV) feature.

NOTE   The "DAV" in WebDAV is pronounced "Dave."

WebDAV is an extension to HTTP and allows remote authors to manage files and directories on a server over an HTTP connection. Because of IIS's integration with Windows XP Professional, WebDAV gets added functionality from Windows security and file access resources.

WebDAV allows remote users to move, search, edit, or delete files and directories from the server. The MMC makes setting up a WebDAV publishing directory easy. Once the directory has been established, authorized users can publish documents to the server and make changes to files. Figure 7-1 shows how documents are shared using WebDAV.

NOTE In order to be able to make changes to a file or files using WebDAV, users must be *authorized*. That is, they must have the necessary permissions in place to make changes.

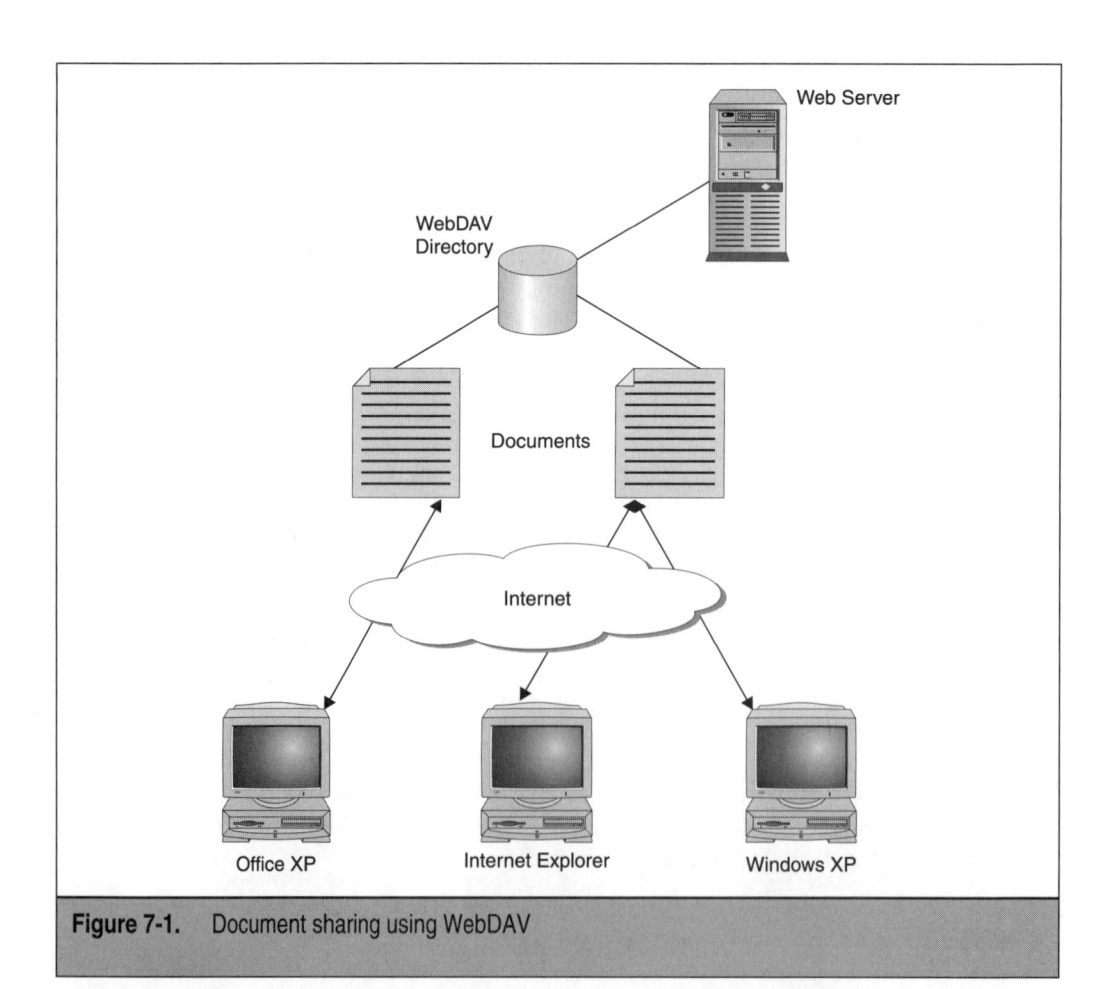

Figure 7-1. Document sharing using WebDAV

Clients using WebDAV can access directories through Windows XP Professional, Internet Explorer 6.0, Microsoft Office XP, or any other client supporting the WebDAV protocol. Connecting to WebDAV is a straightforward process. On a Windows XP Professional client, open My Network Places and use the resulting Add Network Place Wizard (shown in Figure 7-2).

Once the wizard has been started, follow these steps:

1. In the Add Network Place Wizard, follow Windows XP Professional's instructions for creating a shortcut to a web site containing your WebDAV site.
2. Once the shortcut has been created, an icon for the shortcut will appear in the My Network Places folder.
3. Under Other Places, click My Documents.
4. Select the file or folder you want to copy to the web server.
5. Under File and Folder Tasks, click Copy this file or Copy this folder.
6. In the Copy Items dialog box, click the My Network Places folder, and then click the shortcut folder.
7. Click Copy.

Figure 7-2. Use the Add Network Place Wizard in Windows XP Professional for WebDAV connection.

WebDAV support integrated into Windows XP Professional is even more enhanced because it enables any application running on top of it to be WebDAV-enabled as well.

Security

Enhanced security features are a given when any new service comes out. Some of IIS's most interesting security features include Fortezza, Transport Layer Security, Advanced Digest Authentication, and Kerberos version 5 authentication protocol. IIS also includes the latest enhanced versions of tried-and-true security features such as Secure Sockets Layer and (SSL) certificates. Let's take a closer look at the security features of IIS 5.1:

- **Integrated Windows Authentication** This security measure is a holdover from Windows NT, where it was known as Challenge and Response. In IIS 5.1, this feature not only has a new name, but it has also been beefed up to support Kerberos. One of Kerberos's main features is its ability to pass authentication credentials to Windows and non-Windows computers that also support Kerberos. Because authentication duties can be delegated to another computer, scaling a web site with several servers is much improved. Now, establishing certain servers as web servers and others as database servers is easier and more secure.

- **Certificate Server 2.0** The Web Server Certificate Wizard simplifies the certificate setup process and enables SSL communications. Another wizard helps configure Certificate Trust Lists (CTLs). A CTL is a list of certification authorities (CAs) for a site. Finally, the IIS Permissions Wizard assigns web and NTFS permissions to web sites, virtual directories, and files on the server.

- **Server-Gated Cryptography (SGC) and Fortezza** These security features require a special certificate and allow such organizations as financial institutions to use 128-bit encryption. Fortezza is a federal government messaging security standard.

NOTE The name Fortezza is a registered trademark of the National Security Agency.

- **Secure Sockets Layer (SSL)** This protocol is the most prevalent way for Internet browsers and servers to make secure connections. IIS 5.1 uses version SSL 3.0, the latest version of SSL.

- **Transport Layer Security (TLS)** This is based on SSL and provides for cryptographic user authentication. It also gives programmers a way to develop independent TLS-enabled code that can exchange cryptographic information with another process without either programmer needing to be familiar with the other's programming code. TLS is also intended to provide a framework for new and emerging public key and bulk encryption methods.

- **Advanced Digest Authentication** Authentication credentials pass through a one-way process called *hashing*. The result of this process is called a *hash* or *message digest*, and it is not possible to decipher the original text from the hash. The server adds additional information to the password before hashing so that no one can capture and use the password hash.

> **NOTE** Advanced Digest Authentication is supported only by domains with a Windows 2000 or .NET domain controller and can only be used with Internet Explorer version 5 or later.

Management

Management is streamlined over earlier versions of IIS 5.1. First, IIS is easily installed (this is examined in more depth later in this chapter in the section "Installing IIS"). Additionally, IIS 5.1 includes security wizards; the ability to account for time used by processes; flexible remote administration; and custom error message generation.

Like many other Windows XP Professional applications and services, IIS is managed from an MMC snap-in. This is accessed by selecting Start | Control Panel. Next, click Performance and Maintenance, choose Administrative Tools | Computer Management, and then select the IIS snap-in under Server Applications and Services. Alternatively, you can access it by selecting Start | Control Panel. Click Performance and Maintenance, and then choose | Administrative Tools | Internet Information Services.

> **NOTE** Don't forget that you can create your own customized MMC (customization is the whole point of the MMC, after all) and include IIS in your snap-in choices.

Additionally, IIS utilizes a browser-based administration tool, allowing you to remotely administer IIS over an HTTP connection. Because the browser administration tool uses the HTTP protocol, it allows remote management of a server from any browser on any platform.

Application Environment

Developers get a boost from IIS because it extends the web server's application development environment. Active Directory and Component Object Model (COM), along with Active Server Pages (ASP) enhancements, are useful for developers. The primary way to launch dynamic content in IIS is via ASP.

Active Server Pages, which was introduced in IIS 3.0, allows you to mix HTML and scripts using a variety of authoring programs to create new web pages on the fly. Active Server Pages extends the functionality of the basic web server by making it much easier to build dynamic, web-based applications. It provides support for the execution of ASP scripts, which can be written in VBScript, JavaScript, or JScript, as well as other scripting languages. Additionally, ActiveX server components written in C++, Visual Basic, and Java can be incorporated into an Active Server Page. Prewritten objects are also available that can be used to build a complete web application with little or no programming. ASP includes several standard objects that can be used in developing web applications.

In short, ASP scripting is used to generate HTML on the fly. Here is how it works: When a client workstation running a browser hits the IIS server and opens an ASP document, a script is run. The script generates the HTML code based on user input, type of browser, content of cookies stored on client, and so on. As it executes, it may query a database and place the data in a table to be sent back to the client in the HTML stream. Because the server processes requests, executes applications, receives the results, packages them up, churns HTML code, and sends it to the browser, it needs to be a very powerful system. If your server is going to be an "active" server, make sure it is has plenty of processing power.

ASP in IIS 5.1 provides a number of useful tools:

- **Asperror object** This object improves error handling by making it possible for developers to ferret out errors in script files. Flow-control capabilities allow the server to execute pages without the traditional round-trips that are required by server-side redirects.

- **Scriptless ASP pages** These are improved by a new check in the parsing stage. In earlier versions of IIS, sites would use .asp extensions for all their pages, making it possible to keep their links the same if a script was later added to an HTML-only page. The downside of this is that the default scripting engine would be started, even if there was no code. The new check determines when executing requests are waiting for internal components and automatically gives the needed resources to allow other requests to continue processing.

ASP also comes with a number of prebuilt components, to handle such tasks as

- Logging
- Accessing data
- Accessing files
- Using counters

These tools are fast and scalable. The Browser Capabilities tool, for example, can support the capabilities described in cookies sent by the browser. This allows flexibility in running server code based on the features supported by the client.

ASP supports Windows Script Commands. This feature allows scripts to be turned into reusable COM components for use by ASP and other COM-compliant programs.

FrontPage

There is no dearth of HTML authoring tools on the market. Microsoft uses its FrontPage web authoring and management tools extensively in IIS to deploy and manage sites.

With FrontPage's Server Extensions, administrators can manage their web sites with a graphical interface. Authors can create, post, and manage web pages remotely.

Server Extensions

The FrontPage Server Extensions are not limited to Microsoft's offerings. They can be installed on UNIX, SunOS, and other platforms, thereby providing broad availability.

> **NOTE** You can get more information about FrontPage and server extensions at http://www.microsoft.com/frontpage.

FrontPage Server Extensions provide a number of capabilities for web authors and administrators, including the following:

- Allowing authors to collaborate on a web site directly with the server computer
- Adding functions to web sites without programming
- Support for hit counters
- Support for e-mail form handling
- Flexible installation on a number of different platforms
- Automatic update of hyperlinks when a web page has been altered or moved
- Integration of such application packages as Microsoft Office, Visual SourceSafe, and Index Server

FrontPage Snap-In

Like many other tasks in Windows XP Professional, FrontPage Server Extensions are managed through a snap-in to the MMC. The snap-in is used to create and upgrade the server extensions, convert folders into subwebs, reconfigure hyperlinks, and more. In earlier incarnations of FrontPage Server Extensions, management was handled by a tool called Fpsrvwin.

The snap-in allows you to perform the following tasks:

- Install server extensions on a web server
- Fix, upgrade, and remove existing server extensions
- Add an administrator
- Require SSL for authoring
- Reconfigure hyperlinks
- Enable or disable authoring on a web
- Log authoring operations

- Configure e-mail options
- Tune web performance

NOTE As much as the FrontPage Server Extensions MMC snap-in does, it cannot perform command-line scripting or administer the FrontPage Server Extensions from a remote computer. Rather, these can only be administered via the FPREMADM utility and the FPSRVADM utilities, respectively.

You can tell if FrontPage Server Extensions are enabled by right-clicking a virtual server (located in the left pane of the IIS snap-in), and selecting All Tasks. If you see either Configure Server Extensions or commands associated with a server (such as Check Server Extensions or Recalculate Hyperlinks), then server extensions are enabled. If these commands aren't shown, then the server extensions must be enabled. To do this, open the IIS MMC snap-in and perform the following tasks:

1. Click File, and then click Add/Remove Snap-in.
2. If the console menu displays just the Options item, then select Options, and click Always open console file in author mode. Click OK, exit the MMC, and reopen it.
3. Next, from the console menu, click Add/Remove Snap-in. The resulting dialog box is shown in Figure 7-3.

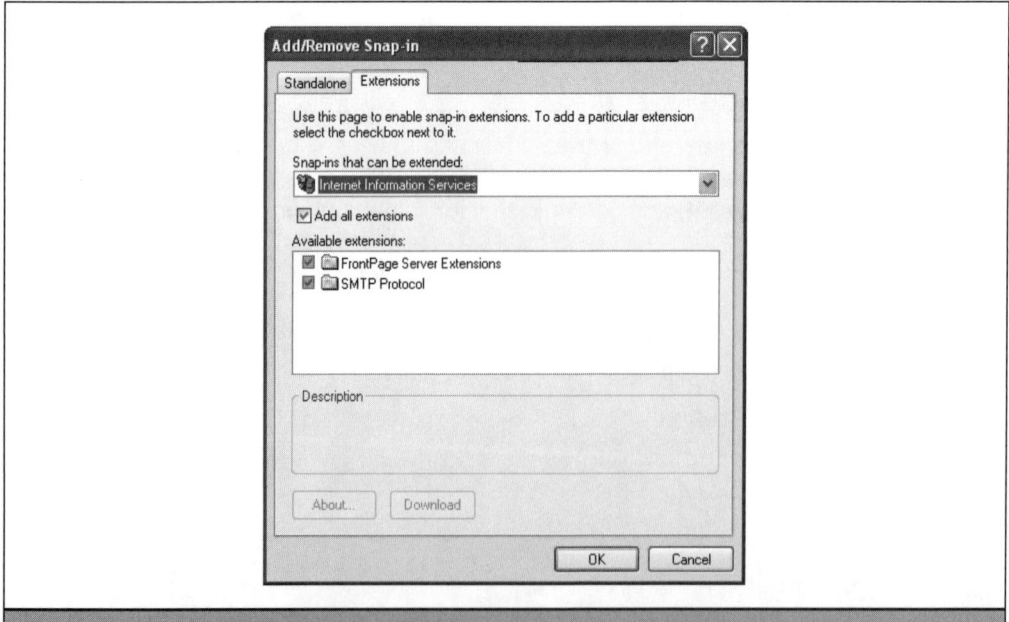

Figure 7-3. Enabling FrontPage Server Extensions

4. Select the Extensions tab, and then choose FrontPage Server Extensions (if it isn't already selected).
5. Click OK.

Intranet Content Management

IIS 5.1 isn't just useful when providing content for the outside world to view. IIS is also a good tool when developing an in-house intranet. In fact, that just might be IIS's best use when employed on Windows XP Professional. For instance, if you have a small LAN in your branch office and plan on developing an intranet as a common bulletin board, establishing one of your Windows XP Professional clients as an intranet server using IIS makes good sense.

Furthermore, some applications will require IIS to be installed in order to function properly. For example, Microsoft's Visual Studio .NET requires you to install IIS if you plan on developing web-based applications.

INSTALLING IIS

Like most other installations that will have an impact on an entire network, there are a couple of steps to the process that should be considered and completed before you start installing IIS on your Windows XP Professional computer. This section examines some issues you should keep in mind and some requirements that you should have in place. Finally, we'll explain the process of installing IIS on Windows XP Professional.

Placement Considerations

Conventionally speaking, IIS would be located on a computer running Windows 2000 Server or .NET Server. However, your organization might not have one of these types of servers, leading you to depend on a client computer to act as the home of IIS. Furthermore, you might find it useful to have IIS on a client for all sorts of reasons, including IIS management or .NET development.

Whether you use a server or a client as the home of IIS, you should consider some physical issues when setting up your IIS. These considerations might seem to be a pain in the neck, but they should be made for the sake of data security, rather than personal convenience. It's best to make sure of the following:

- The server is physically secure
- The server is regularly backed up
- The backup media are rotated to an offsite facility
- IIS has a reliable power supply such as an uninterruptible power supply (UPS)
- The network connections are reliable and have enough capacity to meet demand

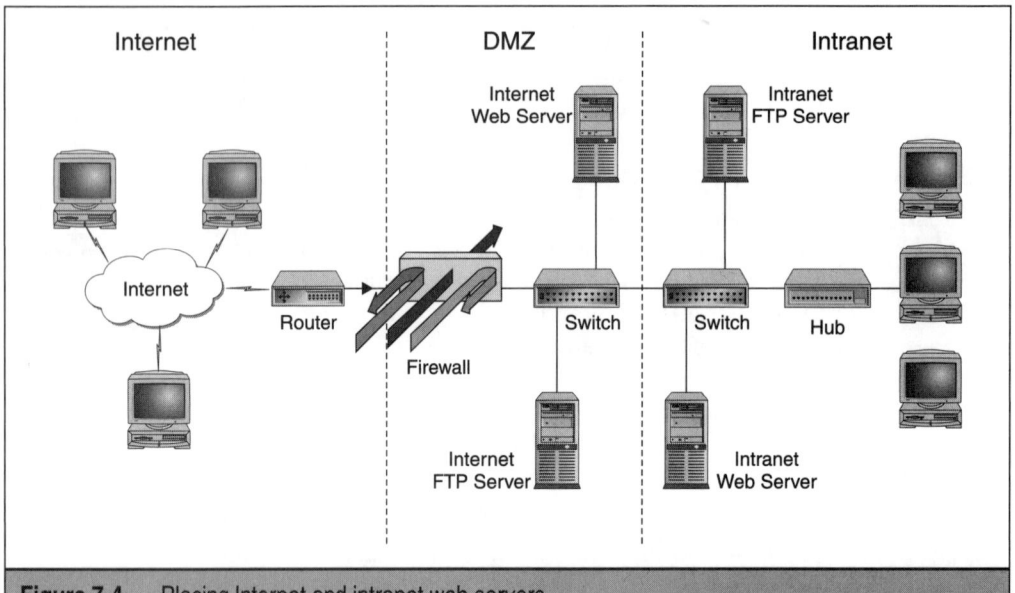

Figure 7-4. Placing Internet and intranet web servers

Naturally, your organization's needs will figure highly in where and how you place your IIS server. For instance, if your branch office uses an IIS-based intranet to keep track of who's bringing in the donuts on Friday, it makes little sense to invest in a $1,000 UPS. On the other hand, if IIS is keeping your dot-com afloat, maybe you want something a little more kicked up than the $1,000 UPS.

Figure 7-4 illustrates typical locations for Internet and intranet web servers. The Internet web server is located after the firewall and terminating router in the demilitarized zone (DMZ). Additional security and filtering can take place at the initial router connecting to the Internet. The intranet server is protected from the outside by the firewalls but offers quick access for local users.

Hardware and Networking Components

In order to install IIS—not only for the computer requirements, but also the infrastructure of the network itself—you'll need to meet some bare minimums. The following lists enumerate the hardware and networking components (for both Internet and intranets) that your IIS solution will require:

- A network interface card (NIC)
- A network connection to your LAN
- An Internet connection to your ISP (Internet)

- Registered IP addresses (Internet)
- Private or registered IP addresses (intranet/Internet)
- A DNS server (recommended: internal DNS and DNS available from your ISP) or a local HOSTS file on every client
- IIS

Software Components

Once you've got the infrastructure in place, you can add additional services on top of IIS. The basics allow you to create and host web pages and document and data stores. However, you can also add these items:

- Active Server Pages (ASP)
- NetShow
- Index Server
- Java Virtual Machine
- FrontPage server extensions
- FrontPage client software
- Seagate Crystal Reports
- SQL Server
- SNA Server
- Exchange Server
- Office XP

Because the Internet is such a huge part of networking and computing, additional components are constantly being developed. You can get the latest information on IIS at Microsoft's web site at http://www.microsoft.com.

Installation Steps

Installation and setup of IIS on Windows XP Professional is a fairly straightforward process. IIS is not part of the regular OS installation, but it is included on the Windows XP Professional CD-ROM. To install and configure IIS, do the following:

1. Place the Windows XP Professional CD-ROM into your CD-ROM drive. Select Start | Control Panel, then select Add/Remove Programs.
2. Click Add Windows Components.
3. Check the box next to Internet Information Services (IIS). Be sure to leave all the default installation settings intact.

4. Installation will take a few minutes. Once IIS is installed, you can view your home page by identifying the site through the Universal Naming Convention. Enter **http://*localhost***, where *localhost* is the name of your computer. If you don't have a web site in the default directory, you'll see the IIS documentation.

NOTE If you don't know the name of your computer, right-click the My Computer icon on your desktop or in the Start menu. Select Properties, and then click the Computer Name tab.

5. Your default web directory is located in the C:\Inetpub\wwwroot folder. However, adding to this directory will overwrite the IIS documentation. To avoid this, you should set up your own virtual directory.

NOTE We explain virtual directories later in this chapter.

6. You can find the IIS console by selecting Start | Administration Tools | Internet Information Services icon.
7. With the IIS console open (as shown in Figure 7-5), you will see any IIS web services you have running on your machine, including the SMTP server and FTP server, if you choose to install them with IIS.

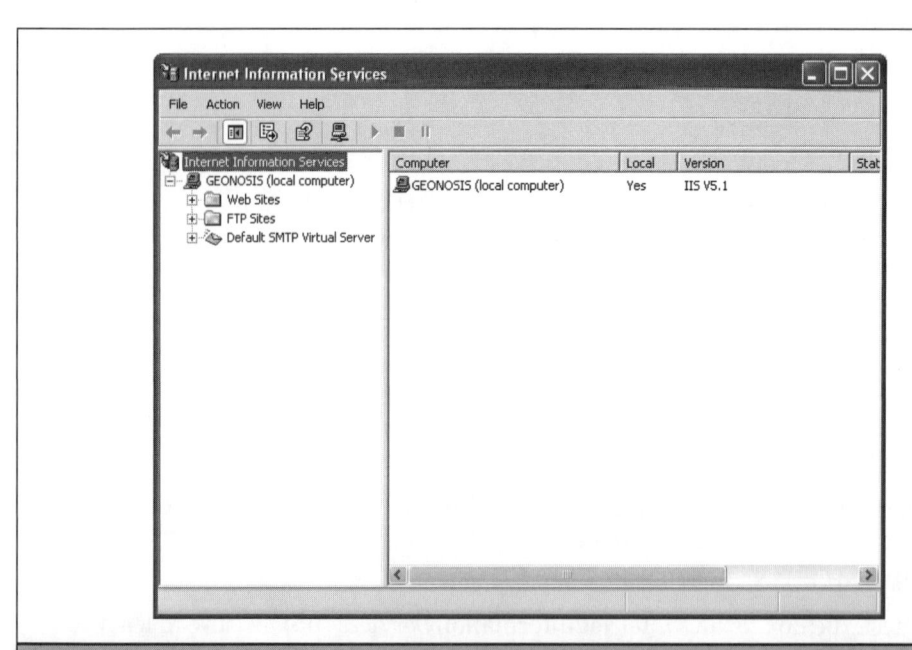

Figure 7-5. The IIS console

CONFIGURING IIS

Installing IIS is one thing (and a fairly painless thing, at that). As you know, once something has been installed, you're still a long way from being fully up and running. Happily, IIS is rather easily configured from its MMC snap-in. This section talks about what tools you can use to perform various configuration tasks.

IIS Management

Windows XP Professional centralizes its resources' management with one tool, the MMC. The tool shows your IIS resources in a tree view, so you can manage everything via a friendly, graphical interface. Services are managed by right-clicking them, and then manipulating the Properties dialog box as needed. The MMC with the IIS snap-in is shown in Figure 7-6.

HTTP IIS Manager

In addition to the MMC, IIS can also be administered from a web browser. The only difference (beside the obvious graphical differences between an application and a browser) is that the browser-based manager cannot start, pause, or stop services.

The HTTP tool is activated by typing **http://<computername>/iisadmin/default.htm** into your web browser's URL address box. From there, management is much the same as it is from the MMC.

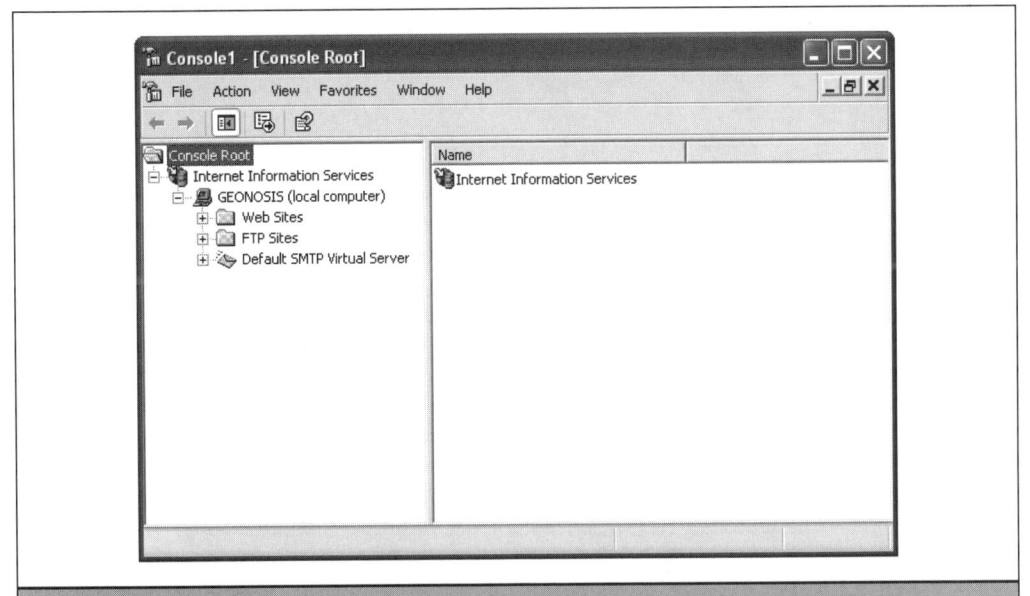

Figure 7-6. An MMC snap-in is used to manage IIS 5.1 in Windows XP Professional.

The IIS default page has a slew of information about IIS features and functions. If you choose to use them, it also has some sample web pages. Additionally, this page includes links to web site resources that you will need an Internet connection to access.

Configuring Web Services

Both IIS management tools allow administrators to manage IIS resources in a familiar manner. Configuring the web services is done by double-clicking the web service listed in the IIS manager main screen and then selecting Properties. The resulting dialog box is shown in Figure 7-7.

Some of the properties you may want to adjust are listed here:

- **Connection Timeout**   Users will be logged off if they have no activity within this period. Shorten this time to eliminate users who hold the connection open without actually retrieving any information.
- **Maximum Connections**   This number represents the maximum users who can be connected at once to your web server. Keep this in agreement with what your hardware and network connection can support.

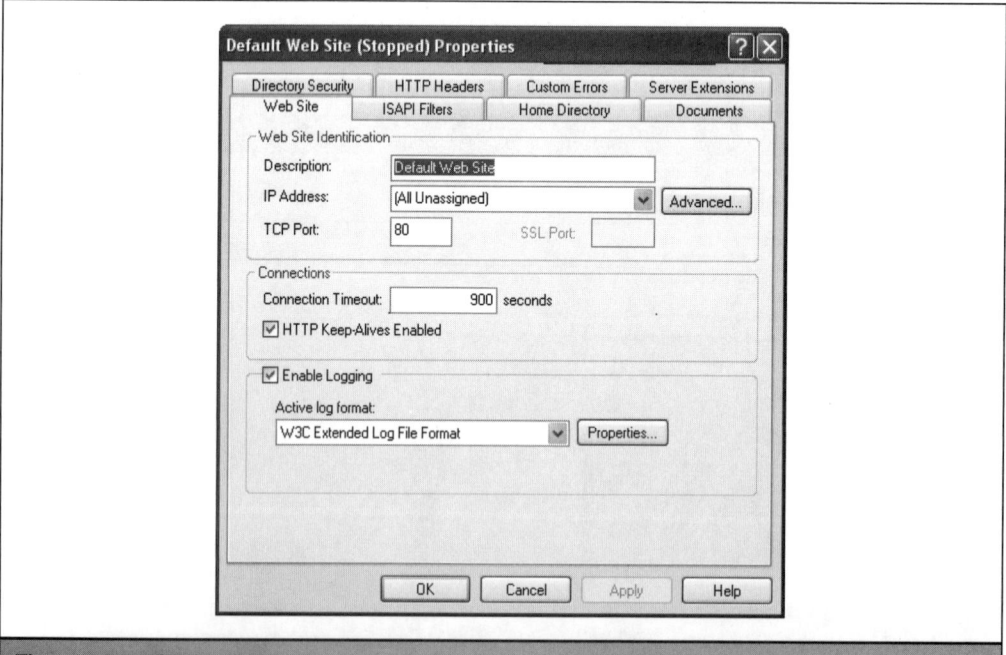

Figure 7-7.   Configuring a web service's properties with the MMC

- **Anonymous Logon** If you would like nondomain users to access your web server, you must allow anonymous logins.
- **Username/Password** This is the account that actually accesses the web pages. Restrict the privileges of this account to allow access only to resources you are willing to share with all users.
- **Password Authentication** If you do not allow anonymous users, you should select users who are required to provide a password via the Windows Challenge/Response method to afford the most secure method of authentication.

Virtual Directories

Based on your installation of IIS, you have more options for creating directories to store your Internet pages in than you might realize. Directories can be created outside of the original directory made during the installation. These are called *virtual directories* and can be located on the same computer or located remotely. To the user, it appears to be a subdirectory of the root Internet directory. In reality, it can be on another machine altogether.

Under IIS 5.1, creating a virtual directory is extremely easy.

1. To add a new virtual directory, right-click a folder beneath the Default Web Site and select New. On the resulting drop-down list, select Virtual Directory.
2. This will spawn the Virtual Directory Creation Wizard. Click Next.
3. Next, you'll be asked to enter an *alias*, which you will use to access the virtual directory from your web browser. This is the name you will type into the web browser after the localhost name to view web pages you place in the directory.
4. Next, a Browse button will appear. Click this button to locate the directory where your web site pages are located on your computer. Then click Next.
5. The last part of the wizard is a series of boxes with security settings, which are shown in Figure 7-8. If you aren't concerned about security, then check them all. If you are and you want to run ASP scripts, then check the first two boxes—Read and Run scripts (such as ASP)—and then click Next.
6. Now the virtual directory has been set up. You can view the web pages in the folder by entering **http://localhost/***aliasname***/**, where *aliasname* is the name you assigned in step 3.

> **NOTE** If you are using NTFS, you can set up a virtual directory by right-clicking a directory in Windows Explorer, clicking Sharing, and then selecting Web Sharing.

Logging

IIS allows tremendous control over what events are logged and how. In addition to letting you log accesses to ordinary text files on a daily, weekly, or monthly basis, or

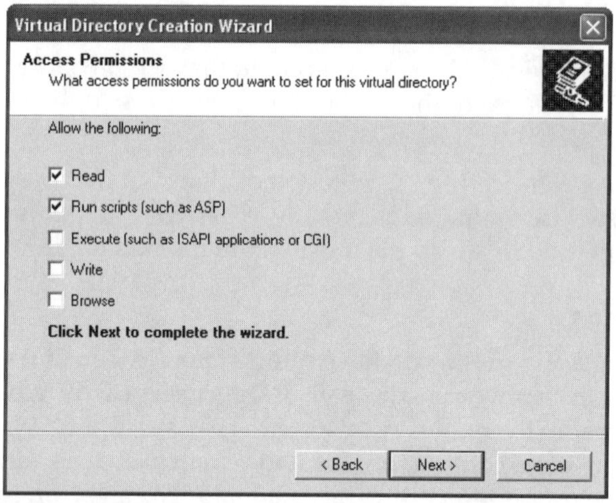

Figure 7-8. Security settings when building a virtual directory

until the log file reaches a particular size, you can export the log files to a Structured Query Language (SQL)/ODBC database.

You can access logging controls by right-clicking the web site you wish to manage, and then selecting Properties. At the bottom of the Web Site tab, in the Enable Logging pane, click Properties. The resulting window is shown in Figure 7-9.

It's most likely that you will use other applications to read your log files and generate reports of web usage. These statistics can show what kind of users are accessing your web server and what they're looking at when they visit. Furthermore, the logs can be extremely useful if your security has been compromised.

NOTE The log files get quite large if IIS server is well used. It's a good idea to locate the log files on a remote machine so that hackers can't wreck them if they manage to mess up your IIS machine.

Access Control

Naturally, the security of your network is important. Trying to allow legitimate users into the system while keeping out the thugs and riff-raff can sometimes be a hard balance to strike. IIS includes a number of security features (which we mention later) that can help achieve that balance.

You can manage access controls by right-clicking the web site you wish to administer in the IIS manager, and then selecting Properties. Click the Directory Security tab and you'll see a number of security options open to you. The resulting window is shown in Figure 7-10.

Figure 7-9. IIS logging options

With IIS you can grant or deny access to specific computers (via IP address). If you wish to grant access to everyone on the Internet, then this sort of access control is of

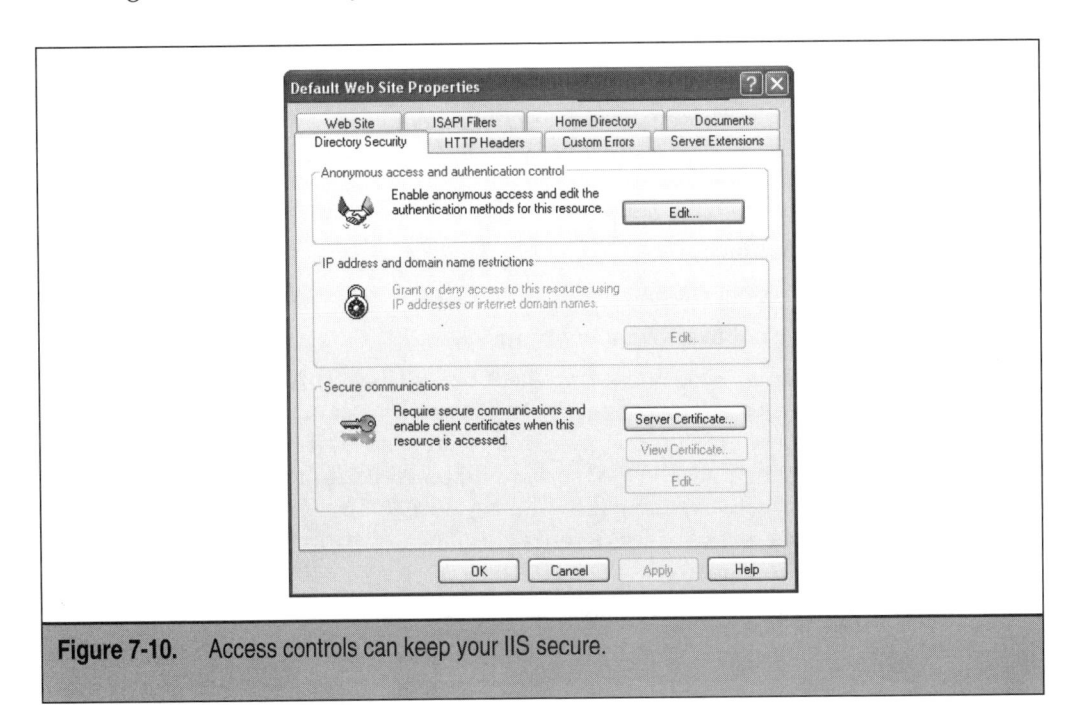

Figure 7-10. Access controls can keep your IIS secure.

little use to you. However, if you have a private intranet, you might want to grant access to users of a specific subnet, say for example, the users of the 10.0.5.0 subnet. To do this, you'd click the Edit button in the IP address and domain name restrictions window pane and input the necessary restrictions.

Configuring an FTP Server

You can share files directly from a web page. However, it's generally faster and more efficient to set up an FTP service if you have many files to share or many people trying to download those files. FTP service shares many of the same configuration options with the web site configuration. Consequently, we'll only talk about where the two differ. First, however, you must make sure that FTP service has been installed with IIS. If it hasn't, you must do so by performing the following steps:

1. In Control Panel, click Add/Remove Programs.
2. Click Add/Remove Windows Components.
3. From the list, select Internet Information Services (IIS), and click Details.
4. Select the File Transfer Protocol (FTP) Service check box.
5. Click OK (Windows XP Professional might ask you to insert the installation CD-ROM).
6. Click Next.
7. Click Finish.

There are several tabs containing various settings that can be customized, depending on your needs. Those tabs are described here:

- **FTP Site**   Under this tab are a number of similar options that have no effect on other services, but are used for the FTP service, including the following:
    - Connection timeout
    - Maximum connections
    - Whether or not to allow anonymous users
- **Security Accounts**   One interesting check box is labeled "Allow only anonymous connections." As the name suggests, this check box should only be enabled if you wish to allow anonymous users into your system. If this box is cleared, then users logging onto the FTP server will be asked for their password (which is sent via clear text, exposing it to interception). If anonymous connections are allowed, then no passwords are sent across the network. However, this setup also allows anyone to access the FTP site.
- **Messages**   The FTP service allows you to send messages to your users when they log on or log off or when the maximum number of users has been reached.

- **Home Directory** This tab allows you to configure virtual directories as you did for the World Wide Web service. You also get the option of displaying the directories in either the DOS or UNIX convention.

The logging and advanced features of the FTP service are similar to the web server and should be configured to fit your specific needs.

USING IIS

We've just given you a quick overview of IIS. To be sure, it is a very intricate tool whose functionality really can't be fully covered in this chapter. There are plenty of books that can provide you with more depth and detail on the ins, outs, ups, and downs of using IIS (such as *Administering IIS 5.0*, by Mitch Tulloch and Patrick Santry, and *IIS 5.0: A Beginner's Guide*, by Rod Trent, both published by Osborne-McGraw Hill).

This final section of the chapter gives a quick-and-dirty look at using IIS to build and manage your resources on Windows XP Professional.

Setting Default Pages

When you install IIS, a default web site and FTP site are automatically created. However, even though the web folders are in place, you still need to publish content to those default folders.

Publishing to Web Folders

Publishing content to web folders is a four-step process:

1. First, you must create your web page using whatever authoring tools you choose.
2. Your home page file must be named Default.htm or Default.asp.
3. Copy your home page into the default web directory for IIS. When you start IIS, the default home directory is located at \Intepub\wwwroot.
4. If your network has a name resolution service, then visitors can enter your computer name in the address bar of the web browser to reach your site. If name resolution is not available, then they must enter the IP address of your computer.

Publishing to FTP Folders

Publishing content to IIS's FTP folder is similar to the process for web folders, with some differences. To publish content to this folder, follow these steps:

1. Move your files to the default FTP publishing directory (the default directory established by IIS is \Inetpub\ftproot).

2. If your network has name resolution service, then visitors can enter the name of your computer, preceded by FTP:// (for example, FTP://www.velte.com). If name resolution is not available, then they must enter the IP address, preceded by FTP:// Better yet, they should use an FTP program like WS_FTP, which makes the transfer process faster and more efficient.

Managing Security

It should go without saying—especially when one puts one's resources onto the Internet—that security is extremely important. IIS 5.1 works in conjunction with Windows XP Professional's security features. This provides an integrated security environment that can be extremely useful.

Permissions

Like so many other Windows XP Professional tools, NTFS provides a means of security at the disk level. IIS is no exception. One of the best attributes of NTFS is its security consciousness. By using NTFS, you can limit access to your IIS files and directories. In fact, you are able to limit which visitors to your site have access to your files based on their user account or membership in a group.

> **NOTE** Before doing anything else, be sure you are using a hard disk that has been converted (or has a partition converted) to NTFS. Without NTFS enabled, believe it or not, NTFS cannot protect anything.

Follow these steps to secure your files with NTFS:

1. Open My Computer and find the folder or file for which you want to manage permissions.
2. Right-click the folder or file, select Properties, and then click the Web Sharing tab.
3. Next to Share On, use the drop-down list to select the web site you wish to use to share this resource.
4. Click the Share this folder radio button. The window this generates is shown in Figure 7-11.
5. Enter an alias name for this folder or file.
6. Set any permissions or restrictions you wish, including the following:
   - Read
   - Write
   - Script source access (this allows users to access source files)
   - Directory browsing

Figure 7-11. Managing NTFS permissions for a folder or file

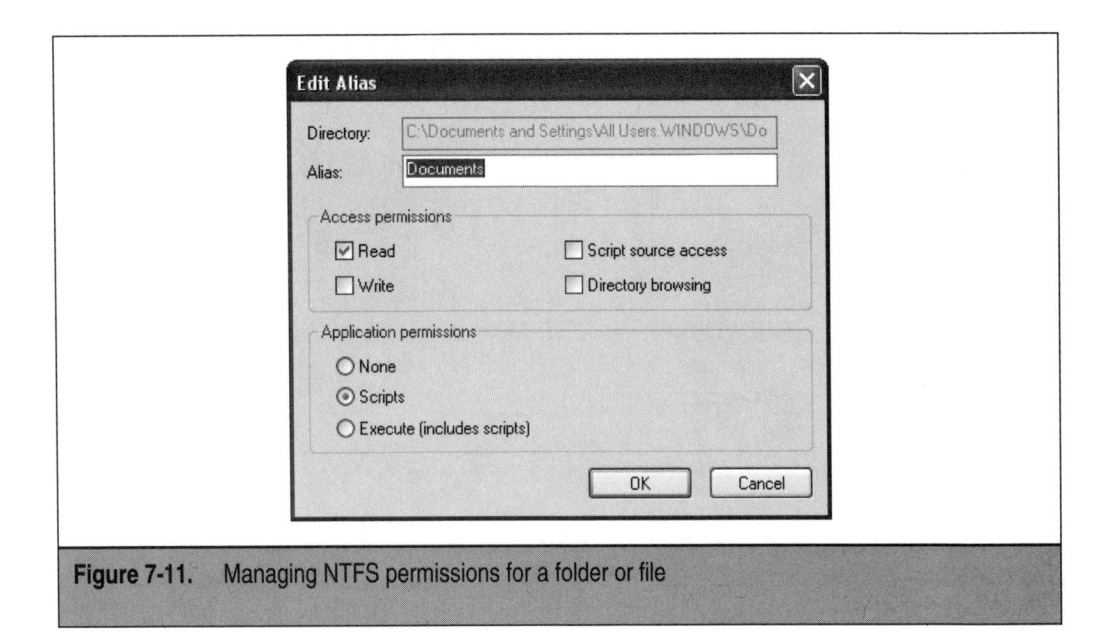

7. You can also set any application permissions:
   - None
   - Scripts
   - Execute (includes scripts)

By following these steps, you can set varying levels of access to your files and folders. It's important to know that you can set one level of permissions for a file folder, but then make the permissions for a particular file (or another folder) within that folder more restrictive.

Authentication

Authentication is the process of making sure a visitor is who he or she claims to be. This is accomplished by using a simple logon box that asks the visitor's username and password. If the user doesn't have the correct information, he or she cannot get into the web or FTP site. You can enable authentication on any web or FTP site. Furthermore, IIS allows authentication to be assigned to a specific virtual directory or file.

Web Authentication   To enable authentication on a web site, follow these steps:

1. First you must create a Windows user account, which will match with the authentication method you're enabling.

2. Configure NTFS permissions for the directory or file you wish to secure.
3. In the IIS manager, pick a web site, directory, or file. Right-click it and select Properties.
4. Select the Directory Security or File Security tab. Under Anonymous Access and Authentication Control, click Edit.
5. Pick the authentication methods you wish to enable in the resulting dialog box, shown in Figure 7-12.

FTP Authentication   Authentication for an FTP service delivers a similar result, but has its own unique process. In order to enable FTP authentication, perform these steps:

> **NOTE**   Whereas web sites allowed you the option of creating authentication based on a file or specific directory, authentication on FTPs can only be enabled at the site level.

1. First you must create a Windows user account, which will match with the authentication method you're enabling.

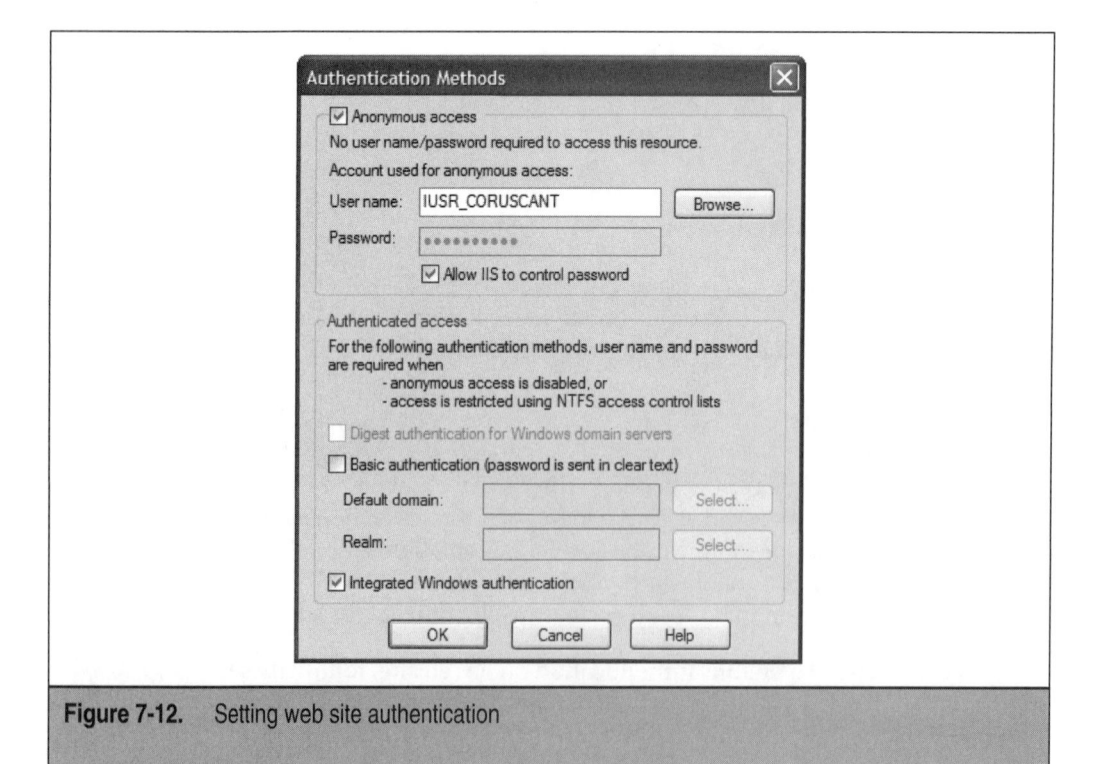

Figure 7-12.   Setting web site authentication

2. Configure NTFS permissions for the directory or file you wish to secure.
3. In the IIS manager, pick an FTP site. Right-click it and select Properties.
4. Click the Security Accounts property sheet, and then select the Allow Anonymous Connections check box.
5. In the Username and Password boxes, type the anonymous logon username and password you will use. The username is typically preset to IUSR_*computername*. If the Allow IIS to control password check box is enabled, clear it to change the password.
6. Recheck the Allow IIS to control password check box so that the passwords are synched with the Windows user accounts.
7. Check the Allow only anonymous connections check box. This requires everyone logging on to log on as an anonymous user.
8. Click OK.
9. Set the requisite NTFS permissions for the anonymous account.

Anonymous Authentication

The default IUSR_*computername* account appears in the Guests file when assigning anonymous access. To vary your level of security by granting permissions to different parts of your web site, you can establish different anonymous accounts, with each providing different access to different groups. Be aware, however, that the anonymous account must have Log On Locally permissions, or IIS will not be able to service any such requests.

> **NOTE** Log On Locally rights are managed by using the Active Directory Service Interfaces (ADSI) snap-in for the MMC.

In order to change the account used for anonymous authentication, follow these steps:

1. In the IIS manager, right-click the site, directory, or file you wish to change, and then select Properties.
2. Select the Directory Security or File Security tab, and under Anonymous Access and Authentication Control, click Edit.
3. This will spawn the Authentication Methods dialog box. Under Anonymous access, click Browse.
4. In the Anonymous User Account dialog box, enter the user account.
5. Clear the Allow IIS to control password check box, and enter the appropriate password for this account.

Encryption

Just because a visitor logs onto your IIS appropriately doesn't mean there isn't some sleazeball out there watching your data flow across the wires. You can have your authorized visitors establish encrypted channels before accessing your information. The only hitch to this is that both your server and your client must support the same encryption scheme used to secure the channel. If both are using up-to-date browsers and server, however, this shouldn't be a problem.

> **NOTE** Encryption is not possible unless you have installed a valid server certificate.

In order to set up encryption, follow these steps:

1. In the IIS manager, right-click the site, directory, or file you wish to change, and then select Properties.

2. Assuming you have not already created a server key pair and certificate request, select the Directory Security or File Security tab. (If you have done this already, skip ahead to step 4).

3. Under Secure Communications, click Server Certificate. This will spawn the Web Server Certificate Wizard, which will take you through the rest of the process.

4. Back in the main Properties window, select the Directory Security or File Security tab, and then under Secure Communications, click Edit.

5. In the resulting Secure Communications dialog box, select Require Secure Channel (SSL).

> **NOTE** Be sure to let your visitors know that they need to enter https:// rather than http://.

Managing Content

As anyone who has spent any time on the Internet knows, developing content and putting it on your web server isn't the end of the journey, but rather the first step. Web sites are moving targets. In fact, that's a big reason that the Internet is so popular. Content no longer needs to be static, as it is in books, magazines, and newspapers. This trait can also be an enormous pain in the neck, if you don't know how to manage your web content.

Once you've gotten the company newsletter posted on your intranet, there will come a time when you have to update it. A number of tools are available to help you manage your IIS content.

Where to Begin

Your first step is to set up your web pages by deciding the directories in which the documents will be maintained. The web pages must be located within these directories so that IIS can publish them. These directories are selected by using the IIS manager.

Assuming all your files are located on the same hard drive where IIS is located, you can publish those documents right away by simply copying the files into IIS's default home directory, C:\InetPub\wwwroot.

> **NOTE** For FTP sites, the default directory is C:\Inetpub\ftproot.

Users on an intranet can access these files by using the URL http// *servername/ filename*; Internet users will enter a conventional URL to get to your page.

Take Me Home

It's in your site's best interests and for your own sanity's sake to have *home directories* established for each web or FTP site. A home directory contains an index file welcoming visitors and linking them to the rest of the pages in your site, and it is mapped to either your domain name (for Internet visitors) or server name (for intranet visitors).

For instance, if you are hosting web content for your four-wheel drive club's annual gala, Internet visitors might enter http://www.mudtacular2002.com. However, members of the club would use the server name—Mr. Mud—to get to the page (in intranet parlance, this would be http://mrmud). Whichever way visitors come to the site, they are taken directly to the home directory. By default, a home directory is created when IIS is installed and a new web site created.

Detour

How many times have you visited a web page only to get a message similar to this one:

```
We're sorry, the page you're looking for is no longer here.
We will redirect you in a moment.
```

As annoying as this is, it is fairly unavoidable, especially at large web sites with intricate file structures. Regrettably, if you have to move pages from folder to folder on your web site, it might not be possible to hunt down and correct all the links. Rather than change all the URLs, you simply make IIS tell the web browser where the new links are. This is called *redirecting a browser request*.

Using IIS, you can redirect requests in several ways:

- From one directory to another
- To another web site
- To another file in a different directory

When the visitor's browser seeks the file at the former URL, IIS tells the browser the location of the new URL (hence, redirection).

The following steps outline how to redirect requests to another web site or directory.

1. Open the IIS manager and right-click the web site or directory you wish to change.
2. Select Properties.
3. Click the Home Directory, Virtual Directory, or Directory tab. The result is shown in Figure 7-13.
4. Choose A redirection to a URL.
5. In the Redirect to box, enter the URL of the new directory.

To redirect requests to a specific file:

1. Open the IIS MMC snap-in and right-click the web site or directory you wish to change.
2. Select Properties.

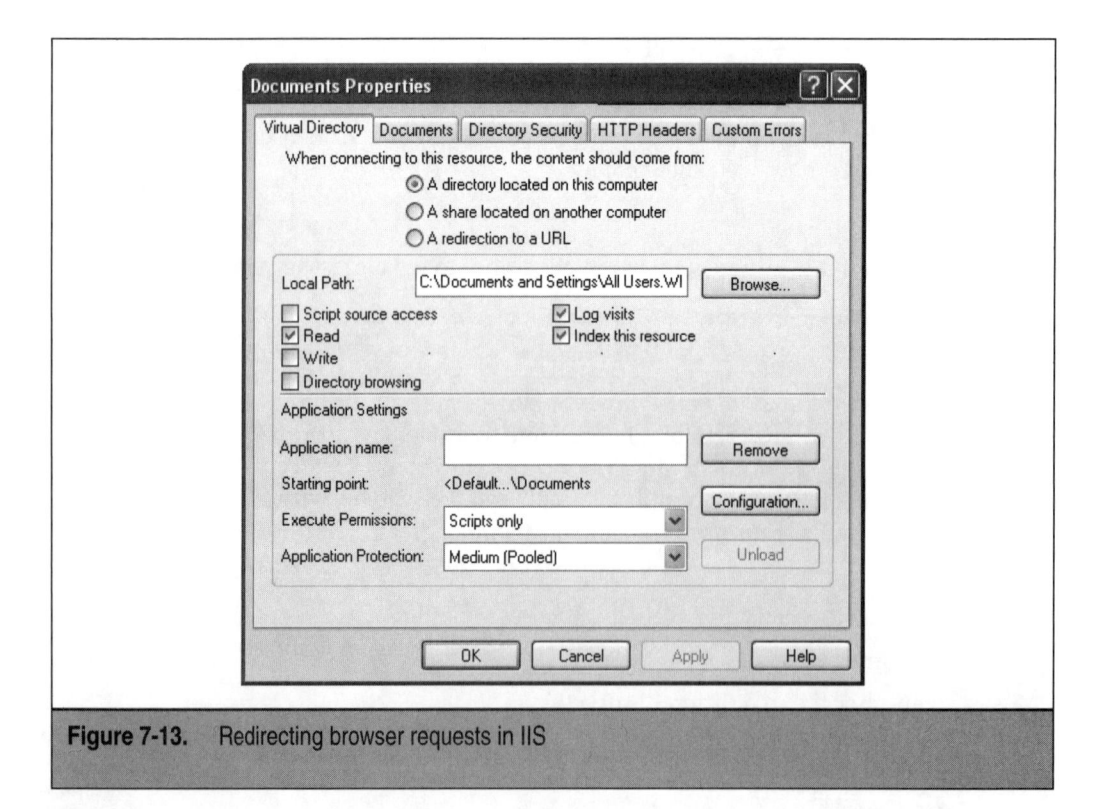

Figure 7-13. Redirecting browser requests in IIS

3. Click the Home Directory, Virtual Directory, or Directory tab.
4. Choose A redirection to a URL.
5. In the Redirect to box, enter the URL of the destination file.
6. Select The exact URL entered above.

Server-Side Includes

Oftentimes, visitors to your web site will need a customized web page delivered to them. So customized, in fact, that there is no way you could anticipate the need and maintain that specific page on your web site. For instance, when you go to Amazon.com and search for a specific title, the resulting information is generated into a page specific to your request. This is called *dynamic* content.

IIS facilitates dynamic content using *server-side includes (SSIs)*. A multitude of web site management activities can be enabled by using SSI. These are called *directives* and are added to web pages when they are designed. When the page is requested, IIS executes the directives on the page.

A popular directive is known as an *include*, which incorporates the contents of a file into a specified web page. For instance, if you have a banner on your web page that links to advertising, then you would use SSI to include the banner's HTML source with the web page. When you need to update the banner, you need not change the whole web page—simply update the banner file.

Enabling SSIs is accomplished by doing the following:

1. Make sure your files containing SSI directives have the appropriate SSI extension (.stm, .shtm, or .shtml).
2. Place the SSI files in a directory with Scripts and Execute access permissions.

Disable SSIs with these steps:

1. Open the IIS manager and right-click the web site or directory you wish to change.
2. Select Properties.
3. Click the Home Directory or Directory tab.
4. Select the application starting point directory.
5. Click the Configuration button, and then click the App Mappings tab. This is shown in Figure 7-14.
6. Choose the extension, and then click the Remove button.

IIS is a very rich subject, and one that doesn't get justice in the little space we have here. Hopefully, this chapter will have given you an idea of the usefulness of IIS and how it is installed and managed. Spend some time getting to know IIS, and you'll find it a useful tool for both Internet and intranet services.

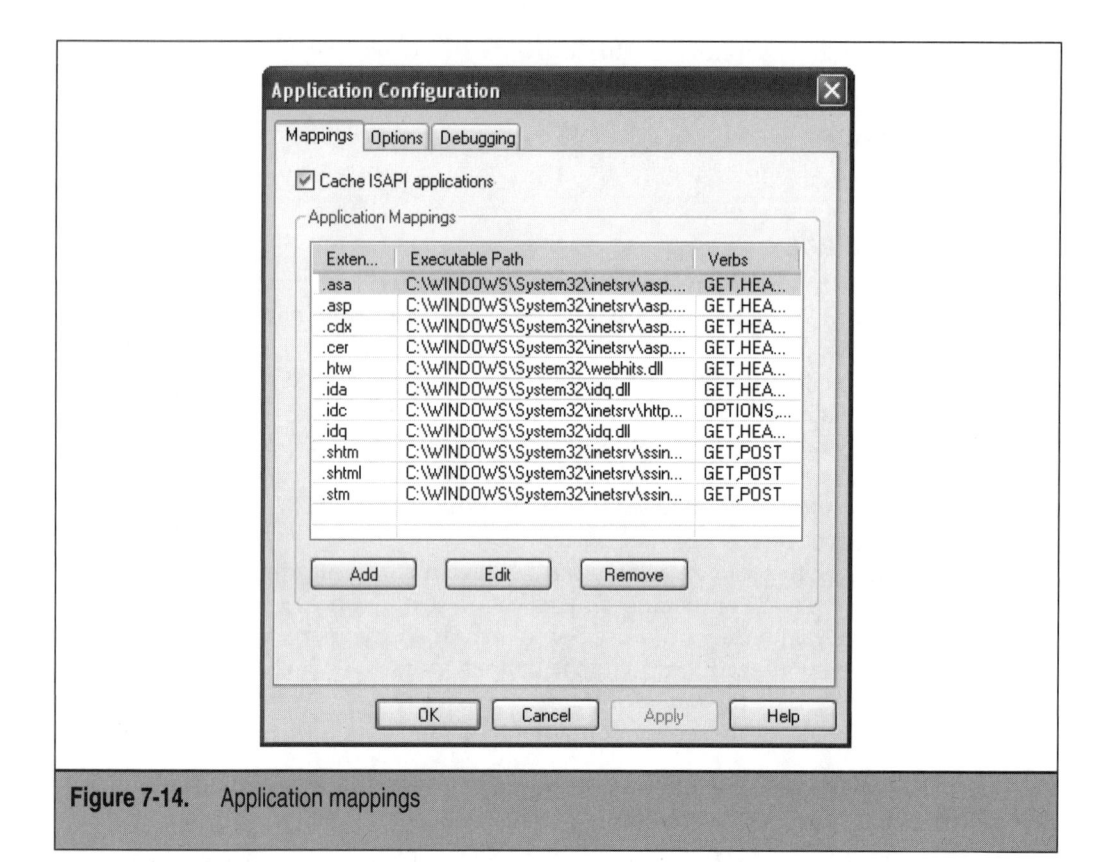

Figure 7-14. Application mappings

CHAPTER 8

Connectivity Problem-Solving Tools and Techniques

Industry has yet to develop the first crashproof computer network. If that ever does happen, look for fortunes to be made and the citizens of the world to join hands in a gesture of universal peace. Until that time, however, you'll have to muddle along, praying that nothing happens to your network. If you do experience connectivity problems (and you will), there are a number of tools in Windows XP Professional that can help you ferret out the source of your dilemma.

This chapter first examines the tools included with Windows XP Professional that can be used to troubleshoot problems with Windows XP itself. From there, we'll talk about troubleshooting Windows XP Professional networks (both local area networks and remote access networks). Finally, we'll take a look at some popular tools used in TCP/IP networks that can be of immeasurable help in hunting down problems with your Windows XP Professional network.

TROUBLESHOOTING WINDOWS XP

A number of tools and techniques can be used to resolve problems with a Windows XP Professional client. Problems come in all shapes and sizes, from the irritation of hanging programs to the worst-case scenario—a computer that won't boot up. This section explains how you can troubleshoot some of these problems and what Windows XP Professional includes to make the process easier.

Startup Modes

If you've ever tried to boot up your computer one day to find that the computer wouldn't start at all, then you know the queasy feeling this causes. However, if Windows is still on your hard drive, Windows XP Professional provides nine ways to get your computer up and running.

Windows XP Professional has a more robust selection of startup modes than earlier versions of Windows and will help track down setup problems more effectively. You can choose from a list of startup modes by pressing F8 during bootup. The Windows XP Professional startup modes are as follows:

- **Safe Mode** Starts Windows XP Professional with minimal drivers (mouse, monitor, keyboard, mass storage, and default system services) and in VGA Mode.

- **Safe Mode With Networking** Starts Windows XP Professional in Safe Mode, but allows network connectivity.

- **Safe Mode With Command Prompt** Starts in Safe Mode, but instead of the traditional desktop, a command prompt is displayed.

- **Enable Boot Logging** Starts Windows XP Professional and logs all drivers and services that were or were not successfully loaded. The list is saved in a file called ntblog.txt and is located in the C:\Windows directory.

- **Enable VGA Mode**   Starts Windows XP Professional with a basic VGA driver. This option allows users to repair their system if they install a video driver improperly.
- **Last Known Good Configuration**   Starts Windows XP Professional using the Registry information from the last time that the system loaded properly. This mode does not repair hardware problems, and changes made since it was last loaded will be lost.
- **Debugging Mode**   Starts Windows XP Professional while sending debugging information via serial cable to another computer.
- **Selective Startup**   This mode isn't shown on the Windows startup menu that appears when you press F8, rather it is enabled by running the System Configuration Utility (which we explain later in this chapter in the section "System Configuration Utility").
- **Normal Mode**   This starts Windows normally.

Each of these modes is useful for different functions. However, there are four modes that you are most likely to use.

Safe Mode

The most basic tool is one that's been around since Windows 95—the Safe Mode. Safe Mode loads the bare minimum set of drivers. Windows' basic functions are still available, but you can tell immediately that you're in Safe Mode, because Windows reverts to a VGA screen (640×480 with 16 colors). The only devices available in Safe Mode are the keyboard, mouse, and hard drive. This mode is used when your computer runs into a problem that prevents it from starting properly—for instance, if a bad software installation causes startup problems.

Safe Mode With Networking

The next startup mode is Safe Mode With Networking. This is, as the name suggests, similar to Safe Mode; however, it allows you to form your network connections. This mode is useful if you need to get on your network to help solve your Windows dilemma—for instance, if you need to find a file on the network, or use Remote Assistance to solve the problem.

Safe Mode With Command Prompt

The previous two modes both featured the stuff that makes Windows so popular in the first place, namely, a graphical user interface (GUI). However, by using Safe Mode With Command Prompt, you won't be able to rely on the safe, point-and-click environment that Windows affords. Rather, you'll be sent to a command prompt and have to use DOS commands to do what you need to do.

This mode can also be started from the Windows XP Professional CD-ROM and is known as the *Recovery Console*. To start the Recovery Console, boot your computer using your installation CD-ROM, and press R when the text mode portion of the setup begins. Furthermore, you can take a proactive step and simply make the Recovery Console part of your Windows XP Professional installation. To do so, put the installation CD-ROM in your CD-ROM or DVD drive, select Start | Run, enter ***d:\i386\winnt32.exe /cmdcons*** (where *d:* is the letter of your CD-ROM drive), and then click OK.

This mode sounds like it is more trouble than it's worth; however, if you know the names and locations of any files that are causing you grief, you can go in and terminate them with extreme prejudice.

> **NOTE** You can get a listing of all the commands in the command prompt environment by typing **HELP** at the prompt and pressing ENTER.

Here are some basic DOS commands that can help you ferret out trouble:

- **DIR** Shows a listing of the contents of the current directory. Entries with a <DIR> next to them are directories. If you are in a particularly large folder and the listing scrolls off the screen, the command DIR /P will pause the output. DIR /W will give you multiple columns of directory information. Or, you can use them in tandem (DIR /P/W) to get multiple columns that pause.

- **CD** What if the file you're looking for isn't in your directory? CD allows you to change folders. Enter **CD**, a space, and the folder name, and you switch to that folder. If there are a number of subdirectories within a folder, add \<*directoryname*> to the end of the folder name. For example:

    ```
    CD windows\desktop
    ```

    will show you the contents of the desktop subfolder within the Windows directory. To back out of a folder, enter

    ```
    CD ..
    ```

- **DEL** Used to delete files. Simply enter **DEL** and the filename, and then kiss it goodbye. You can also use the DEL command to wipe out every instance (in the selected folder) of a particular file type. For example, if you wanted to get rid of all your Adobe Acrobat files, you'd enter

    ```
    DEL *.PDF
    ```

- **CHKDSK** If you don't necessarily need to obliterate a particular file, but are still having bootup issues and suspect hard drive problems, the Microsoft Check Disk tool will check it out for you. It will examine the integrity of the disk and determine space usage. For best results, however, you should run CHKDSK before Windows starts up. To do this, enter **CHKDSK /F**. You'll see an error message and be asked if you want to run it the next time Windows starts. Press Y and then press ENTER, and CHKDSK will run the next time you boot up.

Last Known Good Configuration

Windows XP Professional can also restore your computer to a time when everything was running optimally. By selecting this startup mode, you will likely lose any applications that you were trying to install, but you should also lose the little gremlin that's causing trouble. Unlike System Restore (which we explain later in the section "System Restore"), with the Last Known Good Configuration checkpoint you don't establish the restore point. Rather, the computer looks at its Registry and decides where the restore point is. For the most part, this works fine, but you might not get the results you expect.

The unfortunate reality is that "good" in last known good configuration is a subjective term that you and Windows might not necessarily agree upon. For example, if you are having problems with an application or a driver, yet Windows boots up, then the operating system will consider that a good configuration. However, this won't be good for you, because it won't bring the results you were hoping for.

Boot Floppy Disk

Another sort of startup mode can be made by using a boot floppy disk. This is a disk you keep in a safe place and, in the event of trouble, whip out to restart the computer. In Windows XP Professional, System Restore is meant to make the recovery process easier, but it isn't a bad idea to have a boot floppy disk on hand, just in case.

> **NOTE** We'll explain the System Restore tool a little later in the section "System Restore."

To make a boot floppy disk, do the following:

1. Put a blank floppy disk in your floppy disk drive.
2. Select Start | My Computer.
3. Right-click the icon for your floppy disk drive and choose Format (the resulting screen is shown in Figure 8-1).
4. Select the Create an MS-DOS startup disk check box.
5. Click Start.

If you have to boot your computer from the boot floppy, you'll have an even more basic set of drivers than are afforded with Safe Mode. In fact, you won't be able to use your CD-ROM or DVD-ROM drive. Furthermore, you won't be able to see any NTFS disks, only FAT disks. However, if your hard drive is bad, this is the tool you'll need to get your computer started.

Installation Repair

To quote (and clean up) a popular slogan found on t-shirts and bumper stickers everywhere: "Stuff Happens." If you run into problems during a Windows XP Professional installation, you might have to perform some repairs. To do so, you

Figure 8-1. Creating a boot floppy disk

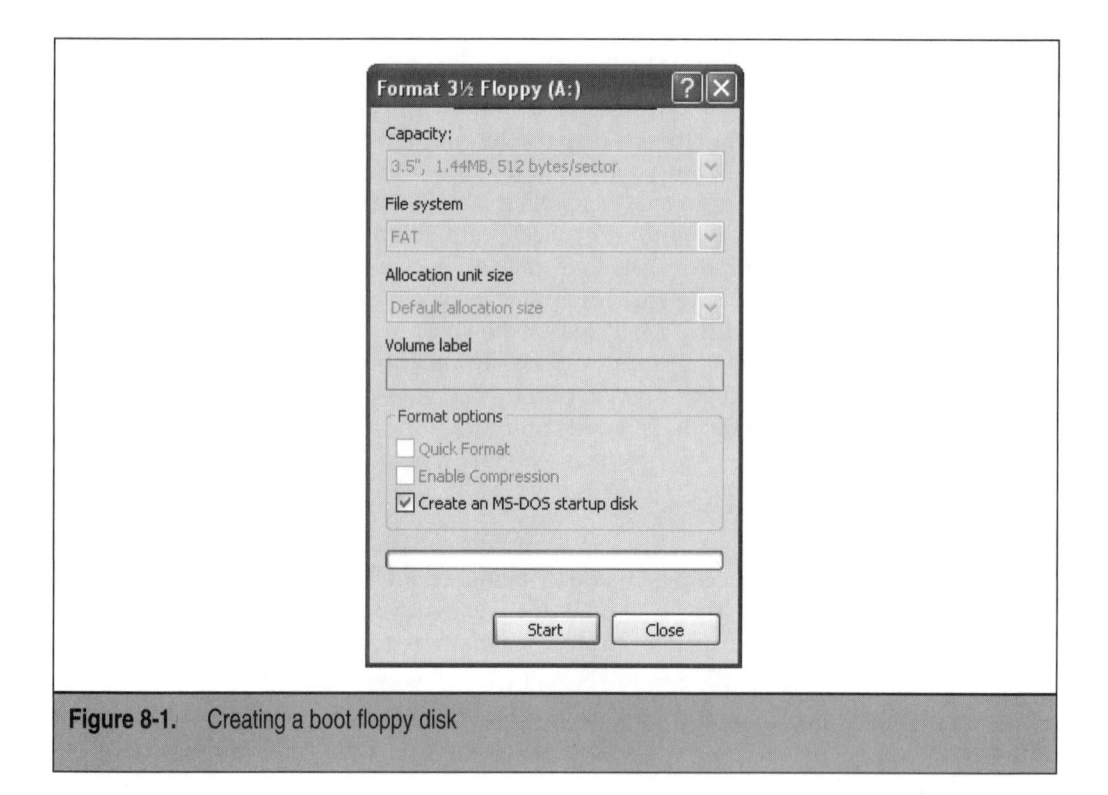

use the Windows XP Professional Setup Wizard. The wizard is invoked by doing the following:

1. Place your Windows XP Professional installation disk in the CD-ROM drive and choose Install Windows XP. The installation process will begin, and after the first reboot it will detect an installation in process. Next, it will ask you if you want to repair the installation.
2. Press R to repair the installation. Once the installation is completed, you will be asked to reboot.
3. Press F3 to reboot, and you'll return to Windows XP Setup. At this point, you can quit the Windows XP Setup Wizard without reinstalling Windows by pressing F3.

Hung Programs

It's happened to the best of us. While running a piece of software, the computer seizes; your data is trapped. It's annoying when playing a video game; it's catastrophic when you've been doing actual work. Sometimes you get lucky and can restore the work you've been slaving away on. Other times, you're not so lucky and have to start from scratch.

When hung programs do occur, Windows XP Professional provides a couple of tools that can help salvage your loss—at least to some extent.

Task Manager

Anyone who's spent much time at all with Windows has experienced a hung program—that is, a program that simply stops responding. Regrettably, when a program hangs, you're pretty much out of luck, and the best you can do is stop the errant program altogether—hopefully without crashing your computer. The Task Manager (shown in Figure 8-2) can be used to stop this errant program.

The Task Manager is invoked by pressing CTRL-ALT-DEL. Under the Applications tab in the Task Manager is a list of currently running applications. If a program is hanging, the entry "Not Responding" will be listed in the Status column. To stop the application, click it, and then click the End Task button.

If your system is really having problems, you might have to reboot completely. To do this, invoke the Task Manager, and then select Shut Down from the menu bar.

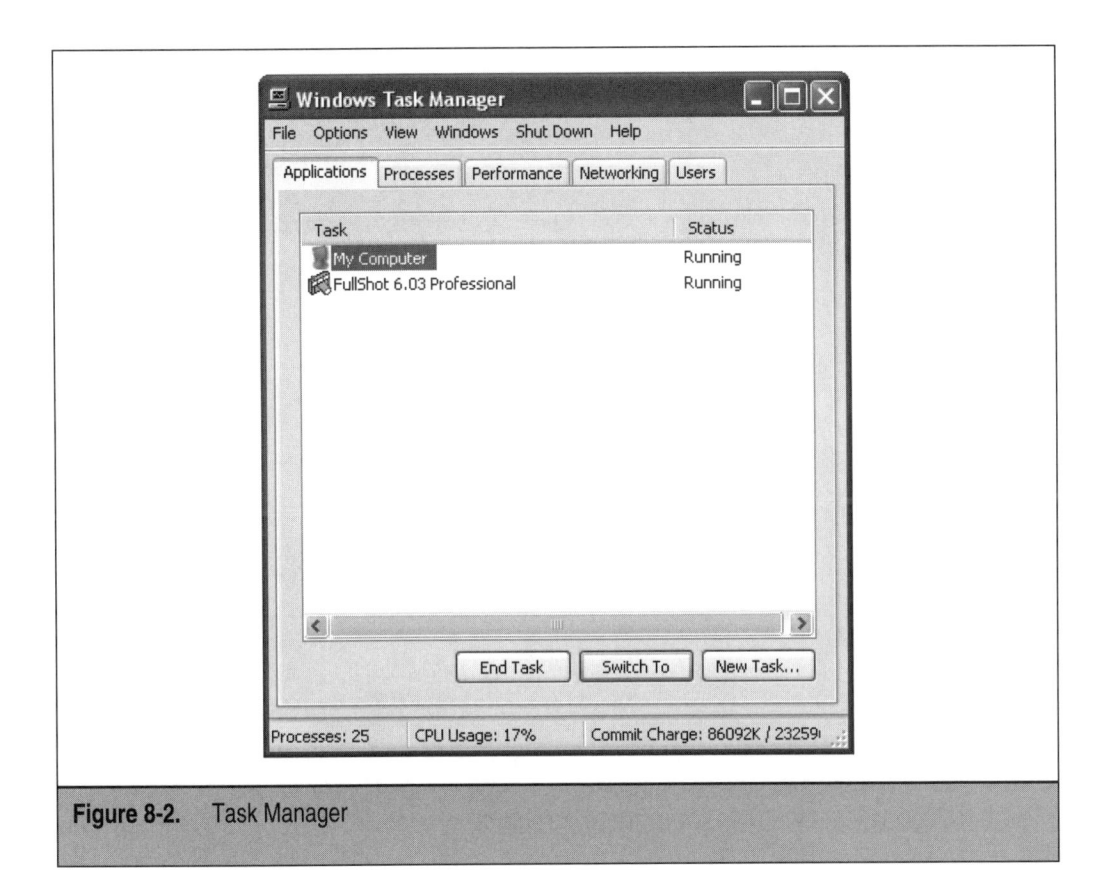

Figure 8-2. Task Manager

Error Reporting

In Chapter 2 we talked about the privacy ramifications of Windows XP activation. Privacy can also become an issue when an application hangs. If your computer runs into trouble, Windows XP Professional can use the Error Reporting feature to generate a report to send back to Microsoft. This feature allows information about crashes to be sent back to Redmond, where Microsoft develops fixes based on the error reports it receives.

However, unlike activation, this feature can be turned off. If you would rather not share error information with Microsoft, do the following:

1. Select Start and right-click My Computer.
2. Select Properties from the resulting menu.
3. Click the Advanced tab.
4. Click the Error Reporting button to display the Error Reporting dialog box (shown in Figure 8-3).
5. You can determine which level of error reporting best suits you:
    - None at all
    - Windows only
    - Applications

Figure 8-3. Configuring Error Reporting options

Stopping Startup Programs

When starting Windows XP Professional, you might experience an automatically launched application that doesn't work and play well with others. Unfortunately, Microsoft doesn't allow auto-starting programs to be turned off very easily at all. If you want to deactivate a particular application, there are three good places to do so, as detailed in the following text.

Startup Folder

The easiest place to deactivate an application is in the Startup folder. To open the Startup folder, select Start | All Programs | Startup. If a shortcut for the application is in this folder, simply delete it.

System Configuration Utility

The System Configuration Utility is a handy tool to display and edit various elements of your system's configuration. The System Configuration Utility (see Figure 8-4) is opened by selecting Start | Run and entering **msconfig**.

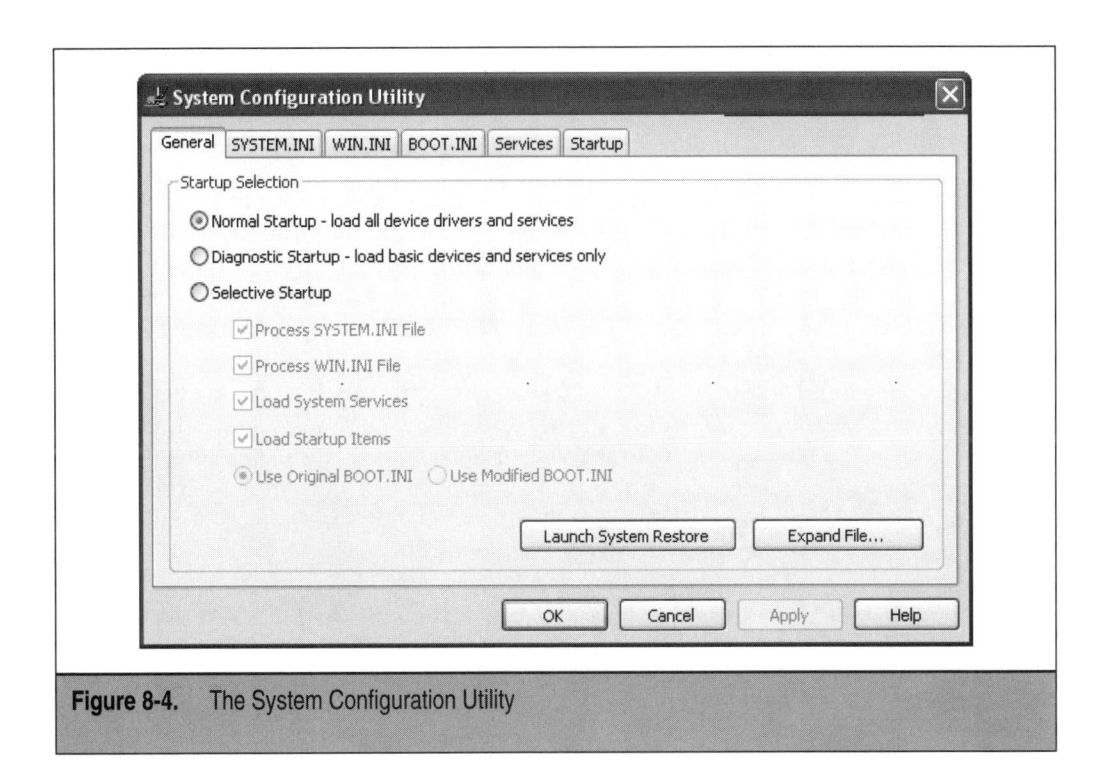

Figure 8-4. The System Configuration Utility

Under the General tab, you can choose Selective Startup to turn on the Selective Startup Mode. This is a mode in which Windows asks for confirmation before running each program in its startup repertoire.

The Startup tab shows a list of programs that start when Windows boots up. If you deselect any item under the Startup tab, then Selective Startup Mode is automatically enabled.

Under the Win.ini tab, you can examine your Win.ini file. This file contains configuration information for Windows. Check this file for a line that activates the application in question. The line will typically start with "run=" or "load=".

Registry

The Registry is a database of program and system setup information for your Windows XP Professional system. Use the Registry Editor (select Start | Run and enter **regedit**) to look for the file. It's a very smart idea to make a backup of the Registry before messing with it. Examine the HKEY_LOCAL_MACHINE\SOFTWARE\Microsoft\Windows\CurrentVersion\RUN group of Registry keys to find the list of programs that run automatically.

CAUTION Win.ini and the Registry are not places to goof around. If you mess up a line you can cause serious problems with your computer. Always take special care when editing these files.

MMC

Microsoft created the MMC in an effort to make management easier by using an extensible, consistent, and intuitive interface for all administrative applications. The MMC is a Windows-based multiple document interface (MDI) that resembles Internet Explorer. Since it's just a framework, MMC has no functionality by itself. You need to apply snap-ins to give it a purpose. For example, there is a snap-in for most of the current administrative tools such as the Event Viewer.

Snap-ins are entirely customizable, can be created from scratch, and can even include web-based interfaces. Once you define the MMC with the snap-ins you want, you save it as a *tool*. An administrator can include in his or her tool only those snap-ins he or she needs to perform all elements of complicated administrative tasks within a single MMC instead of switching between different applications. Later, that administrator can open the tool and it will have just the snap-ins defined earlier.

A basic, empty console looks like Figure 8-5.

The basic layout is the same for almost all snap-ins inside the MMC. At the top of the *parent frame* is the master menu and toolbar. Here you will find familiar items that control file and window management such as the Properties, View, and Help menus. The tools in the toolbar will vary, but they generally offer navigational assistance or perform a function like creating new folders or deleting files.

Figure 8-5. Empty MMC

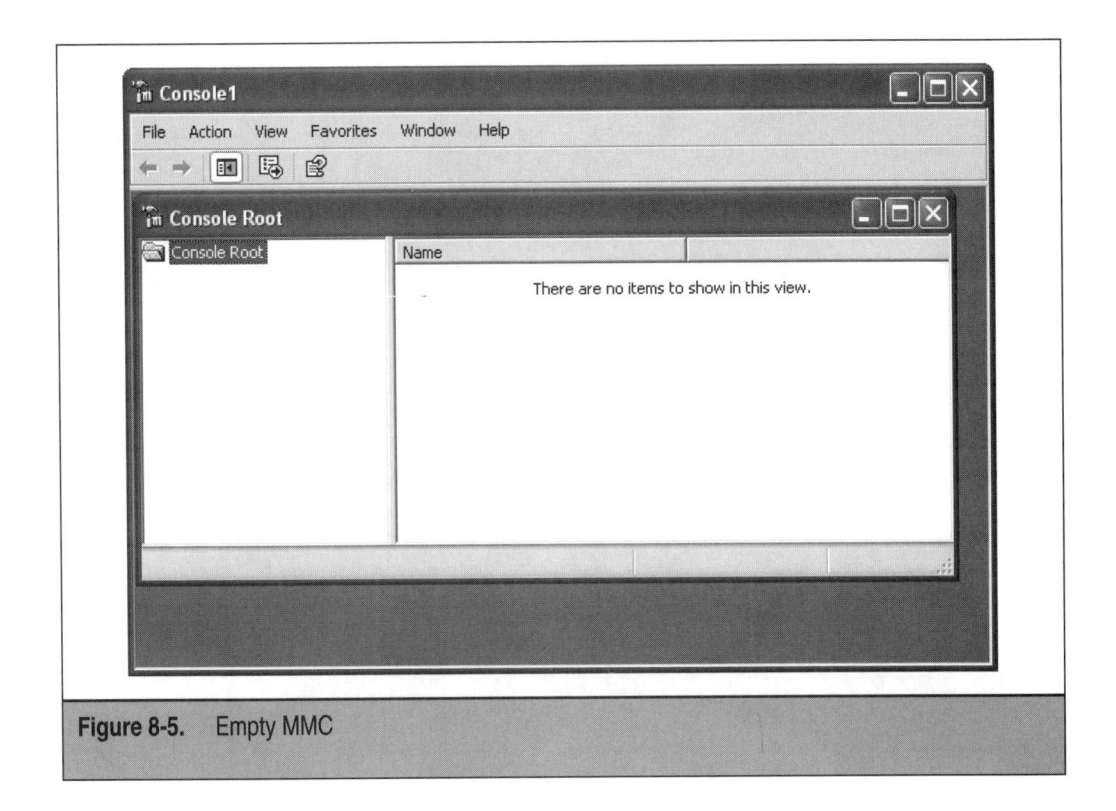

The frames contained within the parent frame are called *children frames*, and they may vary significantly, but generally appear with two frames. The left frame contains the hierarchical organization specific to the snap-in, whereas the right frame presents data specific to the item that is highlighted in the left frame.

To add tools to your MMC, on the Console menu, click Add/Remove Snap-in. This calls up the Add/Remove Snap-in dialog box (shown in Figure 8-6).

In the dialog box, click the Add button, click the snap-in you want to add (in this case, as Figure 8-7 shows, we're adding the Event Viewer, discussed in the next section), and click Add. Use this technique to add as many tools to your MMC as you wish.

Event Viewer

The Event Viewer traces its roots back to Windows NT 3.1. In Windows XP Professional, it can be found as part of the MMC. In a nutshell, what Event Viewer does is keep track of what's going on as Windows runs. It's a pretty powerful tool that might just have the answer if you are having troubles with your system.

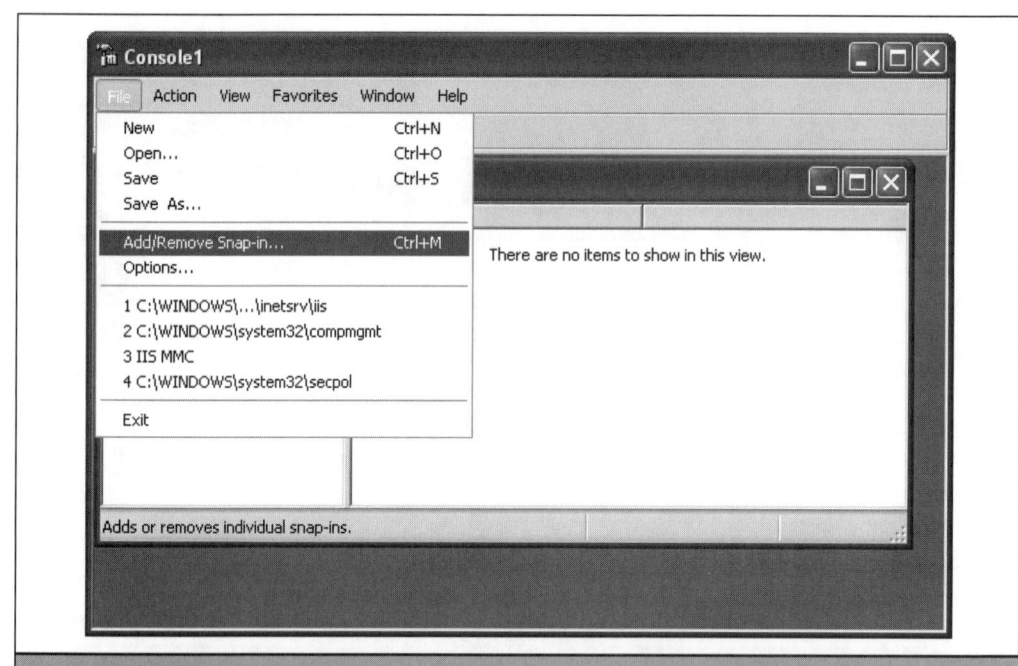

Figure 8-6. Activating the Add/Remove Snap-in dialog box

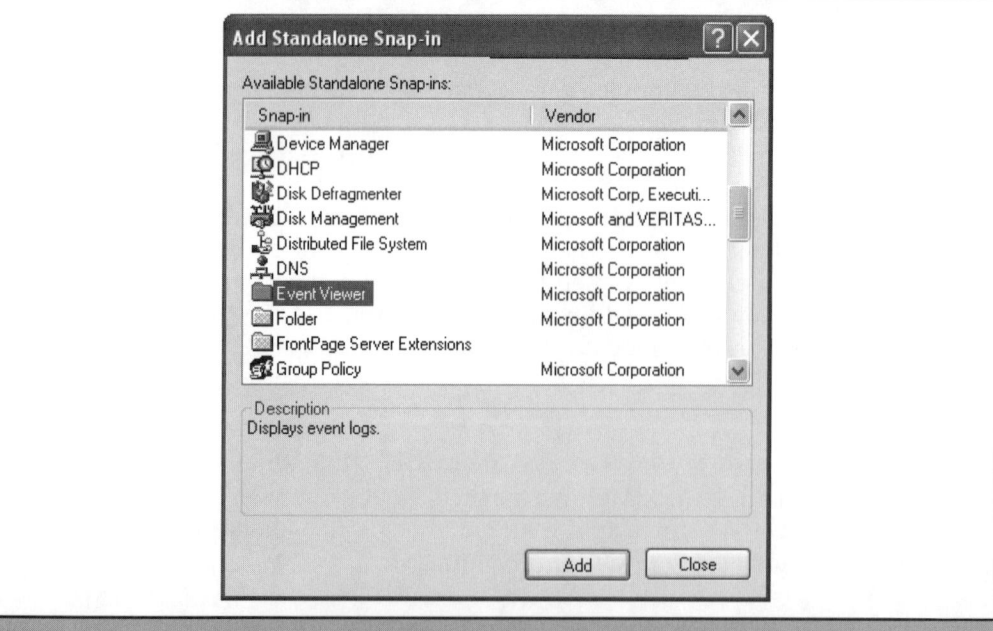

Figure 8-7. Pick your snap-in from the list in the dialog box.

To start the Event Viewer, in the MMC, open System Tools and click Event Viewer. The resulting window (shown in Figure 8-8) displays three items that Event Viewer can track:

- **Application**   Monitors all events generated by applications and programs
- **System**   Monitors system components, such as device drivers
- **Security**   Monitors changes to the security system and alerts you to possible security breaches

Double-clicking a particular event generates a window, which describes the event, when it occurred, and other details and includes an Internet link to describe the event. The properties of one such event are shown in Figure 8-9.

Status Menu Command

If your Windows XP Professional client is meant to accept incoming connections with other devices, an icon with the assigned user name is shown in the Network Connections folder as each user connects. To view the progress of incoming transmissions, right-click a named connection, and then click Status.

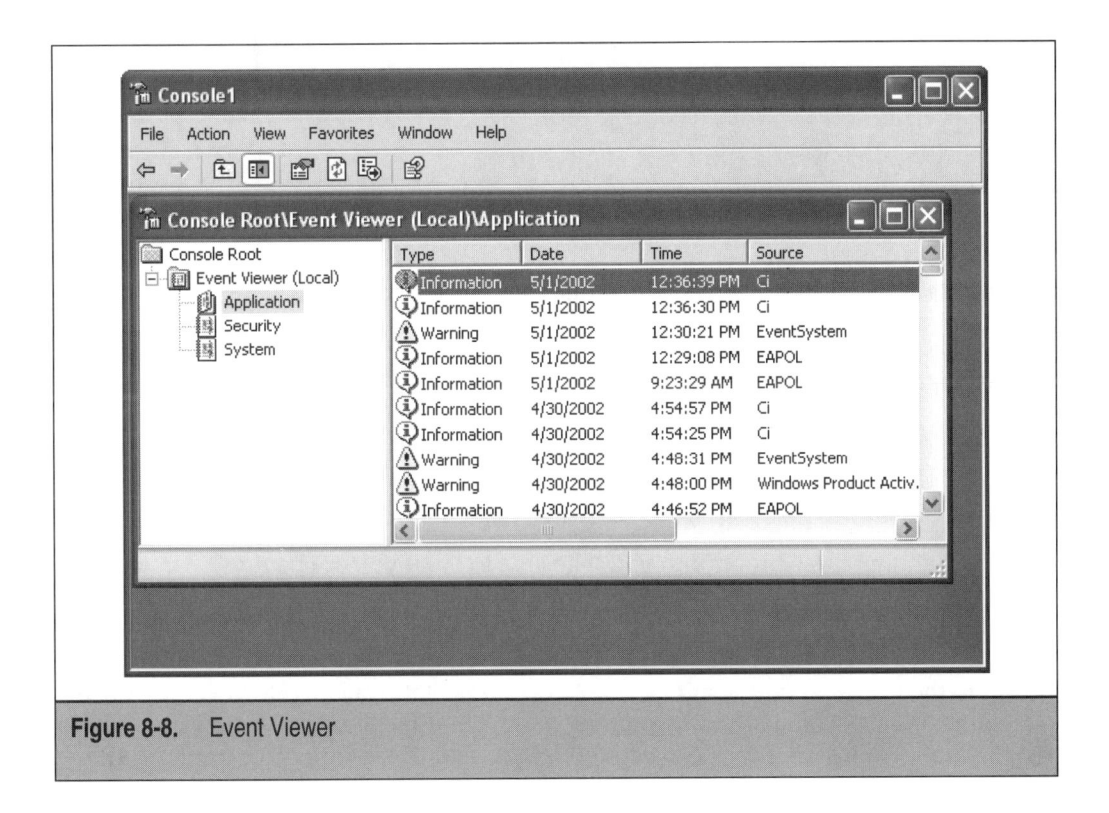

Figure 8-8.   Event Viewer

Figure 8-9. Event properties

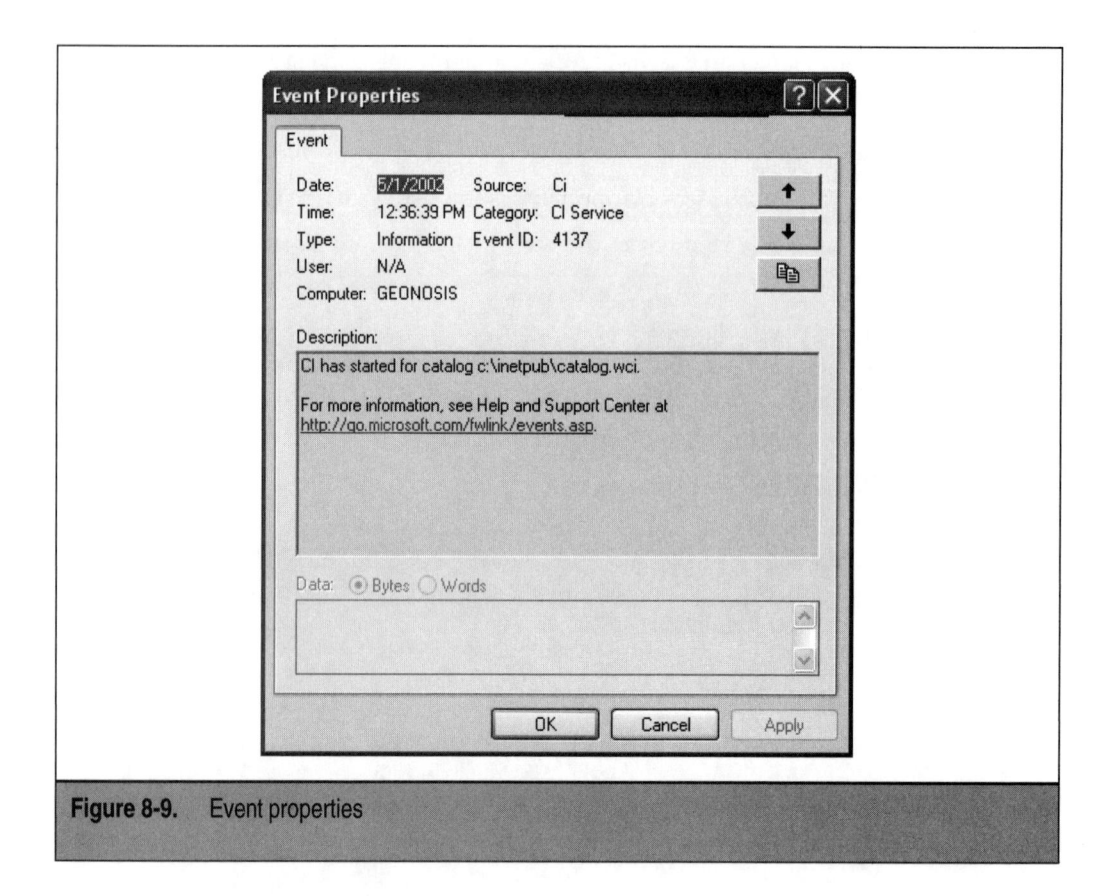

The Status command will show the following information:

- The connection's duration
- The connection's speed
- The number of bytes transmitted and received from a connection
- Diagnostic tools available for a connection

This tool is shown in Figure 8-10.

By examining these properties, you'll be able to tell if you are having a connection issue. For instance, if you are on a Fast Ethernet connection and the speed is only showing 10 megabits per second, you'll know something is not right. Furthermore, and indicative of a larger connection issue, if the connection is disrupted, there will be a red X next to the icon, and you won't be able to open the Status menu. However, text will appear next to the icon that can help point you in the direction you need to go to solve the problem. For instance, the icon caption might read, "Network cable unplugged."

Figure 8-10. Status of a network connection

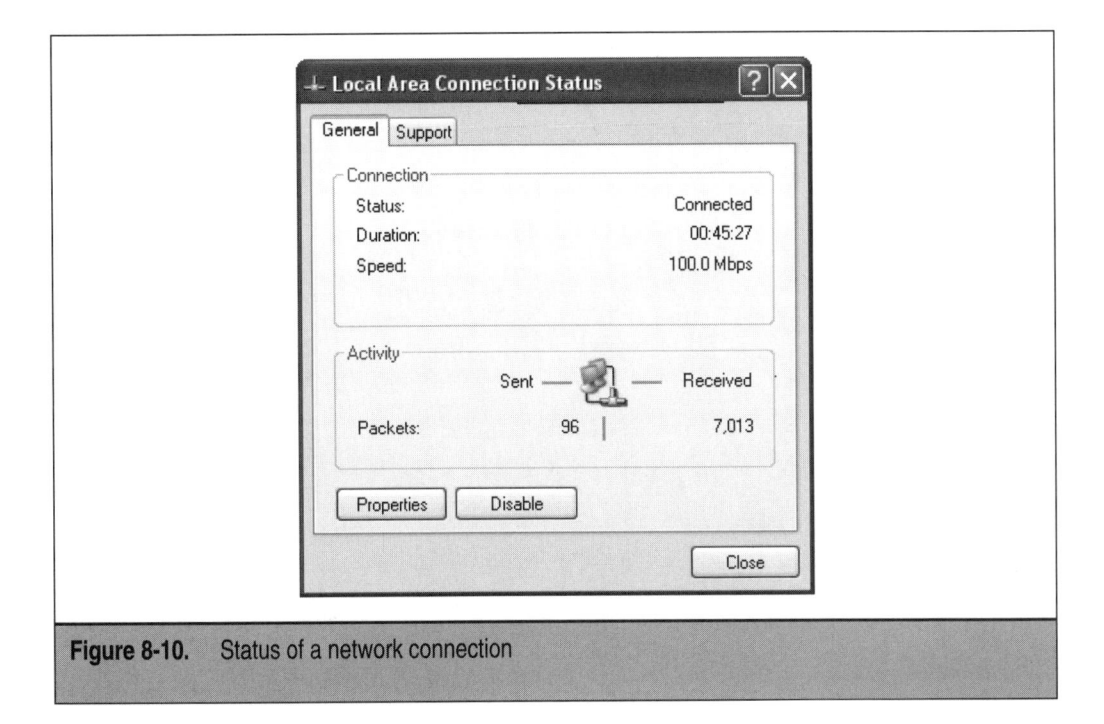

Network Support Help

By opening the Local Area Connection Status dialog box and selecting the Support tab, you can view the address type, IP address, subnet mask, and default address of a connection.

Click the Details button and you can see a detailed summary of the network connection (shown in Figure 8-11), including these items:

- IP address
- Subnet mask
- Default address
- Physical address
- The IP address of its DHCP, DNS, and WINS servers
- The date the DHCP lease of the address was acquired
- The date the DHCP lease is due to expire

Figure 8-11. Network connection details

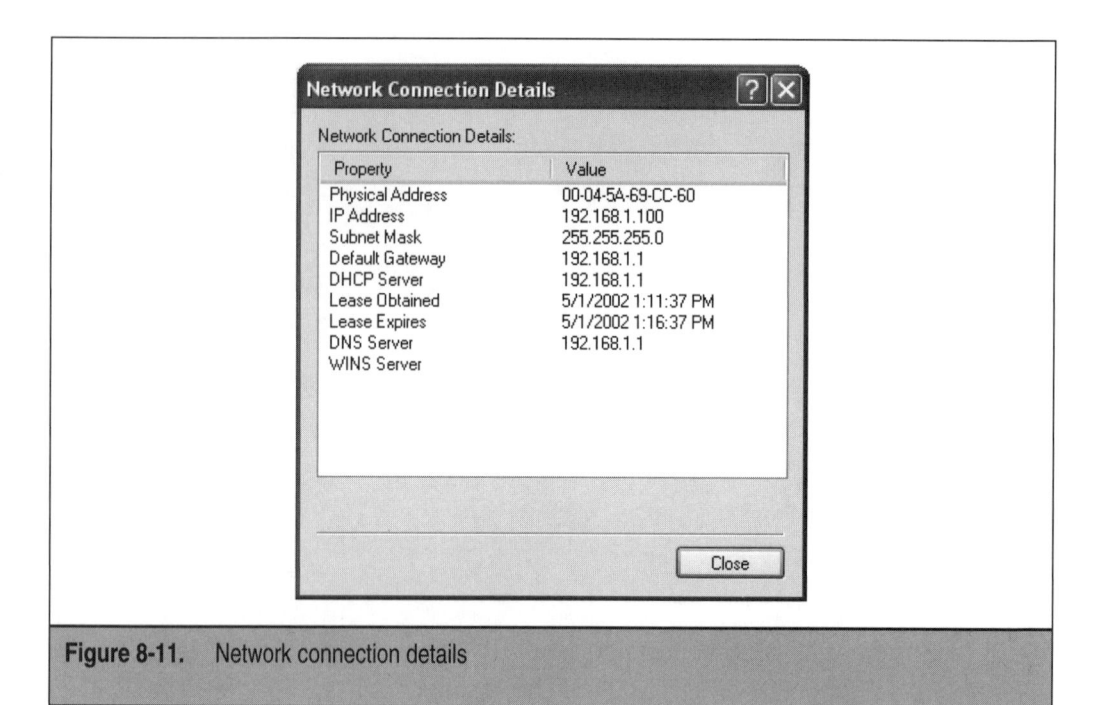

Network Diagnostics

In the Windows XP Professional Help and Support Center, you can use Network Diagnostics (among other helpful, automated tools) to check a number of network settings. To access this feature, open Help and Support Center from the Start menu, and then click Fixing a Problem. A list of problems that can be ameliorated appears in the resulting screen (shown in Figure 8-12).

For example, Windows XP Professional can look at your network and run a battery of automated tests. The tests to be performed can be selected by the user as shown in Figure 8-13.

These tests check a number of issues that might be relevant for your computer and its connection issues. It checks your modems and network cards—among other things—and gives specific details on the devices, applications, and services you're using. For example, details of your network adapter include such items as these:

- When the DHCP lease was obtained and when it expires
- DNS host name
- Whether IPX is enabled
- IP address

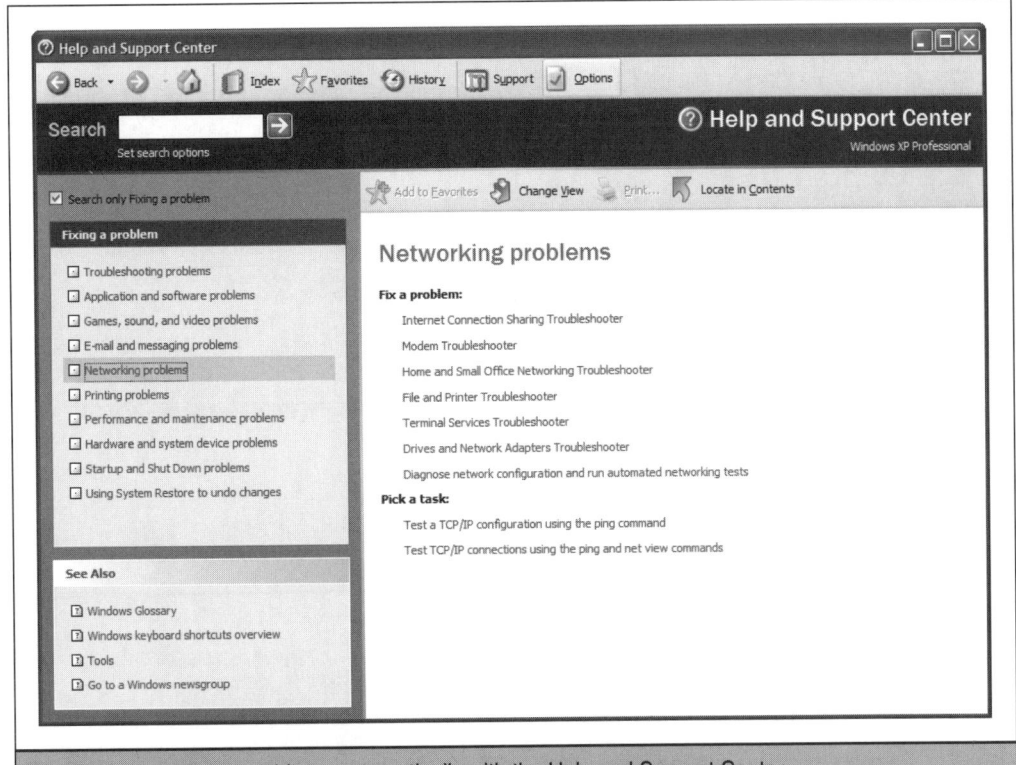

Figure 8-12. Fixing problems automatically with the Help and Support Center

The tool will also show the values of advanced details like the following:

- IPConnectionMetric
- IPSecPermitIPProtocols
- Databasepath

Other troubleshooters will ask you to perform a task, and then click Yes or No, depending on the results that are returned.

Repairing a Connection

If you have a connection that is giving you trouble, Windows XP Professional provides an easy way to restore the connection. Simply right-click a connection in the Network Connections window, and then click the Repair button.

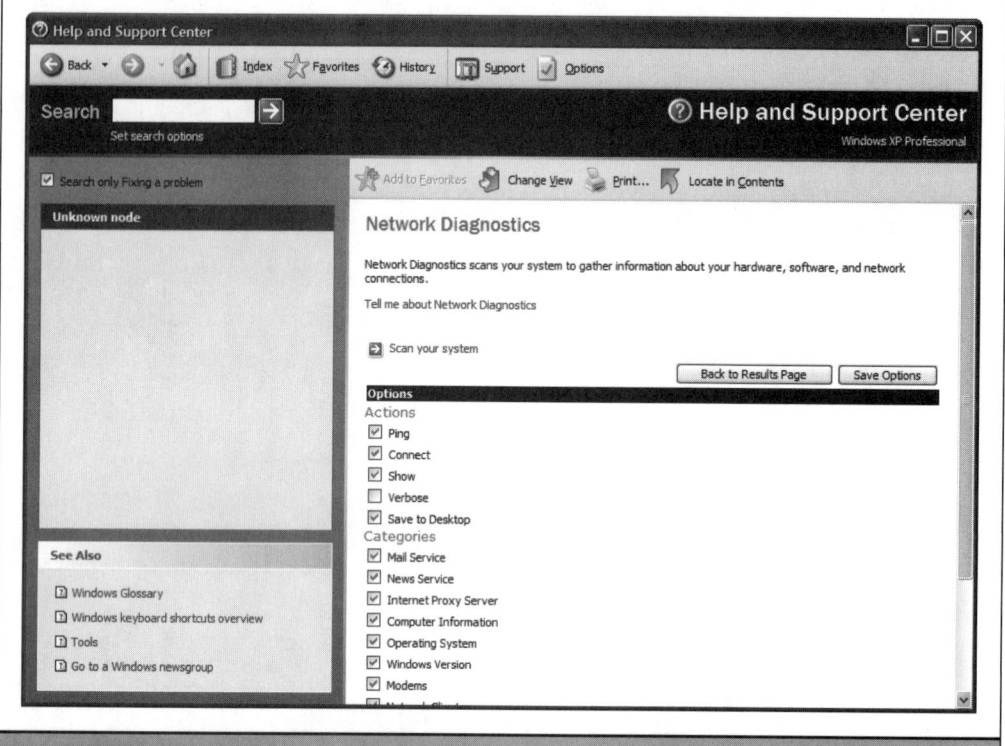

Figure 8-13. Network Diagnostics page within Windows XP Professional Help and Support Center

By clicking the Repair button, you can fix a number of network settings, including the following:

- Releasing current TCP/IP settings.
- Renewing TCP/IP settings.
- Flushing the Address Resolution Protocol (ARP) cache.
- Renewing the IP lease by performing a DHCP broadcast.
- Reloading the remote cache name table of NetBT. (On the command line, this can be accomplished by entering **nbtstat -R**.)
- Sending name release packets to WINS, then refreshing. (On the command line, this can be accomplished by entering **nbstat -RR**.)
- Purging the DNS resolver cache, and then reregistering the DNS information. (On the command line, this can be accomplished by entering **ipconfig /flushdns**.)

System Restore

If you are experiencing trouble with your Windows XP Professional computer, Microsoft provides you with a system-level tool that can help get things back to normal. System Restore is helpful if you have recently installed software that causes your computer to crash or malfunction. It's easy to think of System Restore as a giant "undo" button for your system.

Using System Restore, you can roll back your computer's settings to a time when the computer worked fine. Furthermore, you can manually establish *restore points*. Restore points are created automatically, either on an established schedule or in response to system events, such as installing a new device driver. Additionally, you can manually create restore points whenever you like.

If your computer runs into trouble, you can restore your computer to one of these restore points, which will reset drivers and applications as they were during the creation of the restore point. A restore point contains two types of information:

- A snapshot of the Registry
- Dynamic system files

NOTE System Restore restores programs, not files. If you have to run System Restore, it will not alter Microsoft Office files, web pages, text files, or anything in your My Documents folder.

For instance, information stored at a restore point includes the following:

- User account information maintained in the Registry
- Application and hardware settings maintained in the Registry
- Startup files needed for Windows XP Professional, including those in the systemroot directory and boot files

Enabling System Restore

System Restore is, by default, enabled on your system when you install Windows XP Professional. However, you can turn it off or on as needed. You might elect to turn it off if you are running low on disk space. But remember, you can't use System Restore if it's deactivated. To turn it on or off, follow these steps:

1. In Control Panel, open Performance and Maintenance, and then System.
2. In the System Properties dialog box, click the System Restore tab (shown in Figure 8-14).
3. To re-enable System Restore, clear the Turn off System Restore check box.
4. Additionally, you can specify how much hard drive space System Restore will use by adjusting the Disk space to use slider for each volume.

Figure 8-14. Enabling System Restore

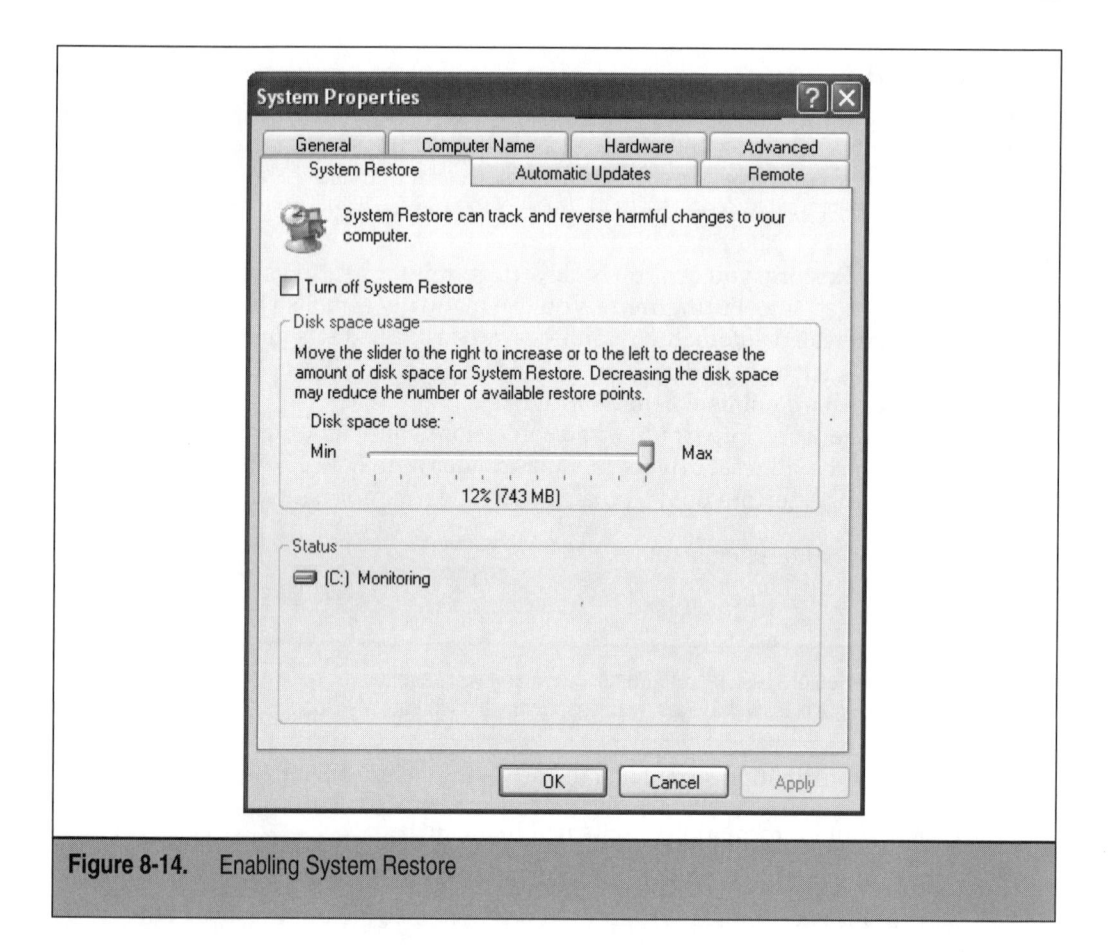

> **CAUTION** Disabling System Restore purges all restore points—so don't disable it without considering future consequences.

Rolling Back to a Restore Point

In order to roll back your computer's settings to a restore point, follow these steps:

1. Click Help and Support Center. Under Pick a task, click Undo changes to your computer with System Restore.
2. On the Welcome to System Restore window, click Restore my computer to an earlier time, and then click Next. (The resulting dialog box is shown in Figure 8-15.)

Figure 8-15. Selecting a restore point

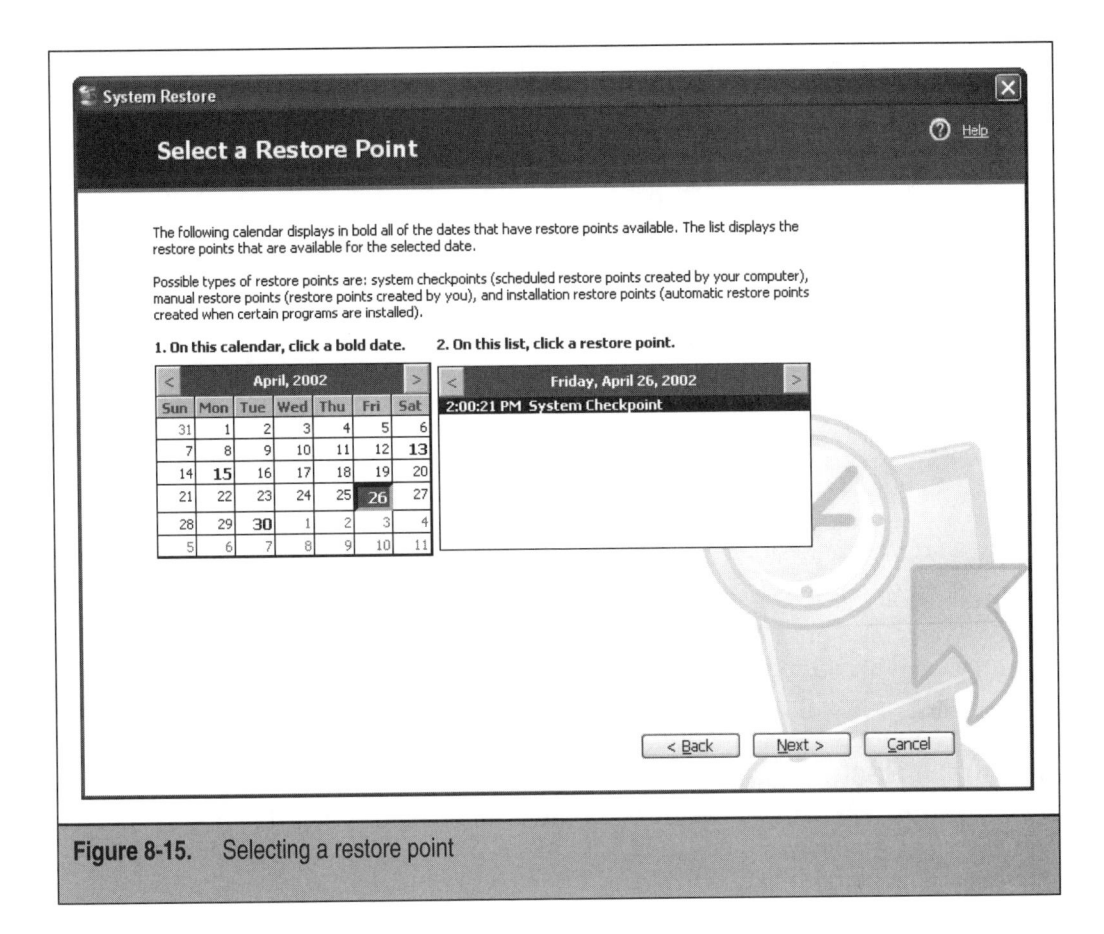

3. Choose a restore point on the Select a Restore Point screen, and then click Next.

NOTE Only go as far back as you need to. If you restore to a time that is too far back, then you might lose some properly working software that you have installed since then.

4. Click Next on the Confirm Restore Point screen.

When you select a restore point, System Restore examines the System Restore change logs and creates a restore map that it uses to revert your system. It uses the map to remove certain files and make changes to the Registry. If it turns out that the restore point did not solve the problem, you might elect to rerun System Restore and select an earlier restore point.

Establishing a Restore Point

When you install an unsigned device driver, Windows XP Professional makes a proactive move and creates a restore point. In addition, Windows XP Professional will also create restore points in these instances:

- When installing System Restore–compliant applications
- Every 10 hours the computer is on or once every 24 hours
- When installing an update by using Automatic Updates
- After a preset interval occurs
- When restoring data from a backup

However, you can also create your own restore points manually by following these steps:

1. Start System Restore.
2. Click Create a restore point, and then click Next.
3. You will be prompted to enter a description for the restore point (this is shown in Figure 8-16).
4. Click the Create button.

Undoing a Restore

It would be great if System Restore was perfect and would solve all your problems. However, it is possible that you won't get the results you wanted with the restore operation. If you aren't happy with the restore, you can undo the restore operation. This is accomplished by clicking Undo my last restoration on the Welcome to System Restore screen. Undoing a restore point is helpful if you wish to move to a restore point that was later than the one you initially selected.

Dr. Watson

Dr. Watson is a program that has been quietly included with Windows operating systems for several years. Dr. Watson (DRWTSN32.EXE) detects errors in programs, diagnoses errors, and logs diagnostic information. The information is found in the DRWTSN32.LOG file. This file can be sent to support personnel for analysis and diagnostics.

Dr. Watson starts automatically when a program error occurs. You can always start the program manually from the Tools menu, or from the command line. Figure 8-17 shows the Dr. Watson tool.

When a program fails, start Dr. Watson right away. Dr. Watson creates a snapshot of the state of your computer, reporting its progress as it goes. You can view a report, showing any trouble spots this tool encountered.

Figure 8-16. Manually creating a restore point

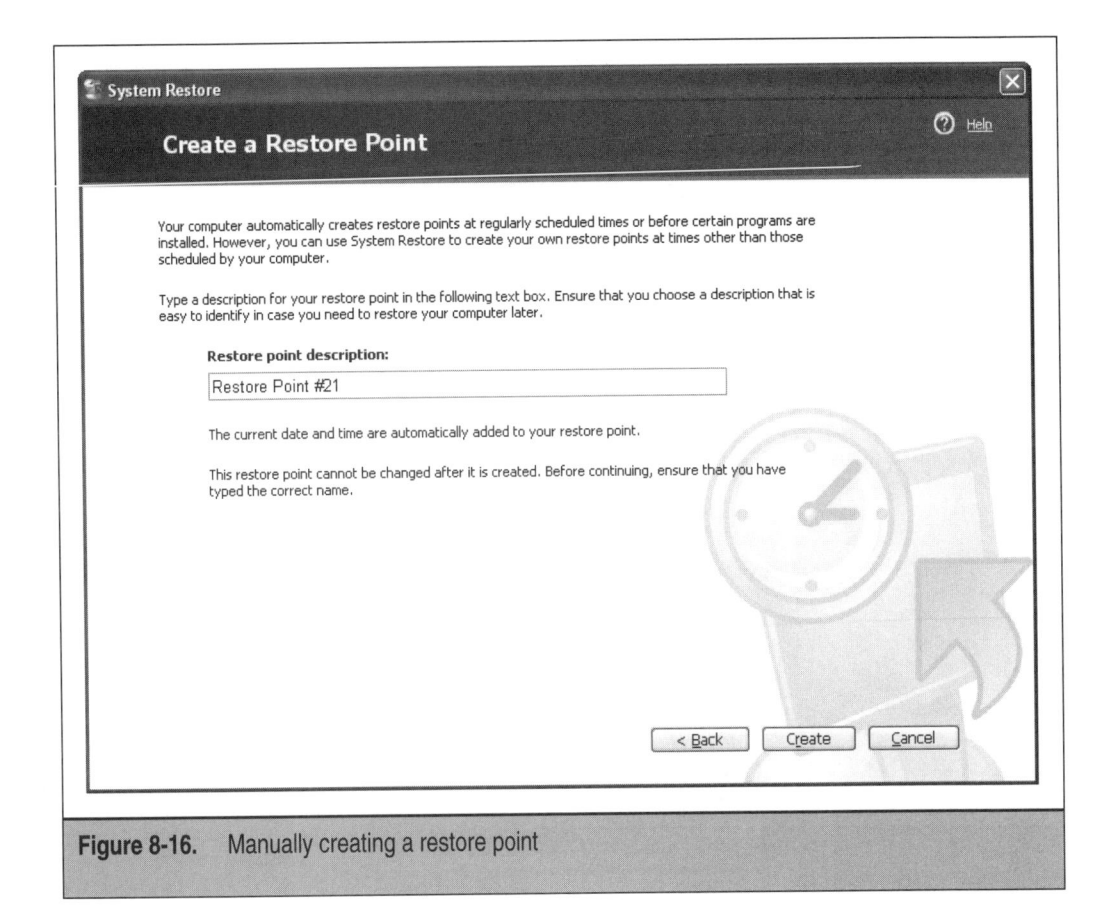

You can save this file, which can be used later for troubleshooting or support. If you care to research the problem yourself, examine the first few lines of the log. Next, go to the Microsoft Support Web page at http://support.microsoft.com and run a search for the names you recorded. You should be able to find some troubleshooting tips at the web site.

PROBLEM SOLVING

Problems don't only occur on a lone computer. As computer networks become larger and more complex, you'll more likely run into problems that are harder and harder to diagnose. This section examines computer networking problems and how you can solve connectivity issues.

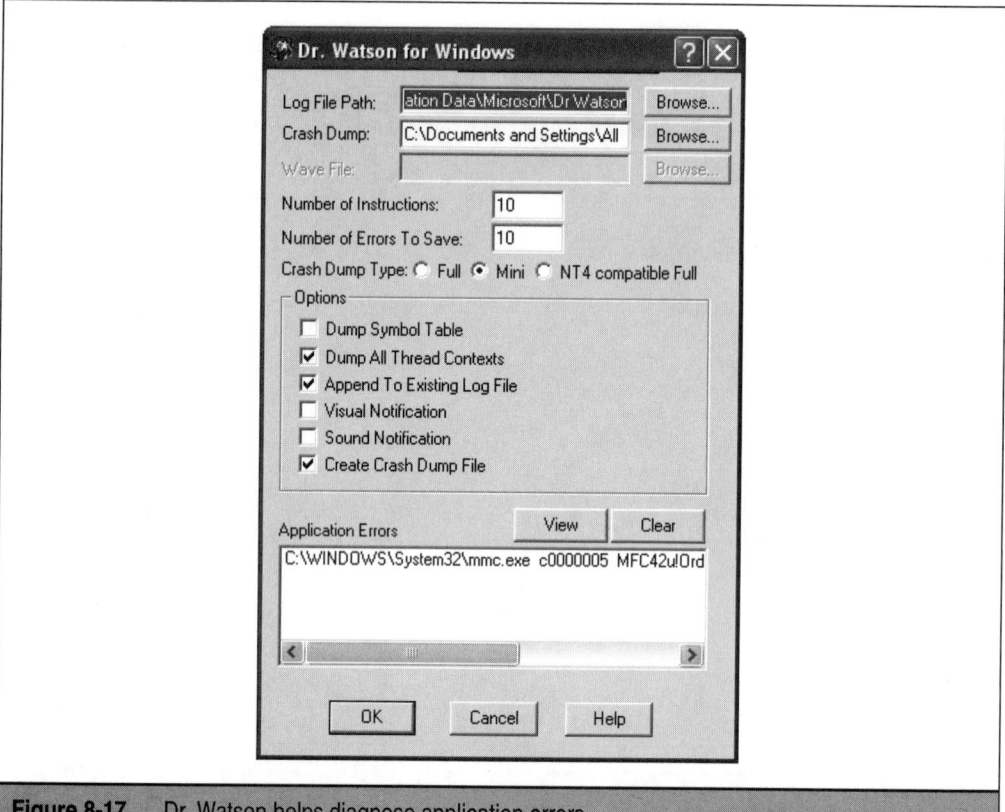

Figure 8-17. Dr. Watson helps diagnose application errors.

LAN Problems

Some common problems with LAN connectivity should be checked out if you encounter trouble. If you are not able to get a response from the LAN, there are two items you should examine first:

- Your network adapter might be having trouble. Check the local area connection icon in the Network Connections folder. If you are not connected, the icon will reflect this state. Use Device Manager to make sure your network adapter is working properly. If it isn't, this tool can be used to attempt to repair the problem.

- Make sure the LAN cable is firmly seated in the network adapter and the network device to which it connects. Did someone bump it? Did it somehow manage to come loose? If it is disconnected, an icon in the task bar will show the connection with a red X through it.

Troubleshooting a network can seem like a complex task (indeed it is), but the task can be made simpler by understanding the four basic places where a network can fail:

- The server
- The networking device (hub, switch, router, and so forth)
- The cabling
- The workstation

By narrowing down where the problem is, you just made your task much easier. For example, if you're able to determine that there is a problem with the server, you've made your job 75 percent easier. But how do you find the place where the problem has occurred?

Where to Start

First, you have to determine which clients are affected. Is there a problem on a single client, or has it radiated to several clients? If the problem is isolated to a single client, you know where to start looking. Next, if the computer has worked before, but has just recently had problems, you should check for a loose connection, a bad cable, or a malfunctioning network interface card (NIC).

If the client computer is new, then you're probably looking at a configuration problem. An easy way to check this connection is to plug another (already functioning) computer into this connection to see if it works properly. Doing this will rule out cabling problems or a faulty switch or hub.

If your problem is with several clients, again, consider what all these clients have in common. For example, if the ones that cannot connect are all new devices, it's likely a configuration issue. If the clients had worked previously, you can narrow the problem down to a faulty cable or a networking device.

If you have organization-wide connectivity issues, most likely there is a problem with the server, and you should concentrate your troubleshooting efforts there.

Client Problems

Troubleshooting a client can be a very complicated task. However, let's take a look at some of the most common sources of trouble for a Windows XP Professional client.

The first and easiest place to look for problems is with the protocol. By and large, your network is probably using the TCP/IP protocol suite. If the client can't see some other devices (or any at all), it's a good idea to check the protocol to ensure that they are all set up with TCP/IP.

This is done in Windows XP Professional by double-clicking the Network and Internet Connections icon in Control Panel. Next, click Network Connections, and right-click the connection you wish to examine. Choose Properties, and you'll see the protocols listed for this connection, as shown in Figure 8-18.

Figure 8-18. Checking your protocols

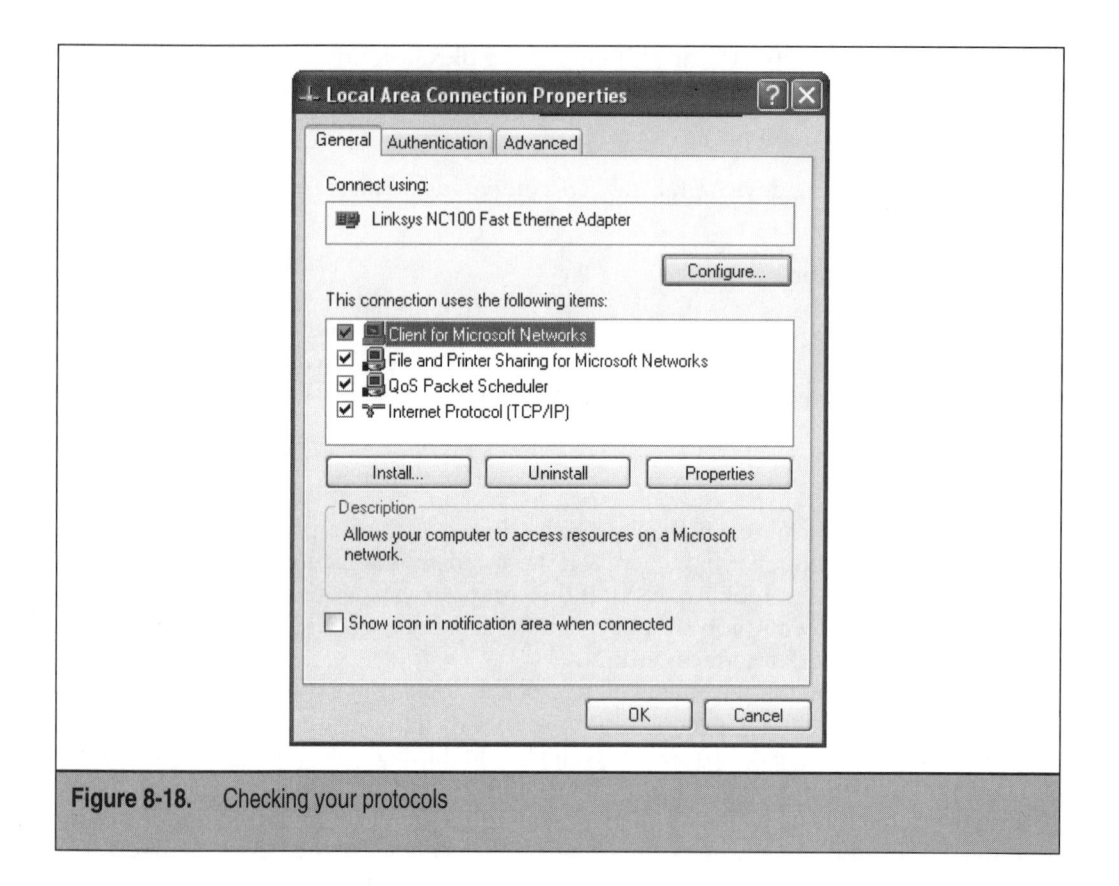

Compare the protocols listed against the protocols used in your network. Do they match? If not, you might have nailed down the source of the problem.

If you are using TCP/IP, you should try to ping your own IP address. If the ping comes back, then this protocol is working all right (but you still might have connectivity issues).

NOTE If you're not familiar with the ping command, we explain it in more detail later in this chapter, in the section "Ping."

Try to ping the address of another computer, your gateway, and another device or two on your network segment. This tests your NIC card. If the ping doesn't come back, then you know the problem is with your NIC. If the ping was successful, try pinging the same computer, but this time with the computer's name. If this test is unsuccessful, then you probably have a WINS or DNS server issue.

If the name ping was successful, try to ping a computer on a different network segment, or somewhere on the Internet. If this test is unsuccessful, then you know you likely have a misconfigured default gateway or a router issue. You should try the ping test with other clients, however. If they are able to ping the outside world, then the problem is likely the default gateway.

Switches and Hubs

If your problem is affecting a number of clients, then you might have problems with a switch or a hub. Consider the network shown in Figure 8-19.

If clients 9 through 16 can't access the network, what do they all have in common? They are all connected to the same hub. In this case, it is worthwhile to check the hub to see if it's having problems. There is another source of potential trouble in this example, however. Since the hubs are daisy-chained to ports on the switch, the problem could be on port 2 of the switch. This is another place to check for trouble.

Servers

If the problem is in your server, don't be overwhelmed by the role of the server in your network. It's a good idea to run through the basics that we mentioned for clients. At the heart of the matter, servers still must use the proper protocol and have functional cabling.

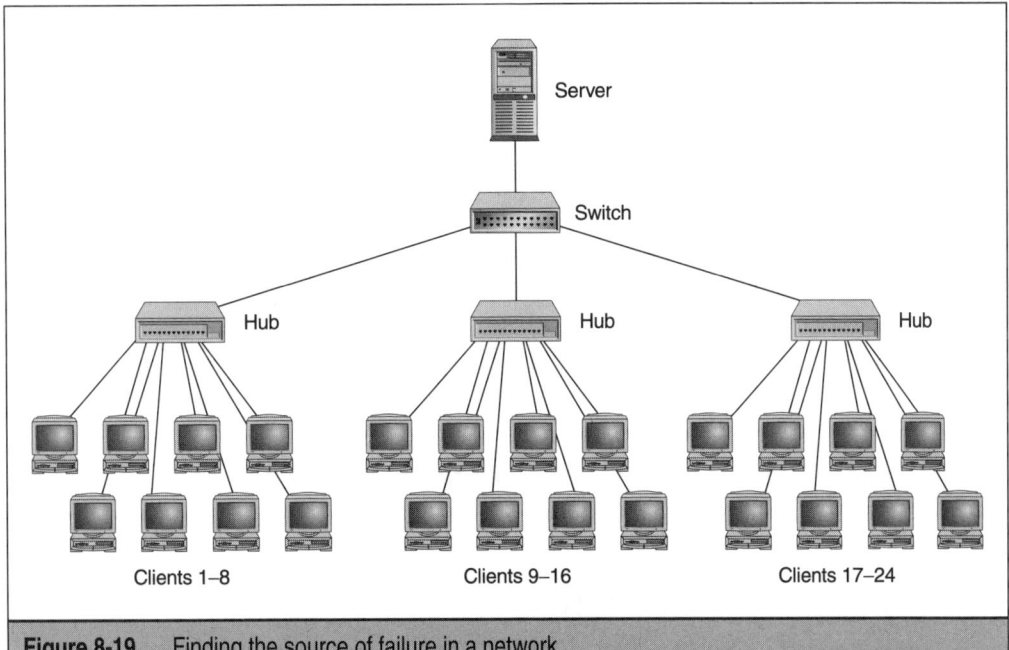

Figure 8-19. Finding the source of failure in a network

Remote Access Problems

Sometimes, the inability to connect to a remote server can be maddening, because you don't know if the problem is on your end or if it is with the remote server. The following lists give you some quick troubleshooting tips for various remote access problems. If you have problems forming a remote connection, you should check for a number of issues.

Modem Not Working

If your modem is not working properly, look into the following issues:

- The modem is not connected properly or it is turned off.
- You are not using the correct dial-in telephone number.
- Your modem is not compatible with Windows XP Professional. Check the hardware compatibility list at http://www.microsoft.com/hcl.
- You do not have a valid user account.
- Your telephone line does not support your connection speed.
- Your telephone line is digital.
- The remote access server is not running.

Connections Keep Dropping

If your connection continually drops off, check these conditions:

- You're getting dropped due to inactivity. Call again.
- Call waiting is interrupting your connection. Disable call waiting.
- Someone else has picked up an extension.
- The modem cable is disconnected.
- Modem software needs to be updated.
- Modem settings are not compatible with the remote access server.
- The remote access server is disconnected.
- Your modem cannot negotiate with the remote access server's modem.

Hardware Messages Appear When Trying to Connect

If you're getting pop-up messages proclaiming hardware problems when trying to make a connection, check the following issues:

- The external modem is turned off.
- Your modem is malfunctioning. Activate modem logging to test the connection.
- Your cable is not compatible with your modem.

ISDN Connections Receive a "No Answer" Message

If you're having problems with an ISDN connection that continually gets "No Answer" messages, check the following conditions:

- The line is busy.
- The line quality is poor.
- Your ISDN switching facility is busy. Try later.
- The phone number is not configured correctly. You might need two telephone numbers for your connection, or you might need just one. Check with your phone company to determine your needs.
- Your Service Profile Identifier (SPID) may not be correctly entered (applies to United States or Canada locations).
- Line-type negotiation is not enabled.
- The remote server is disconnected or turned off.

HELPFUL NETWORK TOOLS AND SCENARIOS

There are several TCP/IP troubleshooting tools that will help you successfully track down problems. These tools are PING, ARP, IPCONFIG, TRACERT, NBTSTAT, and PATHPING. These tools are all executed from the command line, and deliver results in the DOS format. Table 8-1 lists these tools and gives a quick description.

PING

Like sonar in a submarine movie, the PING command lets you know about your neighbors. In this case, however, it's not used for evading depth charges or firing torpedoes. Rather, it can tell you how long it takes for your packets to get from your computer to

Command-Line Tool	Description
ARP	Allows modification of the Address Resolution Protocol table
IPCONFIG	Shows current TCP/IP configuration and allows you to update these values
NBTSTAT	Displays the NetBIOS over TCP/IP connections, reloads the LMHosts cache, and determines the registered name and scope ID
PING	Sends echo requests to target devices
TRACERT	Lists the hops to a target device
PATHPING	Shows the degree of packet loss at any router or link

Table 8-1. TCP/IP Troubleshooting Tools

the destination computer. It does this by sending an Internet Control Message Protocol (ICMP) echo packet to the target device—be it a device on your LAN or a server on the other side of the globe.

If you're pinging a device on your LAN, the device should respond almost immediately. If so, then you know that both computers are working properly. However, if you have problems, there is a five-step process you should undertake:

1. Ping the local loopback address. If you get a reply from this address, then you know TCP/IP is configured on the local computer.

   `ping 127.0.0.1`

2. Next, ping the local IP address to ensure that you are not in contention with another device on the network

   `ping IP_address`

3. Ping the IP address of the default gateway. This checks to see if you can reach your closest router, so you can communicate with computers on other subnets.

   `ping IP_address_of_gateway`

4. Next, ping the address of a target device on another subnet. This checks to make sure that you can reach a device on another subnet.

   `ping IP_address_of_host`

5. Finally, ping the same target device, using its fully qualified domain name. If this fails, but step 4 worked, then you can isolate the problem to an issue with name resolution. From here, you should make sure that DNS servers are available, the Hosts and LMHosts tables are accurate, and WINS (if you use it) is properly configured.

   `ping IP_host_name`

The PING tool is used as follows:

```
ping [-t] [-a] [-n count] [-l size] [-f] [-i TTL] [-v TOS]
[-r count] [-s count] [[-j host-list] | [-k host-list]]
[-w timeout] destination-list
```

Some of PING's arguments include the following:

- **-t** Continues the ping effort until it is stopped (CTRL-C).
- **-n** *count* Pings *count* number of times and then stops.
- **-l** *size* Sends a packet of *size* bytes.
- **-f** Sets a Don't Fragment flag. This means that packets won't be broken into pieces by networking devices.
- **-w** *timeout* Sets the *timeout* value in milliseconds. The default timeout is 750 ms.

ARP

The Address Resolution Protocol (ARP) enables computers to form connections at the physical layer. It doesn't matter if you use NetBIOS or TCP/IP names for computers on your network, they must be converted into media access control (MAC) names of the NIC in the computer. When one station tries to connect to another, it must broadcast with ARP to figure out what the MAC address is. Once the Windows XP Professional computer determines the MAC address, it uses that address to communicate with the device. This IP-to-MAC conversion is stored in the computer's ARP table.

The ARP command allows you to view and edit the ARP table. This is a useful tool when trying to figure out name-resolution problems. The ARP command has the following syntax:

```
ARP -s inet_addr eth_addr [if_addr]
ARP -d inet_addr [if_addr]
ARP -a [inet_addr] [-N if_addr]
```

In these examples, the attributes work as described here:

- **-s** Adds the IP address (inet_addr) or the Ethernet MAC address (eth_addr) to the ARP table. The IP address is in the standard four-octet format, whereas the Ethernet address is six hexadecimal values, separated by dashes.
- **-d** Deletes the specified IP address from the table.
- **-a** Displays the current ARP table. If you include an IP address, only that particular computer's IP-to-MAC address table will be shown.

The [if_addr] argument specifies an IP address other than the default. If you just want to see the ARP table of the computer you're using, you must simply enter **arp -a**. The following listing exemplifies the results of the ARP command.

```
Interface: 192.168.1.101 on Interface 0x2000003
  Internet Address      Physical Address      Type
  192.168.1.1           00-04-5a-d0-b9-67     dynamic
  192.168.1.100         00-04-5a-69-cc-60     dynamic
  192.168.1.102         00-40-96-41-af-29     dynamic
```

IPCONFIG

The IPCONFIG tool is a great place to start tracking down TCP/IP problems. Its syntax is shown here:

```
ipconfig [/all | /release [adapter] | /renew [adapter]]
```

When used without any arguments, IPCONFIG displays just basic TCP/IP settings, including IP address, subnet mask, and default gateway for each network adapter card.

However, by adding arguments you can hone IPCONFIG's usability. Arguments include the following:

- **/all** Displays basic information, plus additional information, such as lease expiration times and name resolution services
- **/release** Releases the IP address for the specified adapter if the adapter used DHCP
- **/renew** Renews the IP address for the specified adapter if the adapter used DHCP

NOTE Entering **ipconfig ?** at the command prompt will generate a complete list of arguments.

```
Windows IP Configuration

        Host Name . . . . . . . . . . . . : geonosis
        Primary Dns Suffix  . . . . . . . :
        Node Type . . . . . . . . . . . . : Unknown
        IP Routing Enabled. . . . . . . . : No
        WINS Proxy Enabled. . . . . . . . : No

Ethernet adapter Local Area Connection:

        Connection-specific DNS Suffix  . :
        Description . . . . . . . . . . . : Linksys NC100 Fast Ethernet Adapter
        Physical Address. . . . . . . . . : 00-04-5A-69-CC-60
        Dhcp Enabled. . . . . . . . . . . : Yes
        Autoconfiguration Enabled . . . . : Yes
        IP Address. . . . . . . . . . . . : 192.168.1.100
        Subnet Mask . . . . . . . . . . . : 255.255.255.0
        Default Gateway . . . . . . . . . : 192.168.1.1
        DHCP Server . . . . . . . . . . . : 192.168.1.1
        DNS Servers . . . . . . . . . . . : 192.168.1.1
        Lease Obtained. . . . . . . . . . : Saturday, April 27, 2002 2:18:33 PM
        Lease Expires . . . . . . . . . . : Saturday, April 27, 2002 2:23:33 PM
```

Using the IPCONFIG tool can give you a great amount of information about your TCP/IP connections and their configuration. A good thing to check is the subnet mask. Make sure that it isn't 0.0.0.0, which indicates a conflict with another device on the subnet.

TRACERT

Trace Route (TRACERT) is a tool that is used to follow a packet as it moves from one device to another. It works by transmitting a packet with a time-to-live (TTL) value of 1. Generally, routers reduce the TTL value by 1 and then send the packet on its way. When a router experiences a TTL value of 0, it sends the packet back to the sender as

Windows XP Professional Network Administration

Table of Contents

Windows 2000/XP Network Model . . . . Pages 2–3

TCP/IP Protocol Suite . . . . Pages 4–5

Windows XP Professional Virtual Private Networks (VPNs) . . . . Page 6

Quality of Service Types . . . . Page 7

Windows XP Professional Internet Connection Sharing. . . . . Page 8

Windows 2000/XP Network Model

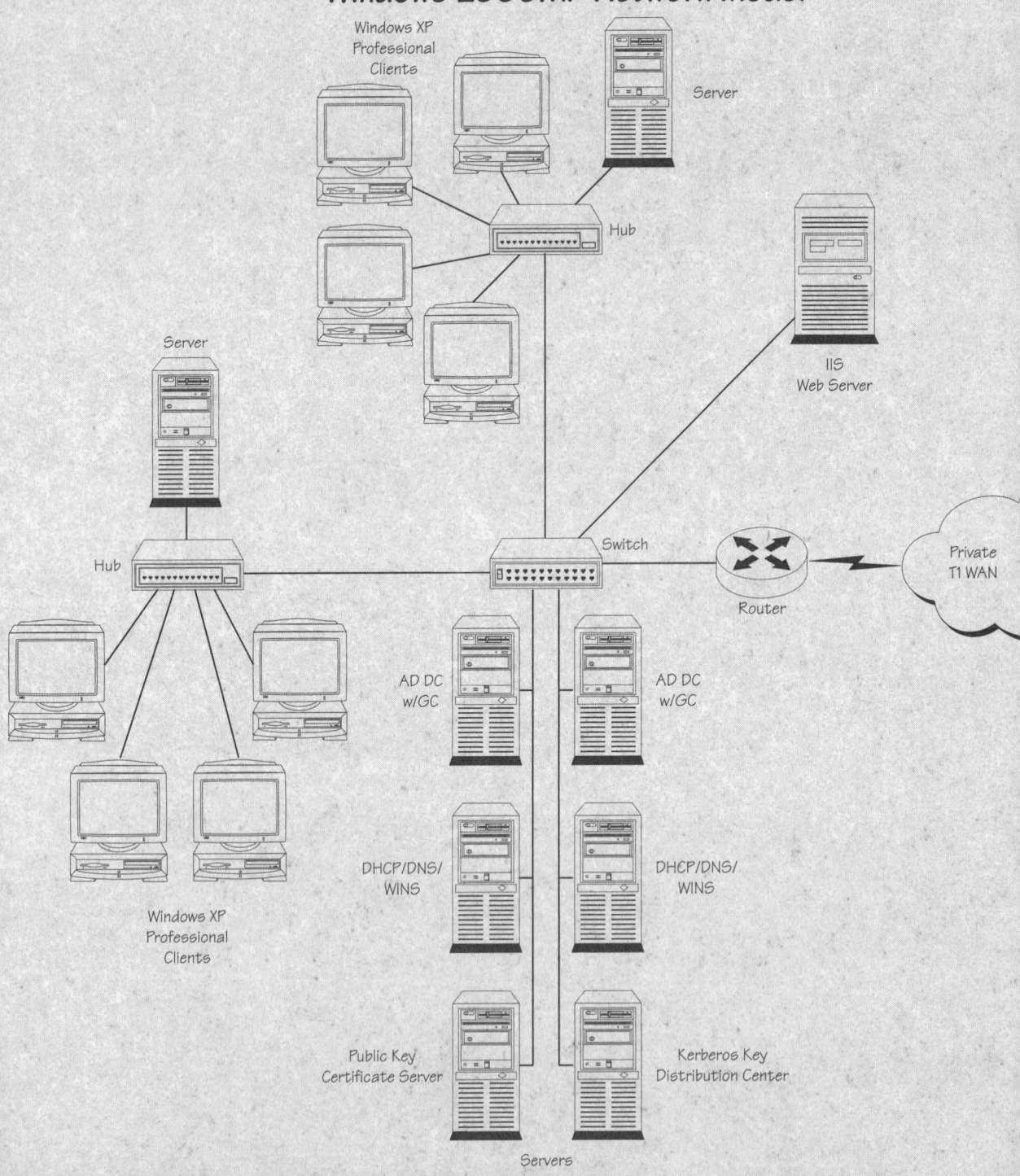

Windows XP Professional Clients

Server

Hub

IIS Web Server

Server

Hub

Switch

Router

Private T1 WAN

Windows XP Professional Clients

AD DC w/GC

AD DC w/GC

DHCP/DNS/WINS

DHCP/DNS/WINS

Public Key Certificate Server

Kerberos Key Distribution Center

Servers

Branch Office A

Branch Office B

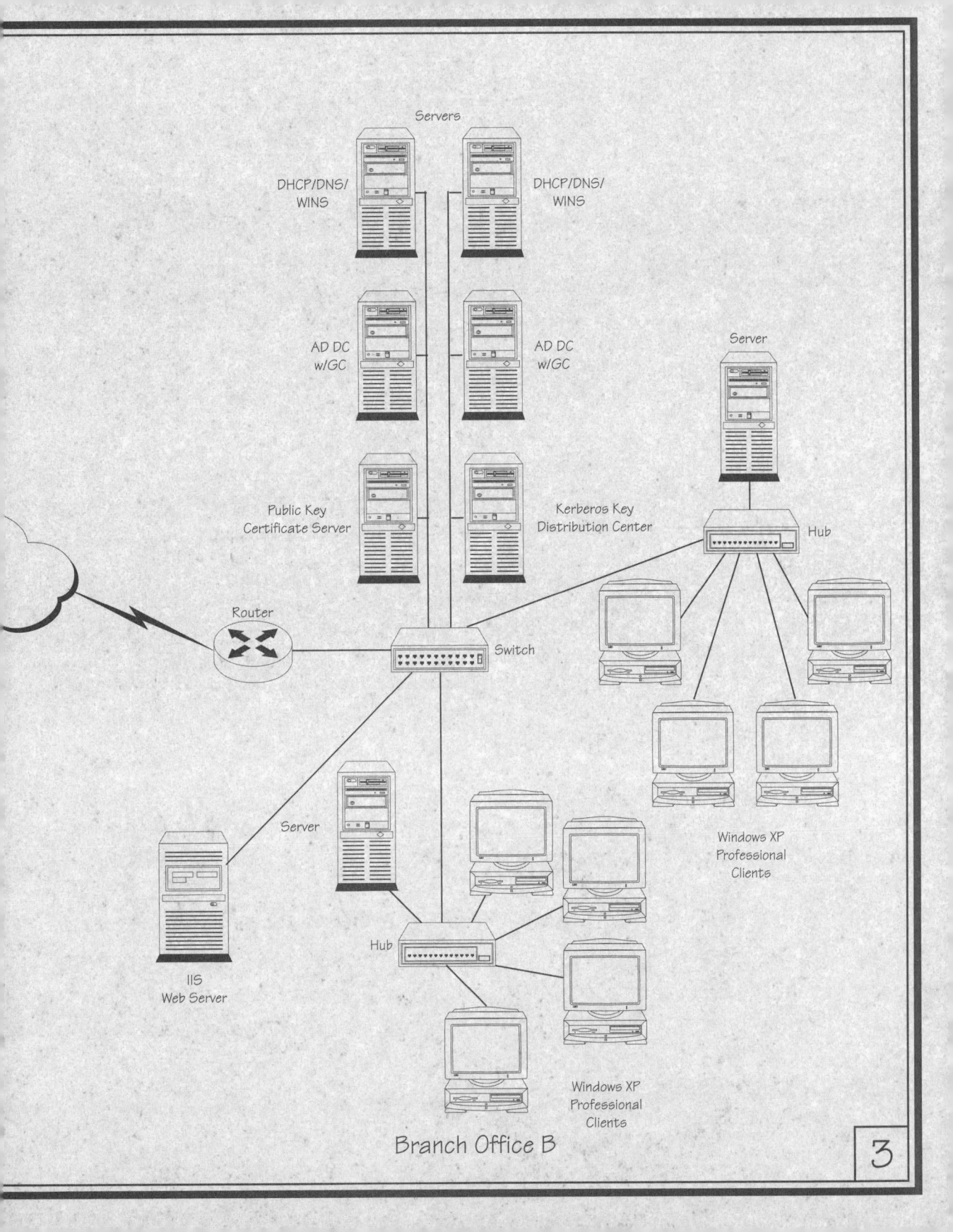

TCP/IP Protocol Suite

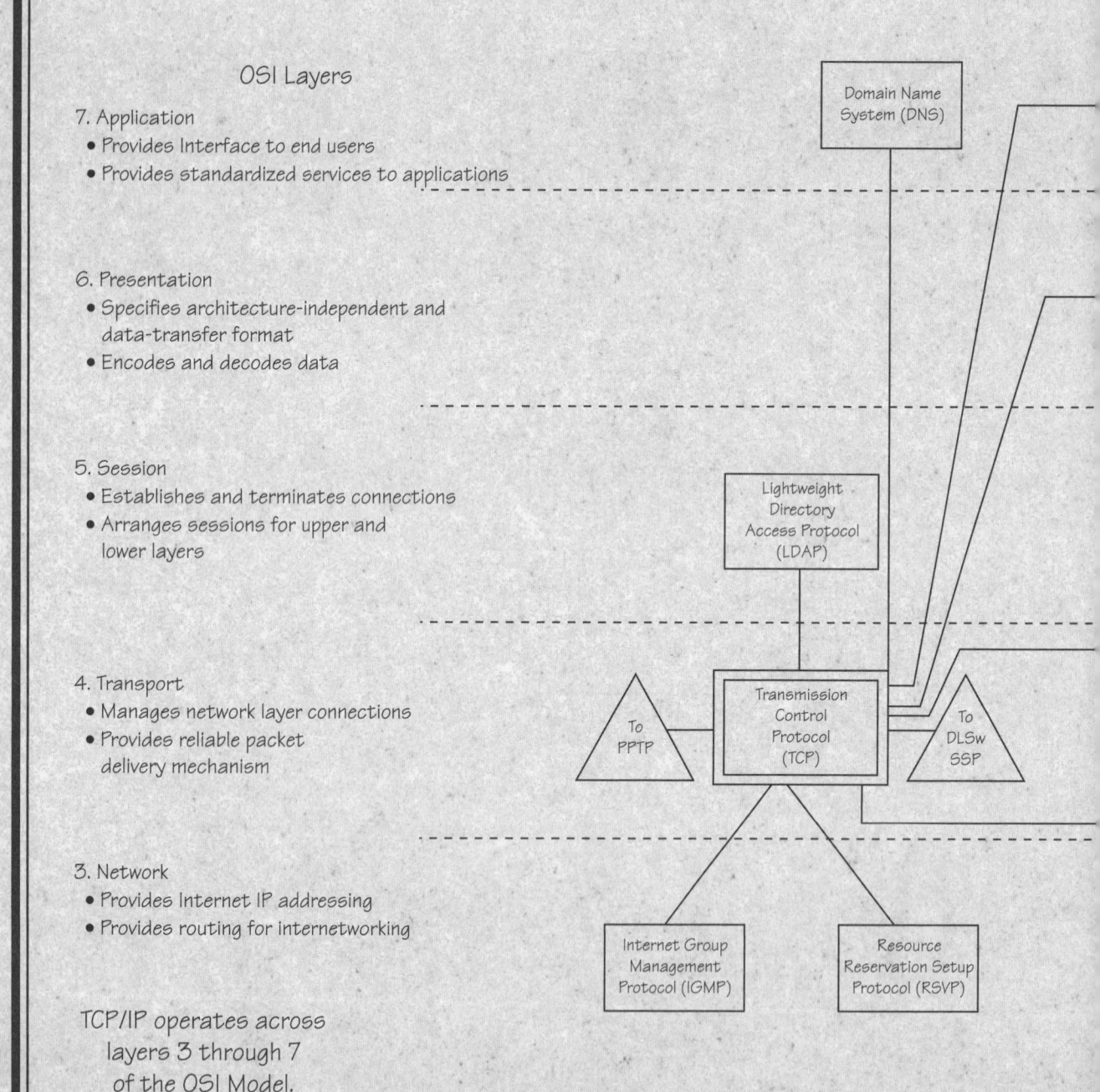

OSI Layers

7. Application
- Provides Interface to end users
- Provides standardized services to applications

6. Presentation
- Specifies architecture-independent and data-transfer format
- Encodes and decodes data

5. Session
- Establishes and terminates connections
- Arranges sessions for upper and lower layers

4. Transport
- Manages network layer connections
- Provides reliable packet delivery mechanism

3. Network
- Provides Internet IP addressing
- Provides routing for internetworking

TCP/IP operates across layers 3 through 7 of the OSI Model.

- Domain Name System (DNS)
- Lightweight Directory Access Protocol (LDAP)
- To PPTP
- Transmission Control Protocol (TCP)
- To DLSw SSP
- Internet Group Management Protocol (IGMP)
- Resource Reservation Setup Protocol (RSVP)

| HTTP | FTP | Telnet | SMTP |

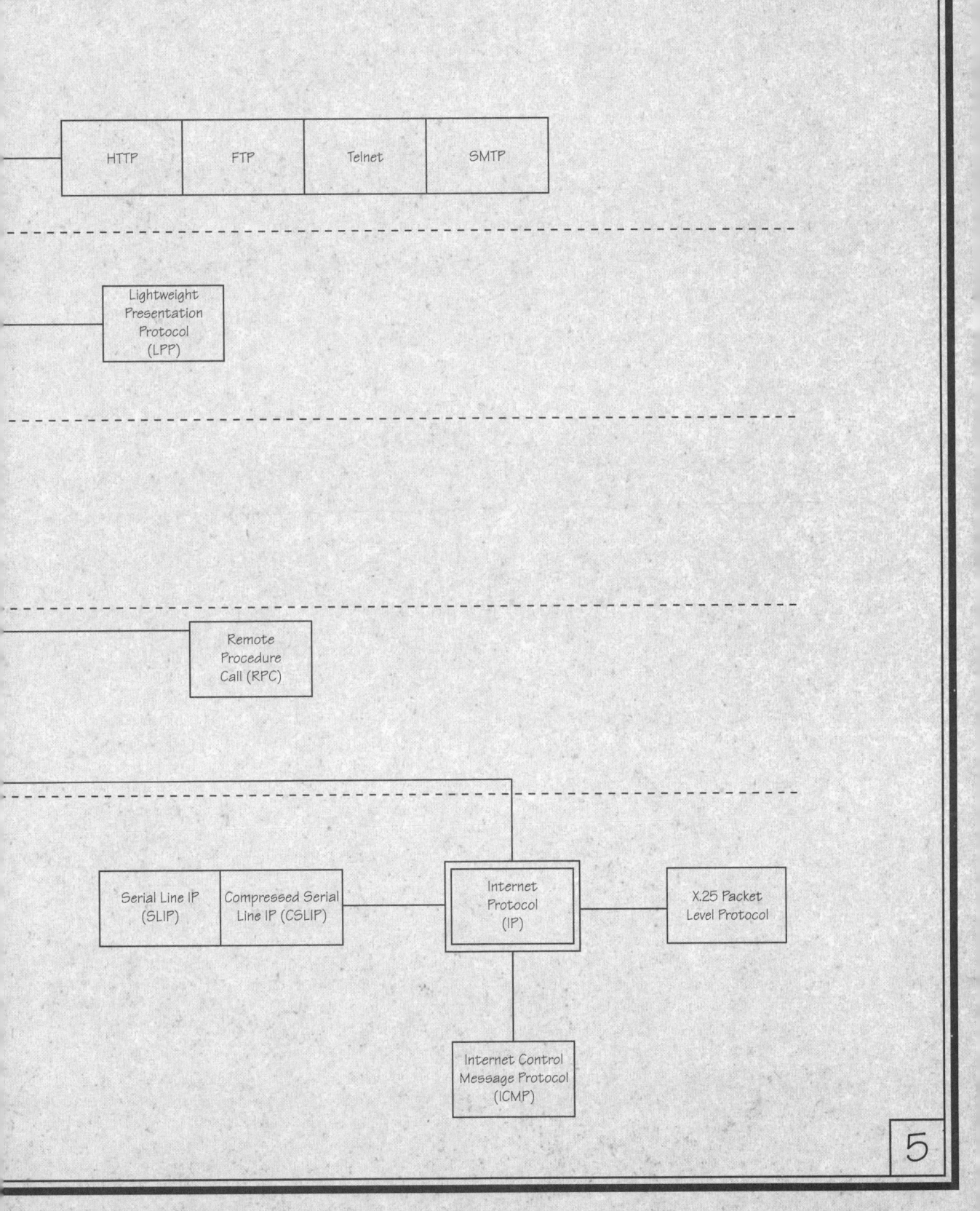

Lightweight Presentation Protocol (LPP)

Remote Procedure Call (RPC)

| Serial Line IP (SLIP) | Compressed Serial Line IP (CSLIP) | Internet Protocol (IP) | X.25 Packet Level Protocol |

Internet Control Message Protocol (ICMP)

5

Windows XP Professional Virtual Private Networks (VPNs)

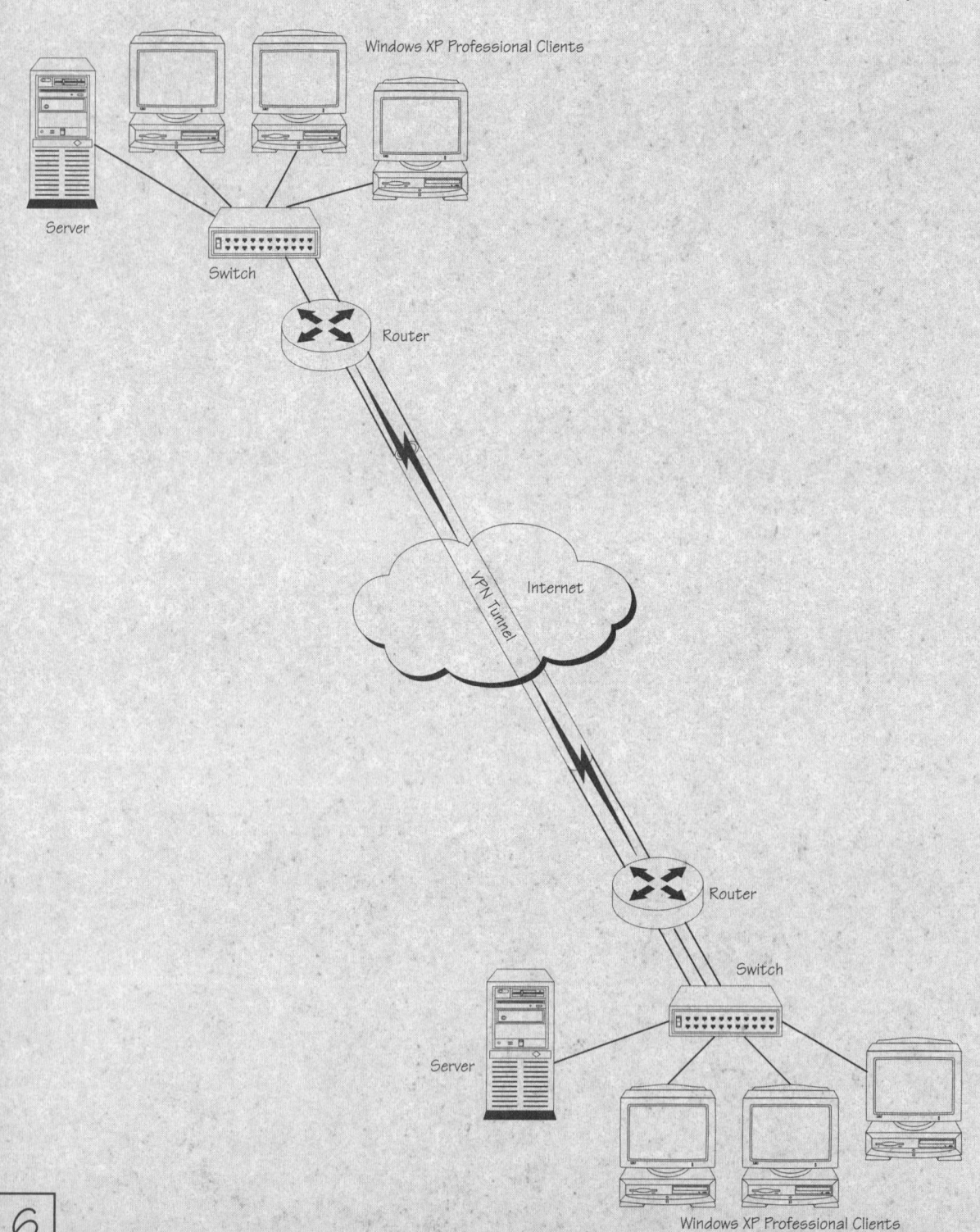

Quality of Service Types

Resource Reservation Setup Protocol (RSVP)

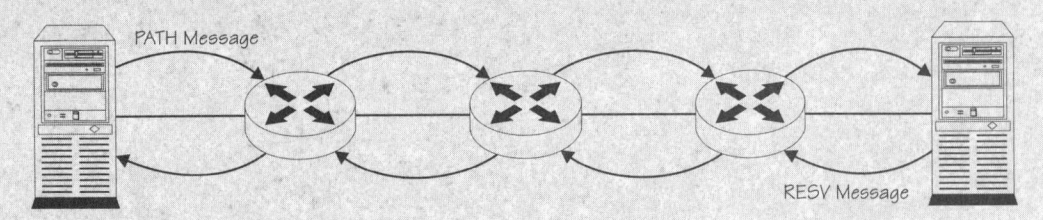

PATH Message

RESV Message

Resources are reserved at each network device in the path.

Differential Services (DiffServ)

Packets are sent out in accordance with QoS policies.

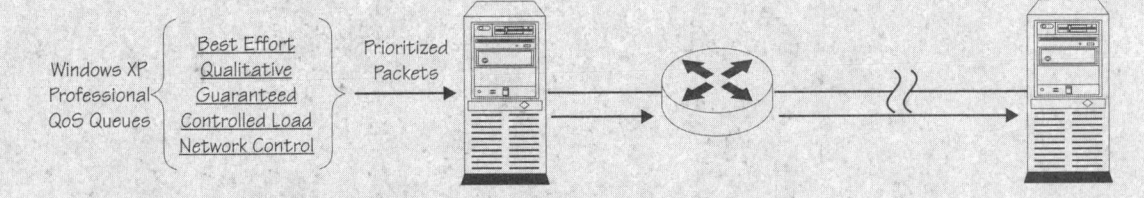

Windows XP Professional QoS Queues:
- Best Effort
- Qualitative
- Guaranteed
- Controlled Load
- Network Control

Prioritized Packets

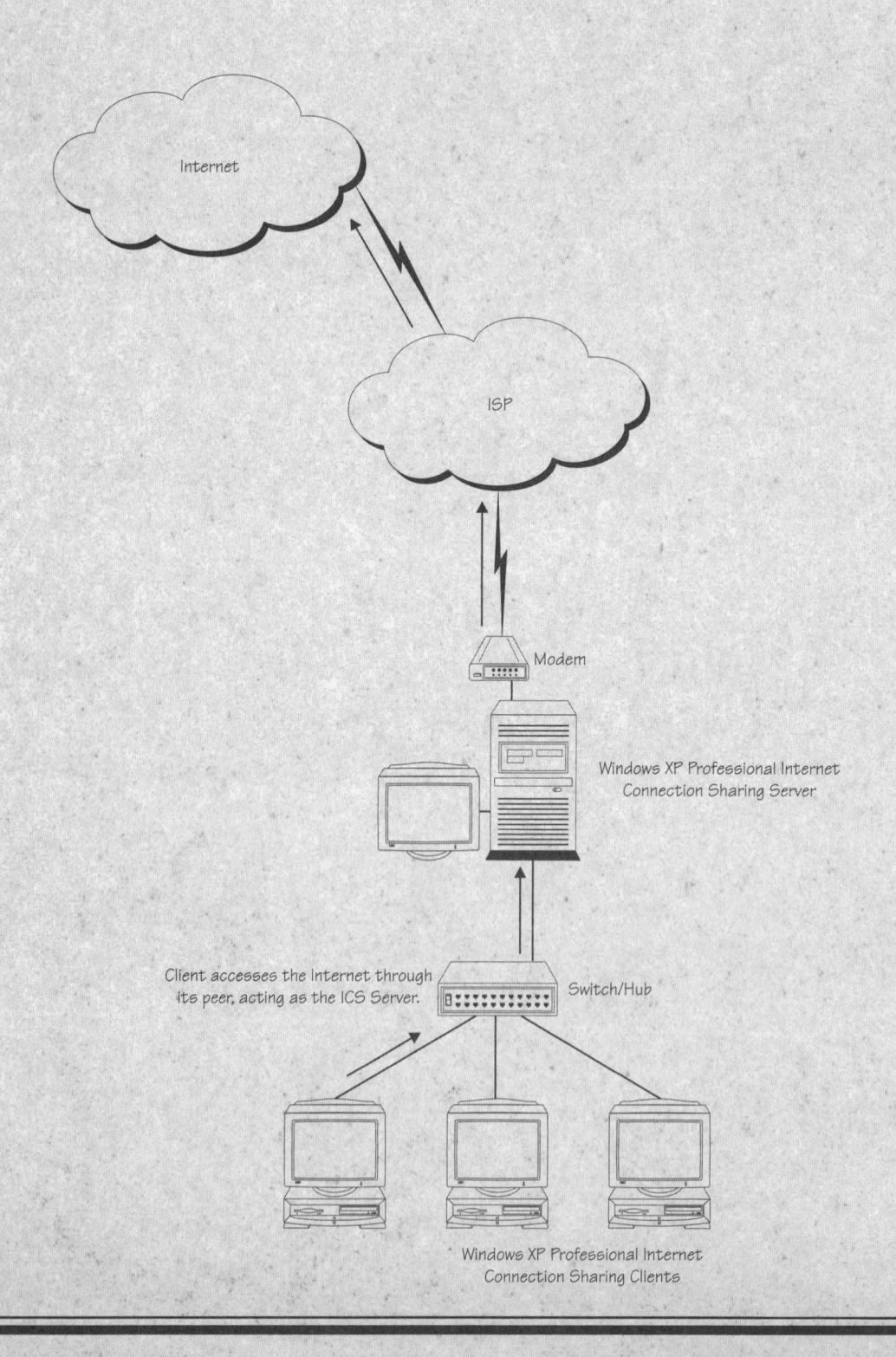

Windows XP Professional Internet Connection Sharing

Internet

ISP

Modem

Windows XP Professional Internet Connection Sharing Server

Client accesses the Internet through its peer, acting as the ICS Server.

Switch/Hub

Windows XP Professional Internet Connection Sharing Clients

expired. This action allows you to learn something about the router. The TRACERT tool does this for the first router in the packet's journey, adds 1 to the TTL, and then sends out another packet. The next packet makes it as far as the second router and then expires. This router returns the packet along with information about itself. This process repeats until the target device has been reached or the maximum number of hops has been reached.

The syntax for TRACERT is as follows:

```
tracert [-d] [-h maximum_hops] [-j host-list] [-w timeout] target_name
```

Some of TRACERT's arguments are described here:

- **-d**   Prevents resolving address to host names
- **-h** *maximum_hops*   Sets the upper limit on the total number of hops the trace can take in search of the target workstation
- **-j** *host-list*   Sets a loose source router along *host-list*
- **-w** *timeout*   Sets the timeout in milliseconds for each hop

You use TRACERT by simply entering **tracert** and the target device. For example:

```
C:\WINDOWS>tracert www.velte.com

Tracing route to www.velte.com [64.66.150.248]
over a maximum of 30 hops:

  1    66 ms    93 ms    63 ms  c6400-1-nrp-6.border.mpls.visi.com [209.98.0.20]
  2    73 ms    62 ms    59 ms  fa4-0-0.core-1.mpls.visi.com [209.98.3.222]
  3    75 ms    59 ms    84 ms  fa1-0-0.core-2.mpls.visi.com [209.98.3.195]
  4    68 ms    62 ms    58 ms  500.POS2-3.GW4.MSP1.ALTER.NET [157.130.98.1]
  5    65 ms    58 ms    63 ms  110.at-1-1-0.CL2.MSP1.ALTER.NET [152.63.67.102]
  6    69 ms    73 ms    69 ms  0.so-7-0-0.XL2.CHI2.ALTER.NET [152.63.145.50]
  7    72 ms    67 ms    83 ms  POS7-0.BR2.CHI2.ALTER.NET [152.63.67.245]
  8    99 ms   116 ms   101 ms  chi-brdr-03.inet.qwest.net [205.171.1.145]
  9   101 ms   101 ms   103 ms  chi-core-02.inet.qwest.net [205.171.20.137]
 10   100 ms   115 ms   100 ms  chi-edge-08.inet.qwest.net [205.171.20.114]
 11   110 ms   109 ms   117 ms  pos-6-0.ons.siteprotect.com [65.112.64.146]
 12   122 ms   115 ms   128 ms  c0-fe0.siteprotect.com [66.113.129.2]
 13   108 ms   107 ms   109 ms  www.velte.com [64.66.150.248]

Trace complete.
```

This is a useful tool to use if you can't run any of the utilities that come with the TCP/IP stack. Once you verify that TCP/IP is installed, and you can't use PING or TRACERT, you should remove and reinstall TCP/IP, which can become corrupted.

NBTSTAT

The NBTSTAT command-line tool is used to troubleshoot NetBIOS name-over-TCP/IP resolution problems. It displays protocol statistics and current TCP/IP connections using NetBIOS over TCP/IP (NetBT). When a network is functioning normally, NetBT resolves NetBIOS names to IP addresses.

The syntax for NBTSTAT is as follows:

```
nbtstat [-a RemoteName] [-A IP address] [-c] [-n] [-r] [-R] [-s] [S] [interval] ]
```

Some of NBTSTAT's arguments include the following:

- **-n** Displays the names that were registered locally by the system using the server or redirector services
- **-c** Lists the name–to–IP address mapping that is cached in the system
- **-R** Causes the system to purge the cache and reload it from the Lmhosts file (only entries with the #PRE designator in the Lmhosts file are automatically reloaded)
- **-a <name>** Returns the NetBIOS name table for the computer <name> as well as the MAC address of its NIC
- **-S** Lists the current NetBIOS sessions, their status, and some basic statistics

NOTE For more information about NBTSTAT, enter **nbtstat /?** at the command prompt.

An example of the NBTSTAT command is shown here:

```
C:\WINDOWS>nbtstat -n
Node IpAddress: [192.168.1.101] Scope Id: []
          NetBIOS Local Name Table

   Name              Type         Status
   ---------------------------------------------
   CORUSCANT        <00>  UNIQUE    Registered
   LAN              <00>  GROUP     Registered
   CORUSCANT        <03>  UNIQUE    Registered
   CORUSCANT        <20>  UNIQUE    Registered
   LAN              <1E>  GROUP     Registered
   DEFAULT          <03>  UNIQUE    Registered
```

Entering **nbtstat –c** produces the following results:

```
Node IpAddress: [192.168.1.101] Scope Id: []
          NetBIOS Remote Cache Name Table
```

```
Name                Type      Host Address       Life [sec]
---------------------------------------------------------------
ENDOR           <00>  UNIQUE     192.168.1.102       180
ENDOR           <20>  UNIQUE     192.168.1.102        60
```

PATHPING

Combining the PING and TRACERT tools is the PATHPING tool. This tool sends regular packets to each router on the way to its destination. It then computes the results based on the packets returned from each hop. Since PATHPING shows the degree of packet loss at any router or link, an administrator can determine which routers or links are causing problems on the network.

The syntax of PATHPING is as follows:

```
pathping [-n] [-h maximum_hops] [-g host-list] [-p period]
[-q num_queries] [-w timeout] [-T] [-R] target_name
```

Some of PATHPING's arguments include the following:

- **-n**   Does not resolve addresses to host names.
- **-h** *maximum_hops*   Specifies the maximum number of hops to search for a target. The default setting is 30 hops.
- **-p** *period*   Specifies the number of milliseconds to wait between pings. The default setting is 250 ms.
- **-q** *num_queries*   Specifies the number of queries to each computer along the route. The default value is 100.
- **-w** *timeout*   Specifies the number of milliseconds to wait for each reply. The default setting is 3000ms (or 3 seconds).

The following example checks the route and path between a computer in the United States and the University of Science and Technology in China, giving a taste of PATHPING's usage and results.

```
C:\pathping 202.38.64.2

Tracing route to www.ustc.edu.cn [202.38.64.2]
over a maximum of 30 hops:
   0  Endor [65.103.23.213]
   1  mplsapanas12poolC254.mpls.uswest.net [65.103.23.254]
   2  www.ustc.edu.cn [207.225.140.29]
   3  min-core-02.tamerica.net [205.171.128.25]
   4  den-core-02.tamerica.net [205.171.8.97]
   5  500.POS4-1.GW4.DEN4.ALTER.NET [157.130.172.41]
   6  175.at-5-0-0.XR1.DEN4.ALTER.NET [152.63.93.202]
   7  177.at-2-0-0.XR1.SLT4.ALTER.NET [152.63.94.46]
```

```
     8  0.so-0-0-0.TL1.SLT4.ALTER.NET [152.63.9.70]
     9  0.so-4-0-0.TL1.LAX9.ALTER.NET [152.63.0.165]
    10  0.so-0-0-0.XL1.LAX9.ALTER.NET [152.63.115.137]
    11  POS6-0.BR3.LAX9.ALTER.NET [152.63.115.1]
    12  if-5-0-1.bb3.LosAngeles.Teleglobe.net [207.45.200.197]
    13  if-2-1.core1.LosAngeles.Teleglobe.net [207.45.220.97]
    14  if-6-0.core1.LosAngeles2.Teleglobe.net [64.86.83.134]
    15  if-0-0-0.bb1.LosAngeles2.Teleglobe.net [64.86.80.38]
    16  64.86.173.34
    17  202.112.61.21
    18  202.112.61.137
    19  202.112.61.193
    20  whbj4.cernet.net [202.112.46.66]
    21  hfwh3.cernet.net [202.112.46.130]
    22  hef1.cernet.net [202.112.38.126]
    23    *        *        *
Computing statistics for 575 seconds...
             Source to Here   This Node/Link
Hop  RTT     Lost/Sent = Pct  Lost/Sent = Pct  Address
  0                                            Endor [65.103.23.213]
                               5/ 100 =  5%    |
  1  172ms    6/ 100 =  6%    1/ 100 =  1%
mplsapanas12poolC254.mpls.uswest.net [65.103.23.254]
                               0/ 100 =  0%    |
  2  167ms    6/ 100 =  6%    1/ 100 =  1%    207.225.140.29
                               0/ 100 =  0%    |
  3  166ms    6/ 100 =  6%    1/ 100 =  1%
min-core-02.tamerica.net [205.171.128.25]
                               0/ 100 =  0%    |
  4  196ms    6/ 100 =  6%    1/ 100 =  1%
den-core-02.tamerica.net [205.171.8.97]
                               0/ 100 =  0%    |
  5  215ms    6/ 100 =  6%    1/ 100 =  1%
500.POS4-1.GW4.DEN4.ALTER.NET [157.130.172.41]
                               0/ 100 =  0%    |
  6  211ms    6/ 100 =  6%    1/ 100 =  1%
175.at-5-0-0.XR1.DEN4.ALTER.NET [152.63.93.202]
                               0/ 100 =  0%    |
  7  215ms    6/ 100 =  6%    1/ 100 =  1%
177.at-2-0-0.XR1.SLT4.ALTER.NET [152.63.94.46]
                               0/ 100 =  0%    |
  8  220ms    6/ 100 =  6%    1/ 100 =  1%
0.so-0-0-0.TL1.SLT4.ALTER.NET [152.63.9.70]
                               0/ 100 =  0%    |
  9  295ms    5/ 100 =  5%    0/ 100 =  0%
0.so-4-0-0.TL1.LAX9.ALTER.NET [152.63.0.165]
                               0/ 100 =  0%    |
 10  293ms    5/ 100 =  5%    0/ 100 =  0%
0.so-0-0-0.XL1.LAX9.ALTER.NET [152.63.115.137]
```

```
                                 0/ 100 =   0%    |
 11   295ms      5/ 100 =  5%    0/ 100 =   0%
POS6-0.BR3.LAX9.ALTER.NET [152.63.115.1]
                                 0/ 100 =   0%    |
 12   294ms      5/ 100 =  5%    0/ 100 =   0%
if-5-0-1.bb3.LosAngeles.Teleglobe.net [207.45.200.197]
                                 0/ 100 =   0%    |
 13   321ms      5/ 100 =  5%    0/ 100 =   0%
if-2-1.core1.LosAngeles.Teleglobe.net [207.45.220.97]
                                 0/ 100 =   0%    |
 14   280ms      5/ 100 =  5%    0/ 100 =   0%
if-6-0.core1.LosAngeles2.Teleglobe.net [64.86.83.134]
                                 0/ 100 =   0%    |
 15   287ms      5/ 100 =  5%    0/ 100 =   0%
if-0-0-0.bb1.LosAngeles2.Teleglobe.net [64.86.80.38]
                                 0/ 100 =   0%    |
 16   442ms      5/ 100 =  5%    0/ 100 =   0%   64.86.173.34
                                 0/ 100 =   0%    |
 17   456ms      5/ 100 =  5%    0/ 100 =   0%   202.112.61.21
                                 0/ 100 =   0%    |
 18   453ms      5/ 100 =  5%    0/ 100 =   0%   202.112.61.137
                                 0/ 100 =   0%    |
 19   444ms      5/ 100 =  5%    0/ 100 =   0%   202.112.61.193
                                 1/ 100 =   1%    |
 20   426ms      6/ 100 =  6%    0/ 100 =   0%   whbj4.cernet.net [202.112.46.66]
                                 0/ 100 =   0%    |
 21   433ms      6/ 100 =  6%    0/ 100 =   0%   hfwh3.cernet.net [202.112.46.130]
                                 0/ 100 =   0%    |
 22   428ms      6/ 100 =  6%    0/ 100 =   0%   hef1.cernet.net [202.112.38.126]
                                94/ 100 =  94%    |
 23   ---      100/ 100 =100%    0/ 100 =   0%   Endor [0.0.0.0]

Trace complete.
```

Troubleshooting can be a very tricky, difficult task. Often, what *should* be the problem isn't the trouble at all. Even though troubleshooting can be a maddening task, between the tips and techniques we've presented here, along with the tools for Windows XP Professional and TCP/IP networks, hopefully, troubleshooting your own networks won't be the cause of too much stress.

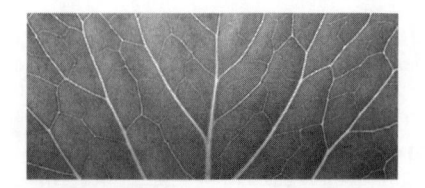

PART III

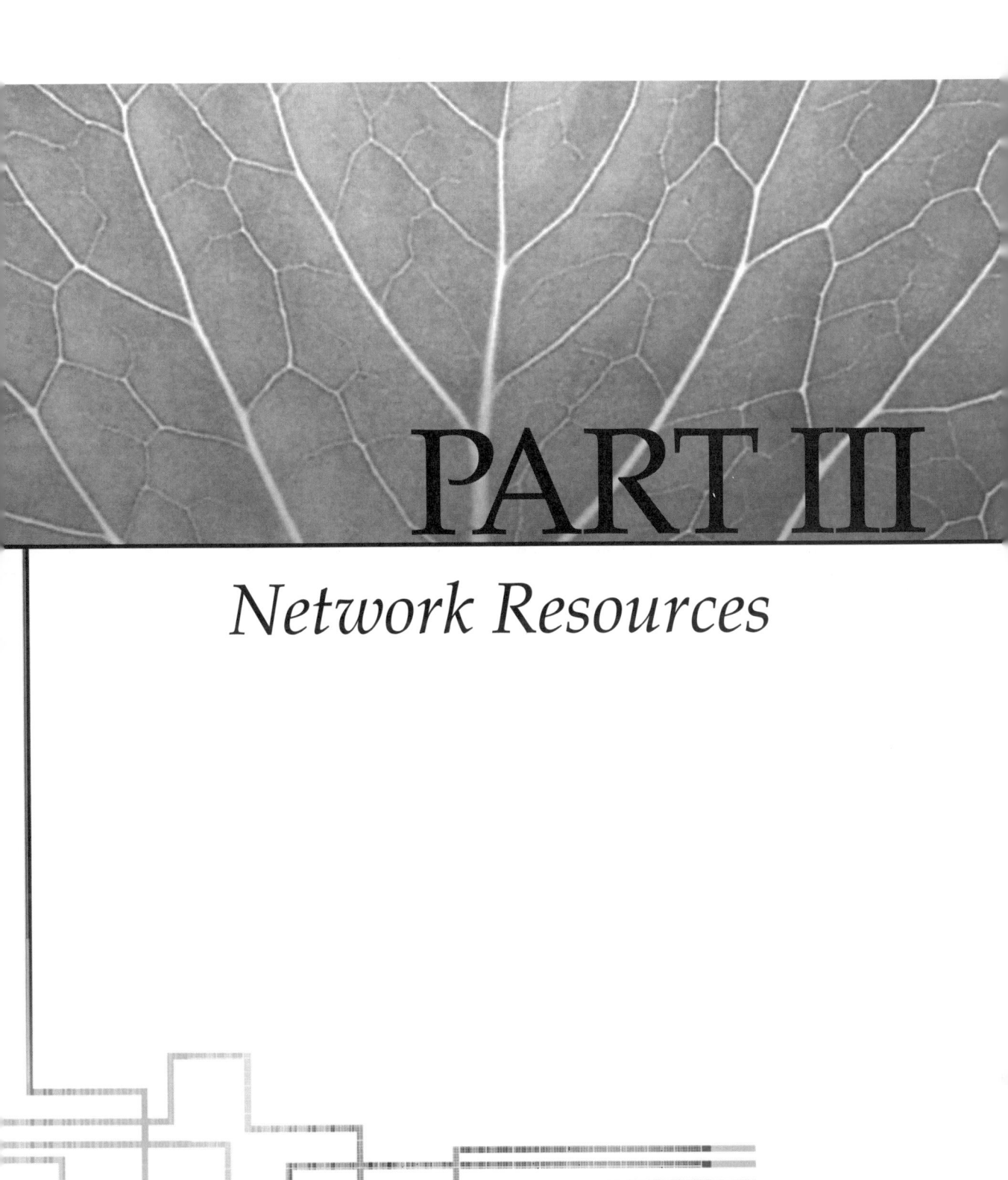

Network Resources

CHAPTER 9

Network Security

When constructing a Windows XP Professional network, security must be managed on two fronts: at the local computer level and at the network level. This chapter examines both areas, first with a discussion of Windows XP Professional, and then with a discussion of server security.

WINDOWS XP PROFESSIONAL SECURITY FEATURES

Windows XP Professional keeps your system safe and secure in a number of ways. Not only are there tried-and-true security measures that are holdovers from earlier versions of Windows, there are also new features that enhance security. We'll talk about managing local security policies, logging, Internet Connection Firewall Security Logs, security templates, the logon process, and finally security configuration and analysis. Not only can these tools be used for managing Windows XP Professional security, but some can be used for managing security settings in a domain as well.

First, however, let's start with an overview of Windows XP Professional's security improvements.

What's New in Windows XP Professional

Windows security is a moving target. That is, whenever a new version of Windows is released, you can expect that it will include significant security improvements as part of the upgrade. Windows XP Professional is no exception.

Windows XP Professional still carries over most of the popular security features found on Windows NT and Windows 2000, but it offers new features, including these:

- **Administrative ownership** In earlier versions of Windows, any resources created by the administrator (such as files and folders) were shared by the entire group. However, in Windows XP Professional, these resources belong to the individual administrator who created them.

- **Encrypting File System (EFS) recovery agent** In Windows 2000, if you try to configure an EFS recovery policy with no recovery agent certificates, then EFS is automatically disabled. In Windows XP Professional, you can encrypt files without a Data Recovery Agent (DRA).

- **Printer installation** Only administrators and power users are able to install local printers. Administrators have this ability, by default, but power users must be granted this privilege.

- **Blank password limitation** Windows XP Professional users can use blank passwords; however, they are only able to log in, physically, at the local computer.

- **Software restriction** Windows XP Professional security policies can be assigned to specified applications based on a file path, Internet zone, or certificate.

- **Fast user switching** On Windows XP Professional machines that are not connected to a domain, the computer can switch from one user to another without having to log off or close applications.
- **Password Reset Wizard** In the event a user forgets his or her password, that user can use a reset disk to access his or her local account.

The following sections examine some of these topics in more depth, whereas others are self-explanatory and occur on the Windows XP Professional system by default.

Local Security Policy

The ability to create and manage security policies on a local computer is accomplished via a snap-in to the MMC. The snap in will allow you to not only view the local security policy, but also make changes to it.

Viewing

To view the security policy settings on a Windows XP Professional computer, select Start | Control Panel | Performance and Maintenance | Administrative Tools. Double-click Local Security Policy. The resulting screen is shown in Figure 9-1.

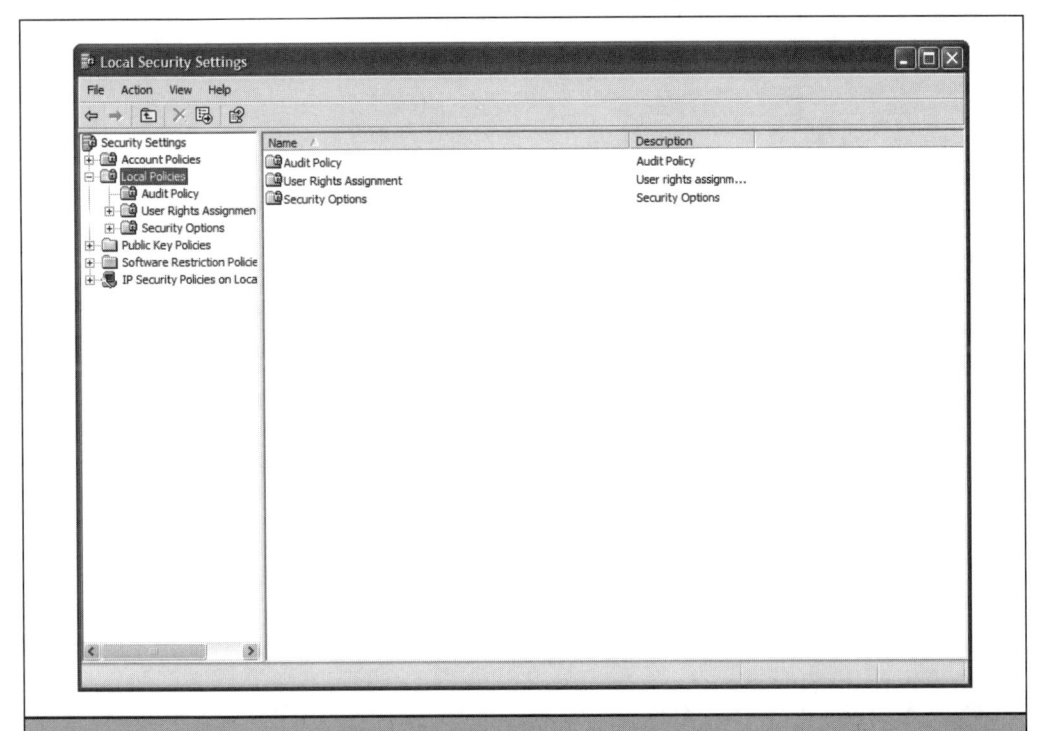

Figure 9-1. Viewing local security policy

> **NOTE** You can also start this tool from the command line by entering **secpol.msc**.

Managing Local Policies

To view individual security policies, double-click the icon of the security topic you wish to examine. For example, the following steps illustrate how to manage security settings under the Security Options folder. Once you've double-clicked Security Options, a list of security settings appears, as shown in Figure 9-2.

Next, click the setting Devices: Unsigned driver installation behavior. As Figure 9-3 shows, there are three choices for this setting's behavior.

- Silently succeed
- Warn, but allow installation
- Do not allow installation

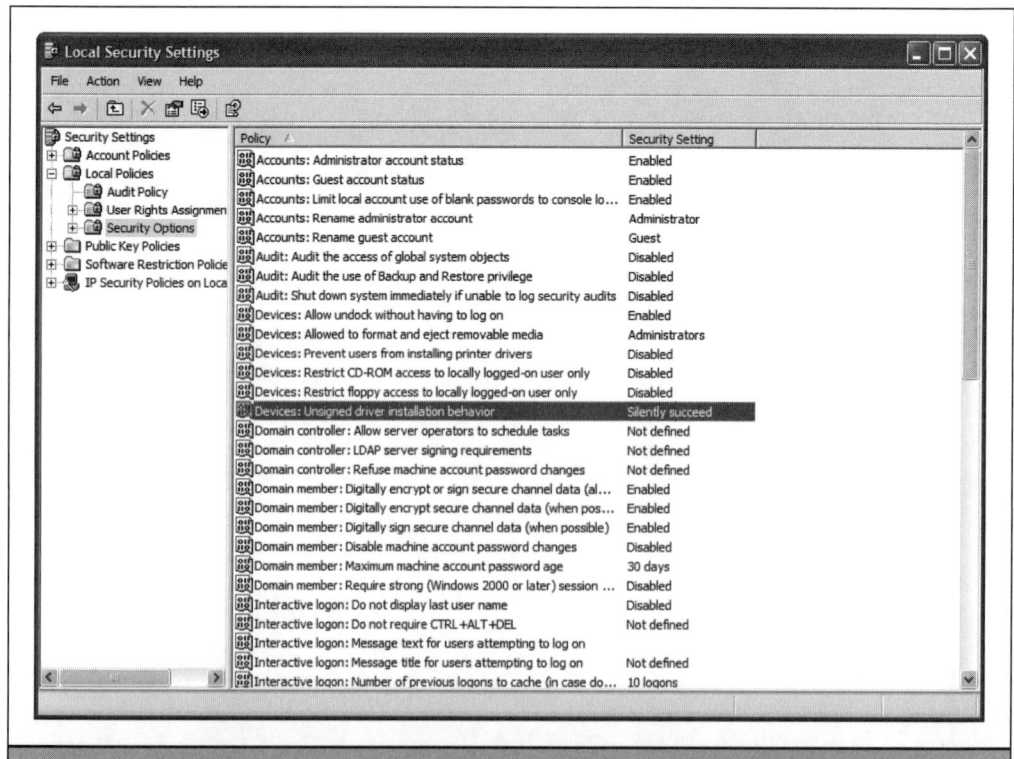

Figure 9-2. Security settings contained in the Security Options local policy folder

Figure 9-3. Expanded setting details

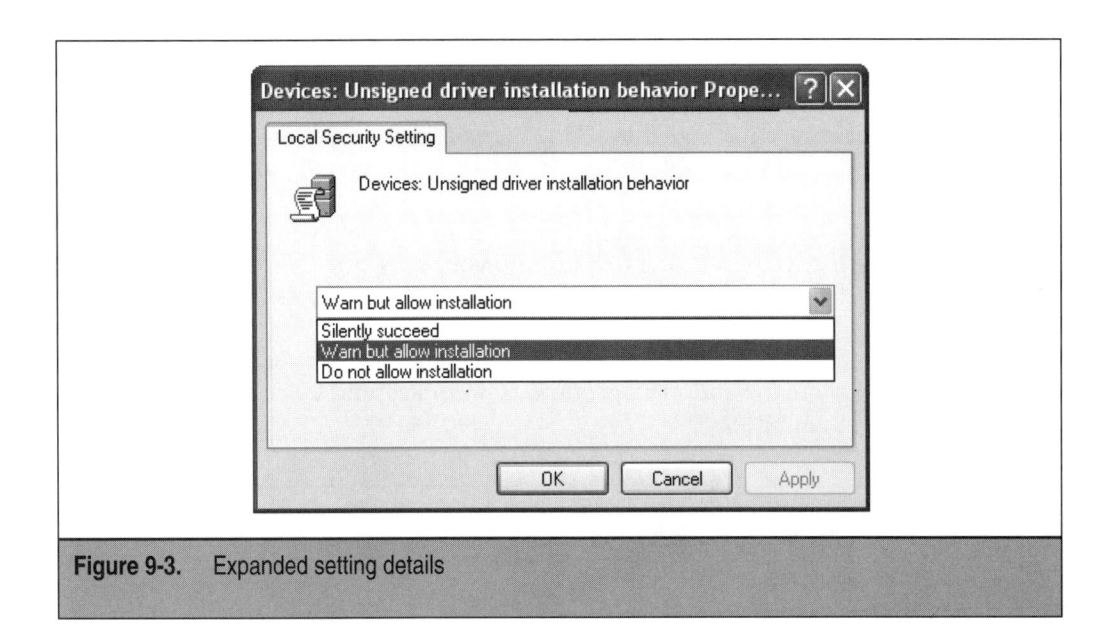

ICF Security Logging

In Chapter 5, we talked about the basic usage and management of Windows XP Professional's Internet Connection Firewall (ICF). Several additional security features in the realm of logging will make your ICF experience more useful.

The ICF security log allows you to generate a list of your firewall's activity—namely, whether traffic is permitted or rejected by ICF. You can customize your ICF's actions by managing different Internet Control Message Protocol (ICMP) rules. For example, ICMP enables you to manage whether or not you wish to allow the following:

- Incoming echo requests
- Incoming timestamp requests
- Incoming router requests
- Redirects

Based on your ICMP rules, various bits of information will be maintained in the ICF security log. The ICMP rules in Windows XP Professional's ICF are helpful in that they don't totally shut off your network from the outside world, although they severely limit access.

The ICF Log File

ICF logs have their own unique format. First is a header listing the version of ICF used, the name of the security log, a note that all log entries are in local time, and a list of fields available for log entries. Table 9-1 explains the entries you are likely to see in an ICS security log.

The ICF security log is useful in that, when used judiciously, you are able to examine it and see if anyone is trying to hack into your network. By examining the action, src-ip, and dst-ip fields, you should be able to tell if anyone is trying to do harm to your network in general, or a specific device in particular.

Now that you know what your security log will contain, let's take a closer look at how you can enable logging and manage various housekeeping functions that can make ICF easier to administer.

Field	Description
action	The operation trapped by the firewall. Entries include: OPEN CLOSE DROP INFO-EVENTS-LOST (this specifies a number of events that occurred, but were not stored in the log).
date	The date of the file entry, stored in the format YY-MM-DD.
dst-ip	The IP address of the packet's destination.
dst-port	The port number of the packet's destination.
icmpcode	A number representing the code field of the ICMP message.
icmptype	A number representing the type field of the ICMP message.
info	An information entry for the event that depends on the type of action.
protocol	The protocol for the communication. When the protocol is not TCP, UDP, or ICMP, then this entry will be a number.
size	The packet's size.
src-ip	The IP address of the packet's source.
src-port	The port number of the packet's source.
tcpack	The TCP acknowledgment number of the packet.
tcpflags	The TCP flag at the beginning of the packet, which can be one of the following: A—Ack (denotes that the acknowledgment field is significant) F—Fin (denotes the last packet) P—Psh (denotes the push function) S—Syn (denotes the synchronize sequence numbers) U—Urg (denotes that the urgent pointer field is significant).
tcpsyn	The TCP sequence number of the packet.
tcpwin	The TCP window size, in bytes.
time	The time of the file entry, stored in the format HH:MM:SS.

Table 9-1. Entries Found in the ICF Security Log

Enabling and Disabling Logging

Because ICF logging is not activated by default when you install ICF, it is necessary to enable it. To open ICF logging, follow these steps:

1. Select Start | Control Panel.
2. Click Network and Internet Connections, and then click Network Connections.
3. Click the connection that is using ICF, and then under Network Tasks click Change settings of this connection.
4. On the Advanced tab, click Settings.
5. On the Security Logging tab (shown in Figure 9-4), you can choose one or both available options.
   - **Log dropped packets**   This makes a log entry whenever inbound connections are attempted, but rejected.
   - **Log successful connections**   This makes a log entry whenever outbound connection attempts are successful.

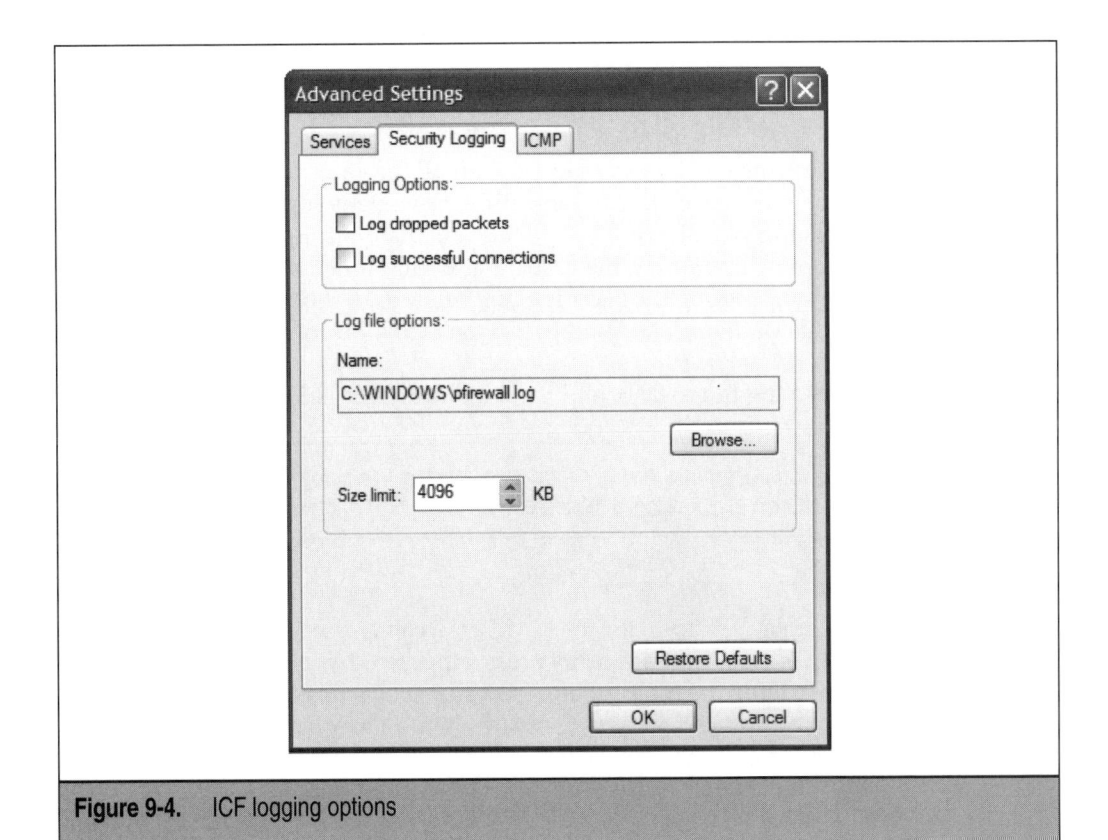

Figure 9-4.   ICF logging options

Conversely, if you decide you no longer wish to track your ICF's activity, you can disable logging. To do so, simply follow the preceding steps, clearing the check boxes next to Log dropped packets and Log successful connections.

ICF Logging File Management

You can also decide to give your ICF log a different filename, and store it on a different path than the default file. This is useful when you wish to generate multiple reports (time of day, day of the week, and so forth). To change the path or filename, under the Security Logging tab (as shown earlier in Figure 9-4), under Log file options, click Browse, and navigate to the file where you want to maintain the log file. Enter the filename of your choice in File name, and then click Open.

> **NOTE** If you leave File name blank, Windows XP Professional will give the log file the default name of pfirewall.log.

Like other ICF tasks, viewing your ICF log is fairly straightforward. On the Security Logging tab, under Log file options, and Name, click Browse, and then find the log. If you haven't saved the log with your own filename, it is stored under the default name of pfirewall.log. Right-click the desired log file, and then select Open to view the contents.

Changing the ICF Log File Size

You might discover that the ICF logging file is too small for your needs. Your file size needs will be based on the size of your organization, how many log entries are made, and how long ICF logging is enabled. If you determine that your log file needs to be beefed up (or toned down, if your log file is sucking up too much hard drive space), you can do it simply by accessing the Security Logging tab, as explained previously. Next, under the Log file options, in Size limit, use the arrow buttons to change the log file size limit.

The default size of a log file is 4MB, and the maximum size is 32MB.

> **NOTE** If you fill up a log file, for instance the default file, logging won't stop. Rather, additional log files will be generated. Once pfirewall.log is maxed out, pfirewall.log.1 is created, and so forth.

Security Templates

Using the Security Templates snap-in for the MMC, you can create text-based files that include all the security settings of the security areas supported by local security policy. These are useful for tweaking the multitudes of security details possible in Windows XP Professional. This section shows you how to create a template, modify an existing template, and then finally apply the template to your Windows XP Professional system.

Chapter 9: Network Security **285**

Creating a Template

To run the Security Templates snap-in to view security policy settings, follow these steps:

1. Open the MMC.
2. On the File menu, click Add/Remove Snap-in, and then click Add.
3. In Available Standalone Snap-ins, pick Security Templates.
4. Click Add, and then click Close.
5. Click OK. The Security Templates snap-in is shown in Figure 9-5.
6. In the left pane, click the + (plus) sign to expand Security Templates.
7. Expand C:\Windows\security\templates (in this example, C: is the letter of the drive where Windows is stored).
8. To create a template, double-click Security Templates, right-click the default templates folder, and then click New Template.

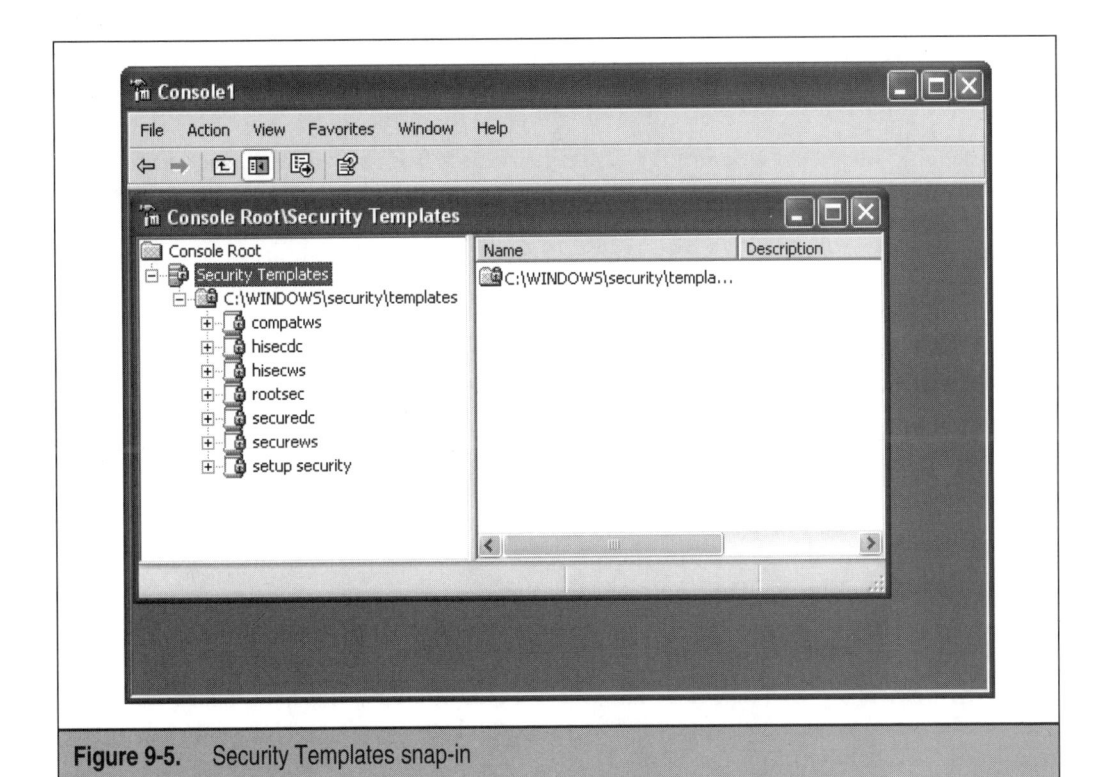

Figure 9-5. Security Templates snap-in

This will generate a blank template that you can fill with whichever security policies best suit your organization. To save the template, simply open the File menu and click Save As.

Editing Existing Templates

Microsoft has included a number of starter templates along with Windows XP Professional. These give a nice foundation on which to build your own security policies. Also, you might have existing security policies you want to fiddle with and apply later.

To open and edit any of these templates, simply double-click them in the left windowpane of the MMC Security Template snap-in.

> **NOTE** Although the Security Template snap-in includes predefined templates, it's a smart idea to check out these templates and make sure they suit the needs of your organization before applying them.

There are four basic types of templates that can be used, depending on your needs:

- Basic
- Secure
- High Secure
- Miscellaneous

These templates represent a range of security needs from standard (Basic) up to strict (High Secure). Furthermore, the Miscellaneous templates provide security settings for some categories that don't easily fall within the Basic, Secure, or High Secure hierarchy. They add security settings for such optional components as Terminal Services and Certificate Services. Some of the templates within each category are listed here:

- **Basicsv**   Establishes a basic level of security for file and print servers
- **Securews**   Establishes the medium level of security for workstations
- **Hisecdc**   Establishes the highest level of security for domain controllers
- **Ocfiless**   Establishes security policies for file servers

Any of the ten sample templates are good places to start for network security. However, if you do change a template, it is a very good idea to save it using a new name, so that the old template is not overwritten.

Applying Security Templates

Creating or editing an existing template does not make changes to your security settings. In order for those changes to be made, you must apply the template to your computer. To apply your newly created or edited template, do the following:

1. Using the Group Policy snap-in, double-click Computer Configuration and expand Windows Settings.
2. Right-click Security Settings, and then click Import Policy (this is shown in Figure 9-6).
3. Choose the template you wish to use.
4. Click OK.

Auditing Security

Since computer networks are constantly being configured, tuned, and reconfigured, it's possible that established, functional security settings will not work properly after changes have been made. In order to keep your finger on the pulse of your network's security issues, it's a good idea to use the security auditing tools provided in Windows XP Professional.

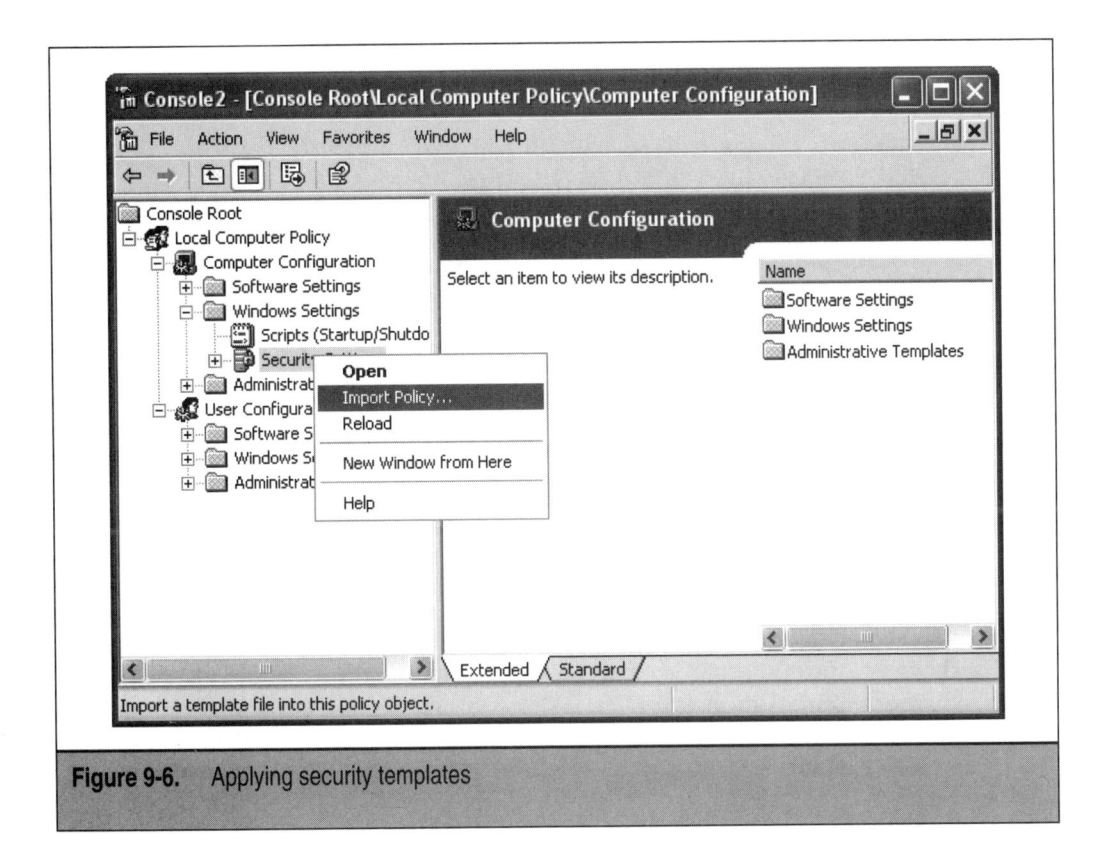

Figure 9-6. Applying security templates

There are a number of useful auditing tools in Windows XP Professional, including the following:

- Event Viewer (which was covered in Chapter 8)
- Audit policies
- The Security Configuration and Analysis snap-in

Auditing is performed from the Group Policy snap-in to the MMC. You can examine the different items that can be audited in Windows XP Professional by viewing the Local Computer Policy\Computer Configuration\Windows Settings\Security Settings\Local Policies\Audit Policy folder in the Group Policy snap-in.

What Can Be Audited

Account logon events make a log entry each time a user tries to log on. The entry might include failed or successful attempts. Failed attempts are further subdivided by whether a user's account has expired, the user is trying to log on locally, the password is invalid, or any other failed attempt has occurred. The following items can be audited:

- **Account management** Makes a log entry each time an account is managed.
- **Logon events** Makes a log entry for logon events over the network.
- **Object access** Makes a log entry each time a certain object (such as a printer or a file folder) is accessed.
- **Policy changes** Makes a log entry whenever a policy is successfully changed on your network. This is useful if you need to reset a policy to a certain state and need reference material.
- **Use of privileges** Makes a log entry whenever a user tries to use special privileges. This entry is made whether or not the user is successful.
- **Process tracking** Makes a log entry each time the user starts a process. This can be used to monitor which applications a user is starting throughout the day.
- **System events** Makes a log entry each time a system event occurs, such as restarting the system.

Before jumping right into auditing, however, it is necessary to develop a solid plan that includes what you'll be auditing and how you can use that information to make positive changes. Auditing significantly taxes system resources, so you'll want to know exactly what you want to audit and what is just overkill.

For example, if you are experiencing performance problems with the network, using process tracking is a good place to start. By comparing the process tracking log to overall system performance, you might be able to tell if certain applications are responsible for a sluggish network. Also, if you are going through toner left and right, you can use object tracking to see which users are using the printer, and for which jobs. Auditing the printer in this way can help you determine if certain users need their printer permissions managed more stringently.

Enabling

To enable auditing, follow these steps:

1. Right-click the object you wish to audit, and then click Properties.
2. On the Security tab, click the Advanced button.
3. This will spawn the Advanced Security Settings for Shared Documents page. Click the Auditing tab. (This is shown in Figure 9-7.)
4. Click the Add button. This will call up a list of users and groups. Select the user or group whose activity you wish to audit.
5. You can select multiple users and groups to monitor. For each one, select whether you want to track successes, failures, or both. (This is shown in Figure 9-8.)
6. Choose whether auditing will be for this object only, or if auditing will include child objects. For instance, if you select the Documents folder, which also contains Administration Documents and Accounting Documents as subfolders,

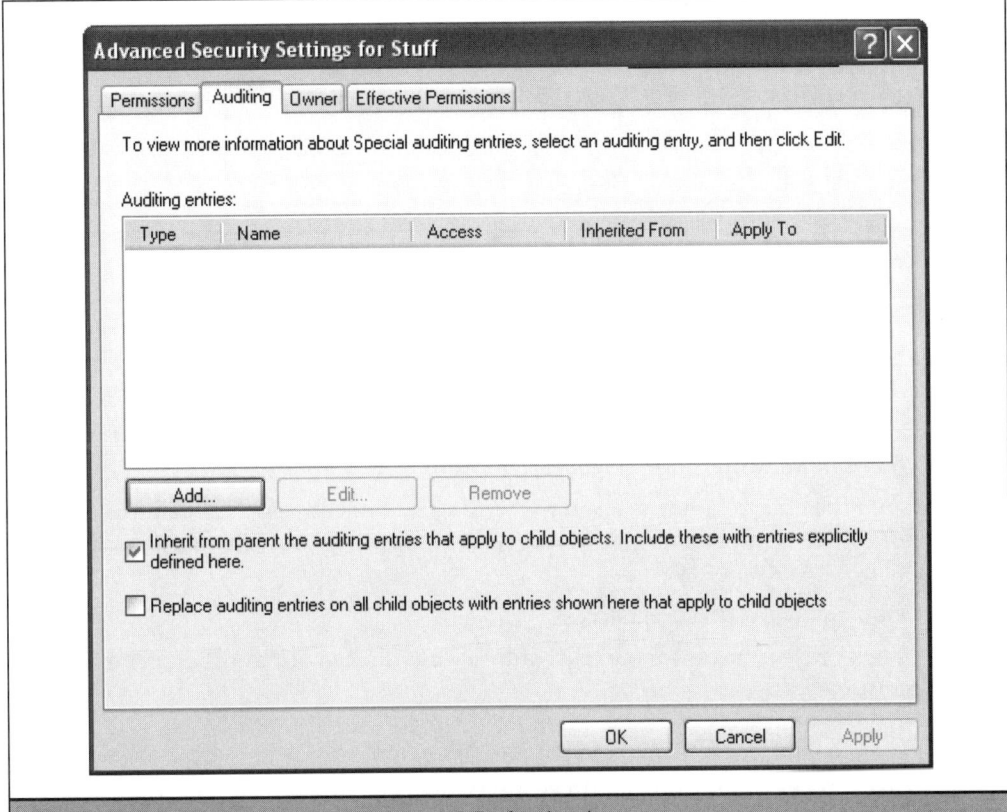

Figure 9-7. Auditing a folder in Windows XP Professional

Figure 9-8. Selecting which items to track

and you wish to monitor their use, select the option Apply these auditing entries to objects and/or containers within this container only.

7. Complete any settings you wish to make for the users, computers, and groups you're monitoring, and then click OK.
8. Open the Group Policy snap-in to the MMC. Navigate to Local Computer Policy\Computer Configuration\Windows Settings\Security Settings\Local Policies\Audit Policy.
9. Double-click Audit object access.
10. Check or clear boxes for success, failure, or both, as your auditing needs require.
11. Click OK.

Auditing can be a time- and resource-intensive task. However, by deciding which properties you need to audit and developing a solid plan for their analysis, you can make sure your system's security settings are what you need.

Security Configuration and Analysis Snap-In

The Security Configuration and Analysis snap-in for the MMC is a good tool to use to analyze your current security settings and compare them against a baseline security template. With the myriad security settings that can be made in a Windows XP Professional environment, it can be difficult to keep track of all the settings, let alone keep track of how they actually function in practice. Performing an analysis will allow you to find any security holes, test the impact of system wide security changes without having to implement them, and identify any deviations from a policy that are present on your system.

For instance, if you have established a security template, and want to compare that template (your ideal security settings) against what is already in place on your system, use the Security Configuration and Analysis tool. If your security template is more restrictive than what is already in place on your system, it will identify which areas need to be beefed up to accommodate the new settings. Furthermore, it will tell you what will happen to your system if those new settings are established.

To start the Security Configuration and Analysis tool, do the following:

1. At the command line, enter **MMC /s**.
2. Under the File menu, click Add/Remove Snap-in.
3. Click Add.
4. In Available Standalone Snap-ins, scroll down to Security Configuration and Analysis and double-click it.
5. Click Close, and then OK.

Now, you will have the Security Configuration and Analysis tool (as shown in Figure 9-9) available, but you still need to perform more configuration steps.

Creating a Database

The Security Configuration and Analysis tool is *database driven*. That means in order to use this tool, you need a security database. You won't have to go so far as to create an Access database; the tool will allow you to create a security configuration and analysis database (also known as a local computer policy database). This database is specific to your computer.

Initially, a database is created when Windows XP Professional is installed. This database contains the default security configurations of your system. If you choose, immediately after installation you can export this database and keep it on hand in case you want to restore your initial settings at some future point.

This database defines the security policy in place for your computer, and your computer runs with the configuration defined in the security policy. However, your security policy might not be sufficient to define the entire configuration. As a result, there will be some holes in your security policy. For example, you might not have

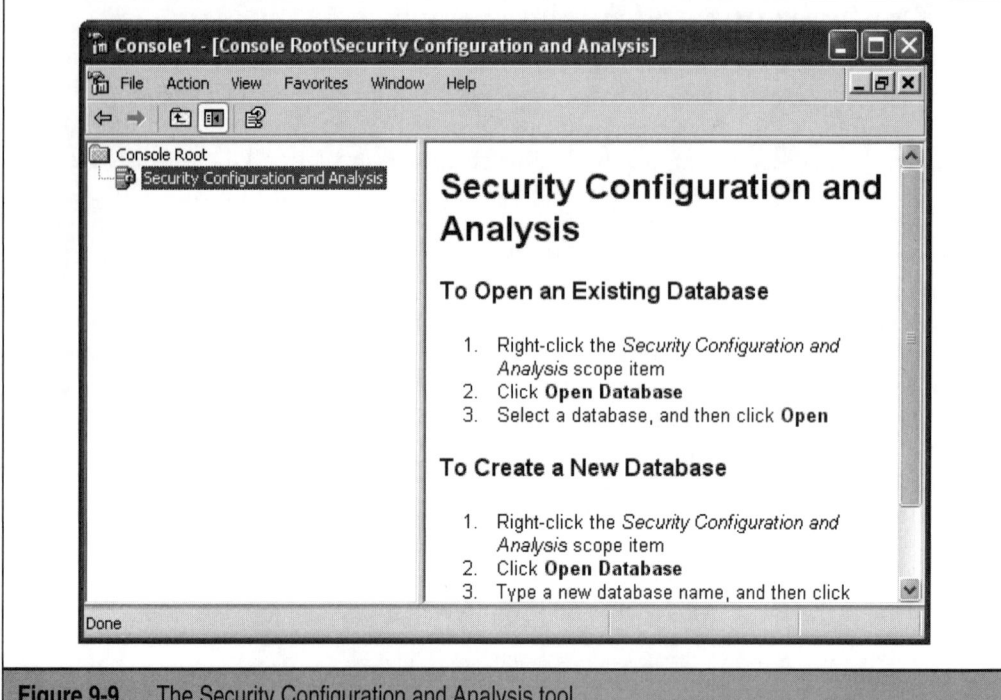

Figure 9-9. The Security Configuration and Analysis tool

security definitions in place for particular files or folders. By running the Security Configuration and Analysis tool, you can find these sorts of security discrepancies.

You can create as many security databases as you like. To create a new security configuration database, do the following:

1. In the left pane of the MMC, right-click Security Configuration and Analysis.
2. Click Open Database.
3. In the Name dialog box, enter the name you wish to use for the new database, and then click Open.
4. Pick an existing security template to import into the database.
5. Click Open.

Analyzing a Database

To analyze a security configuration database, follow these steps:

1. In the left pane of the MMC, right-click Security Configuration and Analysis.

2. Click Analyze Computer Now.
3. In the Error log file path dialog box that pops up, enter the location where you want to send the results of the analysis—for instance, c:\logs\securitylog.log.
4. Click Open, and then click OK. As the tool checks your computer's security settings, a status window will show the progress of the work.

Once the tool has completed its task, you can review the results of the analysis as follows:

1. In the left pane of the MMC, right-click Security Configuration and Analysis.
2. Click View, and then click Customize.
3. Select the description bar to show the database you're working on, and then click OK.
4. In the left pane, click Security Configuration and Analysis.
5. In the right pane, double-click any entry to get a detailed explanation of what was found. This is shown in Figure 9-10.

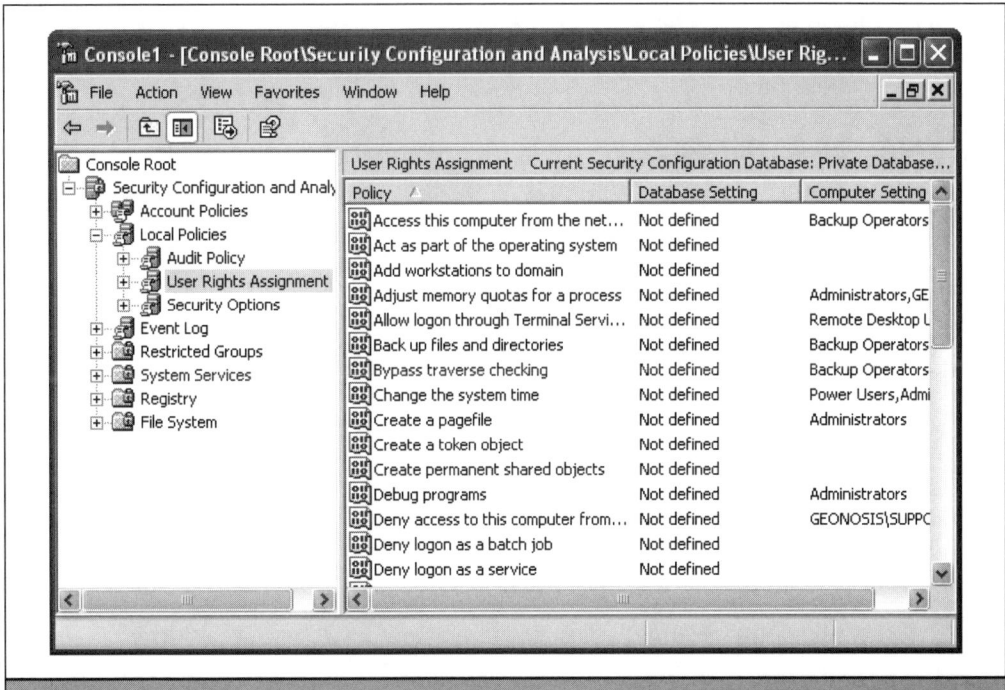

Figure 9-10. Examining the analysis results

Configuration results are shown for the following areas:

- **Account policies**   Displays password, account lockout, and Kerberos authentication policies (on Windows 2000 domain controllers only)
- **Event log**   Displays audit policies, including object access, password changes, and logon/logoff operations
- **Local policies**   Displays audit policies for user rights assignment and computer security options
- **Restricted groups**   Displays group memberships for groups identified as sensitive
- **Object trees**   With Windows 2000 domain controllers, displays directory objects, Registry subkeys and entries, along with the local file system

Other entries include system services, the Registry, and the file system. After reviewing your security analysis, you might decide to change a security setting. If you decide a setting is relevant, then check the Define this policy in the database check box when examining security details. If this check box is clear, then the policy will be removed from the configuration.

To use different configurations and analyses in the future, simply click the Edit Security Settings control to change the existing security definition maintained in the database.

SECURING SERVERS

Although Windows XP does not include a flavor specifically for servers, you should still undertake certain important security tasks on your server (be it Windows NT, 2000, or .NET) when constructing and configuring your Windows XP Professional network. There are also considerations to be made when connecting your server to Windows XP Professional clients. This section examines such server security issues as IP Security (IPSec), security protocols, Group Policy, authentication, and access control lists (ACLs).

IPSec

Windows XP Professional keeps the packets coursing across TCP/IP networks secure by adopting IPSec. IPSec can be used to create an end-to-end security solution that results in encrypted transmission of data. An IPSec solution can offer the following:

- **Confidentiality**   Individuals cannot intercept a message and read it.
- **Authentication**   Messages are sure senders are who they say they are.
- **Integrity**   Messages are guaranteed not to be tampered with along the way.

- **Protection** By blocking certain ports or protocols, IPSec can prevent denial of service (DoS) attacks.

How IPSec Works

Figure 9-11 illustrates, schematically, how IPSec works. A host with an active security policy wants to communicate with another computer running a security policy.

1. Host Computer A attempts to send data. The IPSec driver on Host A communicates with the IPSec driver on Host B to set up a security association (or SA, which is covered in the next section).
2. The two computers conduct a secret key exchange establishing shared and secret keys.
3. Using the methods of security negotiated in the SA, Host A signs and encrypts packets destined for Host B.
4. Host B receives the packets and the IPSec driver checks the signature and key on the packets. If authenticated, the data is passed up the stack to Host B.

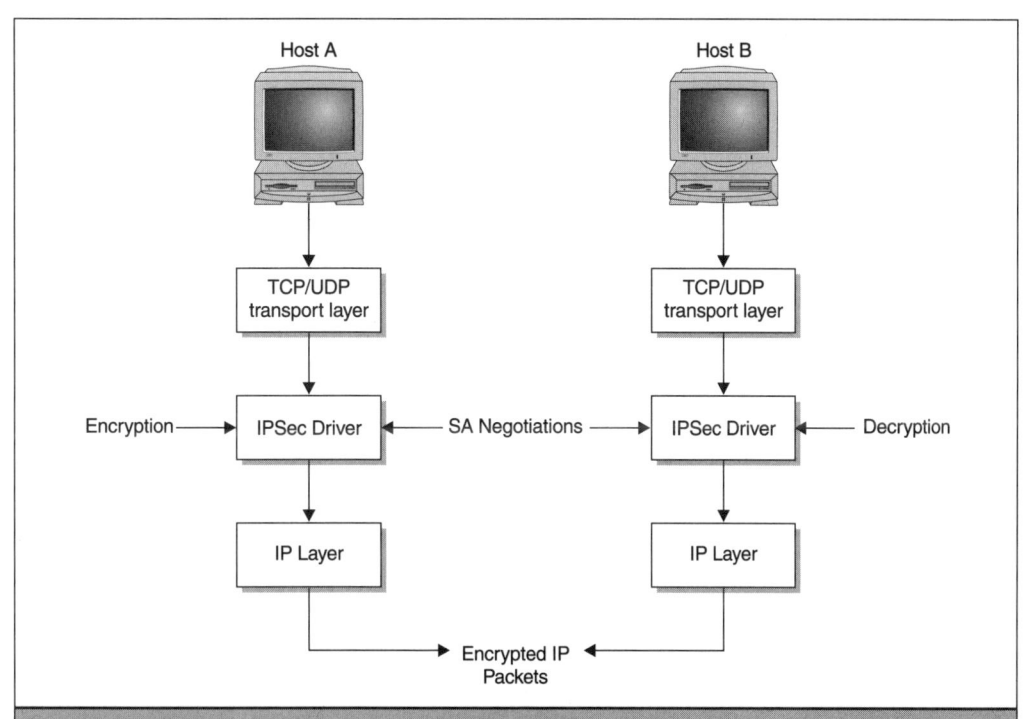

Figure 9-11. IPsec is set up between each communicating host pair.

Of course, the entire process occurs rapidly and without the knowledge of either user at Host A or B. However, additional CPU cycles are consumed encrypting and decrypting these packets.

IPSec Negotiation

An IPSec Policy Agent resides on each computer in a Windows XP/2000/.NET network. Whether it is active or not is up to the administrative policies in place. If the agent is active, it will retrieve the IPSec policy, which describes the local security association and enforces it on the local computer.

An SA is a contract between two communicating computers that is set up before any data is transferred. This negotiation determines specifics about how the two computers will communicate data including these items:

- **The IPSec protocol** Authentication Header, Encapsulating Security Payload
- **The Integrity Algorithm** Message Digest 5, Secure Hash Algorithm
- **The Encryption Algorithm** Data Encryption Standard (DES), Triple DES, 40-bit DES, or none

Establishing IPSec Policies

By default, Windows XP Professional provides three predefined security policies that will satisfy most cases of setting up a policy. You can also start with a predefined policy and customize it to fit your needs. These policies are described in the following list:

- **Client (Respond Only)** Instructs the computer to use IPSec when another computer requests it. It does not request IPSec when initiating communications with another computer. This policy is best for computers that contain little to no sensitive data.
- **Server (Request Security)** For servers that should use IPSec if possible, but won't deny communication if the client does not support IPSec. If total security is required, the Secure Server policy (explained next) should be used. However, this policy is useful in environments where not all the clients can use IPSec—for example, during a migration from Windows NT.
- **Secure Server (Require Security)** For servers containing sensitive data, this policy requires all clients to use IPSec. All outgoing communications are secured and all unsecured requests from clients are rejected.

Choosing the right policy requires careful assessment of the nature of the data. Indiscriminately assigning the highest level of security for all users and servers will unnecessarily put a tremendous strain on the servers and client workstations. This is because of the overhead on the computer to encrypt and decrypt all network traffic. However, allowing any type of client to connect to a secure server opens enormous gates for unsecured information to flow through.

Creating and Applying IPSec Policies

The Microsoft Management Console (MMC) is used to create and configure IPSec policies. The IPSec Policy Management snap-in must be added to the MMC as shown in Figure 9-12.

> **NOTE** Adding IPSec to your MMC is identical to other methods listed in this book for adding a snap-in to your MMC. When scrolling through the list of available snap-ins, select IP Security Policy Management.

When you add the IPSec snap-in to your MMC, you will be asked which computer this snap-in will manage. You can choose from these options:

- This computer
- The Active Directory domain controller of which this computer is a member
- Another Active Directory domain
- Another computer

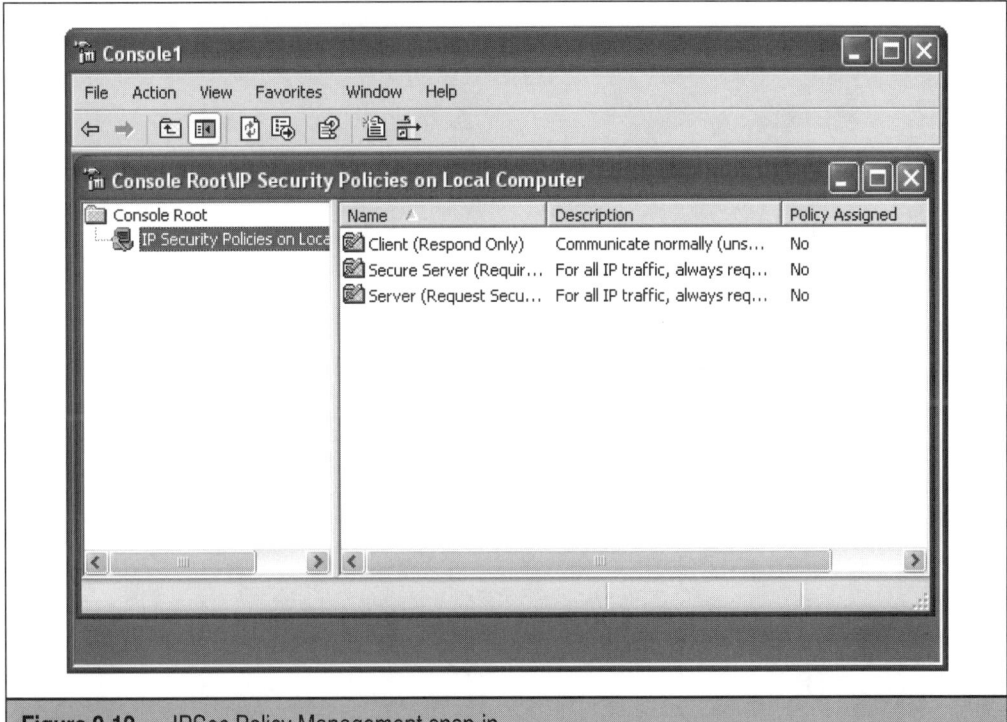

Figure 9-12. IPSec Policy Management snap-in

When the IPSec snap-in is first opened, the three default policies are present for you to alter as you see fit, or you can create your own using the IP Security Policy Wizard. This wizard is started by right-clicking the IPSec snap-in in the left window pane and then selecting Create IP Security Policy.

When the wizard starts, you will be prompted to enter the following information:

- The name and a description of the policy
- Whether this policy will respond to requests for secure communications
- The authentication method (Kerberos, certificate, or preshared key)

The detail of the resulting IPSec policy is shown in Figure 9-13.

You can also adjust settings pertaining to handling of keys and timeout values of shared information. For example, by double-clicking All IP Traffic, you can adjust specific settings for that particular feature. As Figure 9-14 shows, this specific IPSec detail allows you to decide whether you want the filtering rule to apply to all IP traffic, to ICMP traffic, or to both.

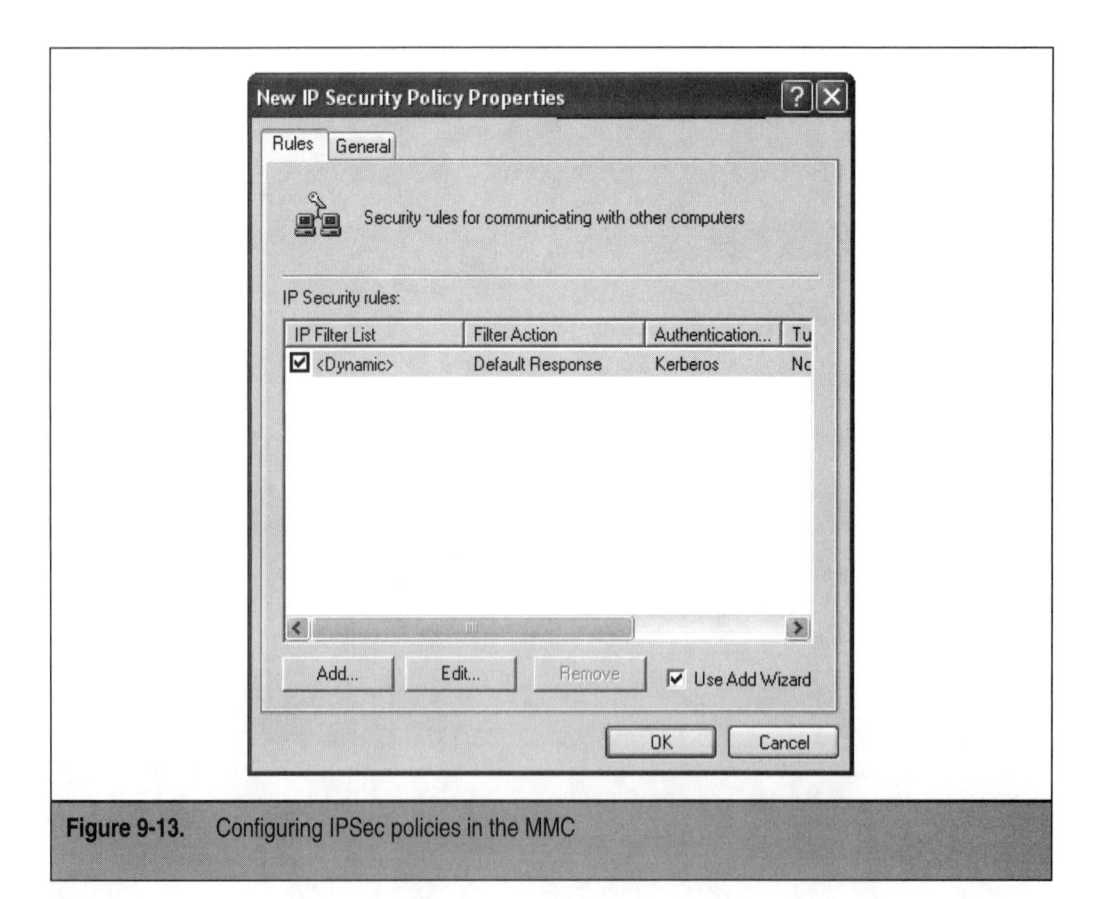

Figure 9-13. Configuring IPSec policies in the MMC

Figure 9-14. Editing IPSec rule properties

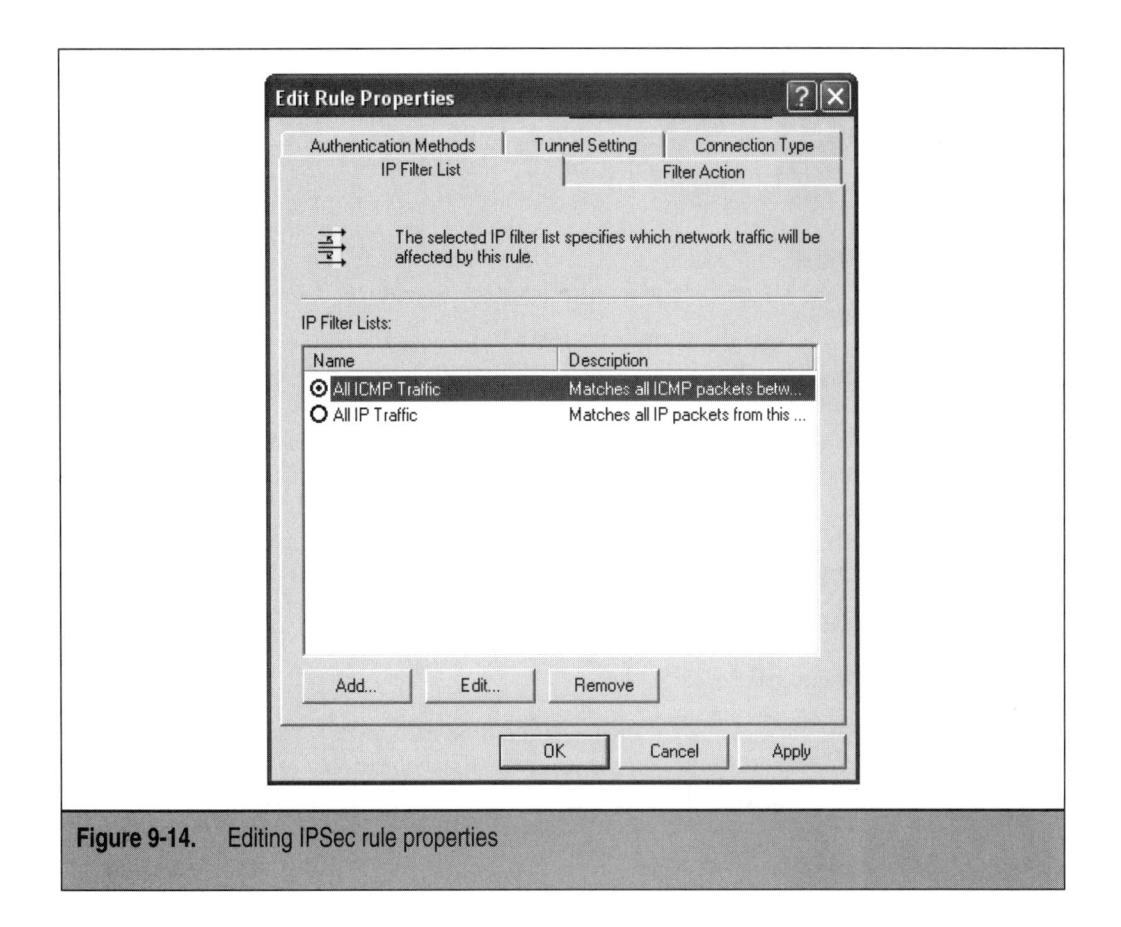

It is also possible to import other security methods as they become available so that you are not stuck using old technology. When you are finished making your changes, the policy is added to the default selections so you can alter or view its properties at a later time.

An IPSec policy can then be assigned to a Group Policy. There it will be applied to all member computers and users of the policy. Unlike many other policies, local policies take precedence over policies higher up the hierarchy. For example, the local Organizational Unit (OU) IPSec policy will override a policy included with the domain.

Logon

The first security step most users encounter is the logon process. When they sit down at their computers and press CTRL-ALT-DEL, they are prompted for their username and password. This section takes a closer look at what is involved with the Windows XP

Professional logon process and how you can switch between two different user accounts once Windows XP Professional has been started.

Types

When using Windows 2000 as a server, Windows XP Professional uses four types of logon processes:

- **Interactive**   This logs on the user to a local computer.
- **Network**   This logs the user onto the network. The Local Security Authority (LSA) of the client's workstation will try to authorize you with the LSA of the remote computer using the credentials employed for logon.
- **Service**   Win32-based services log onto the local computer using the credentials of a local or domain user account or the LocalSystem account. When the LocalSystem account is used (with a Windows 2000 Server), the service would have unfettered access to Active Directory. On the other hand, if a service is running using the security privileges of a local user account, there would be no access to network resources.
- **Batch**   This type of logon is rarely employed in Windows environments, and is used mainly for large batch jobs.

When logging onto Windows XP Professional using the interactive process, the user's credentials can be checked against either the local computer or the domain controller. The process is different, based on where the user's credentials are stored.

> **NOTE**   To log onto a Windows 2000 domain, Logon domain must appear in the dialog box. If it does not appear, click the Options button and select the domain, or enter your username in this format: *username@mycomputer.myorganization*.com.

Interactive Logon

To the end user, the logon process is fairly straightforward: Type your username and password, and then press ENTER. However, quite a lot goes on behind the scenes to make the interactive logon process happen. The following components all take a part in the logon process:

- **Winlogon**   The process responsible for managing logon and logoff operations as well as starting the user's session.
- **Graphical Identification and Authentication (GINA)**   A dynamic link library (DLL) file, called by Winlogon, containing username and password. This is the dialog box that appears at logon.
- **Local Security Authority (LSA)**   The entity on the local device that checks the username and password for authentication.

- **Security Account Manager (SAM)**   The entity that maintains a database of usernames and passwords. The SAM is maintained on both local computers and domain controllers.
- **Net Logon Service**   This service is used in conjunction with NTLM (which is explained later in the chapter) to query a domain controller–based SAM.
- **Kerberos Key Distribution Center (KDC) service**   This service is used when authentication is attempted to Active Directory.

Run As

If you log onto your Windows network, performing *all* your work using your administrator credentials, you open your network to some unnecessary risks. For instance, you could unwittingly download a virus that could propagate to the rest of the network. The best way to minimize the risk is to log on using user or power user rights, and then switch over to your administrator account only when administrative tasks need to be done.

Unfortunately, logging off as a user and relogging on as an administrator is time consuming and inefficient. As such, Windows XP Professional includes a tool called Run As. This allows a user to log on with one set of credentials, and then run an application using a second set of privileges. For example, using user credentials, you could perform your day-to-day work, visit Internet sites, and so forth. Then, if you had to manage a user group, you'd invoke Run As, perform your administrative tasks, and then close out Run As.

Run As allows you to start the following:

- Programs
- Program shortcuts
- MMCs
- Control Panel items

To start Run As, follow these steps:

1. Locate the item you wish to open in Windows Explorer, and then click it.
2. Press SHIFT, right-click the item, and select Run As.
3. In the resulting dialog box (as shown in Figure 9-15), click The following user radio button.
4. Enter your user name and password or the account you wish to use to access the item.
5. In the Domain box, you can do one of two things:
    - To use local administrator credentials, enter the name of your computer.
    - To use domain administrator credentials, enter the name of your domain.

Figure 9-15. The Run As dialog box

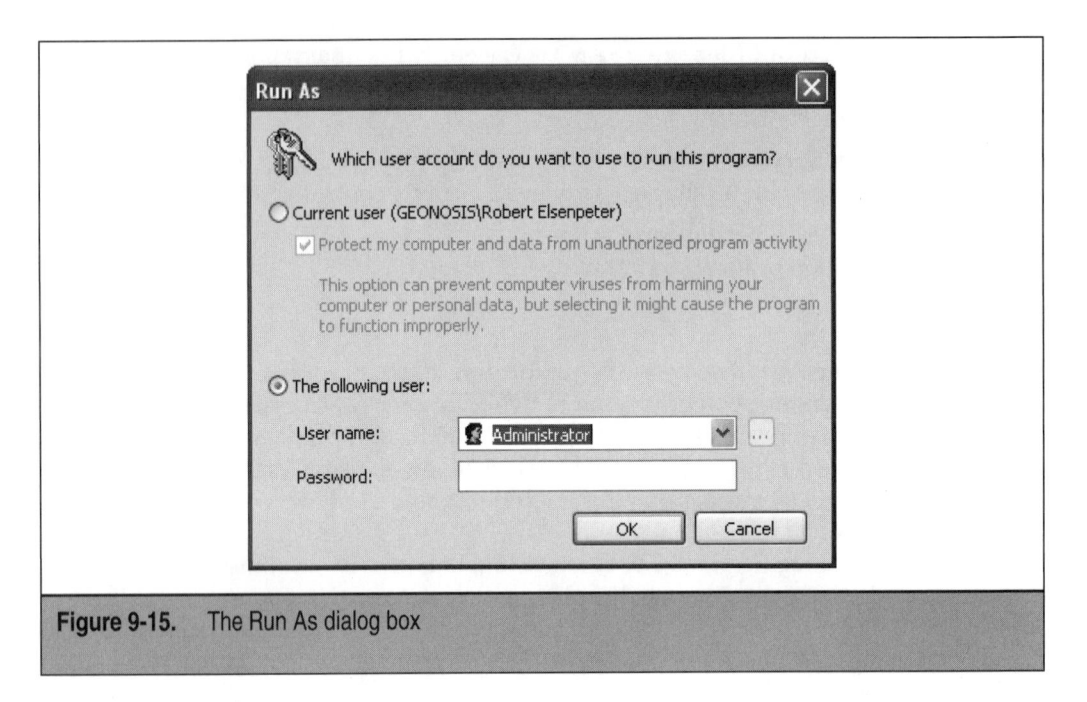

If Run As doesn't work, ensure that the Run As service is enabled by using the Services snap-in to the MMC.

Protocols

Although there are many protocols used for security, Windows XP Professional relies on two of the most prevalent protocols: Kerberos and NTLM. NTLM is used as the default logon protocol for Windows NT networks; Kerberos is used because it is the default protocol for Windows 2000 domains.

The only time Kerberos is employed is when both the domain controllers are using Windows 2000 or .NET and the clients are using Windows XP Professional. In all other scenarios, NTLM is used. The following sections examine what goes on with these security protocols.

Kerberos

We mentioned Kerberos earlier in this book. But because of its importance in Windows 2000 domains (and their connectivity with Windows XP Professional), it deserves further discussion here. Kerberos is the default authentication protocol used in Windows 2000 and Windows XP Professional.

Kerberos was created at the Massachusetts Institute of Technology in 1988. The protocol provides a fast, single logon to Windows network resources, along with other network operating systems that support the Kerberos protocol. Kerberos provides the following features:

- Faster logon authentication in a distributed computing environment
- Interoperability with non-Windows systems that use the Kerberos protocol
- Pass-through authentication for distributed applications
- Transitive trust relationships between domains

Kerberos is a shared-secret authentication protocol. This means the client and another computer (known as the Key Distribution Center, or KDC) know passwords, but no one else does. Kerberos is a faster authentication protocol because it shifts the burden of authentication away from the server and gives it to the client and the KDC.

NOTE The steps involved in a Kerberos logon were illustrated in Chapter 2.

NTLM

NTLM is a protocol that authenticates computers and users based on a challenge/response technique. When the NTLM protocol is initiated, a resource server must contact a domain controller to verify the user or computer's identity.

NOTE NTLM need not only be used in a domain environment; it can also be used in peer-to-peer and workgroup environments.

The following steps explain what occurs with an interactive NTLM logon:

1. The user initiates logon by pressing CTRL-ALT-DEL. This is called the Secure Attention Sequence (SAS).
2. Next, Winlogon calls the GINA DLL, which provides the logon dialog box.
3. Once the user enters his or her username and password, Winlogon sends the information to the LSA.

NOTE The LSA is the entity that receives the username and password from Winlogon and determines if the logon is to take place on the local computer or on the network.

4. If the user's account is stored on the local computer, the LSA uses the MSV1_0 authentication package, comparing the logon information with data in the computer's SAM database. If the user's account is stored on the network, the LSA uses MSV1_0 and Net Logon service to check the SAM on a Windows NT domain controller.
5. If the logon information is valid, the SAM tells the LSA, sending along the user's security identifier (SID). Furthermore, the SAM sends the SIDs of any groups to which the user belongs. This information is used by the LSA to generate an access token that includes the user's SID.
6. The user's session begins when Winlogon receives the token.

Authentication

Don't confuse logon with authentication. Whereas logon allows a user to access a computer (either locally or with network privileges), the process of authentication goes deeper, allowing users to have certain permissions and memberships in groups.

Creating, managing, and deleting *user accounts* and establishing and maintaining *security groups* are important tasks for security management. It is the establishment of these functions that governs what level of access your users will have and how they can use system resources.

User Accounts

Every user on your network has an account. Accounts can be established locally or as part of the larger domain. If a user has a local account, then he or she cannot access network resources (unless anonymous access is authorized on the network); if a user has a domain-based account, then network resources are available via the local computer.

When Windows XP Professional is installed, two user accounts are created:

- **Administrator** Used to configure and manage the system. Once Windows XP Professional has been installed and configured, this account is only needed for the occasional administrative task.

> **NOTE** A good security practice is to log off the administrator account and log on with a user account for day-to-day tasks.

- **Guest** Allows users to log onto the computer without the need for a separate account for each user.

In addition to these accounts, Windows XP Professional allows a number of other types of accounts to be created. These accounts include the following:

- **Backup Operators** Members of this group can perform backup and restore operations on the computer, no matter which permissions are in place.

- **Help Services Group** Members of this group can use applications to help diagnose system problems.

- **Network Configuration Operators** Members of this group are able to provide limited administrative functions, such as assigning IP addresses.

- **Power Users** Members of this group lie somewhere between administrators and users. They can install and modify applications, have read and write functions, and can be granted permission to install local printers (if the administrator delegates that control to the power user).

- **Remote Desktop Users** Members of this group are allowed to log on remotely.

- **Replicator** Members of this group are allowed to replicate files across a domain.
- **Users** Members of this group have limited access to the system and have read and write permissions only to their own profile.

If a certain type of account (such as a user account) is needed for the local computer, the administrator will have to log on and create the account. No one else can create user accounts.

To create, manage, or delete a user account, follow these steps:

1. Select Start | Control Panel.
2. Click User Accounts. The resulting screen is shown in Figure 9-16.

You can also manage additional user traits, as explained in the following sections.

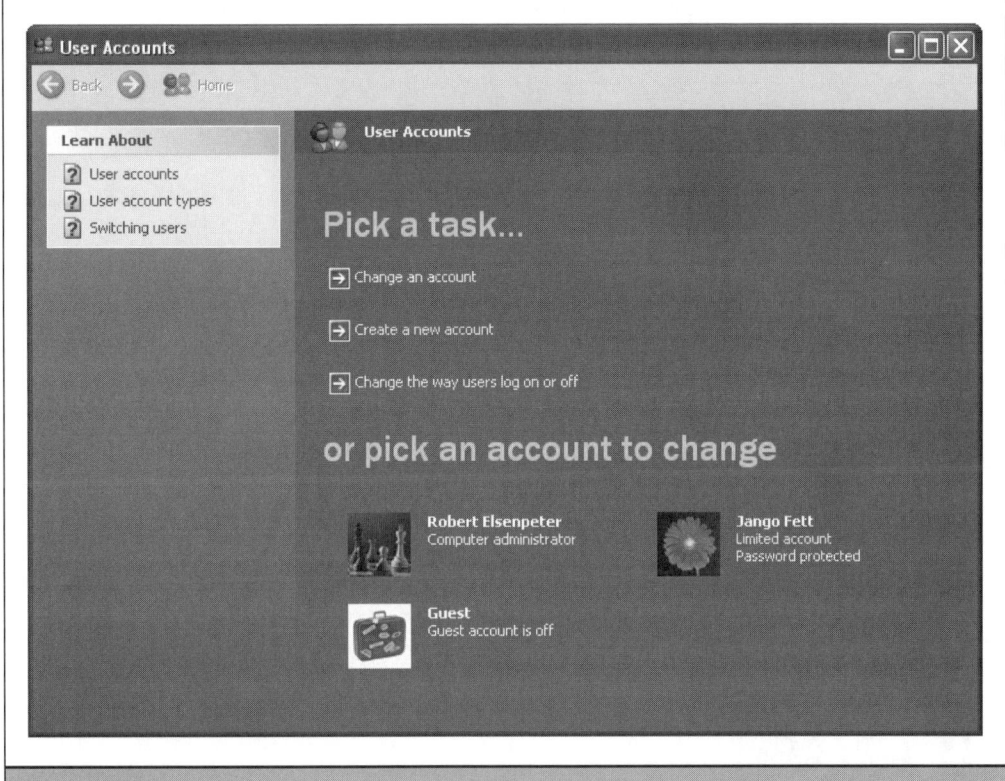

Figure 9-16. Managing user accounts

Password Management

Employees come, employees go (and some employees are *asked* to go). As such, Windows XP Professional provides a way to manage the passwords of your organization's employees. There are two ways in which passwords can be managed in Windows XP Professional:

- **User Accounts**   Located in the Control Panel, this option is used when the computer is *not* part of a domain and passwords need to be managed locally.
- **Local Users and Groups**   This snap-in to the MMC is used when the computer is part of a domain and passwords need to be managed across a number of computers.

Password Tasks

To change a user's password, follow these steps:

1. Select Start | Control Panel, and then double-click User Accounts.
2. In the resulting dialog box (shown in Figure 9-17), click the user's name, and then click Change Password.

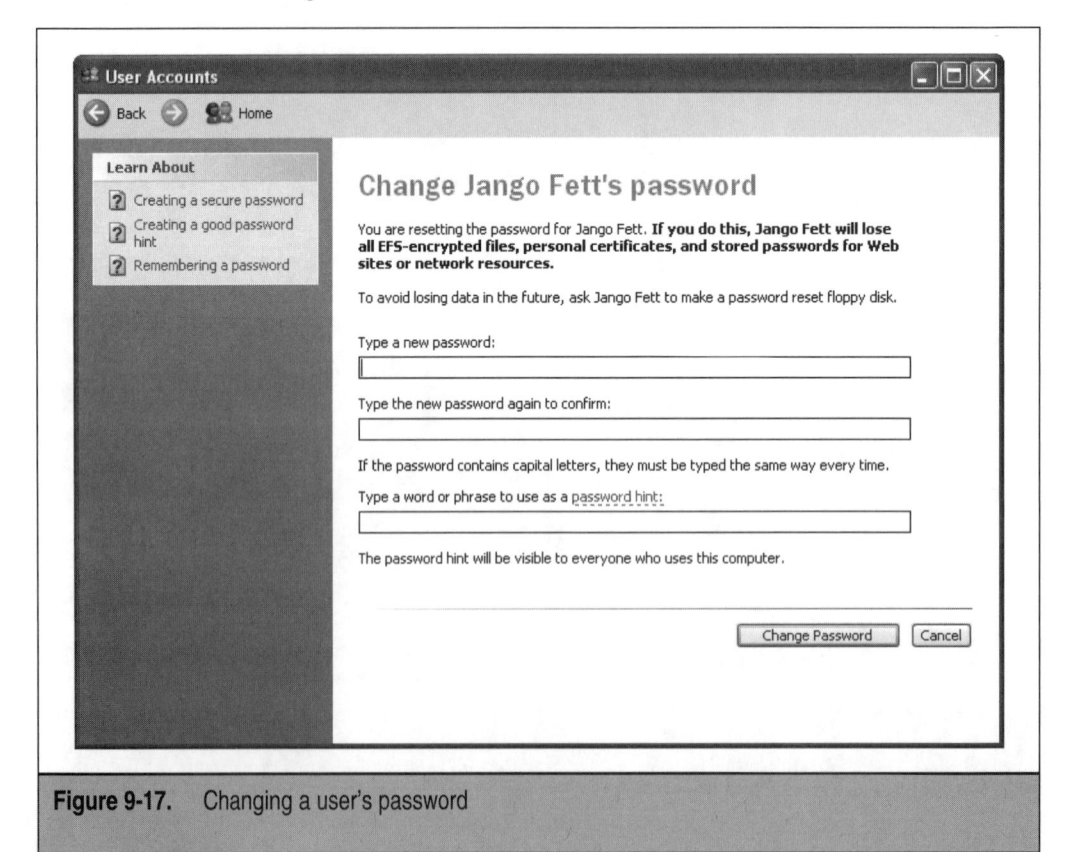

Figure 9-17.   Changing a user's password

3. Type the new password twice in the Reset Password dialog box.
4. You can enter password hints, if you choose, that can help the user in case he or she forgets the password.

Windows XP Professional allows you to set certain rules for password management. For instance, you can make the user change his or her password the next time he or she logs on, you can disable an account, and so forth. To access these rules, follow these steps:

1. Open the MMC and add the Local Users and Groups snap-in.
2. Double-click the Users folder.
3. Right-click the name of the user whose account you wish to manage, and then select Properties.
4. On the Properties page (shown in Figure 9-18), you can establish the following rules.
    - User must change password at next logon.
    - User cannot change password.

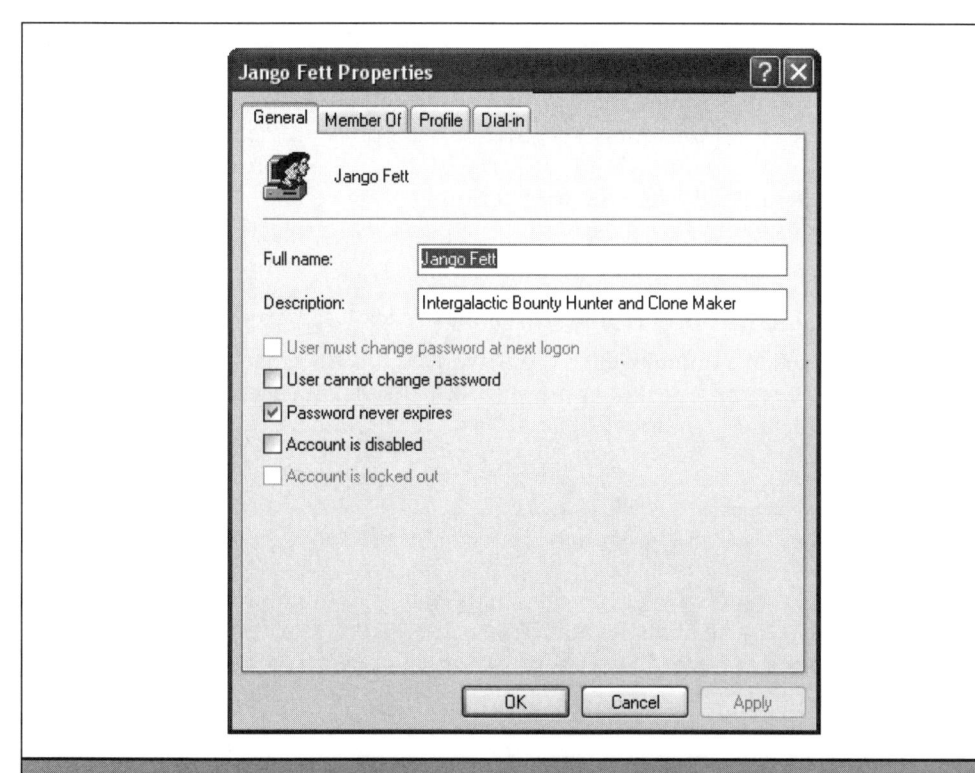

Figure 9-18. Managing password rules

- Password never expires.
- Account is disabled.
- Account is locked out.

NOTE If you need to establish even more sophisticated password rules, this can be accomplished through the Group Policy snap-in. You can set a minimum password length, or a predetermined time when passwords must be changed. Group Policy is discussed later in this chapter in the section "Group Policy."

Stored User Names and Passwords Depending on the complexity and design of your network, you might not want a user to have the same credentials for varying resources. For instance, a user might have power user access to the network, but only user-level access on the server. Whatever your needs, Windows XP Professional can keep track of the user's different credentials using Stored User Names and Passwords, located in the Control Panel.

NOTE Stored User Names and Passwords isn't limited to usernames and passwords. It can also keep track of certificates, smart cards, and Passport credentials.

If a user tries to access a password-protected network resource, his or her logon credentials are used. If those credentials are not sufficient, the Stored User Names and Passwords file is queried. If the requisite credentials are present, then the user can access the resource. If the credentials are not present, he or she is prompted to enter the correct credentials, which will be saved for later use.

To create a new username and password for a password-protected network resource, follow these steps:

1. Select Start | Control Panel, and then double-click User Accounts.
2. If you are part of a domain, click the Advanced tab, and then click Manage Passwords. On computers not part of a domain, click the icon similar to your user account, and then under Related Tasks, click Manage your stored passwords.
3. Click Add.
4. Enter the requested information.

Restoring Passwords If you've ever forgotten a password, you know how frustrating (and embarrassing) it can be to get it reset. To ameliorate this problem, Windows XP Professional includes a Password Reset Wizard, which allows a backup disk to be created that allows passwords to be reset.

> **NOTE** The Password Reset Wizard works only on the local machine. It cannot be used for network accounts. Furthermore, the disk does not actually contain your password, rather it contains a public and private key pair. Since your password is not stored on the disk, it is not necessary to create a new password backup disk each time you change your password.

To back up a password, do the following:

1. Select Start | Control Panel.
2. Select User Accounts, and choose your own account from the list.
3. In the Related Tasks pane, click Prevent a forgotten password. This will invoke the Password Reset Wizard.
4. Click Next.
5. Put a floppy disk into your floppy disk drive.
6. In the Current User Account Password box, enter your password, and then click Next.
7. When the progress indicator shows the task is complete, click Finish, and then keep the disk somewhere safe.

> **NOTE** It's a good idea *not* to put a label on the disk reading "Password Backup" or the like.

Now, if you enter the wrong password, Windows XP Professional will prompt you for your password backup disk. The wizard will ask you in which drive the backup disk is located, and then ask you to enter a new password.

Security Groups

User accounts are the building blocks of security groups. Groups can be established and managed based on your organizational needs. For example, you can place your organization's users into groups for upper management, middle management, and workers. This type of structure is helpful if you wish to give (or take away) a security permission to a specific user group, without giving it to the entire organization. For example, your organization might have just installed a kicked-up color printer, but you only want management to be able to access the printer. By giving that permission to the upper and middle management groups, you don't have to worry that the entire company will be using the printer. Furthermore, because you are able to assign the permission twice (once to each group), you aren't spending all day going through the network's user accounts and applying the permission over and over.

Security groups can be any size. They could govern a lone computer or user, an entire domain, or an entire forest. Windows XP Professional security groups fall into one of the following categories.

- **Computer local groups** These groups are specific to a local computer and not acknowledged anywhere else in the domain.
- **Domain local groups** Permissions are granted to devices only within the domain.
- **Global groups** These are used within a domain to combine user accounts that share a common access need, based on function within the organization.
- **Universal groups** Groups in this category are used in a multidomain setting to combine user accounts that share a common access need, based on function within the organization.

Though not a security group per se, yet sharing the same rules, built-in security principles apply to any account that is using a computer in a specified way. For example, built-in security principles could be set to apply to anyone who uses a dial-up connection to access the computer, or anyone logging onto a computer across a network.

Groups are determined largely by where in the network they are able to use permissions and the amount of traffic the group generates. Another bonus to using groups is that when they are well planned and implemented, network congestion decreases because there isn't as much domain controller replication required.

Whoami

No, Whoami is not an early 1980s world-class breakdancing group. Rather, it is a command-line tool used in Windows XP Professional that allows you to view the permissions and rights that apply to a user.

Whoami is on your Windows XP Professional CD-ROM in the Support/Tools directory. This tool returns the domain or computer name along with the username of the user who is currently logged onto the computer on which Whoami is run. It displays the username and security identifiers (SID), groups and their SIDs, privileges, and status.

To install Whoami, double-click the SETUP.EXE tool in the Support/Tools directory on your Windows XP Professional CD-ROM. Then, complete the steps in the Support Tools Setup Wizard to complete the Whoami installation.

To run Whoami, at the command prompt, enter **whoami**.

Depending on your needs, there are options you can add at the end of Whoami to garner the results you need, as listed here:

- **/all** Displays all the information in current access token.
- **/user** Displays the user associated with the current access token.
- **/groups** Displays the groups associated with the current access token.
- **/priv** Displays the privileges associated with the current access token.
- **/logonid** Displays the logon ID used for the current session.
- **/sid** Displays the SID associated with the current session. This argument must be added to the end of the /USER, /GROUPS, /PRIV, or /LOGONID options.

A couple of examples of Whoami follow.

```
C:\Documents and Settings\Robert Elsenpeter>whoami /user /priv
[User]     = "GEONOSIS\Robert Elsenpeter"

(X) SeChangeNotifyPrivilege         = Bypass traverse checking
(O) SeSecurityPrivilege             = Manage auditing and security log
(O) SeBackupPrivilege               = Back up files and directories
(O) SeRestorePrivilege              = Restore files and directories
(O) SeSystemtimePrivilege           = Change the system time
(O) SeShutdownPrivilege             = Shut down the system
(O) SeRemoteShutdownPrivilege       = Force shutdown from a remote system
(O) SeTakeOwnershipPrivilege        = Take ownership of files or other objects
(O) SeDebugPrivilege                = Debug programs
(O) SeSystemEnvironmentPrivilege    = Modify firmware environment values
(O) SeSystemProfilePrivilege        = Profile system performance
(O) SeProfileSingleProcessPrivilege = Profile single process
(O) SeIncreaseBasePriorityPrivilege = Increase scheduling priority
(X) SeLoadDriverPrivilege           = Load and unload device drivers
(O) SeCreatePagefilePrivilege       = Create a pagefile
(O) SeIncreaseQuotaPrivilege        = Adjust memory quotas for a process
(X) SeUndockPrivilege               = Remove computer from docking station
(O) SeManageVolumePrivilege         = Perform volume maintenance tasks
```

To display my SID, the /user and /sid switches are used in tandem:

```
C:\Documents and Settings\Robert Elsenpeter>whoami /user /sid
[User]     = "GEONOSIS\Robert Elsenpeter"  S-1-5-21-606747145-113007714-17085377
68-1003
```

Access Control Lists

In the last section we gave a quick, back-of-the-envelope sketch about user accounts and how those accounts are managed by their membership in a group. In order to manage your groups (add and remove both users and permissions, for instance), administrators use access control lists (ACLs).

Windows XP Professional uses two types of ACLs:

- **Discretionary access control lists (DACLs)**   Used to identify the users and groups that are allowed (or denied) access
- **System access control lists (SACLs)**   Control how access is audited

ACLs are a handy tool to examine who has access to a specific object, and they provide the means to edit those permissions. For instance, if you determine that an object, such as a new turbo laser printer, isn't to be used by anyone but the marketing department, then an ACL can be used to set and enforce those limits.

Viewing

To view an ACL, right-click a particular object's icon (folder, printer, and so forth), then select Properties. Click the Security tab, and you'll see the groups and users that have access to this object, along with a summary of the permissions granted to that group.

> **NOTE** Computers running Windows XP Professional in stand-alone or workgroup environments won't be able to see the Security tab if simple sharing has been enabled. To disable Simple Sharing, open My Computer. Under the Tools menu, click Folder Options. Next, click the View tab, and then clear the Use simple file sharing (Recommended) check box.

On the Security tab, there are two windows:

- **Group or user names**   This box lists the users or groups that have the requisite permissions for this object.
- **Permissions**   This box lists the permissions granted or denied for the user or group selected in the Group or user names box.

> **NOTE** Only users who have permissions for a particular object are able to view the ACL for the object.

The Add and Remove buttons do as their names suggest: They allow you to add or remove users or groups from the list.

Advanced Settings

By clicking the Advanced button, you can examine more details of particular user and group settings. On the Advanced Security Settings page, you can establish more advanced features for granting permissions, including:

- Managing special permissions for a user or group
- Managing access inheritance options from the object to any child objects
- Viewing attempts to access the object
- Managing the ownership information of an object

When the Advanced Security Settings page appears, it automatically starts on the Permissions tab. This shows the permissions that have been *explicitly* established for this object. A second permissions tab labeled Effective Permissions allows you to examine all the permissions that apply to a user or group for an object, including the permissions that come as being part of a particular group or those established for a particular user.

Group Policy

One of the most powerful administrative tools in Windows XP Professional is Group Policy. Judicious use of this tool can reduce the Total Cost of Ownership (TCO) by locking down users' systems and thus reducing the probability that a user will somehow screw things up. Group Policy is a snap-in for the MMC and can be applied to almost any object. You might, for example, create and apply a Group Policy to a domain, OU, and group within the OU. The policies follow the hierarchy of the domain tree. Therefore, if a policy higher up the tree is in conflict with a lower-level policy, the higher-level policy takes precedence by default.

> **NOTE** By and large, Group Policy is used for Active Directory domains. However, to manage your local computer using Group Policy, you use Local Group Policy. You implement Local Group Policy in the same general way you do Group Policy. However, when you initiate the Group Policy snap-in, you are asked which computer you wish to manage. Rather than a network computer or domain, select Local Computer.

The Snap-In

The Group Policy snap-in, shown in Figure 9-19, includes two major groups: Computer Configuration and User Configuration. These correspond to the System Policy Editor and User Policies, respectively. Each contains three major policy containers.

- **Software Settings** Installs software on specific computers or on users' systems
- **Windows Settings** Sets security settings and runs scripts at startup or shutdown
- **Administrative Templates** Controls how Windows and applications look and behave

Once you have selected the particular policy you want to alter, right-click it and select Properties. You have the choice of disabling or enabling the policy. In this example, we have enabled the Remove Documents menu from Start Menu policy. Now no users in the domain will have the Documents item in their Start menus.

Group Management

If you were in an enterprise with thousands of employees, it would be impossible to manage each user account individually. That's where groups become useful (and necessary). You can apply attributes for a broad range of users with a couple clicks of the mouse.

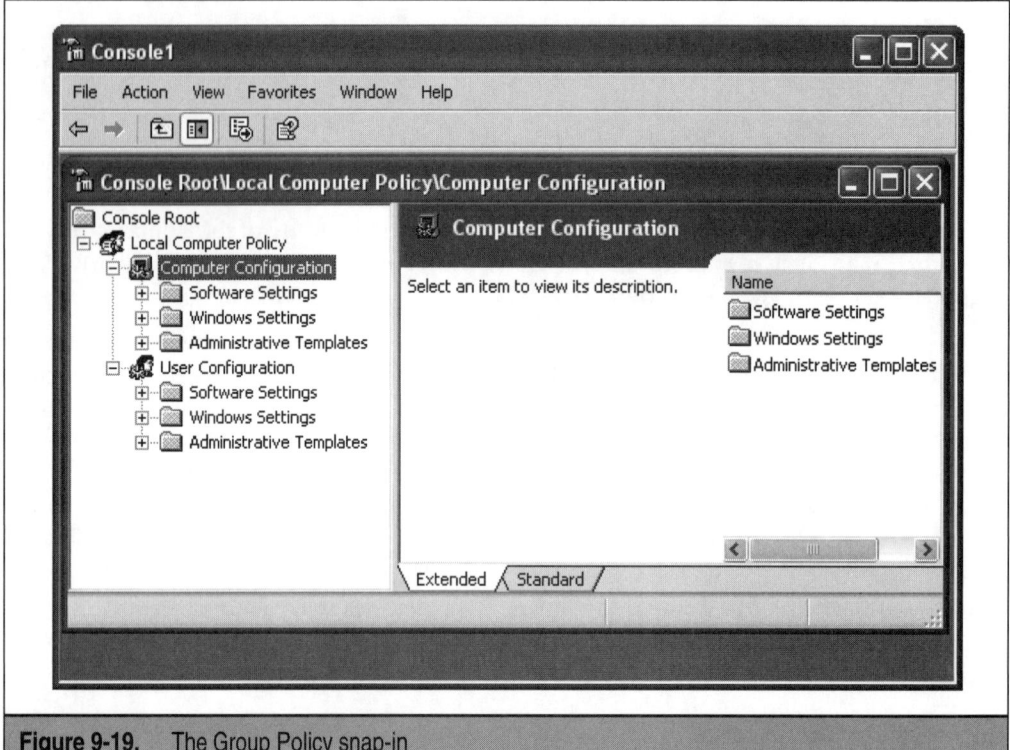

Figure 9-19. The Group Policy snap-in

Creating a Group The first step is to create an OU. This can be done from either the Windows 2000 or .NET server, or using the Windows .NET Server Administration Tools Pack mentioned in Chapter 6 and the appendix. OUs are the basic building block of Active Directory. Open the Active Directory Users and Computers tool by selecting Start | Administrative Tools | Active Directory Users and Computers. Select the domain where you want to locate the OU. Now, choose Action | New | Organizational Unit. Enter the name of your new OU and click OK.

To add a user to your newly created OU, go back to the Active Directory Users and Computers snap-in and pick the OU into which you want to place the user. From the toolbar, choose Action | New | User.

This summons a New Object–User box into which you will enter the necessary user information, and then click Next. You'll be asked for the user's password (which can be changed by the user at the next logon).

Adding a group to your OU follows the same basic steps as adding a user. Again, use the Active Directory Users and Computers snap-in, select Action | New | Group, and follow the dialog boxes to establish your group and its attributes.

You need to pay special attention to where you are creating the new object because it is conceivable to add a new object just about anywhere in the hierarchy. It is possible and encouraged to create OUs within other OUs. If this is what you intend to do and you actually create the new OU under the domain, the results are completely different and will impact all members of that OU. The same can be said for users and groups—the placement of these objects in the Active Directory hierarchy have a dramatic impact on their properties. For example, creating a new user under the domain will give this new user rights over all objects beneath it in the hierarchy, including all member OUs. This is quite different from creating a new user in an OU that has very restricted rights.

NOTE You can easily move users, groups, and OUs around the domain tree using this snap-in. Be aware that a simple move might impact many users.

Editing a Group Groups rarely keep the same information from the time they're created. Active Directory supplies the necessary tools to edit your group and its attributes. Use the Active Directory Users and Computers snap-in, right-click the user or group account, and select Properties. This provides a Properties box containing all the pertinent attributes of your user or group.

As Group Policy shows, security management in Windows XP Professional networks can be rather detailed. Understanding how to manage security can be an important task, and not one that should be taken lightly.

CHAPTER 10

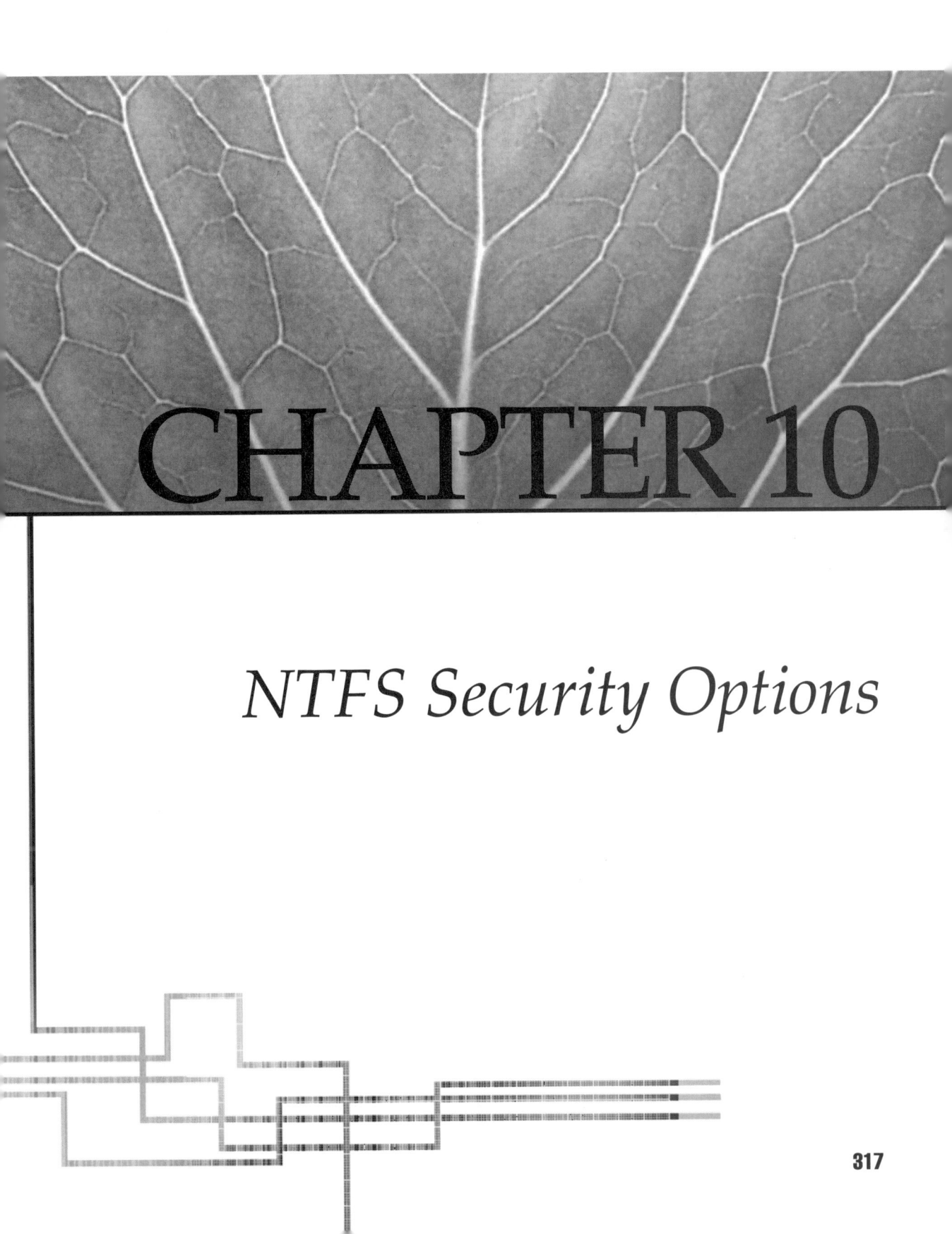

NTFS Security Options

The New Technology File System (NTFS) harkens back to Windows NT. But don't let its age fool you—this file system provides a number of features that promise to keep your hard drives secure, stable, and reliable.

NTFS provides security at the file level, as opposed to the share level (under the file allocation table [FAT] file system). When using FAT, if someone tries accessing your computer over the network, you can allow or forbid access to your share. However, using NTFS, you can establish which specific files and folders can be accessed. Furthermore, using FAT, if a person is sitting at your computer—no matter how that user logs in—he or she can still access your files.

NTFS is an integral part of network and Windows XP Professional security. This chapter examines the security features and usage of NTFS, especially as it applies to Windows XP Professional. First, we'll take a look at NTFS's features, then we'll discuss how NTFS permissions are used. Finally, if you've decided that NTFS is the way to go, we'll talk about how you can convert your FAT drives to NTFS.

NTFS FEATURES

Although we talk about FAT and NTFS, these are used as blanket terms, encompassing several different versions of these formats. For example, there are multiple flavors of FAT (FAT12, FAT16, and FAT32). For the sake of simplicity (and because it really isn't our focus here), we've lumped FAT into a general category. On the other side of the fence, there are two versions of NTFS that you might encounter: versions 4.0 and 5.0.

In this section, we'll talk about the features of NTFS and why it is more useful to your organization (on many levels) than FAT. We'll cover such issues as compression, encryption, quotas, and overall performance notes. First, however, let's take a closer look at the differences between NTFS versions 4.0 and 5.0.

4.0 vs. 5.0

Windows XP Professional offers the newest version of the venerable NTFS. In Windows NT, NTFS version 4.0 was in use. Windows XP Professional uses the version introduced with Windows 2000, version 5.0. Though both versions can read and write to each other's file system, there are a number of new features in Windows XP Professional that Windows NT cannot use when accessing an NTFS 5.0 drive. These features include the following:

- **Reparse points**   Windows NT cannot make use of reparse points.
- **Disk quotas**   Windows NT will ignore disk quotas established by Windows XP Professional.
- **Encryption**   Windows NT cannot read nor write to encrypted files.
- **Sparse files**   Windows NT cannot use sparse files.
- **Change journal**   Windows NT ignores the change journal.

These additions make NTFS version 5.0 a powerful tool with built-in management capabilities that, when used properly, can make your organization more productive and efficient.

Compression

Computer hard disk drives are constantly growing in capacity. This is largely because hard drive costs are coming down and file storage needs are on the increase. Whether you're storing applications, multimedia files, or whatever, there is an ever-present need for larger hard drives. But rather than adding or upgrading hard drives, Windows XP Professional provides a mechanism that can help you make the most of your hard drive's space: folder compression.

Types of Windows XP Professional Compression

Windows XP Professional includes two types of folder compression: *NTFS compressed folders* and *ZIP compressed folders*. The method you use to compress files and folders will depend on what your ultimate goal is. If you are looking to archive data, then zipping a file is the best practice. However, if your day-to-day files are turning into space hogs (or you have files you want to keep on your hard drive, but rarely use), then you should consider NTFS compression. The specifics of these two types of compression are explained next.

ZIP   ZIP compression is the popular compression format that's been around for years as a third-party compression tool. In ZIP compression, a number of files are *zipped* together into one large ZIP folder. In order to compress or decompress the folder, the user must explicitly perform the compression or decompression action. As a result, this type of compression cannot be used transparently by the user. Furthermore, because ZIP files are seen as a unique file type, they cannot be accessed by other applications. ZIP compression is a good idea if you want to send multiple files in an e-mail attachment and size is a consideration, or if you plan on archiving data.

> **NOTE**   ZipMagic is a third-party tool that allows your system to work with ZIP files as if they were system files. For more information on ZipMagic, go to http://www.ontrack.com/zipmagic.

NTFS   What we're more concerned with here is NTFS compression. This type of compression is for both files and folders, but only works on NTFS partitions (another good reason to convert your hard drive over to NTFS). Furthermore, NTFS compression is completely transparent to applications and users. When an application opens a compressed file, NTFS decompresses just the portion of the file being read and copies it to memory. Because it keeps the portion of data in memory still in its compressed state, system performance is not hindered. When data must be saved to the file, then the computer must compress the file. Compression is easy enough with NTFS. Simply enable compression on the file's or folder's Properties menu.

The size of your compressed file or folder will depend on the type of file. For example, if you compress a Word document, then you can expect pretty good compression, from 120KB down to roughly 50KB. On the other hand, if you are compressing a graphic file, you won't get such a good rate of compression. Instead, that 120KB picture of your aunt Mathilda might still consume about 90KB of hard drive space.

Another issue to consider when dealing with compression is that you will likely take a performance hit when accessing a file (though not as much as noted earlier for NTFS compressed files). This is most obvious when the entire drive is compressed, versus a single file or folder. The computer must perform the task of compressing and decompressing a file, so if it has many files to process, your system will be taxed.

Volumes

If you want to squeeze every drop of space out of your hard drive, you can compress the entire volume. Depending on the size of your volume, the number of files in the volume, and the speed of your computer, the process can take several minutes. As compared to compressing files or folders, the task takes longer because Windows XP Professional must go through every folder and change the compression state, then compress (or decompress) every file in that folder.

To compress an entire volume, perform the following steps:

1. Using Windows Explorer or in My Computer, find the volume you wish to compress.
2. Right-click the volume and select Properties.
3. On the General tab (as shown in Figure 10-1) select (or clear, if you wish to decompress a volume) the Compress drive to save disk space check box.
4. Click OK.
5. Next, you'll see a Confirm Attribute Changes dialog box. Select whether you wish to make the compression apply to the entire volume, or just to the root folder.

Files and Folders

Depending on your needs or wants, you might decide that there are only a few folders or files that you care to compress. Rather than compress your entire volume, NTFS allows you to manage the compression of smaller elements, such as files and folders.

In order to enable NTFS compression on select files and folders, follow these steps:

1. Using Windows Explorer or in My Computer, find the file or folder you wish to compress.
2. Right-click the volume and select Properties.
3. On the General tab, click the Advanced button.

Figure 10-1. Compressing an entire volume

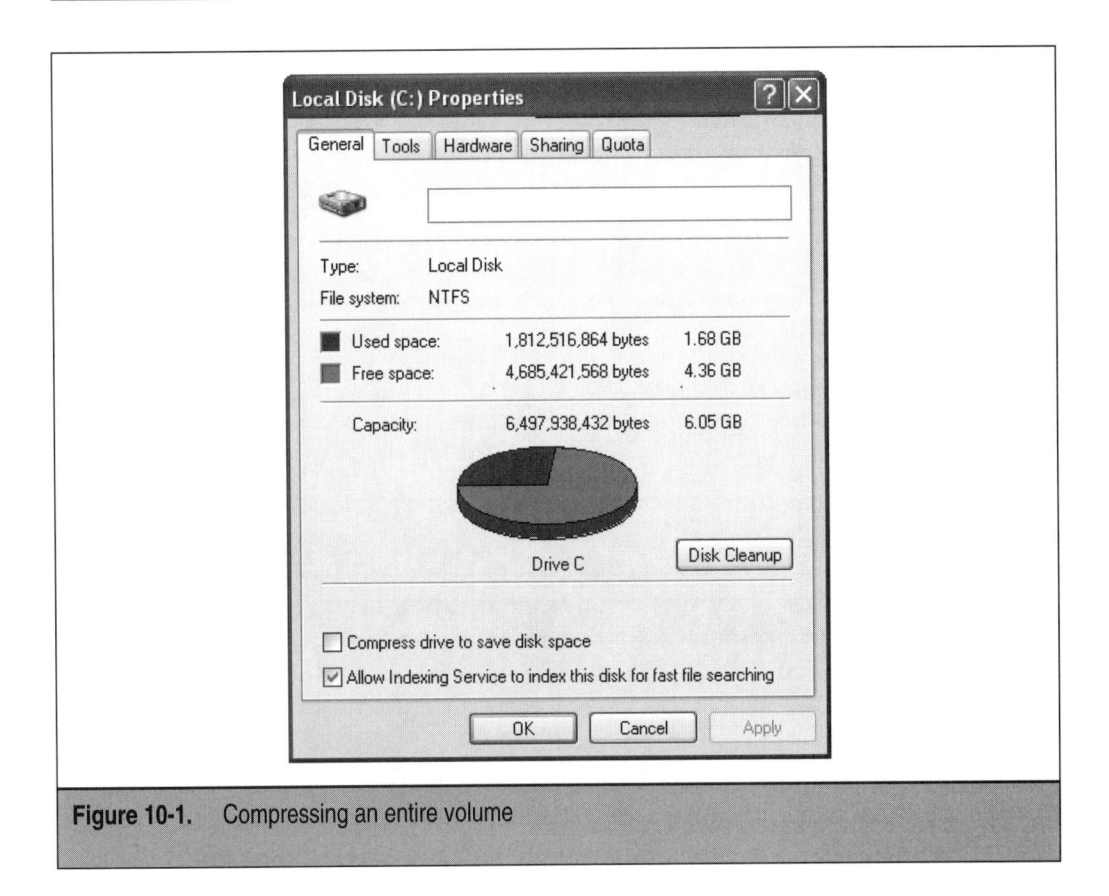

4. In the Advanced Attributes dialog box (as shown in Figure 10-2) select (or clear, if you wish to decompress a volume) the Compress contents to save disk space check box.
5. Click OK.
6. In the Properties box, click OK.
7. If you are compressing a folder, Windows XP Professional will ask you if you want to make the compression apply just to the folder, or to the folder and all its subfolders and files. Make your selection, and then click OK.

When you look at Windows Explorer, you'll notice something a little different on your compressed files and folders. The names of compressed files and folders now appear in a blue font. This is helpful to remind you which files and folders are compressed and which ones are not.

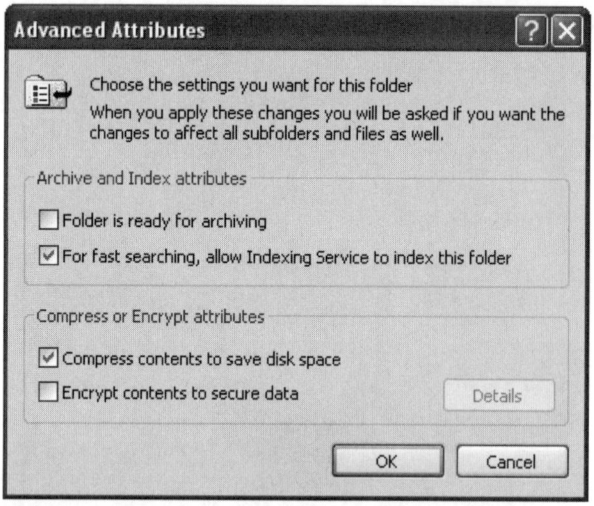

Figure 10-2. Compressing a file or folder

COMPACT.EXE

Like so many other Windows XP Professional tools, you can also compress your files and folders from the command line. The command line might be preferable if you want to perform a batch compression, for instance.

The syntax of COMPACT is as follows:

```
compact /c
```

COMPACT.EXE includes a number of switches that can help customize your compaction duties. In addition to the /c switch (which simply means to compact a file), you can use the /f switch with COMPACT in the event your computer fails during compression, as it allows COMPACT to finish in the background.

Furthermore, COMPACT is useful if you want to compress a certain type of file by using a wildcard. For instance, if you want to compress all your Adobe Acrobat files, you'd enter:

```
compact /c *.pdf
```

From the root folder, you can compress and entire volume by entering:

```
compact /c / i s:\
```

In this case, the switch /i prevents error messages from stopping the compression process.

A complete listing of the COMPACT.EXE switches can be found by entering

```
compact /?
```

at the command prompt.

Performance

Client computers are a good place to use compression, because compression and decompression are performed locally. Conversely, if you place compressed files on servers, the server will spend extra time in the process of compressing and decompressing files. This can cause a performance hit on the server that will radiate into the network, as packets are not being sent out as quickly as they could be.

On the other hand, servers that contain information that is read-only (or files that are infrequently accessed) would be acceptable candidates for compression, because of their access frequency.

Disk Quotas

In this age of MP3s, video clips, and other resource-hungry files, it makes good sense to have a mechanism on hand to limit how much disk space a user can consume. In NTFS, *disk quotas* can be established to limit the amount of hard drive space any one user can fill. But it isn't just worker misbehavior that necessitates disk quotas. For instance, if your hard drive space is very limited, placing quotas will make sure that your hard drive doesn't fill to capacity, closing out mission-critical data that was not able to make it onto the drive.

In Windows XP Professional, disk quotas allow you to do the following:

- Notify users when they have exceeded a warning level (but have not yet reached their quota).
- Prevent writing to the disk if users have reached their quota.

Disk quotas in Windows XP Professional operate on a per-user, per-volume basis. Disk space is charged to each user (the owner of a file is tracked by his or her security identifier, or SID). If a user moves data from one folder of a volume to another folder on the same volume, there is no change in the amount of space the user has occupied. However, if the user *copies* files from one folder to another on the same volume, then the user will be charged twice for that data, because it resides in two locations on the same volume.

Disk quotas are transparent to users. When they look at the available disk space, they are shown how much of their quota is left. As with a full drive, once the quota has been used up no more files can be saved. If a user wants more space, he or she can do the following:

- Delete files
- Have another user assume ownership of files
- Ask the administrator to allot more disk space to the user's quota

> **NOTE** Users cannot "cheat" by compressing their files, thereby allocating more disk space.

When establishing quotas, there are two values that you must be aware of:

- **Warning levels** This establishes a threshold which, when passed, will generate a system log entry that a user has exceeded the warning level.
- **Quota limits** This is the limit of the volume space a user will be allowed to consume. When exceeded, you can tell Windows XP Professional to make a log entry that the quota has been surpassed, or you can simply deny the user the ability to save any more information to the volume. Quota limits can be set as low as 1KB; however, it's a good idea to set the limit to at least 2MB. This allows Windows XP Professional to create a user profile whenever the user logs onto the system.

For example, if you've decided that each user should have a quota of 1GB and you set the warning level at 900MB, when the user has saved 900MB to the volume, an entry is made to the system log. When the user exceeds 1GB, you can set up the quota tool to deny the user any additional disk space, simply make a system log entry, or both.

Enabling Quotas

In order to establish quotas, both the volume must be formatted using NTFS and the quotas must be established by someone with administrator permissions. To enable quotas, follow these steps:

1. Right-click the volume on which you wish to establish quotas.
2. Select Properties.
3. Click the Quota tab (as shown in Figure 10-3).
4. You can make the following settings:
   - Enable or disable disk quotas.
   - Deny disk space to users exceeding their quota.
   - Establish the default warning level and quota limit for new users on the volume.
   - Establish whether to make a log entry when a user exceeds the quota or the warning level.
5. Finally, click OK to establish the quotas.

Quota Management

Once quotas are in place, you can monitor your user's quota levels, warning status, or actual volume space used. Figure 10-4 shows the Quota Entries window, which lists the various users who have access to the computer named GEONOSIS.

Figure 10-3. Establishing disk quotas

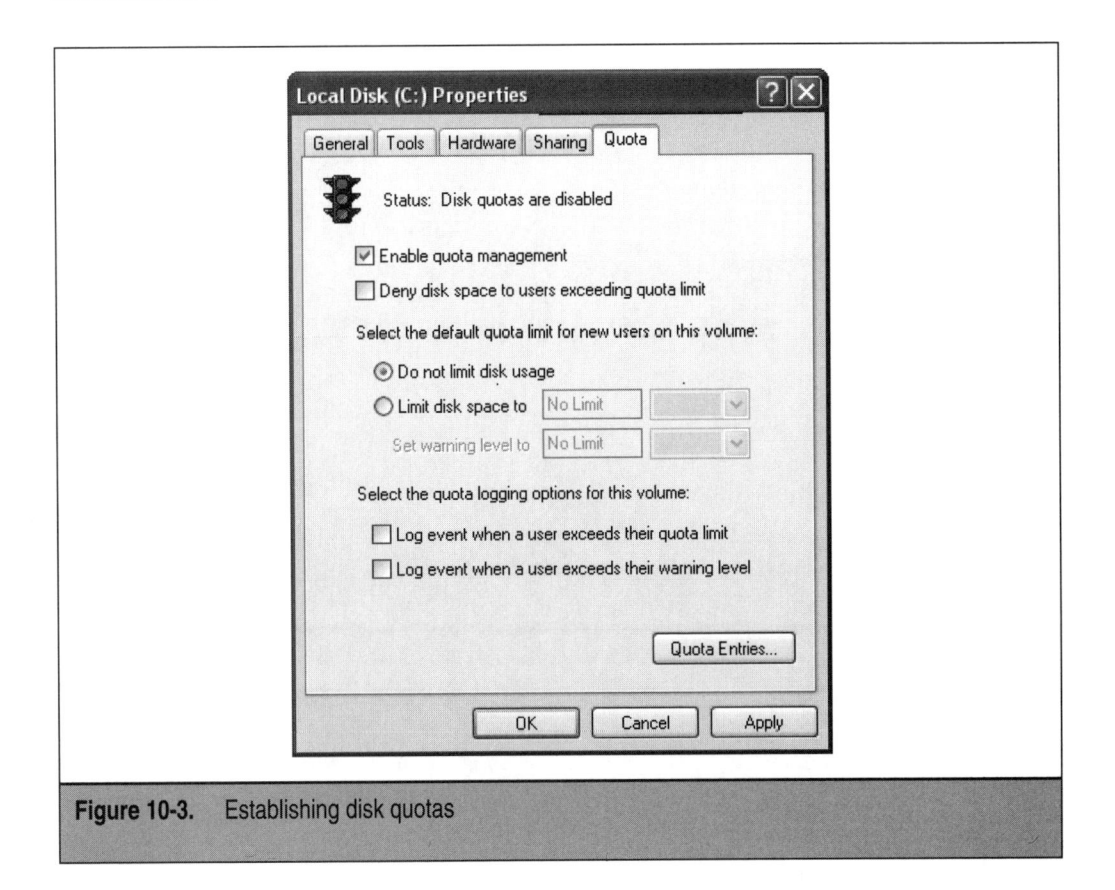

As you can see, of the five users, four are within both the quota limit and warning level. However, the third has exceeded the warning level—this is reflected by the warning icon in the status field.

Let's say that this user needs more disk space made available. To change the quota (either up or down), follow these steps:

1. Right-click the appropriate volume.
2. Select Properties.
3. Click the Quota tab, and then click Quota Entries (this will produce the window shown in Figure 10-4).
4. Right-click the user, and then click Properties to manage that user's quota limit.

The first time you start the Quotas Entries window, however, you will find a blank console. Before establishing any quotas, you must first populate the list with users. This is accomplished by clicking Quota in the menu bar, and then selecting New Quota

Figure 10-4. The Quota Entries window

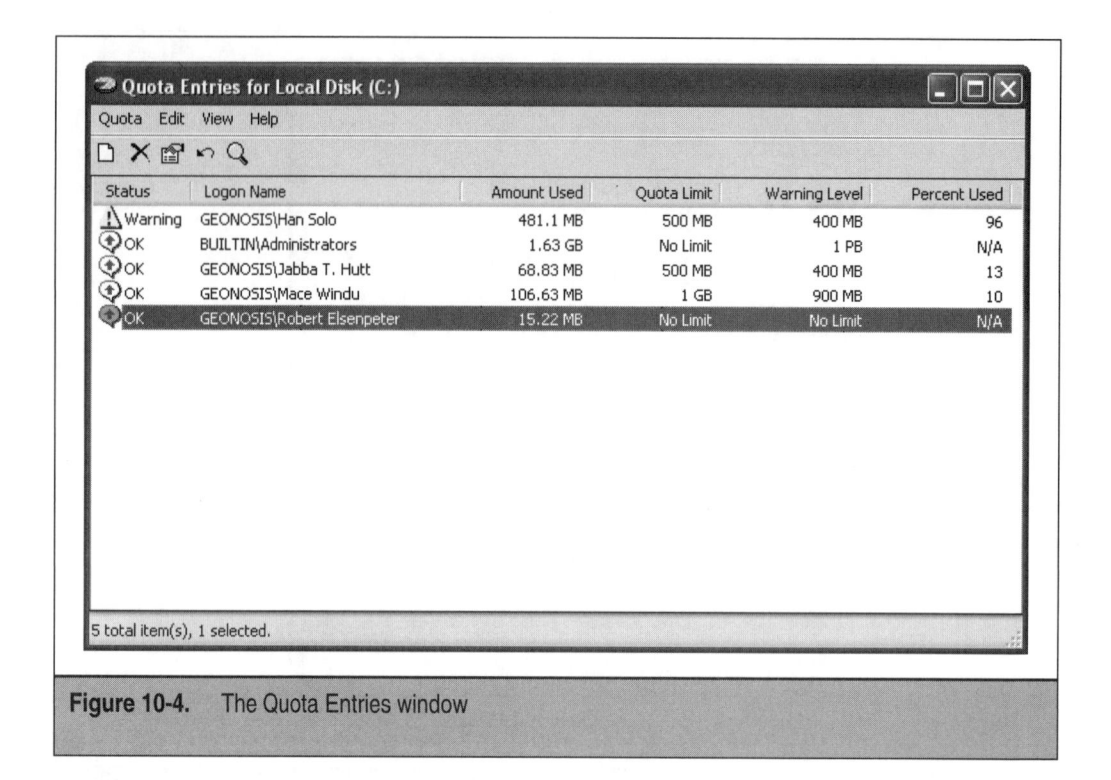

Entry. This generates a window that asks which object you wish to establish a quota for. Enter a username, and the window shown in Figure 10-5 is displayed.

In the Add New Quota Entry window, you establish your quotas. They can be as low as 1 kilobyte (the default amount) or up to a maximum of 6 exabytes.

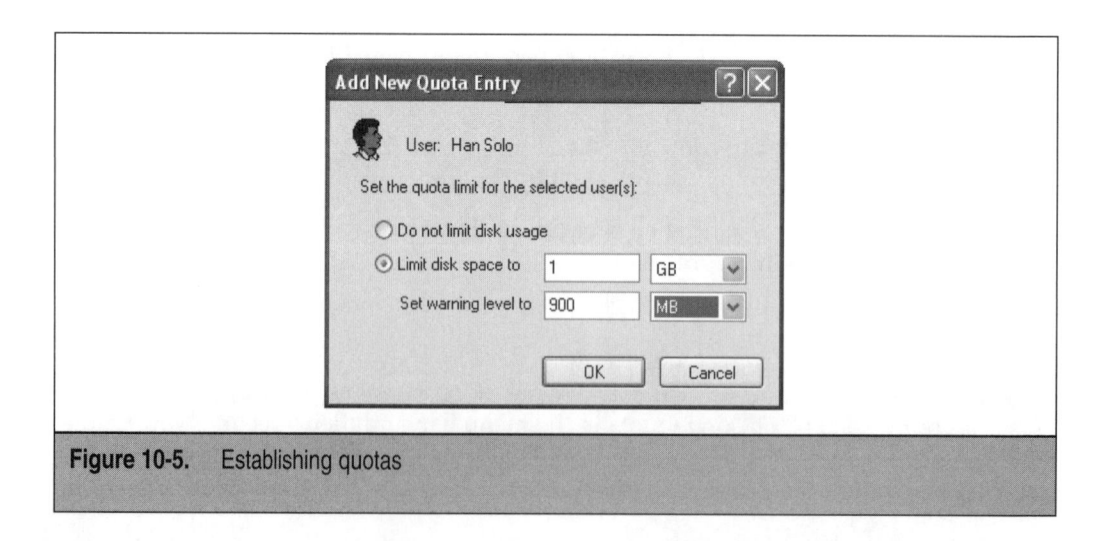

Figure 10-5. Establishing quotas

EFS

When you erase a file from your hard drive, the fact of the matter is you aren't *really* erasing it. Rather, you're simply telling the computer that the portion of the hard drive containing the file is now available for use. In the event something else is written over the file, then it gets wiped out. However, if the file is not replaced, then it is still on the disk and can be resurrected rather easily.

In Windows XP Professional, using the Encrypting File System (EFS) can protect data. Using EFS, when files are saved to disk, they are encrypted, turning them into gibberish unless you've accessed the data correctly.

NOTE EFS can only be used on an NTFS volume.

EFS is a three-step process:

1. A public-private key pair and a per-file encryption key are used to encrypt and decrypt data. When a user first encrypts a file, EFS creates a file encryption key (FEK). The FEK is encrypted with the user's public key. Then, the encrypted FEK is stored along with the file.

2. There are a number of ways a file can be marked for encryption:
   - Manually setting up EFS by changing the file's advanced properties
   - Storing the file in a folder that is already set for encryption
   - Using CIPHER.EXE at the command line

3. To decrypt a file, the user will open the file and remove the encryption or decrypt using CIPHER.EXE. When decrypting the file, EFS first decodes the FEK by using the user's private key, and then decrypts the data using the FEK.

EFS in Windows XP Professional

EFS has been around since Windows 2000, but Windows XP Professional includes some new features, adding to its overall functionality. The new features in Windows XP Professional include the following:

- Offline files can be encrypted.
- Data Recovery Agents are optional.
- The triple-DES (3DES) algorithm can be used in place of Data Encryption Standard XORed (DESX).
- A password reset disk can be used to reset a user's password.
- Encrypted files can be stored in Web folders.

Windows XP Professional enables EFS by default. However, there are some prerequisites to using EFS. First, users must have a public-private key pair and a public key certificate for encryption. However, EFS can use self-signed certificates, so they need not be assigned by an administrator before use.

Encryption and Decryption

When using EFS, it is a good idea to encrypt the entire folder, rather than a specific file. This makes the process much easier and more efficient. Rather than encrypting a file here or there, you need only perform encryption once in a blanket move that can protect multiple files at once. Furthermore, by encrypting the entire folder, any backup files that are created are also encrypted.

NOTE Naturally, only backup files stored in an encrypted folder will be encrypted.

To encrypt a file or folder, follow these steps:

1. In My Computer, select the file or folder you wish to encrypt.
2. Right-click the file or folder and select Properties.
3. On the General tab, click the Advanced button. The resulting screen is shown in Figure 10-6.
4. Select the Encrypt contents to secure data check box, and then click OK.

If you just selected a file to encrypt, Windows XP Professional will ask you if you would like to apply encryption just to that file, or to the entire folder. As we noted previously, it's a good idea to encrypt the entire folder, but you can still encrypt a single file. Once you've encrypted a file, its text will be displayed in green.

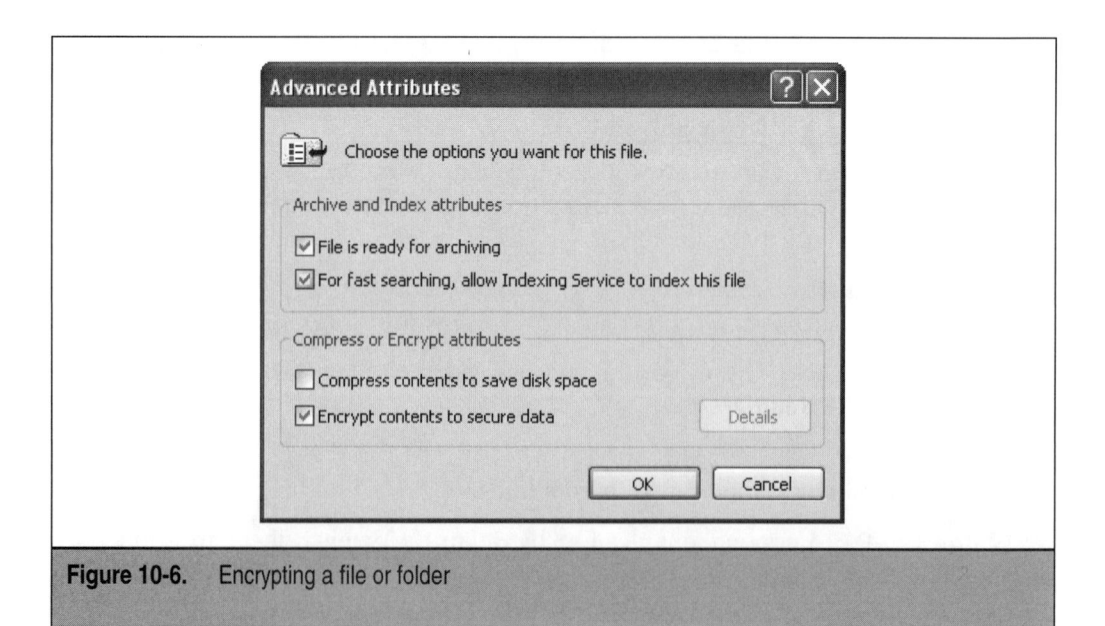

Figure 10-6. Encrypting a file or folder

NOTE Files that are compressed are listed in a blue font. However, a file cannot be both encrypted and compressed.

Decrypting files and folders is a similar process to encrypting them. However, in this case you only need to clear the Encrypt contents to secure data check box.

The CIPHER Command

If you prefer, you can use the command-line tool CIPHER to encrypt and decrypt files and folders. Using CIPHER by itself simply shows the attributes of the files and folders contained in the current folder. However, CIPHER can be used with a number of switches. The following are the most useful:

- /e   Sets a file or folder to be encrypted
- /d   Decrypts a selected file or folder
- /a   Specifies that the action will be performed on all files in a folder
- /?   Displays a listing of all CIPHER's arguments

The following shows two files that had been previously enciphered using the Windows XP Professional GUI, both of which are highly sensitive: Top Secret Plans For World Domination.txt and Aunt Barb's Apple Brown Betty Recipe.txt. By using the CIPHER command, we can see the EFS attributes of the files in this directory. Both of these sensitive files were encrypted. Windows XP Professional tells us this with an "E" next to the filenames. The unencoded folders have a "U" next to them.

```
C:>cipher

 Listing C:\Documents and Settings\Robert Elsenpeter\My Documents\
 New files added to this directory will not be encrypted.

E Aunt Barb's Apple Brown Betty Recipe.txt
U My Music
U My Pictures
E Top Secret Plans For World Domination.txt
```

To decipher these files, we enter the following:

```
C:>cipher /d /a

 Decrypting files in C:\Documents and Settings\Robert Elsenpeter\My Documents\

Aunt Barb's Apple Brown Betty Recipe.txt [OK]
Top Secret Plans For World Domination.txt [OK]

2 file(s) [or directorie(s)] within 1 directorie(s) were decrypted.
```

As a result, the two files were unencoded.

NTFS Optimization

Even though Windows XP Professional and NTFS include many bells and whistles to make file storage and manipulation easy, that simplicity comes at a price. If you need to kick up your hard drive efficiency, there are a number of items you might want to check.

Cluster Size

Deciding to convert your hard drive to NTFS requires some planning—as we will discuss in the section "Converting/Formatting Drives with NTFS" later in the chapter. One way to optimize performance is to think ahead about cluster sizes. If all your files will be largely the same size and less than the default cluster size of 4KB, then you might want to consider changing the default size of your clusters when you convert your hard drive.

Think of your hard drive as being made up of billions of tiny buckets. These are clusters. Let's say these little buckets each hold 4KB of data. If each file only consumes 3KB, then each of these buckets is wasting space. Sure, it's only 1KB, but all those bits add up. Table 10-1 shows the default cluster sizes for various sizes of NTFS hard drives.

On the other hand, smaller clusters result in more fragmentation. That means when you empty one of the little buckets, in order for it to be used again, there must be a file the same size or smaller than the files that used to occupy it. As more files are added to the hard drive (but not written to a previously used series of clusters), fragmentation occurs, because even though there is space on the disk, it is in chunks so small that it cannot be used. If you store large files or they tend to increase in size, it's a good idea to set the default cluster to 16-32KB.

Cluster size is also a concern for volumes converted from FAT to NTFS in Windows 2000 or earlier. This is because the default cluster size is 512 bytes, so there is certain to be fragmentation. For best results, it's a good idea to back up the hard drive, reformat it, specify your desired cluster size, and then put your data back on the volume.

If your hard drive has become fragmented, it's a great idea to run the defragmenting tool that comes with Windows XP Professional. We'll talk about defragmentation and

Hard Drive Size	Cluster Size
512MB or smaller	512 bytes
513MB–1GB	1,024 bytes
1GB–2GB	2,048 bytes
2GB and larger	4,069 bytes

Table 10-1. Default NTFS Cluster Sizes

Windows XP Professional's defragmentation tools in the section "Defragmenting," later in this chapter.

Get Organized

Organization isn't just a good practice for your medicine cabinet or backyard shed—NTFS likes things to be organized, too. In fact, performing a couple of housekeeping tasks on your hard drive can boost NTFS performance.

File Structure   Even though NTFS supports folders with huge amounts of files, it isn't a good idea to chuck everything into one folder. This is especially true if you are constantly reading or deleting files from this folder. Whenever you open this folder, Windows XP Professional spends cycles getting the names and statistics of each file. Your best bet is to put these folders into subfolders whenever possible, to keep the number of reads to a minimum.

Indexing   If your users are constantly searching drives for files and folders, you should turn on the Indexing Service. This cuts search times dramatically. The Indexing Service can also cut down on search times when searching within a document.

Once the Indexing Service is enabled, NTFS tracks changes in the file system in its change journal. This need to update the change journal will cause an initial decrease in system performance; however, in environments where users often search for files and folders, the resulting improvement in search speed will more than make up for the initial performance hit.

Antivirus Shmantivirus

It's common knowledge that you should run some sort of antivirus program on your computer to keep it safe and clean. However, these programs—albeit hazard preventers—also carry with them a lot of overhead. We're not suggesting that you *not* use an antivirus program, but rather that you test a number of antivirus applications, keeping performance in mind while evaluating them. Furthermore, the software vendor probably offers some sort of tuning guide that can help keep overhead to a minimum.

Compression

Earlier, we talked about the ups and downs of compression. Though you might save a few dollars not having to install a larger hard drive, if your volumes are compressed, then you're likely to suffer some performance problems. As we said before, it's a good idea not to compress a server's hard drive. Also, judicious use of compression on client computers isn't a bad idea, either.

Sparse Files

If you have files that contain large amounts of zeros, Windows XP Professional allows you to conserve disk space by specifying the file as a *sparse* file. If an NTFS file is marked as sparse, then NTFS only allocates clusters for the data the application specifically declares. Nonspecified ranges are not allocated, and when the file is read from the disk, the allocated ranges will be returned and the nonallocated ranges will be filled in as zeros. For instance, the Windows Indexing Service uses sparse files on NTFS volumes.

Sparse files are converted using the following syntax at the command prompt:

```
fsutil sparse
```

SPARSE is followed by these arguments:

- **queryflag**   Queries SPARSE
- **queryrange**   Scans a file for ranges that might contain nonzero data
- **setflag**   Marks the indicated file as sparse
- **setrange** *pathname BeginningOffset length*   Fills a specified range with zeros where *BeginningOffset* is the offset within the file to mark as sparse and *length* is the length of the region (in bytes) within the file to be marked as sparse.

Those arguments are followed by the pathname of the file. For example:

```
fsutil sparse setflag c:\sparsesample.txt
```

Sparse files work only on volumes mounted by Windows XP Professional and Windows 2000 computers. If you move a file to a FAT system or to NTFS mounted by another operating system, then the file will revert to its original size. If there isn't enough disk space to accommodate the actual size of the file, then the operation will fail.

NTFS PERMISSIONS

In the last chapter, we talked about network security and the issue of permissions, but it bears more discussion in this chapter because permissions are only available on NTFS drives. In this section, we talk about NTFS's ability to keep unwanted eyes out of your files. Unlike FAT file systems, access to the share isn't either on or off. NTFS affords a level of granularity that keeps out those you want kept out and lets in those you want let in.

Individual User Permissions

Before talking specifically about the permissions that can be established for users and groups, as well as for files themselves, it's important to cover some ground on how permissions do what they're supposed to do. First we'll show you the trickle-down effect of inheritance, and then we'll explore a Windows XP Professional tool that is meant to help, but can be a stumbling block if you aren't aware of its function.

Inheritance

A given network can have a couple of users, or it can have thousands. When establishing user permissions for your NTFS volumes and folders, the task of setting up those permissions isn't too tough for an organization with six people. However, as we noted in Chapter 9, when an organization starts to get big, organizing users into specific groups makes permissions management much easier.

First, you'd establish a set of permissions for a specific group—Engineers, for instance. Then, whenever a new engineer comes into the organization, he or she is added to that group. Immediately, the new engineer *inherits* the permissions of the parent group.

> **NOTE** *Inheritance* is a term that also applies to other objects on an NTFS volume. For instance, if you have established permissions on a certain folder, and then add a subfolder within that folder, inheritance keeps you from having to create a new set of permissions for that folder. Rather, it inherits the permissions from its parent folder.

If, for instance, you decide that the Engineers group needs a certain permission granted or revoked, this is a simple matter to manage. After making the change (which we explain later in this section), the new permission is passed along to everyone in the group.

On the other hand, let's say that a specific engineer needs a permission granted that the other engineers do not need. By going into the Engineers group and making the change on that specific user, only that engineer has the new permission, but he or she hasn't inherited it from the group. As such, the permission won't propagate to everyone else in the group.

Simple File Sharing

New to Windows XP Professional is a feature called *simple file sharing.* When Windows XP Professional is first installed or when you share a volume or folder, simple file sharing is enabled. In order to enable more tools for user access management, you must disable simple file sharing.

You might be wondering why, if simple file sharing needs to be turned off, what good it is in the first place. In essence, simple file sharing makes the process of sharing your files and folders easy. When simple file sharing is enabled, there isn't a lot of configuration that needs to occur for others to have access to your files, printers, and so forth. As such, it provides an easy way to share files. However, if you wish to manage *who* can get access to your files, simple file sharing should be disabled. To deactivate simple file sharing, follow these steps:

1. Select Start | My Computer, then click Tools and select Folder Options.
2. In the Folder Options dialog box, click the View tab.

3. Scroll to the bottom of the Advanced Settings box and either select or clear the check box next to Use simple file sharing.
4. Click OK.

> **NOTE** Disabling simple file sharing alone won't allow you to set permissions for files. You must also have your files and folders on an NTFS volume or partition.

Folder and Volume Permissions

Permissions control what a user or group can do with an object on your network or their local computer. Permissions are supported *only* if simple sharing is deactivated and if NTFS is used. Table 10-2 lists the permissions that can be managed for folders. Table 10-3 lists the permissions that can be managed for files.

Establishing and Managing Permissions

When establishing permissions for your individual files, folders, and NTFS volumes, you have many more security options than on a file system using FAT. The Properties tab for a selected folder or volume includes a Security tab. By clicking that tab, you have access to a number of options for access management.

To set permissions on a given folder or volume, follow these steps:

1. Locate the volume or folder for which you wish to set permissions.
2. Right-click it, and then select Properties.
3. Select the Security tab.

Permission	Allows or Prevents This Action
Change Permissions	Altering the permissions of the folder
Create Files	Creating new files within the folder
Create Folders	Creating subfolders within the folder
Delete	Deleting the folder
Delete Subfolders and Files	Deleting files and subfolders, even if you don't have permissions for those subfolders and files
List Folder	Viewing the contents of the folder
Read Attributes	Viewing the attributes of the folder
Read Permissions	Viewing the permissions of the folder
Take Ownership	Taking ownership of the folder from the present owner
Traverse Folder	Opening the folder to look at subfolders and parent folders
Write Attributes	Altering the properties of the folder

Table 10-2. Folder Permissions

Permission	Allows or Prevents This Action
Append Data	Adding information to the end of the file, without altering existing information
Change Permissions	Altering a file's permissions
Delete	Deleting the file
Execute File	Running a program contained within the file
Read Attributes	Viewing the attributes of the file
Read Data	Viewing the contents of the file
Read Permissions	Reading the permissions of the file
Take Ownership	Taking ownership of the file from its present owner
Write Attributes	Changing the attributes of the file
Write Data	Modifying the contents of the file

Table 10-3. File Permissions

NOTE If your NTFS volume is shared, you should set permissions via the Security tab, rather than using the Permissions button on the Sharing tab.

When the Properties window appears, you will see two windowpanes—the uppermost pane contains a list of users and user groups (as shown in Figure 10-7). The bottommost pane contains a list of permissions that can be set and adjusted for the user. Again, this tab is only available on volumes using NTFS.

By clicking a specific user or user group, you can establish permissions for that user or group in the lower box. The following permissions are available:

- **Full Control**   Allows the user or group to read, create, change, and delete files
- **Modify**   Allows users to delete files and folders, alter permissions, or take ownership of a file or folder from another user
- **Read & Execute**   Allows users to read and run files, but they cannot change the contents of the shared volume or folder
- **List Folder Contents**   Allows users to view folder contents
- **Read**   Allows users to view the contents of the volume or folder. They can also open files, but are not allowed to save changes
- **Write**   Allows users to write to the volume or folder, but not to open files or view a file listing
- **Special permissions**   By clicking the Advanced button, special permissions can be applied

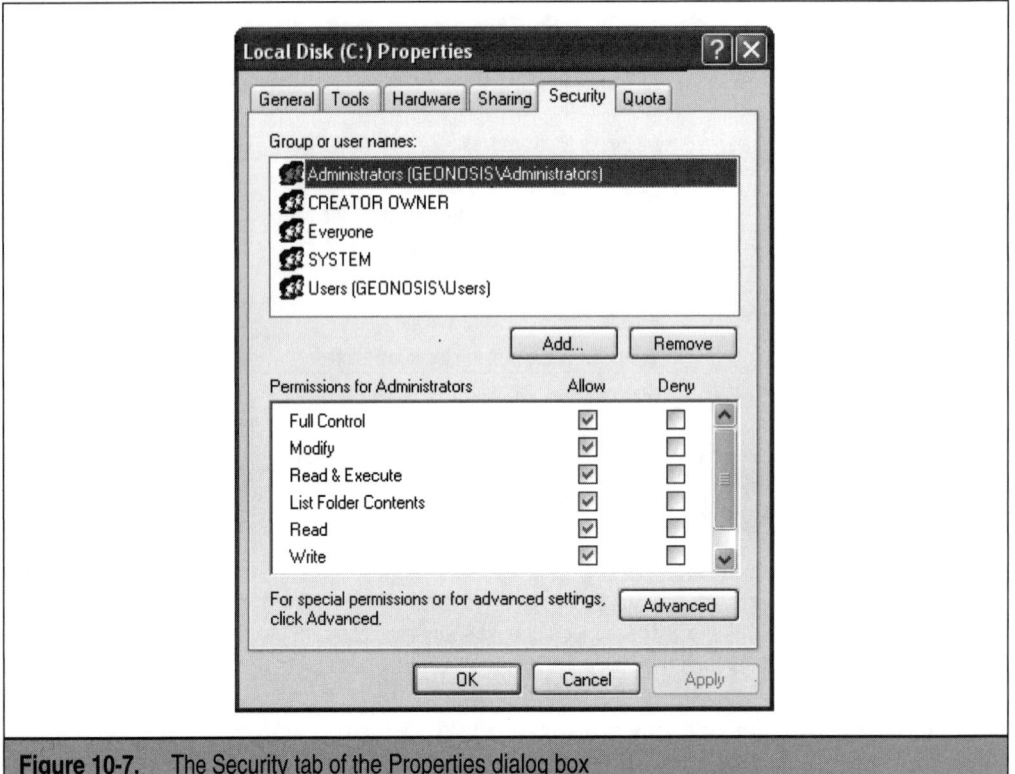

Figure 10-7. The Security tab of the Properties dialog box

Limiting Users

Depending on the size and structure of your organization, you might not want everyone trying to access the same volume simultaneously. If you need to place a limitation on how many users can access a volume or folder at the same time, open the Permissions dialog box (as described previously), and then select the Sharing tab (this is shown in Figure 10-8).

In the User limit section, you can choose either of the following:

- **Maximum allowed**   Allows the maximum number of users the network will support
- **Allow this number of users**   Allows a set number of users that you define

For more information on permissions, flip back to Chapter 9.

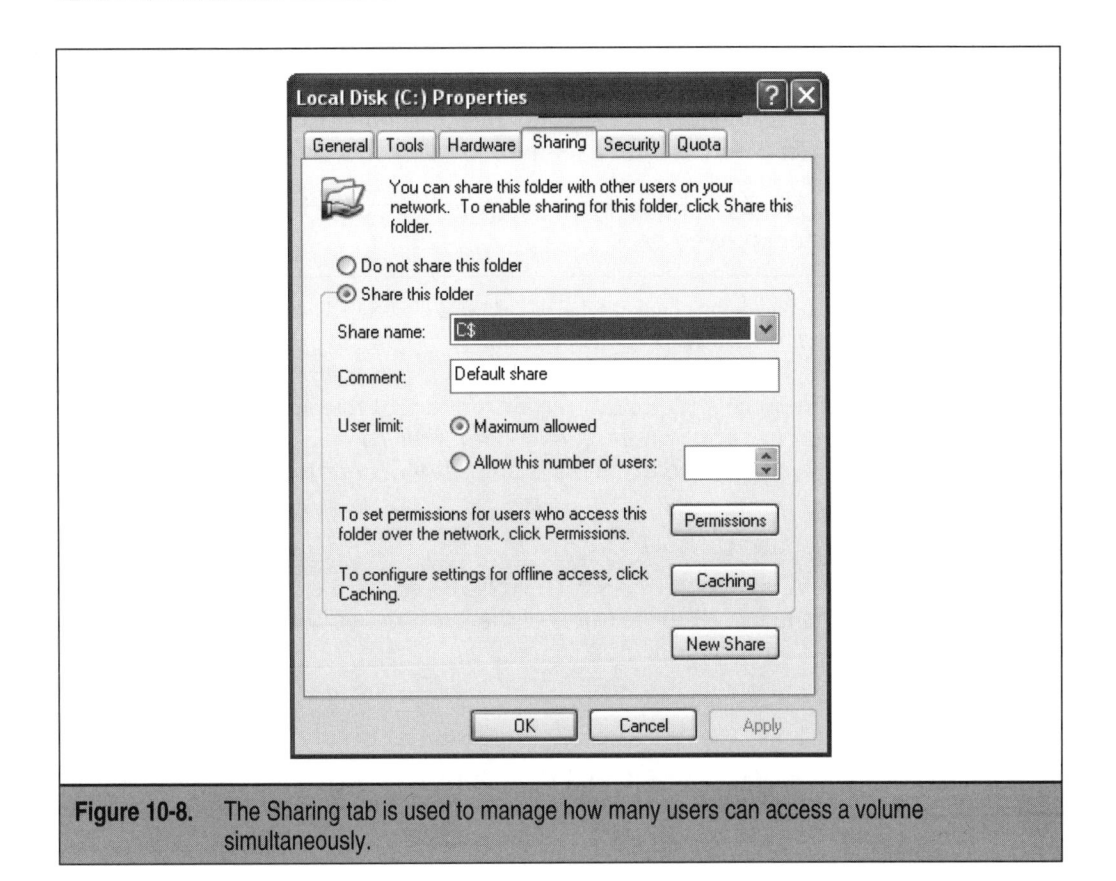

Figure 10-8. The Sharing tab is used to manage how many users can access a volume simultaneously.

CONVERTING/FORMATTING DRIVES WITH NTFS

In order to take advantage of all the features we've talked about, hard drives must use the NTFS file format. This is an easy enough process when the computer comes with Windows XP Professional preinstalled, because the drive is already in the NTFS format. However, when migrating from a computer using FAT (such as Windows 95 or Windows 98), it is necessary to convert the hard drive or partition.

This section examines the steps you should take when converting your drive to NTFS, or when formatting a hard drive. First, we'll discuss some of the issues surrounding a FAT-to-NTFS conversion, then we'll talk about the command-line tool—CONVERT.EXE—and the switches that can be used to convert your drive.

Issues

Although NTFS provides excellent functionality over FAT, there are still a number of issues one must consider before deciding to make the conversion:

- Converting to NTFS is a one-way street. Once you make the conversion to NTFS, you cannot convert back.

NOTE There are some third-party products that will allow you to convert back to FAT, but it's best to stick with one format, rather than switching back and forth.

- The conversion process requires a certain amount of free space on the drive or partition in order to perform the conversion. If the conversion tool deems that there isn't enough space to make the change, it will not proceed.
- You might be operating in a dual-boot environment. As such, you should be aware of the following issues:
    - Although Windows NT uses NTFS (NTFS version 4.0, to be exact), it will not be able to use all the features of the latest flavor of NTFS—NTFS 5.0, introduced with Windows 2000.
    - Windows Me, 9X, and earlier cannot access NTFS files.
- If you convert to NTFS, Windows XP Professional cannot be uninstalled.
- The possibility of data corruption during conversion exists. As always, back up your data.
- Conversion can take some time. Because the first step is to run the CHKDSK.EXE tool, time is needed for more than just the conversion.

NOTE No matter what operating system you're using, floppy disks will always use FAT.

Protecting Data

Converting a drive from FAT to NTFS can be a stressful process, especially when the issue of data integrity is considered. Although it is strongly recommended that you back up your files before performing such a conversion, Windows XP Professional performs the following steps to protect data from corruption.

First, CONVERT.EXE runs CHKDSK or AUTOCHK to make sure the file system is not damaged. If any files are found to be corrupt, you must use the CHKDSK /F command to repair any problems, then run convert again. AUTOCHK, on the other hand, tries to fix the problem itself, and proceeds with the conversion process. Next, the existing FAT clusters are relocated (to make way for the new NTFS structure), and then the file allocation table is rebuilt. If the sectors are unreadable, then the conversion process fails and the FAT volume remains as it was before the conversion.

An *elementary* NTFS structure is formed in the FAT free space. These structures are fixed-size tables that are used in all NTFS volumes. Following the elementary structure, an NTFS master file table and directory are generated in the FAT free space. The amount of space needed will vary, depending on the total number of files and folders to be converted. The next step is to indicate in the NTFS bitmap that the FAT clusters in use during the conversion process are now free. The FAT metadata overhead can be freed up and used as free space for NTFS.

Finally, the NTFS boot sector is written. It is this action that causes the drive to be seen as an NTFS volume. If there is any error in the conversion up to this point, the drive is still considered a FAT drive. Throughout this process, all writing is performed to free space. If there is a problem with the conversion, the FAT data will still be usable.

Defragmenting

As part of your routine maintenance on a Windows XP Professional NTFS hard drive, it's a smart idea to defragment the drive regularly. There are two ways to defragment your NTFS drive in Windows XP Professional.

First, you can use the Disk Defragmenter snap-in, shown in Figure 10-9.

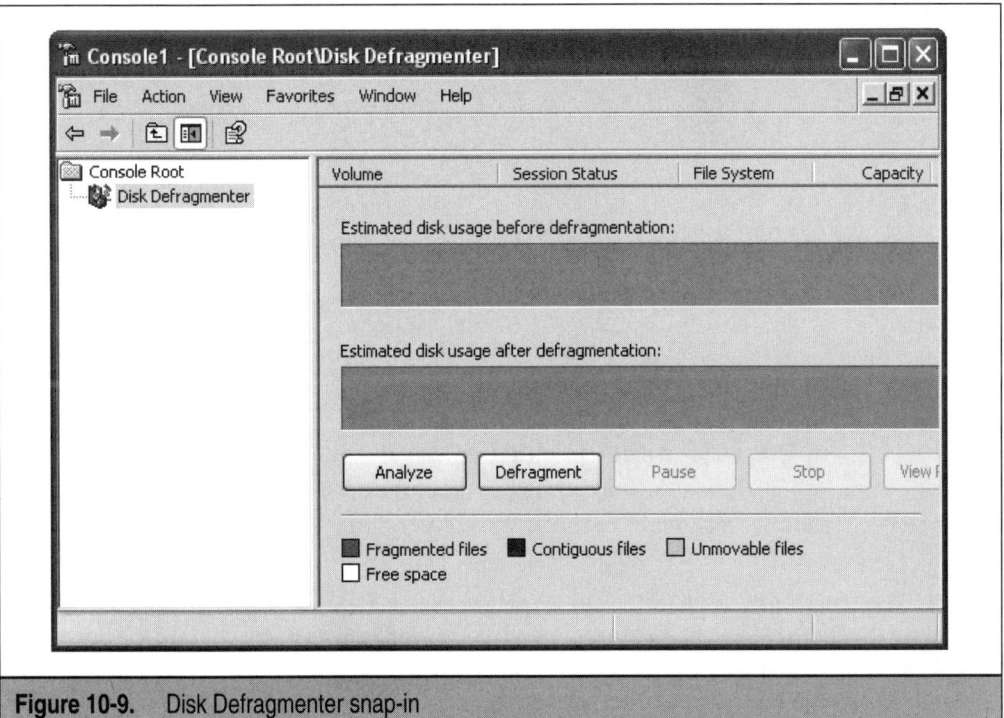

Figure 10-9. Disk Defragmenter snap-in

Alternatively, you can use the command-line tool DEFRAG, new to Windows XP Professional, as follows:

```
defrag <volume> [-a] [-f] [-v] [-?]
```

The attributes are as follows:

- **volume** Drive letter to be defragmented
- **-a** Analyze only
- **-f** Force defragmentation even if free space is low
- **-v** Verbose output

Both methods of defragmentation provide new functionality in Windows XP Professional. First, Windows XP Professional allows NTFS volumes with clusters of any size to be defragmented. This is in contrast to Windows 2000, where only clusters in sizes of 4KB or smaller could be defragmented. Also, files contained in fewer than 16 clusters can be defragmented. In Windows 2000, free space smaller than 16 clusters was ignored.

Converting

There are three ways to convert your drives into NTFS:

- Format while installing Windows XP Professional
- Convert using Disk Management
- Convert using command prompt

Format While Installing Windows XP Professional

The easiest time to convert your hard drive to NTFS is while installing Windows XP Professional. Conversion is accomplished as part of the migration. As you might imagine, conversion is even less troublesome if it is performed on a clean system—that is, a system with no files that need backing up. Although ideal, this is rarely possible.

Convert Using the Disk Management Snap-In

If you've already installed Windows XP Professional, but chose not to convert to NTFS for whatever reason, you can still perform the conversion. Windows XP Professional includes a snap-in called Disk Management that allows the process in a GUI environment.

> **NOTE** Disk Management allows the conversion of any drive or partition, except CD-ROM and DVD-ROM drives and the system drive.

Once you've started the snap-in (as shown in Figure 10-10), select the partition you wish to reformat. Right-click the partition, and then select Format. Another pop-up dialog box will appear, allowing you to choose the following items:

- Volume name
- File system
- Cluster size

There are two check boxes at the bottom of the pop-up dialog box: Perform quick format and Enable file and folder compression. It's best to leave the quick format box clear (as quick formats can result in errors) and check the other box if you wish to use file and folder compression.

NOTE The biggest limitation to converting a hard drive to NTFS is that it cannot run on the current system disk.

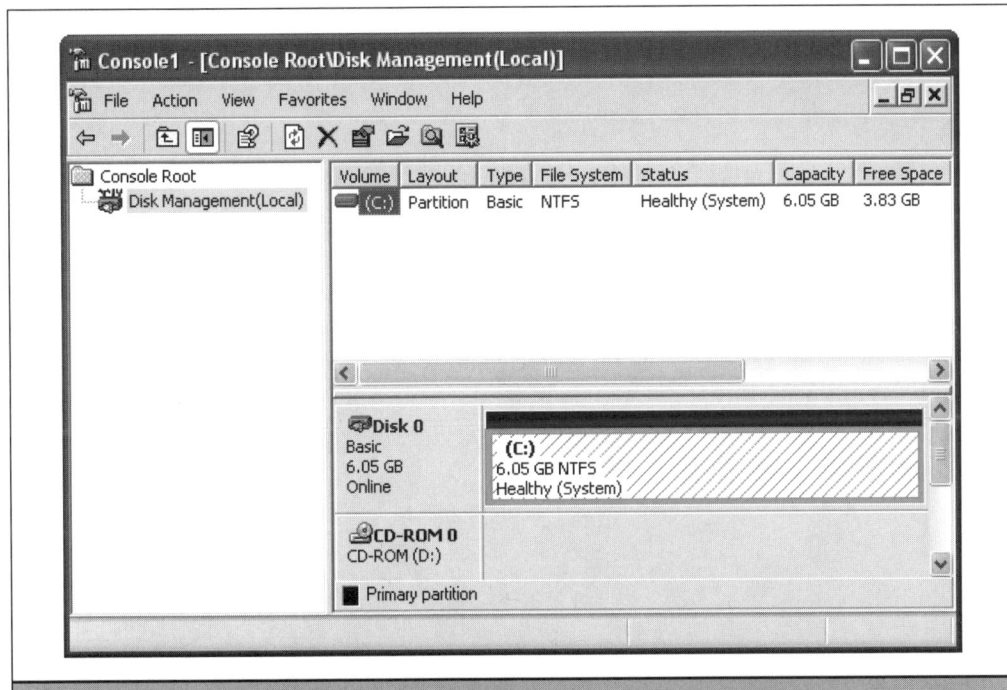

Figure 10-10. The Disk Management snap-in

Convert Using the Command Prompt

The third way to convert your computer to NTFS is similar to the last method; however, this method uses the command prompt. This is ideal when you have no backup storage devices and have large files that won't fit onto another partition. The tool used in Windows XP Professional is called CONVERT.EXE.

The syntax for CONVERT is as follows:

```
convert volume: /fs:ntfs [/v] [/x] [/cvtarea: filename] [/nosecurity] [/?]
```

where *volume* is the drive letter, mounted drive, or volume name you wish to convert. These are the switches used with CONVERT:

- **/fs:ntfs**   Indicates that you want to convert the drive to NTFS
- **/v**   Activates the verbose mode, which displays all messages generated by Windows XP Professional during the conversion
- **/x**   Dismounts the volume before it is converted if necessary
- **/cvtarea:*filename*** Denotes that NTFS metadata files are written to a placeholder file. This file must be located in the root folder of the converted volume
- **/nosecurity**   Does not apply default NTFS permissions to the converted volume. This switch mimics a Windows 2000 conversion
- **/?**   Displays CONVERT help

You might get an error message telling you that the drive is in use and cannot be formatted. Don't worry, this doesn't mean that the conversion can never take place. Rather, Windows XP Professional will ask if you wish to perform the conversion on the next reboot. If you choose OK, then you should reboot the computer to complete the conversion.

NTFS allows you a level of robust file management. Whether you need to compress, encrypt, or manage file quotas, NTFS provides a means to accomplish these goals. Furthermore, if you are using the FAT file system, conversion is an easy process. Although Windows XP Professional includes a number of tools to enhance security (such as Internet Connection Firewall and Group Policy), NTFS allows you to manage resources of individual files.

CHAPTER 11

Network Shares

Windows XP Professional allows you to share just about anything on a network—whether it's files and folders, printers, or even applications. In this chapter, we talk about how you can share your network's resources.

First, we cover the specifics of sharing applications, files and folders, drives, and printers. Additionally, once you've enabled your sharing, we'll talk about the ways you can manage your shared resources. Finally, we'll dip our big toes back into the waters of network security and talk about the specific ways you can keep your shares secure, be it via permission management or administering users once they've accessed your network resources.

UNDERSTANDING SHARES

By enabling sharing on Windows XP Professional, you can share your files, folders, printers, and other network resources. These resources can be shared either with other users on a local computer, or users on a network. This section explains how to set up sharing on your Windows XP Professional system.

First, we'll talk about sharing folders and drives. Then, we'll turn our attention to printers before rounding the section out with a discussion of application sharing using the Windows Messenger application.

Folder and Drive Sharing

The ability to share information is what networks are all about. Without being able to access the same files and folders, there would be little reason for a network. Windows XP Professional allows folders and drives to be shared in a number of ways. Essentially, enabling sharing is quite simple. However, the way in which items are shared will differ, depending on how your Windows XP Professional system is set up.

Be aware that this section discusses folder and drive sharing. The folder level is the most basic level at which you can manage sharing. You cannot enable sharing for a single file. It must be moved to or created within a folder that has sharing enabled.

Enabling Sharing

If you decide to enable file sharing, the process is very simple. Simply navigate to the desired folder, right-click it, and select Properties from the menu that appears. Click the Sharing tab, and then make the requisite settings. The settings you choose are dependent on a number of issues: First, whether you have Simple File Sharing enabled or disabled will present you with different options. Furthermore, the file system you're using—NTFS or FAT—will also affect your sharing options. We'll explain these various settings later in this chapter.

In order to share your resources on the network, you must first have File and Printer Sharing for Microsoft Networks enabled in your network dialog box. If you don't see the Sharing tab in your folder's Properties dialog box, then you do not have this service enabled. Normally, this service is automatically installed by the Network Setup Wizard. However, if you need to install this service, follow the steps presented in this section.

> **NOTE** File and Printer Sharing for Microsoft Networks only needs to be installed on peer-to-peer networks of Windows computers. If you are in a domain environment, then the permission must be set up on the server.

1. Click Start, right-click My Network Places, choose Properties, right-click Local Area Connection, and choose Properties.
2. Click the General tab.
3. Click the Install button. This calls up the Select Network Component Type dialog box.
4. Select Service and click the Add button.
5. Select File and Printer Sharing for Microsoft Networks and click OK.
6. You will be returned to the Local Area Connection window and might be asked to insert the Windows XP Professional CD-ROM.
7. Click OK to save your changes.
8. You might be asked to restart your computer.

Access Levels

Windows XP Professional offers five levels of access, which govern file and folder access. These are useful to know so that, depending on your organization's sharing needs, you can make the requisite settings. The levels are as follows:

- **Level 1** My Documents. This is the most restrictive level. The only person who can read these documents is the person who created them.
- **Level 2** My Documents. This is the default level for local folders.
- **Level 3** Files in shared documents are available to local users.
- **Level 4** Shared Files on the Network. At this level, everyone on the network can read these files.
- **Level 5** Shared Files on the Network. At this level, not only can everyone read these files, but they can also be written to.

> **NOTE** Files at levels 1, 2, and 3 are only available to users who log on locally.

The following paragraphs explain the specifics of these levels in greater detail. To exemplify configuring these access levels, the process of establishing this level of security is shown on a system with Simple File Sharing enabled.

Level 1 The first level, Level 1, is the most stringent level of file security. At this level, only the owner of the file can read or write to it—not even the network administrator can access these files. Furthermore, all subfolders within a Level 1 folder maintain the tight level of privacy that the parent folder establishes. If the owner wishes to make any files or subfolders within this folder available to others, then the security settings must be changed.

The ability to establish a Level 1 folder is only available to a user account and within its own My Documents folder. To set a folder at Level 1 security, follow these steps:

1. Right-click the desired folder, and then click Sharing and Security.
2. Click the Make this folder private check box.
3. Click OK.

Level 2 At Level 2, the owner of the file and administrators have read and write privileges to the file or folder. This is Windows XP Professional's default setting for each user's My Documents file.

To establish Level 2 security on a folder, its subfolders, and files, follow these steps:

1. Right-click the desired folder, and then click Sharing and Security.
2. Clear the check boxes next to Make this folder private and the Share this folder on the network.
3. Click OK.

Level 3 Level 3 allows files and folders to be shared with users who log onto the computer locally, but not across the network. Depending on a user's type (for more information on user types, flip back to Chapter 9), he or she can or cannot do certain things with Level 3 files in the Shared Documents folder:

- Local computer administrators and power users have full access.
- Restricted users are limited to read access.
- Remote users cannot access Level 3 files.

Establishing Level 3 permissions involves moving the desired folders or files into the Shared Documents folder.

Level 4 At Level 4, files are available for everyone to read across the network. Local users are restricted to read access (this includes the Guest account) and cannot write or modify the files. At this level, anyone who can access the network can read these files.

To establish a folder with Level 4 permissions, follow these steps:

1. Right-click the desired folder, and then click Sharing and Security.
2. Check the Share this folder on the network check box.
3. Clear the Allow network users to change my files check box.
4. Click OK.

Level 5 Finally, Level 5 is the most permissive level of file and folder security. Any user anywhere on the network has *carte blanche* to files and folders at Level 5. Because anyone on the network can read, write, or delete files and folders, it's a good practice to allow this level of security only in closed, trusted, and protected networks.

To establish a folder with Level 5 permissions, follow these steps:

1. Right-click the desired folder, and then click Sharing and Security.
2. Check the Share this folder on the network check box.
3. Click OK.

Drive Mapping

If you find yourself accessing a specific drive often, you can make the process easier by enabling drive mapping. This process assigns the shared drive a letter on your system, much like your own local drives have. As such, you won't have to spend an inordinate amount of time navigating through the My Network Places windows to find your frequently accessed drive.

For instance, your computer probably has its hard drive designated as the C: drive. If you continually access the accounting department server's C: drive, by using drive mapping, you can establish that drive as Z: (or some other available letter you like). Once mapped, the drive appears as though it is a drive on your computer (it will appear in drive pull-down boxes and so forth), even though it is a network resource.

Mapping a Drive

To map a drive, follow these steps:

1. Select Start | My Computer.
2. From the menu bar, select Tools | Map Network Drive. The resulting window is shown in Figure 11-1.
3. From the drop-down list, select the drive letter of your choice. Only drive letters that are available will be shown in the list. Letters that are already associated with drives on your computer (A:, C:, and so on) won't be listed. Letters that are already mapped to a network drive are also listed, but with the share name next to them.
4. Click the Browse button next to the Folder box and find the resource you wish to map. The list will be presented in the Universal Naming Convention (UNC) format and show all the shared resources on your network
5. To enable this mapping each time you restart Windows, leave the Reconnect at logon check box selected.
6. Click Finish to complete the mapping. If the resource requires a password, you'll be prompted to supply it.

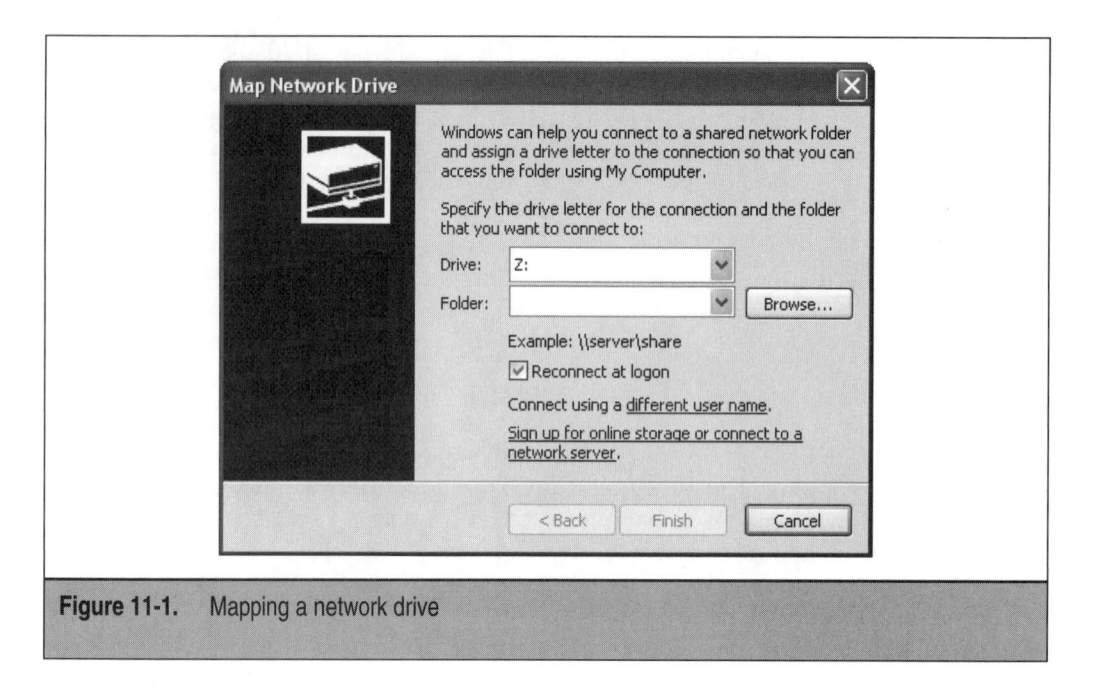

Figure 11-1. Mapping a network drive

> **TIP** You can display a Map Network Drive button on the Windows Explorer toolbar. To do so, right-click the toolbar, select Customize from the menu, and then click Map Drive from the Available Toolbar Buttons list. Click Add, and then click Close.

When you have a mapped drive, it will be shown with an icon in Windows Explorer and when you open My Computer. When you map a drive, you enable those settings only for the local computer. Mapping is not a networkwide affair. If you want the drive mapping to be on every computer in your organization, you must implement it at each computer.

Unmapping a Drive

To unmap a drive, the process is fairly straightforward. Follow these steps:

1. In Windows Explorer, right-click the drive you wish to unmap.
2. Choose Disconnect from the shortcut menu (alternatively, on the menu bar, you can go to Tools | Disconnect Network Drive, and then choose the drive to disconnect).

You will still have access to the shared resource; however, the drive letter is no longer associated with the share.

Mapping via the Command Prompt

If you prefer to use the command prompt, you can map drives using the NET USE command. This is especially useful if you want to perform a batch operation, mapping several drives at once. The syntax for this command is as follows:

```
net use d: \\computername\sharename
```

In this case, *d* should be replaced with the letter you wish to map, followed by the UNC of the shared resource.

Printer Sharing

Even though you can buy a printer for $1 with most new computer purchases, really good printers can still cost hundreds, or even thousands, of dollars. Furthermore, when such a piece of equipment is used only occasionally, it makes sense for network users to share it.

Additionally, different printers can have different functions in your organization. For instance, you probably don't want users printing off the 250-page reports on the color printer, depleting the color ink. On the other hand, the laser printer—though speedy—won't produce the color graphics the folks in marketing are looking for. As such, it is a costly proposition to suggest each user have his or her own printer (maybe even two, depending on their role in the organization). The best solution, as you probably guessed, is to share these printers.

The task of sharing a printer involves two steps:

1. Configuring the computer with the printer to share the device
2. Configuring other devices on the network to see the printer

Sharing Your Printer

The first step in sharing your printer is ensuring that it is properly connected to act as a *local* printer. Plug and Play makes this easy enough—ideally, you should be able to plug in the printer and wait for Windows XP Professional to notice that there is a new printer available, maybe answer a few questions about it, and insert the CD-ROM with the printer driver to finish the installation.

Plug and Play Printers   Virtually all new printers support Plug and Play. What's more, if Windows XP Professional already has a copy of your printer's driver, then setup is extremely simple. If Windows cannot identify your printer (or locate a driver for it), then it will start the Found New Hardware Wizard. Just answer its simple questions and be ready with the CD-ROM containing the device driver.

If Windows XP Professional does not see the new printer, then it is likely that your printer does not support Plug and Play. It's always a good idea to check the manufacturer's instructions and make sure there isn't anything unique to the printer that is preventing you from forming the connection.

> **NOTE** If your printer is not Plug and Play–compliant, it is a good idea to visit your printer manufacturer's web site and see if a recent copy of the driver is available.

Non–Plug and Play Printers   If your printer simply is not Plug and Play–compatible, you will have to do more manual work to get everything up and running. To add a non–Plug and Play printer, do the following:

1. Plug in and turn on the printer.
2. Connect the printer to your computer (either with USB or parallel cabling).
3. Select Start | Printers and Faxes | Add Printer.
4. Choose Add a Printer from the Printer Tasks list, and then click Next.
5. Windows XP Professional will ask you a series of questions about your printer, including the following:
   - The port to which you're connecting
   - The printer's manufacturer and model number
6. If the printer's manufacturer and model number are not listed, then click the Have Disk button, insert the disk containing your printer's driver, and use the driver supplied by the manufacturer.

Sharing Printers   Once you've got your printer connected, you can share it. The computer that is connected to the printer is called the *print server*. Depending on the size of your organization, the print server might be on a coworker's PC, or in a large organization it could be its own dedicated computer.

The printer should be given a share name (similar to the naming process used for client computers added to a network). Once it has a share name, others on the network will be able to see it and easily recognize it. The share name can be whatever you choose. It could be the make and model of the printer (BROTHER, in our example) or part of your naming scheme.

To share the printer, follow these steps:

1. Select Start | Printers and Faxes.
2. Right-click the printer you want to share, and then choose Sharing from the menu (the resulting Properties dialog box, with the Sharing tab selected, is shown in Figure 11-2).
3. Select the Share this printer radio button.

Figure 11-2. Sharing a printer

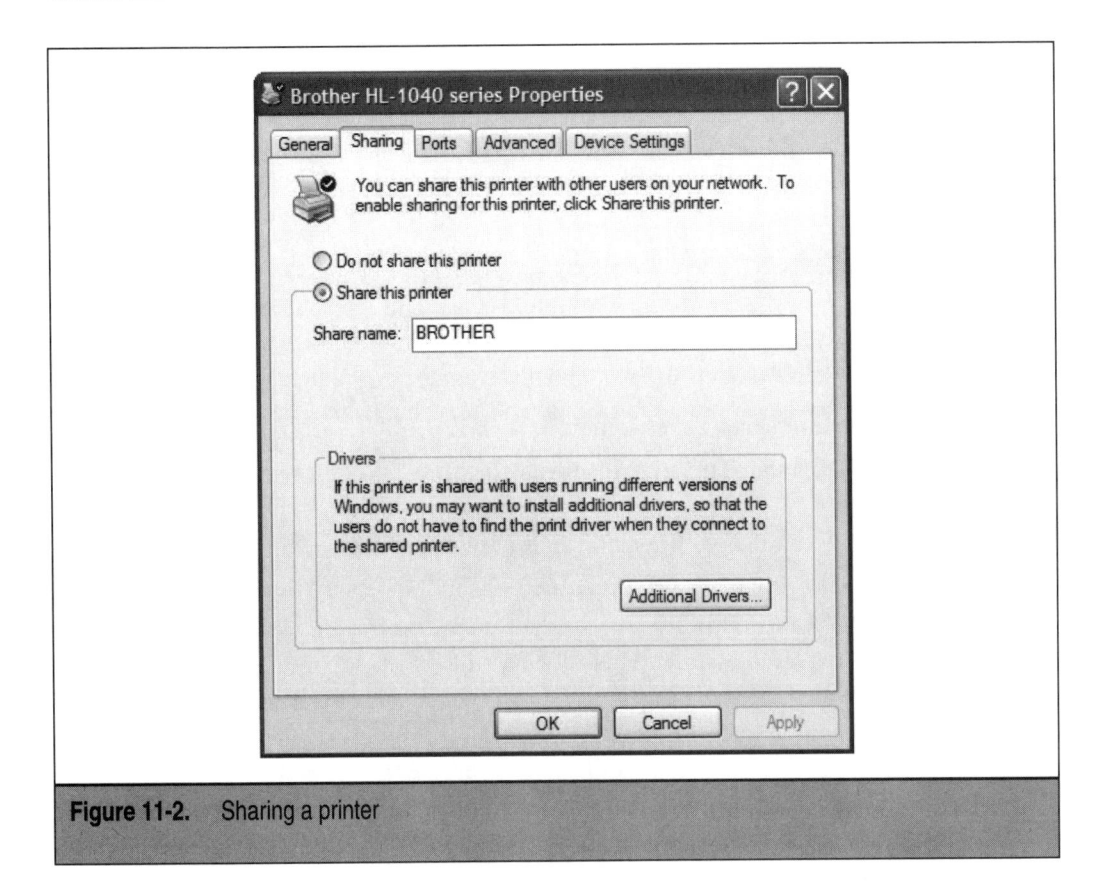

4. Name your printer so it can be found on the network.
5. If you have deactivated Simple File Sharing (which is explained in more detail in Chapter 10), then the Security tab is shown in the Properties dialog box. Selecting the tab allows you to manage access to the shared printer by user. On the tab, there are two settings that are of interest:
   - Manage Printers gives the user administrative control over the printer.
   - Manage Documents allows the user to start, stop, and rearrange the order of print jobs.
6. Click OK. Now the printer is shared and should have a little hand under its icon to indicate as much.

If you decide to turn off printer sharing, follow the same steps just listed, except this time, on the Sharing tab click the radio button next to Do not share this printer.

Using the Networked Printer

The next step in sharing a printer is to make sure other computers on the LAN can see it. When Windows XP Professional sees a shared printer on another computer within the LAN, it tries to install that printer's driver automatically. So, when users are trying to access a printer, it may be just as simple as checking the list of available printers on your application.

To check within Windows XP Professional to see if a printer is already available, select Start | Printers and Faxes to display the Printers and Faxes folder. If a printer is shared, there is a cable underneath it. If the shared printer is not on the list, and a driver needs to be installed, follow these steps:

1. Open the Printers and Faxes folder.
2. Click Add a printer. This invokes the Add Printer Wizard, which asks you these questions:
   - **Whether you're installing a local or network printer** Select network printer.
   - **The network path for the printer** Using the browse button, find the printer on your network.
   - **Which driver to install** This allows you to use a previously installed driver, update it with a more current driver, or install a new driver altogether.
   - **What name you want to call the printer** Providing a descriptive name is helpful in case you have multiple printers on the network.
   - **Whether you want this printer to be your default printer** If you select Yes, this is the printer to which all print jobs will be sent.

After these steps have been completed, the printer has been set up successfully and can be printed to at any time (assuming the print server is turned on).

Application Sharing

Printers, files, and folders aren't the only things that can be shared in Windows XP Professional. Included with Windows XP Professional (and available free from Microsoft's web site) is Windows Messenger. This application is conventionally used as a chat device on the Internet. However, it includes several built-in features that allow you to share applications—across your LAN or the Internet.

Before you can use Windows Messenger, you must have a .NET Passport account. The first time you run Windows Messenger, the .NET Passport Wizard will pop up and eagerly sign you up.

> **NOTE** Naturally, by requiring everyone to sign up for a .NET Passport account, Microsoft can use the number of users to market its .NET e-commerce initiative. However, if you don't mind being a number in Microsoft's ledger, then read on.

We won't delve too deeply into the inner workings of Windows Messenger here. Rather, we'll just explain how to share applications using the tool. Windows Messenger's Application Sharing feature can allow you to use an application while others watch, or others can take control of your application via the network while you watch. Furthermore, this tool allows you to share applications collaboratively, but without requiring that everyone in the conversation have the application.

NOTE Even though not everyone in the conversation has to have the application being used, they do need to have a version of Windows Messenger that supports application sharing. It's a good idea to visit http://www.microsoft.com to get the latest version of Windows Messenger.

Enabling Application Sharing

Before sharing an application, you must first sign in to Windows Messenger, add users with whom you will share the application, and so forth. Once you begin the Windows Messenger setup process, it can walk you through the steps needed to make these settings.

To enable application sharing, in the Windows Messenger Conversation window (shown in Figure 11-3) select Actions | Start Application Sharing. Once you do this,

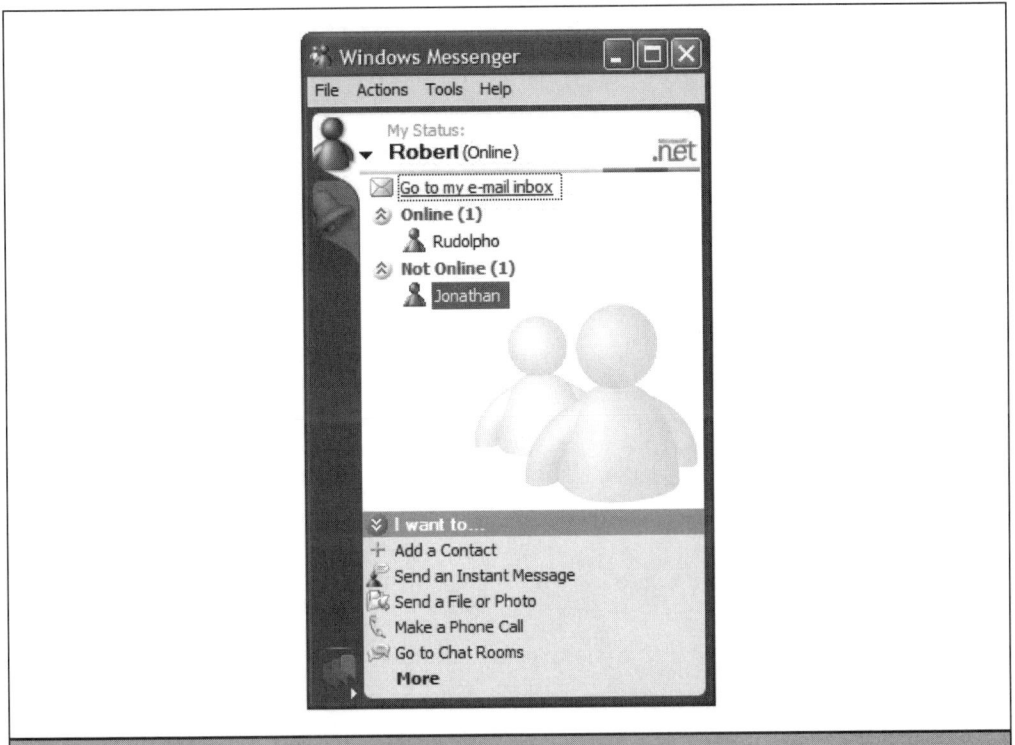

Figure 11-3. The Windows Messenger Conversation window

Windows Messenger sends an invitation to the other people in your conversation to share an application with you. If they click Accept, the Sharing session window opens, as shown in Figure 11-4.

When the Sharing window appears, choose the application you wish to share with the other members of your conversation. For instance, if you want to share an Excel spreadsheet, you open Excel and load the spreadsheet. Then, click Share. This causes the application to appear on the screens of everyone in your conversation.

> **NOTE** Make sure your shared application screen is active or it runs the risk of being blocked by another window. This blocked view will be retransmitted to everyone sharing the application.

When you decide to share an application, it's a good idea to make sure everyone has the same screen resolution. This prevents the screen from jumping around while the cursor or mouse moves around the screen. On a LAN, sharing the application won't pose a speed problem. However, if you are sharing the application with some users via dial-up connections, it will take a while for the screens to download to their desktops.

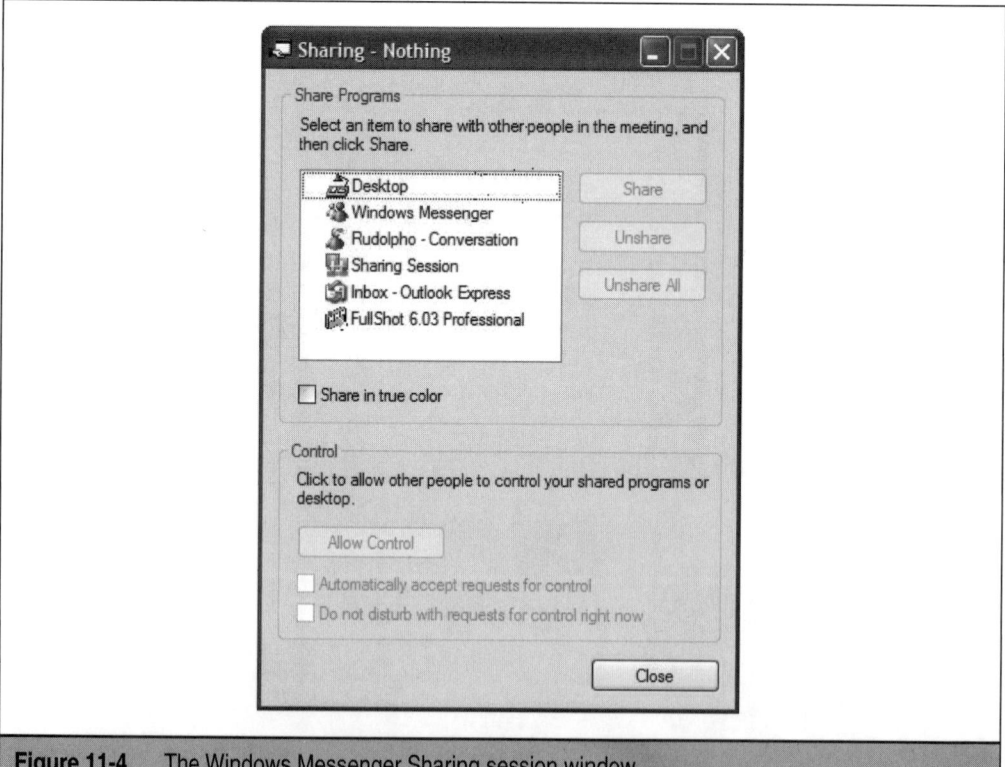

Figure 11-4. The Windows Messenger Sharing session window

Allowing Others to Control the Application

Once you've established the application sharing session, you can hand off the controls to someone else by switching back to the Sharing window, and then clicking Allow Control. This is shown in Figure 11-5.

If someone else double-clicks the window in which your application is displayed, a Request Control window pops up on your screen, indicating who wants to take control of the application. You can click Accept or Reject, depending on whether you want to give up control or not.

If you click Accept, then that person has control of the mouse and keyboard for that application. You can stop them by pressing any key. When you're done sharing control of the application, switch back to the Sharing window and click the Prevent Control button. When you're done with the application sharing session, simply close the application.

You can manage your application control rules by selecting the Automatically accept requests for control check box. By doing so, you won't be interrupted with requests for control. If you don't want to be pestered with requests for control and

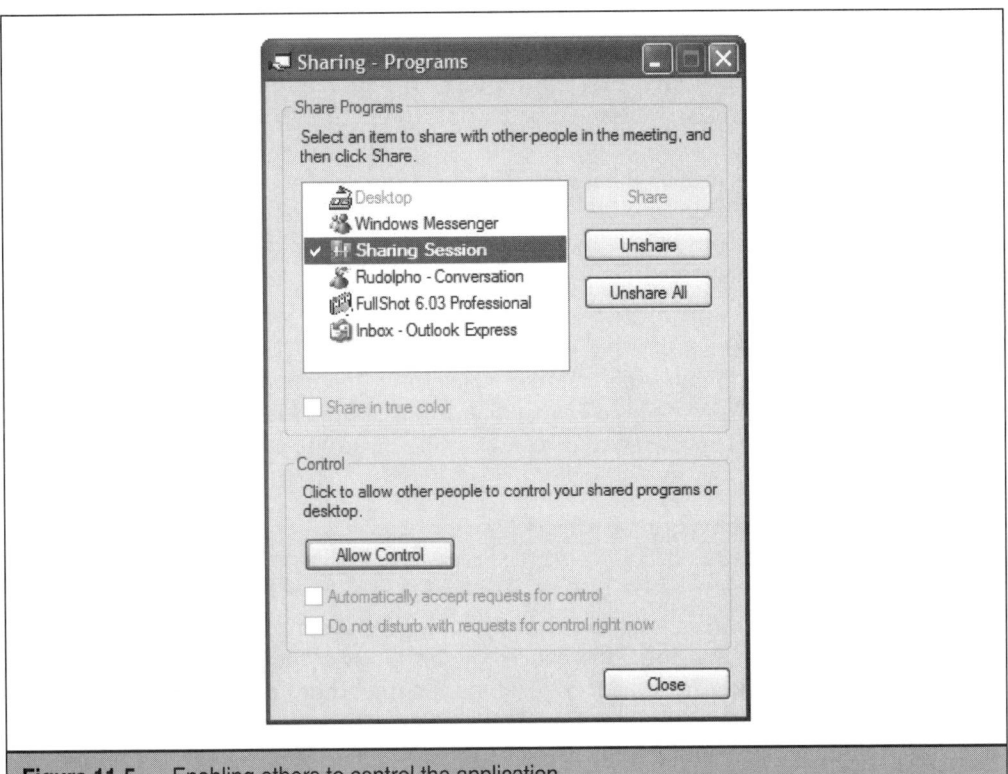

Figure 11-5. Enabling others to control the application

you don't intend to give up control, select the Do not disturb with requests for control right now check box.

> **NOTE** Be aware that if you share Windows Explorer, then all Explorer windows will be shared with the other members of your conversation.

CONTROLLING SHARED ACCESS

You can manage access to your shared Windows XP Professional resources via two methods: by having solid security practices in place and by utilizing the Computer Management snap-in to the Microsoft Management Console (MMC). In this section, we talk about methods you can use to control access to your shared resources.

In the realm of security, access to your shared resource is proactive, meaning that with the proper security settings, you can keep unauthorized users out of your shared resources or set varying levels of access for authorized users. By using the Computer Management snap-in, you become reactive. That is, it can be used to examine current user access, disconnect users, or send messages, if necessary.

Security

We talked about security in the preceding two chapters. However, when it comes to managing shared resources, the issue bears more coverage. A number of factors are involved when you manage security for your shared resources. The options you have are governed by such issues as what type of file system you're using and whether or not you are using Windows XP Professional's Simple File Sharing. In this section, we look at the issue of Simple File Sharing and file system usage as they apply to the security of network shares.

Simple File Sharing

As we've noted earlier, Simple File Sharing is a setting that can allow you to manage the levels at which you share files. Because the use of Simple File Sharing presents different scenarios for securing shared resources, it's useful to talk about Simple File Sharing in more depth.

> **NOTE** For instructions on enabling or disabling Simple File Sharing, flip back to Chapter 10.

With Simple File Sharing enabled, sharing resources is simplified. In fact, that's the point of Simple File Sharing. However, that simplicity comes at the cost of security flexibility. When Simple File Sharing is disabled, on the other hand, Windows XP Professional allows you a number of security options. Those options, however, are dependent on whether your drive is FAT or NTFS. When you select a file or folder to share, you'll see a different window generated depending on whether or not you have Simple File Sharing enabled or disabled. Figures 11-6 and 11-7 show the sharing tab for folders on a computer with Simple File Sharing turned on, and turned off, respectively.

By looking at these windows, you can see why Simple File Sharing is called "simple." There are only three settings to be made on the window with Simple File Sharing enabled—and those are just check boxes. With Simple File Sharing disabled, however, there is a lot more that you can do to manage your shares:

- Choose whether or not to share the folder.
- Give the share a name.
- Add a comment about the share (for example, Janet's Printer).
- Limit the number of users who can access the resource.
- Set permissions for users who access the resource.
- Configure offline access settings.

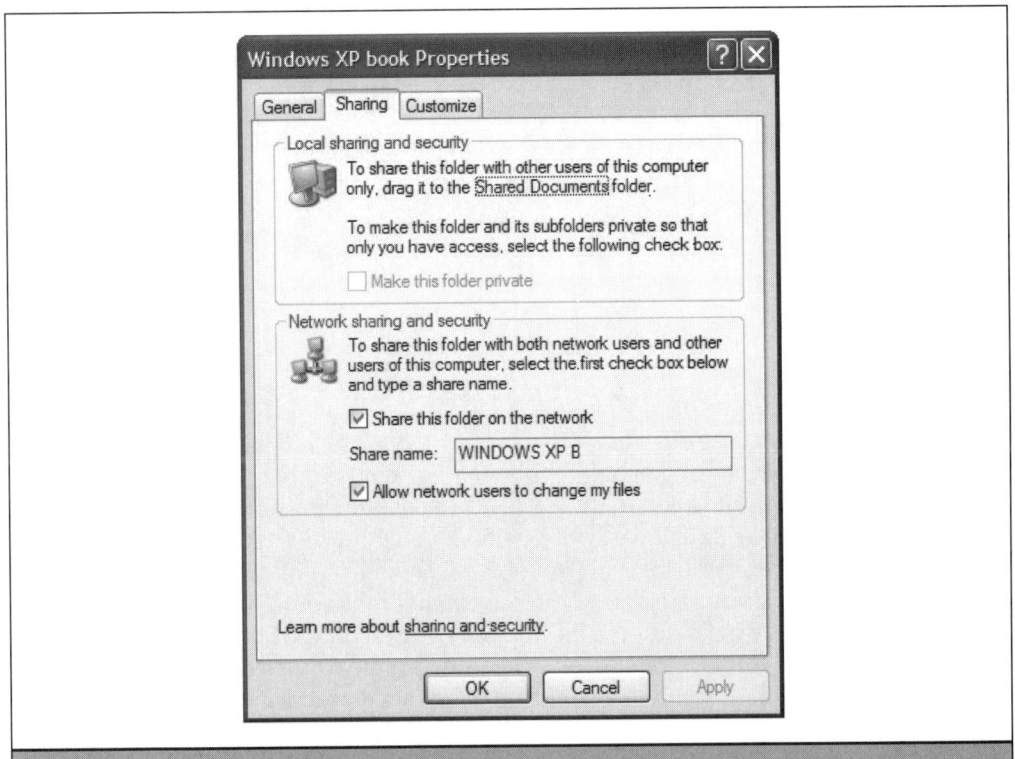

Figure 11-6. Sharing a folder with Simple File Sharing turned on

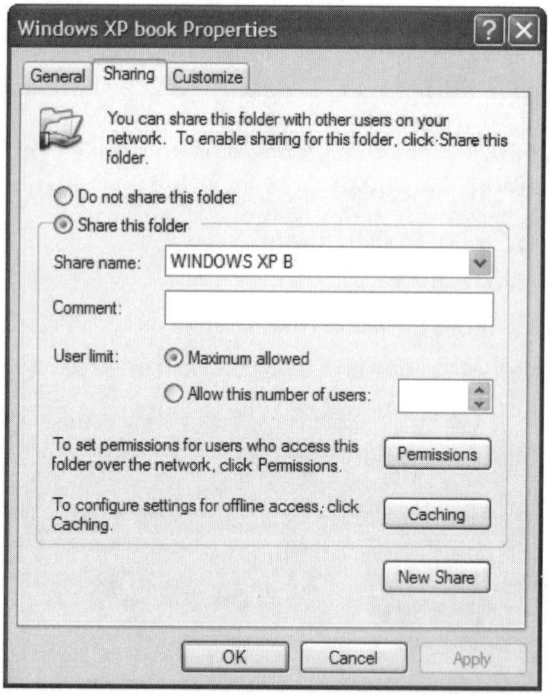

Figure 11-7. Sharing a folder with Simple File Sharing turned off

NOTE We talk about offline files in more detail in Chapter 12.

Permissions

If you have Simple File Sharing enabled, then there is really only one security option: whether or not you want to allow network users to change the contents of your file. Because Simple File Sharing allows everyone to access your files, you can't be selective about who is looking at them, but you can prevent them from making changes.

With Simple File Sharing disabled, you have many more options, as we noted in the preceding section. By clicking the Permissions button on the Sharing tab, you can establish permissions for your resource. Depending on the drive's file system (FAT or NTFS), you have different settings that can be established and managed.

FAT Drives If you are trying to establish permissions on a FAT drive, or on a FAT partition, you have only limited options, as compared to an NTFS drive. Permissions are established and managed in the Permissions dialog box, as shown in Figure 11-8.

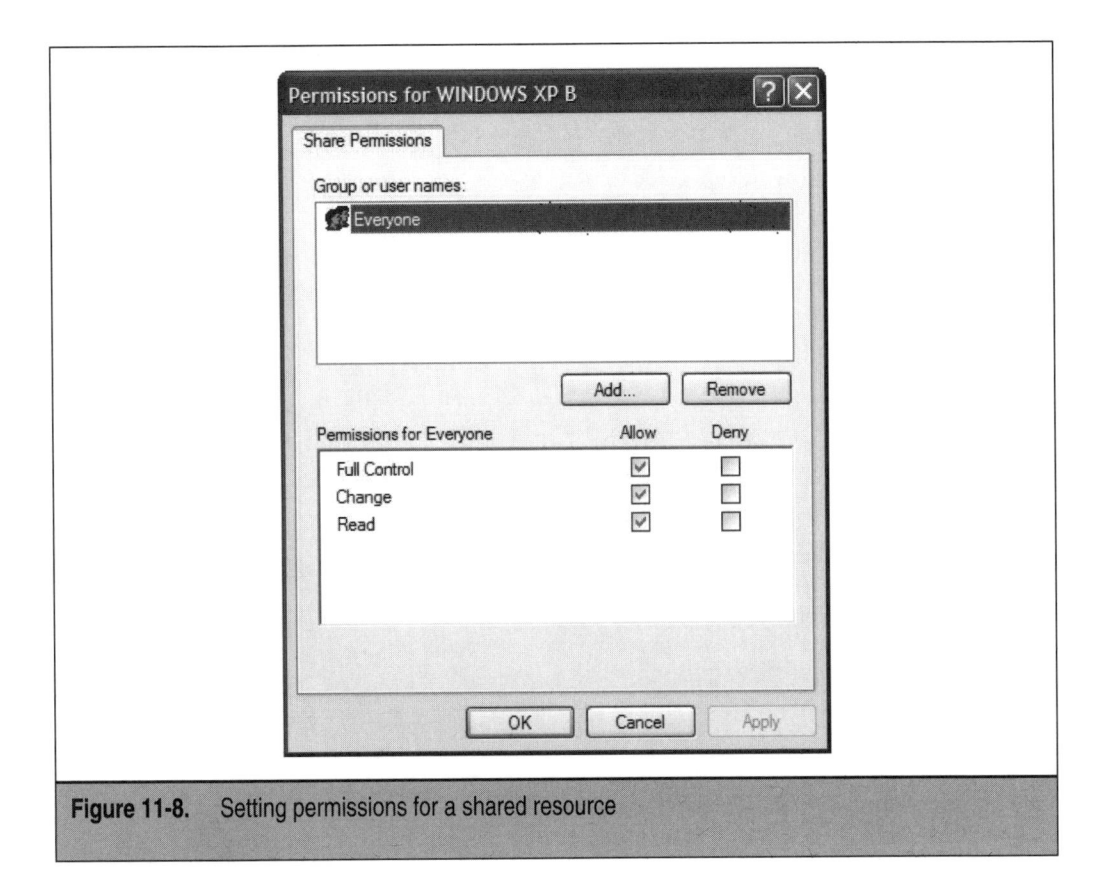

Figure 11-8. Setting permissions for a shared resource

In the Permissions dialog box, you select the group or user, and then use the check boxes at the bottom of the window to establish permissions. With FAT, there are only three permissions that can be managed:

- **Full Control**   Allows or denies the user or group the ability to read, write, delete, create, or change files. This setting allows the network user to do whatever the computer user can do.
- **Change**   Allows or denies users the ability to delete resources, change permissions, or take ownership of a resource.
- **Read**   Allows or denies users the ability to open and read files.

Be aware, however, that you don't have six settings, you really only have three. By denying one type of access, you are automatically changing the setting for the other two, as well. For instance, if you deny full control, then the change and read permissions are automatically denied.

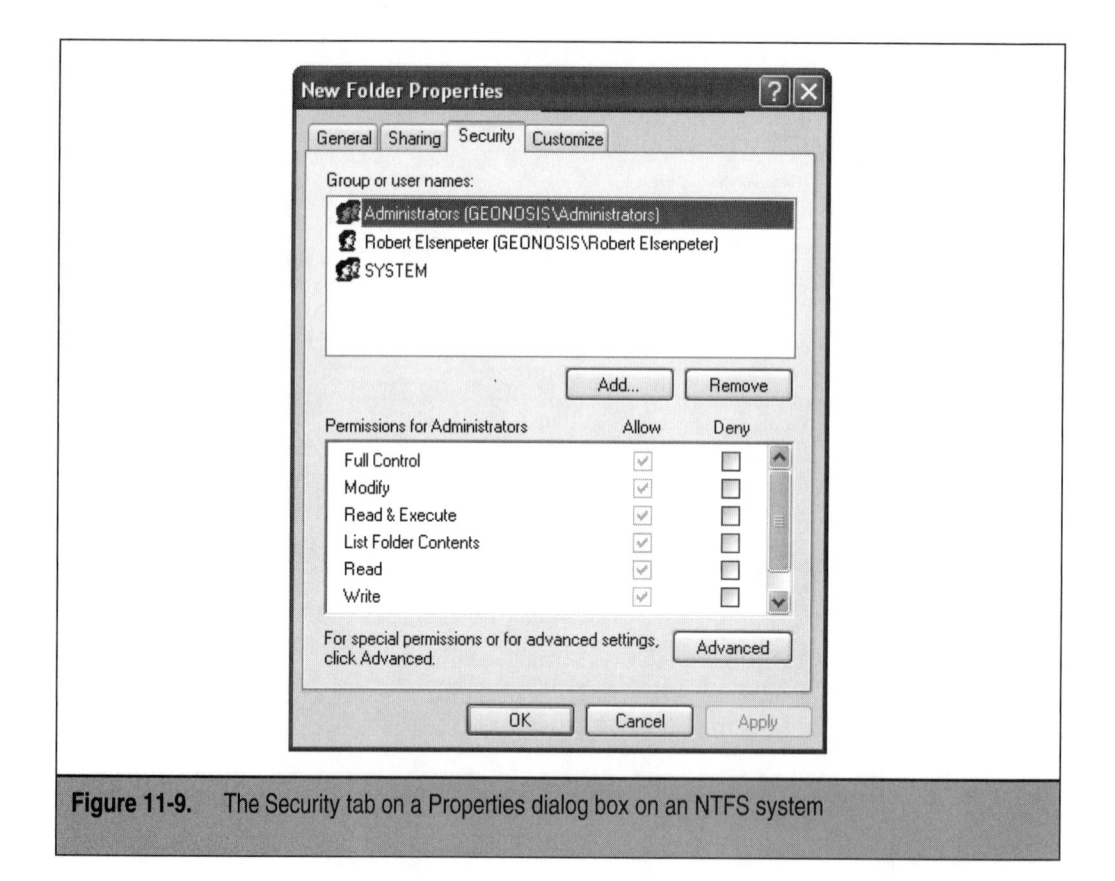

Figure 11-9. The Security tab on a Properties dialog box on an NTFS system

NOTE You can add or remove users and groups to this share by using the Add and Remove buttons.

NTFS Drives If you are managing permissions for a shared resource on an NTFS drive or partition, you have significantly more options than when doing so on a FAT drive or partition. As Figure 11-9 shows, NTFS drives add a Security tab to a file's or folder's Properties box.

NOTE When managing access to shared files on an NTFS volume, it's a better security practice to use the Security tab rather than the Sharing tab.

The Security tab's controls are much the same as the Permissions dialog box for a FAT system. First, you select a user or group, and then establish or manage permissions. The permissions available on an NTFS system include the following:

- **Full Control** Allows or denies the user or group the ability to read, write, delete, create, or change files. This setting allows the network user to do whatever the computer user can do.

- **Modify** Allows or denies users the ability to delete folders and files, alter permissions, or take ownership of a file or folder.
- **Read & Execute** Allows or denies users the ability to read and run files. They cannot change the contents.
- **List Folder Contents** Allows or denies users the ability to examine the contents of the folder.
- **Read** Allows or denies users the ability to see the contents of the drive or folder and open files. They cannot save changes.
- **Write** Allows or denies users the ability to write to the drive or folder. They cannot, however, open the folder and examine its contents.
- **Special permissions** Click the Advanced button to apply special permissions.

Using the Computer Management Snap-In

Sharing files, folders, and other resources is a helpful way to allow multiple users to access your network's resources. However, there might be times when it is necessary to see who is accessing what resources. For instance, if you are performing server maintenance, it's a good idea to see who's using a resource before you have to cut them off—it's also nice to be able to send users a message to let them know they need to log off, without unceremoniously pulling the plug. Also, there are a number of security issues that necessitate checking out who's using what; you might also need to check out the network's resource usage to plan for network expansion. Whatever your reasons, Windows XP Professional provides a useful tool to monitor your shared resources called Computer Management.

In-Depth View

As you can tell by looking at the Computer Management snap-in, there is more functionality than simply disconnecting users. Let's take a closer look at the different folders within the Shared Folders portion of the Computer Management tool. There are three subfolders in Shared Folders:

- Shares
- Sessions
- Open Files

By using the Computer Management tool, you can supervise user access to your shares by viewing the files being accessed, the individual user's session, or the share itself.

Shares The Shares folder contains a list of information about your shared resources. The columns and the data they contain include the following:

- **Shared Folder** Lists the shared resources on your computer. This can be a shared file, folder, printer, or an unrecognized type of resource.
- **Shared Path** The path to the shared resource.

- **Type** The type of network connection (that is, Windows, NetWare, and so forth).
- **# Client Connections** The number of users who are connected to the shared resource.
- **Comment** A description of the shared resource.

Figure 11-10 shows an example of this view.

Sessions A session contains information about all the network users who are connected to the computer. Information in the Sessions folder includes the following:

- **User** The network users connected to the computer
- **Computer** The computer name of the connected user
- **Type** The type of network connection
- **# Open Files** The number of resources that the user has open
- **Connected Time** The hours and minutes that the user has been connected
- **Idle Time** The hours and minutes since a user last initiated an action
- **Guest** Whether or not this user is connected to the computer as a guest

Figure 11-11 shows an example of this view.

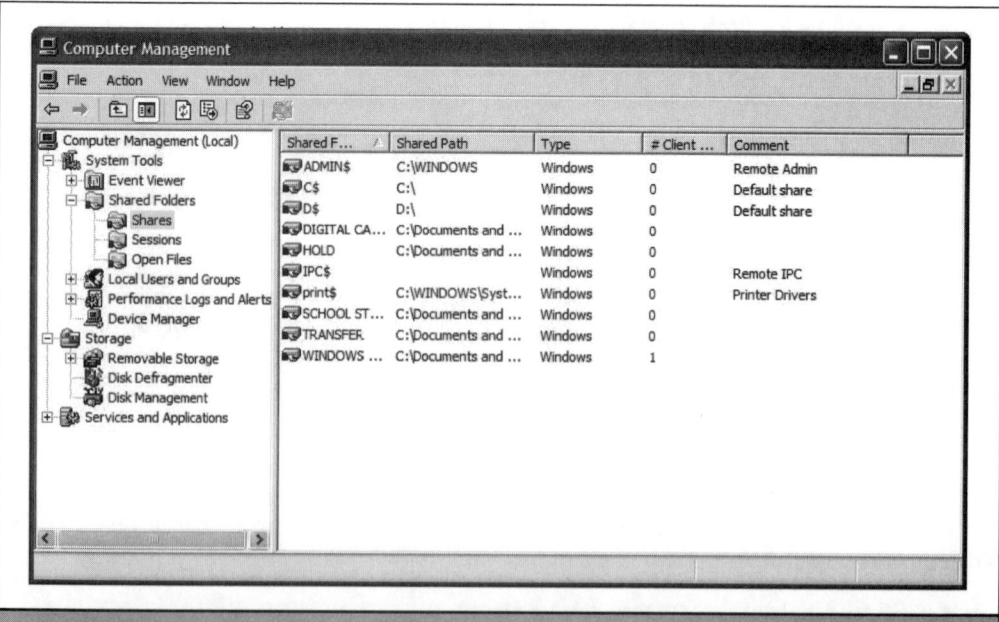

Figure 11-10. The Shares view of Computer Management

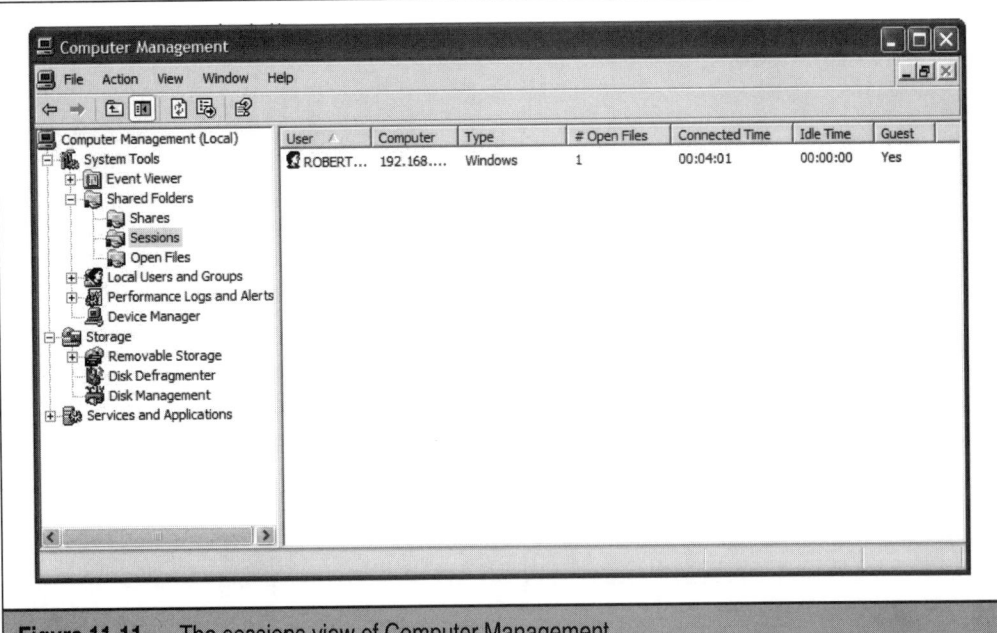

Figure 11-11. The sessions view of Computer Management

Open Files   Finally, the Open Files folder lists information about all the open files on your computer. Its information includes the following:

- **Open File**   The names of open files. Open files could be a print job or an unrecognized type of file.
- **Accessed By**   The name of the user accessing the file.
- **Type**   The connection type.
- **# Locks**   The number of locks on the resource.
- **Open Mode**   The permission that was granted when the resource was opened.

Figure 11-12 shows an example of the Open Files view.

Using the Computer Management Snap-In

Computer Management can be activated several ways:

- On your desktop, right-click My Computer and select Manage.
- From the start menu, select Programs | Administrative Tools | Computer Management.
- If you prefer to use the MMC, you can add Computer Management to your console.

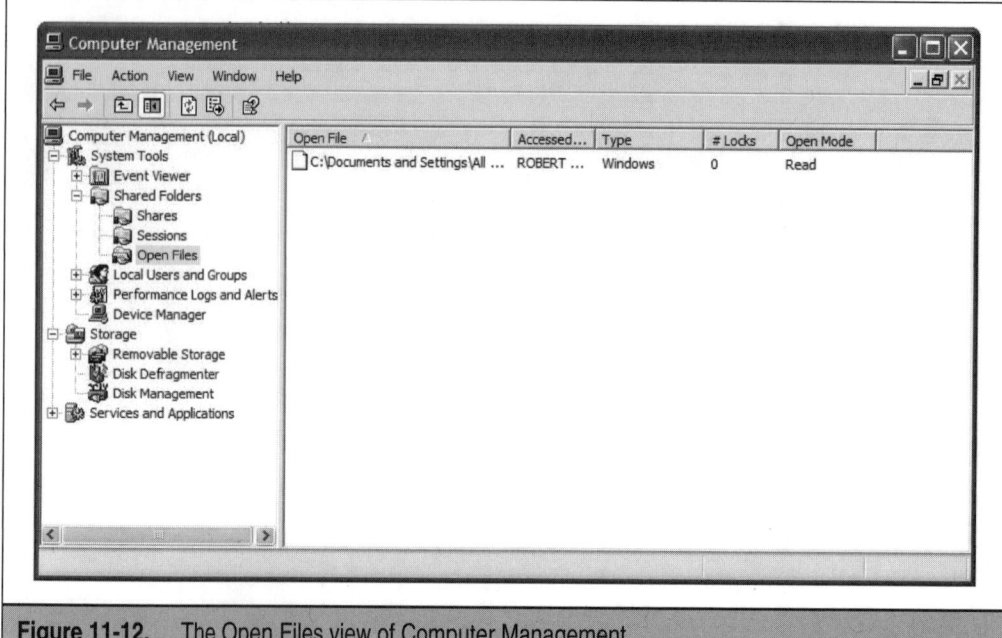

Figure 11-12. The Open Files view of Computer Management

Once you've started the Computer Management tool (as shown in Figure 11-13), to manage shared resources navigate to Computer Management | System Tools | Shared Folders | Shares. This section of the console shows all the shares that exist on your computer. You can view such details as share name, the physical location of a shared folder, and comments related to the share. What is of most importance here is that you can see how many clients are attached to a share under the # Client Connections column.

If a certain share is giving you problems, for instance, you can examine how many clients are accessing that share. You can then right-click the share and select Properties from the resulting context menu. When you do, you'll see the share's properties sheet. This window will show you the same basic information that you've already seen, but will also display the maximum number of clients that are allowed to access the share point. You can use this number to determine if you're having trouble with the share because too many people are trying to use it. You can also use this properties sheet to view things like the share's security and cache settings.

Figure 11-13. The Computer Management tool

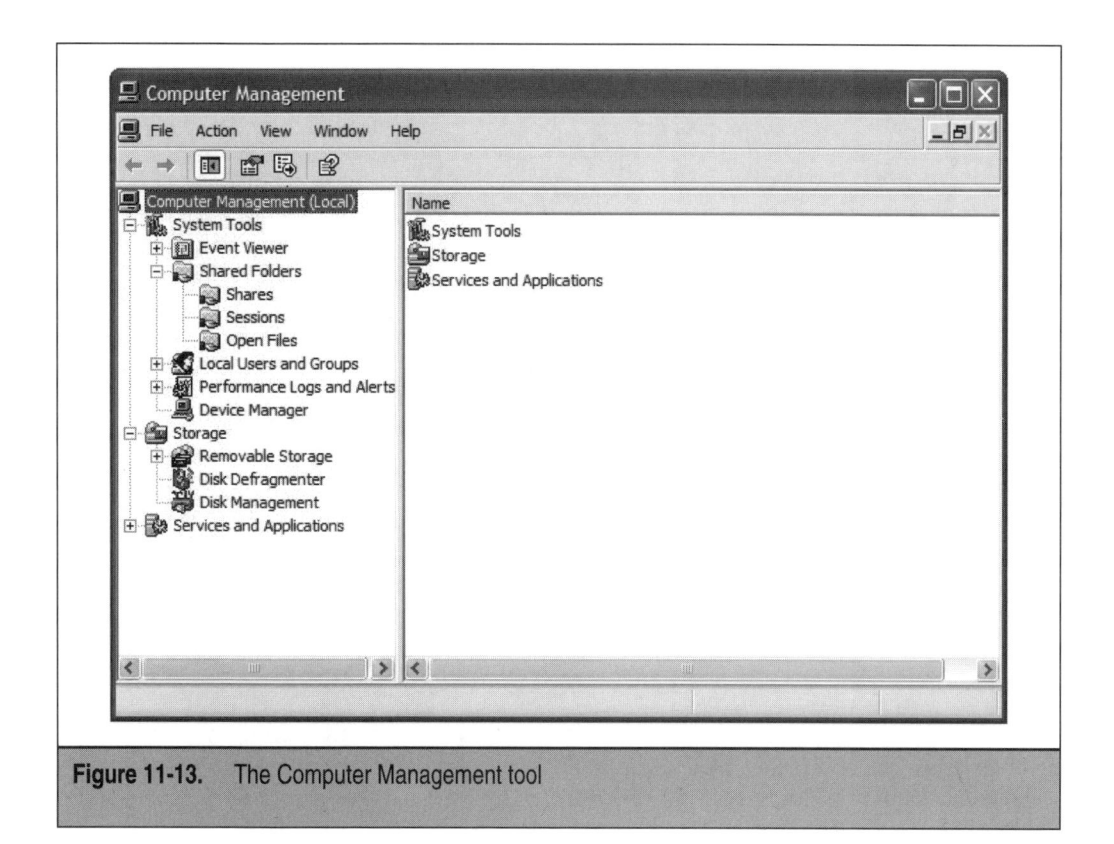

Send a Message

At the beginning of this section we noted that it might be helpful to send a message to a user who is accessing a shared resource that you might have to disconnect. Frankly, you can send a message for any reason to someone accessing one of your shares.

To send a user a message, navigate through the console to Computer Management | System Tools | Shared Folders and then right-click Shared Folders. Next, select All Tasks | Send Console Message. A dialog box will open in which you can type your message and select a message recipient. The dialog box in which you type a message is shown in Figure 11-14. The resulting message popping up on the user's screen is shown in Figure 11-15.

Figure 11-14. Sending a user a message

If your message requesting that the user disconnect doesn't work (the user might be away from the computer, for example) and you need him or her to disconnect right away, then you might have to be a little more forceful and disconnect that user. This can be done by navigating to Computer Management | System Tools | Shared Folders | Open Files. Then, right-click Open Files and select All Tasks | Disconnect All Open Files.

Sharing resources is the heart of computer networking. Windows XP Professional not only provides you an easy way to share files and folders (via Simple File Sharing), but it also offers a means to manage those resources. Not only can you take preventive action to manage your resources, but you can also keep an eye on what's going on after users have started accessing each other's resources.

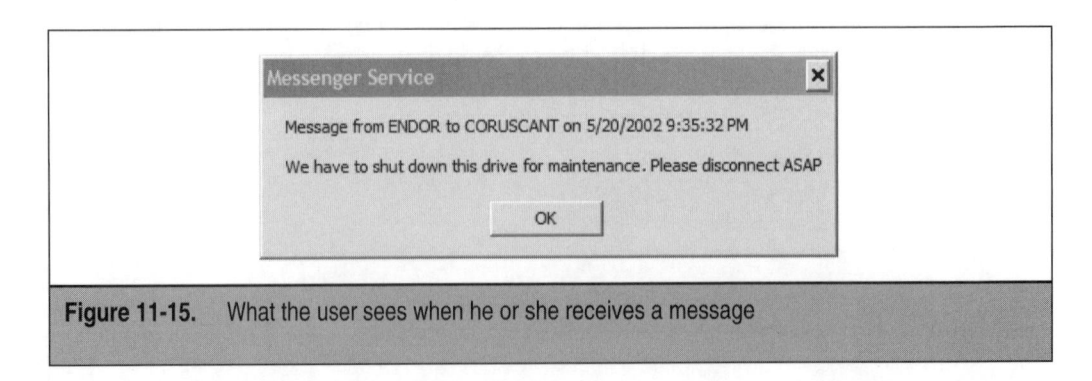

Figure 11-15. What the user sees when he or she receives a message

CHAPTER 12

Offline Files and Folders

It's 10:30 P.M. on Sunday night. One of your coworkers has been at the office most of the weekend finishing up the big report that's due first thing Monday morning. In the middle of a crucial part of the report, a pop-up window tells this user that he or she has been disconnected from the network. That means your coworker can't finish the report, let alone access the database with this quarter's financial data and performance numbers. All attempts to reconnect meet with failure. What can the user do?

Unfortunately, the user in this scenario is going to have trouble in a few hours when the report is due. However, this problem could have been avoided if the user had enabled Offline Files. This Windows XP Professional feature allows you to continue working on a network file, even after the connection to the network has been lost.

As the last chapter illustrated, Windows XP Professional networks provide an excellent means to share files, folders, and applications. A user can access folders maintained on the server or in another user's shared folders, which provides a good way to collaborate on documents, or access a common data store. However, there are times when it is simply not feasible for a user to connect to the local area network (LAN). The absence of a network connection doesn't mean, however, that a user cannot access his or her files.

Windows XP Professional's Offline Files tool is one way of providing connectivity for users who need access to shared and centrally stored materials. Offline Files allows access to files for users who have to detach their computers from the network (for instance, a user who travels) or someone who works primarily detached from the network, connecting only occasionally (for instance, a telecommuter). Furthermore, the use of Offline Files is also helpful when the server is taken offline for maintenance, or the user becomes disconnected, for whatever reason.

Travelers or telecommuters can access the files that they would when part of the network; however, they need not be physically tethered to the network to work with these files. Obviously, this presents a data integrity issue. With files on the network and others on users' local computers, there needs to be a means in place to reconcile these documents. To avoid having different versions of files creating confusion, Windows XP Professional allows Offline File users to reconnect to the network and "synchronize" their files. This can be done either when users come into the office or remotely (for instance, over a dial-up connection from the road).

This chapter examines the issues related to Offline Files and folders. We cover such topics as simple offline file and folder setup, management of these files, and synchronization. We'll also discuss the use of the Windows Briefcase, which provides another tool to help manage offline files. Finally, we'll talk about troubleshooting problems with offline files and folders.

USING OFFLINE FILES AND FOLDERS

Offline Files is not just useful for so-called road warriors. As the user at the beginning of this chapter learned, Offline Files can be a lifesaver. For instance, if the server is to be taken offline for maintenance, yet users still need access to network files, they can simply designate their files as Offline Files and continue working, synchronizing them when they reconnect.

For more enhanced file availability, Offline Files can be paired with Folder Redirection. For instance, if a user is trying to access a folder on another user's computer, enabling Folder Redirection will send the contents of that folder to a location on the server. By default, Windows XP Professional makes any redirected folder available offline. As such, if Dave in accounting is trying to access a folder on the computer of Larry in production, but Larry has turned it off, Dave can still access Larry's folder if it has been redirected and a copy is located on the server.

NOTE If you choose to disable Folder Redirection in your organization, use the Group Policy snap-in to the Microsoft Management Console (MMC), and change the Do not automatically make redirected folders available offline setting.

In Active Directory environments, Group Policy settings are used to manage the Offline Files feature. We will explain these settings later in this chapter.

Enabling

The first step in using Offline Files is to enable the feature on the local computer. To configure your computer to use Windows XP Professional's Offline Files feature, do the following:

1. Select Start | My Computer.
2. Under the Tools menu, select Folder Options.
3. Click the Offline Files tab (this is shown in Figure 12-1).
4. Select the Enable Offline Files check box, and then click OK.

NOTE You will not be able to use Offline Files if Fast User Switching is enabled on your machine. To disable Fast User Switching, go to User Accounts in the Control Panel. Select Change the way users log on or off, and then clear the Use Fast User Switching check box.

Making Files and Folders Available Offline

After enabling the Offline Files feature, you can start selecting which files and folders you will need for offline use. Like so many other Windows XP Professional tasks, you can invoke a wizard (in this case the Offline File Wizard) to help select the files and folders you wish to manage. Once you've selected the files for offline use, there is a specific way they should be accessed to ensure that they are properly synchronized when you reconnect to the network. The following sections explain these procedures.

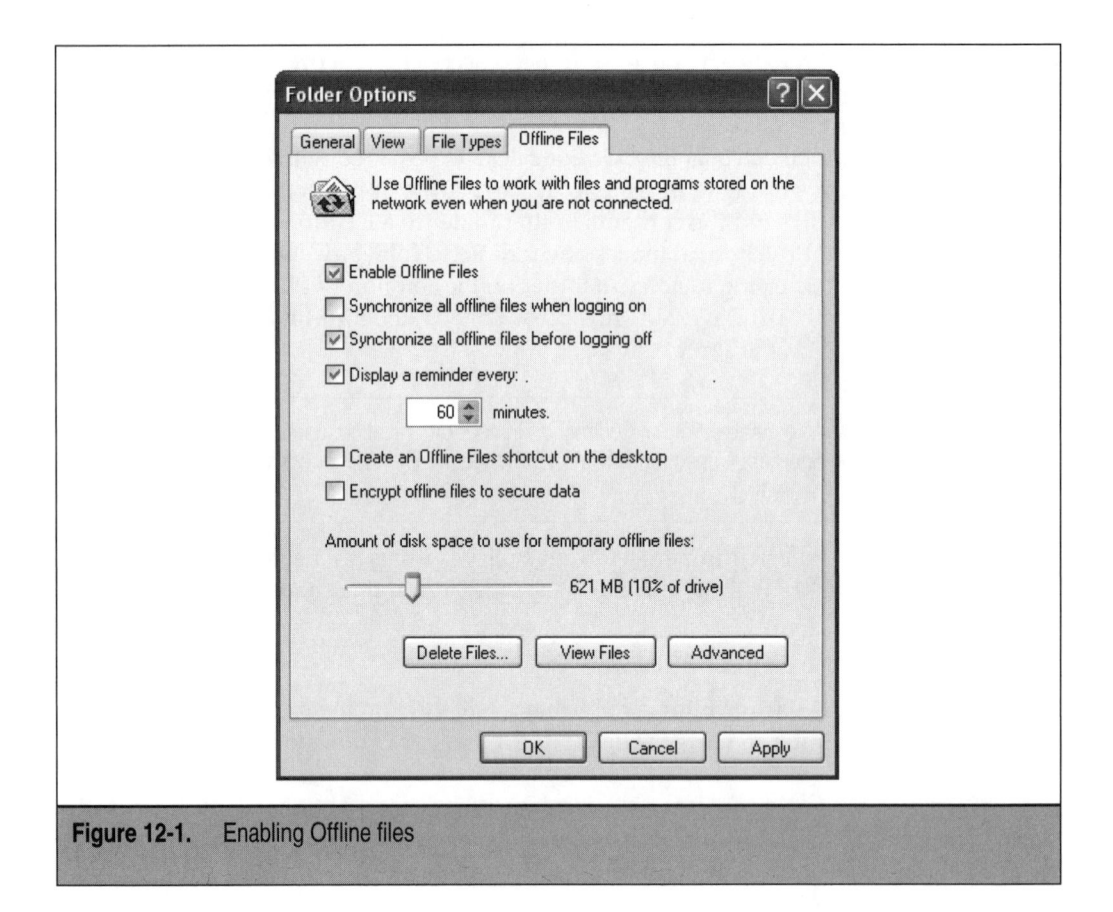

Figure 12-1. Enabling Offline files

Offline Files Wizard

To set up a file or folder for offline use, follow these steps:

1. Using Windows Explorer, navigate to the file or folder on the network you wish to use offline.

2. Right-click the file or folder, and then choose Make Available Offline from the shortcut menu. This activates the Offline Files Wizard, which is shown in Figure 12-2.

3. Click Next. The wizard will ask you if you wish to automatically synchronize the offline files the next time you log on or log off. Make your selection, and then click Next.

Figure 12-2. The Offline Files Wizard

4. Next, the wizard will present you with two options. The first, Enable Reminders, displays a reminder in the notification area whenever you are working offline. The second asks if you wish to create a shortcut to your offline files on the desktop. This provides a quick way to get to your offline files. Make your selections, and then click Finish.

NOTE For simplicity's sake, it's a good idea to create the shortcut to your Offline Files. This makes accessing them much easier.

---

5. If you have selected a folder containing subfolders, a dialog box will pop up asking if you want the subfolders to be made offline as well. Make your selection and click OK.

While Windows XP Professional is moving your files and folders to the Offline Files folder of your computer the Synchronizing dialog box is displayed.

Offline files are not restricted to Windows servers. If a third-party sever is using the Server Message Block (SMB) protocol, then offline files can be accessed from other types of servers, such as UNIX servers.

To use this feature on third-party servers, make sure the SMB protocol has been set up on the server. Once the SMB protocol is enabled, you can use Windows XP to connect to those files and make them available offline.

Using Offline Files

Using Offline Files seems like it should be simple enough—and to a degree it is—but you should also take care to ensure that you're using them properly. This will prevent data loss, which is the whole point of Offline Files in the first place.

If you choose to create a shortcut to your offline files and folders while running the Offline Files Wizard, then using offline files is an easy task. Simply double-click that shortcut, and then open your files from the resulting window.

If you did not create the shortcut, you can find your offline files by opening Windows Explorer and selecting Tools | Folder Options. Next, click the Offline Files tab and click View Files. Figure 12-3 shows the window that appears regardless of which way you access these files.

When using Offline Files, make sure you save them back to the Offline Files folder so that they can be properly synchronized when you reconnect to the network share.

Downloading Files for Offline Use

Once you've selected which files and folders you wish to use offline, Windows XP Professional goes about the task of downloading them to your local computer in a

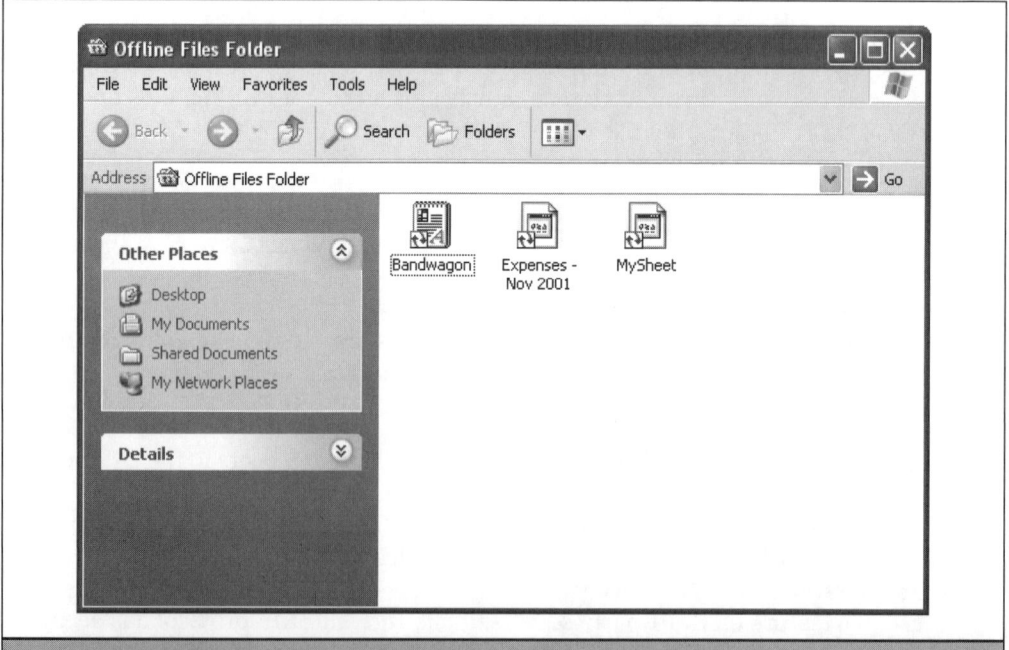

Figure 12-3. Offline files contained in the Offline Files folder

couple of different ways. Specifically, the means of download is dependent on how you indicate to Windows XP Professional that you will be using these files. Additionally, files can be downloaded to the local computer when you reconnect to the network, assuming certain conditions are met.

Offline Files

There are two ways in which files are cached for offline use. Either you can specifically tell Windows XP Professional which files you want to use offline, or you can make a sort of general statement to Windows XP Professional, hoping it includes your file when it performs some housekeeping chores. The two means of specifying offline files are as follows:

- **Manually** Files are manually cached when a computer *pins* a file or folder as an Offline File. You pin a file or folder by navigating to it, and then on the File menu selecting Make Available Offline. These types of files are always available offline.

- **Automatically** Files are automatically cached when the server indicates that the file or folder must be made available offline. As such, some files might be available offline, but there is no guarantee that they will be.

You can establish automatic caching for select files and folders by right-clicking the folder, selecting Properties, clicking the Sharing tab, and then clicking Caching. In the resulting Settings box, click Automating Caching of Documents. This method also allows you to disable caching.

By default, the size allotted to automatically cached files is 10 percent of your hard drive's space. This default can be adjusted to anything between 0 and 100 percent. This amount is not affected by files manually cached by the user or files that the administrator has selected to be pinned. Manually cached files can use as much disk space as is available, in total.

Conditions for Reconnection

In order for a network share to become available after it has been offline (in addition to the presence of a stable network connection), three conditions must be present:

- No offline files are open.
- No offline files from the network share need to be synchronized.
- The network connection is not a slow link.

NOTE A *slow link* is a threshold that you set for a connection's speed. If the connection falls below this threshold, then the link is considered "slow."

When these conditions are present, a user can open a file and begin work on it, and it will be saved both to the network share and to the Offline Files folder. If any one of the aforementioned conditions is not met, then the user will access the offline file, even though the version on the network share is available. Any changes that the user makes to his or her file must be synchronized with the version on the network share.

NOTE We talk about synchronization in more depth later in this chapter, in the section "Synchronization."

Deleting Offline Files

When you moved into your abode, after unpacking there were probably a few boxes that you never bothered with. Maybe they had Christmas tree ornaments in them, maybe they contain stuff you keep meaning to sort through and organize. No matter what their contents, they probably wound up in an attic or a corner of the garage. After a while, more and more boxes and miscellaneous items have wound up in the attic—so many that you don't even remember putting them away. Offline files can present a similar problem, except they don't clutter up your attic, they clutter up your hard drive.

After a period of time, the Offline Files Folder can become filled with files that you no longer use. This congestion doesn't just make for a cluttered work environment; it also sucks up hard drive space. It's a good idea to remove these files from your system when they are no longer needed.

Deleting offline files can be accomplished in one of two ways. You can either delete a file or files from your Offline Files folder, or you can delete all the files associated with a particular share by using the Delete Files feature from the Offline Files Properties page.

CAUTION Do not delete, move, or alter any files located in the *systemroot*\CSC folder.

Not to worry: Deleting offline files using the following methods only removes them from the local cache, not from their original location on the network.

Using the Offline Files Folder

To delete offline files from your local cache using the Offline Files folder, follow these steps:

1. Navigate to the desired folder in Windows Explorer, and then on the Tools menu, select Folder Options.
2. Click the Offline Files tab.

3. Click View Files.
4. Select the files you wish to delete, and then on the File menu click Delete.

Deleting from a Network Share's Cache

To delete offline files from a cache on a network share, follow these steps:

1. Using Windows Explorer, navigate to a shared network folder, and then on the Tools menu select Folder Options.
2. Click the Offline Files tab.
3. Click Delete files.
4. A dialog box will ask you to confirm the deletion request. You can select whether you want to delete only the temporary versions of offline files (files that are automatically cached) or if you want to delete both temporary versions and versions that are always available offline (files that are manually cached).

Wiping Out the Cache

You might discover that your efforts to delete files from the cache are not working. If this happens, you can make a more aggressive move and wipe everything out of the cache by reinitializing it. Be aware that this will wipe *everything* out of the cache. So if there are files that have not been synchronized, it is a good idea to do that first, otherwise you might lose everything. To reinitialize the cache, follow these steps:

1. Navigate to the desired folder in Windows Explorer, and then on the Tools menu select Folder Options.
2. Click the Offline Files tab.
3. Press CTRL-SHIFT, and then click Delete Files.
4. You must restart the computer for the reinitialization to occur.

NOTE Restarting the computer is one of those Microsoft quirks that can pose a speed bump to your productivity. It's a good idea to keep on top of your cached files as you work, deleting them when they are no longer needed. However, if you decide to do some spring cleaning and purge everything from the cache, maybe you want to plan to do this task during a time when you can spare the few minutes it takes to restart your computer.

Security

Offline files are *cached* in the Offline Files folder. There is only one Offline Files folder per computer, no matter how many users have access to the computer. To prevent unauthorized access to the folder, it is protected by administrator permissions. As you remember from our discussion of NTFS files, this level of permission is only available on file systems formatted with NTFS. Several other means of protecting offline files and folders are available, either via permissions, the Group Policy snap-in, or encryption.

Permissions

Offline files are protected via permissions, like any other file on an NTFS system. That is, they maintain the same permissions in the Offline Files folder that they had on the network share from which they originated. For example, let's say Larry and Dave are both using the same computer to access the network. Larry has created a spreadsheet on the network share, setting permissions for the file so that only he can access it. After transferring an offline copy onto the computer, he leaves for the day. When Dave comes in for the next shift, the spreadsheet is available in the shared Offline Files folder; however, he cannot access the version on the network share, nor can he access the version in the Offline Files folder, because the permissions set by Larry have carried over.

The establishment and carrying over of permissions occurs regardless of file system type. That is, if you establish permissions on a network share using NTFS, and then make that file available offline on a FAT drive, in Windows XP Professional the permissions will carry over, even though the drive is not using NTFS.

Group Policy Setting Impacts

As we noted earlier, in Active Directory settings, Offline Files settings and permissions are managed via the Group Policy snap-in to the MMC (shown in Figure 12-4). The Offline Files settings can be managed in two locations on the Group Policy snap-in, depending on your Offline Files management needs:

- **Computer** You can manage specific Offline Files settings for an individual computer by following Computer Configuration\Administrative Templates\Network\Offline Files.
- **User** You can manage specific Offline Files settings by user and groups by following User Configuration\Administrative Templates\Network\Offline Files.

Figure 12-5 shows the setting dialog box for a specific offline file setting.

Table 12-1 lists the Group Policy Offline Files settings and a brief description of their functions.

Chapter 12: Offline Files and Folders

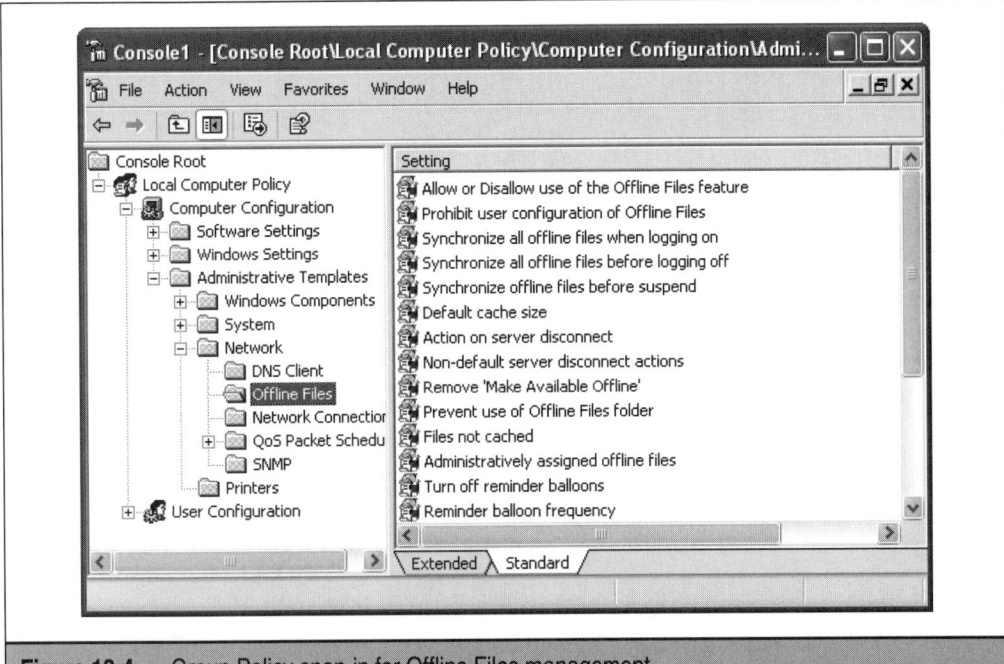

Figure 12-4. Group Policy snap-in for Offline Files management

Setting	Description
Allow or Disallow use of Offline Files feature	Establishes whether or not Offline Files is enabled.
Prohibit user configuration of Offline Files	Establishes whether users will be able to manage Offline Files settings.
Synchronize all offline files when logging off	Synchronizes files when a user logs off.
Synchronize all offline files before logging on	Synchronizes files when a user logs on.
Synchronize offline files before suspend	Synchronizes files when a computer enters a suspend mode.
Default cache size	Sets a limit on how much disk space can be used by Offline Files.
Action on server disconnect	Determines if network files remain available if the computer is suddenly disconnected from the network.

Table 12-1. Group Policy Settings for Offline Files

Setting	Description
Non-default server disconnect actions	Establishes how computers will react when they are disconnected from servers. Depending on the name of the server, different actions can be established.
Remove "Make Available Offline" tab	Prevents users from making a specific file or folder available offline by removing the Make Available Offline tab from the file menu and all shortcut menus.
Prevent use of Offline Files folder	Disables the View Files button on the Offline Files tab. This keeps users from viewing or opening files by using the Offline Files folder. However, it does not prevent them from working on offline files or using Windows Explorer to navigate to their offline files.
Files not cached	Excludes certain types of files from caching. This setting is useful when you have files that should not be separated, such as database components.
Administratively assigned offline files	Allows administrators to establish which files and folders are available offline.
Turn off reminder balloons	Enables or disables the reminder balloon that usually pops up when a network connection is lost to let users know that they are working on a local copy of the file.
Reminder balloon frequency	Establishes (in minutes) how often the reminder balloon will pop up.
Initial reminder balloon lifetime	Establishes (in seconds) how long the initial reminder balloon will be visible.
Reminder balloon lifetime	Establishes (in seconds) how long subsequent reminder balloons will be visible.
At logoff, delete local copy of user's offline files	Deletes files from cache when a local user logs off. (Note: This setting does not automatically synchronize files. Unless the local user synchronizes his or her files, they will be lost when the cache is emptied.)
Event logging level	Establishes which Offline Files events will be recorded in the event log.
Subfolders always available offline	Makes any subfolders available if a parent folder is made available offline.
Encrypt the Offline Files cache	Encrypts offline files stored in the cache.
Prohibit "Make Available Offline" for these files and folders	Allows administrators to establish which files and folders they do not want available offline.
Configure slow link speed	Establishes the speed Offline Files will consider to be too slow, thus preventing excess traffic from slowing down the connection.

Table 12-1. Group Policy Settings for Offline Files *(continued)*

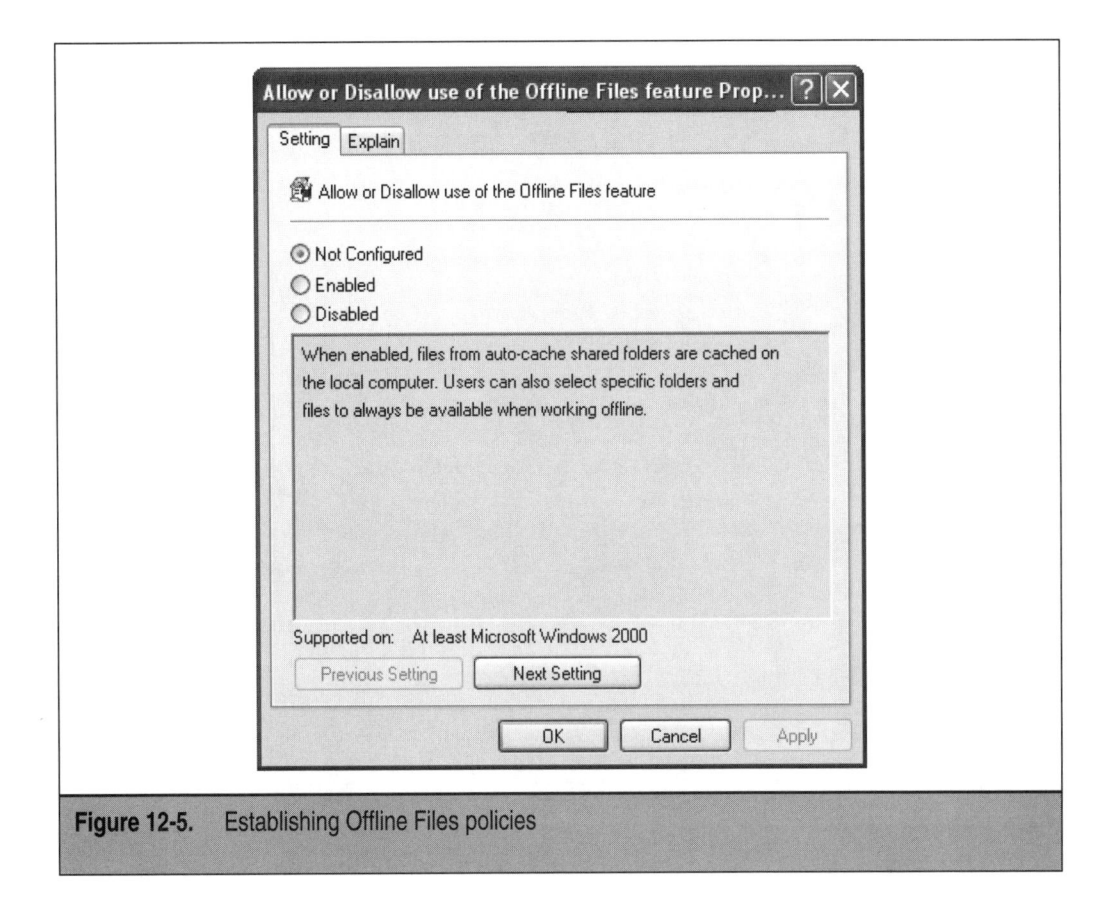

Figure 12-5. Establishing Offline Files policies

Some of the settings in Table 12-1 are just for the computer, whereas others are just for users. However, when the same setting is configured for both the computer and the user, then the computer's configuration takes precedence.

Encryption

The Encrypting File System (EFS) can also be used on your offline files to keep them safe from prying eyes. As long as your offline files are maintained on an NTFS volume, they can be encrypted. To enable Offline Files encryption, in the Folder Options dialog box, click the Offline Files tab, and then select the Encrypt offline files to secure data check box (this is shown in Figure 12-6).

Figure 12-6. Encrypting offline files

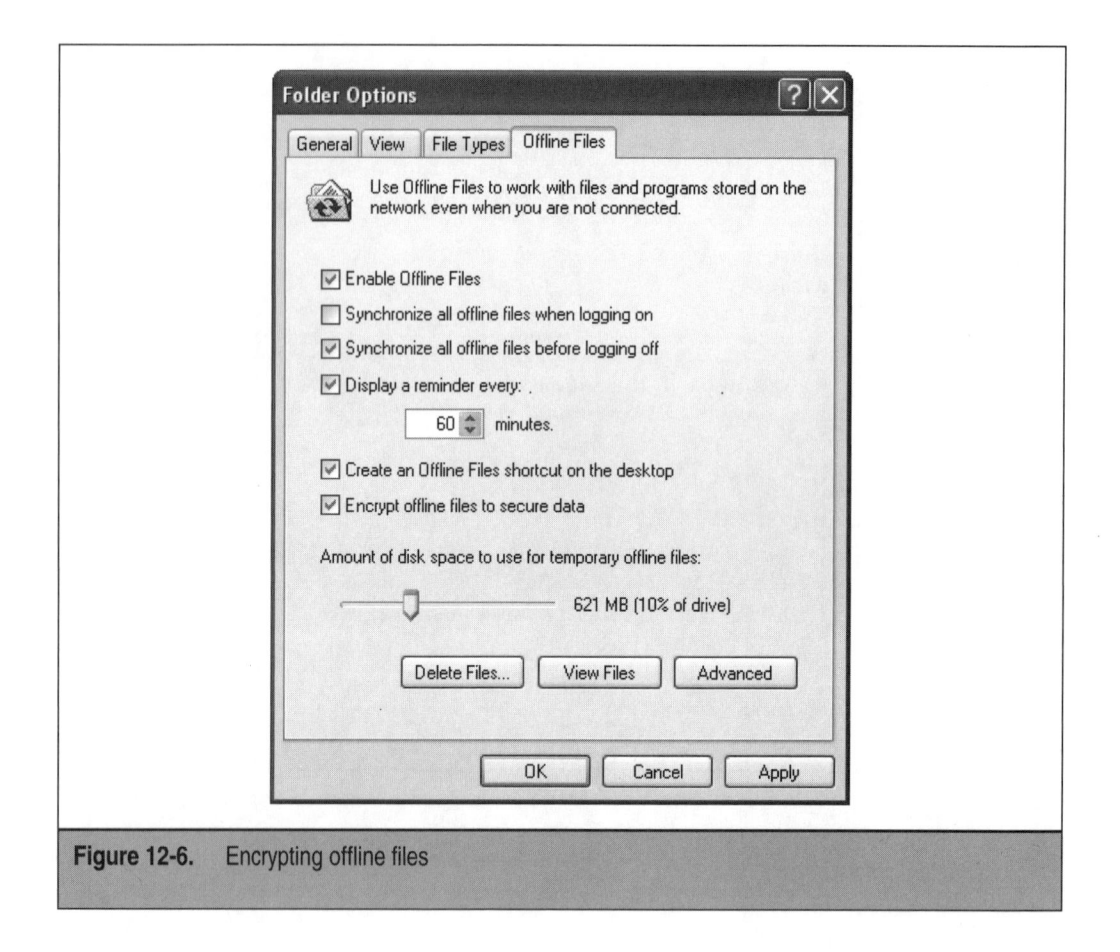

For a group of users, this setting can be established via Group Policy, as we illustrated in the previous section. Using the Group Policy snap-in, enable the Encrypt the Offline Files cache setting. Since this setting is being made by an administrator for a group of users, it cannot be overridden by a user via the Offline Files tab on the local computer.

Printing in Offline Mode

Two of the most likely reasons you would be using Offline Files is because you (or another user) are using a laptop, or the connection to the network share has been disconnected, for whatever reason. In the event you are using a network printer, this means that you won't be able to print files as long as you are disconnected from the network.

Depending on how important it is to print a document, you might find yourself either waiting to print your document, or tracking down a printer that you can use temporarily. Let's examine both of these scenarios and explain how Windows XP Professional handles them.

Printing Without a Printer

If you have a printer set up for your computer but it is not currently connected, you can use Windows XP Professional's *deferred printing* option. This allows you to execute a print command; however, the print job will be stored on your hard drive until the printer is reconnected. When you reconnect—either to the network or to a local printer you will see a message that print jobs are waiting. At this point, you can start the print jobs or cancel them altogether.

If when you reconnect, you don't see the aforementioned message, you can manually start the print job by following these steps:

1. Select Start | Printers and Faxes.
2. Right-click the offline printer. A check mark will appear next to the Use Printer Offline option on the shortcut menu.
3. Select Use Printer Offline. This clears the check mark and starts the waiting print jobs.

If you are anxious to print a given file, you might connect to another printer that you don't normally use.

Using a Different Printer

Assuming you have the correct software on hand, you can temporarily change the printer used on your Windows XP Professional machine. The biggest hurdle will be finding the correct driver for the printer. If the driver is included on the Windows XP Professional CD-ROM, Windows should be able to locate it because it copies most of the drivers to your hard drive during installation. However, you might have to use the CD-ROM or floppy disk containing the printer's driver. If you have an Internet connection, you can go to the printer manufacturer's web site and download a copy of the driver.

Assuming the planets are in alignment and you have the necessary printer driver, follow these steps to install the new temporary printer driver:

1. Select Start | Printers and Faxes.
2. Open your default printer (if you have print jobs pending, they will be listed).
3. Right-click the printer window, and select Properties from the shortcut menu.
4. If necessary, change the port to which the printer is connected on the Ports tab.
5. Click the Advanced tab, and then select the driver you need. If your temporary printer isn't listed, click the New Driver button and pick the type of printer you have.

6. Exit out of all the dialog boxes. Windows XP Professional might ask you for the installation CD-ROM (though you should be able to use the CAB files to complete the installation in lieu of using the installation CD-ROM).

Once you return to your normal work environment, it will be necessary to follow the preceding steps to reset your normal printer as the default.

Installing a temporary printer is a pain, and it assumes a lot of conditions are present. First, it assumes that you have access to a second printer; next, it assumes that you have the proper driver; finally, it assumes you have the Windows XP Professional installation CD-ROM (or at least the necessary CAB files). Especially if you're on the road, you might not have access to these resources.

SYNCHRONIZATION

When a computer comes back to the network (for instance, a road warrior is connecting his or her laptop to the LAN, or users have been working on files while the server is down for maintenance), it is necessary to synchronize the offline files with the originals, stored on the network. This is accomplished in Windows XP Professional by using the Synchronization Manager.

Using Group Policy, administrators can establish when offline files for a computer are to be synchronized. This can be done in the following situations:

- When users log on
- When users log off
- When the computer enters a suspended state

This section examines the specifics of Offline Files synchronization and the settings you can establish to manage your synchronization behavior.

Synchronizing Offline Files and Folders

As we've already noted, the point behind Windows XP Professional's Offline Files feature is to allow users to take their computers away from the network and still use online files. This allows any shared folder available on the network to be made available offline.

When the user reconnects, the offline files must be coordinated with the files in the network share. This is accomplished via the Synchronization Manager.

Synchronization Manager

Synchronization Manager scans the system and, if changes are detected, the files are automatically updated. By updating just the files that have changed (rather than all offline files), time and computing cycles are saved.

Using the Synchronization Manager, Windows XP Professional allows your offline files and designated web pages to be synchronized in one of three ways:

- During logon or logoff
- During times when the computer is idle
- At scheduled times

In addition to automatic synchronization times established with the Synchronization Manager, a user can manually initiate synchronization. Furthermore, during synchronization, you can tell Windows XP Professional to perform one of two types of synchronization:

- **Full synchronization** Synchronizes every file in the local cache with the network share
- **Quick synchronization** Simply ensures that all files in the cache are complete, but doesn't concern itself with whether or not the files are up-to-date

For instance, with quick synchronization, let's say you've got a 1MB file named Test.doc. When synchronization first occurs, the client computer will start downloading Test.doc in increments until it is fully downloaded. However, if something happens to prevent Test.doc from being fully downloaded to the client, then it will not be available offline. Quick synchronization is used to complete these files.

Full synchronization occurs by default whenever the user logs off. The Group Policy snap-in for the MMC is used to manage synchronization settings, and if you choose to disable the setting Synchronize all offline files before logging off, then the system will automatically perform quick synchronizations.

When synchronization takes place, Windows XP Professional compares the original file on the network share against the version in the local cache. If there is a difference, you can examine both files, and then decide which one you want to keep. During synchronization, the Resolve File Conflicts box appears, presenting you with three options:

- **Keep both versions** Both versions of the file are saved. However, the locally cached version is saved to the network using the format *filename(username* v*x).ext*, where *filename* is the original filename; *username* is the user's name; *x* is the version number; and *ext* is the file's extension.
- **Keep only the version on my computer** The network version is replaced with the locally cached version.
- **Keep only the network version** The locally cached version is replaced with the network version.

Configuring Synchronization

To synchronize your Offline Files folder, follow these steps:

1. Select Start | All Programs | Accessories | Synchronize.
2. In the Items to Synchronize dialog box, click Setup. The resulting screen is shown in Figure 12-7.
3. Click Setup. In the When I am using this network connection box, choose the connection for which you want to specify offline web pages and files to be synchronized.
4. All offline web pages and offline files are displayed in the Synchronize the following checked items box. Select the items you want to be synchronized when you reconnect to the network.
5. Repeat Steps 3 and 4 until you have configured the synchronization settings for each of your network connections.

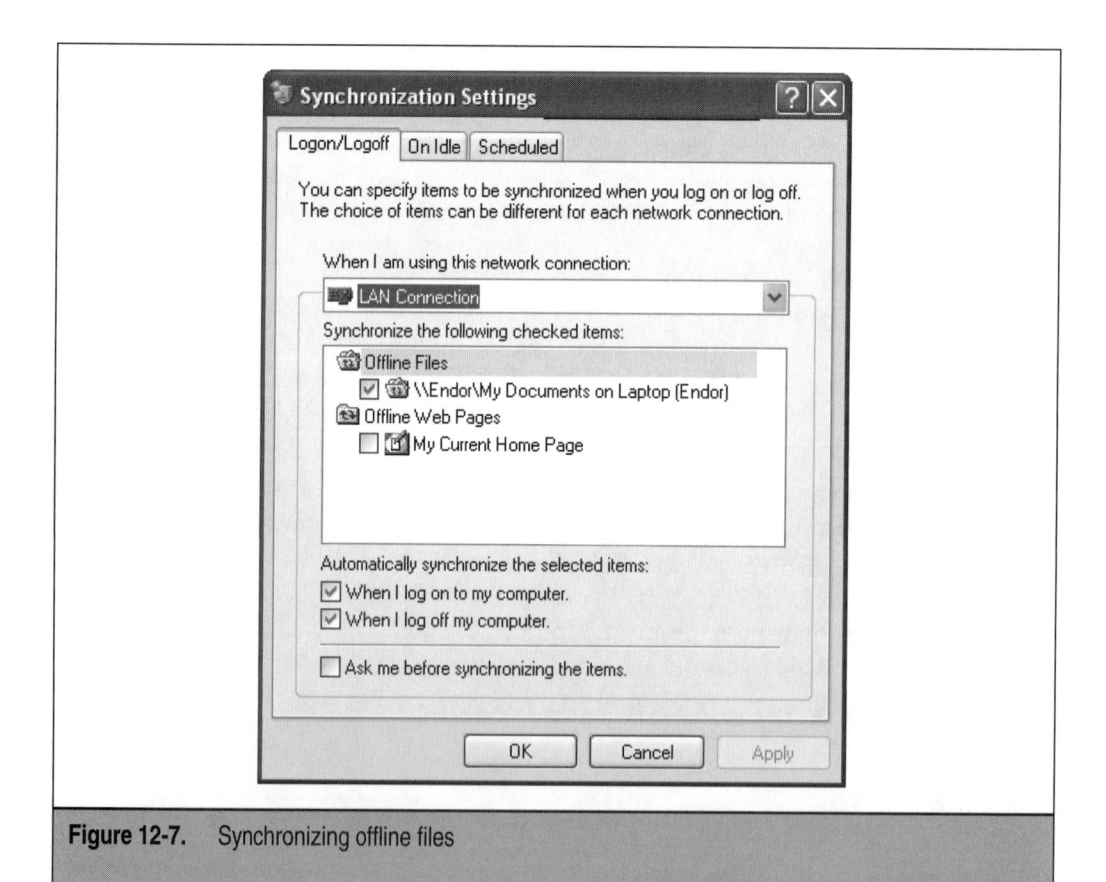

Figure 12-7. Synchronizing offline files

6. Indicate whether you want items to be synchronized when you log on or log off Windows, or if you want to be notified before synchronization occurs.
7. Click OK.
8. Click Synchronize to complete the synchronization immediately, or click Close to close the Items to Synchronize dialog box.

Scheduling Synchronization

With your offline files (or web pages), you can determine a specific time when they will be synchronized. This is useful if you work offline regularly and need to synchronize your offline files with the network share. To establish a scheduled synchronization time, follow these steps:

1. Select Start | All Programs | Accessories | Synchronize | Setup.
2. Click the Scheduled tab.
3. Click Add. This starts the Scheduled Synchronization Wizard, as shown in Figure 12-8.
4. Select the connection you wish to use.

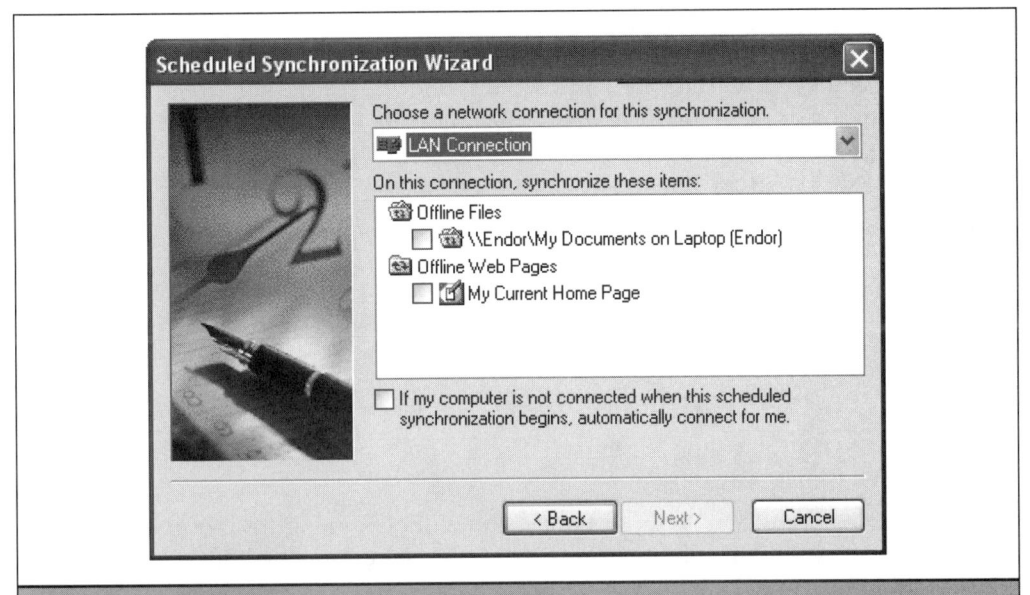

Figure 12-8. The Scheduled Synchronization Wizard

5. Click Next.
6. From the drop-down box, click the network connection that will be used for the synchronization.
7. In the On this connection, synchronize these items pane, select the check box next to each item you wish to synchronize. Also, if you will not necessarily be connected at the time of synchronization, check the box next to the option If my computer is not connected when this scheduled synchronization begins, automatically connect for me.
8. Click Next.
9. The wizard allows you to set a time for the scheduled synchronization. You can also tell it to perform the synchronization every day, every weekday, or every x number of days. You can also pick a start date when the scheduled synchronization will begin.
10. Click Next, and then give the task a name.
11. Click Finish to complete the scheduled synchronization task.

If you need to delete or edit an existing scheduled synchronization, when you get to step 3, select the scheduled synchronization, and then click the Delete or Edit button as necessary.

Laptop Synchronization Options

If you or a user is using Offline Files on a laptop, certain settings will prove helpful when performing (or planning for) synchronization. The following sections examine different practices that you can use for optimizing your laptop's synchronization behavior, especially as they relate to laptops running on battery power.

During an Idle State

When a laptop is in an idle state, and running on battery power, synchronization does not take place. This is a default setting used to conserve battery power. If you want to disable this setting, follow these steps:

1. Select Start | All Programs | Accessories | Synchronize | Setup.
2. In the Synchronization Settings dialog box that appears, click the On Idle tab, and then click Advanced.
3. In the resulting Idle Settings dialog box (as shown in Figure 12-9), clear the Prevent synchronization when my computer is running on battery power check box.

As Figure 12-9 shows, synchronization can be set up for specific times to coincide with your computer's idle time.

Figure 12-9. Enabling or disabling synchronization when an idle laptop is running on battery power

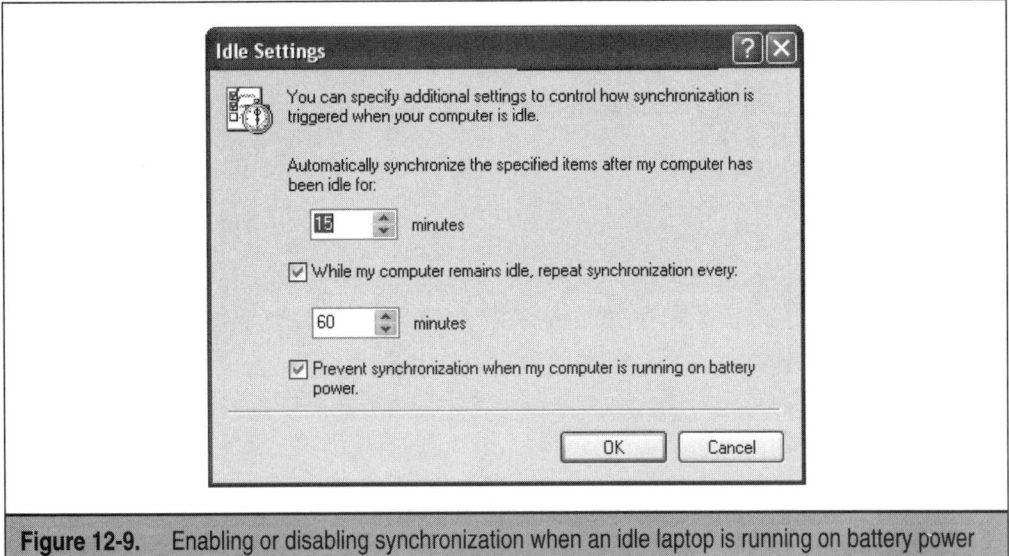

Halting Scheduled Synchronization

If you've already established a scheduled time to perform synchronization, you might want to disable the scheduled synchronization effort, especially if the laptop is running on battery power, or when the battery power is low.

When Running on Battery Power   If you are running on battery power, you might not want to start a scheduled synchronization, which has the potential to deplete your battery level. To prevent the synchronization, follow these steps:

1. Select Start | All Programs | Accessories | Synchronize | Setup.
2. In the Synchronization Settings dialog box, click the Scheduled tab.
3. Select a scheduled task, and then click Edit.
4. Click the Settings Tab (shown in Figure 12-10). Under Power Management, select the check box. Don't start the task if the computer is running on batteries.

When Battery Power Is Low   If your laptop's battery is especially low, running a prescheduled synchronization might not be desirable. To prevent it, follow these steps:

1. Select Start | All Programs | Accessories | Synchronize | Setup.
2. In the Synchronization Settings dialog box, click the Schedule tab.
3. Select a scheduled task, and then click Edit.
4. Click the Settings Tab. Under Power Management, select the check box. Stop the task if battery mode begins.

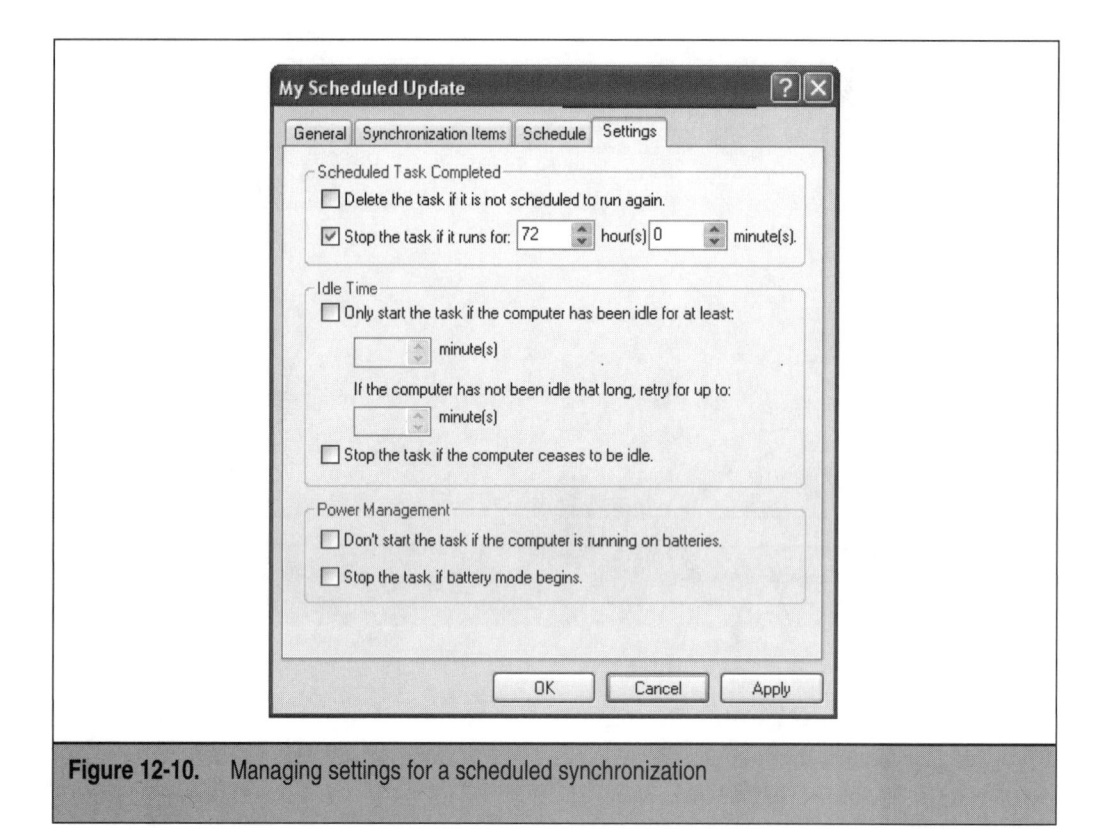

Figure 12-10. Managing settings for a scheduled synchronization

WINDOWS BRIEFCASE

Another way to coordinate offline files is through the Windows Briefcase tool. Whereas Offline Files is useful for working with network files on a desktop or laptop computer, Windows Briefcase is especially well suited when you need to take a file from one computer (your desktop computer, for example) and use it on another (a laptop, for instance). When you come back to your desktop computer, you use Windows Briefcase to synchronize the two files, thus allowing you to have the most current file, wherever you're working.

This tool works by creating *briefcases*, which are nothing more than folders containing the files and subfolders you are transferring between your desktop and laptop computers. To coordinate these files, you simply connect the laptop to the network and make the transfer. You or your user might not have a second network drop at the desktop. You can still synchronize files by using a floppy disk; depending on the size of your briefcase, you might need more than one floppy disk to transfer everything.

You should see a briefcase icon on your desktop (it's been a staple on Windows desktops since Windows 95). If it isn't there, you can create a new briefcase by right-clicking the desktop and choosing New | Briefcase. You can also create multiple briefcases, which can be useful when organizing offline files for varying needs.

When you create a new briefcase, and then open it, Windows XP Professional welcomes you to it with an informative dialog box, as shown in Figure 12-11. You needn't do anything with this screen other than read the tips and click Finish.

Once you've created a new briefcase, simply drag and drop the files you wish to work on into the briefcase, as shown in Figure 12-12.

Using the Briefcase

Using Windows Briefcase involves these general steps:

1. Move your desired files to the briefcase.
2. Copy the briefcase to the laptop (either via a network connection, floppy disk, or other means).
3. Use your files.

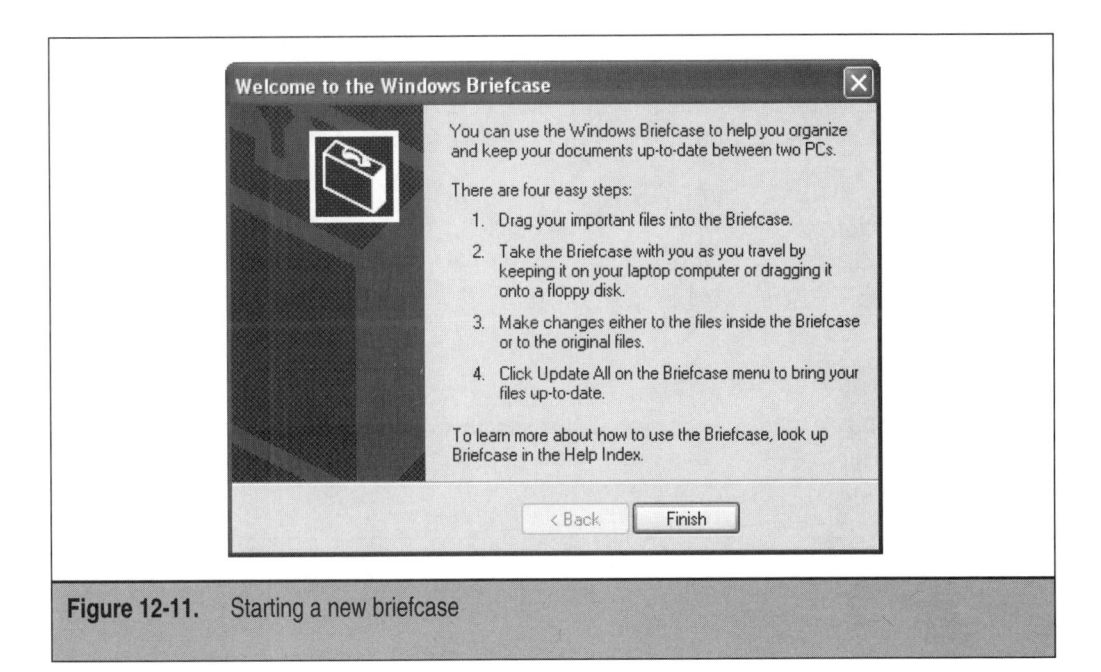

Figure 12-11. Starting a new briefcase

Figure 12-12. A briefcase with some files

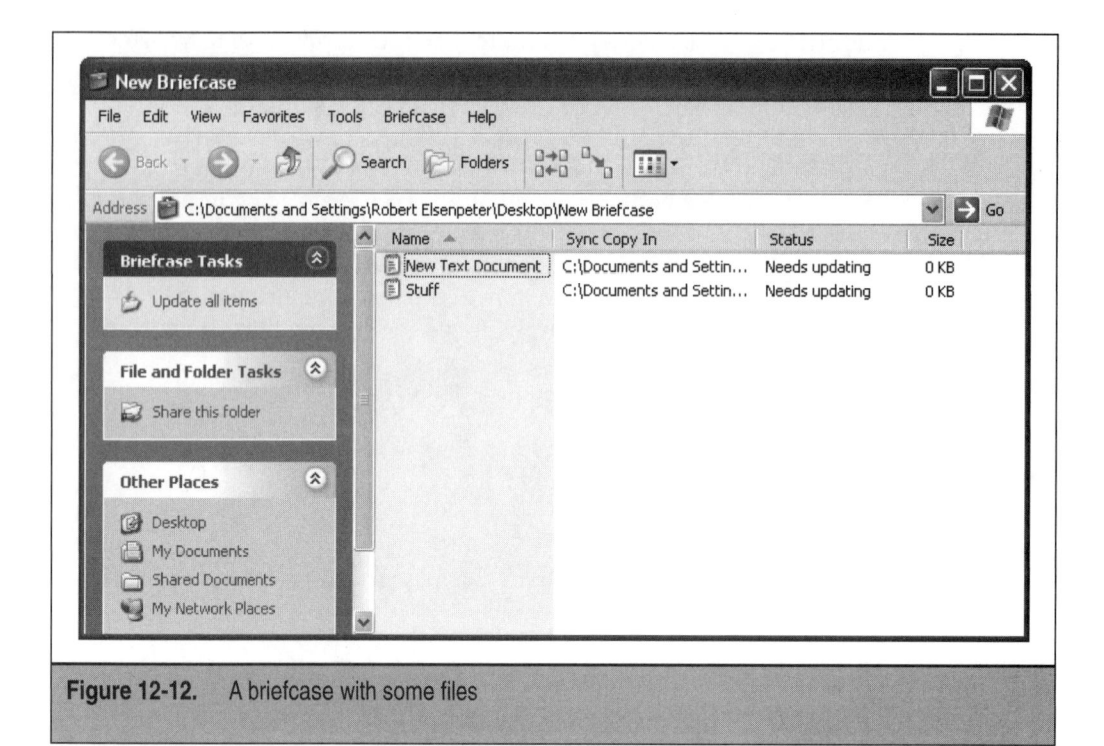

4. Once you're ready to transfer your files back to your desktop computer, click the Update All or Update Selection icon, shown just under the menu bar.

These steps will differ slightly, depending on whether you are transferring your briefcase via a LAN or with floppies. Using floppies, you transfer the files from your computer's A: drive; using a LAN, you drag your files from the desktop to the laptop's briefcase. The preceding steps are explained in more detail in the following sections.

Moving Files to the Briefcase

First, you must take the files you want to transfer from your desktop computer and move them to your briefcase. This can be done by locating them in Windows Explorer and dragging them to your desktop's briefcase.

NOTE You can drag the files to either the briefcase icon or the open Briefcase window.

Alternatively, select one or more files, right-click, and then select Send To | My Briefcase from the shortcut menu.

If you're using a LAN, simply locate your files on the network and drag them to your laptop's briefcase—there's no need to transfer them to a desktop briefcase first. If you are using a floppy disk, create a briefcase on your desktop computer, drag the files to it, and then drag the briefcase to your floppy drive. Or, you can right-click the briefcase and select Send To | Floppy. If your briefcase is larger than 1.44MB, then you'll be prompted for additional disks.

Copying the Briefcase to a Laptop

Once the files are located in your desktop's briefcase (or on the floppy disks), they must be transferred to your laptop. This step can be skipped if you are using a LAN, because you already set up the briefcase on the laptop. However, if you are transferring your briefcase with floppy disks, you must follow these steps:

1. Insert the first floppy disk into the laptop's floppy disk drive.
2. Open that drive in Windows Explorer.
3. Drag the briefcase onto your laptop's desktop.

This places the briefcase on the desktop where the files can be easily accessed.

Using Briefcase Files

Once your briefcase files are offline, it's important that you use the files while they are located in the briefcase. To use them, double-click the briefcase icon and make your selection from the window as you would with any other file.

If you prefer, you can use an application's Open command. Once you select Open, navigate to the briefcase and pick your file from the list. When saving your files, again make sure that you are saving to your briefcase.

> **CAUTION** If files aren't saved back to the briefcase, then they cannot be synchronized when you reconnect to the network.

One of the shortcomings of Windows Briefcase is that you cannot synchronize files that have been updated on both the network and the laptop. For instance, if a road warrior edits a Word file, and someone else has edited or added to the original file in the meantime, then Windows Briefcase won't be able to synchronize them. You'll be able to keep one or the other, but cannot merge the two.

Windows Briefcase allows you to manage some of your offline files' traits. For instance, you can check the update status of each file in the Status column of the briefcase. The status of a particular item can also be checked by selecting it in the briefcase window, right-clicking the desired file, selecting Properties from the shortcut menu, and clicking the Update Status tab. This view is shown in Figure 12-13.

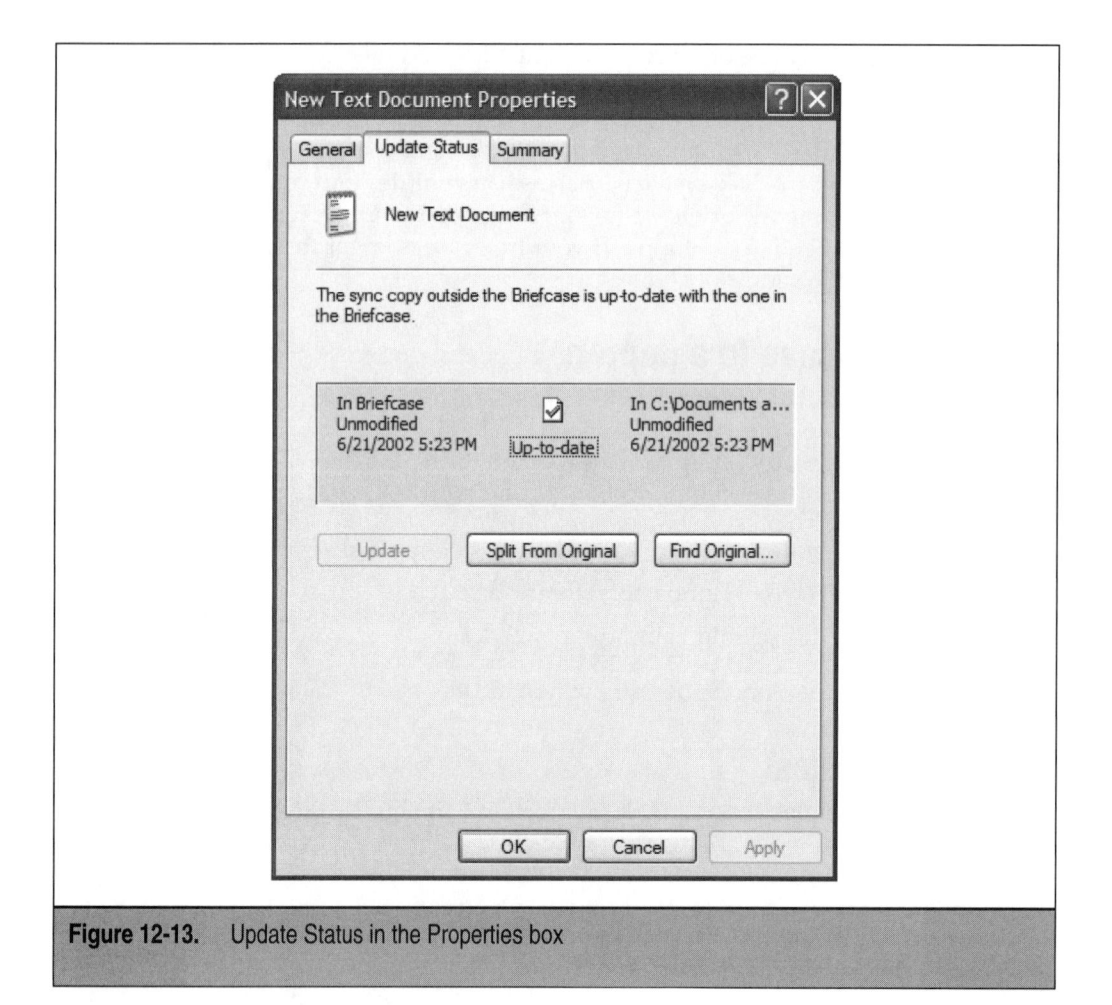

Figure 12-13. Update Status in the Properties box

The original copy of a file located in the briefcase can be found by opening the file's Properties box, selecting the Update Status tab, and then clicking the Find Original button. Windows XP Professional will show the folder in which the original file is located.

If you're working on a file from the briefcase and decide that it has changed so much that it should not be synchronized with the original, you can elect to keep the files separate. This is done by selecting the file in the briefcase window, and choosing Briefcase | Split From Original in the menu bar. This task can also be accomplished from the Update Status tab by clicking the Split From Original button.

Briefcase Synchronization

The point of this section has been to show you how to manage offline files via Windows Briefcase. When it comes time to synchronize your laptop with your desktop, you should follow these steps:

1. Connect your laptop to your network or desktop computer. If you're using floppy disks to transfer the briefcase, move the briefcase from the laptop back to the floppy disk, insert the floppy disk into the desktop computer, and move the briefcase back to the original computer's desktop.
2. Open the briefcase. The status of each file will be listed in the Status column as one of the following three states:
   - **Orphan**   The file exists only in the briefcase and not in the original computer. For instance, it might have been deleted or moved while the briefcase was in use.
   - **Up-To-Date**   The file does not differ from the copy on the original computer.
   - **Needs Updating**   The file in the briefcase differs from the one on the computer and should be updated.
3. In the briefcase's toolbar, click the Update All button. A dialog box will appear (as shown in Figure 12-14) that shows how each file must be updated. There are three ways in which a file can be updated:
   - **Replace (with an arrow pointing to the right)**   The briefcase will replace the original file with the briefcase's copy.

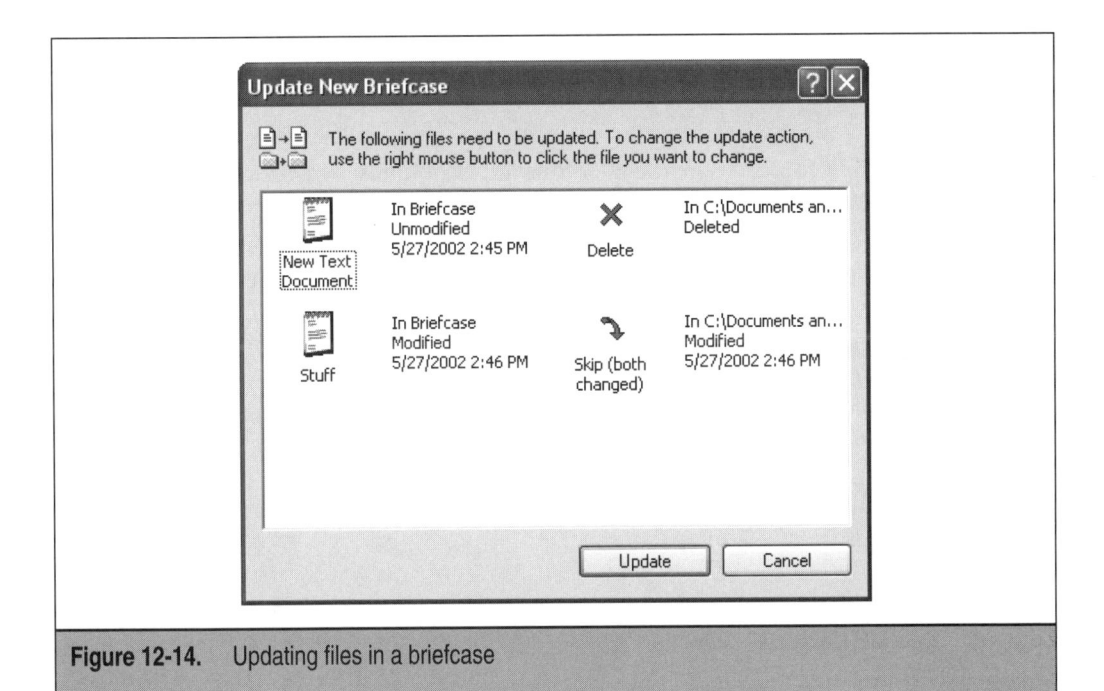

Figure 12-14.   Updating files in a briefcase

- **Replace (with an arrow pointing to the left)** The briefcase's copy of the file will be replaced with the one on the original computer.
- **Skip (both changed)** Both files have been changed, and the briefcase cannot tell which one should be used. In this case, you need to make the decision as to which file is the most current.

4. If the methods shown don't appeal to you, right-click the file and select a method from the resulting shortcut menu.
5. Click the Update button to update the files.

If there are files in your briefcase that you don't want to bother trying to synchronize, rather than click the Update All icon in Step 3, click the Update Selection icon.

TROUBLESHOOTING OFFLINE FILES

If you remember all the Group Policy settings in Table 12-1, it should come as no surprise to you that Offline Files, while powerful, has a lot of nooks and crannies through which problems can seep. The last section of this chapter endeavors to help you resolve problems that might occur when you're trying to make Offline Files and synchronization work properly.

Inability to Make a Folder an Offline Folder

If the user right-clicks a file or folder, but cannot see Make Available Offline, the following are good places to check:

- **Local file or folder** The file or folder might actually be a local file or folder and not on the network in the first place.
- **My Documents redirection** If the user is trying to redirect access to his or her My Documents folder, but does not have access to the file share, first make sure that the Make Available Offline option is available. If it is, but not when My Documents is right-clicked, then make sure that the My Documents folder has been redirected appropriately and is on a network share, not the local computer. Next, make sure that the user has the appropriate permissions to read and write to that share.
- **Group Policy settings** Check your Group Policy settings to make sure that Offline Files is enabled.

Files Available Online Are Not Available Offline

When a user tries to access files that were previously available online but cannot be found in the Offline Files folder, then check the following situations:

- **Windows flavor**   Offline Files is only available in Windows 2000 and Windows XP Professional environments. If the server is a different flavor of Windows, automatic caching is not available.
- **Enabling Offline Files**   Offline Files might be disabled on the computer. Right-click the file or folder and look for the Make Available Offline option. If it is not there, then Offline Files must be enabled.
- **Caching of shared folders disabled**   Offline Files may not be available because the Allow caching of files in this shared folder option is not enabled. To check this setting (and enable it, if necessary) follow these steps:

    1. On the server housing the desired file, use Windows Explorer to navigate to the file.
    2. Right-click the shared folder, and then choose Properties.
    3. Click the Sharing tab, and then click Caching.
    4. Make sure the Allow caching of files in this shared option box is checked.
    5. Select either Automatic Caching for Documents or Automatic Caching for Programs, depending on whether the folder contains documents or applications.

Fast User Switching Enabled

If you have Fast User Switching enabled, you won't be able to use Offline Files. In fact, if you attempt to use Offline Files with Fast User Switching enabled, you'll see the message shown in Figure 12-15.

If you cannot access your offline files, you must first disable Fast User Switching. To turn off Fast User Switching, follow these steps:

1. Select Start | Control Panel.
2. In Category view, click User Accounts.
3. Select Change the way users log on or off.
4. Clear the Use Fast User Switching check box, and then click Apply Options.
5. Click OK to exit User Accounts and the Control Panel.

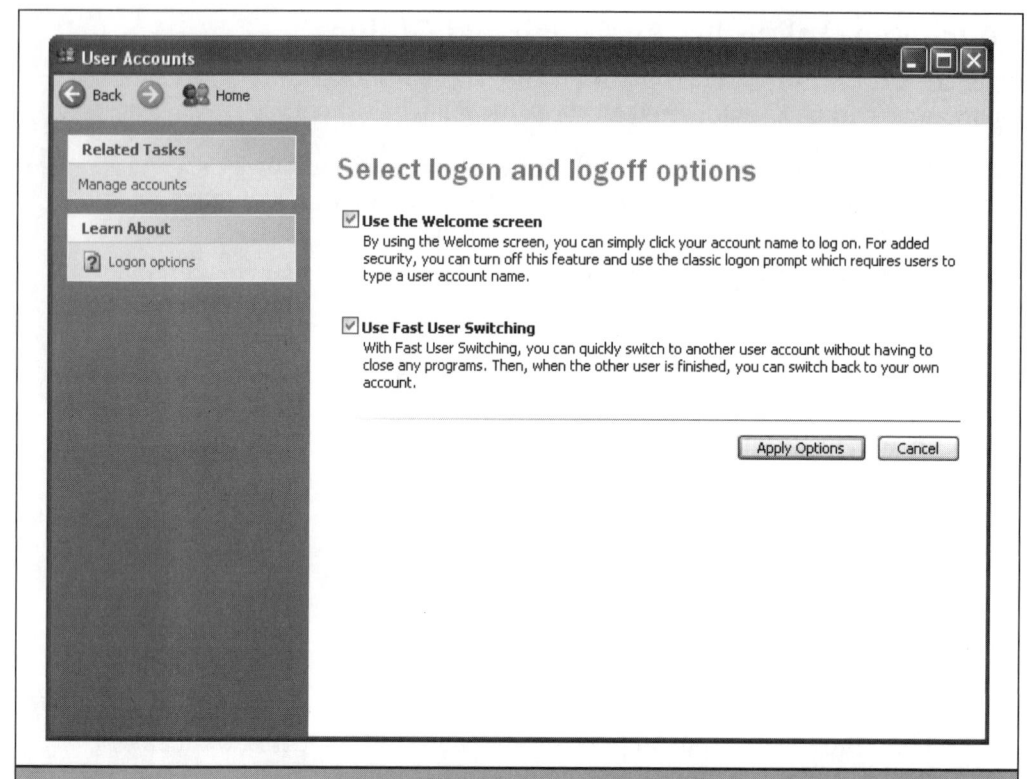

Figure 12-15. You cannot use Offline Files with Fast User Switching enabled.

Resolve File Conflicts Message Appears

If while you're trying to synchronize offline files a Resolve File Conflicts message appears, it's most likely that both the online and offline copies have been changed, and Windows XP Professional isn't sure how to synchronize the files. To ameliorate the problem, select the method of file resolution you want, and then click OK.

If you have multiple online and offline files that were altered since your last connection and you want to perform the same synchronization method for all of them, select the Do this for all conflicts check box.

Inability to Synchronize Offline Files

If a user is unable to synchronize his or her offline files and folders, there are a number of issues you should check:

- **Extensions** The first items to check for problems are the extensions on the filenames. Files with the extensions .db, .ldb, .mdb, and .mde are not synchronized, by default. To resolve this, you can use the Group Policy snap-in to make these extensions synchronizable. Furthermore, the administrator might have set Group Policy to prevent a certain file type from being synchronized. These settings can be checked in Group Policy by following Computer Configuration\Administrative Templates\Network\Offline Files\Files Not Cached.

- **Network connectivity** Connection problems might be preventing synchronization from occurring. Check the connection between the client and the server by pinging the server's IP address, and then ping its name to check DNS name resolution. Additionally, you can use the command

    ```
    net view \\servername
    ```

    to see the share where the file is located. This will also show if the user has the correct permissions to access the share.

- **Disk space** There might not be enough room on the client disk drive to perform the synchronization. Check the hard drive and make sure it has sufficient room.

- **Access rights** The user may not have the requisite rights (read and write) to access the file. Check permissions to make sure that the user has the appropriate level of rights.

Most of the problems you might encounter with Offline Files can be managed by examining the state of the organization's Group Policy settings. With about two dozen different settings, it is easy for something to be inadvertently set (or overlooked), which then affects users attempting to use and synchronize offline files.

PART IV

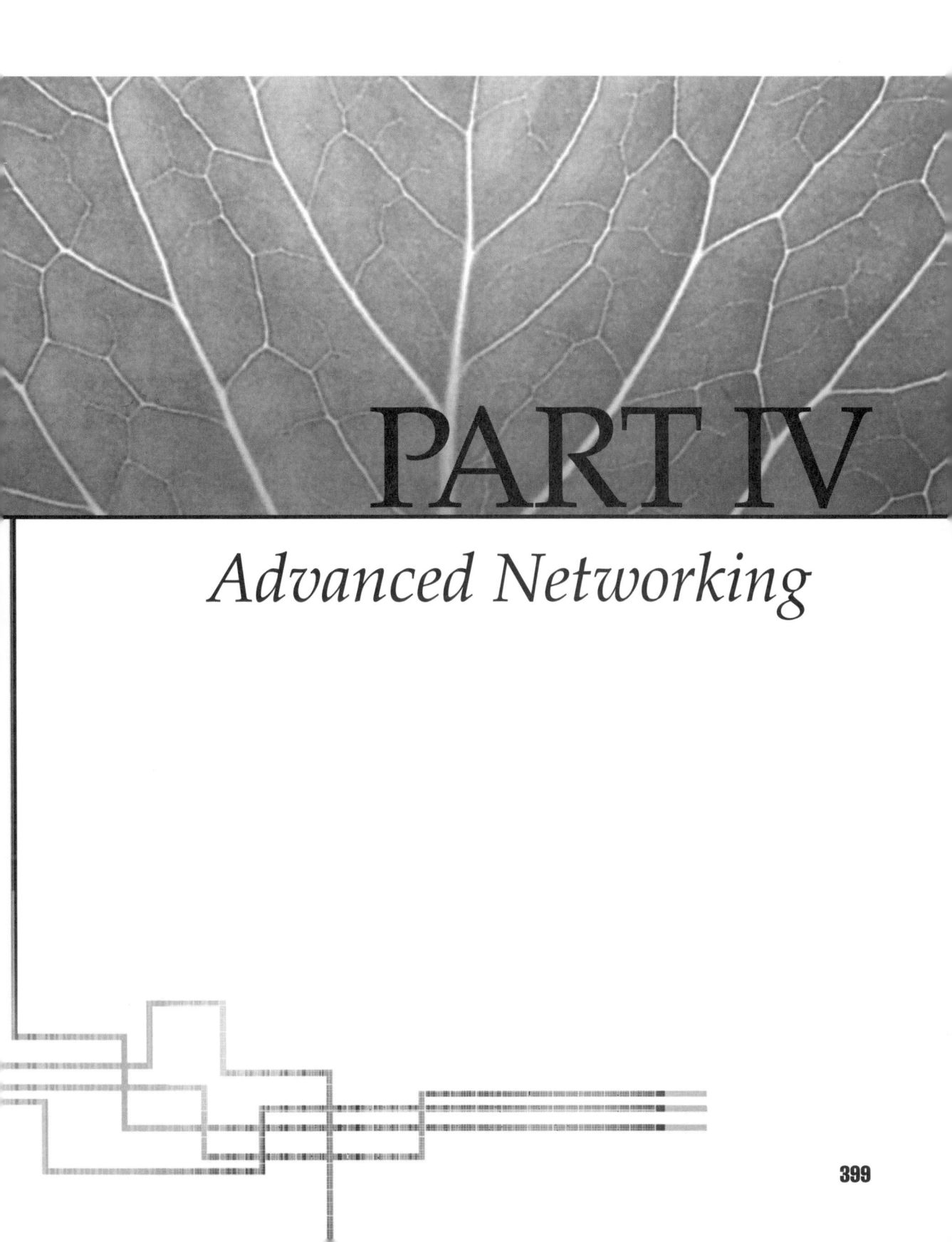

Advanced Networking

CHAPTER 13

Remote Desktop and Remote Assistance

For years, support technicians have used programs that allow them to look at and fix a user's computer without having to visit that user's office, or even his or her cubicle for that matter. Such programs as Carbon Copy and pcAnywhere have made it possible for these technicians to perform remote control and assistance tasks directly from their own computers. In Windows XP Professional, Microsoft integrated its own version of remote access features.

Windows XP Professional comes with two different tools designed for remote control and assistance. The first is Remote Desktop, which allows someone else to use your computer via a network or dial-up connection. Remote Assistance is a more aid-oriented tool, which you use when you need help getting your computer or an application to work properly.

This chapter examines both Remote Desktop and Remote Assistance. First, we talk about the functionality of Remote Desktop and how to set it up and use it. Next, we'll shift our attention to Remote Assistance and examine how it works and how you can use it to help (or be helped by) a friend.

UNDERSTANDING REMOTE DESKTOP

Windows XP Professional's Remote Desktop tool allows you to control one computer, remotely, from another. For instance, if you need to access your office computer from home (and assuming you had the foresight to set up your work computer before leaving the office), you could use Remote Desktop to access everything on your work computer—including files, applications, and network connections. You can even hear the dorky sound the remote computer makes when a file is opened.

In fact, Remote Desktop not only allows you to access the remote computer's files, but you also actually see the desktop as it appears on that machine. Furthermore, if the remote computer is running Windows 2000 or .NET Server, more than one person can use the remote computer simultaneously.

Remote Desktop is based on *Terminal Services technology*. This means that Remote Desktop allows you to run applications on a remote computer using Windows XP Professional from any other client using a Windows operating system.

As we'll see later in this chapter, Terminal Services technology is also the basis for Remote Assistance, which allows you to invite a friend or technical expert to connect to your computer, view your desktop, and control your computer.

Remote Desktop connections are formed using a LAN, a virtual private network (VPN), or an Internet connection. As you might expect, the speed of your connection will have a significant effect on your Remote Desktop experience.

NOTE We talk about VPNs and Windows XP Professional in more detail in Chapter 14.

There are two components to a Remote Desktop connection:

- **Server** This is the remote computer to which you will be connecting. It could be your desktop computer at the office, or it could be a computer set up for road warriors to remotely access when they're traveling.
- **Client** This is the computer you will use to form your connection with the server. For example, a road warrior's laptop.

There are two different versions of Remote Desktop you can use, depending on your need:

- **Remote Desktop** The first version is for use on a LAN and requires that you install software on the client computer.
- **Remote Desktop Web Connection** This version only requires that the client computer be using Internet Explorer, but it necessitates more software to be installed and set up on the server.

Features

Remote Desktop affords a number of features that make the Remote Desktop session more usable and functional for the user. Its main features include console security, color support, and resource redirection.

Console Security

When you use Remote Desktop, you need not worry that someone will sit at the remote computer and watch what you're doing. Remote Desktop uses *console security*. That is, when a Remote Desktop session has been initiated, the session is not played out on the client computer screen *and* the server computer screen. Rather, Windows XP Professional disables the display on the remote computer, preventing anyone from monitoring your activities.

Color Support

Remote Desktop supports up to 24-bit color. That is, whatever is displayed on the Remote Desktop server is what is displayed on the Remote Desktop client. The amount and depth of color displayed can be adjusted by the user as needed.

Resource Redirection

The important part of any Remote Desktop session is the ability to actually *use* the components of a remote computer. Remote Desktop employs *resource redirection*, allowing the remote user to function as if he or she were sitting in front of the remote computer. Resource redirection applies to several aspects of a remote computer's assets, including the ability to use the remote computer's file system as if it were a shared network resource.

Audio redirection allows the client computer to play sounds that are produced on the server computer. In the event there are two applications playing sound, the two streams are combined to deliver a mix of both. Remote Desktop also takes available bandwidth into consideration when playing sound. Rather than choke the connection with sound, Remote Desktop will renegotiate the sound stream quality, if bandwidth changes.

Remote Desktop Protocol

Remote Desktop uses the Remote Desktop Protocol (RDP) as the basis of its connections. RDP is a presentation protocol that allows a Windows client to communicate with a Windows XP Professional–based computer. RDP works across any TCP/IP connection, which makes it an ideal protocol to function across a broad range of connections.

RDP version 5.1 is the version used in Windows XP Professional. Any client using RDP 5.1 is able to employ the following attributes of another computer also using RDP 5.1:

- **File system** The file system of a remote computer is fully accessible, as if it were a network drive.
- **Audio** Any audio output that would be heard on the Remote Desktop server is heard through the Remote Desktop client's speakers.
- **Port** Access to serial, parallel, and USB ports on the client computer is still permitted while using an application on a server. This allows any peripheral device to still be used while the session is in progress.
- **Printer** The default printer for the client computer is used for the session (assuming the server has the requisite driver installed).
- **Clipboard** Both the Remote Desktop server and client share a common clipboard. This allows information to be cut and pasted freely between them.

Security Issues

Obviously, security is an important issue with Remote Desktop. Not only is the specter of unauthorized use of your computer present, but there is also the need to manage what authorized users are allowed and not allowed to access.

Security in Remote Desktop can be managed through several techniques. The following sections explain how you can keep your system secure—at varying levels—using Remote Desktop. These settings are managed using the Terminal Services section of the Group Policy snap-in to the Microsoft Management Console (MMC).

Terminal Services is located by activating the MMC, adding the Group Policy snap-in, and then double-clicking Computer Configuration. Next, click Administrative Templates, click Windows Components, and then click Terminal Services. This tool is shown in Figure 13-1.

Figure 13-1. Terminal Services portion of the Group Policy snap-in

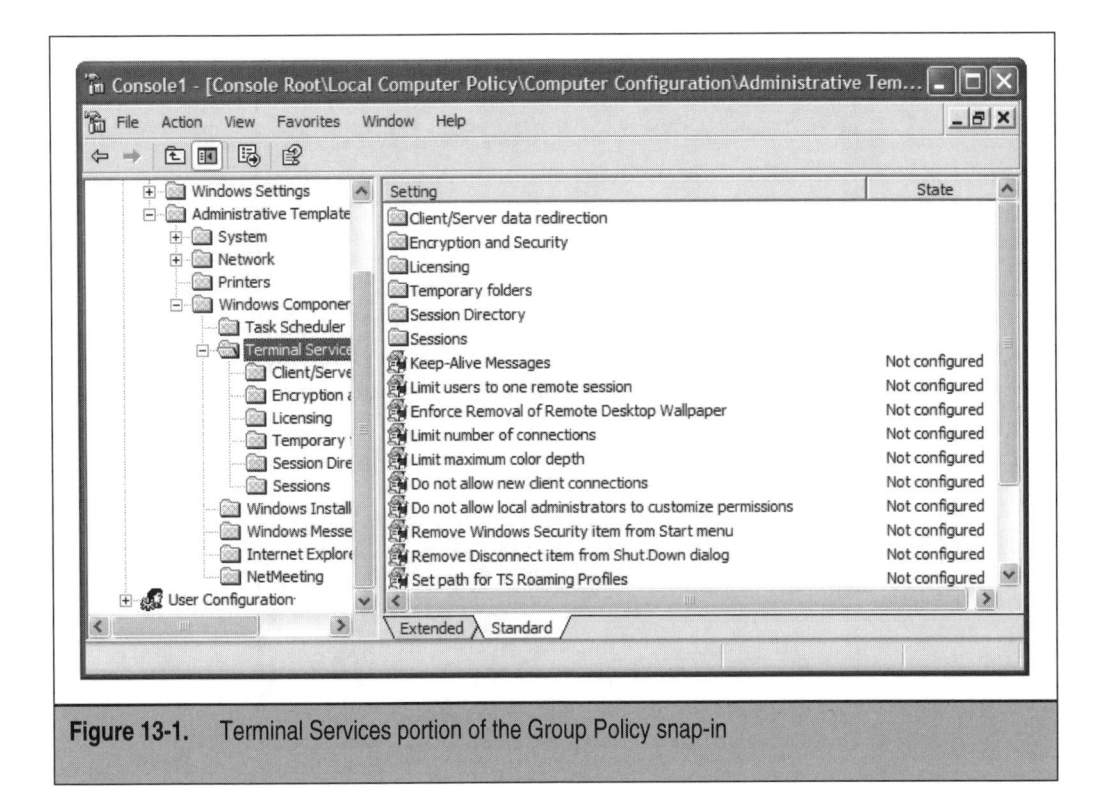

Encryption

You can enable and manage encryption levels between your Remote Desktop client and server by using the Terminal Services Group Policy setting. There are two encryption levels that you can choose between (as shown in Figure 13-2):

- **High Level** This level encrypts data between the client and server using strong 128-bit encryption. This level should only be chosen if you are certain that both computers can use 128-bit encryption (for instance, if both computers are using Windows XP Professional). If your client does not support this level, it will not be able to connect.

- **Client Compatible** This level encrypts data at the highest level supported by the client computer.

If your encryption settings are incompatible—for instance your server is using strong 128-bit encryption and the client can only handle 56-bit encryption, the connection will not be established.

Figure 13-2. Setting encryption levels for Remote Desktop

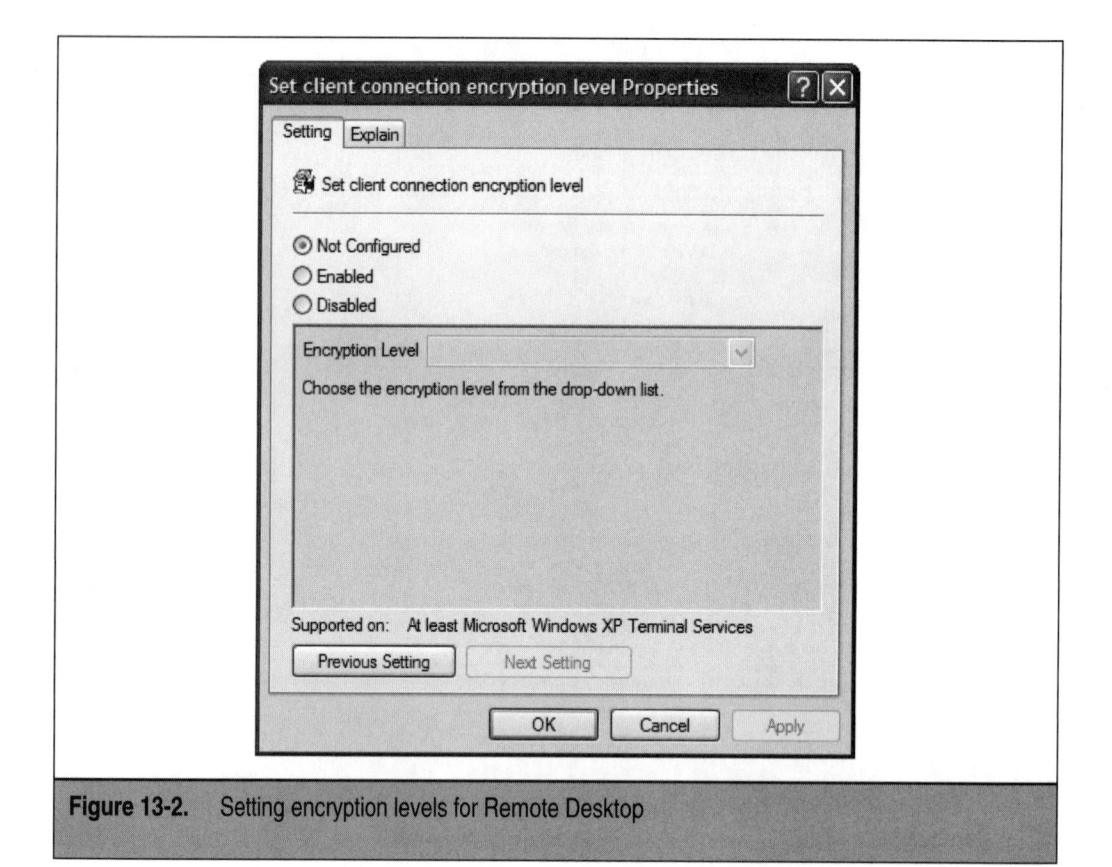

Password Authentication
Rather than allowing a password to be automatically passed during a client logon, it's a good idea to prompt the user for the password when he or she tries to log on. In the Terminal Services Group Policy setting, this is managed under Always prompt client for password.

Disabling the Clipboard
If you elect to prevent users from sharing a clipboard between the Remote Desktop client and server, this can be disabled in the Terminal Services Group Policy setting under Do not allow clipboard redirection.

Disabling the Printer
Disabling printing is also possible and is a security setting you might wish to set. To prevent users from using printer redirection, in the Terminal Services Group Policy setting, enable the option Do not allow printer redirection.

Disabling Files

If you don't want remote users to be able to rummage through the file system connected to the Remote Desktop server, in the Terminal Services Group Policy setting, enable the option Do not allow drive redirection policy.

USING REMOTE DESKTOP

Once you decide that you will be using Remote Desktop, you should make sure that the server is properly configured for remote access. It's also a really good idea to test your connection to make sure everything is working properly. After all, once you're away from the server, the computer cannot be accessed to perform any tweaks or tuning. Proper setup and testing is necessary no matter if you are using Remote Desktop or Remote Desktop Web Connection.

Configuring a Server for Remote Desktop

Now that you understand some of the basics of Remote Desktop and its functionality, it's time to talk about how to set up your Remote Desktop server. As noted earlier, there are two different ways to connect remotely. The first is via a LAN connection, and the second is via a Web connection. Each method is explained in the following sections.

LAN Connection

When you configure a Remote Desktop server, you will also indicate the user accounts that will be allowed to form Remote Desktop connections to your server. These user accounts must have passwords, which naturally will be used to keep evildoers out of your system. If you don't usually use a password to sign on to your system, Windows XP Professional requires you to create one for Remote Desktop.

When you configure your server for Remote Desktop, you will enter the user account name when Windows XP Professional asks for the Object Name in the Select Users dialog box. To configure a Remote Desktop server, follow these steps:

1. Select Start | Control Panel. Then click Performance and Maintenance and choose System.
2. Click the Remote tab.
3. In the Remote Desktop portion of the dialog box, select the check box Allow users to connect remotely to this computer. You might see a box warning you about user accounts needing passwords. If so, click OK.
4. Click the Select Remote Users button. This calls up the Remote Desktop users dialog box, in which you will add users who will be allowed to remotely access this computer. Administrative accounts are automatically given access.
5. Click Add. This calls up the Select Users dialog box, as shown in Figure 13-3. User accounts have three identifying components: object type, location, and name.

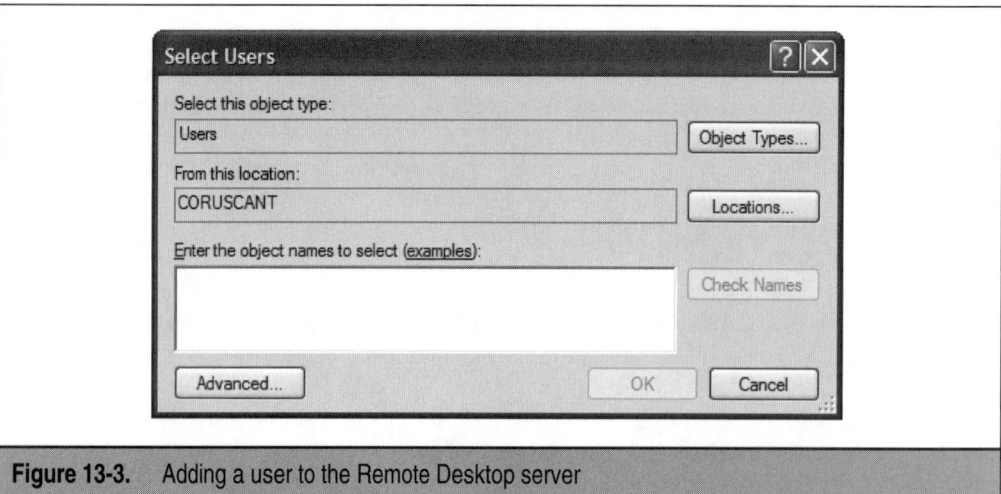

Figure 13-3. Adding a user to the Remote Desktop server

6. If you want to locate a user account from the Remote Desktop server, make sure the Select this object type option is set to Users, and type an account name in the Enter the object names to select box. If you wish to enter a user from another computer on an Active Directory–based LAN, click the Locations button and select the domain, and then enter the user account name.

7. Click Check Names. This gives Windows XP Professional a chance to enter the name, in *computername\username* format.

8. Click OK. The user you just indicated will be added to the list of users permitted to remotely access your Remote Desktop server. To add more users, repeat steps 5 through 8.

9. Click OK twice to exit all the dialog boxes.

10. Finally, if your Remote Desktop server is protected by a firewall, make sure that the firewall allows remote connection traffic.

Internet Connection

To access a Remote Desktop server via the Internet, it is necessary to install the Remote Desktop Web Connection on the server. This tool is part of Microsoft's Internet Information Services (IIS), which comes with Windows XP Professional. The good news is that any client using Internet Explorer 4.0 or later can access the remote server.

NOTE For more information about IIS, flip back to Chapter 7.

When IIS is installed, the files are copied to the C:\Windows\Web\TSWeb folder. To use Remote Desktop Web Connection, you must follow these steps, which ensure that the tool is installed on the Remote Desktop server.

> **NOTE** These steps must be performed by a user who logs on with an administrative account.

1. Select Start | Control Panel.
2. Select Add or Remove Programs.
3. From the list of optional Windows components, select Internet Information Services, and then click Details.
4. Select World Wide Web Service, and then click Details.
5. Select both Remote Desktop Web Connection and World Wide Web Service, as shown in Figure 13-4.
6. Click OK to close dialog boxes until you return to the Windows Components Wizard.
7. In the Windows Components Wizard window, click Next. This will start the installation process. During this process, you might need to insert the Windows XP Professional CD-ROM.
8. When installation is completed, click Finish to close the Wizard.
9. Close the Add or Remove Programs window
10. Click Start, and then right-click My Computer and select Manage.
11. Click the + (plus) box to the left of the Services and Applications item in the left pane of the Computer Management window.
12. Click the + (plus) box to the left of Internet Information Services. Keep following the + boxes until you reach Internet Information Services\Web Sites\TSWeb.
13. Right-click the TSWeb folder and choose Properties. This calls up the TSWeb Properties window
14. Click the Directory Security tab.
15. In the Anonymous Access and Authentication Control portion of the dialog box, click the Edit button. This opens the Authentication Methods dialog box.
16. Select the Anonymous Access check box.
17. Click OK.

Whew! Microsoft didn't make that any too easy, did it? The upshot of those 17 steps is that the Remote Desktop Web Connection has been installed on your computer, and you can now access your computer across the Internet. Whether you're choosing to

Figure 13-4. Installing Remote Desktop Web Connection

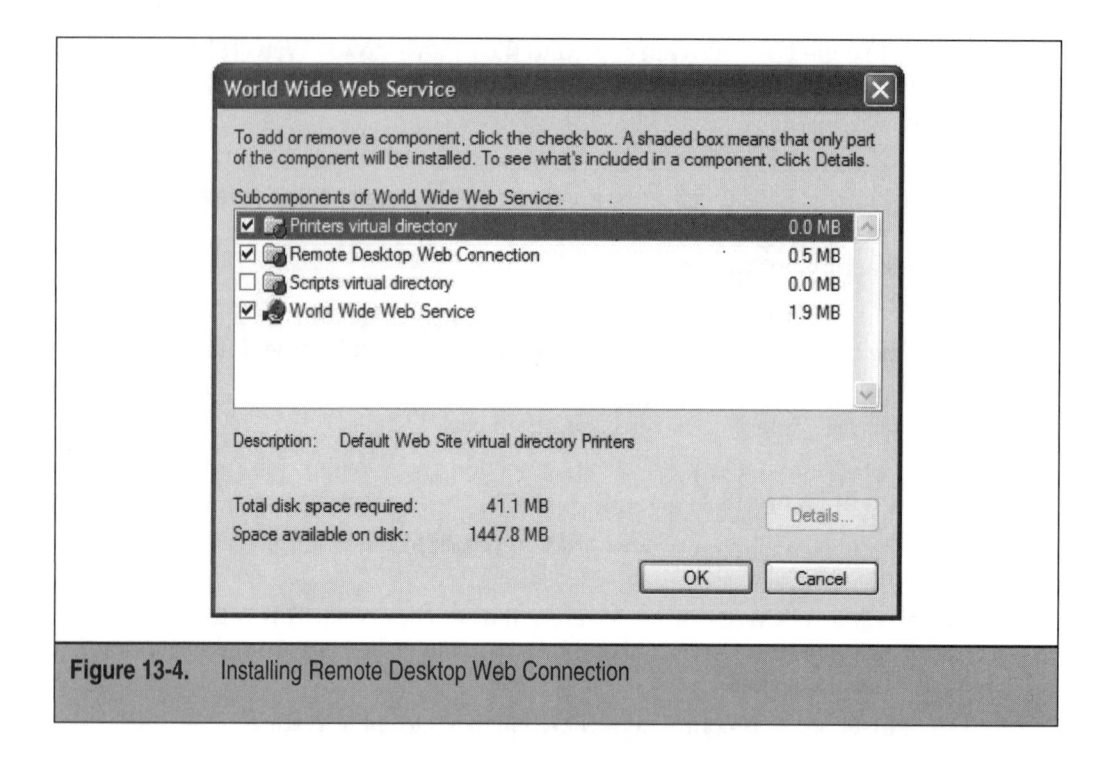

access your computer across the Internet or a LAN, the next step is to configure the Remote Desktop client.

Configuring a Client for Remote Desktop

As we noted earlier in the chapter, if you want to use Remote Desktop Web Connection, then all you need on your client is Internet Explorer. However, if want to use Remote Desktop (the LAN flavor), then your Remote Desktop client must have the Remote Desktop Connection tool installed.

Remote Desktop Connection Tool

The Remote Desktop Connection tool is generally installed by default. If you've not used this tool before, it's a good idea to make sure that you actually have it installed before setting up your Remote Desktop server, packing up your laptop, and heading for a branch office somewhere. You can check that the Remote Desktop Connection tool is installed by selecting Start | All Programs | Accessories | Communications | Remote Desktop Connection. When the program starts, your screen should look like the one shown in Figure 13-5.

Figure 13-5. The Remote Desktop Connection tool

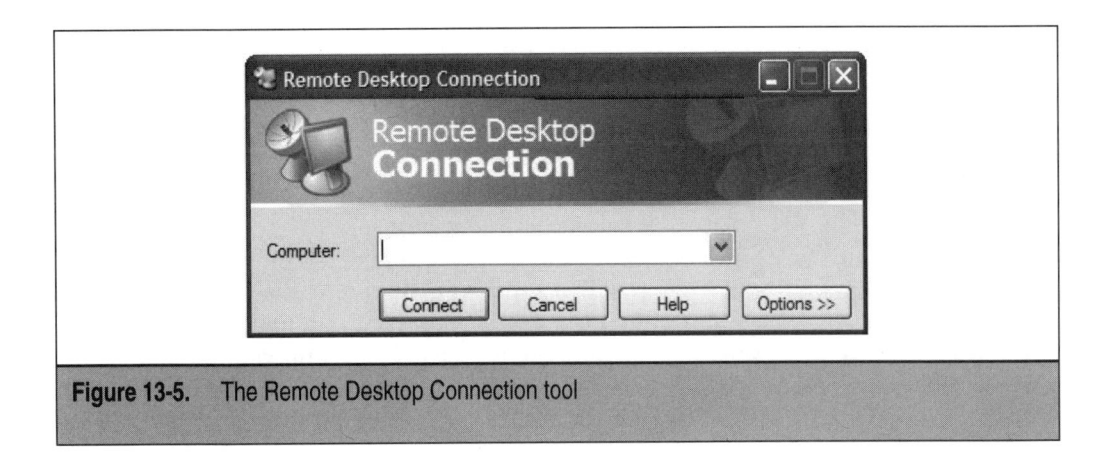

If for whatever reason the Remote Desktop Connection tool hasn't been installed on your computer (for instance, during a mass migration to Windows XP Professional, the administrator chose not to include it as part of the upgrade), it can be installed from the Windows XP Professional CD-ROM. Simply insert the disk into your CD-ROM or DVD-ROM drive and when the welcome page appears, click Perform Additional Tasks. Next, choose Set Up Remote Desktop Connection. This will start the Remote Desktop Connection InstallShield Wizard.

This wizard allows you to choose who is allowed to use the remote connection. You can pick one of the following two options:

- Anyone using the computer
- Just the currently logged-in user

When the installation is finished, simply close the installation program.

Again, if you are using Remote Desktop over an Internet connection, the only requirements are that TCP/IP be installed and that you have Internet Explorer 4.0 or higher (Windows XP Professional comes with Internet Explorer 6.0).

Remote Desktop Client for Older Flavors of Windows

Although we're specifically discussing Remote Desktop connections using Windows XP Professional, earlier versions of Windows (particularly Windows 95, Windows 98 and 98 Second Edition, Windows Me, Windows NT 4.0, and Windows 2000) can install a free Remote Desktop client from Microsoft. The Remote Desktop client is a 3.4MB file that you can download from http://www.microsoft.com/windowsxp/pro/downloads/rdclientdl.asp. When installed, this client allows older versions of Windows to connect to a Windows XP Professional Remote Desktop server.

Establishing Remote Desktop Connections

After you have configured the setup tasks for your Remote Desktop server and client, you should test the connection. First, make sure the Remote Desktop server is turned on and connected to the network (either your LAN or the Internet). The Remote Desktop server can accommodate multiple remote connections; however, no one can be logged onto the computer locally.

If in fact someone is logged on locally, you'll see a message telling you that if you wish to connect, the local user must first disconnect. Furthermore, the locally logged on user will see a message that allows him or her to prevent the Remote Desktop session from taking place. If he or she fails to respond within a predetermined amount of time, the connection takes place and he or she is logged off.

Next, turn on your Remote Desktop client. The following two sections explain the steps required to form either a Remote Desktop connection or a Remote Desktop Web Connection.

LAN Connection

If you wish to connect to the Remote Desktop server across a LAN, follow these steps:

1. Select Start | All Programs | Accessories | Communications | Remote Desktop Connection.
2. From the Computer drop-down list, pick the name of the server computer or enter its IP address. If the drop-down list does not contain any computer names, then click Browse For More to see the available computers in your domain or workgroup. This list will only show computers that have been enabled for Remote Desktop.

> **NOTE** If you don't know a computer's IP address, you can find it by selecting Start | My Network Places, and then clicking View Network Connections. Right-click your LAN or Internet connection, choose Status, and then click the Support tab.

3. Click Connect.
4. In the Log On To Windows window, enter your username and password to access the Remote Desktop server.
5. Click OK.
6. The connection has now been formed, and you'll see the remote desktop as shown in Figure 13-6.

As you have no doubt noticed, the desktop looks exactly the same as if you were sitting at that computer and using it locally. At the top of the desktop is a special toolbar. This can be used to minimize, maximize, or close the Remote Desktop view. For example, if you wish to work on your client computer, you click the minimize button. To return to the Remote Desktop connection, click the maximize button. The pushpin icon locks the menu in place.

Figure 13-6. A Remote Desktop connection over a LAN

Internet Connection

To connect to a Remote Desktop server using Remote Desktop Web Connection, any computer with Internet Explorer 4.0 or later and an Internet connection can be used. The server computer can be accessed by following these steps:

1. Open Internet Explorer.
2. In the address box, enter the URL for the Remote Desktop computer. The URL will typically be in this format: http://*computeraddress/path*. For the value *computeraddress*, use the address of your Remote Desktop's server—this can either be the LAN's name or the computer's IP address. For the value of *path*, use the path containing the Remote Desktop files. By default, the Remote Desktop files are located in C:\TSWeb.
3. Press ENTER. This calls up the Remote Desktop Web Connection page, as shown in Figure 13-7.

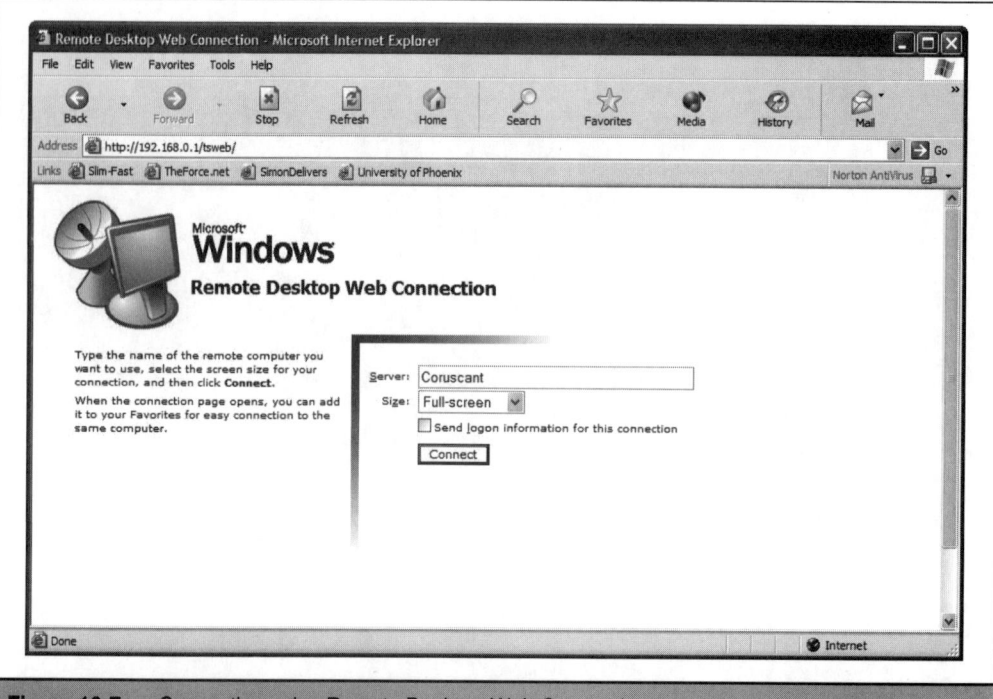

Figure 13-7. Connecting using Remote Desktop Web Connection

4. Enter the Remote Desktop server computer's name or IP address in the Server box.
5. Select the size of your Remote Desktop window.
6. Click connect.
7. The first time you use Remote Desktop Web Connection, Windows XP Professional will ask if you want to install the Microsoft Terminal Services Control program. If this message appears, click Yes. This will spawn a Remote Desktop Connection Security Warning dialog box.
8. Select or clear check marks, as needed, for the following options:
   - **Connect your local disk drives to the remote computer**   This allows the drives on your client computer to be available on the remote computer. This option enables you to see not only the hard drives on your server, but also those on the client.
   - **Connect your local ports to the remote computer**   This allows the ports on the client computer to be available on the server computer. For example, this option enables you to see and use any locally installed printers and other peripherals in the Remote Desktop Web Connection window.
9. Enter the username and password needed to use the Remote Desktop server.

If you chose to access the Remote Desktop server in full-screen view, you'll see a desktop similar to the one shown in Figure 13-8. If you chose another size, the desktop will look like the one in Figure 13-9. You can control the size and location of the window as you would any other Windows application. When you have finished your Remote Desktop session, close the Internet Explorer window.

Remote Desktop Function

Now that you've formed a Remote Desktop connection (or Remote Desktop Web Connection), you can use the server computer locally just as you would if you were sitting in front of it. If you are using a Remote Desktop session, you might find it necessary to mix and merge components from one system to another. For instance, you might need to include a spreadsheet located on the Remote Desktop server with a document stored on your Remote Desktop client.

Figure 13-8. Full-screen Remote Desktop view

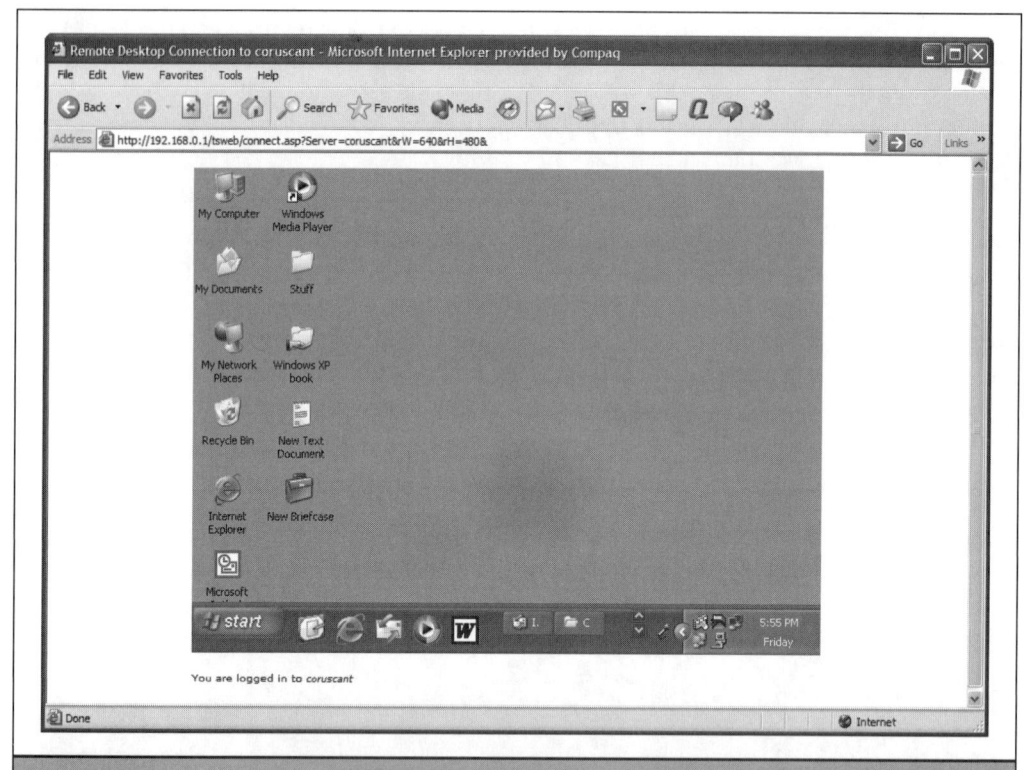

Figure 13-9. The size and location of a Remote Desktop view can be customized.

Remote Desktop provides a number of ways in which you can use your Remote Desktop client in conjunction with your Remote Desktop server, as described here:

- **Cut and paste**   Information displayed on your Remote Desktop window can be cut and pasted into an application on the client computer, or vice versa.

- **Use local files**   Local files can be used in the Remote Desktop session in one of two ways. If you are using the Remote Desktop Connection program, by default you can use local files. If you are using the Remote Desktop Web Connection, this feature must be activated. This is accomplished by selecting the Connect your local disk drives to the remote computer option when you log on (this is explained in the previous section). When this option is enabled, your local drives will appear in My Computer under Other. They will also be in any Open and Save dialog boxes of your applications.

- **Use a local printer**   Printing is a little convoluted when using Remote Desktop. Here's how it works: A print job will be sent to the default local printer—as long as the server computer contains the driver for your client computer's printer.

Other Remote Desktop Settings

When you connect to a Remote Desktop server, the Remote Desktop Connection dialog box appears. In addition to username and password, a number of other preferences can be set by clicking the Options button. The resulting window is shown in Figure 13-10.

Table 13-1 explains the tabs, settings, and a description of each.

As soon as you have set your preferences, you can save them under a specific name. This is helpful if you use multiple Remote Desktop servers and have preferred settings for each. Your preferences are saved by clicking the Save As button on the General tab of the Remote Desktop Connection dialog box.

UNDERSTANDING REMOTE ASSISTANCE

In the first part of this chapter we talked about Remote Desktop, which is a useful tool for allowing access to a remote computer. Remote Assistance, on the other hand, shares some of the same attributes, but they are used for two different purposes.

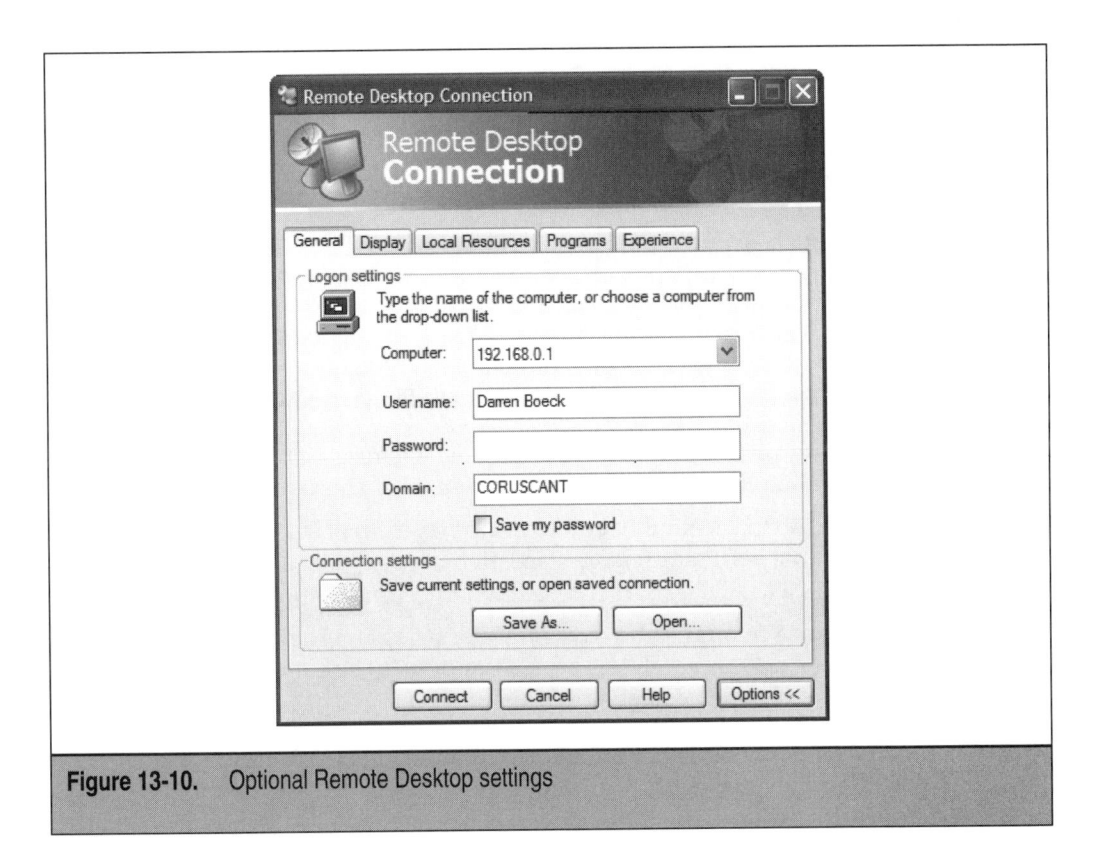

Figure 13-10. Optional Remote Desktop settings

Tab	Setting	Description
General	Save my password	Establishes whether or not your password will be maintained on the computer, or if you will enter it whenever you wish to form a Remote Desktop connection.
Display	Remote desktop size and colors	Establishes the size and colors used on your screen for Remote Desktop.
Local Resources	Remote computer sound	Denotes whether the Remote Desktop client will play the sounds that the Remote Desktop server would play.
Local Resources	Keyboard	Denotes whether ALT-key combinations apply to the Remote Desktop server, or the Remote Desktop client.
Local Resources	Local devices	Denotes which devices you can connect to on the Remote Desktop server.
Programs	Start the following program on connection	Automatically runs a specified program when you connect to the Remote Desktop server.
Experience	Allow the following (Desktop background, Show contents of window while dragging, Menu and window animation, Themes, and Bitmap caching)	Denotes which items will appear in your Remote Desktop server view. You can select or deselect the items you wish.

Table 13-1. Optional Remote Desktop Settings

First, and most relevant, is that Remote Assistance can be called upon when a user needs help with his or her computer. Remote Desktop, on the other hand, is used when a user needs to access resources on a remote device. Other important distinctions between Remote Desktop and Remote Assistance include the following:

- Remote Desktop establishes new connections, whereas Remote Assistance requires someone connecting remotely to be part of an existing session.
- Remote Desktop locks out the remote computer from being used locally while the remote session is taking place. Remote Assistance, on the other hand, requires a local user to be present while getting help.
- Remote Desktop clients can be any computer using Internet Explorer 4.0 or later. Remote Assistance requires both computers to be running Windows XP (Professional or Home versions).

In this section, Remote Assistance and its functionality are explained in more depth. Additionally, we'll explain how to use Remote Assistance and how connections are formed.

Features

Remote Assistance offers a number of features that are useful in ferreting out and solving problems. Not only can a friend or expert access your computer and provide help, but that person can also use a number of troubleshooting tools in his or her endeavors to assist you.

Desktop Control

Remote Assistance allows you to invite a friend or expert to remotely and interactively help you solve a problem with your Windows XP Professional computer. Conversely, if a user is having problems with his or her computer, you could be called upon to provide help. Remote Assistance is useful in a number of scenarios:

- **Problems that are hard to reproduce**   It's happened to anyone who's taken his or her car to the shop. That nauseating grinding noise that you heard on the freeway doesn't reproduce itself when you're in the shop talking to the mechanic. It's the same for computer users. Given the endless ways a computer can be configured, sometimes the only way to really understand a problem is to view it on the user's computer. Using Remote Assistance, the user can show the expert exactly what's happening (or not happening for that matter).

- **Resolutions that are complicated**   If you've ever given instructions to someone and five seconds into your explanation, that person's eyes glaze over and you can hear the "Mexican Hat Dance" spilling from his or her ears, you'll understand how useful it is to be able to perform the steps yourself. Using Remote Assistance, you can show the user the steps to fix the problem. Who knows? Maybe it'll sink in for future reference.

Troubleshooting Tools

In addition to allowing a friend or expert to help diagnose and solve problems, Remote Assistance also provides the following tools that are useful in troubleshooting and problem solving:

- **File transfers**   The user and expert can send files between their respective computers.
- **Chat**   The user and expert can enter text messages to each other.
- **Voice over IP**   Provided the connection has enough bandwidth—and a speaker and microphone are attached to each computer—the user and expert can talk to each other over the connection.
- **Bandwidth management**   Depending on the speed of the connection between the user and the expert, Remote Assistance will manage settings to make the best use of the available bandwidth. That is, color depth and quality of the voice connection will be enhanced or reduced, depending on the bandwidth available.

Security Issues

Naturally, giving your computer over to a friend or expert for assistance is meant to ameliorate problems, not create new ones. With that in mind, there are some security issues that you should consider when using Remote Assistance.

First, when a friend or expert accesses your computer remotely, all the actions are performed using the user's security level, not the helper's. That is, if the network administrator is attempting to help a user, he or she will not be able to use permissions that are granted only to the administrator. Rather, he or she will be limited to what the user is able to do.

Second, if you're seeking help from someone who will use an Internet connection to access your computer, it's a good idea to use a VPN connection. This is a safe method, because it does not allow traffic through your organization's firewall, which could pose a security breach.

> **NOTE** Chapter 14 contains information about establishing VPN connections.

USING REMOTE ASSISTANCE

When using Remote Assistance, you invite a person (be it a friend or your help desk) to take control of your computer. This can be accomplished via either Windows Messenger or e-mail. If the person accepts your invitation, he or she can control the mouse and type as if sitting in front of your computer. Additionally, Remote Assistance lets you share information either by typing in comments or by using microphones for a voice chat.

Configuring Remote Assistance

One of the first steps to using Remote Assistance is to ensure that it is enabled on your computer. To check this, open the Control Panel, and then click System. On the Remote tab (shown in Figure 13-11), under Remote Assistance, select the Allow Remote Assistance invitations to be sent from this computer check box, and then click OK.

Sending Invitations

In order for someone to help you out via Remote Assistance, it is first necessary to send an invitation. There are two ways to send an invitation and seek assistance. You can send the invitation via conventional e-mail or with Windows Messenger.

The most common way to initiate Remote Assistance is via an invitation. However, the process can also work in reverse. That is, a person can offer to help, rather than waiting for an invitation.

Figure 13-11. Enabling Remote Assistance

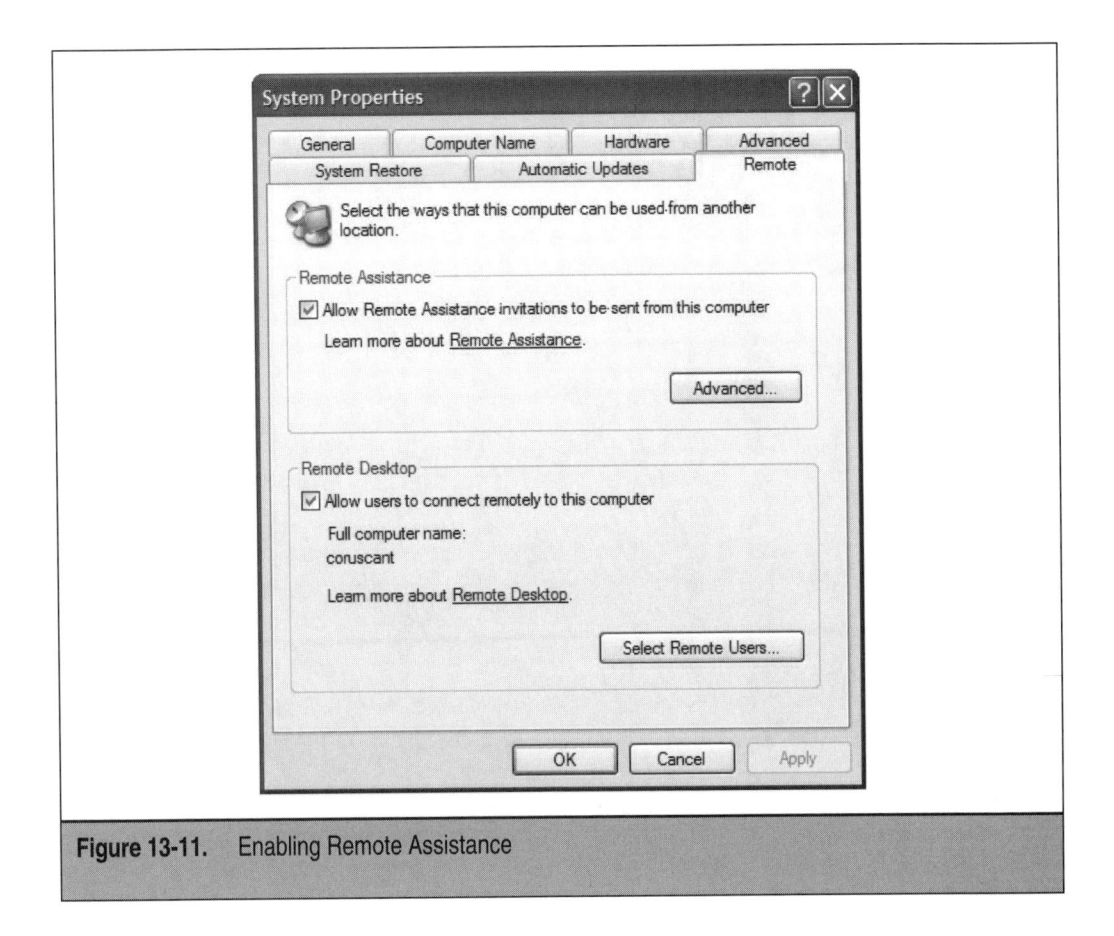

Sending Remote Assistance Invitations

To send an invitation, follow these steps:

1. Select Start | Help and Support to open the Help and Support Center window.
2. In the toolbar, click Support, and then click Ask a friend to help in the resulting task list.
3. Click Invite someone to help you in the next window.
4. Next, as Figure 13-12 shows, choose whether you want to send your invitation via e-mail or Windows Messenger. Identify from whom you wish to get assistance, and then click Invite.

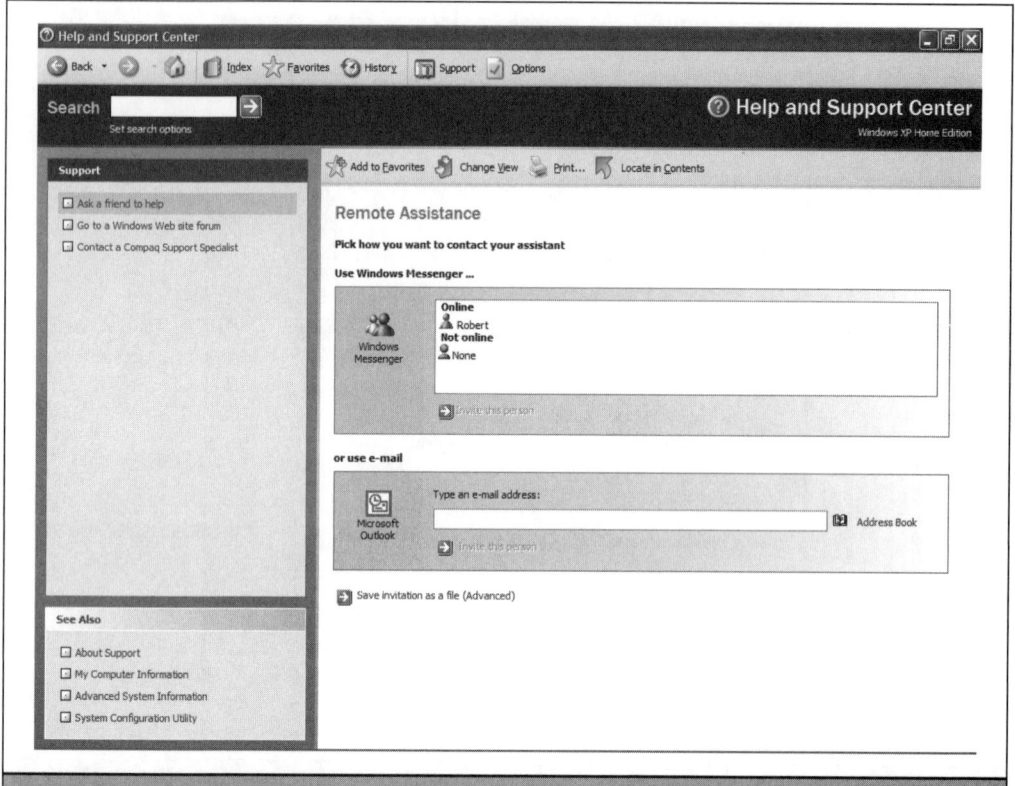

Figure 13-12. Inviting a friend to remotely assist you

5. As you proceed through the invitation process, you are given the opportunity to send a message to your helper, describing the problem, or any other information you care to send. You can also determine how long you'll leave the invitation open in the Set the invitation to expire box.
6. It's a good idea to leave the check mark in the Require the recipient to use a password check box. Otherwise, anyone managing to get a hold of the invitation can take control of your computer. You'll need to enter a password that the invitee will have to type in for access.
7. Click Send Invitation.
8. If you are using an e-mail program that lets you know when another application tries to send an e-mail, you'll be notified that an e-mail is being sent. Click Send, or whatever else is used to approve outgoing e-mail.

9. Call your helper and tell him or her that an invitation is on the way. This is a good time to share the password with your helper.
10. When your helper gets the invitation and enters the password to access the invitation ticket, you'll see a dialog box asking "Do you want to let this person view your screen and chat with you?" Click Yes to proceed.
11. As Figure 13-13 shows, the Remote Assistance window appears. You can chat with your helper on the left side of the window.
12. If you didn't already explain the problem you're experiencing, you can share the specific details in the Message Entry area in the lower-left corner of the Remote Assistance window.

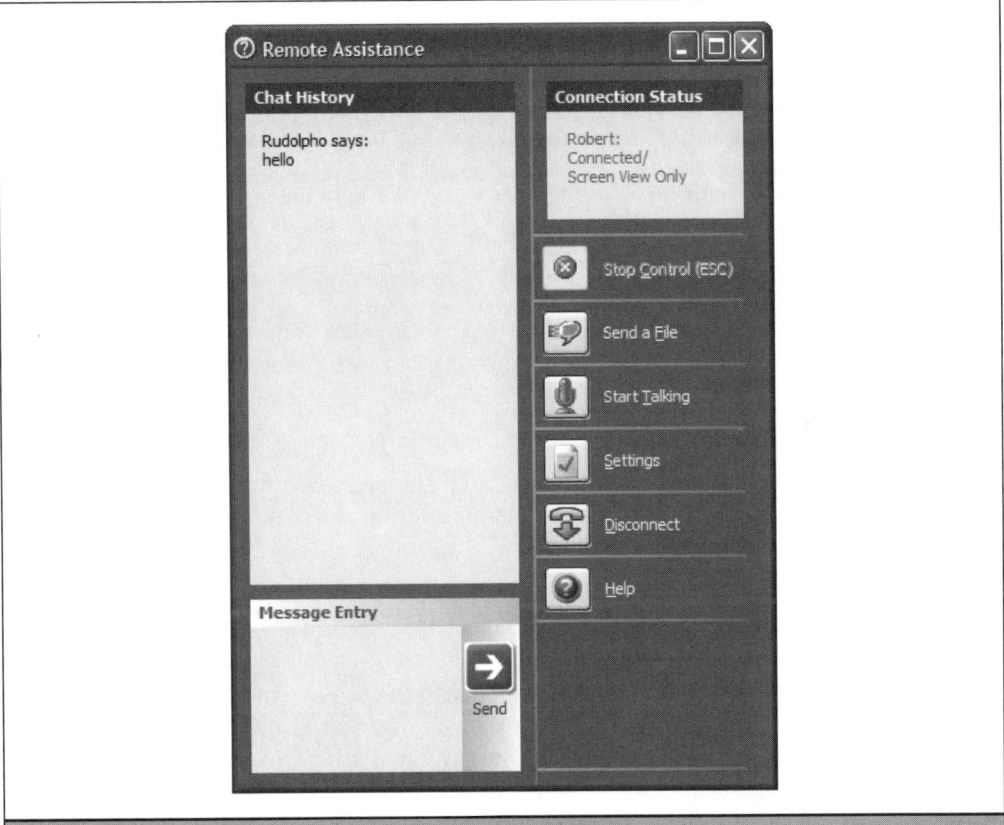

Figure 13-13. Remote Assistance enabled

When your helper establishes a Remote Assistance session, there are three things you can do:

- **Share control of your computer**   This enables your helper to take control of your computer, and is the last step before control is taken. When you are using Remote Assistance, it's a good idea not to type or move the mouse. Since someone else is trying to use these controls, it can be troublesome for both parties when you are trying to use them at the same time. To stop sharing your computer—but to maintain the connection—either press ESC or click Stop Control.

- **Send a file**   This allows you to send a file to the person with whom you are sharing your computer. When you click this button, you'll need to enter the filename you wish to send.

- **Voice chat**   If both you and your helper have microphones and speakers installed (and have a fast enough connection), you can chat about your computer problem. You can manage the audio quality by clicking Settings. When you or your helper clicks the Start talking button before you do, a message is sent to the other computer, to ask if a voice chat is desired.

When you're done with the session, either you or the helper can click Disconnect to wrap things up.

Invitation Restrictions

When a friend or expert gets your invitation for help, he or she needs only respond and use the invitation ticket (which can be used multiple times). However, for the ticket to be valid, two conditions must be present:

- *The ticket has not expired.* The time limit on a ticket is established by the user. If the user anticipates that help is needed just once, the ticket can be set to expire in a day. If the user wants to keep the invitation open longer, that period can be adjusted accordingly.

- *The IP address of the expert's computer has not changed since the ticket was issued.*

Offering Assistance

Typically, the user initiates a Remote Assistance session with a friend or expert. However, Windows XP Professional offers another feature to bolster Remote Assistance's functionality. Offer Remote Assistance allows anyone with administrator privileges to initiate a Remote Assistance session without first having to be invited.

Enabling Offer Remote Assistance   Offer Remote Assistance is disabled by default, but it can be activated by following the steps in this section.

NOTE Offer Remote Assistance can only be used within an organization, not across the Internet.

1. Open the Group Policy snap-in to the MMC.
2. Expand Local Computer Policy.
3. Expand Computer Configuration.
4. Expand Administrative Templates.
5. Expand System.
6. Expand Remote Assistance.
7. Double-click Offer Remote Assistance.
8. Click Enabled.
9. Click OK.

The preceding steps grant Offer Remote Assistance privileges to administrators; however, others in the organization can be granted this privilege. Follow these steps to grant the privilege to others:

1. Open the Group Policy snap-in to the MMC.
2. Expand Local Computer Policy.
3. Expand Computer Configuration.
4. Expand Administrative Templates.
5. Expand System.
6. Expand Remote Assistance.
7. Double-click Offer Remote Assistance.
8. Click Enabled.
9. Click Show, and then click Add.
10. In the Add Item dialog box, enter the name of the user or group to whom you want to grant this privilege. The entry should be made in either of the following formats: *domain\username* or *domain\groupname*.
11. Click OK.

Offering Help Once you've enabled Offer Remote Assistance, you first tell the user that you are offering help. Then, follow these steps:

1. Click Start.
2. Select Help and Support Center.
3. Click Pick a Task.

4. Click Use Tools, and then click Offer Remote Assistance.

5. Enter the name or IP address for the computer to which you wish to connect.

6. A message will appear on the user's screen informing the user of the connection attempt, telling him or her who is trying to connect, and asking if he or she wishes to permit it. If the user clicks Yes, the session is initiated.

NOTE The user must be present at his or her computer to accept the connection attempt. Remember, Remote Assistance is a joint effort.

Accepting an Invitation

In the previous section, we talked about the steps taken on your part to initiate a Remote Assistance session. In this section, we'll talk about what happens when someone asks you for Remote Assistance.

If you get an e-mail seeking help, it will include this text:

```
Robert Elsenpeter would like your assistance.
A personal message may be included below.

You can easily provide assistance from your computer
by following the instructions at:

http://windows.microsoft.com/RemoteAssistance/RA.asp


Caution:

* Accept invitations only from people you know and trust.
* E-mail messages can contain viruses or other harmful attachments.
* Before opening the attachment, review the security precautions
and information at the above address.

Personal message:
Please help!
```

The message will also include an attached file (named rcBuddy.MsRcIncident—the first part might be different, however) containing the *invitation ticket*. If need be, you can click the link within the message, which will call up a web page explaining how Remote Assistance works.

NOTE Antitrust alert! This message only works in Internet Explorer.

If you'd like to accept the invitation, and you have the password the user has entered, follow these steps:

1. Make sure you are connected either to the Internet or the LAN (assuming the person you are helping is on the LAN with you).
2. Open the attached file. The Remote Assistance dialog box appears.
3. Enter the password and click Yes to connect. Remote Assistance handles the niggling details of forming the connection across your LAN or the Internet. The resulting window is shown in Figure 13-14.
4. In the Message Entry area in the lower-left corner of the screen, you can enter text messages that will be shared with the other computer. Once you've entered your message, click Send to speed the message on its way.

When you establish a Remote Assistance session, there are three things you can do:

- **Share control of your computer** This enables you to take control of the remote computer, and is the last step before control is taken. When you are using Remote Assistance, it's a good idea not to type or move the mouse. Since someone else is trying to use these controls, it can be troublesome for both parties when someone else is trying to use them at the same time. To end the Remote Assistance session, press ESC or click Stop Control.
- **Send a file** This allows you to send a file to the person with whom you are sharing your computer. When you click this button, you'll need to enter the filename you wish to send.

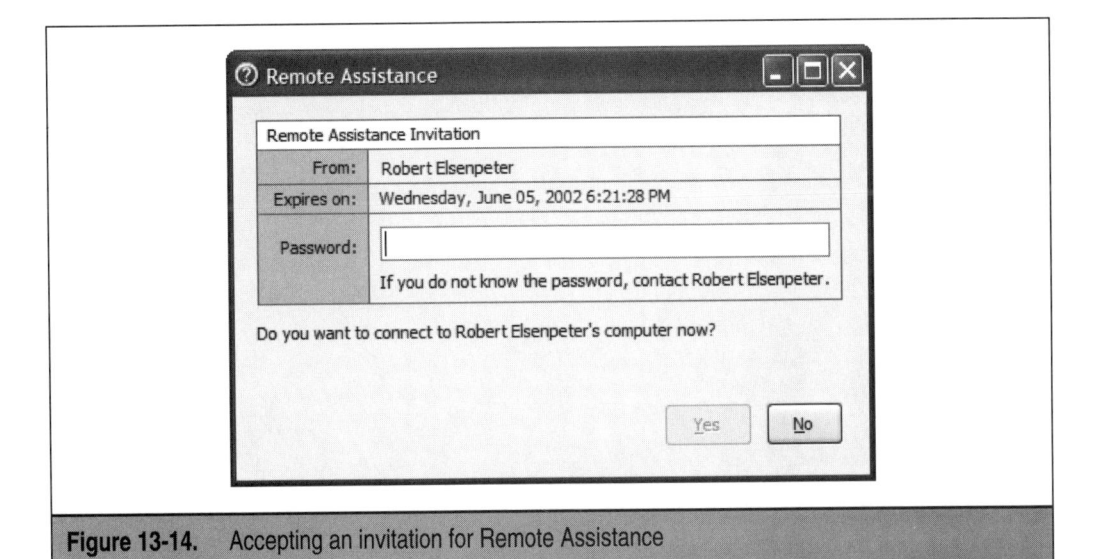

Figure 13-14. Accepting an invitation for Remote Assistance

- **Voice chat**   If both you and the person you are helping have microphones and speakers installed (and have a fast enough connection), you can chat about your computer problem. You can manage the audio quality by clicking Settings. If your helper clicks the Start talking button before you do, you'll get a message asking if you'd like to start a voice chat.

When you're done with the session, either party can click Disconnect to wrap things up.

Remote Assistance and Remote Desktop are both tools meant to improve productivity—whether you are seeking help from a friend, or trying to access your computer from the road or at home, these tools can help. As useful as these tools are, however, it cannot be stressed strongly enough that these tools must be set up and enabled in advance, otherwise they will be of limited benefit.

CHAPTER 14

Remote Access and Virtual Private Networks

Windows XP Professional provides a number of different ways to use your computer from a remote location. In the last chapter, for instance, we talked about how you can use a laptop or desktop computer to directly access and manage another computer. Remote Assistance and Remote Desktop are both useful tools, but you might find that you don't need to use another computer remotely. Rather, you simply need access to another computer or your local area network (LAN).

This chapter examines the two tools you are most likely to use in such events. The first, remote access, allows you to use a dial-up connection to access a computer or your LAN. The second tool is the virtual private network (VPN), which uses the infrastructure of the Internet, rather than a dial-in connection, to form a secure network link.

REMOTE ACCESS

The first tool we'll discuss is remote access. This is an implementation that allows clients using Windows XP Professional to call into the network (or a local computer) and access it as if they were a client on the LAN. In this section, we talk about the basics of remote access using Windows XP Professional, and then show you how to configure your remote access server and clients.

Understanding Remote Access

The term *remote access* seems self-explanatory enough—in essence, one accesses a computer or the network from a remote location. To be sure, it's a simple enough concept. However, there are different ways in which a remote connection can be made. The methods that you are most likely to use are dial-in technologies.

Furthermore, like so many other facets of computer networking, security cannot be stressed strongly enough. Security encompasses a couple of areas, specifically the means to prevent unauthorized users from accessing the remote resource and preventing hackers from listening in on the connection once it has been made.

Dial-in Connection

One of the simplest means of connecting to a remote computer is through a dial-in modem. Since most people only use their modems to dial out, you might be shocked to learn that the modem can actually take *incoming* calls as well. Even if you weren't blown away by that bit of information, Windows XP Professional facilitates the use of accepting incoming calls to your computer.

There is some tradeoff that comes with dial-in modems. Dial-in modems are very slow connections that offer just a fraction of the speed of a local network connection. On the other hand, the pervasiveness of telephones makes this means of connecting extremely useful.

ISDN

Integrated Services Digital Networking (ISDN) is another technology used for remote access. This method still utilizes a dial-up connection; however, special ISDN equipment is needed at both the remote access client and remote access server. Furthermore, a line must be set up specifically for ISDN use. Because of the line limitation, ISDN is not the best solution for "road warriors."

Even though ISDN is faster than a dial-in modem (128 Kbps vs. 56 Kbps), the availability of the ISDN line and its equipment can be problematic. To use ISDN as a remote access technology, it is probably best if deployed in a branch office or some other scenario where a dedicated ISDN line can be installed and the requisite hardware can be purchased.

Security

You've done a lot to ensure your network has a solid security policy in place. From setting and establishing user permissions, to establishing a policy for passwords, your network is as bulletproof as it can get without being dipped in Kevlar. When developing a remote access solution, the connection becomes another way for an intruder to gain access to your network. These dial-in access points are often called *back doors* into the network and are the nemesis of security managers. Dial-in connections and VPNs can be set up with Windows XP Professional to enforce authentication at two levels:

- **Interactive** The interactive logon procedure ensures a user's identity to either a domain account or local computer. Depending on where he or she is logging on, the user will have different levels of access:
  - **Domain** When a user logs onto a network using credentials that are stored in Active Directory, this is known as a *domain account*. Logging on with a domain account allows the user to access resources anywhere in the domain and trusted domain (within the boundaries of his or her user permissions).
  - **Local account** When a user logs onto a local computer, he or she can only access the resources of the local computer (again, within the boundaries of his or her specific user permissions). Logging on with a local account will not allow the user to access the LAN or any trusted networks.
- **Network access control** Network access control is used to confirm a user's identity when he or she tries to access a network service or resource. Network access control works primarily with the aforementioned local accounts when a user tries to use a network resource. Each time the user tries to use a network resource, he or she might be prompted for his or her credentials.

These differing types of permissions and accounts can be managed with the Group Policy snap-in to the Microsoft Management Console (MMC). For more information on managing user permissions, flip back to Chapter 9.

Configuring a Computer to Accept Remote Access Calls

Back before the Internet (but slightly after fire, the wheel, and indoor plumbing), people connected to electronic bulletin boards by using their modem, as they do now to dial into an Internet service provider (ISP). Bulletin board operators configured their computers to answer their phone and connect the user via a telephone line to access the bulletin board's content.

The Internet has made this practice less and less common—now, if you want to get your content online, you simply build a web page and upload it to your ISP. However, it is still possible (and for any number of reasons, necessary) to configure your computer so that it can communicate with others via a modem. For instance, maybe your company feels more comfortable about allowing road warriors to connect to the company server via a dial-up connection than allowing access over the Internet. Maybe you work for a small company that doesn't need a complex remote access service via the Internet, and a quick-and-easy dial-in connection will suffice.

A dial-in connection allows you to use the resources of the computer to which you will be dialing in. For instance, if you are on the road and use your laptop to dial into your desktop computer, you can access your hard drive, the printer, and the network (if the desktop computer is connected to a LAN).

Like the Remote Desktop configuration we talked about in Chapter 13, there are two components to a remote access solution:

- **Remote access server** When you dial into a computer, the computer you call is known as the *remote access server*. This can be any type of computer, but most often it is a desktop computer that, obviously, has a telephone line(s) connected to it. This computer is the one containing the resources that dial-in users want to use—be it files, printers, or a network connection.

- **Remote access client** This is the computer connecting to the remote access server via the dial-up connection. Most often this computer will be a laptop; however, it doesn't have to be. For instance, if you forgot something on your office computer and have remote access enabled, you could call into your office computer from a home computer and get the files you need. The terminology becomes a little more refined when the remote access client calls into a computer that is connected to the LAN. In this configuration, the remote access client is known as a *remote node*. The configuration allows your remote client to act as if it were in the same building as the rest of the LAN. That is, not only can you access the LAN, but the contents of your remote access client are visible on the LAN.

NOTE Even though, as a remote node, you are technically part of the LAN, don't forget that you are connecting across a telephone line and won't come close to experiencing the speeds you would with an Ethernet or WiFi connection.

It should go without saying that your computers need modems and telephone lines to form dial-up connections.

Server Setup

Setting up the remote access client is a fairly straightforward process—as the task tends to be on most client-server configurations. The process of configuring the remote access server, on the other hand, is a little more involved. Happily, Windows XP Professional manages to streamline the process (again using the New Connection Wizard), so setting up a remote access server isn't overly burdensome.

In essence, the remote access server must have an *incoming* dial-up connection configured. When this connection is in place, it tells Windows XP Professional to answer the phone when it rings and connects the client to the computer. To set up the remote access server, follow these steps:

1. Click Start | Connect To | Show all connections.
2. Click Create a New Connection to invoke the New Connection Wizard.
3. Click Next.
4. Select Set up an advanced connection, and then click Next
5. Pick Accept incoming connections and click Next.
6. The resulting dialog box (as shown in Figure 14-1) displays a list of devices for incoming connections.
7. Choose the modem from the list. If your computer has more than one modem, then you can select more than one device from the list.
8. The next window you see is the Incoming Virtual Private Network (VPN) Connection window. It doesn't matter whether you choose to allow VPN connections, so click Next.
9. In the next screen (as shown in Figure 14-2) you can select which users you wish to allow to remotely access this server. Make your selections, and then click Next.

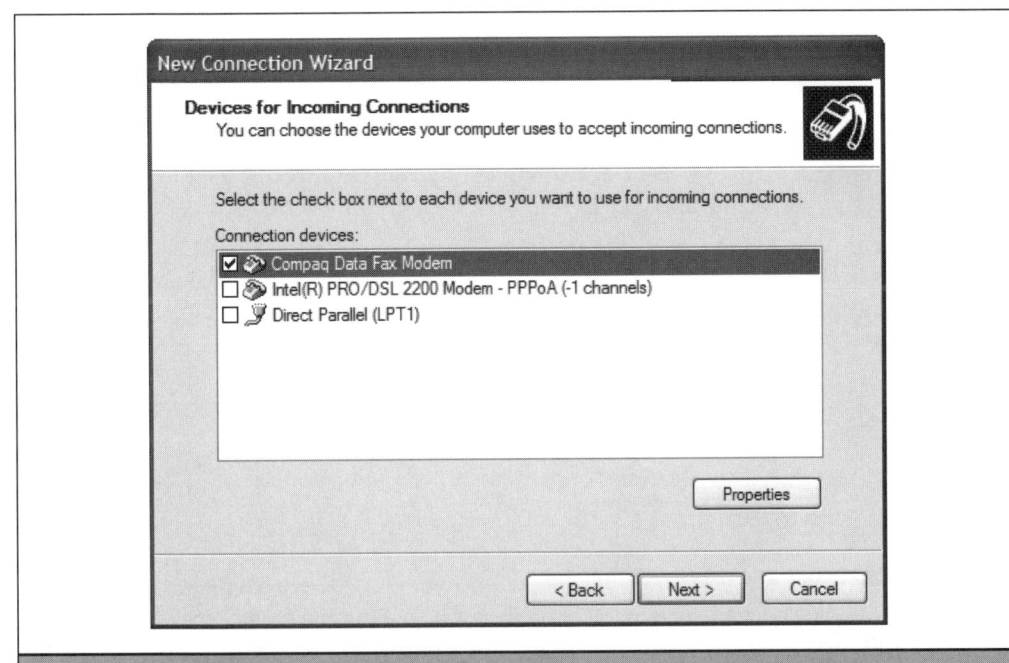

Figure 14-1. Select your dial-in modem from the Devices for Incoming Connections dialog box.

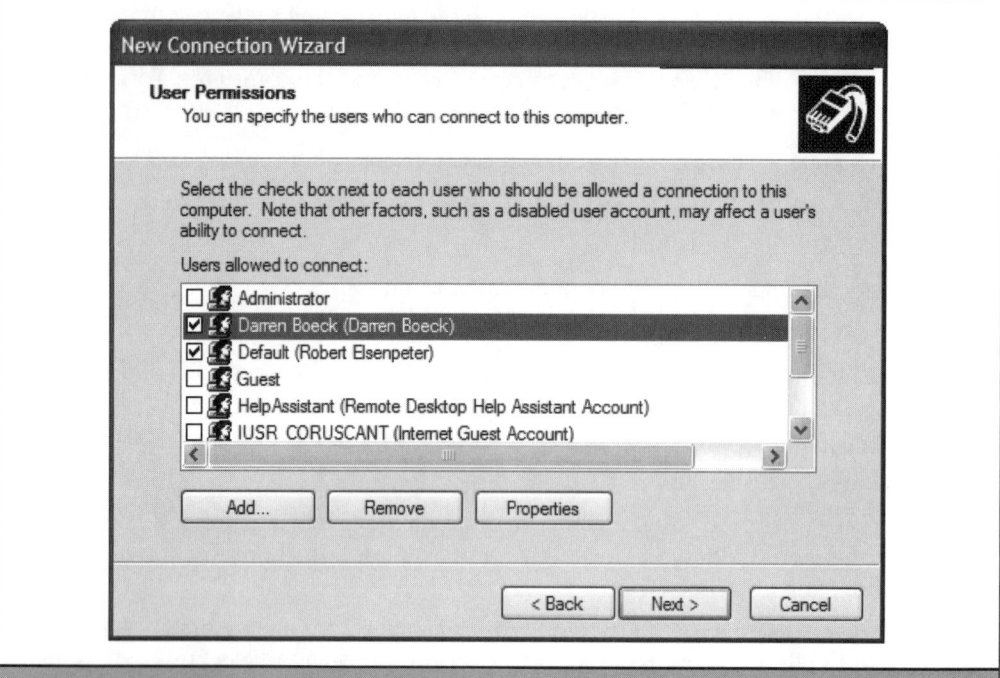

Figure 14-2. Select which users you will allow to use remote access on this computer.

10. Next, a list of Microsoft's recommended networking components is shown. Clear the check boxes next to any components you *don't* want to use. That having been said, it's best not to change anything in this list, as it is a listing of such components as TCP/IP and others that you will likely need.
11. Exit the New Connection Wizard by clicking Finish.

Once the preceding steps are completed, a new icon called Incoming Connections is placed in your Network Connections window.

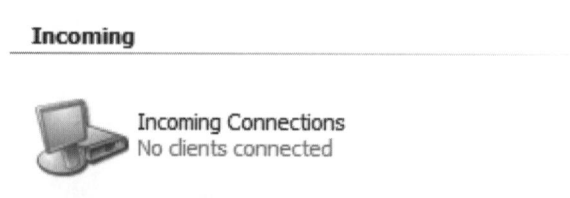

NOTE If you already have an Incoming Connections icon (or try to add another one), the properties of the existing icon are edited, merging both your old and new access selections.

Laptop ("Road Warrior") Connections

Remote access connections are quite useful for users who have to disconnect their computers from the network and travel. Since there is no continual connection to the network, they need some way to access network resources, such as shared documents and so forth.

Windows XP Professional affords these so-called road warriors a number of different means to connect to network resources. As we've already explored, road warriors can make use of Offline Files, Windows Briefcase, and Remote Desktop.

In order for road warriors—or anyone needing remote access to a network, for that matter—to configure their laptops as remote access clients, there is a basic series of configuration steps that they can follow. Furthermore, Windows XP Professional provides advanced features that administrators can access to make the remote access process even more useful.

New Connection Wizard on the Remote Access Client

Setting up a client to make a call to a remote access server is virtually identical to the process used to create a dial-up connection to an ISP. The task invokes the New Connection Wizard (which we discussed in greater detail in Chapter 4). To make a dial-up connection for your remote access server, follow these steps:

1. Click Start | Connect To | Show all connections.
2. Click Create a New Connection in the task pane. This starts the New Connection Wizard.
3. Click Next.
4. Select Connect to the Network at my workplace, and click Next.
5. Select Dial-up connection, and click Next.
6. Select the device you'll use to connect to the remote access server—in this case, your modem.
7. Enter a name of your choosing to identify this connection, and click Next.
8. Enter the phone number you will use to connect to the remote access server (this is shown in Figure 14-3).
9. If you want this connection to be accessed via a shortcut on your desktop, make your selection, and then click Finish.

When you double-click this connection (either from a desktop shortcut or in the My Network Places window), Windows XP Professional dials the telephone and waits for the remote access server to pick up and form a connection.

CompuGlobalMegaWare Dial-in
Disconnected
Compaq Data Fax Modem

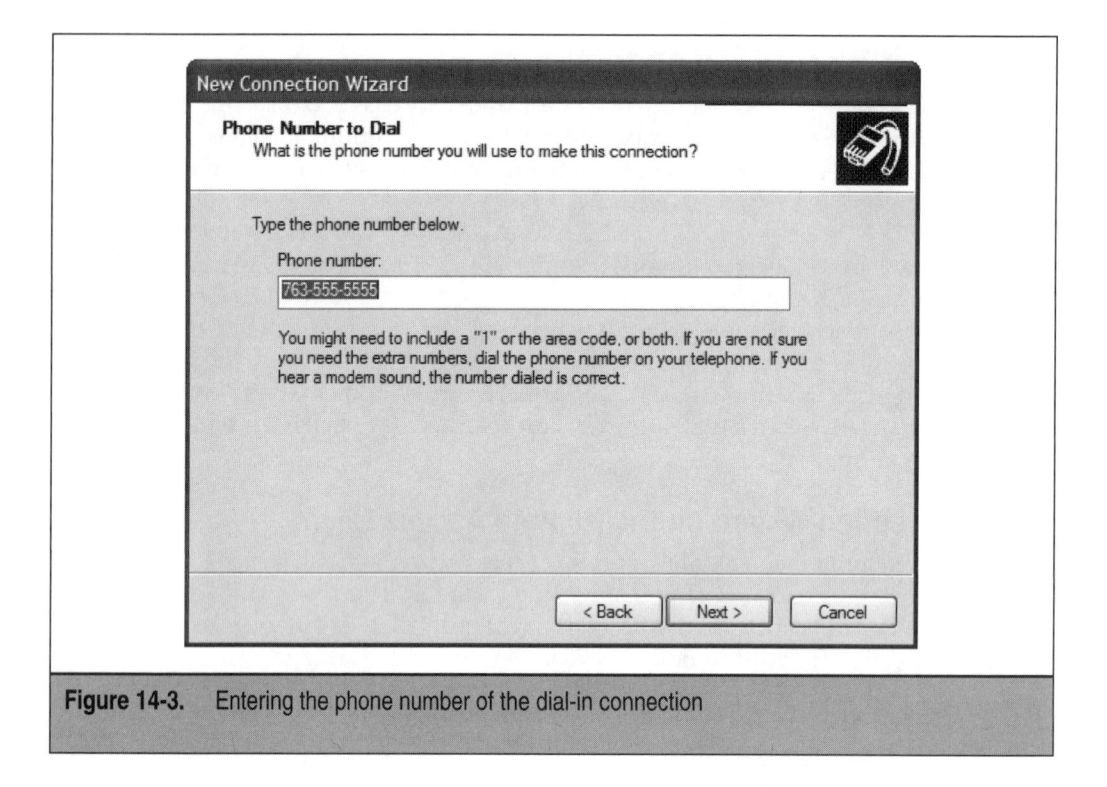

Figure 14-3. Entering the phone number of the dial-in connection

If you have more than one remote access server to which you will be connecting, repeat the preceding steps and create different dial-in connections. Also, if your remote access server gets a different phone number, or you want to change its name or any other configuration information, just right-click the icon, select Properties from the pop-up menu, and make your adjustments.

Advanced Settings

Configuring your remote access server and client is a fairly easy process. Microsoft has included some additional features that you might find useful, depending on your organization's need. These advanced settings provide additional layers of security and functionality.

These features are accessed on the Network Connections folder by clicking Dial-up Preferences under the Advanced menu option. This screen is shown in Figure 14-4.

The functionality of the tabs is explained in the following sections.

NOTE Dial-up Preferences can be enabled or disabled on client computers by using the Group Policy snap-in to the MMC. The policy to enable or disable is Enable the Dial-up Preferences on the Advanced Menu.

Figure 14-4. Dial-up Preferences dialog box.

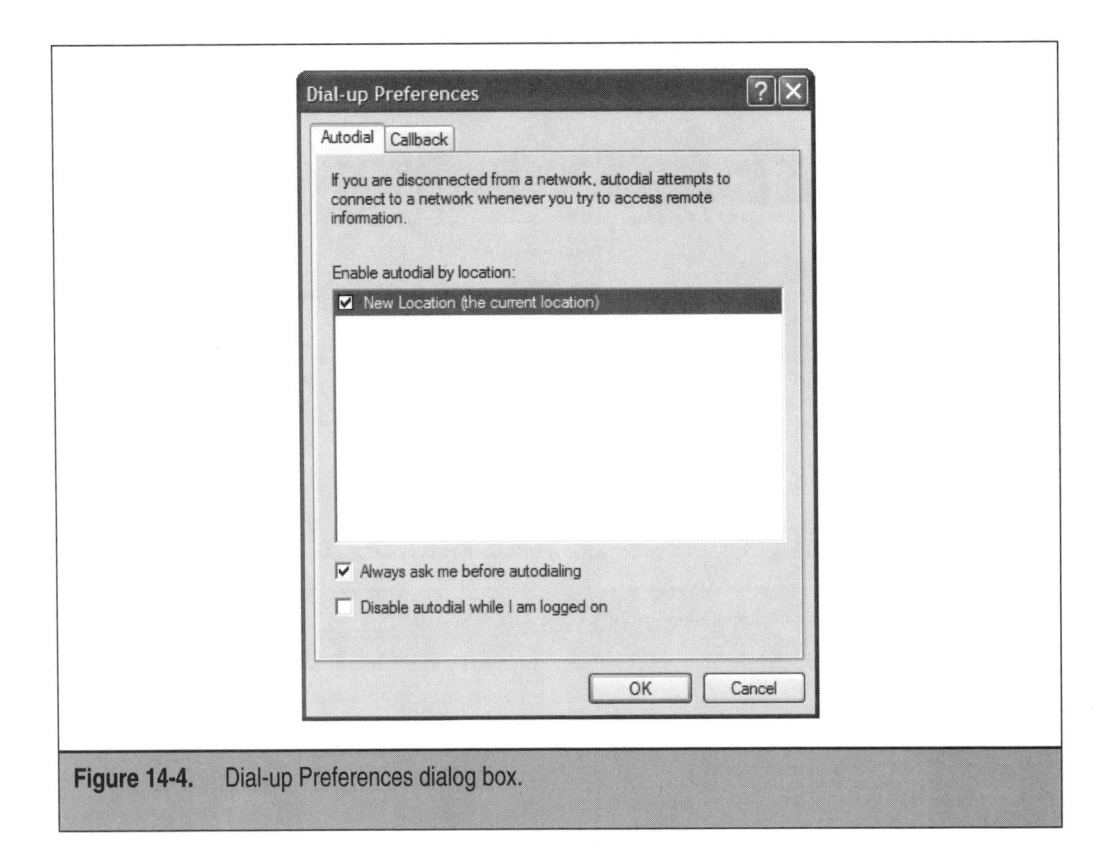

Autodial The Autodial tab is used to enable your computer to automatically dial a connection. This option maintains a list of network addresses and their matching connection destinations, which allows a destination to be automatically dialed when it is viewed.

For example, if you are looking at an application with embedded web links, and you click one of the links, you need to access the Internet. Windows XP Professional will ask you which connection you wish to use to access your ISP. The next time a link is clicked, Windows XP Professional remembers the choice you made and automatically dials that number.

Enabling or disabling autodial is as simple as checking or clearing the check box next to the connection. Autodial can only be used when the Remote Access Auto Connection Manager service is on. By default, this feature is turned on in Windows XP Professional clients that are not part of a domain. To activate Remote Access Auto Connection Manager, follow these steps:

1. Right-click My Computer, and click Manage from the pop-up menu.
2. Double-click Services and Applications, and then click Services (this is shown in Figure 14-5).

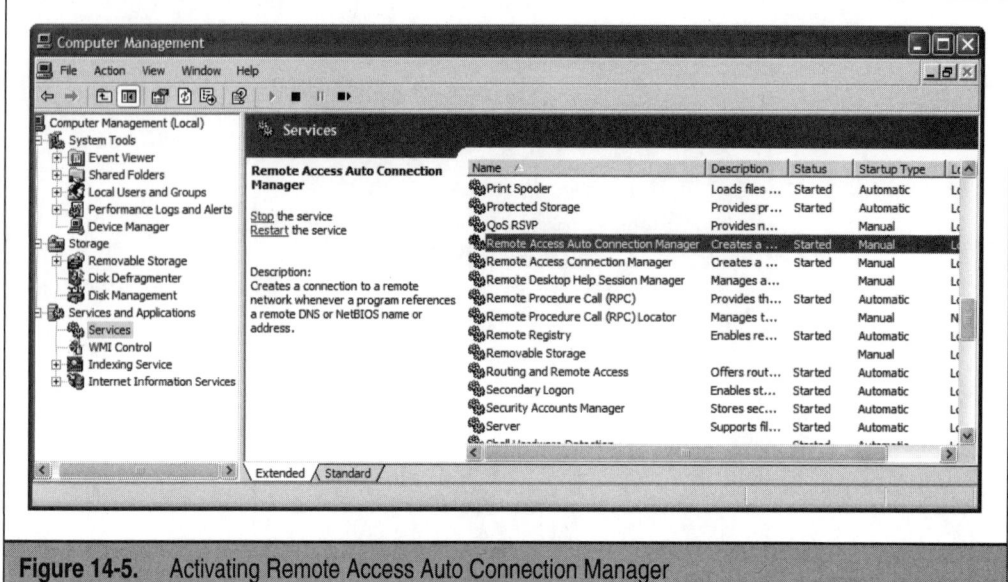

Figure 14-5. Activating Remote Access Auto Connection Manager

3. Right-click Remote Access Auto Connection Manager, and then click Start.

Callback If you've ever placed a call from a hotel room, you know just how criminally expensive the calls can be. One way to enable road warriors to call into a remote access server, but not have to pay an arm and a leg, is by enabling *callback* on the remote access server. With callback enabled, the caller logs onto the remote access server and, if the login is accepted, the server disconnects and calls the remote access client back.

The callback feature is enabled by performing the following steps:

1. Click Start | Connect To | Show all connections.
2. Double-click the Incoming Connections icon to show the Incoming Connections Properties box.
3. Click the Users tab.
4. Pick the user for whom this feature will be enabled.
5. Click Properties.
6. Click the Callback tab (as shown in Figure 14-6).

Figure 14-6. Enabling the callback feature

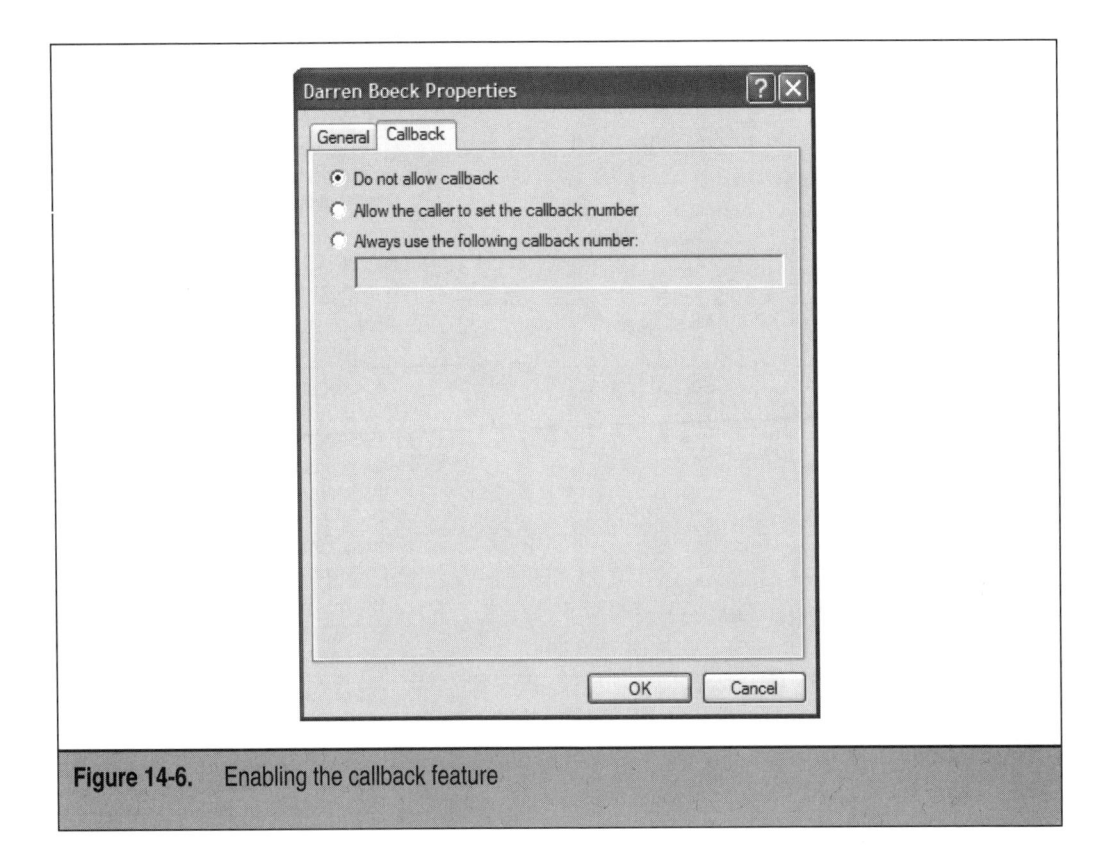

7. Choose either Allow the caller to set the callback number or Always use the following callback number, and then make sure you enter the phone number to be used.
8. Click OK.

Your callback behavior will vary, depending not only on the settings of your Remote Access client, but also on the settings established on the remote access server. Table 14-1 details the various callback behaviors.

Although callback is also useful in keeping phone bills down, it is even more useful as a security measure. By requiring clients to call back to a certain number, only users who know the correct phone number can access the network. Then, when the connection is dropped and the server calls the user back, it makes the process of tricking the server much more difficult.

Remote Access Client Setting	Remote Access Server Setting	Callback Behavior
Do not allow callback	No callback	The connection stays in place.
Do not allow callback	Set by caller	The server will offer a callback, the client will decline, and the connection will remain.
Do not allow callback	Always callback to	The server will offer a callback, the client will decline, and the server will disconnect.
Ask me during dialing when server offers	No callback	The connection stays in place.
Ask me during dialing when server offers	Set by caller	A dialog box will appear asking for the callback number. Enter the callback number, and then wait for the connection to disconnect and the server to call back. To keep the connection in place, press ESC. This cancels the callback procedure.
Ask me during dialing when server offers	Always callback to	The remote server will disconnect and call back to the number specified in Network Connections.
Always call me back at the number(s) below	No callback	The connection stays in place.
Always call me back at the number(s) below	Set by caller	The server disconnects and calls back to the number specified in Network Connections.
Always call me back at the number(s) below	Always callback to	The server disconnects and calls back to the number specified in Network Connections.

Table 14-1. Callback Behavior, Based on Client and Server Settings

VPN CONNECTIONS

If you need to connect to your office or any other computer remotely, you might discover that the dial-up sessions are taking their toll on your wallet. Because dial-up connections take place over a conventional telephone line, long-distance bills can become a large, uncomfortable fact of life. A very easy way around this is to use infrastructure that's already in place—specifically, the Internet. By using a virtual private network (VPN), you or another user can connect a client computer—across the Internet—to your LAN. To form a secure connection, the VPN *tunnels* through the Internet to connect to the LAN.

This section examines the process of configuring a VPN and how you can connect your clients across the Internet to the LAN. One of the first considerations when connecting to a LAN with a firewall is that the organization's firewall must support Point-to-Point Tunneling Protocol (PPTP). PPTP allows the VPN to connect through the firewall. Furthermore, a VPN server must be configured to handle incoming connections. A VPN server is the application that provides PPTP. Also, both the VPN server and VPN client must have active Internet connections.

If your organization already has a VPN server in place, no further configuration needs to be done to accommodate Windows XP Professional clients. All you need is the IP address of the VPN server for your VPN client. If you need to configure both the VPN server and VPN client, those steps are explained later in this section.

In either event, the VPN server must have a *routable* IP address. That means the IP address must be on the Internet. If the VPN server connects to the Internet via a shared connection, or is behind a firewall, then the server does not have a routable IP address. However, a way around this is to configure the server with a nonroutable address, and the firewall with the routable address. The firewall is then given a rule that directs VPN traffic from the firewall to the server.

Understanding Virtual Private Networks

Before delving into the specific implementation of a Windows XP Professional VPN connection, let's take a closer look at some of the components involved in a VPN connection.

VPNs create a secure link between your LAN and a computer out in the field somewhere. This is illustrated in Figure 14-7. The connection allows someone in Massachusetts to work on the LAN as if he or she were onsite with the other computers in Idaho, for instance.

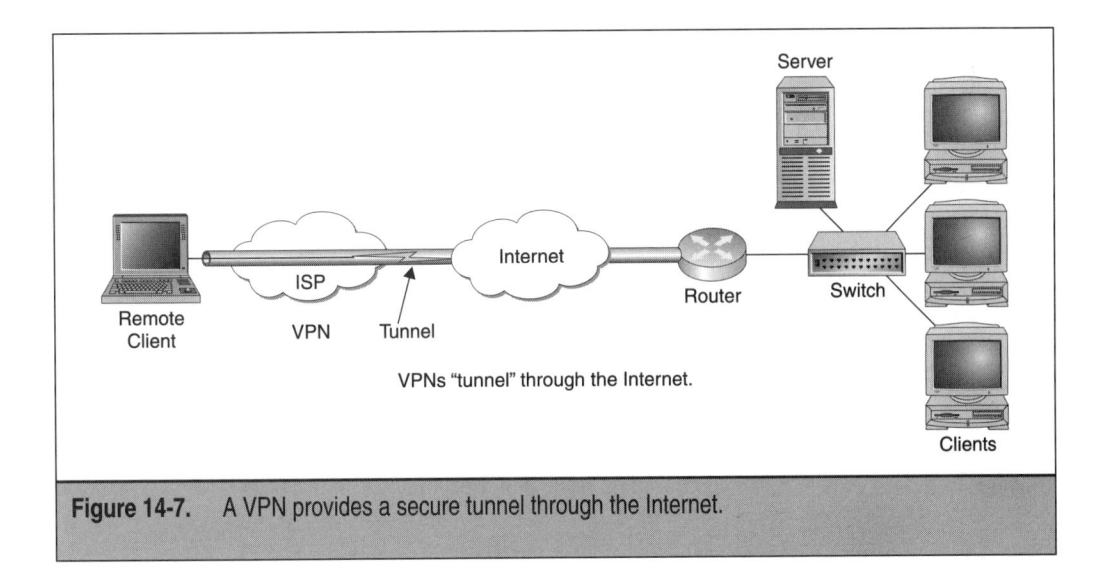

Figure 14-7. A VPN provides a secure tunnel through the Internet.

A VPN is a private connection between two different locations. This connection is encrypted, thereby creating a tunnel through the Internet. The Point-to-Point Protocol (PPP) remote access protocol acts to encrypt the data passing over the VPN. Once the data is encrypted, it is routed over a dial-up or LAN connection.

IPSec

IPSec is the set of protocols that supports secure exchange of packets at the IP layer. Because IPSec operates at the network layer (layer 3), it can provide secure transport capable of supporting any application that uses IP.

IPSec provides three main areas of security when transmitting information across a network:

- Authentication of packets between the sending and receiving devices
- Integrity of data when being transmitted
- Privacy of data when being transmitted

IPSec operates in two modes—transport and tunnel:

- In *transport* mode, Encapsulation Security Protocol (ESP) and Authentication Headers (AHs) reside in the original IP packet between the IP header and upper layer extension header information. For instance, Windows XP IPSec uses transport mode to provide security between two end systems, such as a Windows XP Professional client and a Windows 2000 Server.
- In *tunnel* mode, IPSec places an original IP packet into a new IP packet and inserts the AH or ESP between the IP header of the new packet and the original IP packet. The new IP packet leads to the tunnel endpoint, and the original IP header specifies the packet's destination. You can use tunnel mode between two security gateways, such as tunnel servers, routers, or firewalls.

IPSec tunnel is the most common mode; it works like this:

1. A standard IP packet is sent to the IPSec device with the expectation that the packet will be encrypted and routed to the destination system over the network.
2. The first of the two IPSec devices, which in this case would probably be either a firewall or a router, authenticates with the receiving device.
3. The two IPSec devices negotiate the encryption and authentication algorithms to be used.
4. The IPSec sender encrypts the IP packet containing the data and then places it into another IP packet with an AH.
5. The packet is sent across the TCP/IP network.
6. The IPSec receiver reads the IP packet, verifies it, and then unwraps the encrypted payload for decryption.
7. The receiver forwards the original packet to its destination.

Point-to-Point Tunneling Protocol

The Point-to-Point Tunneling Protocol (PPTP) enables the secure transfer of data from a remote client to an organization's server. PPTP supports multiple network protocols, including IP, IPX, and NetBEUI. You can use PPTP to provide a secure virtual network using dial-up lines, over LANs, over WANs, or across the Internet and other TCP/IP-based networks. In order to establish a PPTP VPN, you must have a PPTP server and a PPTP client. Windows XP Professional software includes the necessary parameters to configure PPTP communication.

Layer Two Tunneling Protocol (L2TP)

PPTP is a Microsoft technology that establishes a virtual connection across a public network. PPTP, together with encryption and authentication, provide a private and secure network. Cisco Systems developed a protocol similar to PPTP, called Layer Two Forwarding (L2F), but it required Cisco hardware at both ends to support it. Cisco and Microsoft then merged the best features of PPTP and L2F, developing the Layer Two Tunneling Protocol (L2TP). Similar to PPTP, L2TP provides a way for remote users to extend a PPP link across the Internet from the ISP to a corporate site.

Security

When putting your network resources on the Internet, you probably develop a slight tick in your cheek, hoping that some hacker doesn't figure out how to invade your network and meddle with private, proprietary information—not to mention introduce destructive viruses. But security isn't a concept that just encompasses the marauders on the Internet waiting to exploit your goodies. Security policies need to be in place within the organization as well. Naturally, when setting up a remote access solution, you must make sure your VPN or dial-in connection is as secure as possible.

When you configure a VPN server or dial-in server to accept connections, you open a door for not only authorized users, but also unauthorized users. Although logon ID and password are required to get onto your network, why leave the door open in the first place?

If you aren't expecting any incoming connections to your VPN or dial-in servers, it's a good idea just to disable the connection. To do so, follow these steps:

1. Click Start | Connect To | Show all connections.
2. Double-click the Incoming Connections icon to show the Incoming Connections Properties box.
3. To disable dial-in connections, deselect the modem in the Devices box. To disable VPN connections, deselect the Virtual Private Network option.
4. Click OK.

When you need to reconnect your modem or VPN, repeat the same steps, except select the modem or VPN connection.

Naturally, if you use dial-in or VPN connections, there will come a time when you need to enable them. To keep your network safe, take some preventative measures to bolster security. For instance, don't print the modem's phone number on your corporate web site or on a company phone list. Keep it safe. Also, you should change passwords often. Finally, it's a good idea to use the callback feature.

Creating a VPN Connection

To configure your VPN client, you use the venerable New Connection Wizard. VPN client configuration is accomplished by following these steps:

1. Make sure you're connected to the Internet.
2. Click Start | Connect To | Show all connections.
3. Click Create a New Connection. This starts the New Connection Wizard.
4. Click Next.
5. Select Connect to the Network at my workplace.
6. Click Next.
7. Select Virtual Private Network Connection.
8. Click Next.
9. Give the connection a unique name to help identify it.
10. Click Next.
11. In the Public Network window, as shown in Figure 14-8, indicate which connection to use for the Internet connection. Windows XP Professional allows you the choice of connecting automatically or making the connection yourself. If you'd rather establish the Internet connection manually, choose Do not dial the initial connection.
12. Click Next.
13. In the VPN Server Selection window, shown in Figure 14-9, enter the name or IP address of your VPN server (for instance, pptp.widgetech.com).
14. Click Next.
15. You can place a shortcut to the connection on your desktop if you so choose. Make your selection, and then click Finish.

A new section of your Network Connections window is established: Virtual Private Network. Within this section appears the VPN connection you just configured. When you want to connect via VPN, all you need to do is double-click this icon, and Windows XP Professional will log onto the Internet and connect to your VPN server. Remember, however, if you choose to manually form your Internet connection in Step 11, you'll have to log onto the Internet first and then click the VPN icon.

Virtual Private Network

CompuGlobalMegaWare VPN Client
Disconnected

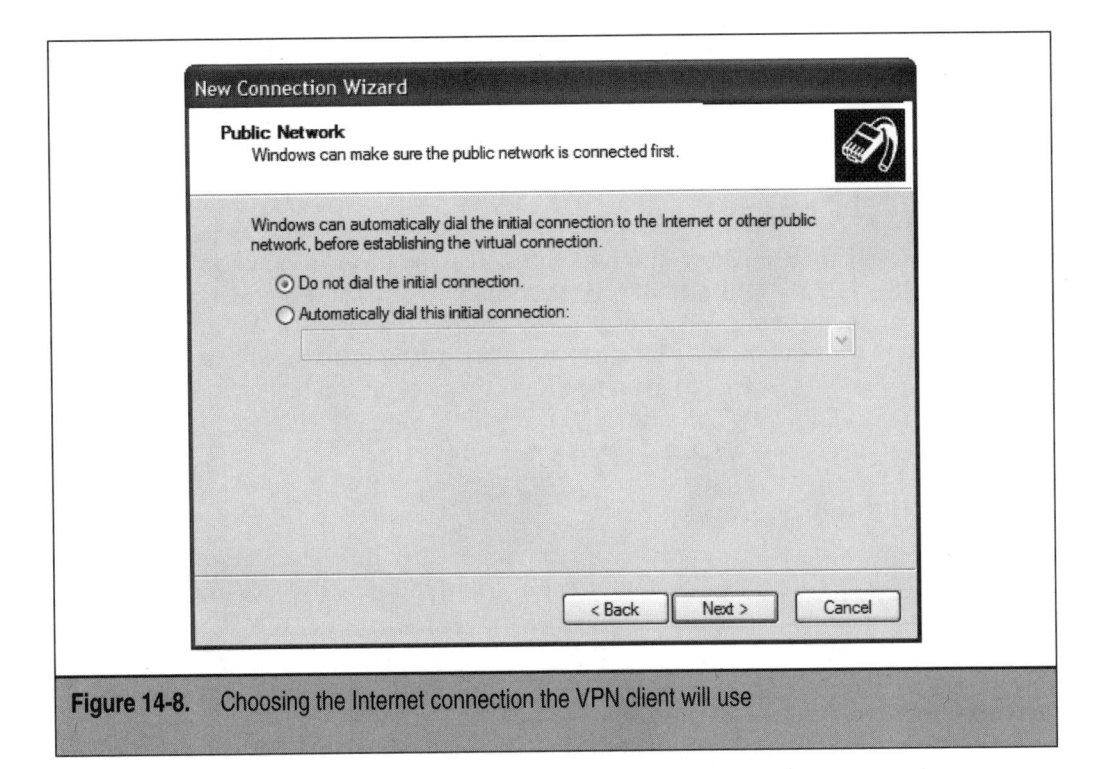

Figure 14-8. Choosing the Internet connection the VPN client will use

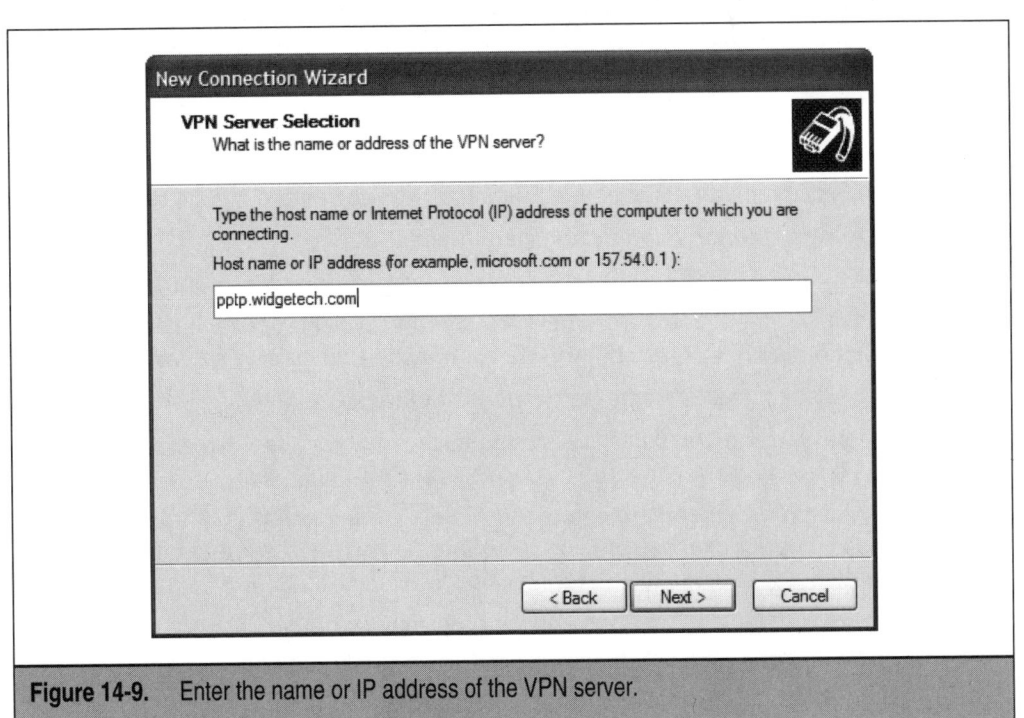

Figure 14-9. Enter the name or IP address of the VPN server.

NOTE If your VPN server connects to the Internet via a dial-in connection and has its IP address assigned dynamically by the ISP, you'll have to change the IP address in the VPN Properties dialog box on the client before you attempt a connection.

Receiving a VPN Connection

VPN connections can be made to different types of servers. For instance, in a large corporation, the need for multiple VPN servers might exist. These servers would do nothing but handle incoming VPN traffic and would probably use a Windows 2000 or .NET Server. On the other hand, a smaller organization might have a client set up as its VPN server so that the occasional incoming VPN connection can be made.

Since we're dealing with Windows XP Professional here, let's talk about how these types of VPN servers are configured for remote users.

Configuring the VPN Server

For your computer to act as a VPN server, you must have an Incoming Connections icon in your Network Connections folder. If this icon is already in place (for instance, you already have a remote access configured), double-click it. This displays the Incoming Connections Properties dialog box. Make sure that the Allow others to make private connections to my computer by tunneling through the Internet or other network check box is selected.

If you do not have the Incoming Connections icon in your Network Connections folder, follow these steps:

1. Click Start | Connect To | Show all connections.
2. Click Create a New Connection to invoke the New Connection Wizard.
3. Click Next.
4. Select Set up an advanced connection, and then click Next.
5. Pick Accept incoming connections, and then click Next.
6. The resulting dialog box shows a list of devices for incoming connections.
7. Deselect all the modems from the list, as you will be accepting incoming connections only through the Internet connection, not a dial-up connection.
8. Select Allow virtual private connections, and then click Next.
9. In the next screen you can select which users you wish to allow to remotely access this server. Make your selections, and then click Next.
10. Next, a list of Microsoft's recommended networking components appears. Clear the check boxes next to any components you *don't* want to use. It's a good idea just to leave these settings alone.
11. Complete the New Connection Wizard by clicking Finish.

Once the preceding steps are completed, a new icon called Incoming Connections is placed in your Network Connections window. If you already have this icon and you started the New Connection Wizard, then the existing connection is edited to accommodate your new settings.

Configuring a VPN Connection

Over time, you might find that your VPN settings need to be adjusted or changed. For instance, in the scenario we already mentioned, if your VPN server's IP address is dynamically assigned, you'll have to change that setting on your VPN client each time the VPN server connects to the Internet.

To make changes to your VPN connection, navigate to the Network Connections window, right-click the VPN or Incoming Connections icon, and select Properties from the pop-up menu. Depending on whether your computer is configured as a client or a server, you will be presented with a different set of options.

The Properties dialog box for a VPN client is shown in Figure 14-10. The Properties dialog box for a VPN server is shown in Figure 14-11.

On the VPN client, the options on the General tab are used to manage the host name or IP address of your VPN server or the Internet connection you'll use. The options on the Advanced tab are used to manage your Internet Connection Firewall and to share the VPN connection.

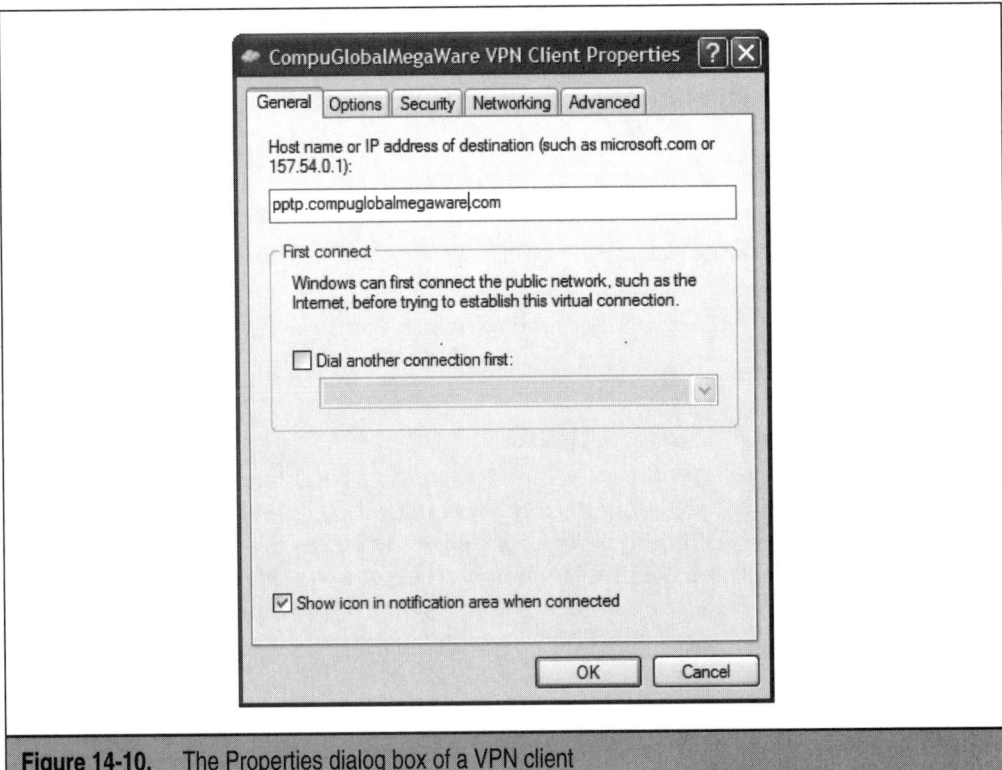

Figure 14-10. The Properties dialog box of a VPN client

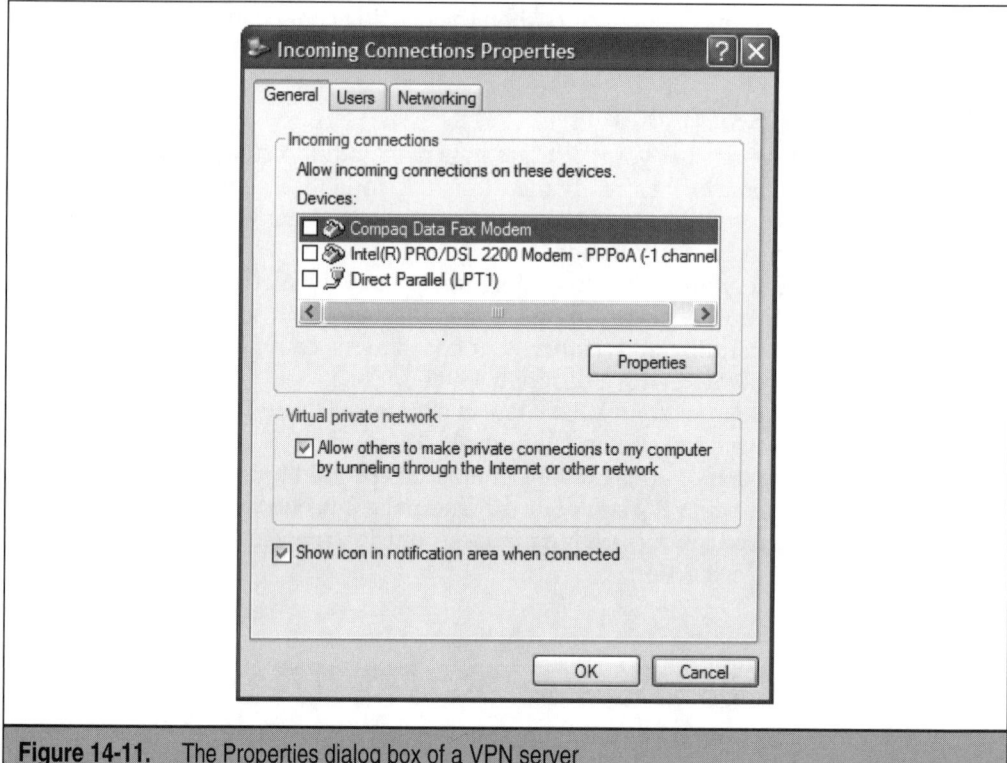

Figure 14-11. The Properties dialog box of a VPN server

On the VPN server, you can make changes to the settings you established with the New Connection Wizard. You can turn the VPN on or off, elect to display an icon in the taskbar when you're connected, or manage which users can and cannot use the VPN connection.

Troubleshooting VPN Connections

As simple as Windows XP Professional makes the process of establishing VPN connections, there are still some pitfalls that you can find yourself in. Troubleshooting a VPN connection is difficult because there are so many pieces to the puzzle. Is the problem on the client? Is there a problem with the server's connection to the ISP? Is the server misconfigured? Is there a problem with a router? A firewall? You get the idea.

To this point, we've discussed VPNs as existing between Windows XP Professional clients. That is, not only is the VPN client a Windows XP Professional computer, but so is the VPN server. It is quite likely (though outside the scope of our discussion here) that the VPN termination point will be a router or firewall, and the VPN server will actually be located on your Windows 2000, NT, or .NET Server.

For a VPN connection to take place, the VPN client calls to the ISP using PPP. At this point, the ISP issues the client a TCP/IP address, a DNS server address, and a default gateway.

When the client tries to form a VPN connection (using PPTP), it causes a second TCP/IP session to be created. This session, the tunnel portion of the VPN connection, is embedded within the first TCP/IP session and provides packet encryption and encapsulation. When the client successfully connects to the VPN server, the VPN server issues a second IP address, a second DNS server address, and another gateway.

At any step along the way, a problem can occur and cause connection issues.

Server Considerations

Although a bit outside the scope of this book, there are some server issues you should keep in mind when building your VPN solution. Let's touch on them just briefly:

- Use a server that has a minimum number of services installed. Limit the protocols it uses to just TCP/IP and PPTP.
- If your VPN server is located inside your firewall or in the DMZ, you'll need to redirect traffic from the server's outside routable IP address to the VPN's inside address. This is usually done with a special configuration on the firewall called Network Address Translation or use of a conduit (in Cisco parlance).
- If you must place your VPN server behind a firewall, make sure that your firewall software can accommodate PPTP packets. Some firewall software packages don't accept PPTP packets, and if you're running one of these, you will be unable to use your VPN.

Client Troubleshooting

The next place to look for problems is at the VPN client. The process of a VPN client connecting to the VPN server follows several steps. First, a VPN client needs to have two sets of TCP/IP settings for proper functioning: One is used with the ISP and the Internet connection, one is used for the VPN connection. Additionally, the VPN client must also have two entries in its routing table: one that directs network packets to the ISP for any web browsing, and another to send packets to the VPN server for LAN access.

Some of the most prevalent VPN connectivity problems, as they relate to clients, include the ones described in the following sections.

Inability to Connect to the Server If the VPN client cannot connect to the server, there are a series of settings to check. Make sure that the VPN server is connected to the Internet. To do this from the client, ping the server with its IP address. Your firewall might block the ping message, but if you get a "request timed out" message, then you know something's wrong with the server. Also, if your server gets its IP address dynamically (if it's using a dial-up connection, and so forth), make sure you change the VPN server's IP address in the VPN icon located in the Network Connections window.

If your VPN server responds to a ping of its IP address, ping its name. If it does not respond by name, then your server might not have a registered domain name, or your ISP DNS server might be malfunctioning.

Check PPTP filtering. If your server has PPTP filtering enabled, you might see an error message indicating the server isn't responding. Disable PPTP filtering on the server and try to form a nonfiltered connection.

If you can connect with filtering disabled, check your server to see if UDP ports 137 and 138 or TCP port 139 have been disabled. If so, reenable them, as NetBIOS packets can't pass through the network without these ports. Furthermore, these ports must be enabled on all routers and firewalls between your VPN server and client.

If you've done all the preceding steps and you still cannot connect, you should check the routers between the VPN client and server to ensure they are not filtering out generic routing encapsulating (GRE) packets. It's a good idea to check this with your ISP, because they oftentimes use GRE internally for router management.

Client Connects, but Cannot Log On   Another common problem is the ability of the VPN client to connect to the server, but not to log onto the network. If the VPN server is configured as a domain controller, make sure the user has an account and that the account allows remote access. If the server isn't a domain controller, make sure the client has the requisite permissions to log onto that server.

Winsock Proxy Client   If a Winsock Proxy client is active, then the VPN connection cannot be established. A Winsock Proxy redirects packets to the proxy server before they can be encapsulated for transmission across the VPN link. Make sure your Winsock Proxy client is deactivated.

Name Resolution   If you suspect problems with name resolution that prevent you from resolving names to IP addresses, use the fully qualified domain names and IP addresses in the connection.

Other Places to Check

Other sources of VPN problems tend to be more advanced than what a user can (or should) check. The following sources are general network conditions that should be examined if the source of trouble cannot be pinned down to a client or a server issue.

Network Address Translation Issues   If the VPN client is behind a network device performing Network Address Translation (NAT), the L2TP session will fail, as the encrypted IPSec ESP packets can become corrupted. On the other hand, if your VPN client is on the same computer as Internet Connection Sharing or NAT, then the client should be able to establish an L2TP connection. This is because NAT does not perform any IP address or port translation on packets that come from its own node.

ESP Issues   Another source of problems can be the ESP. The ESP might be blocked if the NAT is in front of the client or if the routers are in front of the VPN. In this case, the server might not allow ESP through. Outbound ESP traffic will appear, but incoming

ESP packets from the gateway will not. Furthermore, the ESP might be modified. This occurs if the NAT (possibly a malfunctioning network device) is corrupting packets. Packets can also be corrupted by a network interface that has IPSec offload capabilities. To check for this, enter the following on the command line:

```
netsh in tip show offload
```

If you suspect that a NIC's IPSec offload capability is the source of trouble, start a Network Monitor capture and use the IPSec Monitor to analyze each connection attempt. Check the Confidential Bytes Received counter to see whether bytes are being lost when they're received. You can turn off the IPSec automatic policy to see if that enables the connection to be made.

Windows XP Professional allows you to connect to your LAN or a local computer using different methods. If you want to connect remotely via the Internet, a VPN allows you to do so securely. You can also enable a server or local computer to automatically answer a dial-in line, allowing users to remotely connect via the telephone. Whichever method you prefer, these means of remote connection allow you to provide greater network availability for your users.

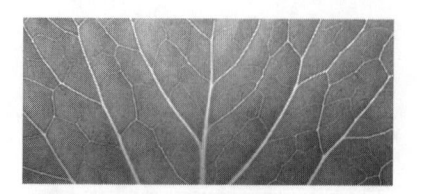

CHAPTER 15

Quality of Service

As networks continue to grow, and as the applications that run across those networks demand more and more bandwidth, a mechanism needs to be in place that ensures important network traffic gets where it needs to go, without becoming bogged down in the chaff. *Quality of Service (QoS)* is such a mechanism. It ensures that networks have the resources they need, without having to add more bandwidth to them.

This chapter examines QoS from different angles. First, we'll talk about QoS basics so you can get a better understanding of what it does and how it does it. Then, we'll focus on how Windows XP Professional manages QoS. Finally, we'll talk about how you can monitor your system to prepare for a QoS implementation, and then make the necessary adjustments to keep packets flowing.

WHAT IS QOS?

Internet Protocol (IP) networks are a "best-effort" service. That is, they provide their resources to users on a first-come, first-served philosophy. This means that the CEO's packets course across the network with the same speed and importance as those of the new guy in accounting. Not only are both their networking access needs duking it out for the same bandwidth, but they are also contending with Larry in production, who is downloading a ton of MP3s. Because of this best-effort philosophy, organizations have had to tolerate dropped packets and slow networks.

It might sound like this is a problem with the design of the Internet. The fact of the matter is that it was designed this way on purpose. When it was planned, the Internet's architects knew that the network had to be kept simple so that it could be used on a global scale. As such, designers knew that they had to keep the Internet straightforward, pushing its complexity to the network's edges.

Even though the Internet was designed with simplicity in mind, it has grown beyond its humble beginnings. Not only has the Internet gotten big, but so has its character. These are all reasons why QoS is so important.

This section serves as a primer on QoS, its need, and its implementation.

Raw Bandwidth Is Not Enough

The resolution to the Internet congestion problem seems simple enough: Throw more bandwidth at it. For a while, this philosophy solved most problems. With more bandwidth applied to the problem, network user satisfaction increased. Now, however, the amount of data coursing through networks isn't the only issue. Timing and coordination are just as important as raw throughput for acceptable service quality.

Applications don't just need gobs of bandwidth; they also need packets delivered in a timely manner. Consider, for instance, voice over IP (VoIP). Sure enough, it consumes a lot of bandwidth, but it also imposes an operational requirement on the IP network—packets must arrive in the order they were transmitted. Furthermore, they must arrive in a timely manner. If there is packet delay in a VoIP conversation, the call will be a garbled mess.

The packet delivery delay that causes a signal to lose its timing references is better known as *jitter*. If a VoIP call is affected by jitter, it is apparent to the users and is regarded as unacceptable.

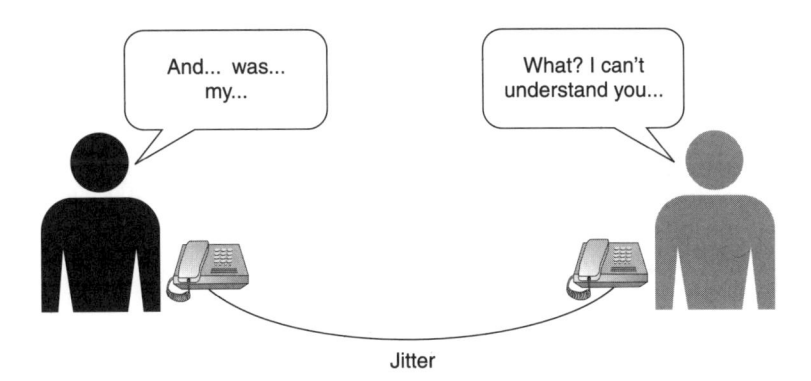

Jitter is only applicable to applications in which timing and speed are important, such as VoIP or streaming audio or video. On the other hand, applications such as e-mail, web browsers, and File Transfer Protocol (FTP) aren't affected by jitter. If the packets arrive out of sequence, with half-second delays here and there, it isn't noticeable or bothersome to the end user. These services are not sensitive to timing issues. (*Delay* refers to a message that arrives in the proper order, yet there is a lengthy impediment between packets.)

Opening a wider pipe for media applications like VoIP won't necessarily help the problem, because sudden bursts of traffic can still cause jitter. The more sensitive a network application's signal pattern is to delivery delay, the more difficulty it has with IP's best-effort delivery scheme. Table 15-1 illustrates different traffic types and their sensitivity to packet delay or jitter.

For the most part, Internet applications tend to be asynchronous and are very tolerant to jitter. For instance, a user might not like that a web site is taking 15 seconds to download, but functionally speaking there's nothing wrong with the web browser. On the other hand, applications that need their packets delivered quickly and in the proper order won't be so forgiving of a slow connection.

For the Internet to evolve to its next level, the industry is convinced IP must be tweaked to provide reliable network service levels. QoS is the answer to this need.

Tolerance to Delay	Traffic Type	Effect of Packet Delay on Network Application
Very Tolerant	Asynchronous	Fully elastic; delay has no effect.
	Synchronous	Delay can have some effect, usually just slowness.
Somewhat Tolerant	Interactive	Delay annoys and distracts users, but application is still functional.
	Isochronous	Application is only partially functional.
Not Tolerant	Mission-critical	Application is functionally disabled.

Table 15-1. Jitter Is a Function of the Traffic Type

QoS Concepts

There are two basic kinds of QoS, and they differ sharply:

- **Prioritization**   Individual packets are treated differently according to the service class to which they are assigned. Simple prioritization QoS is packet based. In other words, the treatment the packet deserves is in one way or another signified inside the packet itself. Although all QoS is priority-driven and operates packet by packet, prioritization QoS is distinguishable in that its implementation is constrained to a device inspecting packets. In other words, routers treat prioritization independently of other routers. Prioritization, specifically *Differentiated Services*, is the method of QoS used in Windows XP Professional.

- **Resource reservation**   A connection is allocated a certain amount of bandwidth negotiated with routers and switches along its path. Reserved connections, by contrast, are far more complex. Reservation schemes must get all routers along a connection's path to agree on a QoS regimen before transmission can begin. Moreover, the path itself must be defined before the reservations can be made. Reserved path bandwidth may also need to make real-time adjustments to changing operating conditions, further adding to complexity. Resource Reservation Setup Protocol (also known as RSVP) is the method that Microsoft has embraced for QoS in Windows 2000.

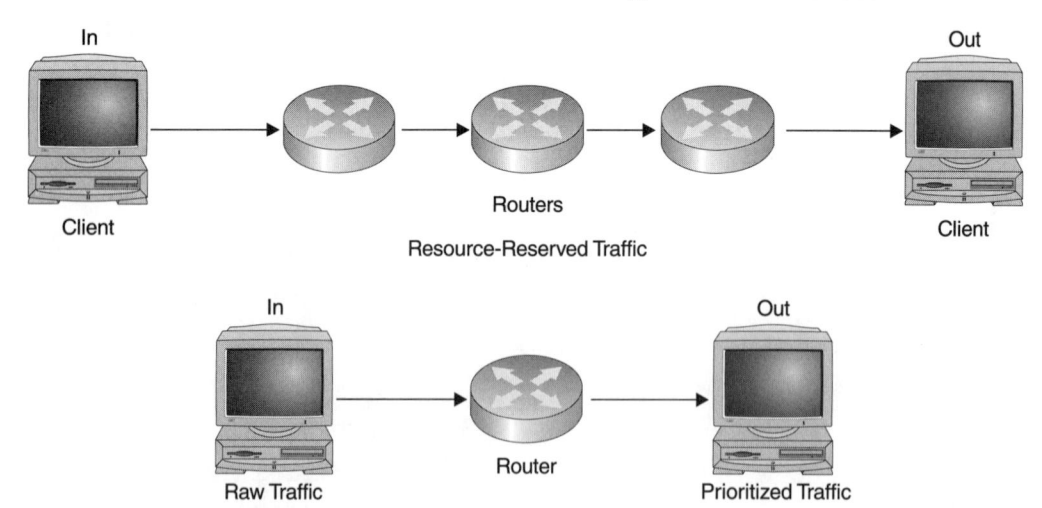

Compare and Contrast

The primary difference between these types of QoS strategies comes in their management of packets. Prioritization requires the transmitting server or network device to establish a queue in which packets are organized. Then, the packets are sent out in order of their importance. RSVP, on the other hand, necessitates that routers between the sender and receiver be dynamically configured so that important packets are given precedence over other packets coming into the router.

In packet-prioritized networks, if operating conditions change because packets from another flow—with the same or higher priority—enter the same router, the original flow's packets are simply adjusted in its queue.

On the other hand, in an RSVP environment, reserving bandwidth requires all devices in the path to converse and cooperatively arrive at a QoS service-level commitment. As you can surmise, this presents quite a problem with resources, especially when differing QoS levels are demanded by different flows. Furthermore, older routers that do not possess QoS capabilities will be the weak link in the chain, ruining any chance for QoS.

When QoS is contained in the packet itself, there is no need to establish and monitor flows across routers, routing areas, and autonomous system boundaries.

NOTE An *autonomous system* is a collection of routers under a single administrative authority using a common interior gateway routing protocol. For instance, an ISP is an autonomous system.

Flows and Connections

A *flow* is a packet stream moving between two IP addresses identified by a Transmission Control Protocol (TCP) or User Datagram Protocol (UDP) network application port number. A packet stream moving between the same two hosts, but in the opposite direction, is a separate flow. It is quite common for multiple simultaneous flows to run between two hosts. For example, if a user has multiple web browser screens open, then each of those sessions has its own flows. These flows are kept separate by using different port numbers.

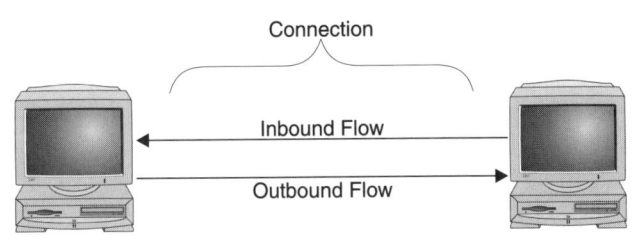

Flows are elemental to QoS because they tell every packet stream the *where* (the path connecting the hosts), the *when* (the connection's sequence and direction), and the *why* (the application being run). Flows are identified using some or all of these packet data elements:

- **Source host address**   The network address of the originating host (specific to a layer 3 protocol such as IP or IPX)
- **Destination host address**   The network address of the receiving host (also specific to a layer 3 protocol such as IP or IPX)
- **Protocol**   Network and transport protocols such as IP, TCP, UDP, IPX, SAP, and so on
- **Source protocol port**   Network application protocol from the source host, such as HTTP, FTP, and so on

- **Destination protocol port** Network application protocol dependent on the destination host network address
- **Source device interface** The network interface through which the traffic entered the device, usually a router

Any combination of the aforementioned flow definition criteria is known as a *tuple*. In QoS, functions use tuples to identify different flows. When flows are aggregated between two hosts, a *connection* is formed. A connection simplifies the task of service-level management by reducing the number of flow management instructions. Another term for a connection is a *session*. Sessions are most often employed in the context of people using a connection.

A flow identification is a very basic QoS enabler, because it is used by network devices to determine to what connection a packet belongs. This allows the appropriate level of service to be applied to that packet.

RSVP

RSVP delivers QoS on a per-flow basis. As the name suggests, RSVP "reserves" bandwidth resources along a path connecting source and destination devices so as to ensure a minimum level of QoS. Applications running on IP end systems will use RSVP to indicate the nature of the packet streams they want to receive, thereby "reserving" bandwidth that can support the required QoS. This is done by defining parameters for such characteristics as minimum bandwidth, maximum delay jitter, and the like.

RSVP is the QoS mechanism used in Windows 2000. A discussion of it is included here in the event your Windows XP Professional clients will be connecting to a Windows 2000 Server, which uses RSVP for QoS. Additionally, Windows XP Professional includes tools to enable the monitoring of RSVP attributes in System Monitor, which is explained later in this chapter.

RSVP is considered the enabling protocol for what is called *integrated services* QoS architecture, or *IntServ* for short. The "integrated" part comes from the notion that all devices—end hosts and interim devices alike—are integrated into a single QoS service regimen to be maintained in both directions for the life of the QoS-serviced flow.

How It Works

RSVP is a complex process. It defines a *sender* and a *receiver* host for each flow. The sender transmits a *PATH* message downstream to the receiver, with the PATH collecting a roster of devices along the route. Once the PATH message is received, the receiver sends a request called a *RESV* message back upstream along the same path to the RSVP sender. The RESV message specifies parameters for the desired bandwidth characteristics. Once all the interim devices are signed on to support the QoS levels, the session may begin. When the connection is terminated, an explicit tear-down mechanism is used to free up resources on the reserved devices. The RSVP process is depicted in Figure 15-1.

For the reservation to be fully guaranteed, each hop between network hardware must grant the reservation and physically allocate the requested bandwidth. By granting the reservation, the hop commits to providing the requested resources.

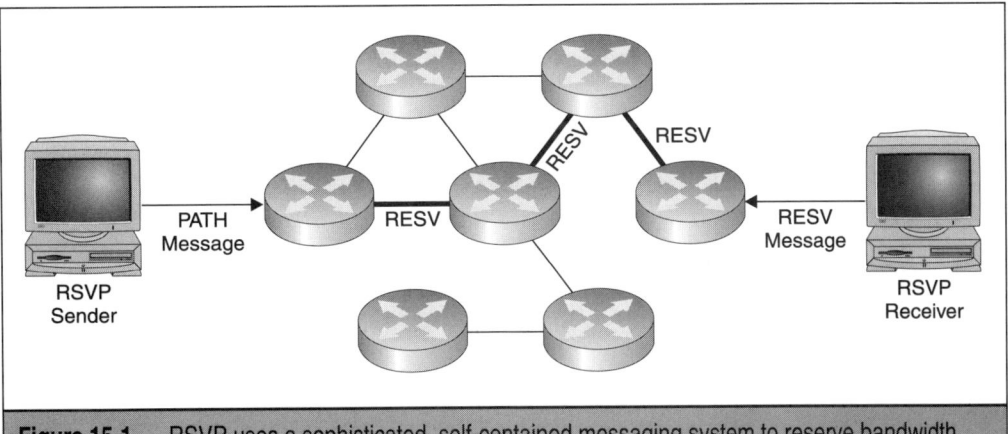

Figure 15-1. RSVP uses a sophisticated, self-contained messaging system to reserve bandwidth.

If the reservation is denied, the program receives a response that the network cannot support the amount and type of bandwidth or the requested service level. The program determines whether to send the data now using best-effort delivery or to wait and try the request again later.

RSVP is a *soft-state protocol,* which requires the reservation to be refreshed periodically. The reservation information, or *reservation state,* is cached at each hop. If the network routing protocol alters the data path, RSVP automatically installs the reservation state along the new route. If refresh messages are not received, reservations time out and are dropped, and the bandwidth is released.

NOTE Many legacy routers and switches are not RSVP compliant. In these cases, the reservation messages pass through each hop. End-to-end and low-delay guarantees for the requested service level are not available.

Route aggregation partially ameliorates RSVP complexity and overhead. For example, if thousands of RSVP receiver hosts were to receive a multicast (say, a Web TV videocast), the RESV messages would be rolled up and combined at aggregation points. Conversely, only one stream would be sent downstream from the videocaster, replicated at aggregation points to worm out to all end-point destinations.

RSVP Messages

We talked about RSVP messages in the last section, but let's take a closer look at the specific messages that RSVP uses to establish and maintain a reserved path for QoS traffic on a subnet:

- **PATH** Carries the data flow information from the sender to the receiver. The PATH message reserves the path that requested data must take when returning to the receiver. PATH messages contain bandwidth requirements, traffic characteristics, and address information.

- **RESV** Carries the reservation request back to the sender from the receiver. RESV messages contain the actual bandwidth reservation, the service level requested, and the source IP address.
- **PATH-ERR** Indicates an error in response to a PATH message.
- **RESV-ERR** Indicates an error in response to the RESV message.
- **PATH-TEAR** Removes the established PATH state along the route.
- **RESV-TEAR** Removes the established RESV state along the route.

RSVP can get amazingly complicated. Some experts openly question whether RSVP is even feasible, in light of the seemingly unbounded complexity the large number of potential variables implies, and the overhead likely to be incurred to set up and operate bandwidth reserved in this way.

DiffServ

A better prioritization model is called *Differentiated Services*, or *DiffServ* for short. DiffServ is meant to provide a relatively coarse but simple way to prioritize traffic. DiffServ redefines the original IP Type of Service (ToS) field bits (as shown in Figure 15-2) into its own scheme, where 2 of the 8 ToS bits are used for congestion notification, and the remaining 6 bits for packet markings. This new scheme implements so-called *code points* within the 6-bit marking space. Packets are marked for DiffServ class as they enter the DiffServ QoS network.

DiffServ attempts only to control so-called "per-hop" behaviors. In other words, policy is defined locally, and DiffServ as a mechanism executes within a device to influence when and where the packet's next hop will be. Once policy is set across a topology, everything takes place in-device. DiffServ supports two service levels (traffic classes):

- **Expedited Forwarding (EF)** Minimizes delay and jitter. Packets are dropped if traffic exceeds maximum load threshold set by local policy.

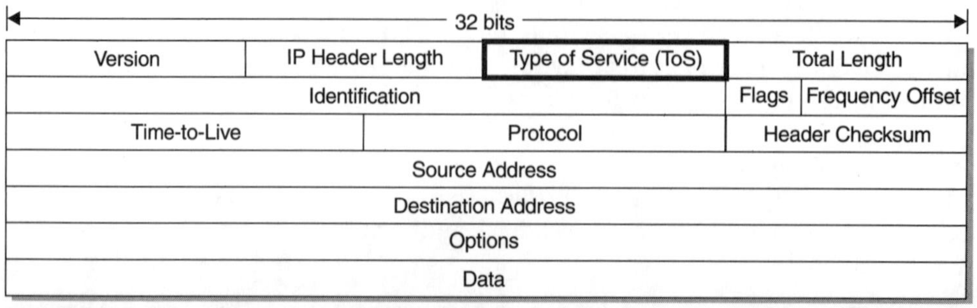

Version	IP Header Length	Type of Service (ToS)	Total Length
Identification			Flags	Frequency Offset
Time-to-Live		Protocol	Header Checksum
Source Address			
Destination Address			
Options			
Data			

Figure 15-2. ToS bits are used to assign priority levels to packets.

- **Assured Forwarding (AF)**   Provides for four subclasses and three drop precedences within each subclass, for a total of 12 code points. If traffic load exceeds local policy, excess AF packets are not delivered at the specified priority but are instead demoted to a lower priority (but not dropped). This demotion procedure cascades through any configured drop-precedence code points.

QOS IN WINDOWS XP

In Windows XP Professional, QoS is used to provide traffic shaping, smoothing bursts and peaks in traffic to an even flow. Packet marking (802.1p marking for layer 2, and DiffServ Code Point [DSCP] marking for layer 3) is used to shape traffic. The QoS Packet Scheduler enforces QoS rules for data flow. The QoS Packet Scheduler retrieves the packets from the queues and transmits them according to the established QoS rules. The marked packets receive priority over nonmarked packets when processed by network devices such as switches and routers along the data path.

In Windows XP Professional, QoS is managed in a number of ways. First, QoS must be installed and configured. Installation is accomplished via a simple service installation. Configuring and managing QoS is accomplished via the QoS Packet Scheduler.

Once you've gotten your QoS settings at the levels you want (or if you need to establish QoS levels), you can use the powerful System Monitor to keep track of the various attributes of a TCP connection, or an RSVP session if you are connecting to a Windows 2000 Server. This section examines these tools and processes for setting up, using, and managing QoS on Windows XP Professional.

Windows XP Usability

In Windows XP Professional, QoS can be used to aid in a variety of network configurations and issues. Overall, your individual needs will vary; however, the following are some scenarios in which QoS can be especially helpful in Windows XP Professional networks.

QoS with ICS

Internet Connection Sharing (ICS) is a means of connecting several computers to the Internet via a single link or connection, usually a dial-in or digital subscriber line (DSL) connection. This is a good way to connect several computers to the Internet; however, it also presents a problem when traffic delay permeates the link. This delay occurs because of the speed difference between what the ICS clients are capable of and the ICS server's link to the Internet.

NOTE   For a refresher on ICS terms and concepts, flip back to Chapter 5.

For example, if the ICS client's network connection is fast (such as a 100 Mbps Fast Ethernet connection) and it connects to the Internet through an ICS server that is connected behind a remote access to a fast network, then this bottleneck is present. In this setup, the ICS client's receive window is set at too large a value, based on the speed of the link to which it is connected. The ICS server sends at a slow rate, but if packets aren't lost, then the rate increases.

Ultimately, this can affect the performance of other TCP connections that have to move across the same network, because their packets will have to wait longer and longer to be transmitted across the LAN. If packets have been lost, then they must be retransmitted, which congests the link even more.

To resolve this, the ICS server should set its receive window to a smaller size that conforms to the slow link. This overrides the receiver's speed specification. Ultimately, this has a throughput result as if the ICS client were directly connected to the slow link. This QoS setting should be made on the ICS server.

QoS with Modems and Remote Access

In a small office or home office environment, it is not uncommon for access to remote connections (the Internet or remote access to a LAN, for instance) to be accomplished through dial-in modems. Even though this speed is rather slow, in comparison to DSL or LAN links, users still wind up employing several applications that use the link at the same time. For instance, they might open a web browser, their e-mail, an online chat program, another browser, and so forth. These programs all use TCP as the transfer protocol, each forming its own connection.

The first program that uses the dial-in link has exclusive use of it. When the next application starts, it is subjected to a slow start algorithm. This algorithm restricts the volume of unacknowledged data that can be in transit. As the first application has a more established connection than the second application, packet transfer will be much slower.

When multiple TCP applications are running at the same time, Windows XP Professional uses a fairness scheme called *deficit round robin (DRR)* when it is operating on a slow link. DRR assigns several data flows and assigns new data streams to those flows. These flows are automatically tended to in a round-robin fashion, which provides improved responsiveness and performance. Since this is handled automatically, the user need not perform any manual configuration.

NOTE DRR was included in Windows 2000, but in Windows XP Professional it is turned on by default.

Setup Steps

The QoS Packet Scheduler is the tool used to manage QoS in Windows XP Professional. It is not installed with Windows XP Professional by default; it must be added later. To install the QoS Packet Scheduler, follow these steps:

1. In the Network Connections window, right-click the desired network connection.
2. From the pop-up window, select Properties.
3. Click the Networking tab.

4. Click Install.
5. Select Service and click Add.
6. Select QoS Packet Scheduler and click OK.
7. You are returned to the connection's Properties box and might be prompted to restart your computer.

Additionally, Windows XP Professional QoS relies on 802.1p. This must be enabled on all the network adapters on which you plan to use QoS. To configure your adapter to use QoS, under the Properties screen for the network adapter (located in the Device Manager), select the option for QoS support, as shown in Figure 15-3.

Furthermore, your network adapter must compatible with 802.1p.

NOTE The Institute of Electrical and Electronics Engineering (IEEE) 802.1p signaling method is used for traffic prioritization at OSI Reference Model layer 2. It is implemented in network adapters and switches for best-effort QoS and does not require resource reservation setup.

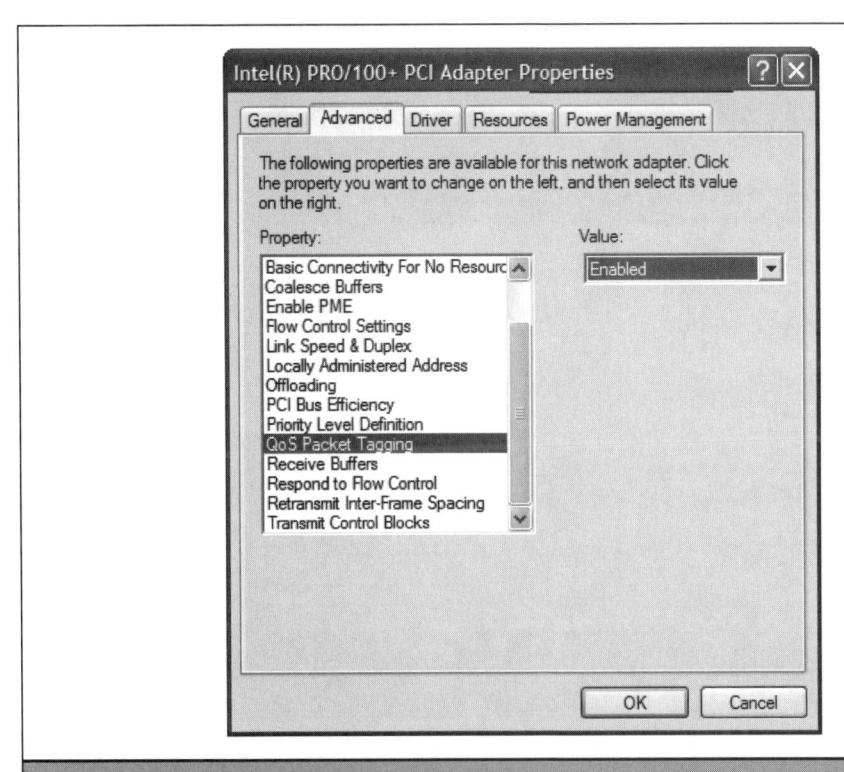

Figure 15-3. Enabling QoS (802.1p) on a network adapter

Management

Managing and establishing QoS levels is accomplished through the Group Policy snap-in to the MMC.

> **NOTE** You can either add the Group Policy to the MMC, or you can enter **gpedit.msc** at the command prompt.

Once you've got the Group Policy snap-in open, the QoS Packet Scheduler is located by doing the following:

1. Expand Computer Configuration.
2. Expand Administrative Templates.
3. Next, expand Network.
4. Click QoS Packet Scheduler.

The main QoS Packet Scheduler is shown in Figure 15-4.

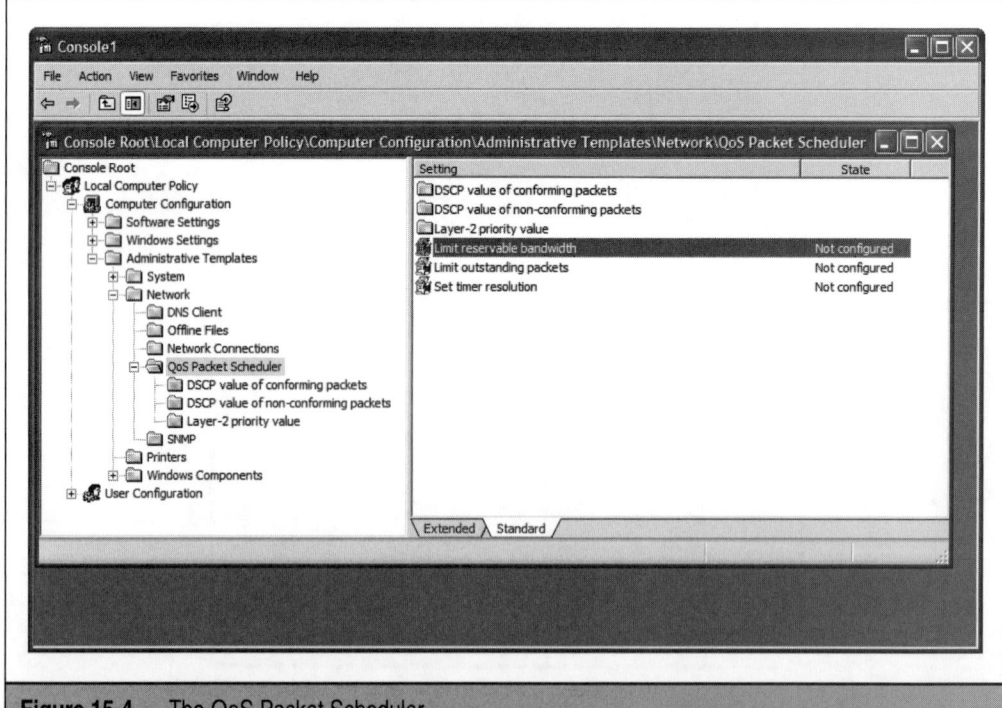

Figure 15-4. The QoS Packet Scheduler

Main View

Within this view are six items. The folders (DSCP value of conforming packets, DSCP value of nonconforming packets, and layer 2 priority value) are explained in more depth later in this section.

> **NOTE** For all of these settings, if a value is defined in the Registry, that value supersedes any settings made in the Group Policy snap-in.

Each of the settings contained in the QoS Packet Scheduler allows you to give each type of packet a specific level of precedence. For instance, depending on your criteria for packets (traffic to a certain address or port, packets belonging to a certain user or application, and so on), differing levels of priority can be established. The lower the precedence, the lower the packet is in the queue for transmission.

In addition to the aforementioned folders are three manageable settings, discussed next.

Limit Reservable Bandwidth   This setting is used to determine what percentage of connection bandwidth can be reserved by the system. When you enable this setting, it is established, by default, at 20 percent. This amount can be adjusted lower or higher, depending on your QoS needs. If this setting is disabled or not enabled, then it uses the system default value of 20 percent of the connection.

Limit Outstanding Packets   *Outstanding packets* are packets that the Packet Scheduler has sent to a network adapter for transmission, but that have not yet been transmitted. This setting is used to establish the maximum number of outstanding packets that your system will permit. Once the number of outstanding packets reaches this threshold, the Packet Scheduler postpones all outgoing data headed for network adapters until the amount falls below this threshold. Enabling this setting allows you to limit the number of outstanding packets and adjust the threshold to your desired limits. Disabling or not enabling this setting makes no impact on the system.

Set Timer Resolution   This setting is used to establish the smallest amount of time that the Packet Scheduler uses when scheduling packets for transmission. This threshold establishes how often packets are transmitted. Packet Scheduler cannot send packets more frequently than this setting. Enabling this setting allows you to establish the rate at which packets are transmitted and is adjustable in increments of 10 microseconds. Disabling or not enabling this setting has no impact on the system.

DSCP Value of Conforming Packets

Key to DiffServ QoS deployments is the Differentiated Services Code Point. Essentially, when traffic enters the network's ingress interface, it is classified and subjected to a preconfigured admission process and then *shaped* to meet policy requirements based on settings established by the organization. The data stream is then assigned to a behavior aggregate. The DSCP value initiates a specific Per-Hop Behavior (PHB) in devices in the network and classifies the packet service level.

The folder DSCP Value of Conforming Packets within the QoS Packet Scheduler contains the following settings (applicable at layer 3 of the OSI Reference Model) that are used to vary the DSCP value for the various attributes of conforming packets. *Conforming packets* are those that match flow specifications.

There are five service types used for QoS in Windows XP Professional:

- **Best Effort** This service type does not make any guarantees that requested QoS parameters will be implemented or enforced, but can be used by senders to specify traffic control objects.

- **Guaranteed** This service type is used for applications that require a specific service level. The guaranteed service type is designed to transmit packets within an established delay boundary.

- **Controlled Load** This service type is used to define service levels similar to Best Effort under *unloaded* conditions.

- **Qualitative** This type of service is used for applications that require better than Best Effort service, but cannot quantify their QoS needs.

- **Network Control** This service type is reserved for use by critical traffic management applications.

Best Effort Service Type Packets that are designated as Best Effort type of service packets can be given an alternate DSCP value. The QoS Packet Scheduler inserts the adjusted DSCP value into the IP header of the packets. Enabling this setting allows you to change the default DSCP value associated with the Best Effort service type. If this setting is disabled, then the default value of 0 is used. The Properties screen for this setting is shown in Figure 15-5.

Controlled Load Service Type Packets that are designated as Controlled Load service type packets can be given an alternate DSCP value. The QoS Packet Scheduler inserts the adjusted DSCP value into the IP header of the packets. Enabling this setting allows you to change the default DSCP value associated with the Controlled Load service type. If this setting is disabled, then the default value of 24 is used.

Guaranteed Service Type Guaranteed type of service packets are given alternate DSCP values using this setting. The QoS Packet Scheduler inserts the adjusted DSCP value into the IP header of the packets. Enabling this setting allows you to change the default DSCP value associated with the Guaranteed type of service. Disable this setting, and the default value of 40 is used.

Network Control Service Type Network Control type of service packets can be given an alternate DSCP value using this setting. The QoS Packet Scheduler inserts the adjusted DSCP value into the IP header of the packets. Enabling this setting allows you to change the DSCP value associated with the Network Control type of service. If this setting is disabled, the default value of 48 is used.

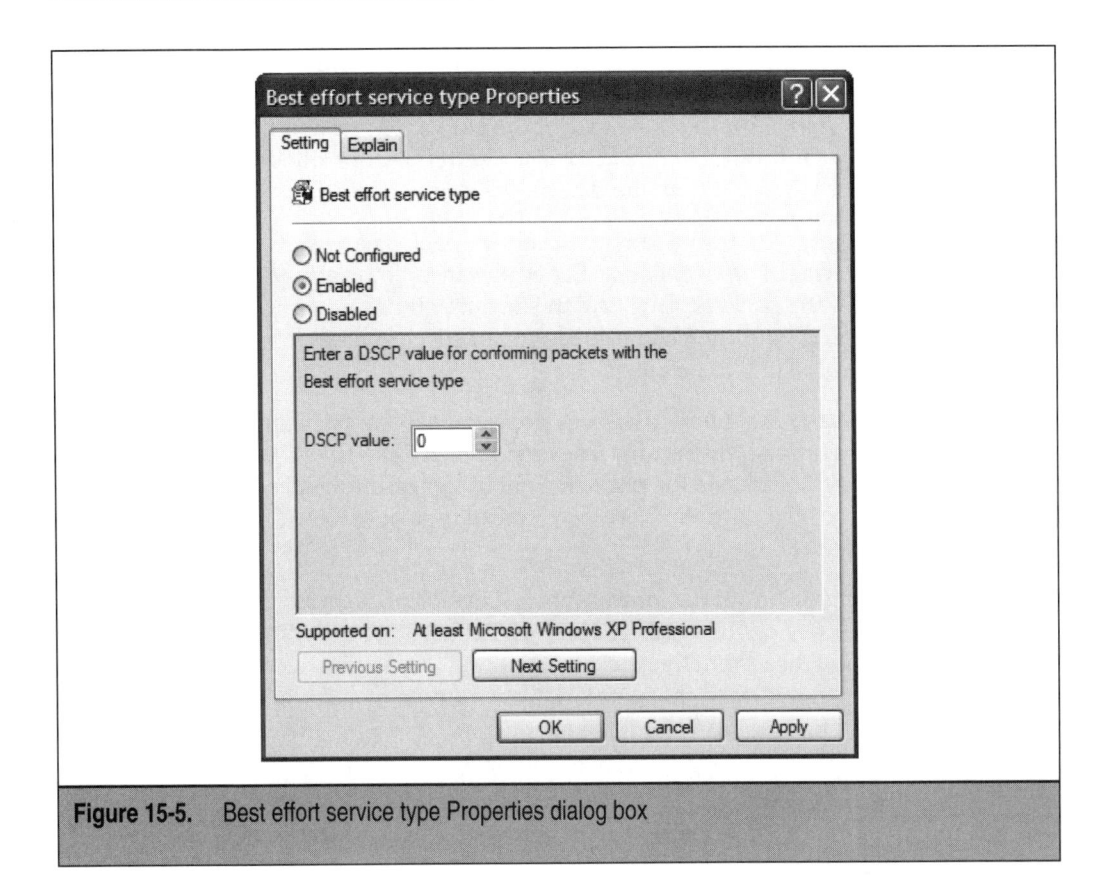

Figure 15-5. Best effort service type Properties dialog box

Qualitative Service Type   Network Control type of service packets can be given an alternate DSCP value using this setting. The QoS Packet Scheduler inserts the adjusted DSCP value into the IP header of the packets. Enabling this setting allows you to change the DSCP value associated with the Network Control type of service. Disable this setting, and the default value of 0 is used.

DSCP Value of Nonconforming Packets

The following settings are quite similar to those in the previous section. However, they differ in that their default values are all the same—0—and that these settings only apply to packets that do not conform to the flow specification.

Best Effort Service Type   Packets that are designated as Best Effort type of service packets can be given an alternate DSCP value. The QoS Packet Scheduler inserts the adjusted DSCP value into the IP header of the packets. Enabling this setting allows you to change the default DSCP value associated with the Best Effort service type. If this setting is disabled, then the default value of 0 is used.

Controlled Load Service Type   Packets that are designated as Controlled Load service type packets can be given an alternate DSCP value. The QoS Packet Scheduler inserts the adjusted DSCP value into the IP header of the packets. Enabling this setting allows you to change the default DSCP value associated with the Controlled Load service type. If this setting is disabled, then the default value of 0 is used.

Guaranteed Service Type   Guaranteed type of service packets are given alternate DSCP values using this setting. The QoS Packet Scheduler inserts the adjusted DSCP value into the IP header of the packets. Enabling this setting allows you to change the default DSCP value associated with the Guaranteed type of service. Disabling this setting causes the default value of 0 to be used.

Network Control Service Type   Network Control type of service packets can be given an alternate DSCP value using this setting. The QoS Packet Scheduler inserts the adjusted DSCP value into the IP header of the packets. Enabling this setting allows you to change the DSCP value associated with the Network Control type of service. Disable this setting, and the default value of 0 is used.

Qualitative Service Type   Network Control type of service packets can be given an alternate DSCP value using this setting. The QoS Packet Scheduler inserts the adjusted DSCP value into the IP header of the packets. Enabling this setting allows you to change the DSCP value associated with the Network Control type of service. Disabling this setting causes the default setting of 0 to be used.

Layer 2 Priority Value

The attributes in this section are used to manage the layer 2 priority values for the various types of packets. The QoS Packet Scheduler inserts the appropriate priority value in the layer 2 headers of the packets.

Nonconforming Packets   This setting establishes an alternate link layer value for packets not conforming to the flow specification (the other service types apply to packets that conform to the flow specifications). By enabling this setting, the default priority value of nonconforming packets is used. If this setting is disabled, then the default value of 1 is used.

Best Effort Service Type   This setting establishes an alternate link layer value for packets designated as Best Effort type of service to the flow specification. By enabling this setting, the default priority value of Best Effort packets is used. If this setting is disabled, then the default value of 0 is used.

Controlled Load Service Type   This setting establishes an alternate link layer value for packets designated as Controlled Load type of service to the flow specification. By enabling this setting, the default priority value of Controlled Load packets is used. If this setting is disabled, then the default value of 4 is used.

Guaranteed Service Type   This setting establishes an alternate link layer value for packets designated as Guaranteed type of service to the flow specification. By enabling this setting, the default priority value of Guaranteed packets is used. If this setting is disabled, then the default value of 5 is used.

Network Control Service Type   This setting establishes an alternate link layer value for packets designated as Network Control type of service to the flow specification. By enabling this setting, the default priority value of Network Control packets is used. If this setting is disabled, then the default value of 7 is used.

Qualitative Service Type   This setting establishes an alternate link layer value for packets designated as Qualitative type of service to the flow specification. By enabling this setting, the default priority value of nonconforming packets is used. If this setting is disabled, then the default value of 0 is used.

Monitoring QoS

To monitor your system's QoS, you can set up the System Monitor tool (PERFMON.EXE) and add TCP to the list of items you wish to monitor.

> **NOTE**   System Monitor (formerly known as Performance Monitor in Windows NT) is a very powerful tool that can be used to monitor hundreds of system events. System Monitor is explained in more detail in Chapter 17.

Once the System Monitor is started, as shown in Figure 15-6, you add *performance objects* by clicking the + (plus) sign from the row of icons shown in the right-hand windowpane. The resulting dialog box is shown in Figure 15-7.

If your Windows XP Professional client is connected to a Windows 2000 server, or to another server using RSVP for QoS, the following performance objects can be added to System Monitor:

- RSVP interfaces
- RSVP service

These objects track such RSVP-based issues as the following:

- Failed QoS sends
- Failed QoS resends
- QoS clients
- QoS-enabled senders
- QoS-enabled receivers
- RSVP sessions
- RESV-ERR messages sent
- RESV-ERR messages received
- RESV-TEAR messages sent

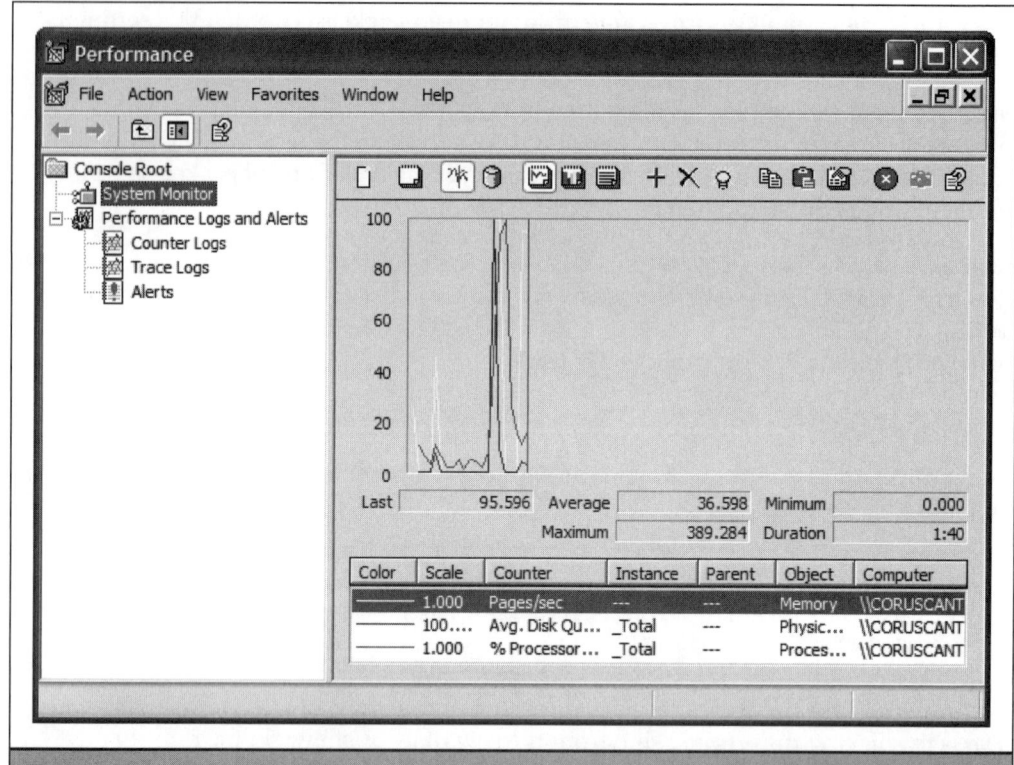

Figure 15-6. The System Monitor tool

- RESV-TEAR messages received
- Signaling bytes sent
- Signaling bytes received

When using Windows XP Professional's DiffServ-based QoS mechanism, the following performance objects can be added to your System Monitor:

- Segments received/sec
- Segments retransmitted/sec
- Segments/sec
- Segments sent/sec

In addition, the Internet Control Message Protocol (ICMP) and User Datagram Protocol (UDP) object counters can be useful for more detailed TCP/IP network monitoring. The ICMP performance object includes counters that measure the rates at which ICMP messages are sent and received using the ICMP protocol. Furthermore, it also includes counters that monitor ICMP protocol errors.

Figure 15-7. Adding a performance object

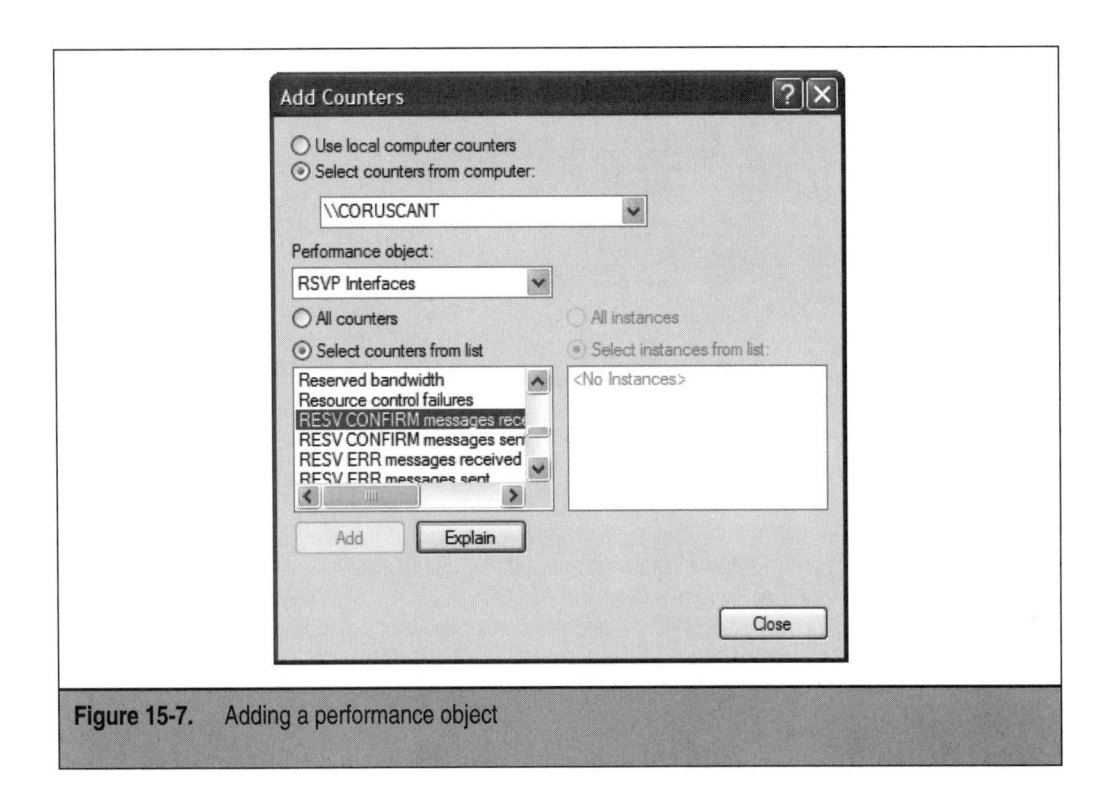

The UDP performance object consists of counters that measure the rate at which UDP datagrams are sent and received using UDP. It includes counters for measuring UDP errors.

NOTE For more information on setting up and using System Monitor, flip ahead to Chapter 17.

QoS can be a lofty concept to wrap one's brain around. Hopefully, its usefulness and necessity has been made apparent in this chapter. Happily, Microsoft has opted to forgo RSVP QoS for Windows XP Professional and has, instead, decided to utilize DiffServ-based QoS. This decision takes QoS from a notional concept to something you can practically deploy in your Windows XP Professional network.

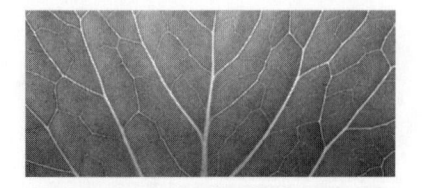

CHAPTER 16

Interconnectivity with Other Systems

Networks tend to be heterogeneous environments. That is, even though most of your client computers are Windows machines that probably connect with other Windows servers, there may also be servers running other operating systems to which your clients might need to connect. Two of the most prevalent operating systems are Novell NetWare and UNIX.

This chapter examines how you can connect your Windows XP Professional clients to other systems. Because Windows XP Professional is used on network clients, we'll examine various network designs using Windows XP Professional, along with scenarios in which Windows XP Professional will connect with Windows 2000 Server, or a UNIX or NetWare server.

NETWARE CONNECTIONS

Windows XP Professional comes with built-in tools to connect with Novell NetWare resources. The first tool we will discuss is the Client Service for NetWare (CSNW). This allows Windows XP Professional clients to access NetWare servers and is a good mechanism for small environments or scenarios in which Windows XP Professional–NetWare connectivity is frequent.

Another tool that provides Windows-NetWare interoperability is located on a Windows 2000/.NET Server and is called Gateway Service for NetWare (GSNW). This tool acts as an intermediary between the Windows XP Professional client and your NetWare servers.

Client Service for NetWare

To access NetWare resources, Microsoft includes a tool called Client Service for NetWare with Windows XP Professional. This service allows you to access file and print resources on NetWare servers that are running Novell Directory Services (NDS), NetWare 3.x, 4.x, or bindery security from your Windows XP Professional client.

> **NOTE** CSNW does not support the IP protocol that is present in NetWare 5.x and later. To connect with CSNW, the IPX protocol must be loaded onto the NetWare 5.x server.

CSNW does not support the Internet Protocol (IP) and cannot be used to access NetWare in an IP-only environment. As such, you must install the Internetwork Packet Exchange (IPX) protocol to communicate with NetWare servers. To install the IPX/SPX protocol, follow these steps:

1. Open Network Connections.
2. Right-click the desired local area connection, and then click Properties.
3. Click the General tab, and then click Install.
4. The Select Network Component Type dialog box appears. Click Protocol, and then click Add.

5. In the Select Network Protocol dialog box, as shown in Figure 16-1, click NWLink IPX/SPX/NetBIOS Compatible Transport Protocol, and then click OK.

Once the proper protocols have been installed, you can install the CSNW tool. This is accomplished by following these steps:

1. Open Network Connections.
2. Right-click the desired local area connection on which you wish to use Client Service for NetWare, and then click Properties.
3. Click the General tab and then click Install.
4. The Select Network Component Type dialog box appears. Click Client, and then click Add.
5. In the Select Network Client dialog box (as shown in Figure 16-2), click Client Service for NetWare, and then click OK.

Once the NWLink IPX/SPX/NetBIOS Compatible Transport Protocol has been installed, you must configure it. This is accomplished by following these steps:

1. Open Network Connections.
2. Right-click the desired LAN, and then click Properties.
3. Click the General tab, click NWLink IPX/SPX/NetBIOS Compatible Transport Protocol, and then click Properties. The resulting screen is shown in Figure 16-3.

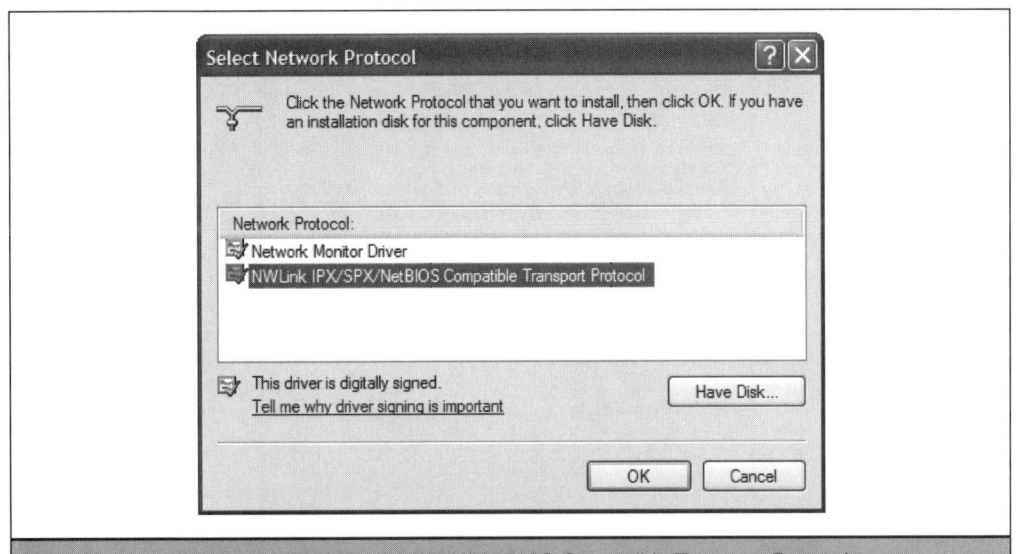

Figure 16-1. Installing the NWLink IPX/SPX/NetBIOS Compatible Transport Protocol

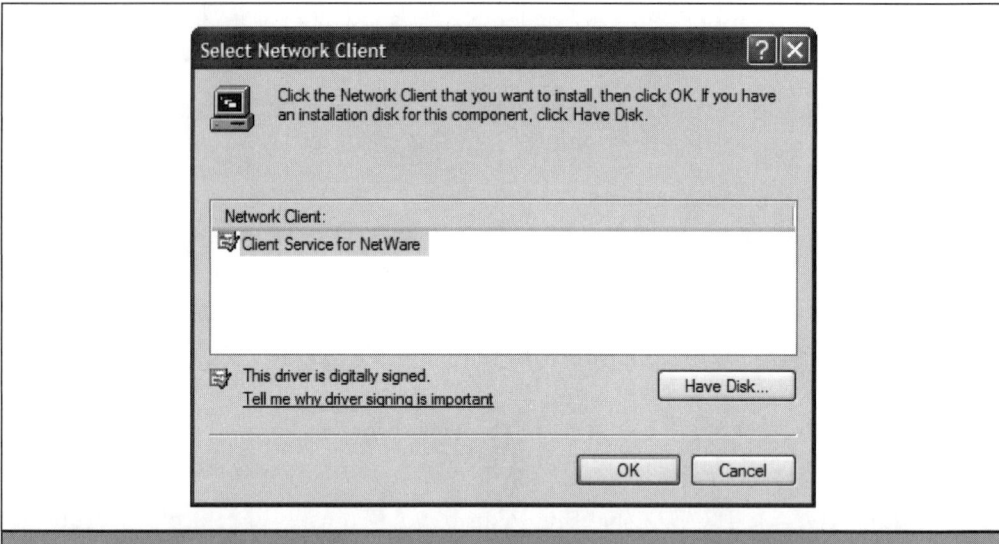

Figure 16-2. Installing the Client Service for NetWare tool

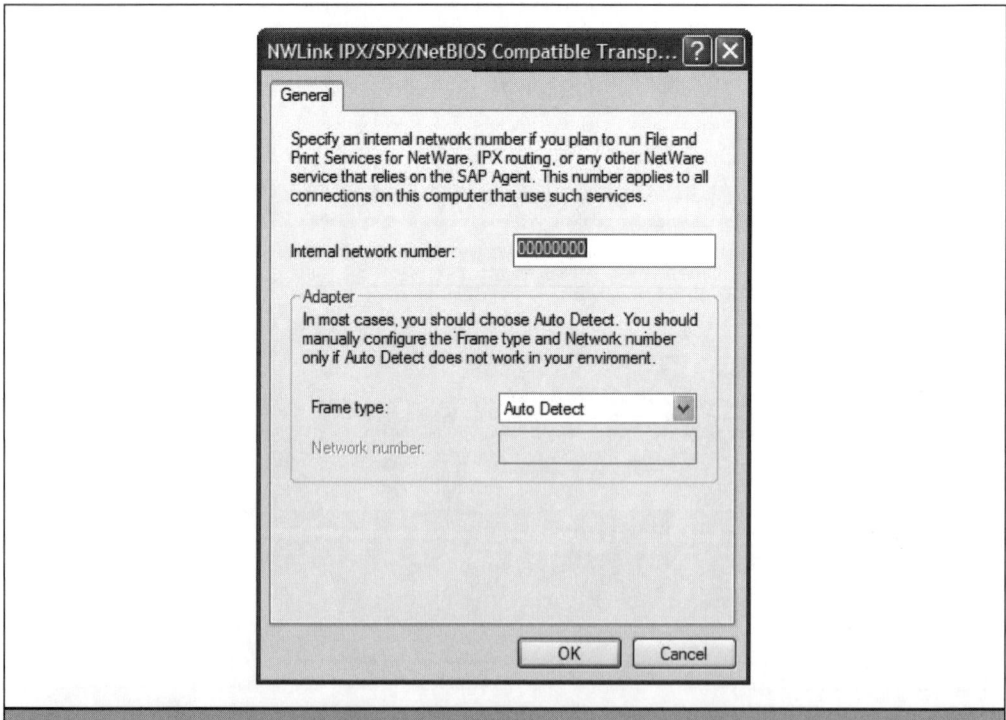

Figure 16-3. Configuring the CSNW tool

4. Enter a value for Internal network number, or leave this value at the default of 00000000.
5. Next, you must establish the *frame type* of this connection. This can be done automatically by clicking Auto Detect and clicking OK, or by clicking a frame type, entering a network number, and then clicking OK.
6. Click OK to save your settings.

Gateway Service for NetWare

Earlier in this chapter, we examined the CSNW tool for Windows XP Professional (actually, it comes with all implementations of Windows, not just Windows XP Professional). However, depending on your network and organization's need, you might find it better *not* to install CSNW on all your clients, but rather to set up a gateway. A gateway (as we will explore with other tools) serves as an intermediary between your organization's clients and your NetWare servers, as shown in Figure 16-4. CSNW would not likely be selected for implementation in an organization where the more elaborate server tools are available.

> **NOTE** When connecting to NetWare resources, use CSNW for frequent access and GSNW for less frequent access. If you use GSNW to provide a gateway to NetWare resources, you do not have to install NWLink IPX/SPX/NetBIOS Compatible Transport Protocol on clients or enable IPX on your networking gear.

The following sections discuss the NetWare integration tools available in Windows 2000, which can be used in conjunction with Windows XP Professional clients. Before getting to these tools, it's important to note that you should be sure to stay abreast of any patches released by both Novell and Microsoft. These patches will ensure enhanced connectivity and performance and are therefore important, especially in mixed environments.

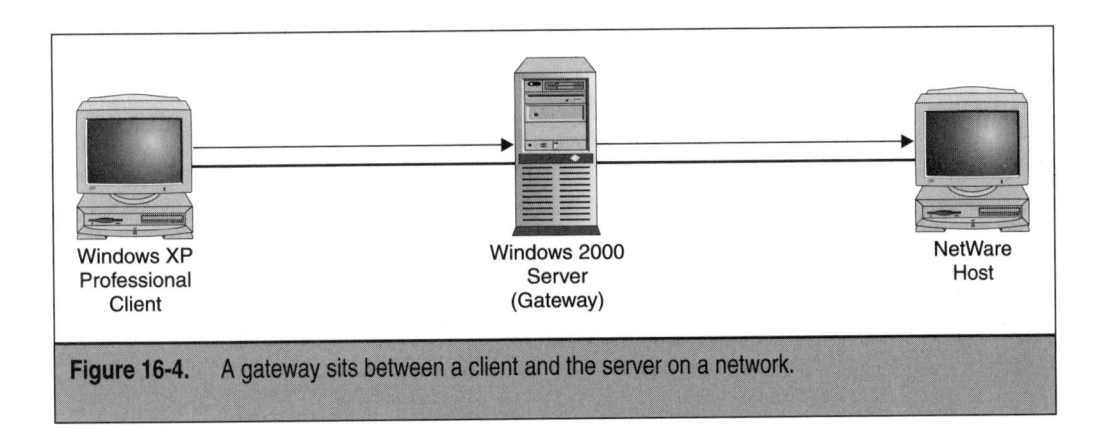

Figure 16-4. A gateway sits between a client and the server on a network.

Windows 2000 Gateway Services for NetWare

Windows 2000 includes GSNW, enabling Windows 2000 Servers to connect with computers running NetWare 3.*x* and 4.*x*. GSNW can be used by administrators to provide a gateway between client computers (like Windows XP Professional) and file and printer resources. These features are all implemented on the Windows 2000 Server, and no changes need to be made on the NetWare server or the Windows XP Professional clients.

Creating a Gateway   To create a gateway on Windows 2000, you must meet a few requirements. First, your NetWare server must have a group named NTGATEWAY. Second, you must have a user account on both the NetWare network and the NTGATEWAY group, along with the necessary rights to access it.

To install Gateway Service for NetWare, follow these steps:

1. Open Network and Dial-up Connections by selecting Start | Settings | Network and Dial-up Connections.
2. Right-click a local area connection, and then click Properties.
3. On the General tab, click Install.
4. In the Select Network Component Type dialog box, click Client, and then click Add.
5. In the Select Network Client dialog box, click Gateway (and Client) Services for NetWare, and then click OK.

Enabling Gateway Services   Once Gateway Services are installed into Windows 2000, they must be enabled. This is accomplished by following these steps:

1. Open Gateway Service for NetWare by selecting Start | Settings | Control Panel and double-clicking GSNW.
2. Click Gateway, and then select the Enable Gateway box.
3. In Gateway Account, type the name of your gateway account.
4. In Password and Confirm Password, enter the gateway account password.

Activating Printer and File Gateways

In order to access NetWare files and printers, a gateway to each volume or printer must be activated. The process of gateway activation establishes the resource and share for the Windows XP Professional clients' use.

Activating a Gateway to Files   To activate a gateway file, do the following:

1. Open Gateway Service for NetWare by selecting Start | Settings | Control Panel and double-clicking GSNW.

2. Select Gateway, and then choose the Enable Gateway box.
3. Click Add. In Share Name, enter the share name clients will use to access the resource.
4. In Network Path, enter the network path of the NetWare directory you want to share.
5. In Use Drive, enter the drive your want to use as a default.
6. Click Unlimited, and then click OK.

Activating a Gateway to Printers   To activate a gateway to printers, do the following:

1. Open Printers by selecting Start | Settings | Printers.
2. Select Add Printer, and then click Next.
3. Select Network Printer, and then click Next.
4. Under Name, enter the name of the printer in this format:

   `\\servername\sharename`

5. If you need to find the NetWare printer in Shared Printers, click Next.
6. Follow the resulting instructions in the wizard to complete the process.
7. Select the printer you just created and, under the File menu, click Properties.
8. On the Sharing tab, select Shared. In Shared as, enter a name for the printer.

Setting Permissions for NetWare Resources

You can manage the availability of your network's NetWare resources once GSNW has been installed and activated by establishing and managing the resource's permissions. On your Windows 2000 Server, permissions for GSNW are managed by following these steps:

1. Open Gateway Service for NetWare by selecting Start | Settings | Control Panel and double-clicking GSNW.
2. Select Gateway.
3. Click the share on which you want to set permissions, and then click Permissions.
4. To add users or groups, click Add. In Names, select the user or group, and then select Add. In Type of Access, click the permission for this user or group.
5. To remove users or groups, select the user or group in the list of allowed users, and then click Remove.
6. To change permissions for users or groups, select the user or group, and then select the level of access in Type of Access.

Accessing NetWare Resources

Once installed, the CSNW is used to access resources located on a NetWare server. There are two ways in which you can access your NetWare resources—either via the Windows interface or via the command prompt.

Windows Interface

Accessing NetWare resources from a CSNW-enabled Windows XP Professional computer is just like locating a resource on a Windows network. Essentially, it's a simple matter of pointing and clicking. To connect to a NetWare resource using a Windows graphical user interface, follow these steps:

1. Open My Network Places.
2. You then do one of the following:
   - Double-click NetWare or Compatible Network.
   - Double-click Entire Network, and then double-click NetWare or Compatible Network.

   This will display the Novell Directory Services tree or trees from which you can pick.
3. Double-click your selected tree or volume. Next, double-click the resulting contents to further drill down and see other computers and volumes.

Ultimately, when you find the folder or volume that you wish to access, double-click to expand it. If you want to map a local drive to the volume or folder, click the volume or folder, and then under the Tools menu, click Map Network Drive. This will invoke the Map Network Drive Wizard (shown in Figure 16-5), the use of which is explained in Chapter 11.

Command Prompt

If you prefer to use the command prompts, there are a number of ways to manage NetWare resources from a Windows XP Professional client. The following are various commands and usages to access and manage NetWare resources.

Accessing a NetWare Volume   Most tasks make use of the NET USE command. If you wish to access a specific NetWare volume, for instance, you would enter:

```
net use drive: [UNCname|NetWareName]
```

To use the Universal Naming Convention (UNC) format to redirect drive H to a directory named \plans\getoffisland off the Minnow volume on the Castaways server, you'd enter:

```
net use H: \\castaways\minnow\plans\getoffisland
```

Figure 16-5. Mapping a NetWare resource

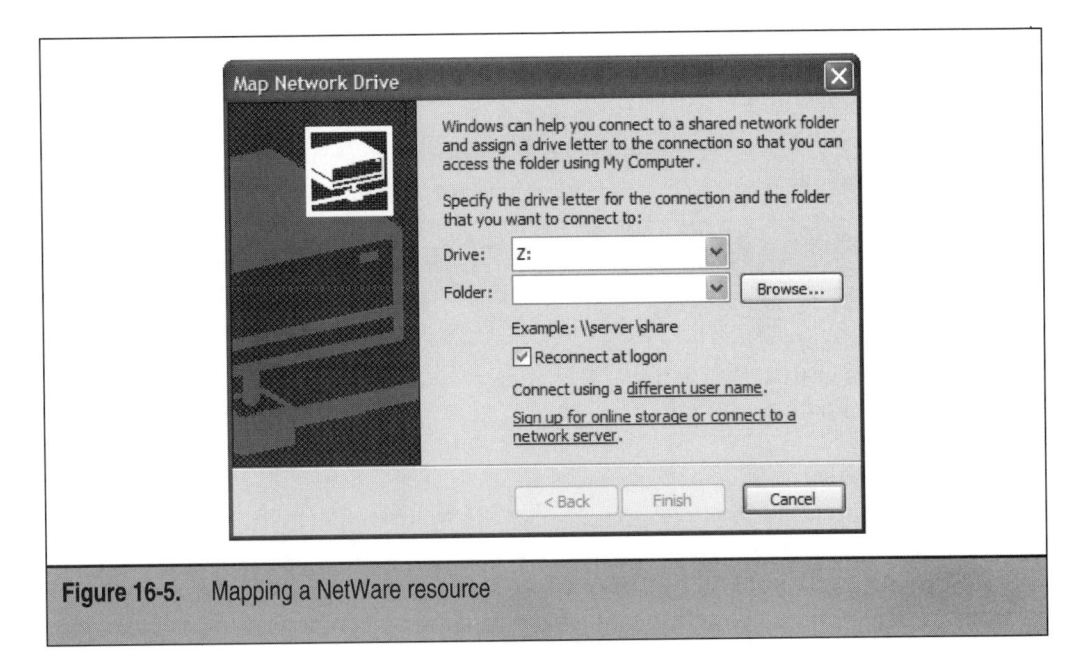

Login Depending on the NetWare server's security settings, it might be necessary to enter your username and password to access a shared resource. To log into a NetWare server from the command prompt, you enter your username and password by entering:

`/user: UserName Password`

This command can be used in conjunction with other commands to provide access to protected resources. For example, if user Gilligan with the password littlebuddy needs to log onto a directory named \plans\getoffisland off the Minnow volume on the Castaways server on drive H, he'd enter:

`net use H: \\castaways\minnow\plans\getoffisland /user:gilligan littlebuddy`

Connecting to an NDS Tree Connecting to an NDS tree using a Windows XP Professional client is accomplished using the following command:

`net use drive: \\TreeName\volume.OrgName.OrgName [/u:UserName.OrgName.OrgName [password]]`

Table 16-1 lists the components of the login command.

Displaying NetWare Servers To display the NetWare servers your Windows XP Professional client can access, use the following command:

`net view /network:nw`

Component	Description
TreeName	Name of the tree
OrgName	Tree location to which you wish to connect
UserName.OrgName.OrgName	The user name and context of this tree

Table 16-1. Components of the NDS Tree Connection Command

Displaying Volumes on a NetWare Server To display the volumes on a particular NetWare server, use the following command:

```
net view \\NWServerName /network:nw
```

Displaying the Contents of a Directory To display the contents of a given directory, use the following command:

```
dir \\DirectoryPath
```

Displaying the Contents of a NetWare Server Using NDS To view the contents of a NetWare server that is using NDS, you must enclose the directory path in quotation marks. For example:

```
dir "\\NDStree\volume.unit.group"
```

Printing

Once your Windows XP Professional client is connected to a NetWare server, connecting to a printer connected to a NetWare server is done by following the same steps you would use when connecting to a printer connected to a Windows server. The simplest way is to start the Add a New Printer Wizard.

Alternately, you can use the command line to perform various printing tasks.

Redirecting Port Output to a Print Queue

To redirect output from a port to a print queue, use the following command:

```
net use ServerName \\PrintQueue
```

For instance, to redirect output from your LPT1 port to a NetWare print queue named Printing on the GroupA server, you'd enter:

```
net use lpt1 \\groupa\printing
```

Sending Files Not Requiring Formatting to LPT1

If you have files to print that do not need to be formatted (that is, they do not have any special fonts, spacing, or layout needs), first redirect the output with the NET USE command (as explained in the section "Redirecting Port Output to a Print Queue"), and then, at the command prompt, enter:

copy *FileName ServerName*

Copying a File to a Print Queue

If you want to copy a file to a print queue, first you must redirect the output with the NET USE command, and then, at the command prompt, enter:

copy *FileName* *PrintQueue*

Connecting to a Printer in an NDS Tree

To connect to a printer that is connected to an NDS tree, the command is similar to the process of accessing any resource located on an NDS tree. Specifically, use the NET USE command as follows:

net use drive: *TreeName**printer.OrgName.OrgName*
[/u:*UserName.OrgName.OrgName* [*password*]]

Table 16-2 lists the components of the connection command.

LINUX/UNIX CONNECTIONS

The first half of this chapter examined NetWare connections that are made possible using the CSNW and GCNW tools included with Windows XP Professional and Windows 2000 Server. However, for Windows XP Professional–UNIX connections, Microsoft does not include a tool as part of Windows. Rather, to use Microsoft's solution, you must purchase it as an add-on. In order to provide interoperability between Windows XP Professional and UNIX environments, Microsoft uses the Services for UNIX 3.0 tool.

Microsoft and UNIX use two different protocols for client access to files and printers. Windows XP Professional uses the Common Internet File System (CIFS) protocol for file and print services, whereas UNIX predominantly uses the Network File System (NFS) protocol for file services and the Line Printer (LPR)/Line Printer Daemon (LPD) protocol for print services.

Component	Description
TreeName	Name of the tree
OrgName	Tree location to which you wish to connect
UserName.OrgName.OrgName	The username and context of this tree

Table 16-2. Components of the NDS Tree Printer Connection Command

Services for UNIX 3.0

Windows Services for UNIX (SFU) 3.0 is a tool that allows Windows XP Professional to interoperate with Solaris 2.7, HP-UX 11, AIX 4.3.3, and Red Hat Linux 7.0 (the tool has been specifically designed for these platforms, but Microsoft says it will work with other major UNIX platforms and versions). SFU provides a number of cross-platform services that allow Windows clients to be integrated into an existing UNIX environment.

> **NOTE** An evaluation version of SFU 3.0 can be ordered from Microsoft by going to http://www.microsoft.com/windows/sfu/productinfo/trial/default.asp.

Interix

Prior versions of SFU had to be used in tandem with an application called Interix. Interix allows you to run UNIX-based applications and scripts on Windows XP Professional and Windows 2000 Server. In SFU 3.0, however, Microsoft has merged the two tools. This is the single biggest change to SFU 3.0, as it includes not only the Interix subsystem, but also its slate of more than 300 tools and the Interix software development kit. The Interix subsystem technology provides an environment in which both Windows and UNIX applications can be run on a single system. Interix runs on top of the Windows kernel, enabling UNIX applications and scripts to run natively on the Windows platform alongside Windows applications. The Interix subsystem and utilities replace the earlier Korn Shell and utilities that were part of previous incarnations of SFU. Figure 16-6 shows an example of the Interix tool.

The Interix subsystem is a fully integrated POSIX subsystem that runs natively under Windows XP Professional and 2000. This subsystem provides the necessary support for compiling and running UNIX applications in Windows.

Interix provides both the Korn Shell and C Shell, which behave exactly as they do in a UNIX environment. An advantage SFU 3.0's version of Interix has over earlier versions is that both shells use a single rooted file system. That is, it is no longer necessary to convert scripts to support drive letter syntax. This change makes it easier to port scripts from UNIX to Windows XP Professional because there is a single rooted file system, as in UNIX, and the colon character retains its UNIX meaning as a field separator.

Another feature of this version of Interix is that it is much more user friendly than previous versions. For example, in earlier versions of Interix, case sensitivity was strictly enforced. This made scripting difficult if the writer did not know the precise case of the Windows utility. This has been changed in SFU 3.0, along with the need to add extensions to executable programs.

System Requirements

Table 16-3 lists the minimum system requirements needed for SFU 3.0.

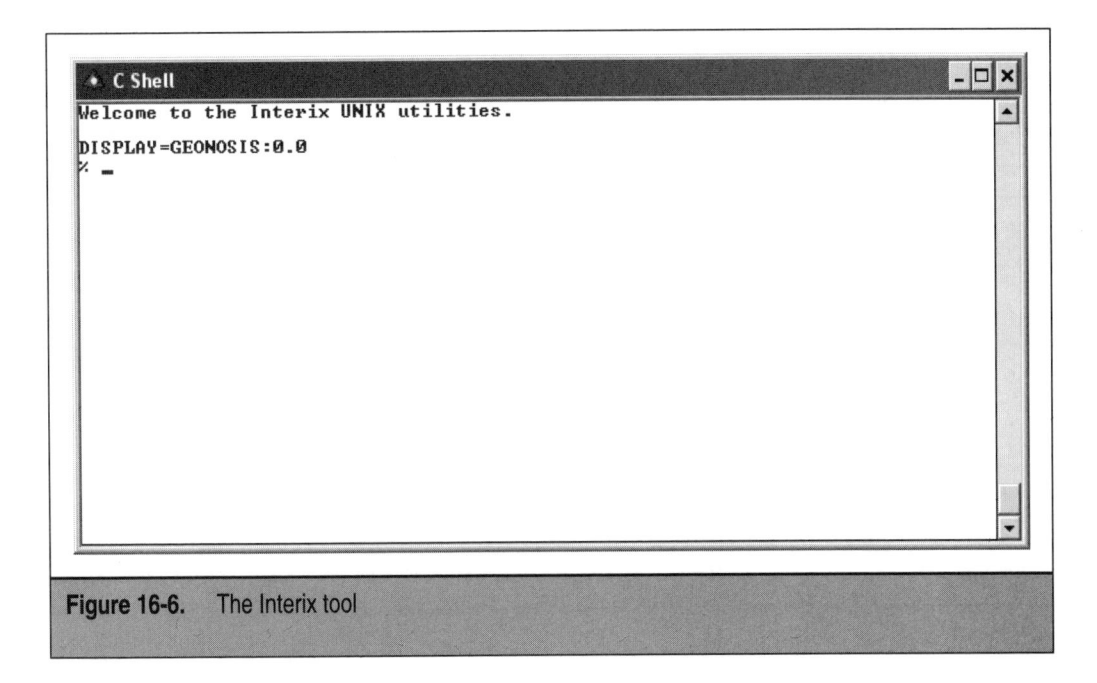

Figure 16-6. The Interix tool

Network File System Components

SFU 3.0 utilizes three Network File System components:

- Client for NFS
- Server for NFS
- Gateway for NFS

In the latest release of SFU 3.0, all have additional enhancements, primarily as they relate to performance and internationalization.

Component	Minimum Requirement
Memory	16MB RAM
Hard drive space	184MB
Browser	Internet Explorer 5 or later
Other components	Network adapter and CD-ROM drive

Table 16-3. Minimum requirements for SFU 3.0

> **NOTE** The three NFS components support Korean and Chinese character sets.

Client for NFS Client for NFS allows Windows computers to act as clients to gain file access on an NFS server. To implement the Client for NFS component, it needs to be installed on each Windows XP Professional system that needs access to NFS files.

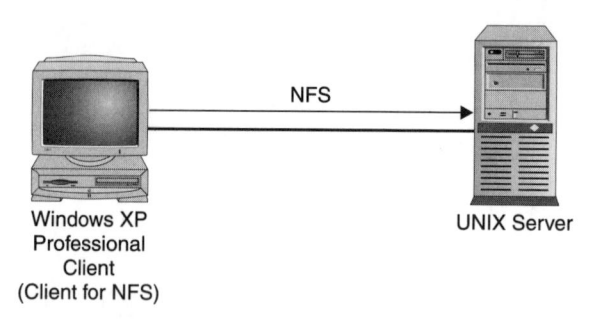

```
Windows XP              NFS           UNIX Server
Professional    ───────────────────▶
Client
(Client for NFS)
```

In SFU 3.0, changes in the Client for NFS make the client faster and more efficient in mixed environments. Improvements include the following:

- Ability to set setuid/gid/sticky bits
- Ability to create symbolic links
- Support for mount and file system traversal syntax, which is expected by UNIX users

Client for NFS improves performance by directory caching at the client, providing a faster machine. Figure 16-7 shows an example of the SFU 3.0 Client for NFS.

Server for NFS Server for NFS allows a Windows computer to serve as an NFS server. Computers running NFS client software (Windows or UNIX systems) can access files on the NFS server. To implement the Server for NFS component, it must be installed on your Windows XP Professional computer.

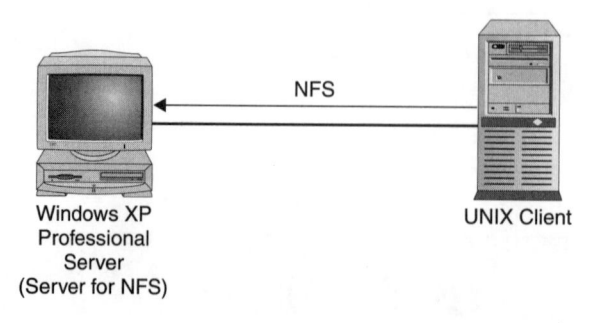

```
Windows XP              NFS           UNIX Client
Professional    ◀───────────────────
Server
(Server for NFS)
```

The Server for NFS portion of SFU 3.0 has also been improved by enhancing the performance of individual servers and by making Server for NFS cluster aware.

Figure 16-7. SFU 3.0 Client for NFS

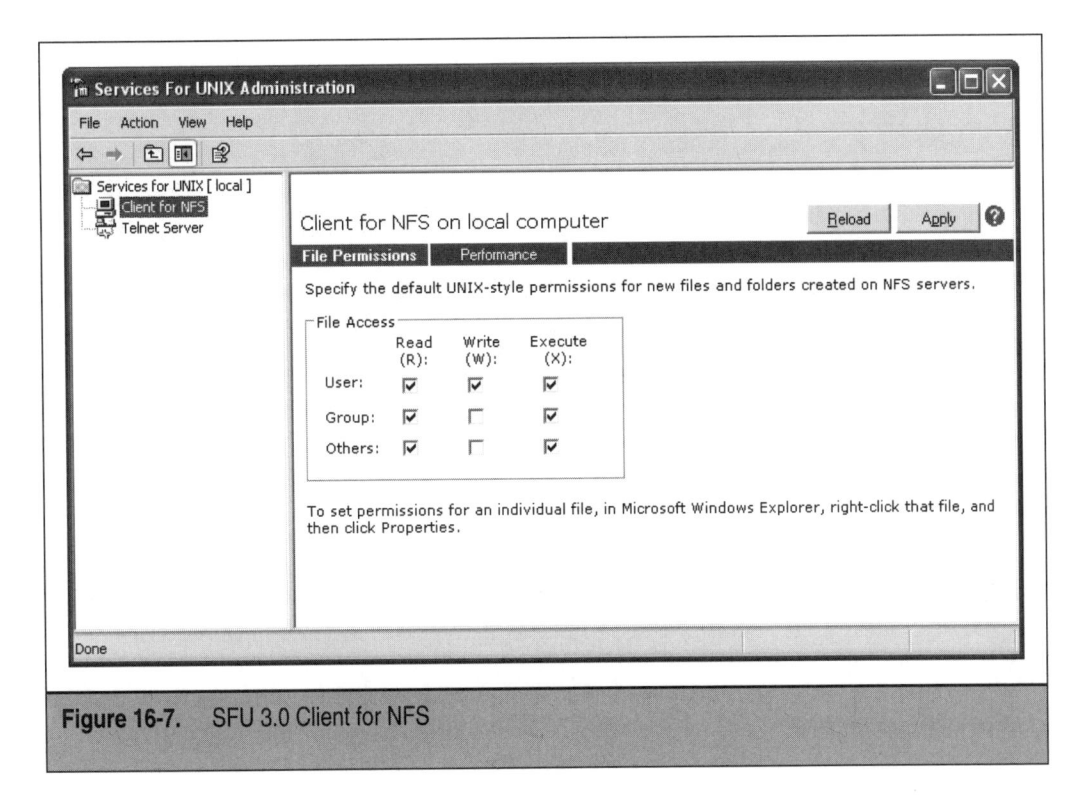

Security is also enhanced, because translation of Windows 2000 permissions into UNIX or NFS shares has been improved, maintaining consistency with the security models present in Windows 2000 and .NET Servers.

Gateway for NFS Finally, Gateway for NFS allows a Windows XP Professional computer to act as a gateway through which Windows computers *without* NFS client software can access NFS file and print resources. The gateway acts as an intermediary between the Windows Server Message Block (SMB) protocol and the UNIX NFS protocol. The translation process is slower using Gateway for NFS than using Client for NFS. If frequent access to an NFS resource is needed, then it is best to use Client for NFS than to go through Gateway for NFS.

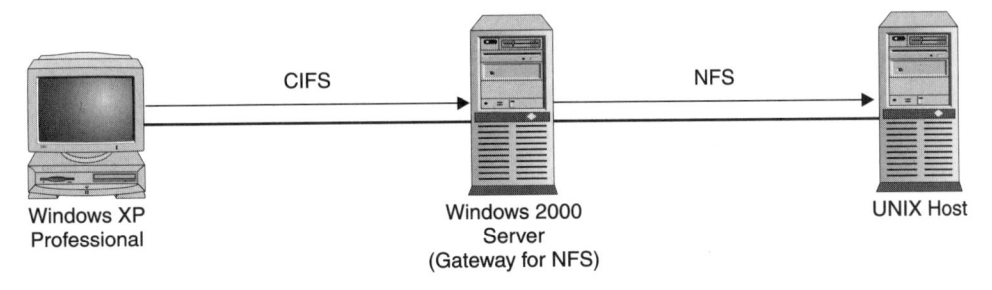

In SFU 3.0, Gateway for NFS also shows improvements, including better command-line and GUI administrative controls, international character set support, and clustering support improvements.

SAMBA

Microsoft's Services for UNIX 3.0 isn't such a bad deal—it sells for US$99. However, if the thought of shelling out any money to connect your UNIX devices with your Windows network makes you cringe, SAMBA is another solution, and the price is right—it's free.

The SAMBA server package is a very popular means of providing Windows clients with access to UNIX resources. This freeware runs on UNIX servers and provides Windows clients access to UNIX resources. Don't let the thought of using freebie software in your organization be a turnoff. SAMBA has been in existence for quite a while and has been widely used in both academic environments (where it was developed) and several large corporate sites.

SAMBA is built on the Server Message Block (SMB) protocol that Windows uses for file sharing. SAMBA creates UNIX support for the SMB protocol. When SMB requests are sent out from Windows XP Professional clients, the SAMBA daemon becomes a server, responding to those requests.

It's important to note that SAMBA is installed and maintained entirely on UNIX systems—there is no additional software installed on the Windows XP Professional client. Though this makes the Windows portion of set up much easier, a UNIX system administrator must install the SAMBA server. Also, given the seemingly endless versions of UNIX out there, it's good to know that SAMBA is compatible with all major versions of UNIX (such as products from Apollo, HP, DEC, NeXT, SCO, Sun, and SGI, among others).

NOTE For more information about SAMBA, visit its web site at http://samba.anu.edu.au/samba/.

Windows Network Client Requirements

Although there are no SAMBA client files that must be installed in Windows XP Professional machines, these computers must have appropriate network protocols and services installed and running to be able to connect to the UNIX machines that they will gain access to. These required elements are the TCP/IP protocol suite and DNS services.

NOTE If DNS is unavailable, the UNIX machine's DNS names and IP addresses can be placed in the HOSTS file located in the %Systemroot%\System32\drivers\etc directory.

UNIX Configuration

On the UNIX machine, configuration is established in the SMB.CONF file. This is a text file that looks a lot like a Windows SYSTEM.INI file, and carries the same basic structure.

The file is subdivided into different sections, each of which handles the individual shares that will be created to handle such tasks as setting valid users, read-write privileges, and public access. The following is an example of a SMB.CONF file:

```
[global]
workgroup = ACCOUNTING
server string = Accounting Department's SAMBA Server
encrypt passwords = True
security = user
smb passwd file = /etc/smbpasswd
log file = /var/log/samba/log.%m
socket options = IPTOS_LOWDELAY TCP_NODELAY
domain master = Yes
local master = Yes
preferred master = Yes
os level = 65
dns proxy = No
name resolve order = lmhosts host bcast
bind interfaces only = True
interfaces = eth0 192.168.1.1

hosts deny = ALL
hosts allow = 192.168.1.4 127.0.0.1
debug level = 1
create mask = 0644
directory mask = 0755
level2 oplocks = True
read raw = no
write cache size = 262144

[homes]
comment = Home Directories
browseable = no
read only = no
invalid users = root bin daemon nobody named sys tty disk mem kmem users

[tmp]
comment = Temporary File Space
path = /tmp
read only = No
valid users = admin
invalid users = root bin daemon nobody named sys tty disk mem kmem users
```

There are two sections of the file that are very important for use in an organization with a large number of clients. The [homes] section automatically allows users that already have accounts on the UNIX system to connect to their home directories without the need to create individual shares for every account. The [global] section establishes several inclusive properties of the server. The most important are the security options that determine the method of user authentication. There are three security modes that can be specified in the [global] section under the security= entries:

- **Security=share** The valid users entry in each share section can specify specific users and their privileges within that share. This is a relatively insecure method and is limited to users who already have UNIX accounts, so it is a poor method for general access for Windows network users within the enterprise.

- **Security=user** In this mode, all authentication occurs via the UNIX user accounts. In those cases where all Windows network clients also have accounts on the UNIX system, this is a secure and efficient system. For those enterprises that already have UNIX accounts for every user of the network, this is a viable option.

- **Security=server** This mode is the clear choice when all users do not have or should not have UNIX accounts. In this mode, user access is authenticated through a server other than the UNIX SAMBA server—for example, a Windows 2000 DC. This could allow a single Windows machine to grant access to both Windows 2000 and SAMBA resources using a single database of usernames and passwords. It also has the great advantage of not requiring users to change their passwords on two different systems. When this entry is made in the [global] section, the name of the server that will perform the authentication must be added in the password server= entry.

NOTE This name will be the NetBIOS name of the server. For that machine to be found, it will have to be added to the /etc/hosts file on the UNIX system.

A drawback to SAMBA is that it is only useful if your clients use SMB protocols. This will include Windows 9X, 2000, XP, and NT, but not NetWare or Macintosh clients.

NFS Servers

A different approach to Windows-UNIX file access is called NFS and was developed by Sun Microsystems, Inc. NFS differs from other cross-platform tools in that it does not use the SMB protocols and instead relies on two different means to provide file access:

- **Remote procedure calls (RPC)** Used between the server and clients; function at the session level

- **External Data Representation (XDR)** The protocol that actually handles the data transfer

The end result—whether using SAMBA or NFS—is largely transparent to the end user. It's all the same—UNIX resources are browseable, and data can be read from or written to UNIX resources (assuming the correct permissions are in place). The difference is in the placement of the translation application.

XP Client Configuration

In a SAMBA deployment, you'll remember, client software is not needed. NFS, on the other hand, requires client software to be installed that will provide file sharing services. This is because RPC and XDR protocols are not part of the Windows platform, as is SMB.

Installing NFS client software can also be advantageous, in that it opens a gateway to other operating systems. For example, NFS for the Macintosh exists, and there is an NFS Gateway for NetWare. The long and the short of this is that more platforms have NFS support than SAMBA support.

On the NFS client, authentication is handled on the Windows XP Professional computer via a login window that takes a username and password that is checked against the UNIX accounts database. If the logon is authenticated, then a series of UNIX resource *mounts* can be accomplished (normally, these mounts are preconfigured by the user). This is similar to the "Reconnect At Logon" option for network drives in Windows XP Professional networking. If new resources are sought, the username and password that were entered at logon will be checked against the user permissions for the shared resource. The mounted NFS resource will appear as a new drive letter in the File Manager or Explorer, as with any Windows share.

The NFS daemon on a UNIX system might stop operating. When this occurs, the Windows XP Professional client will be unable to view files on the UNIX system, but it is not always clear that the failure to connect is due to a problem at the client or the server. It used to be that a failure of the NFS daemon would hang the client if it requested resources, but this is not always the case in recent versions of the NFS client software. When connections cannot be made, you need to be sure that the NFS daemon is running and that the resources have been exported by the server, as discussed in the next section.

UNIX Configuration

In one important way, NFS is quite like SAMBA in that there is less work to be done by the system administrator. This is because NFS is the standard method of file transfer used on UNIX systems. To share UNIX resources, the UNIX administrator must configure the resources to be shared. This process should be given considerable thought because it is easy to produce a chaotic NFS organization, prone to frequent failures.

Most UNIX systems are planned so that the NFS server comes online when the UNIX machine is booted, so long as the server has been configured to provide *exports*. These are the resources physically located on one or more computers that are placed into the /etc/exports file.

The general steps to make a UNIX resource available involve creating the correct entries in the /etc/exports file. Once that is done, the resources are made available by invoking the command that activates the exports (the exact form will vary across UNIX systems). The contents of the /etc/exports file include the pathname of the resource to be shared and can also include information regarding access privileges (such as read-only or which workstations are permitted access).

Given the mix of operating systems in play in most modern organizations, it's important for a mechanism to exist to allow connectivity to resources maintained on different machines. Happily, Microsoft has seen fit to include such a mechanism for NetWare resources and—at additional cost—has another tool for UNIX connectivity. If you need to connect to UNIX resources, however, it might not be a bad idea to investigate SAMBA or NFS to see if either is a tool that would fit into your organization.

CHAPTER 17

Monitoring XP Network Performance

Once your Windows XP Professional network is up, running, and configured properly, you might think your work is over. Don't exhale in relief too quickly. Now that everything has been set up and configured, you must start the ongoing task of maintaining and tuning your network, while planning for the inevitable future expansion that will come sooner than you might expect.

This last chapter helps you maintain and tune your Windows XP Professional network, and allows you to get ready for expansion. To address these topics, this chapter first covers an overview of network performance, including some general tips for keeping everything running smoothly. Next, we'll talk about an extremely useful tool included with Windows XP Professional called System Monitor. System Monitor keeps tabs on thousands of processes that go on with your Windows XP Professional computer and network. From there, we'll get you ready to think about the future of your network with a discussion of capacity planning. Finally, we'll offer some third-party tools that might be helpful for your organization's maintenance and tuning needs.

NETWORK PERFORMANCE OVERVIEW

Ensuring your network is optimized for peak performance is a battle to be fought on many fronts. It isn't simply a matter of fine-tuning your hardware, nor is software alone where fingers should be pointed because of a slow network. Instead, performance is an issue of balancing network hardware and software, in addition to managing your organization's use of the network.

Network performance management is a lot like owning a race car. If you want to win races (or at least *finish*), in addition to a fast car, you also need a skilled driver and a pit crew that can do its job well. Without any one of these attributes, your racing team won't even be able to win a sponsorship from Uncle Elmo's Mule Rentals, let alone compete with other racers. The same is true of Windows XP Professional networks. You can have the best networking equipment available, but if it is misconfigured, or users are abusing it, you might as well have bought your gear out of the back of some shady character's van.

Concepts

The bulk of this chapter will focus on tools and techniques you can use to optimize and monitor your system's performance. However, there are a few basics to keep in mind when designing, tweaking, and maintaining your network.

Know Your Network

First, it's important to have an accurate diagram and documentation of your network. This includes the most current topology diagrams and detailed information about the network equipment, its configuration, protocols in use, IP addresses, wide area network (WAN) links, servers, and user local area network (LAN) segments. Without this information encompassing the entire network, it will be hard to know what needs to be changed or what has changed from one network configuration to the next.

Baseline Your Network

When you start making changes to your network, it's necessary to know—and be able to quantify—what kind of performance you are currently experiencing. *Baselining* is the process of recording your network's performance so that when changes are made, you'll be able to determine if those changes were for the better, for the worse, or had no impact at all. You can baseline your network using a tool such as System Monitor (which we'll explain later, in the section "System Monitor"). Then, when you collect all the pertinent information, you can build a picture of your network's capacity.

Simplify Your Efforts

When you tune your network, make sure you're making changes that are reasonable and fall into understandable parameters. Especially within organizations that have hundreds or thousands of computers, there will be many people involved in the process of maintenance and tuning. If you make bizarre changes to the network, not only do you run the risk of screwing up the network, but you also have the potential to affect the work others are doing. Also, make sure that you keep good documentation of the changes you're making.

Maintain a Flat Topology

As larger networks evolve, resist the temptation to hang hubs off of hubs and add additional routers that hang off of user LAN network segments, for example. This nesting of network components creates single points of failure that may not be well documented and are likely to be difficult to manage. You also increase the likelihood that you and others will spend additional time troubleshooting and leave yourself less time to spend planning for the future needs and requirements of your users. There are also security issues associated with allowing "seat of the pants" engineering on the network. An undocumented router hanging off of a remote part of the network can be a wide-open door to unauthorized individuals.

Reduce Administrative Traffic

In Windows XP Professional, the Internet Protocol (IP) is the protocol of choice. As we've examined in earlier chapters, IP is the most popular networking protocol, used by most computer platforms these days. As such, you should endeavor to stick to this one protocol. Naturally, if you're interconnecting different kinds of computers (old Novell NetWare, or IBM mainframes, for instance), multiple protocols might be unavoidable. However, do your best to keep the number of protocols in play to a minimum. Furthermore, keep an eye on so-called *administrative* traffic, such as WINS replication, domain name system (DNS) zone transfers, and other server-to-server types of traffic. This will allow you to find traffic patterns that you can adjust as you see fit. For instance, if your servers are synchronizing with each other every half hour and the network is congested, maybe changing settings so that synchronization occurs once every hour or so is more effective for your network's needs.

Keep an Eye on the Users

Network congestion and other problems can often be tracked back to a user (or users) who is abusing the network. That is, the user is sucking up network resources for his or her own personal, nonbusiness purposes. Especially with the Internet being located on everyone's desktop, the opportunity for abuse is more prevalent than ever. Whether it's a user downloading MP3s during peak business hours or an online gaming server popping up on the network, the impact can be felt all across the network as packets are delayed due to this excess traffic burden. Managing users may be as simple as establishing a solid Internet access policy, or as stormtrooperish as setting up proxy servers or filters to restrict user access to the Internet.

Networking for a Better Network

The previous section suggested heavy-handed tactics to oppress your workers. However, this does not mean that the network administrator need be an ogre. By maintaining an open, communicative atmosphere between yourself and users, you can find out if there are performance issues with the network before something becomes a mission-critical problem.

Network Construction

Previously, we focused on some basic rules of thumb that are important for good network functionality. However, there should be no confusion—optimizing your network will largely be an issue of hardware and software configuration. This section focuses on the specific hardware issues that you need to keep in mind when constructing or, more likely, expanding your Windows XP Professional network. Additionally, we'll discuss some strategies to help improve network performance, including network segmentation and planning.

Most of the performance problems you'll encounter will come from four areas: your servers' memory, processor speeds, disk systems, and network systems. Network systems will be addressed later in the chapter, but an examination of the other three suspected performance culprits first is useful.

RAM

When checking system performance, the first place to check is to ensure your network servers have enough random access memory (RAM). Without enough memory, your system will be slow and sluggish. On a Windows 2000 Server, the *minimum* memory is 128 megabytes (MB) (Microsoft recommends 256MB). On a Windows XP Professional machine, the minimum memory is 64MB (Microsoft recommends 128MB). Generally speaking, however, you can't have too much memory. Especially in recent years, as RAM has dropped in price, this can be an easy, cost-effective way to improve network performance.

Processor

The next issue to consider when beefing up your network is your servers' processors. Are they powerful enough to get the job done? The minimum processor speed for a Windows XP Professional client is 233 megahertz (MHz), but at least 300 MHz is recommended. The minimum for a Windows 2000 Server is 133 MHz. However, this is just a minimum (you're not even going to find new servers running at 133 MHz)—you should have at least 700 MHz processors. This assumes you've got Windows 2000 Servers; if you have Windows NT (or even Windows for Workgroups, for that matter), your servers are probably chugging along with a microprocessor that has less juice than the latest handheld video game.

High-speed processors are very important, especially as the nature of networks changes. For instance, as bigger, beefier files are transferred around the network, and as the timing of packet delivery becomes more important, you need a fast processor.

Storage

When warehousing files in a mass storage environment, it's important that your servers can get at the necessary information as quickly as possible. You can run into problems if you've got your virtual memory jacked through the roof, such that the hard drive is spending an excessive amount of time on paging file swaps and it takes forever to access the resource. Of course, having enough RAM ameliorates the virtual memory problem, but it's also a good idea to have large enough hard drives that performance doesn't lack. Like memory, hard drives are inexpensive, so buy the biggest ones you can afford.

Additionally, you should make sure you have fast enough hard drive interfaces so that there isn't a bottleneck between the server and the hard drive. SCSI and FireWire drives are great hard drives to consider adding to your network. Prices for SCSI drives have come down a great deal and are extremely affordable. Connecting a FireWire drive couldn't be easier—you simply plug it into an open FireWire port and continue without having to shut down or restart your computer. Furthermore, you experience excellent performance because both SCSI and FireWire are very fast.

Network Segmentation

The easy, kill-a-fly-with-a-sledgehammer approach to increasing network performance is to spend a stack of money and kick your computers' resources up a million notches. That's certainly an option, but a more refined way to make things run smoothly is to think out your network and develop the most efficient, logical network possible. One key component of a well-designed network is *network segmentation*.

Segmentation separates your network into functional portions, increasing performance, security, and reliability. Segmentation is generally accomplished via a router or a switch. Before breaking your network into pieces, you should understand what types of traffic are coursing through your system and what paths they take. Finally, you should minimize the number of devices between the data's origination point and its destination.

Segmentation via Router

A common way to segment a network is to use routers and servers between a network's segments. This is so prevalent because it is an inexpensive and easy thing to do—all you really need to do is add a few network adapters, rather than redesign an entire network.

Consider the network shown in Figure 17-1. This is a very simple, two-server network. Each server has two network adapters and two user segments. Even though this is a very basic design, its principles still apply to networks with hundreds of clients.

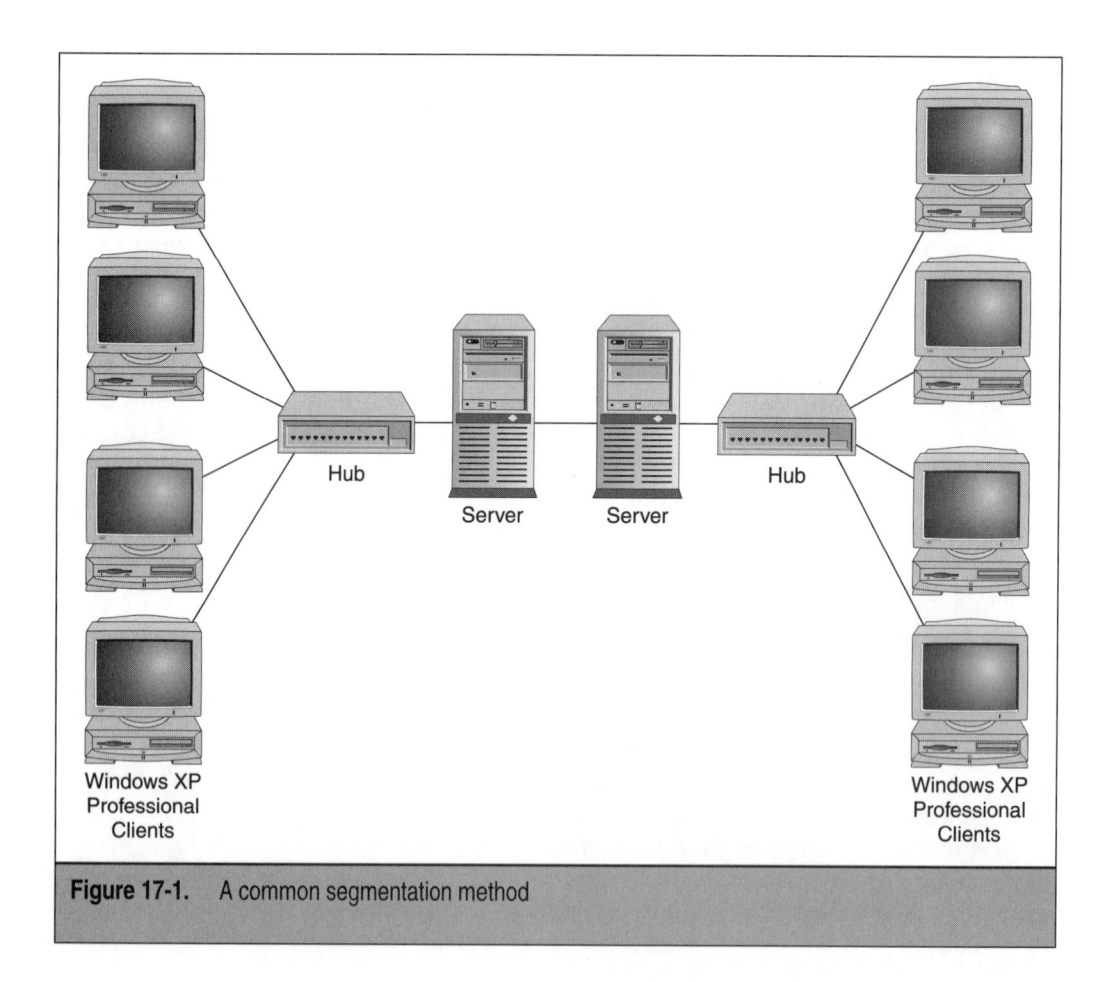

Figure 17-1. A common segmentation method

The problem with this design is that the servers have a performance burden. Not only must the servers provide resources to users, but they must also route data between the network segments. Furthermore, both servers must be available to all the clients in the organization as backup devices in case one or the other fails. These problems can be fixed, as shown in Figure 17-2, by locating a router between the two segments.

Each server will be located on the segment it will use most often. Also, because routers do not retransmit packets that don't need to pass through, traffic is lightened without adding any overhead to the servers. Redundancy is still present, and in the event one of the servers crashes, that segment's traffic can be redirected to the other server with little or no trouble.

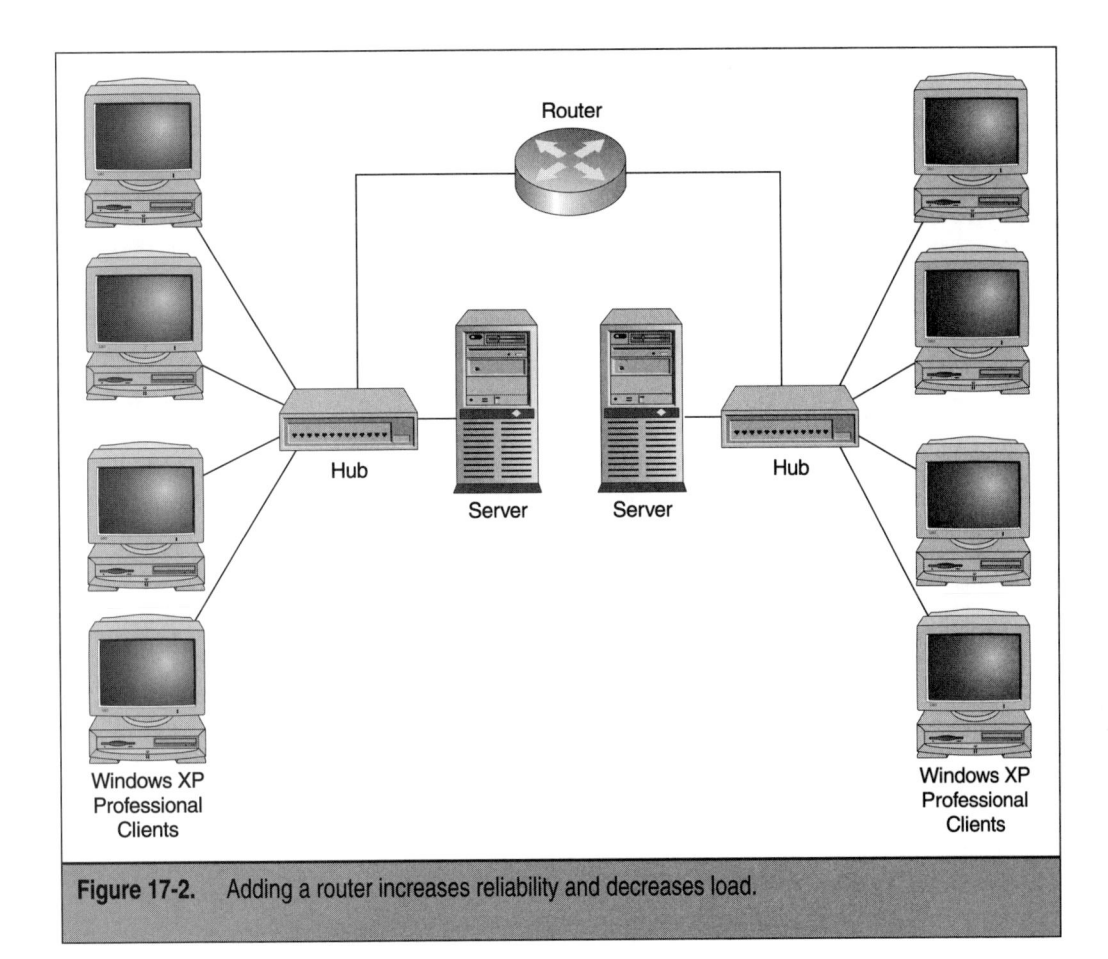

Figure 17-2. Adding a router increases reliability and decreases load.

Segmentation via Switch

Another way to segment your network is by using a switch. This method is similar to the aforementioned router method—that is, data is routed to the port where the destination device resides. The difference, however, is that switches work on a larger scale. To design a switching-based network, you should start with a switch positioned on your network's backbone. This switch will feed a layer of hubs and more switches. The advantage of a switched-based configuration is that security and performance are improved more than with any other segmentation plan. This configuration is becoming more popular, especially as (at the time of this writing) the price of switches continues to drop. However, it is still a more expensive option when per-port costs are considered.

To keep costs down somewhat, many organizations will connect hubs to the central switch, rather than connecting the central switch to another layer of switches. If you decide to pursue this option, there are a few ways in which you can improve network performance.

Position Devices Together That Communicate Most Often   Positioning devices that need to talk to each other most often is a smart way to keep excess traffic off your network proper. For example, if 80 percent of a given server's traffic comes from the production department, then it only makes sense to position that server on the same segment as the users. This will improve not only users' access to that server, but will reduce traffic on the central switch and will cut down the path along which the traffic must flow.

Switch Port Load Balancing   Conventional thought says 24 to 48 devices can run on the same 10 Mbps network segment. However, a better way to calculate the number of devices on each segment is to look at how much traffic and what kind of traffic each device generates. The production department, for instance, probably uses much more bandwidth than the accounting and administration departments. Rather than putting all three departments on one 24-port hub, buy two 12-port hubs—one for the high-traffic production department and one for the low-traffic accounting and administration departments. This design does little for the administration department but will do a lot for the production department's network performance.

Don't Overload Your Devices   One of the most useful reasons to employ switching-based segmentation is to reduce the bottlenecks in your network. On the other hand, if you don't spend a little time up front figuring out your network's design, you might wind up creating a slew of new bottlenecks. The network shown in Figure 17-3 illustrates how well-intended network segmentations can produce unfortunate results.

The switch shown in Figure 17-3 has 12 ports. Of those ports, 8 are connected to 10 Mbps hubs and 4 ports are connected to servers. During peak usage, clients on each of these hubs use between 2 and 3 Mbps of bandwidth. In total, this scenario results in between 16 and 24 Mbps of traffic, which is a bottleneck, moving straight to the servers that only have 10 Mbps links to the switch.

Figure 17-3. Too much traffic coming from a segment can choke your servers.

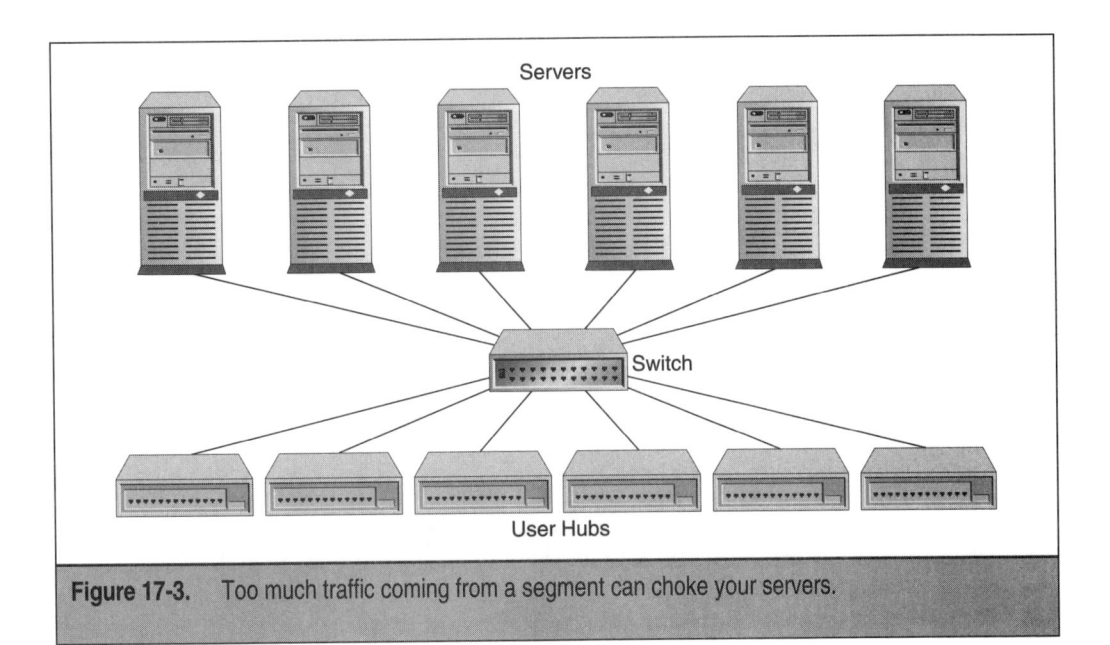

SYSTEM MONITOR

One of the most powerful tools that comes with Windows XP Professional is the System Monitor. This tool provides current, accurate information about thousands of different attributes of your Windows network. In this section, we will take a closer look at System Monitor, explain how to use it, and cover some essentials, including what you should monitor on your system.

Basics

A crucial part of performance and tuning is knowing what the problem is and, once you've made changes, how successful those changes have been. System Monitor is a tool that has been included since Windows NT. In Windows NT, however, the tool was called Performance Monitor. When Microsoft released Windows 2000 a couple of years ago, they renamed the tool System Monitor, but didn't change anything else about it except for its look, which fits in with the Microsoft Management Console (MMC) look that all system tools have. In fact, from the command line, System Monitor is started exactly the same way as Performance Monitor—you simply enter **perfmon** at the command prompt.

> **NOTE** System Monitor can also be added as a snap-in to your MMC.

System Monitor gathers information provided by various software components running on your system. Information comes from a broad range of sources, including the operating system, workstation and server hardware, peripherals, network interfaces, and other software services.

When System Monitor is first started (as shown in Figure 17-4), it is in an inactive state and is not monitoring anything. Don't be deceived by its meek appearance; System Monitor is a very powerful tool. The amount of information that System Monitor can access is impressive, to say the least. A little exploration using the tool can give you information about the state of your machine, helping you to find bottlenecks and tune for performance.

Views

System Monitor can best be understood if you think of it as an application with four distinct tools. These tools are known as *views*. Each of these views allows you to do such things as display, perform actions on, store, and generate reports on the data monitored by System Monitor. Table 17-1 explains these views in more detail.

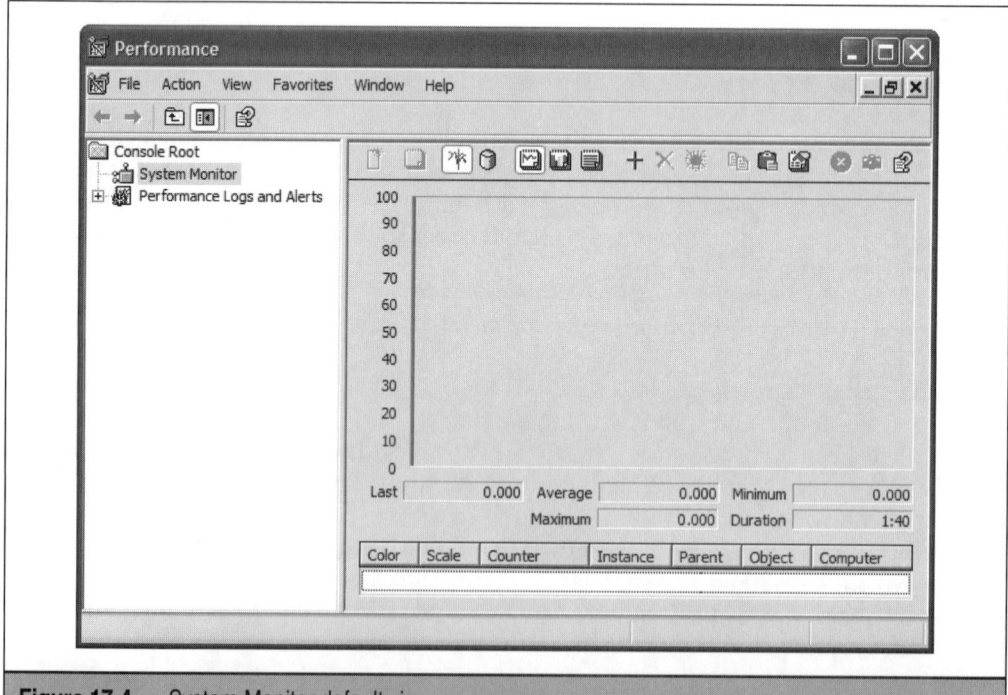

Figure 17-4. System Monitor default view

View	Description
Chart	Displays monitored system data as line graphs or histogram formats. These display options are referred to as *Gallery* settings
Alert	Allows you to create alert events based on counter thresholds. Alerts can be set to perform actions according to when a counter exceeds or drops below user-specified values. Actions include network user notification using the Alerter and Messenger services; they can also be set to execute an application as defined in the Run Program on Alert box in the Alert Entry and Add to Alert windows
Log	Allows you to create or open an existing log file and write object data to the file. You can use the log to create reports in the Report view. You can also export the log in .tsv and .csv text formats (tab- or comma-separated values) for use in applications such as Microsoft Excel
Report	Allows you to list objects and their associated counter data in a report using values derived from current activity or from a log file

Table 17-1. System Monitor Views

All these views read information about local and remote systems. The information is organized into computers, objects, instances, and counters:

- **Computers** Local or remote machines on which there are many objects. This allows you to view system performance on multiple computers with System Monitor.

- **Objects** A physical, logical, or software component associated with a particular computer. For instance, an object could be the processor or an FTP server. Each object may have more than one instance and may contain a number of counters relevant to the object.

- **Instances (of an object)** The attribute to be measured and tracked by System Monitor. Instances can be created for each physical, logical, or software component. For example, if there are two physical disks in the computer, there are two *instances* of the physical disk object. When objects and their associated counters have multiple instances, you can monitor the counters associated with each individual instance separately. In some cases, you have the option of displaying counter data that is based on the total values of all instances.

- **Counters** The information that is defined for each instance of an object. For example, for Physical Disk, % Disk Read Time is the percentage of elapsed time that the selected disk drive was busy servicing read requests. Disk Transfers/sec is the rate of read and write operations on the disk. There may be many counters defined within an object.

Figure 17-5. The drop-down object list

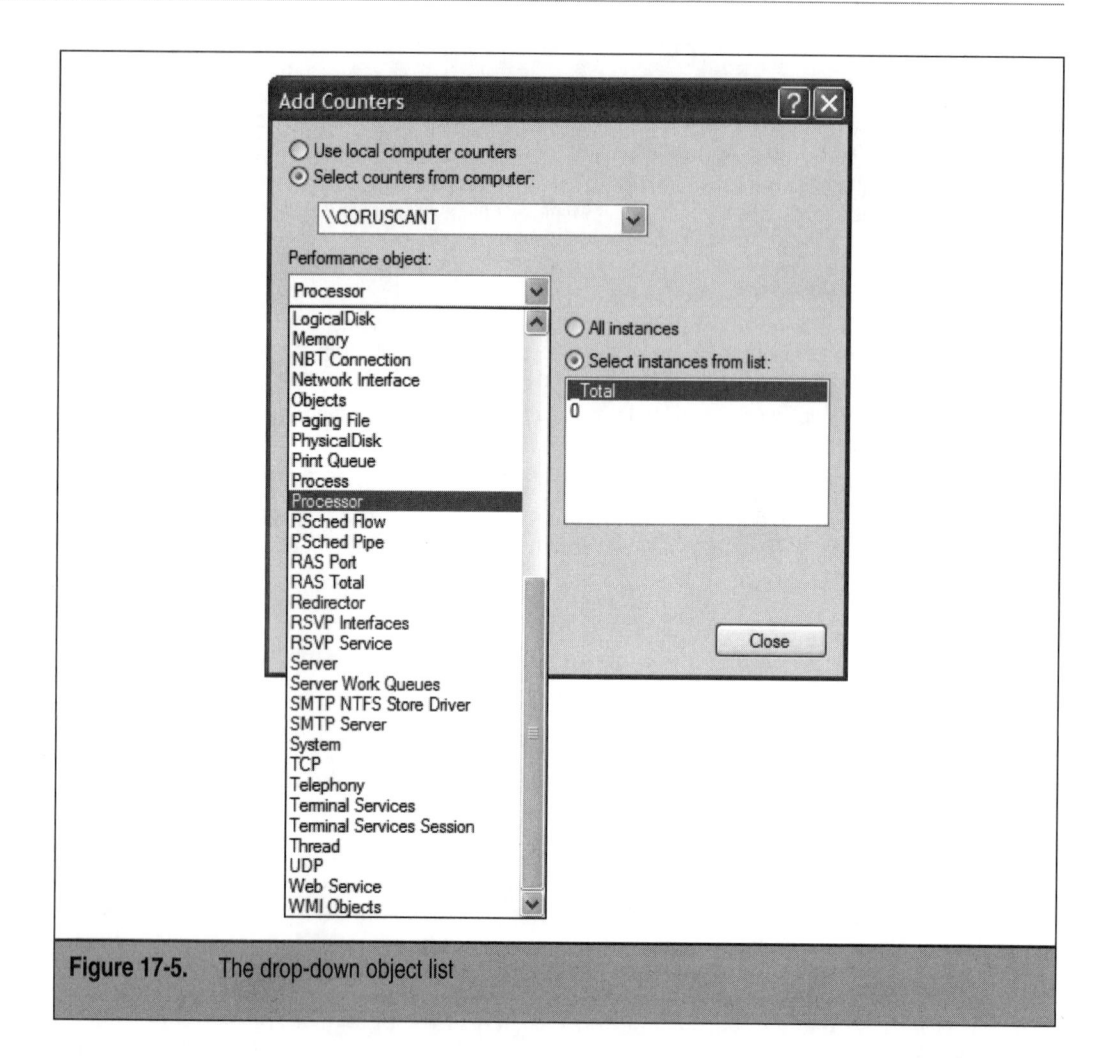

Computers, objects, and counters can be viewed in any of the four ways you wish when selecting the counters you wish to monitor. Once you've selected a computer, you will see a list of objects available to be monitored on that computer. Figure 17-5 shows part of the drop-down object list for the computer CORUSCANT.

The list of objects in System Monitor isn't set in stone. Rather, it is a dynamic environment that can add or remove objects depending on your system's configuration. Some are added manually, some are listed by default. If you want to know more about

Object	Function/Description
Cache	File system memory cache information including cache hits
LogicalDisk	Logical drive information including disk read/write times, transfer rates, and free space measured in megabytes
Memory	Physical memory information, including committed bytes in use and page reads/writes
Objects	Software objects that provide information about OS events, processes, semaphores, threads, and so on
PagingFile	Page file usage and usage peaks
PhysicalDisk	Physical disk information including disk read/write times, transfer rates, and disk queue length
Process	A software object that allows you to set counters to monitor the behavior of selected applications or the total of all running applications
Processor	Hardware processor information
Redirector	Network redirector information including bytes received/sent, connections, file reads/writes, packet data, and network errors
System	Counters that provide general system information including Registry quotas in use, total processor time, systems calls, and system uptime
Thread	Information about threads as a total or within a particular process

Table 17-2. Some Default System Monitor Objects

a certain object and its counter, click the Explain button for a brief clarification of the counter's function.

The default items are listed in Table 17-2.

The best way to understand System Monitor is to do some hands-on work and actually monitor something. First, let's create a chart that will display information about our Windows XP Professional client.

Chart View

In Figure 17-6, we have selected the Chart view and clicked Add on the toolbar to bring up the Add Counters dialog box. We then selected CORUSCANT and selected the highlighted Processor object. We kept the default %Processor Time Counter. Because CORUSCANT has only one processor, instance 0 is the only instance option available to us. If CORUSCANT had two processors, we could select between instances 0 and 1. Before clicking Add to add this counter to the chart, we clicked Explain to get a detailed description of the highlighted counter—%Processor Time.

Figure 17-6. Adding a counter to the chart

We added one more counter, this time Interrupts/sec, so we could get a look at the processor utilization and the number of interrupts on the same chart. After letting System Monitor run for a while, we had a comparison of the processor utilization and interrupts, as shown in Figure 17-7.

The view of the %Processor Time counters can be changed between a line graph and a histogram by clicking the line graph or histogram icons at the top of the System Monitor window, which makes changing the Chart Options a one-click process.

You can manage how your chart appears by right-clicking the chart and selecting Properties from the pop-up menu. Alternatively, you can click the icon shown here:

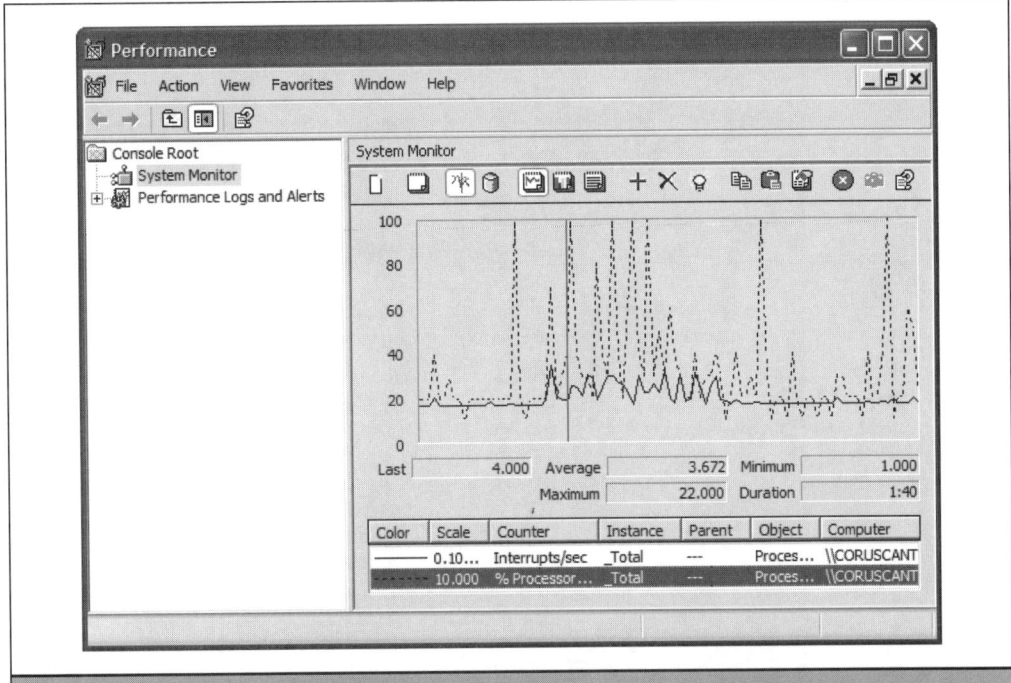

Figure 17-7. Chart view of %Processor Time counters

The System Monitor Properties dialog box (shown in Figure 17-8) allows you to select whether you want the Legend, Value bar, Grids, and Labels to be displayed. You can also define the Vertical Maximum number to be displayed on the left-hand side of the chart. Additionally, you can change the Update interval time or set it to Manual if you want to take attended readings.

As with the other views, Chart view can be set up for a wide variety of counters that can be read in real time or from previously saved log files. The uses for the Chart view range from quick performance spot-checks to long-term analysis of data. The information bar below the graphs provides Last, Average, Minimum, Maximum, and Duration data on the selected counter. When captured to a log file, this information is stored and can be read later.

Alert View

Alert view is helpful when you want to monitor specific counters but have better things to do than sit and stare at a graph all day. You can set thresholds and have System Monitor send you a message if the threshold either rises above or falls below a predefined value. For example, you might monitor the free space on a disk drive and have an alert sent if the free space falls below a specific value. You can also specify a

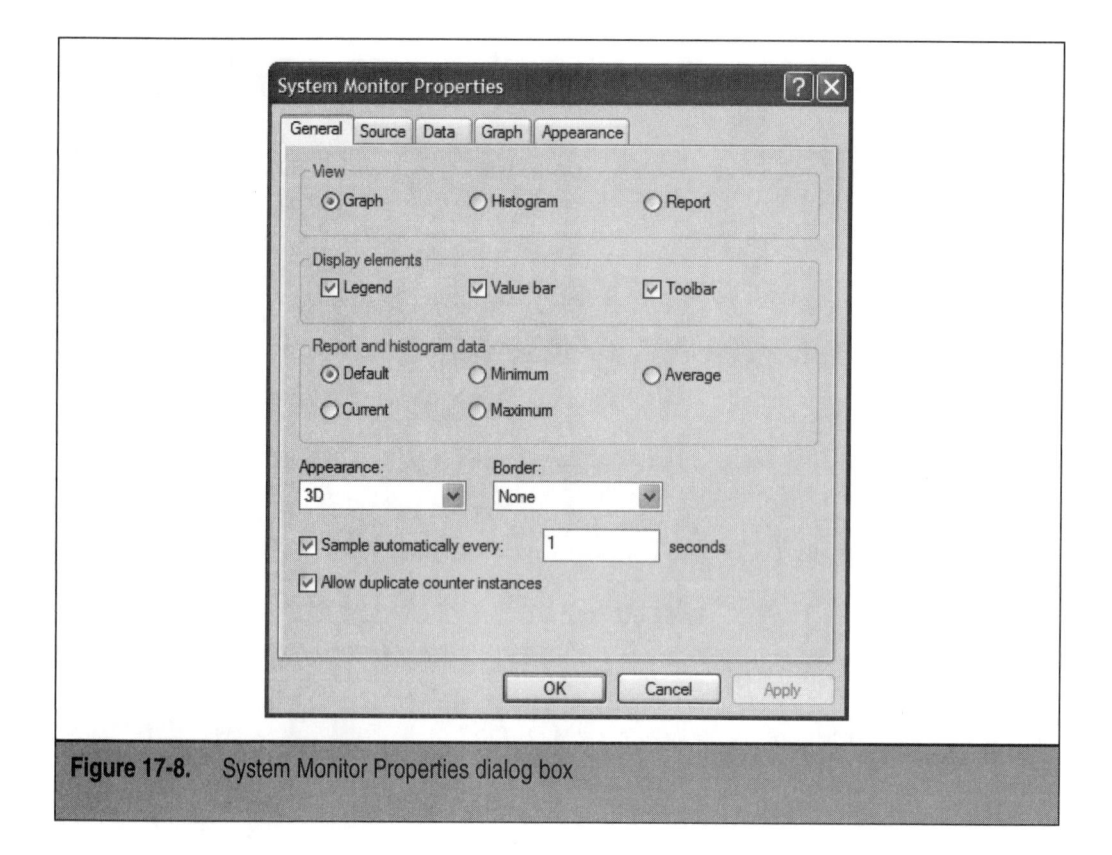

Figure 17-8. System Monitor Properties dialog box

command-line executable that will be run if the monitored counter falls above or below the predefined threshold.

Adding alert counters is done in the same way as it is in the Chart view. The Alert view is located in the left pane of the MMC while running the System Monitor snap-in. Right-click the Alert icon, and then select New Alert Settings from the pop-up menu.

Figure 17-9 shows the alert that we have set up. This MMC view shows a single alert; however, it can contain multiple alerts that can be customized and included for whatever your needs are. In the example shown in Figure 17-9, the included alerts are:

- Available bytes of RAM
- % Free Space on the hard drive
- TCP Segments Received/sec

[Figure 17-9 screenshot of Performance console showing the Alert view with Console Root > System Monitor, Performance Logs and Alerts (Counter Logs, Trace Logs, Alerts) in the left pane and an "Alerts - Various alerts" entry in the right pane.]

Figure 17-9. The Alert view

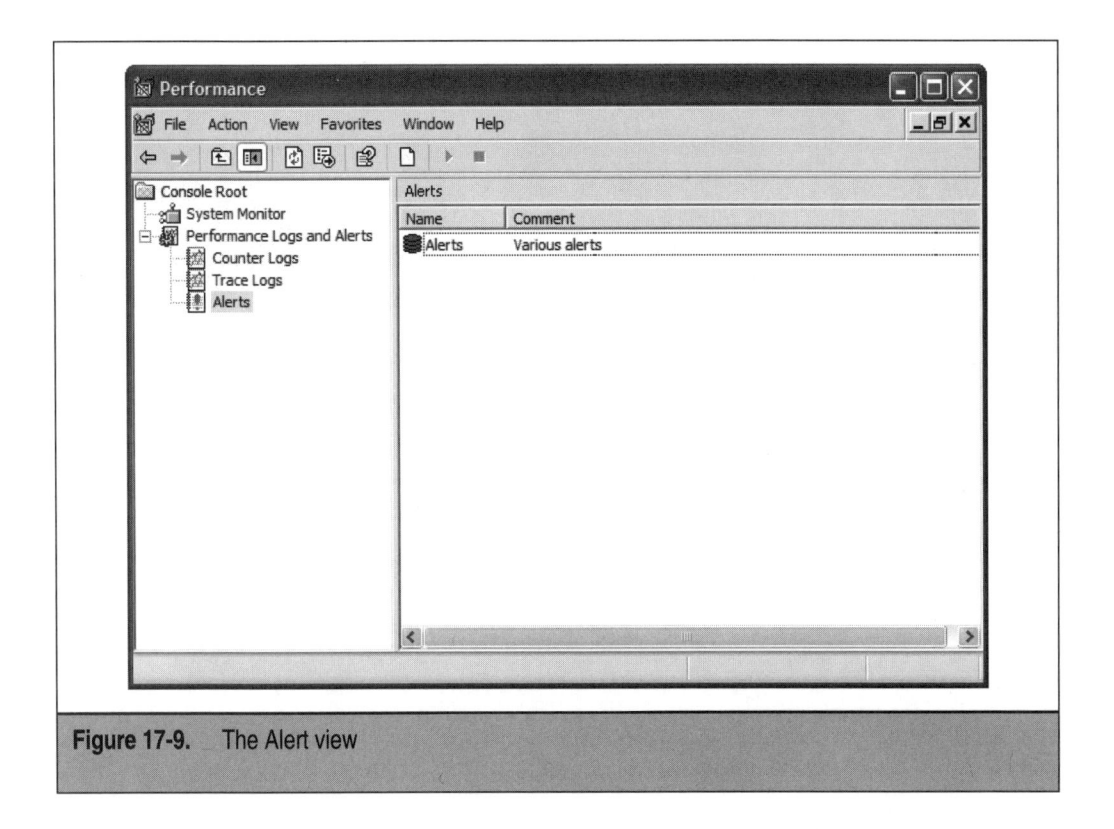

In order to have System Monitor send an alert message, it must be configured to do so. You should note that for the message to be delivered, the defined Net Name must be a registered NetBIOS name and the Alerter and Messenger services must be running. You can register a NetBIOS name at a specific computer such as "letmeknow" by entering **net name letmeknow /add** at the Windows XP Professional computer's command prompt. Once the name is registered, the alerts will be displayed on that computer.

The General, Action, and Schedule tabs within the Alerts Properties dialog box (shown in Figure 17-10) are used to define several settings, including having the following occur:

- Logging the alert event into the Application Log so that it can be read in the Event Viewer
- Sending a network message via the alert event to a specific network name listed in the Net Name dialog box
- Setting the Update Time to Manual Update or Periodic Update at a defined interval

Figure 17-10. The Alerts Properties dialog box

Log View

The third view is the Log view. This view allows you to sample data at predetermined intervals so you can review and analyze it later. The other views can then read the log file and perform their various functions as if the logged data were happening in real time.

For each selected object, the selected counters are written to the log. To write data to the log, you must add selected objects to the Log view. The Log view can be easily selected from a row of icons at the top of the window. The Log view icon looks like this:

Once you have added the objects you wish to log, open the Log Options dialog box, and then indicate the location of the log file, the name of the log file, and your update time settings.

NOTE Be careful when establishing the time interval—some objects can generate a huge amount of data for the log, and you might find yourself running out of hard drive space quickly.

Once these parameters are established, click OK. At this point, System Monitor will capture data for all displayed objects (as shown in Figure 17-11) and will allow you to monitor the log file size.

Report View

The Report view displays the same sort of counter information available in the Chart view. The difference between the two is that the Report view displays the information in a tabular format based on computer, objects, and counters. This view can be accessed by clicking this icon from the toolbar:

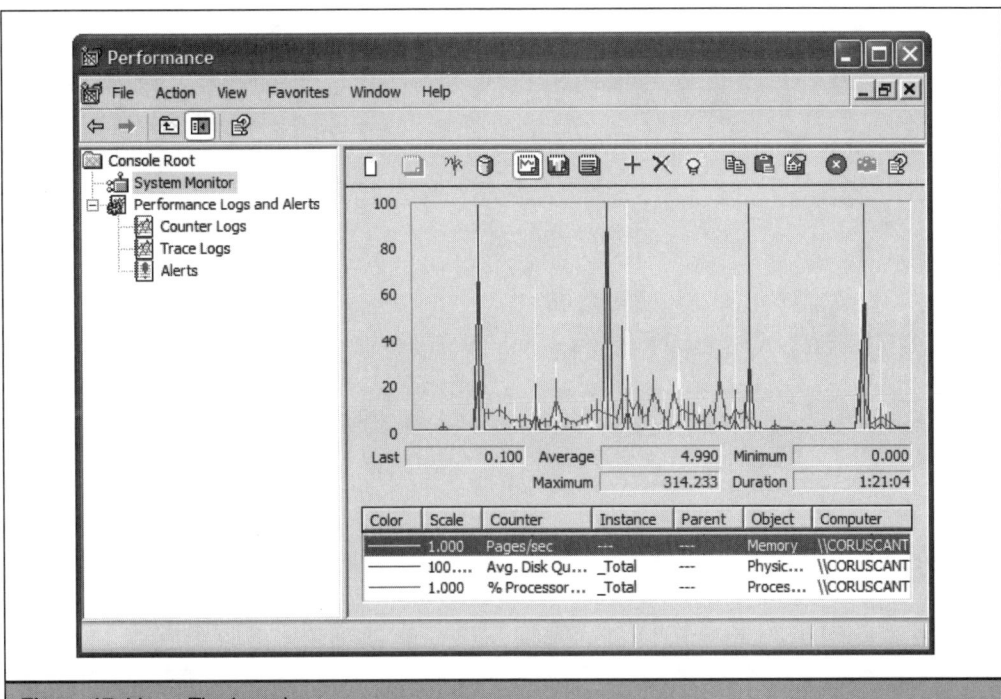

Figure 17-11. The Log view

The values are all aligned on the right-hand side of the report, with multiple instances shown in consecutive columns to the right. Figure 17-12 shows the Report view for a single computer.

System Monitor does not allow you to print your own reports from the application (which is too bad because it's all formatted nicely), but you can export the data to be viewed in another application, such as Excel. This allows you to print, manipulate, and manage the data as you see fit. Depending on your mastery of Excel, you can create some pretty attractive charts and graphs, or even display them on an intranet for in-house perusal.

What to Monitor

System Monitor can track thousands of bits of information. This powerful tool can track and report on nearly any statistic you can think of and hundreds more that would never have occurred to you. It's great that System Monitor allows you to keep an eye on so many statistics. The only problem, however, is that all the details System Monitor can track can quickly turn into information overload. You might have specific monitoring needs (like Quality of Service, or QoS, which we discussed in Chapter 15), but for the

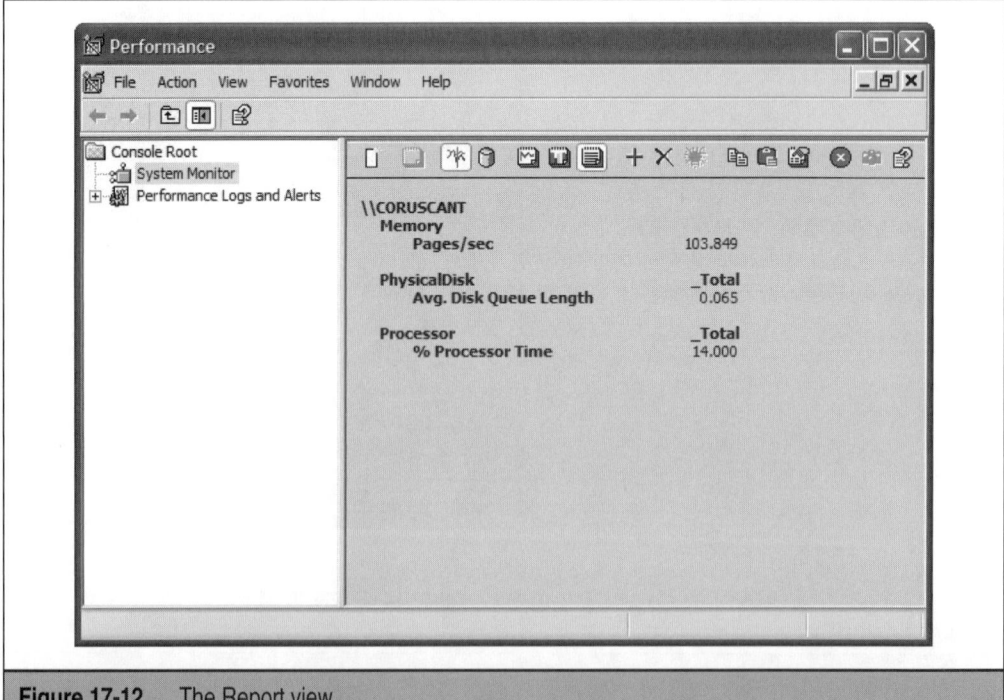

Figure 17-12. The Report view

most part, there are four key places you should monitor—the sites of the most common network bottlenecks:

- Memory
- Processor
- Disk subsystem
- Network subsystem

Additionally, you should keep an eye on resources that have a particular impact on your network. For example, let's say you've got a Windows XP Professional computer set up to handle print functions for your network. Because it handles printing, it is a good idea to monitor its duties. When you develop a monitoring scheme that includes the aforementioned areas, your computer's usefulness and performance will greatly increase.

RAM

The two most important memory counters you should keep an eye on are:

- Page Faults/sec
- Pages/sec

When used together, these counters can tell you if your system is configured with enough RAM. They do this by showing the amount of paging activity in your Windows XP Professional system.

Virtual memory is used to trick your computer into thinking that it has more RAM than it actually does. Virtual memory creates a *paging file* on the hard drive that serves as additional memory. Your applications have no idea that part of the available RAM is actually only available as a portion of the hard drive.

Page Faults/sec includes both hard and soft faults. An appropriate level will be much higher than that for the Pages/sec counter. Most systems can tolerate Page Faults/sec levels of about 250 before system performance takes a noticeable hit. Pages/sec, which is often above 20, however, shows that the system is not configured with enough RAM. Once Pages/sec exceeds 10, you should start thinking about adding more memory.

Two other counters to keep an eye on are:

- Commit Limit
- Committed Bytes

These two counters work in tandem, so it's necessary to look at both sets of values to establish whether the system is utilizing virtual memory appropriately. The Commit Limit counter shows the total amount of available virtual memory. The Committed Bytes counter shows the total amount of virtual memory that the system has already committed from its resources. When the size of the Committed Bytes closes in on the Commit Limit value, then you know the system is about to run out of virtual memory.

You might need to adjust your minimum and maximum paging file sizes to suit your specific needs, based on system usage. Microsoft's recommendation for a minimum paging file is the amount of your physical RAM, plus 11MB (if your system has 256MB, you should set your virtual memory to 267MB). A better way to figure out your paging file needs is to determine the typical usage requirements of the paging file for a given computer, and then specify that amount (so long as it doesn't fall below Microsoft's formula).

> **NOTE** Windows XP Professional allows you to let the computer decide how big the paging file should be. However, if you decide to let the computer do that, you'll take a performance hit. It's best to set the size of the paging file manually.

The maximum size of the paging file should be the highest value you ever expect the paging file to grow. Yes, that's fantastically vague, so a good rule of thumb is to set the maximum value to 150 percent of the minimum value, monitor the Commit Limit and Committed Bytes values, and adjust accordingly.

Processor

Your system's processor contains several items that can be monitored. The most critical item to monitor is the %Processor value. This counter shows the amount of time that the processor is doing *productive* work, which is the amount of time the processor is executing nonidle threads or servicing interrupts.

Each instance of %Processor should not exceed a value of 50 (that is, 50 percent use). So what happens if this counter consistently meets or exceeds 50 percent use? The next step is to check the Interrupts/sec counter. If the value exceeds 3,500 or more, then the system is experiencing 3,500 (or more) interrupts every second. More than likely this means that a device or device driver is taxing the processor.

Disk Subsystem

For your disk subsystem, the two most relevant counters to watch are:

- %Disk Time
- Disk Queue Length

These are found in either the LogicalDisk or the PhysicalDisk object. Ideally, the best values will be less than 55 percent and 2, respectively.

> **NOTE** The drivers needed to monitor disk performance are disabled, by default, to avoid the overhead of the process. To gather hard disk statistics, load the monitoring drivers by entering **DISKPERF -Y** at the command prompt. When you're done monitoring, enter the command **DISKPERF -N** at the command prompt to disable the drivers.

When monitoring the disk subsystem, it's important to understand its reliance on physical memory. As we mentioned earlier, a system that does not have adequate memory can cause disk performance problems. This is because the system is trying to compensate for a lack of RAM by using paging. If you notice an inordinate amount of disk activity and your %Disk Time and Disk Queue Length values are high, check to see if your paging file is appropriately configured and if the system has enough RAM.

Network Subsystem

The final place to check is the network subsystem. This is often the most difficult area to troubleshoot and optimize, because the network is such a complex, dynamic environment. For instance, the operating system, network applications, NICs, and protocols all play crucial roles in the network. However, that shouldn't be taken to mean the network subsystem is far too complex to monitor.

The Bytes Total/sec counter in the Server object shows the amount of network activity experienced by the server. An acceptable value for this counter is 0.8 MBps for 10 Mbps Ethernet-based networks and 0.5 MBps on 16-Mbps Token Ring networks. If values exceed this level, chances are that the network will start getting sluggish. If you are regularly exceeding this level, you should consider segmenting the network, increasing your network speed, or using switches instead of hubs.

CAPACITY PLANNING

It's been said elsewhere in this book and it bears repeating: Networks are moving targets. Rarely is a network completed once it's designed and built. Networks are dynamic entities, constantly evolving and changing based on your organization's needs.

To build your network and help it grow, it is helpful to understand your organization's needs and plan for future growth and expansion. This section examines different tools and techniques that you can use to keep your Windows XP Professional network from getting stale and how you can add on to it in the future. The best way to understand your needs is to understand your current network environment and then plan accordingly.

Network Simulation

Even though the government pays $725 for toilet seats, that doesn't mean that it's *completely* frivolous with money. Case in point: fighter jet training. Rather than stick a rookie pilot in a multimillion dollar fighter jet, the military lets the pilot learn his or her chops on terra firma before dropping him or her into the cockpit of a stealth fighter.

The same is true of network design. It would be extremely expensive and wasteful to buy a boatload of switches, routers, servers, and clients without knowing how many (and what capacities of each) you need. As with fighter jet training, this can be achieved through simulation. Network simulation is a great way to make sure that your network has been properly designed and constructed. Because networks are dynamic in nature, network simulation can show how a new device will affect the overall network.

Unlike the fighter jet version of the simulator (which are giant, cool video games), network simulators are simply pieces of software that allow your to build your test network with various configurations, and then apply different loads to see how it behaves. Simulation is a very useful tool, because as your network grows and as routes are transformed, it would be otherwise impossible to anticipate how a single, small change would impact the entire network.

A solid model of your network will encompass as many of its details and nuances as possible. Traits to be mindful of include the following:

- Router characteristics
- Switch properties
- Traffic patterns
- Design characteristics

Network simulators use two methods for traffic modeling:

- **Discrete** Examines each packet to determine its behavior, but is slower than the analytical method
- **Analytical** Makes assumptions and summarizations about network traffic

Even though the analytical method makes assumptions about network traffic, some analysts believe that it is just as accurate as discrete modeling. In organizations with more than 50 routers or switches, it's preferable to use the analytical method. This is because each packet is examined using the discrete modeling method, which can take a lot of time.

The following items discuss some of the important network issues that should be considered and how they can be simplified for modeling.

Topology

When modeling your network, the first step is to create a depiction of the network that includes both its topology and traffic. *Topology* is the framework of your network; it means both its physical construction as well as its logical configurations. Some of the devices on your network that should be included in your topological representation are listed here:

- Routers
- Computers
- Switches
- WAN links
- LANs
- Point-to-point connections

Some of the logical settings you should take into consideration include the following:

- Router interface settings
- LAN speeds
- WAN speeds
- Router capabilities
- Routing protocols
- Naming conventions

If the thought of having to gather all this information is causing your eyes to glaze over, don't worry. You don't need to head into the server room with a clipboard, sleeping bag, and freeze-dried food. There are programs (a couple of which we'll mention later) that use the Simple Network Management Protocol (SNMP) to query your network, discovering all your network's physical and logical settings.

Traffic

The last section talked about building the basic roadmap of your network. Now, let's add some traffic to those roads. It is necessary to show where the traffic occurs on your network, because the traffic generated by existing applications will have an impact on the traffic generated by a new application, and vice versa. The best way to see where traffic exists is by placing network probes at points where traffic originates and terminates. Unfortunately, network probes don't come cheap (costing upwards of $15,000), and they can take a long time to set up.

Generally speaking, probes are simply PCs with probe software installed on them. They can also be pieces of hardware that are smaller than a PC and have no monitor or keyboard attached. In either case, they function the same, sitting quietly and unobtrusively, gathering data from your network.

Even though probes are expensive and a pain in the neck to set up, the information they gather is priceless. Table 17-3 lists some vendors for network probes.

Company/Product	Solution Format	Cost	Contact
Compuware/NetworkVantage	Software	$3,000–$12,000	http://www.compuware.com
NetScout/NetScout	Software and hardware	$1,500 for software; $3,000–$15,000 for hardware	http://www.netscout.com
HP/OpenView Network Node Manager	Software	$5,000	http://openview.hp.com

Table 17-3. Third-Party Network Probes

Good probes gather information about traffic all the way up to the application layer and generate statistics based on applications. Information you should expect from your probes includes the following:

- Network protocols
- Application name
- Source computer
- Destination computer
- Number of packets flowing in each direction
- Number of bytes flowing in each direction
- Application latency
- Conversation duration

When all this information has been gathered, it is useful when building your network model. However, even if you aren't building a topology and traffic model of your network, this information can be quite helpful on its own. For example, you can use a probe to check application latency to see if your applications are meeting your minimum QoS policies. You can also see how much bandwidth is being used by each application, and so forth.

Testing Considerations

Once you're ready to run your simulation, expect the test to take several hours. This isn't such a bad prospect, however, when you consider the longer you run your simulation, the better the image of your network you'll receive. If you want to increase the performance of your simulation, you can remove or consolidate traffic conversations.

Reducing Conversations Naturally, if you remove conversations from your network, this will artificially reduce the amount of traffic on your network and return skewed results. However, that doesn't mean that it can't be done without impeding progress. When you have a number of probes capturing data at the same time, several probes will pick up the same conversations. Normally, the probes' software will eliminate duplicate conversations, but if the software does not catch them, you should eliminate them manually. Also, conversations with small byte counts have a negligible impact on the network and can be removed without skewing the results. In all likelihood, you can remove about 40 percent of the conversations and lose only 3 percent of the network traffic.

Conversation Consolidation Another way to streamline the process is to consolidate conversations that have the same source and destination and are the same type. All packets and bytes are added to this consolidation, so no traffic load is lost. It's a good idea to define a specific amount of time in which both conversations must occur before consolidation. In total, you should enjoy a 40 to 70 percent reduction in the number of conversations by eliminating small conversations and consolidating those remaining.

Running the Simulation

Once you've got a detailed blueprint of your network's topology and traffic patterns, you're ready to start your simulation. Before you begin, you should have a specific question in mind like, "If I add another bank of users to this server, what will the impact be on the network?" When the simulation is run with this question in mind, and you notice a change in performance, some changes to consider include the following:

- Changing or adding WAN links or LANs
- Changing or adding routers
- Changing routing protocols
- Moving or adding servers
- Moving or adding users
- Adding or removing an application

Network Simulation Tools

The following vendors offer third-party network simulation tools that will help you model your network. For more information about each of these products, contact the vendor. Their respective web addresses are listed at the end of each product description.

NetScout nGenius

NetScout's nGenius Capacity Planner predicts application, network, and device traffic patterns by analyzing information from a number of data sources, including network probes, SNMP manageable devices, and custom MIBs.

> **NOTE**   MIB is an acronym for Management Information Base. MIBs are a formal description of a set of network objects that can be managed by SNMP.

The use of all these information-gathering tools allows nGenius to have timely and accurate information about the network's state. nGenius uses NetScout's application-aware probes, which return information on bandwidth consumption based on user and application.

Additionally, nGenius examines application traffic details, allowing you to understand how much of your network's resources your applications are consuming. nGenius also uses the nGenius NewsStand to deliver customized reports for specific users or groups of users. The reports can also be exported to an intranet for internal use.

nGenius allows you to do the following:

- Identify the most- and least-used network segments, circuits, and virtual LANs.
- Drill down to network specifics to locate the specific source of demand.
- Use NetScout probes to receive accurate, up-to-date data on network conditions.

nGenius Capacity Planner allows you to look at the current state of your network; then—using its Traffic Signature technology—it plots maximum, 90th percentile, and average baselines. Traffic Signature allows nGenius to provide the following information:

- Reports for each hour of the day, compared against maximum, 90th percentile, and average baselines
- Recurring patterns
- Use of alarms, when traffic deviates from normal traffic patterns

For more information about the nGenius Capacity Planning tool, visit the NetScout web site at http://www.netscout.com.

Compuware Predictor

Compuware's Predictor allows you to see the impact of a traffic or topology change across your entire network. Predictor uses delay and utilization metrics, as well as predictions of where bottlenecks and applications response time issues will occur.

Predictor can be used for:

- Switching out devices
- Modeling protocol changes
- Planning for network outages
- Server centralization
- Bandwidth management
- Upgrade management
- Locating bottlenecks
- Adding new users, user groups, and applications

Predictor provides a number of metrics and reports for such issues as WAN bandwidth and latency, and delay and utilization. Furthermore, Predictor employs warnings, alarms, and overload information to show where bottlenecks and application response problems are likely to occur.

In addition to network patterns, Predictor can also be used to track network behavior that will change based on application transactions. This can be overlaid on live background traffic to model how a new application will affect the network if it is applied to the existing configuration. This allows you investigate alternatives to minimize response times, including bandwidth increases, server relocation, and processor speed upgrades.

Finally, and of most importance in Microsoft environments, is Predictor's interoperability with .NET applications. Predictor allows detailed analysis of .NET applications' impact on your local network, as well as on a WAN. Because of Microsoft's .NET architecture, applications will behave differently than "conventional" applications.

For instance, some .NET applications will take random paths through the Internet, whereas others will deploy across dedicated WAN links. Whatever the case, bandwidth requirements and link capacities should be analyzed before the applications are deployed across your organization. Predictor allows .NET users to model their .NET infrastructure and then calculate how specific links will be affected by the deployment.

For more information about Compuware Predictor, visit Compuware's web site at http://www.compuware.com.

THIRD-PARTY TOOLS

Earlier in this chapter we talked about Microsoft's System Monitor, which is a pretty robust piece of software. However, you might find it necessary to use a third-party tool to help with your network performance monitoring. To be sure, there is no dearth of products on the market to help you monitor your network. The following are just a few of the available applications.

Lucent VitalSuite

Lucent's entry into the network performance monitoring game is its VitalSuite application. VitalSuite is an integrated collection of software modules for monitoring network activity, applications, and their transactions. For capacity planning and other needs, VitalSuite stores a year's worth of data in the included Microsoft SQL Server database (both SQL Server 7.0 and 2000 are included with VitalSuite).

My Vital merges views from the three primary VitalSuite components—VitalNet, VitalAnalysis, and VitalHelp—into a single display. This provides a high-level summary that shows how the system is performing.

But where other performance tools look at the network with an eye to network links, processor performance, and so forth, My Vital can be set up with various reports custom tailored not only to the IT department or the network administrator, but also to other individuals in the organization.

The display can be customized based on your particular monitoring needs. For instance, it can show performance for the entire network, for a specific user, or for any other object within the network. Because the VitalSuite product family is web based, individual My Vital reports and displays can be generated for anyone in the organization.

This ability allows different members of the organization to take the appropriate action based on their particular role. For example, the accounting department doesn't need to know how well the routers are performing; however, the department does need to know how well specific applications and business transactions are performing. As such, employees in accounting can set up My Vital to monitor those applications and transactions, and then generate the appropriate report with the end results.

For more information about Lucent's VitalSuite in general, or My Vital in particular, visit the VitalSuite web site at http://vital.lucent.com.

Concord eHealth

Concord's eHealth is a four-part suite of network monitoring components consisting of the following:

- **Network Health**   Monitors the performance and availability of WAN interfaces, routers, switches, Frame Relay circuits, and remote access equipment.
- **Live Health**   Polls SNMP-manageable devices, determining their status and condition. It then displays faults and potential outages.
- **System Health**   Monitors servers and selects clients to alert administrators to application performance problems, server crashes, and disk shortage problems.
- **Application Health**   A transaction-oriented collection of tools for determining the cause of poor application response times. One tool, called the Application Assessment component, watches over such software as Microsoft Exchange, Internet Information Server, and SQL Server, looking for problems.

eHealth can deliver its collected performance data via a browser-based interface, a server console, or Adobe Acrobat–formatted files. Furthermore, eHealth comes with its own web server for rendering management data and reports as web pages.

When eHealth is first activated, it spends its time baselining the network, characterizing "normal" behavior. When it's done baselining, it points out extraordinary events, like high traffic or low traffic through a router or switch, based on a number of rules. When an anomaly is detected, eHealth's SystemEdge component can e-mail or page someone.

For more information on Concord's eHealth application, visit Concord's web site at http://www.concord.com.

HP OpenView

Hewlett-Packard's line of monitoring tools includes its OpenView line of products. The OpenView line contains 56 different tools for monitoring a variety of networking environments. OpenView products are used to monitor web activity, UNIX environments, and OS/400 environments, among others. The most germane to a Windows XP Professional environment is HP's OpenView Operations for Windows.

OpenView Operations for Windows is a distributed solution, meaning it is installed on a number of your network's hosts. Its central operations, performance management console, and database automatically do the following:

- Discover your network
- Deploy management rules and policies
- Collect and automatically respond to events
- View and handle messages

- Generate reports and graphs
- Display business-critical services in color-coded topology maps

A combined event and performance agent monitors multiple platforms and can be remotely deployed from the management console. For heterogeneous environments, OpenView Operations for Windows allows you to manage not only your Windows computers, but also machines running the following software:

- Solaris
- AIX
- HP-UX
- NetWare
- Tru64
- Linux

From a single OpenView Operations for Windows management server, hundreds of nodes and thousands of events can be monitored. Because OpenView Operations for Windows uses Microsoft-native technologies, it has received Windows 2000 certification. Since there are so many products in the OpenView line, each serving a specific function, OpenView Operations for Windows can be linked with various other OpenView products to enhance the capabilities of both tools. Some of the other products include the following:

- **OpenView Operations for UNIX**   Useful for managing large, heterogeneous environments
- **OpenView Network Node Manager**   Useful for network element discovery, layout, inventory, and performance
- **OpenView Problem Diagnosis**   Supplies a map of two network elements and the points in between for root-cause analysis
- **OpenView Reporter**   A web-based, near-time and historical reporting of all network elements
- **OpenView Internet Services**   Software that simulates the user experience with applications and Internet services

For more information about Hewlett-Packard's OpenView product line, visit the product's web site at http://openview.hp.com.

Compuware NetworkVantage

Compuware's performance monitoring solution is a product called NetworkVantage. It monitors your network passively, meaning that its activity does not add to your network's resource consumption. NetworkVantage monitors the amount of traffic generated by your network's various applications (it can automatically discover over 2,000 applications and protocols throughout the 7-layer OSI stack), and then associates that traffic load back to the originating client. This allows network administrators to see which applications are using the most bandwidth and which users are generating the most traffic.

In the event network traffic exceeds the threshold established by the organization, NetworkVantage sends an alert so that network administrators can take appropriate action to prevent the network from becoming bogged down. The notification is made via the NetworkVantage Interactive Viewer, a user interface that profiles the applications that are slowing down your network. The viewer is also used to drill down to specific performance characteristics of the network, servers, and clients.

NetworkVantage is also useful for growth management. It generates reports that identify trends in network usage by inputting topology and utilization data to Predictor (which we mentioned in the last section).

In addition to identifying applications and bandwidth hogs, NetworkVantage can also tell you specific details about the traffic on your network. For example, it can differentiate between bandwidth contention, latency, and client or server response time issues.

Like some of the other tools we've looked at, NetworkVantage also allows you to examine your network's data in different, useful ways. NetworkVantage can display network and application performance readings in various ways. For instance, the data can be organized by application, client, or server. This can help show if network issues are due to a specific client, a greedy application, or a misconfigured server.

For more information on Compuware's NetworkVantage, visit Compuware's web site at http://www.compuware.com.

Monitoring your network's performance is extremely important. Not only is it necessary to ensure that the system is functioning optimally, but it is also useful to observe changes when planning modifications to the network—be it a new bank of users, a new networking device, or even an application. Performance monitoring requires a multidiscipled approach, taking into consideration the impact of hardware and software, as well as the users.

APPENDIX

Windows .NET Administration Tools

You can administer different aspects of your Windows Active Directory network from a Windows XP Professional client with the Windows .NET Server Administration Tools Pack. This amalgam of more than two dozen applications provides server management tools allowing administrators to remotely manage Windows 2000 and .NET Servers from Windows XP Professional machines.

As of this writing, the Windows .Net Administration Tools Pack is in the beta 3 stage of testing. If you wish to download it and install it on a Windows XP Professional computer, the tool pack can be found at Microsoft's web site at http://www.microsoft.com/downloads/release.asp?ReleaseID=34032&area=search&ordinal=1.

NOTE The Windows .NET Server Administration Tools Pack will only work on Windows XP Professional (other versions are available for other flavors of Windows).

This application pack provides a number of commonly used tools for administering network servers and services remotely. The administration tools pack is provided as a set of snap-ins to the Microsoft Management Console (MMC), or the tools can be launched from a newly created Start menu icon called Administrative Tools. The server administration tools include the following applications:

- Active Directory Domains and Trusts
- Active Directory Sites and Services
- Active Directory Users and Computers
- Certification Authority
- Cluster Administrator
- Component Services
- Computer Management
- Connection Manager Administration Kit
- Data Sources (ODBC)
- DHCP
- Distributed File System
- DNS

- Event Viewer
- Local Security Policy
- .NET Framework Configuration
- .NET Wizards
- Network Load Balancing Manager
- Performance
- Remote Desktops
- Remote Storage
- Routing and Remote Access
- Server Extensions Administrator
- Services
- Telephony
- Terminal Server Licensing
- Terminal Services Manager
- WINS

The following sections explain and demonstrate some of the functionality of each of these tools.

NOTE You might notice some familiar faces in this list of tools (such as Event Viewer and Performance, aka System Monitor). Although these tools appear elsewhere in your Windows XP Professional system, they are included here for management of not only your local resources, but also those of the domain.

ACTIVE DIRECTORY DOMAINS AND TRUSTS

The Active Directory Domains and Trusts snap-in is used to manage and administer domain trusts and user principal name suffixes, and to change the domain's mode.

Figure A-1 shows the dialog box used to connect to your domain.

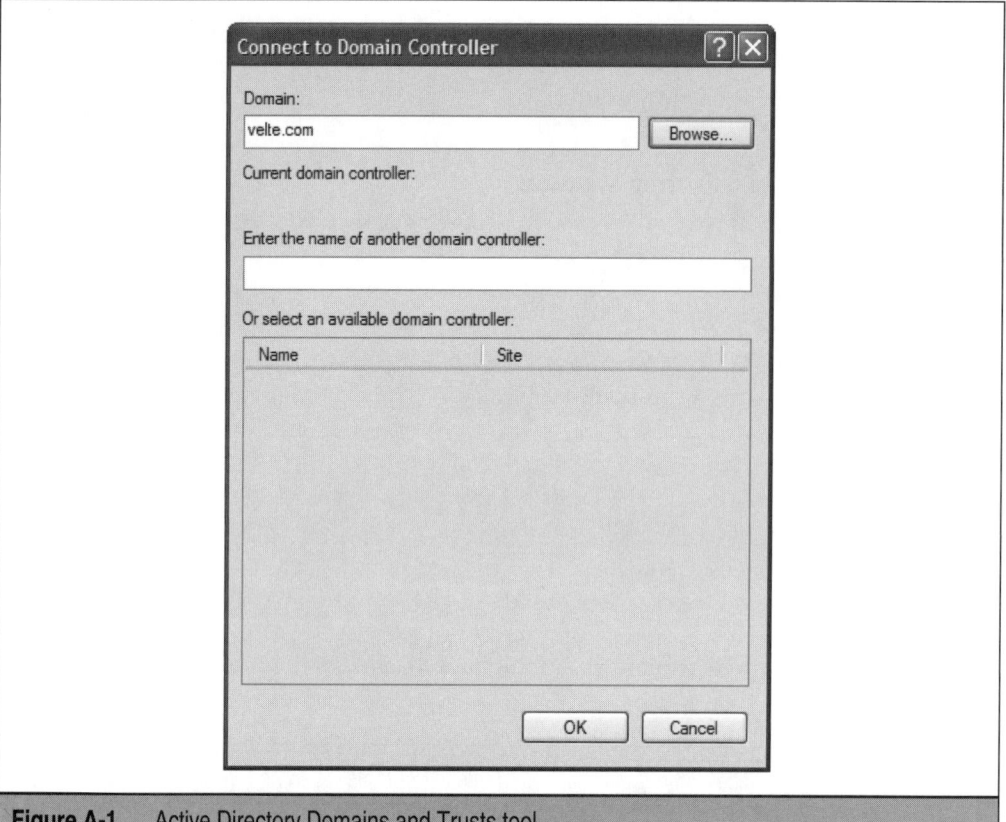

Figure A-1. Active Directory Domains and Trusts tool

ACTIVE DIRECTORY SITES AND SERVICES

The Active Directory Sites and Services tool is used to administer the replication of data. This includes information about domain controllers, replication between sites, and replication of network services. A *site* is the term used to define the topology and schedules used for Active Directory replication. *Services* allow the administration of selected organization-wide Active Directory services. The Active Directory Sites and Services tool is shown in Figure A-2.

Figure A-2. Active Directory Sites and Services tool

ACTIVE DIRECTORY USERS AND COMPUTERS

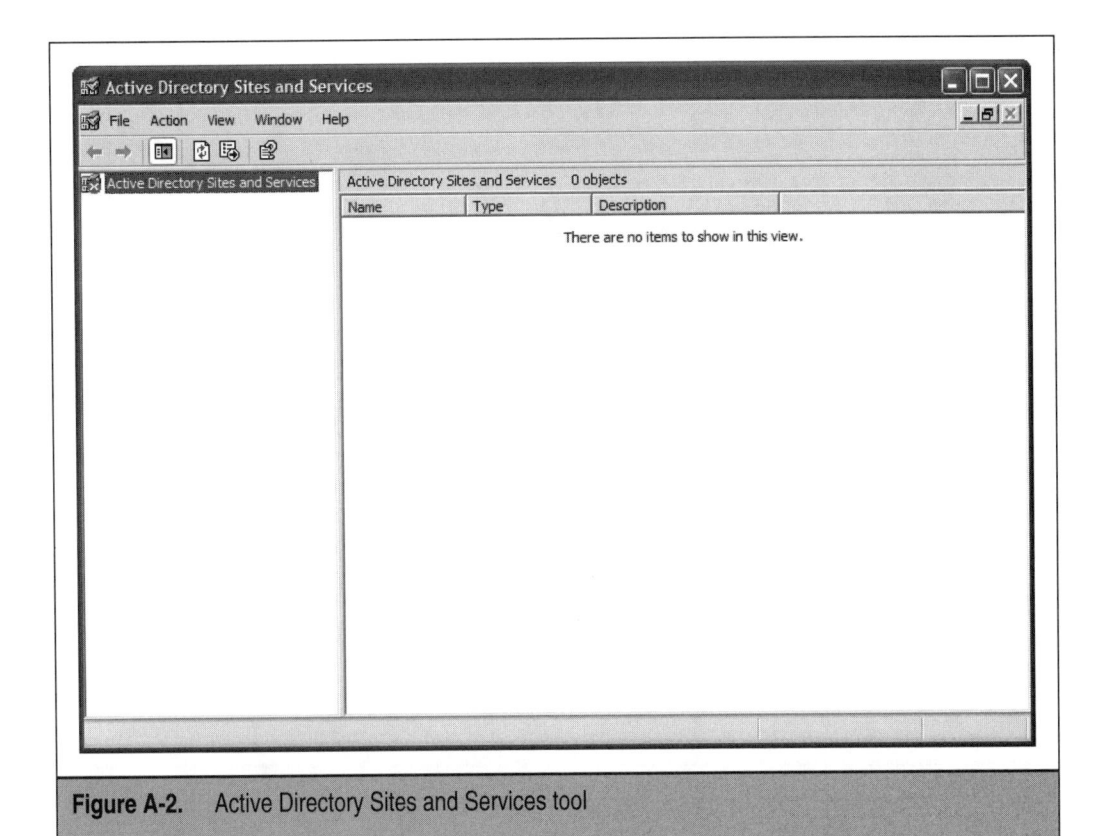

The Active Directory Users and Computers tool is used to manage users and computers within an Active Directory domain. This includes individual users, computers, groups, organizational units, and all other Active Directory objects. Figure A-3 shows the Active Directory Users and Computers snap-in.

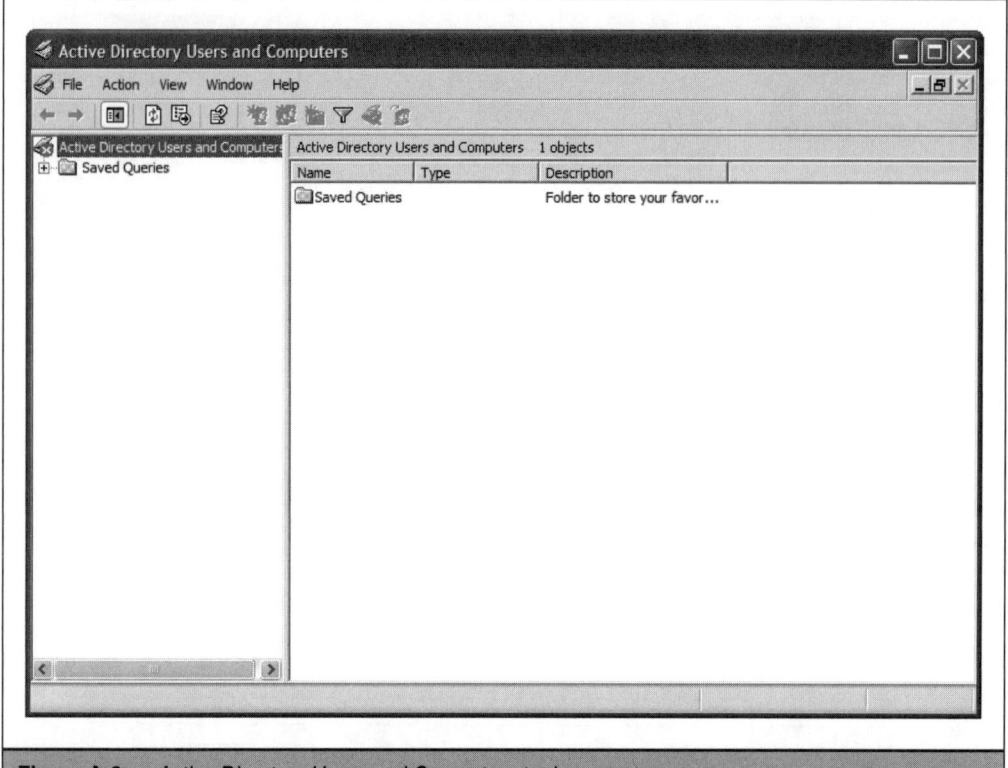

Figure A-3. Active Directory Users and Computers tool

CERTIFICATION AUTHORITY

The Certification Authority tool is used to revoke licenses, change policy settings, display a list of all certificates issued, and perform sundry other tasks on servers with a Certificate Service installed. A certification authority vouches for the authenticity of a user's public keys or those keys belonging to other certification authorities. The Certification Authority tool is shown in Figure A-4.

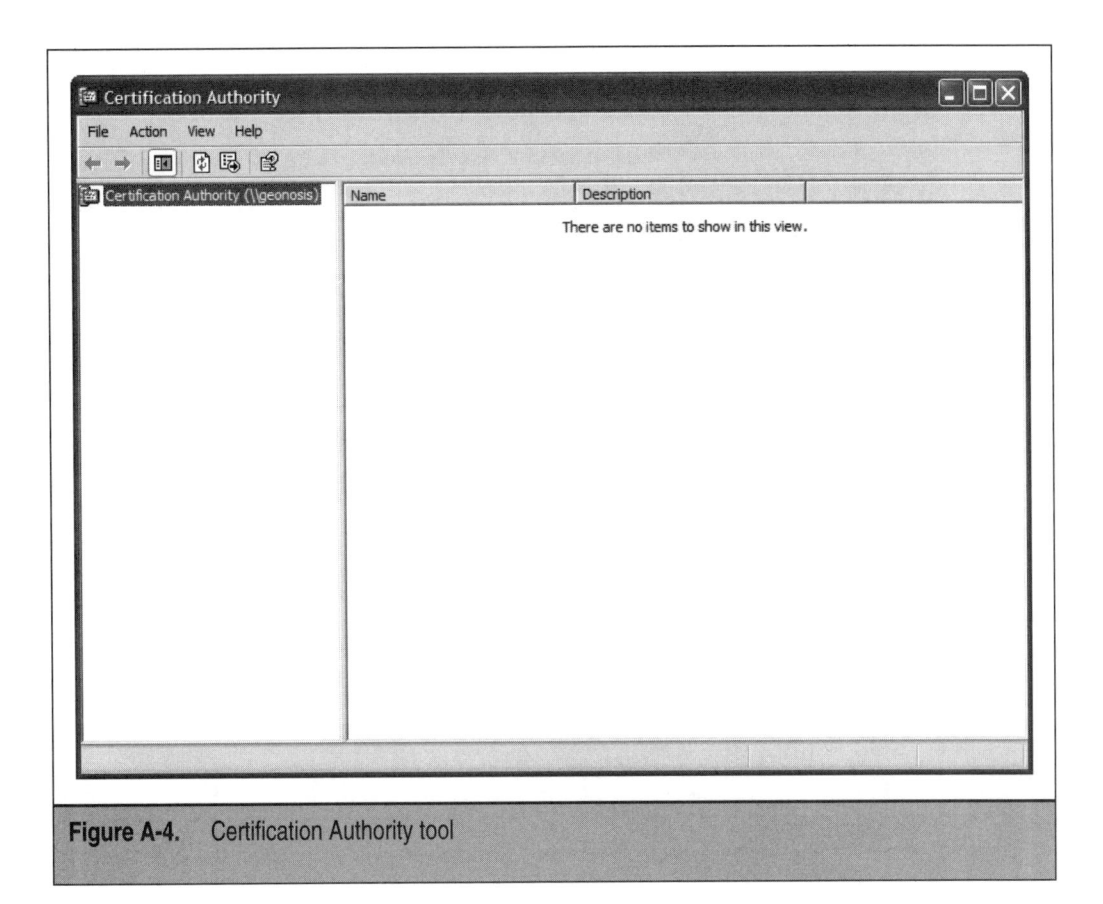

Figure A-4. Certification Authority tool

CLUSTER ADMINISTRATOR

Server clusters are groups of independent computer systems working together as a single unit. Clustering ensures that important programs and resources are available to clients. There are two types of software that run the cluster. The first is called *clustering software* and is responsible for making the cluster run. The second, the Cluster Administrator tool, administers the cluster. Figure A-5 shows the New Server Cluster Wizard that is activated when you create a new cluster with the Cluster Administrator.

Figure A-5. New Server Cluster Wizard

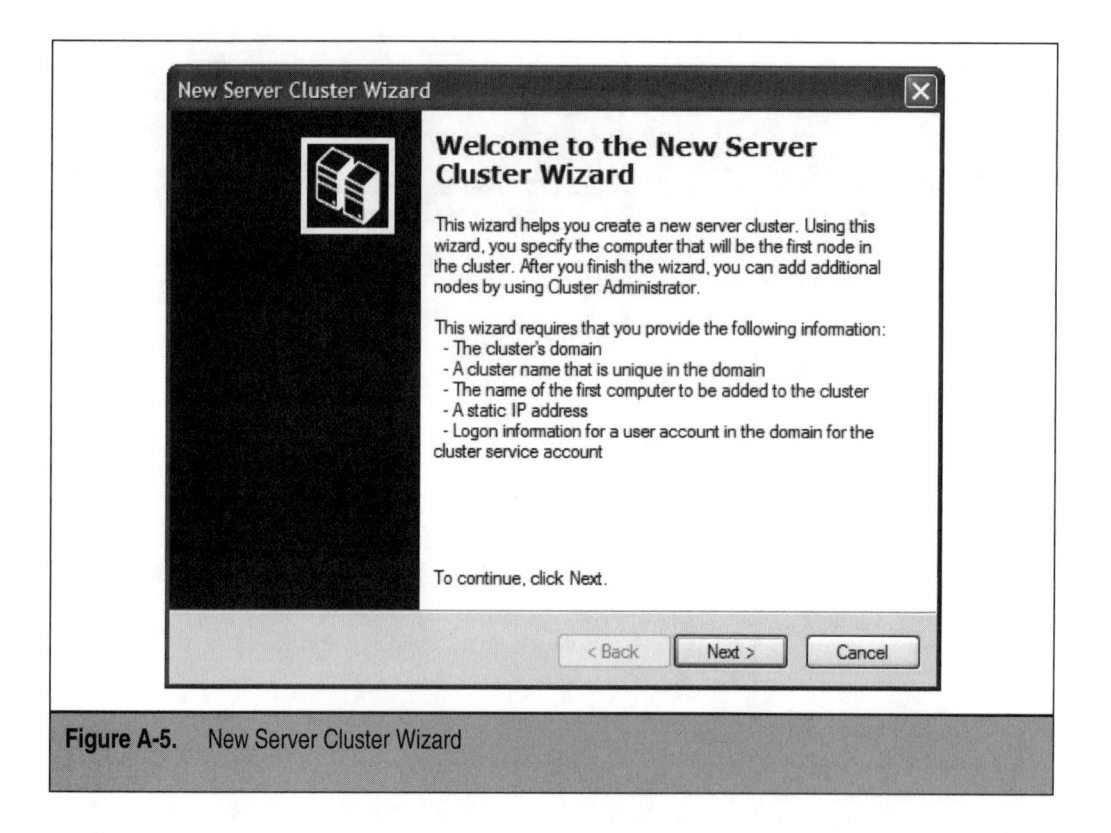

COMPONENT SERVICES

The Component Services tool is used for four purposes:

- Configuring your system for Component Services
- Forming initial services settings
- COM+ application installation and configuration
- Monitoring and tuning component services

The Component Services tool is shown in Figure A-6.

Figure A-6. Component Services tool

COMPUTER MANAGEMENT

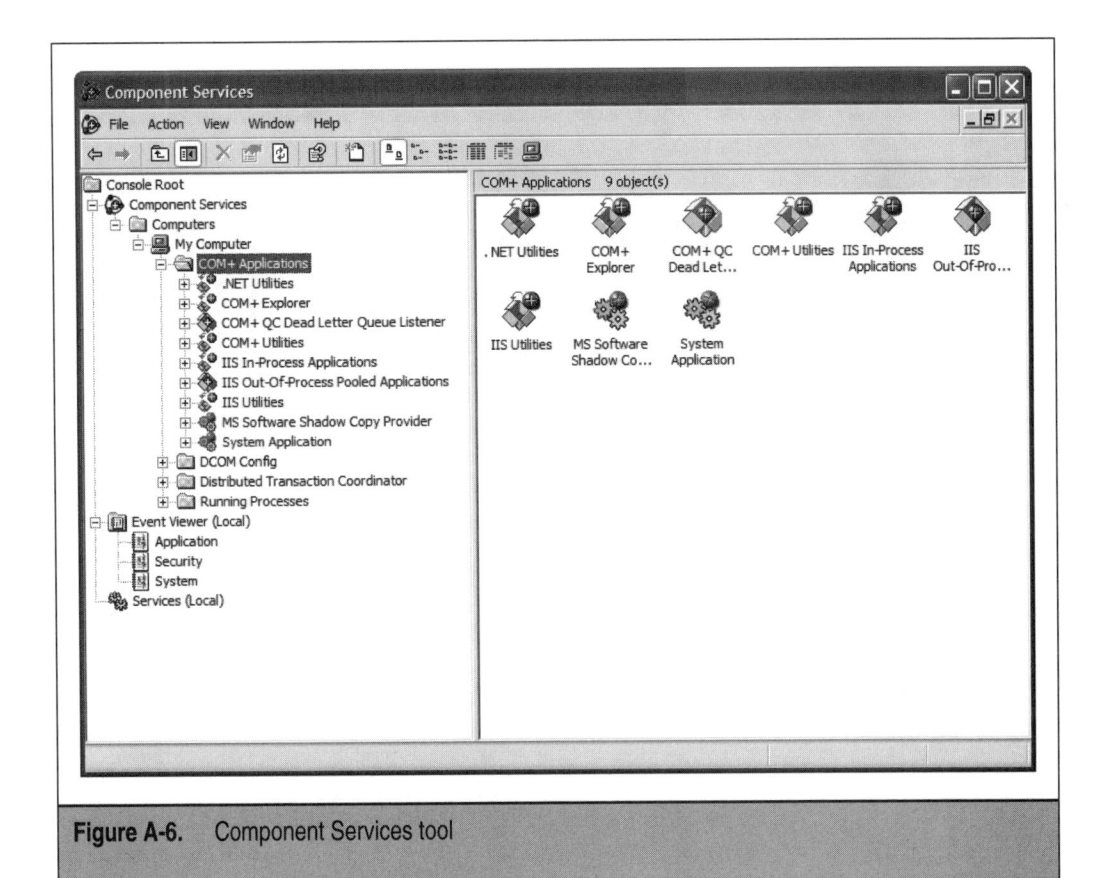

The Computer Management tool provides a number of snap-ins for the MMC that perform computer management tasks and gather useful information about local and remote computers for troubleshooting. The Computer Management tool allows you to view information about:

- Event Viewer logs
- Shared folders
- Local users and group accounts
- Performance logs and alerts
- Device Manager
- Storage devices
- Services and applications

The Computer Management tool is shown in Figure A-7.

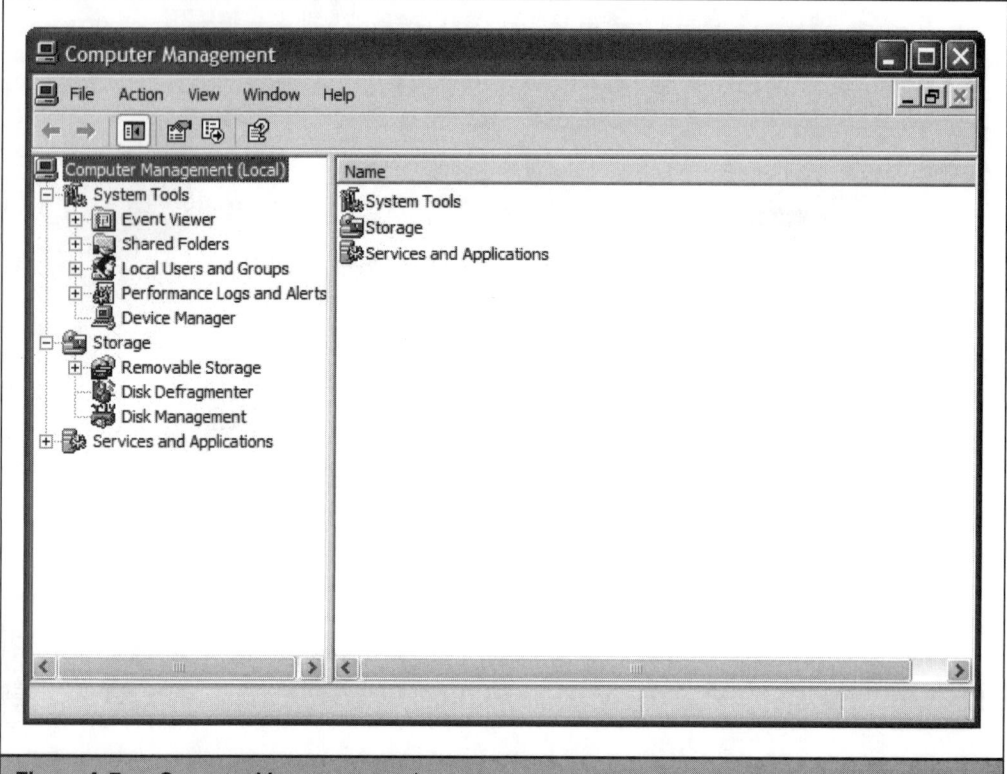

Figure A-7. Computer Management tool

CONNECTION MANAGER ADMINISTRATION KIT

The Connection Manager is a client dialer and connection software customized by using the Connection Manager Administration Kit. To use the kit, first you must run the Connection Manager Administration Kit Wizard (shown in Figure A-8). You answer the wizard's questions and provide information about your client's configuration. Then, the wizard builds a service profile. This profile is a conglomeration of files that you distribute to users so they can install and run the premade version of Connection Manager.

DATA SOURCES (ODBC)

The Data Sources (ODBC) tool stores information about the sources of various forms of data. For instance, it defines how you can connect to a selected data provider. The

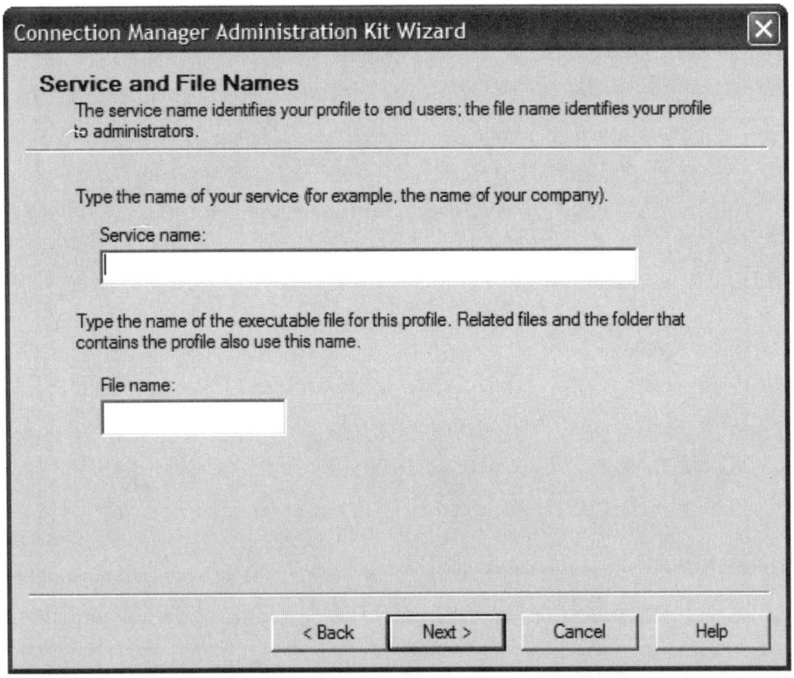

Figure A-8. Connection Manager Administration Kit Wizard

Data Sources (ODBC) tool allows you to manage such data connectivity settings as the following:

- User Data Source Name (DSN)
- System DSN
- File DSN
- Drivers
- Tracing (allows you to create logs of calls to ODBC drivers)
- Connection Pooling (allows applications to reuse open connection handles, thus saving round-trip access to the server)

NOTE ODBC is a programming interface that allows applications to access data in database management systems using Structured Query Language (SQL).

The Data Sources (ODBC) tool is shown in Figure A-9.

Figure A-9. Data Sources tool

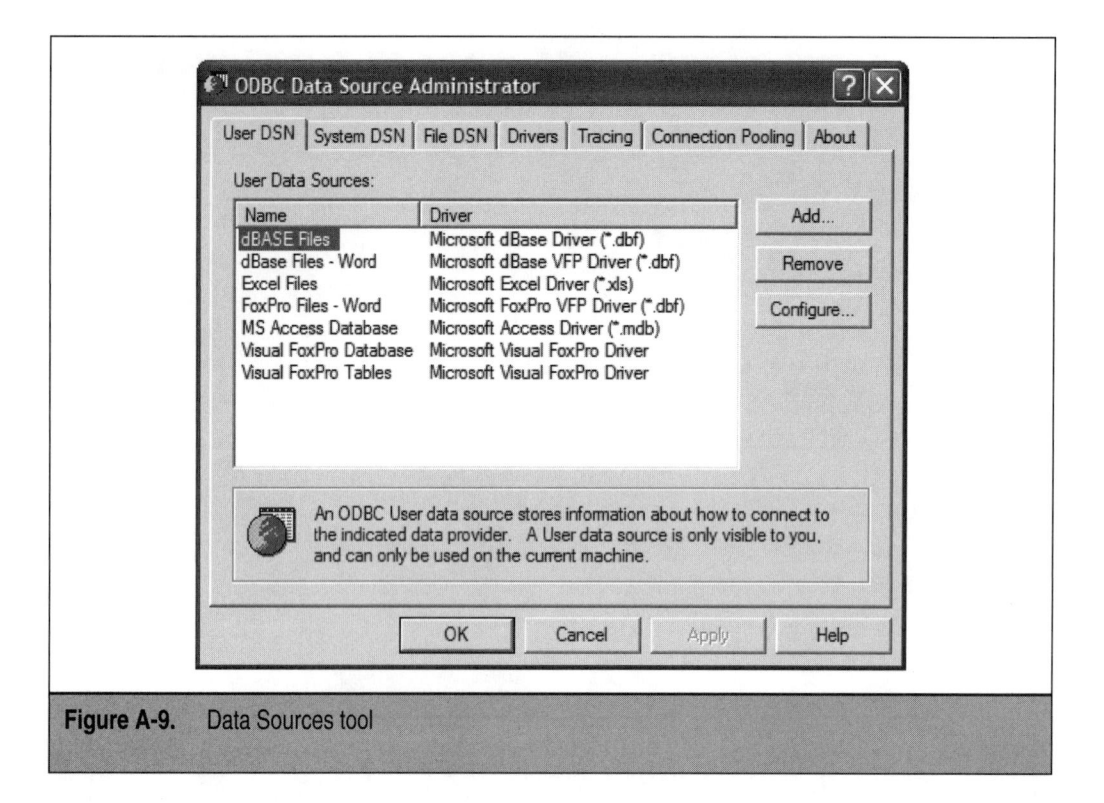

DHCP

Dynamic Host Configuration Protocol (DHCP) is a Transmission Control Protocol/ Internet Protocol (TCP/IP) standard used to simplify the administration of IP addresses. Once a server on your network is set up to centrally manage IP addresses, the DHCP snap-in is used to manage your domain's DHCP service. Figure A-10 shows the DHCP snap-in.

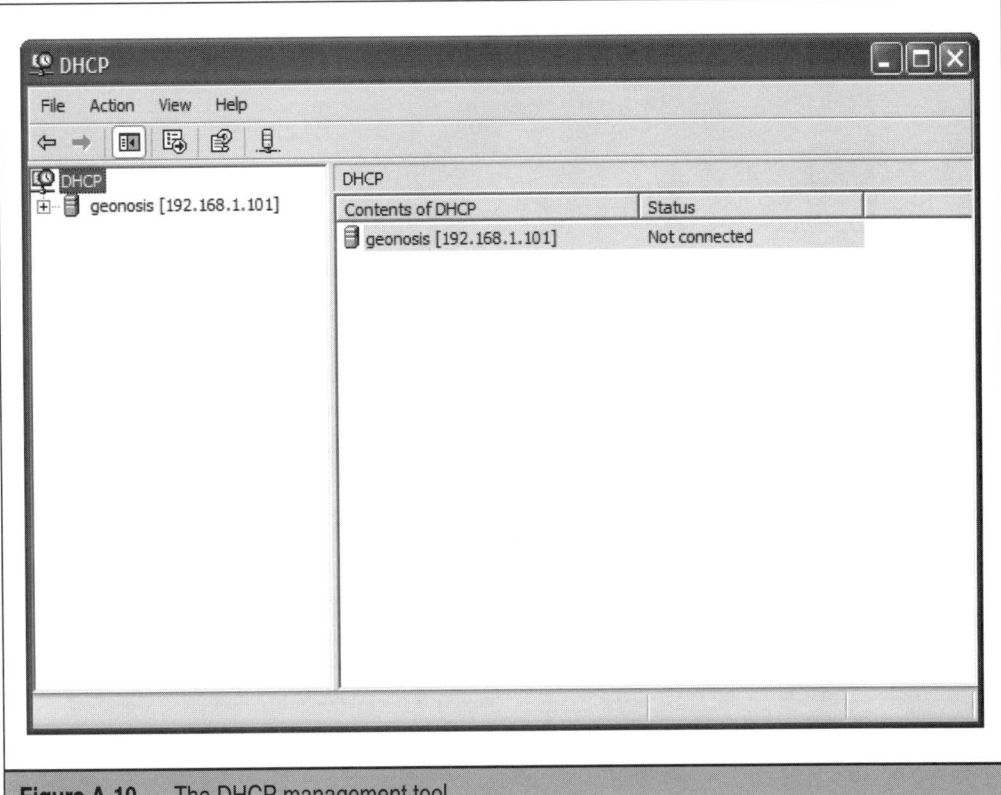

Figure A-10. The DHCP management tool

DISTRIBUTED FILE SYSTEM

The Distributed File System (DFS) takes all the contents of your network's file systems and combines them into a single hierarchical file system. DFS provides a logical tree structure for the file system—in which a resource can be located anywhere on the network. Using the DFS, you need not know the exact, physical location of files distributed across the network. Figure A-11 shows the DFS tool when it is first activated. You can add roots to the tool by clicking Action in the menu and selecting Add Root.

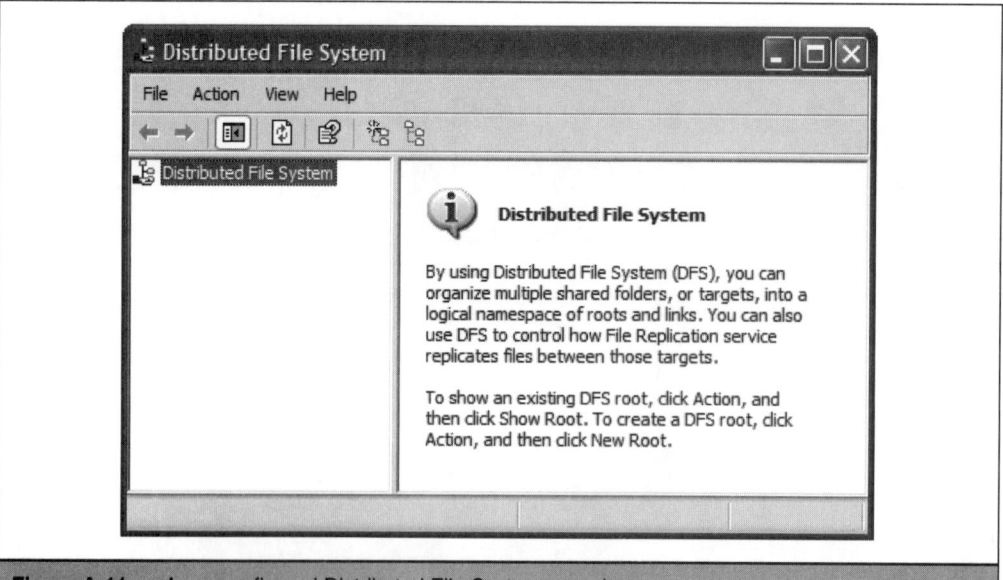

Figure A-11. An unconfigured Distributed File System snap-in

DNS

The Domain Name System (DNS) is a standard for Internet and TCP/IP naming. A DNS service enables the server to act as a DNS server, allowing client computers to register and resolve domain names from IP addresses. The DNS snap-in is used to administer the DNS server and is shown in Figure A-12.

Figure A-12. The DNS tool

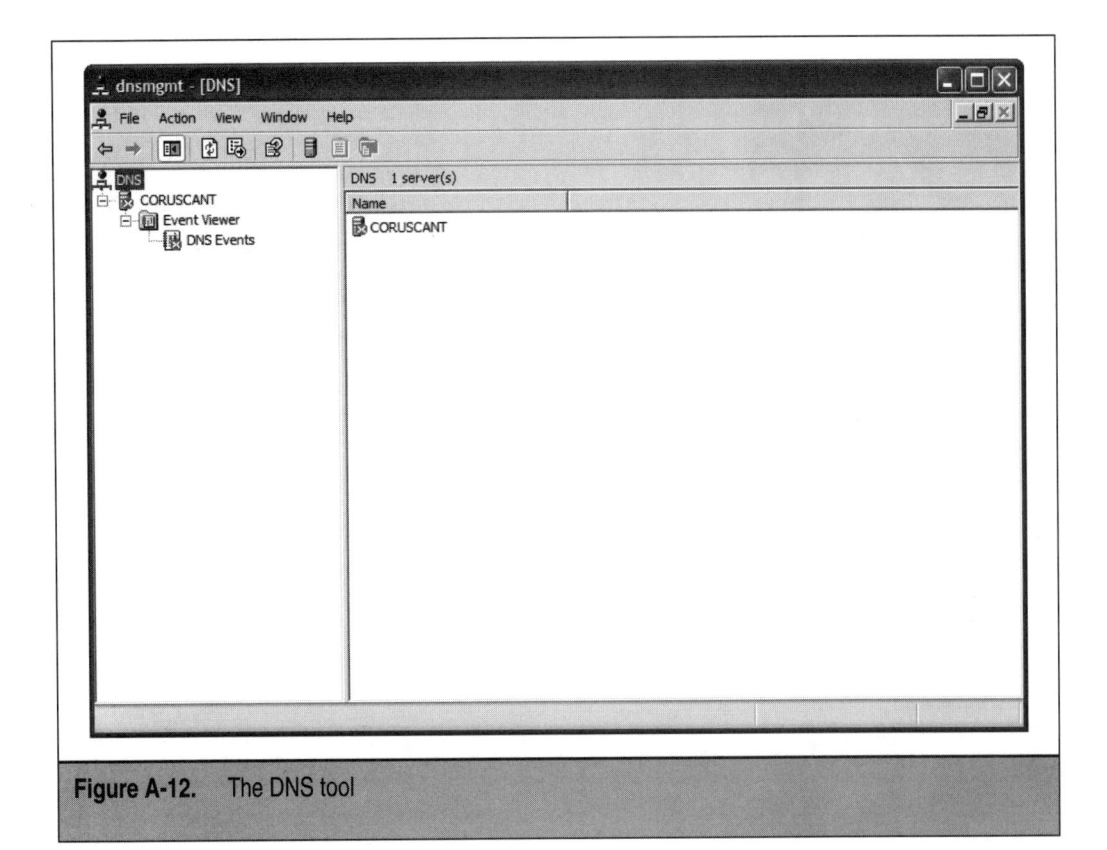

EVENT VIEWER

The Event Viewer tool is an MMC snap-in that allows you to view three different types of logs that are stored in Windows XP Professional:

- **System Log**   A log of Windows XP Professional's system components, including drivers and other components that failed to activate during startup.
- **Application Log**   A log application or program information. Such services as DHCP and DNS use this log.
- **Security Log**   A log of security events, including valid and invalid logon attempts.

The Event Viewer, as shown in Figure A-13, is used to manage and view these event logs.

Figure A-13. Event Viewer tool

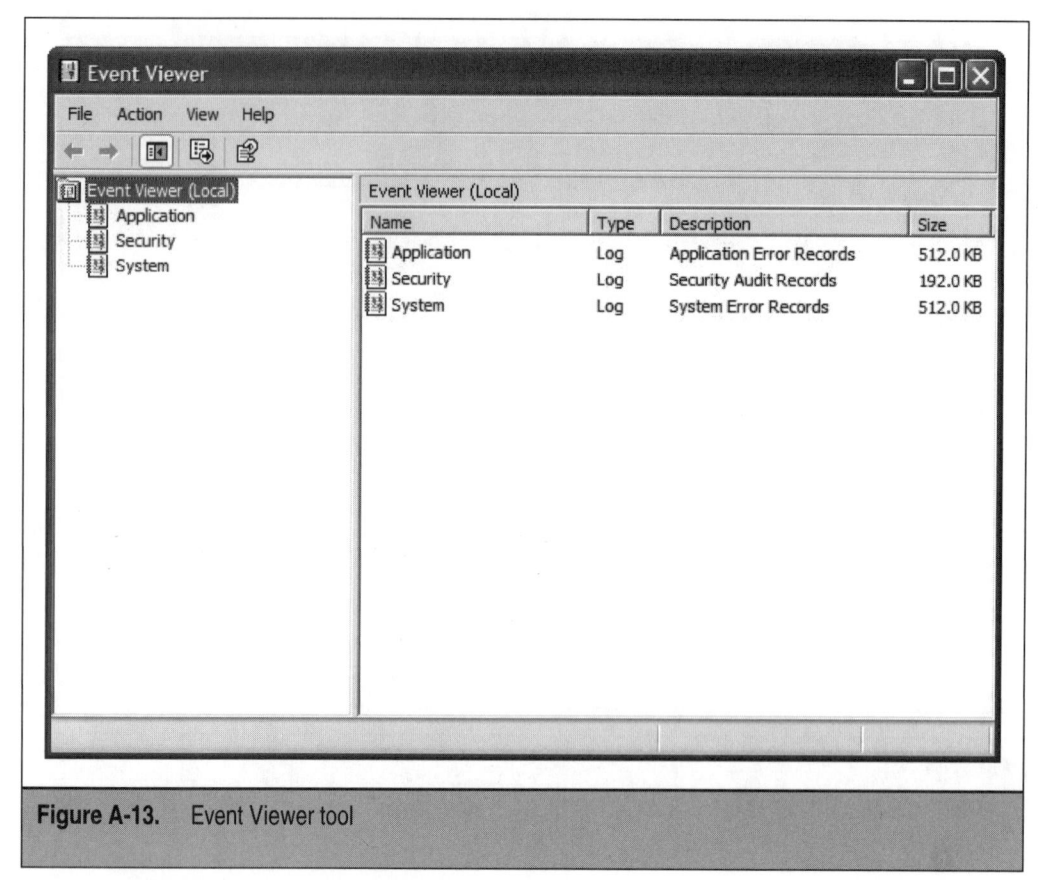

LOCAL SECURITY POLICY

The Local Security Policy snap-in is an extension of the Group Policy snap-in and helps you establish and manage security policies across your domain. The name of the tool seems to imply that it affects only the local computer, but it is used for domainwide security management. The Local Security Policy tool is shown in Figure A-14.

.NET FRAMEWORK CONFIGURATION

The .NET Framework Configuration tool is used to configure assemblies, remoting services, and code access. The tasks you can perform through this tool include the following:

- **Managing the assembly cache**   This cache stores assemblies that are shared by several applications.
- **Managing configured assemblies**   This is a set of assemblies from the assembly cache that have an associated set of rules.
- **Configuration of code access security policy**   This policy manages applications' access to protected resources.
- **Adjusting remote services**   This task manages communications channels for all applications on a computer.
- **Managing individual application**   Unique applications get their own individual assemblies and remoting services with this task.

The .NET Framework Configuration tool and the launch point for each of the preceding tasks is shown in Figure A-15.

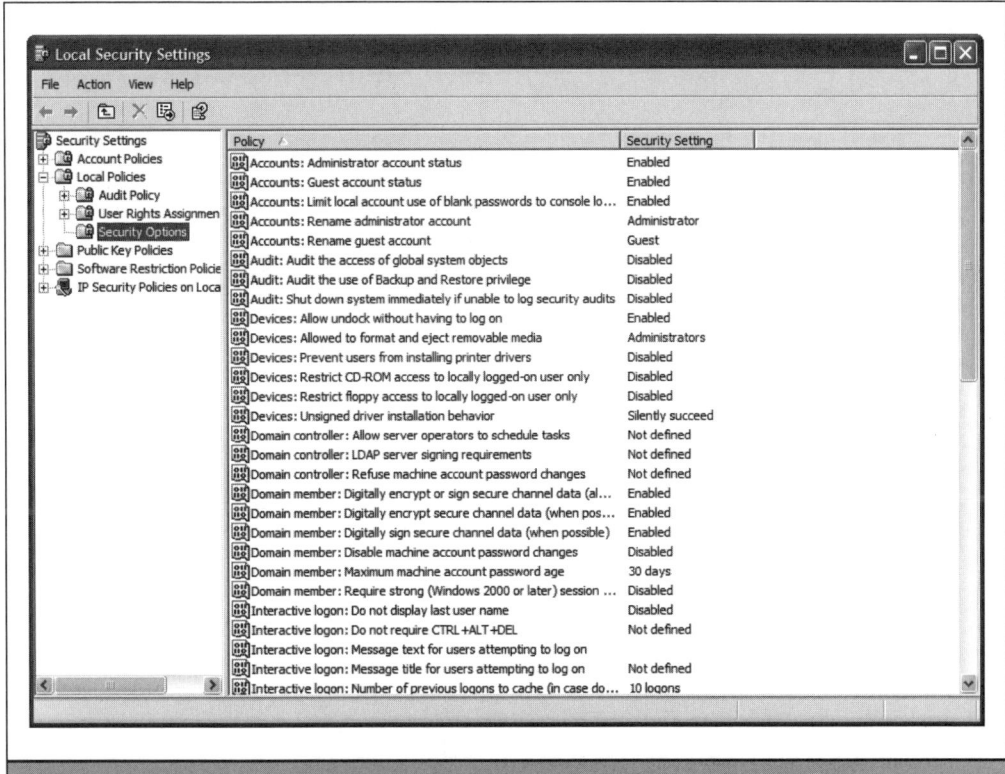

Figure A-14.   The Local Security Policy tool

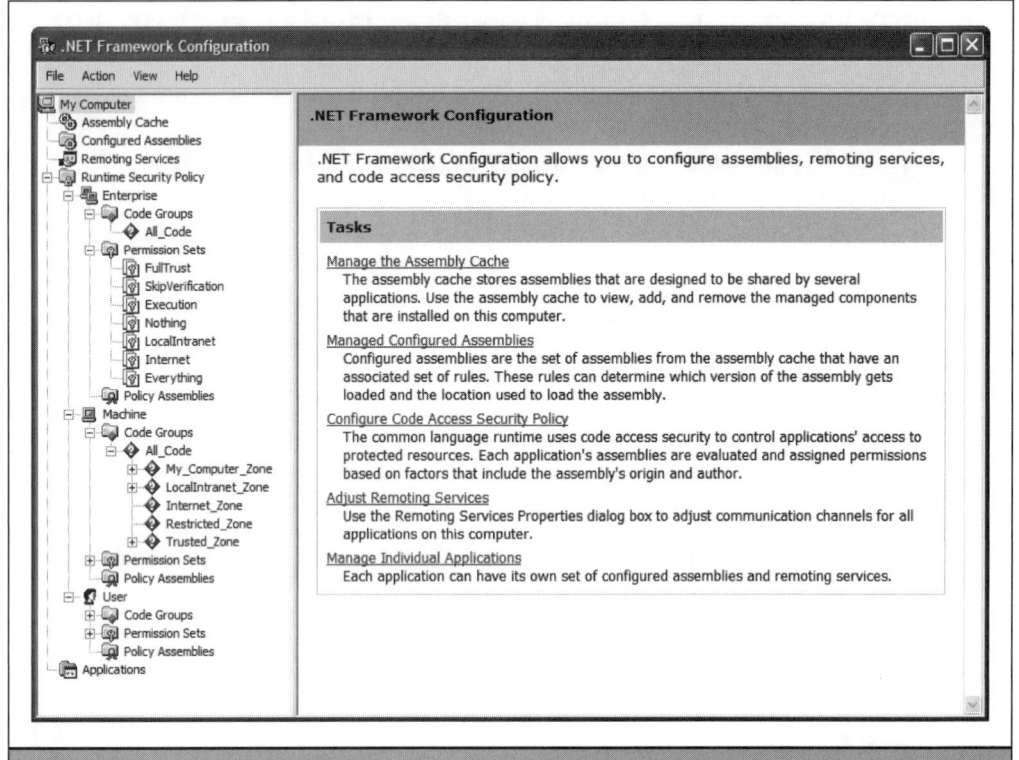

Figure A-15. .NET Framework Configuration tool

.NET WIZARDS

The .NET Wizards tool is a launching point for three individual .NET Wizards:

- Adjust .NET security
- Trust an assembly
- Fix an application

The .NET Wizards tool is shown in Figure A-16.

NETWORK LOAD BALANCING MANAGER

The Network Load Balancing Manager is a tool used for managing server clusters. In a nutshell, load balancing ensures that requests of the TCP/IP-based server cluster are met with equal attention across the cluster. That is, no one server winds up bearing the

Figure A-16. .NET Wizards tool

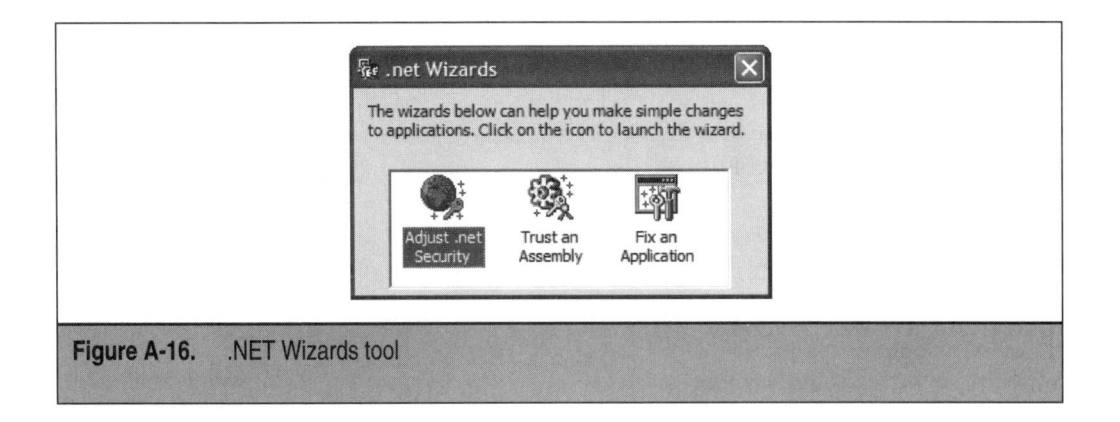

brunt of the service requests; rather, they are spread equally over all the servers of the cluster. Clusters with up to 32 servers can be managed via the Network Load Balancing Manager. This tool is shown in Figure A-17.

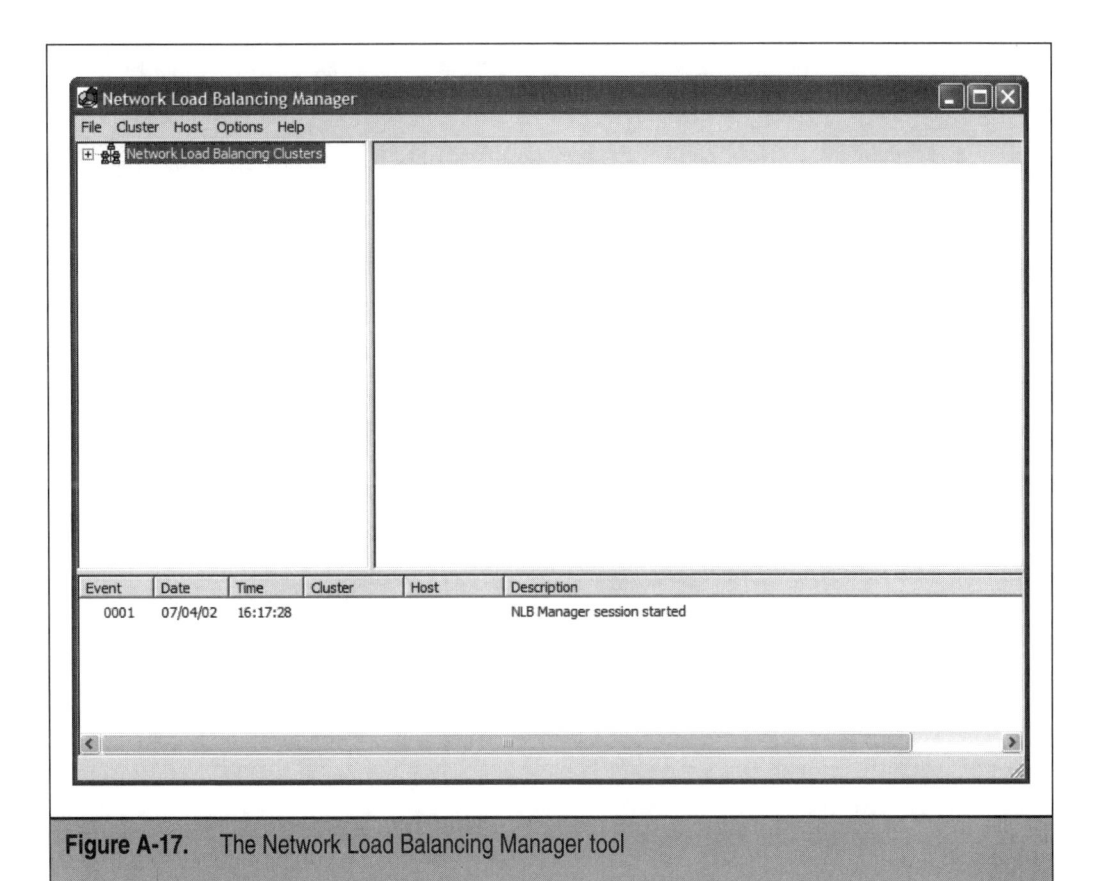

Figure A-17. The Network Load Balancing Manager tool

PERFORMANCE

The Performance tool is another way to invoke the System Monitor. For more information on System Monitor, flip back to Chapter 17. When started, System Monitor looks as shown in Figure A-18.

REMOTE DESKTOPS

The Remote Desktops tool is used to manage multiple terminal servers. Once connected, remote computers can be configured to run certain programs. A tree view on the left pane of the MMC allows easy switching between connections. This tool is useful for administrators who must remotely manage several Windows servers or terminal servers. Figure A-19 shows the process of creating a new remote desktop connection using the Remote Desktop tool.

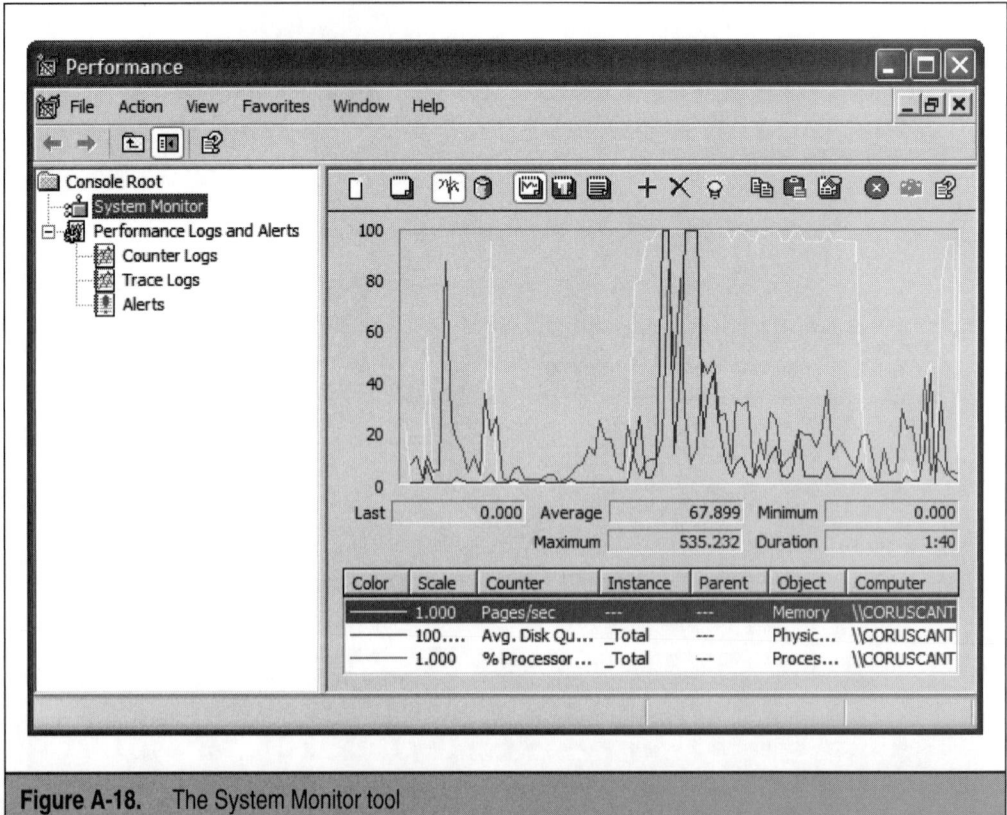

Figure A-18. The System Monitor tool

Figure A-19. Creating a new remote desktop connection

REMOTE STORAGE

Disk space on a computer can be extended by using the Remote Storage tool. This tool allows you to establish a threshold for disk space. If the drive level ever drops beneath this threshold, Remote Storage automatically copies the infrequently used files on your local computer to a tape library, opening space on your hard drive. This tool is shown in Figure A-20.

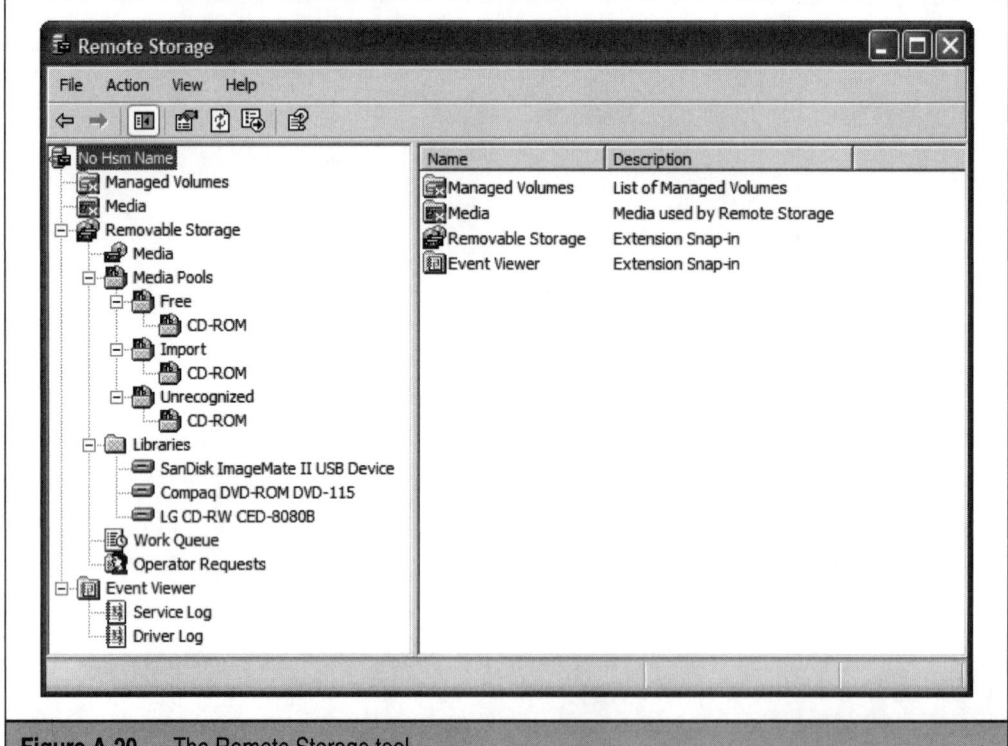

Figure A-20. The Remote Storage tool

ROUTING AND REMOTE ACCESS

The Routing and Remote Access tool is used for managing user permissions and ports on Routing and Remote Access Service (RRAS) servers. An RRAS server employs a user account database. This allows you to create an application that can be used to perform such tasks as the following:

- Listing users who have established RRAS permissions
- Assigning and revoking RRAS permissions for given users
- Listing configured ports on a RRAS server
- Gathering information and statistics about a port on an RRAS server

The Routing and Remote Access tool is shown in Figure A-21.

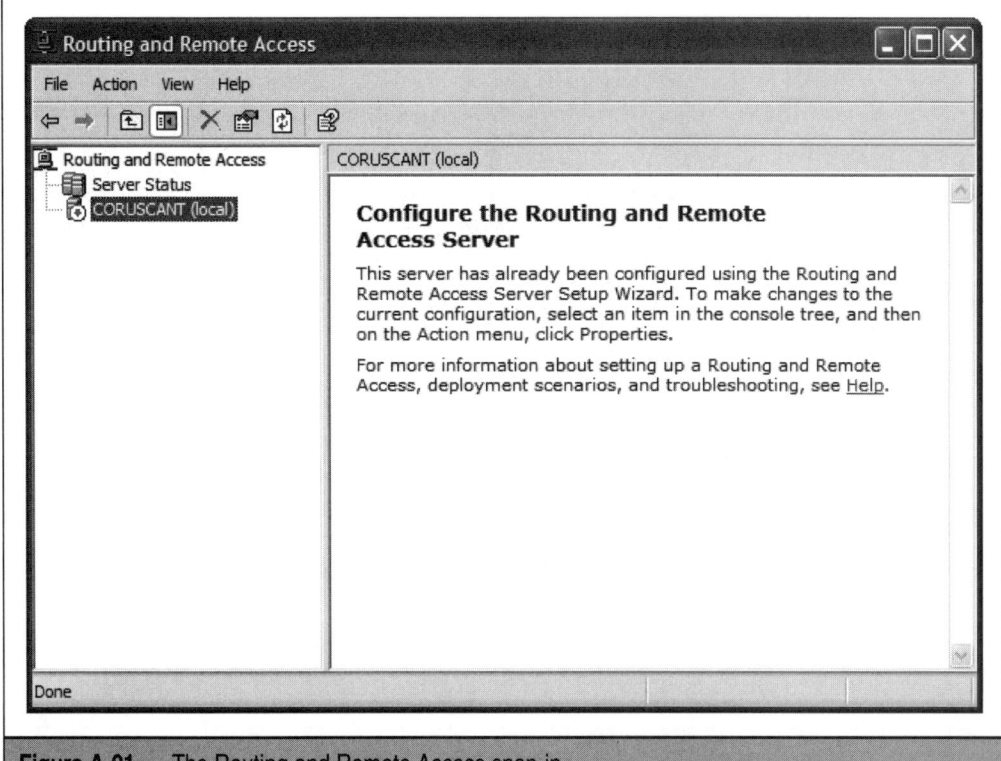

Figure A-21. The Routing and Remote Access snap-in

SERVER EXTENSIONS ADMINISTRATOR

The Server Extensions Administrator tool is used to manage FrontPage Server Extensions. For more information about FrontPage Server Extensions, flip back to Chapter 7. Figure A-22 shows the Server Extensions Administrator tool.

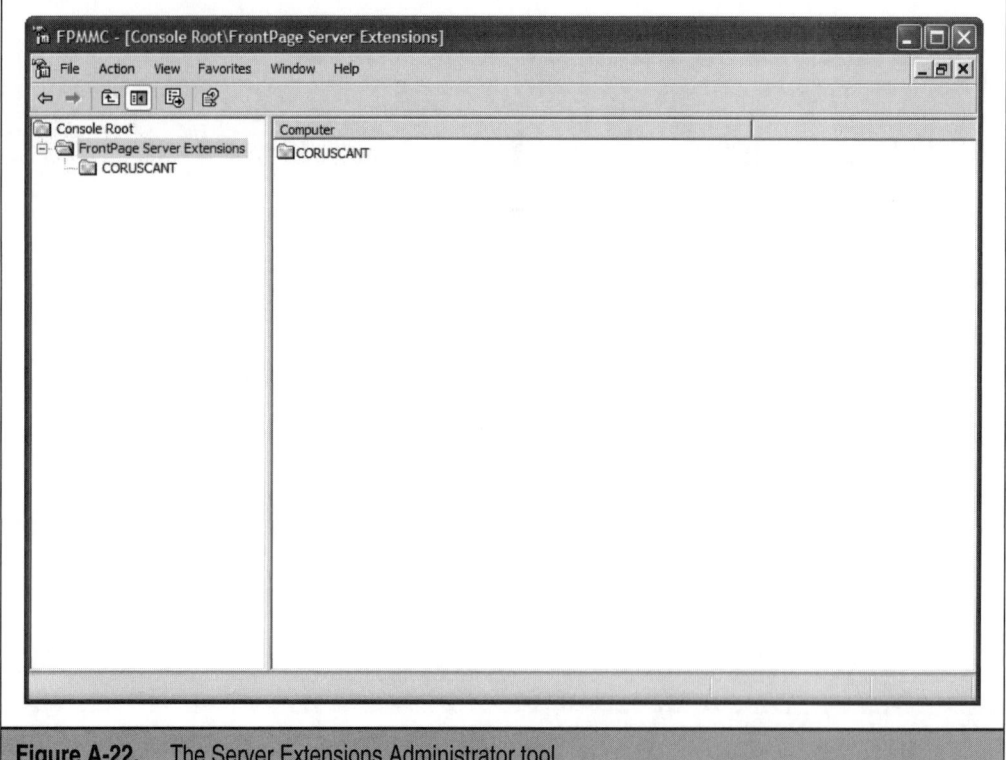

Figure A-22. The Server Extensions Administrator tool

SERVICES

The Services snap-in is used to start, stop, and manage Windows services. Some included services are:

- Alerter
- COM+ Event System
- DHCP Client
- Indexing Service
- QoS RSVP

The Services tool is shown in Figure A-23.

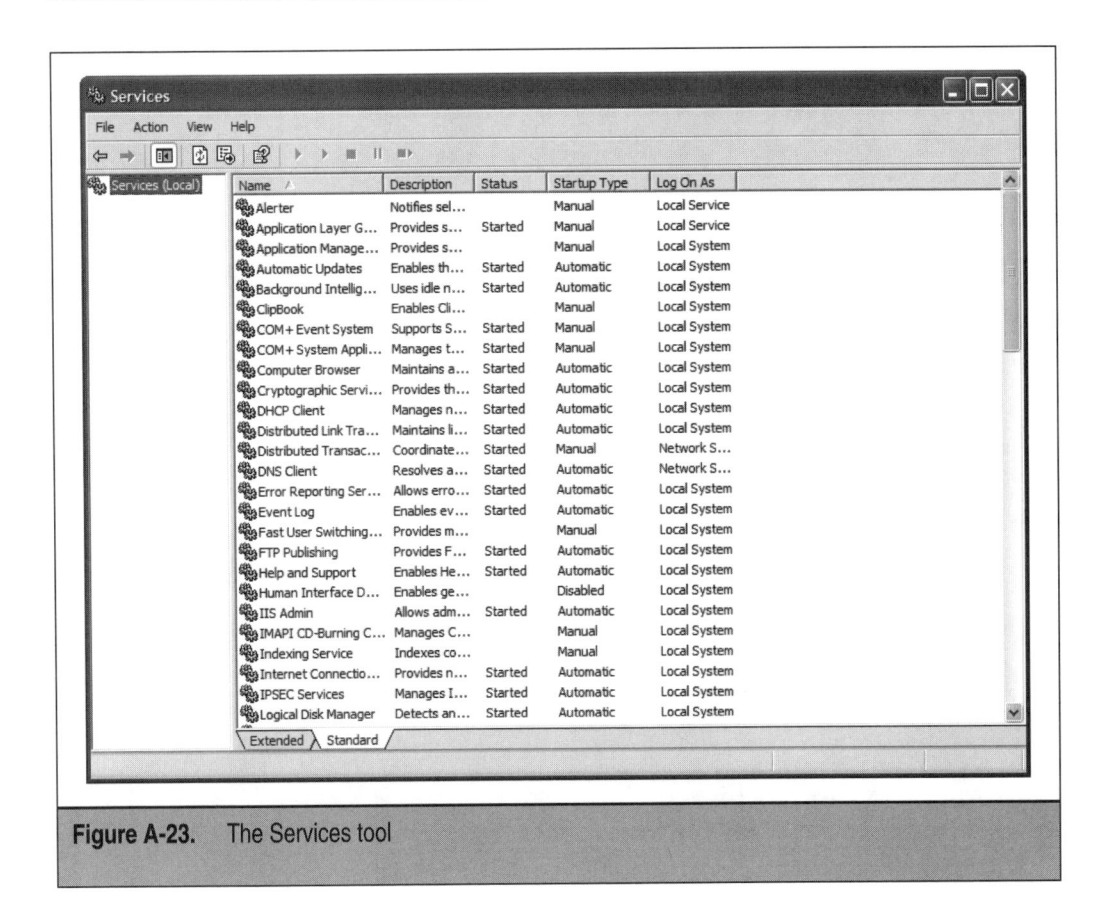

Figure A-23. The Services tool

TELEPHONY

The Telephony tool is used to integrate telecommunications technologies with your network. It provides a management tool for client-server voice and data, and video support for voice, fax, IP, and multicast video. This tool allows telephony programs installed on Windows .NET Server systems to communicate over conventional phone lines, LANs, WANs, and the Internet. The Telephony tool is shown in Figure A-24.

Figure A-24. The Telephony tool

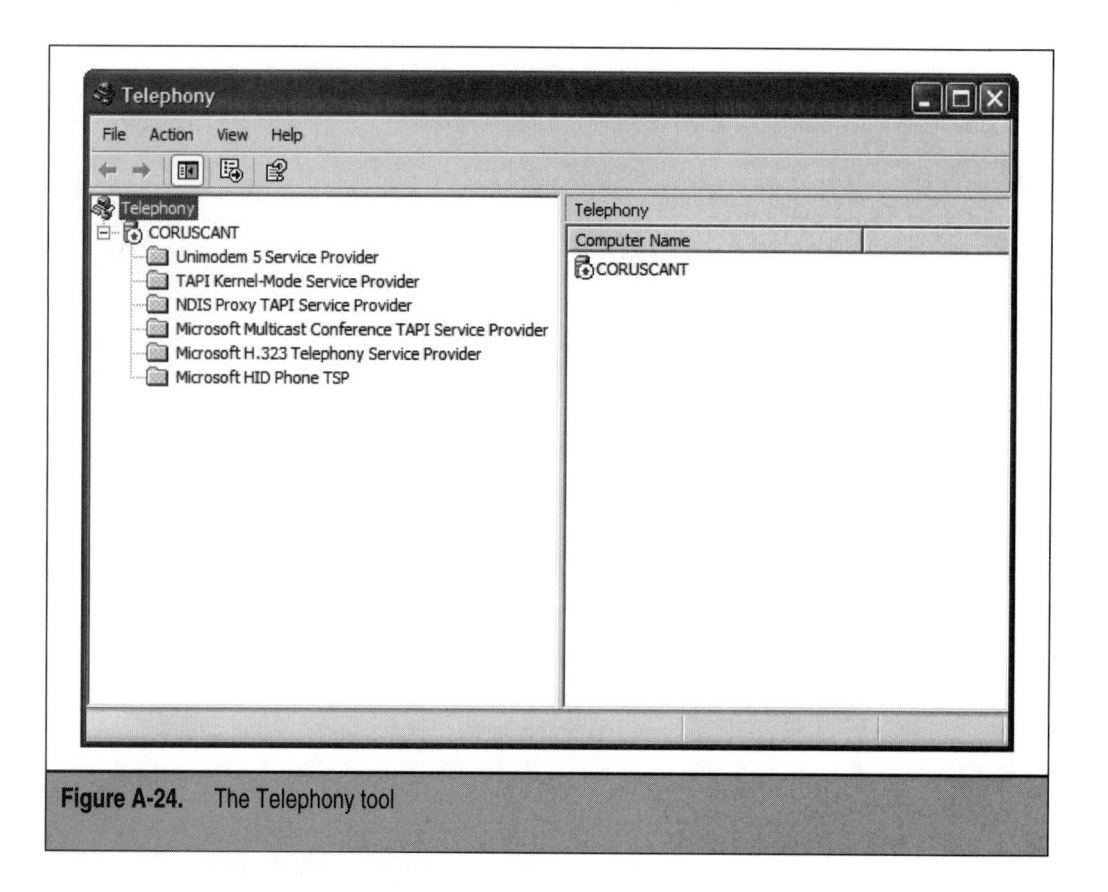

TERMINAL SERVICES MANAGER AND TERMINAL SERVER LICENSING

Both the Terminal Services Manager and the Terminal Server Licensing tools are used to manage multisession environments in which computers are able to access a server desktop through thin client software. These tools allow you to manage servers and the connections with Client Connection Manager.

Figures A-25 and A-26 show these tools.

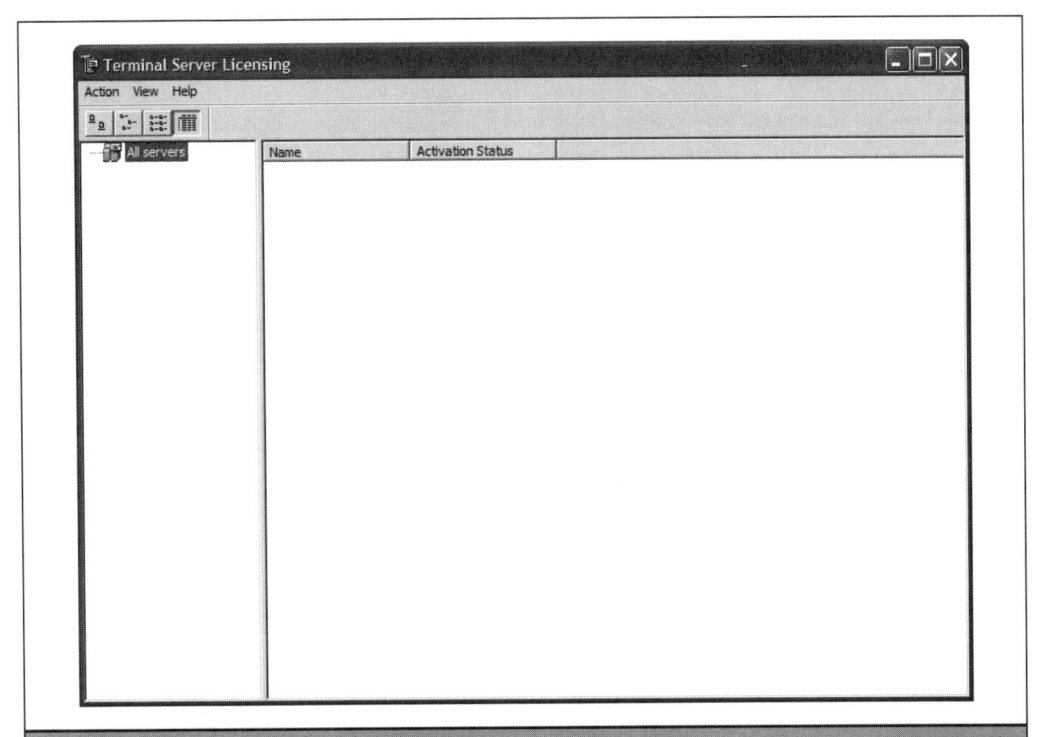

Figure A-25. The Terminal Server Licensing tool

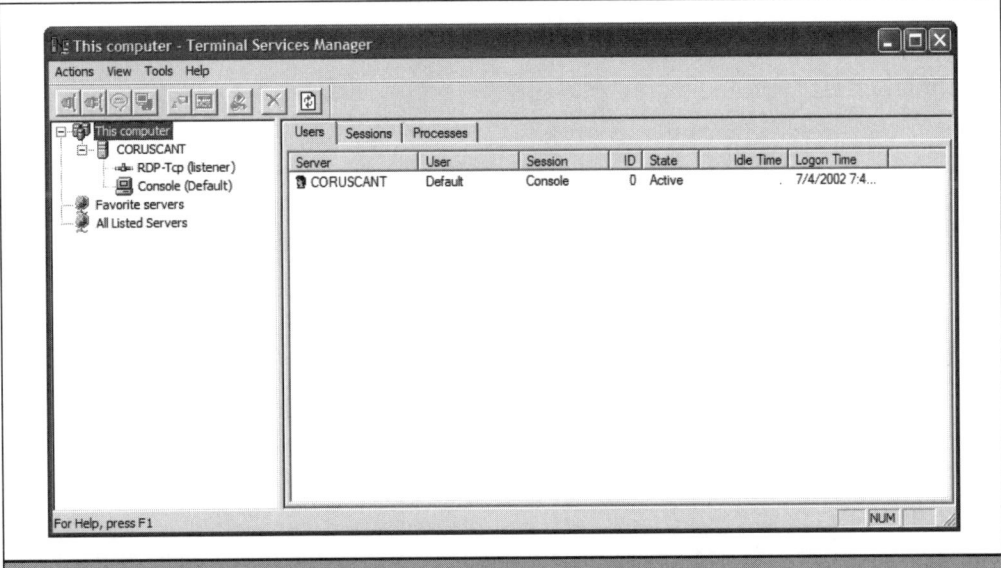

Figure A-26. The Terminal Services Manager tool

WINS

Phased out in Windows 2000, but still present in many Windows networks, is the Windows Internet Name Service (WINS). This provides a name resolution service akin to DNS. The WINS server registers and resolves names for WINS-enabled client computers. The WINS tool, shown in Figure A-27, is used to manage these devices.

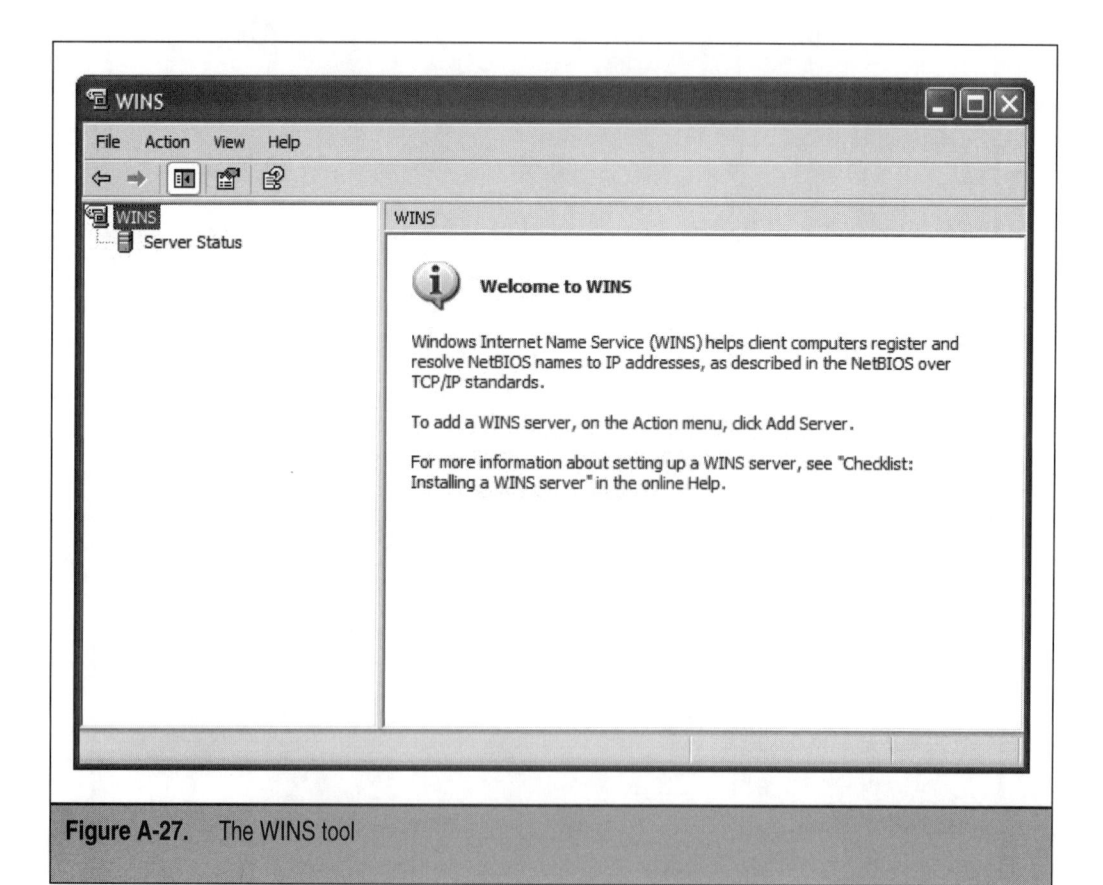

Figure A-27. The WINS tool

INDEX

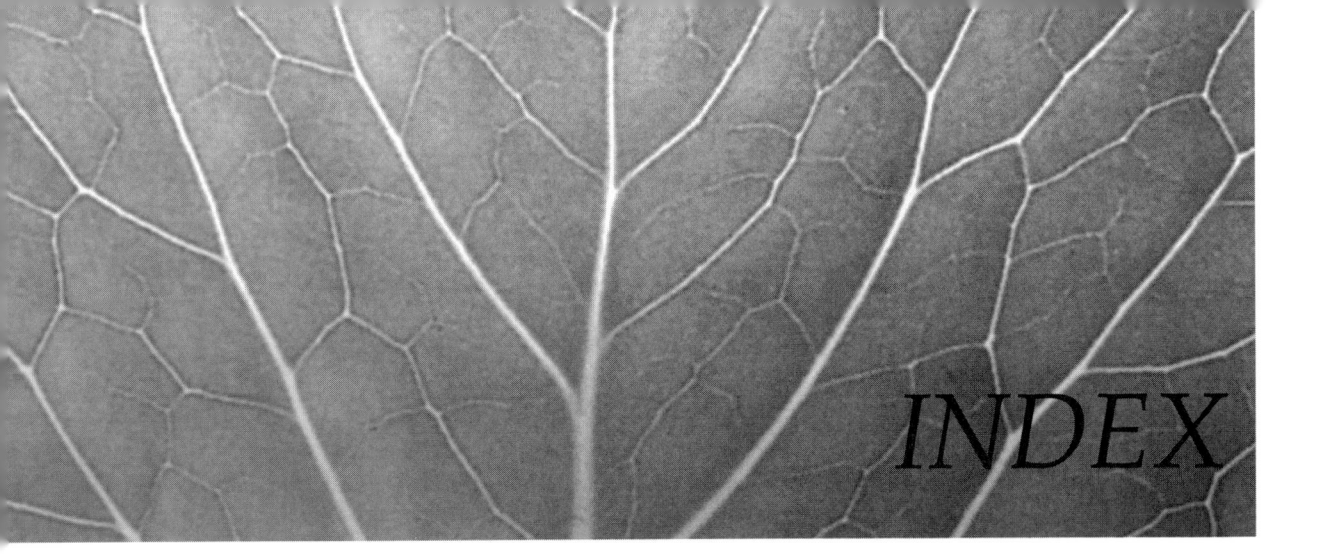

❖ A

Abstract layering, 14
Abstraction layer, 7
Access control (IIS), 224-226
Access LANs, 17-18
Access levels, file and folder, 345-347
Access points (APs), WLAN, 24, 34, 172-173, 175
Account logon attempts, auditing, 288
Accounts, types of, 304
ACLs (access control lists), 311-312
Activation (Windows XP), 68-70
Active Directory (AD), 62, 64-65, 198-205
Active Directory (AD) hierarchy, 201
Active Directory Domains and Trusts, 527-528
Active Directory schema, 200
Active Directory Sites and Services, 528-529
Active Directory Users and Computers, 314-315, 529-530
ActiveX server components, 213
Ad hoc networks, 179
Add Network Place Wizard, WebDAV connections, 211
Add New Hardware Wizard, 155
Add New Quota Entry window, 326
Add Standalone Snap-in dialog box, 248
Add/Remove Snap-in dialog box, 216
Administrative ownership, 278
Administrative Templates (Group Policy), 313

Administrative Tools (Windows .NET), 203-205, 525-552
Administrative traffic, reducing, 495
Administrator account, switching to from user, 301
Adminpak.msi, 203-204
Adobe Acrobat files, compressing all, 322
ADSI (AD Service Interfaces), 231
ADSL (Asymmetrical DSL), 28-29
Advanced Digest Authentication, 213
Advanced TCP/IP Settings dialog box, 102
AF (Assured Forwarding) traffic class, 461
AHs (Authentication Headers), 442
Alert counters, 508
Alert Properties dialog box, 509-510
Alert view (System Monitor), 507-510
Alias (to access virtual directories), 223
Alternate DNS servers, 108-109
Alternate IP addressing, 94, 103-104
Analog circuits, 26
Analog modems, 120-125
Analog telephone lines, 26
Analytical traffic modeling, 516
Anonymous authentication, 231
Anonymous Logon property (IIS), 223
Antivirus software, 47, 331
APIPA (Automatic Private IP Addressing), 91, 93-94, 98-100

Application Configuration dialog box, Mapping tab, 236
Application errors, diagnosing, 258-260
Application layer (TCP/IP), 14, 72
Application log events, viewing, 539
Application mappings, 236
Application permissions (NTFS), 229
Application protection (IIS 5.1), 209
Application server, defined, 10
Application sharing, 352-356
Applications
    enabling others to control, 355-356
    hung, 242-244
    viewing details of, 252
Area code rules for Dialing Locations, 141-143
ARP (Address Resolution Protocol), 267
ASP (Active Server Pages), 213-214
ATM (Asynchronous Transfer Mode), 20, 22-23
ATM cells, 22
Auditing security, 287-290
Authentication, 179-180, 304-311
    anonymous, 231
    IIS, 229-231
    Kerberos, 47-48, 212
    vs. logon, 304
    vs. WEP key, 179
Authentication hashing, 213
Authentication protocol (Kerberos), 47-48, 193, 212, 302-303
Autodial, enabling and disabling, 437-438
Automatic update feature, 41
Automatic wireless configuration, 177-178
Auto-starting programs, turning off, 245-246

❖ B

Backbone LANs, 17-18
Backing up and restoring files, 41-42
Backup Operators, 304
Bandwidth
    Ethernet vs. Token Ring, 22
    raw, 454-455
    reserved, 458-459
    split by switches, 11
Bandwidth management (Remote Assistance), 419
Baselining your network, 495

Batch logon, 300
B-channels, ISDN, 27
BDCs (backup domain controllers), 184-185
Best-effort service, 454, 466-468
Binary file, defined, 5
Binary messages, 4-5
Binary transmission, explained, 5
Binding protocols to clients and services, 157-158
Bits, 4-6
Blank password limitation, 278
Boot floppy disk, making, 241-242
Bootable CD-ROM, 59
BRI (Basic Rate Interface), ISDN, 27
Briefcases. *See* Windows Briefcase
Broadband connection, 135, 138
Browser Capabilities tool (ASP), 214
Browser request, redirecting, 233-235
BSS (basic service set), 176
Bundling of ISDN connections, 138-139
Bus support for Plug and Play, 119
Bytes, 5-6

❖ C

CAB (cabinet) files, 130
Cable adapter, configuring, 129-130
Cable hardware, 129-130
Cable modem, 30
    configuration, 129-130
    installation, 129
Caching files and folders, 373-375
Callback feature
    enabling, 438-439
    remote access settings, 440
Calling cards, 144-147
Capacity planning, 515-521
Carrier sensing, Ethernet, 19
CAs (certification authorities), 212
CD command (DOS), 240
CD-ROM
    bootable, 59
    installing Windows clients from, 152
Cells (ATM), 22
Cells (802.11 LAN), 176
Cells (WLAN), 24
Certificate Server 2.0, 212
Certification Authority tool, 530-531
Challenge and Response (Windows NT), 212

Index

Change permission (FAT), 359
Chart view (System Monitor), 505-507
Chat (Internet), 352
Chat (Remote Assistance), 419
Checksum, explained, 76
CHKDSK command (DOS), 240, 338
CIFS (Common Internet File System) protocol, 483
Cipher command, 327, 329
Class B IP addresses, 82, 84-87
Class B whole octet subnet example, 84-87
Class C IP address octet ranges, 81-82
Class C partial octet subnet example, 88
Clean installation (automatic), 58
Client compatible encryption (Remote Desktop), 405
Client computers. *See* Windows XP clients
Client For Microsoft Networks, 156
Client for NFS (SFU 3.0), 486-487
Clipboard, disabling in Terminal Services, 406
Clock (computer), setting correctly, 193
Cloning, 58-59
Cluster Administrator, 531
Cluster sizing, to optimize performance, 330
Clustering software, explained, 531
Clusters, explained, 330
CO (Central Office), 127
Code points, defined, 460
COM (Component Object Model), 213
Compact.exe, 322-323
Compatibility check process, 52-53
Compatibility Mode, 40-41
Component Services tool, 532-533
Compressed volumes, 320-322
Compression, 319-323
Computer local groups, 310
Computer Management snap-in, 356, 361-366, 533-534
    activating, 363
    Open Files view, 364
    Sessions view, 363
    Shares view, 362
Computer words (bits), 6
Computers, System Monitor views of, 503
Computing architectures, 6-7
Compuware NetworkVantage, 523-524
Compuware Predictor, 520-521
Concord eHealth, 522
Conforming packets, explained, 466

Connect to Wireless Network dialog box, 181
Connection Manager Administration Kit, 534
Connection Manager Administration Kit Wizard, 534-535
Connection status, viewing, 249-251
Connection Timeout property (IIS), 222
Connections
    flows and, 457-458
    managing, 139-147
    repairing, 253-254
    that keep dropping, 264
    troubleshooting, 237-273
    workgroup, 149-181
Connection-specific domain names, 107-108
Console security (Remote Desktop), 403
Contention, Ethernet, 19
Controlled load service type (QoS), 466, 468
Conversation consolidation, 518
Convert.exe tool, 44, 338, 342
Converting FAT drives to NTFS, 44, 337-342
Copy command, 483
Cost of ownership (WLAN), 171
CPU, 6
CSMA/CD, 14, 19
CSNW (Client Services for NetWare), 474-477
CTLs (Certificate Trust Lists), 212
Cycles (Hz), 5

❖ D

DACLs (discretionary access control lists), 311
DARPA (Defense Advanced Research Projects Agency), 72
Data, from computer's perspective, 4-7
Data frame, 17
Data integrity, when converting to NTFS, 338-339
Data Sources (ODBC) tool, 534-536
Database driven, explained, 291
Datagrams (IP), 16, 73, 75-77
Data-link layer (OSI), 14, 16-17
D-channel (delta channel), ISDN, 27
Dcpromo.exe, 63
DCs (domain controllers), 184-185.
    See also Domains
    changes to one replicated to all, 186
    changing from mixed mode to native mode, 68

checking for secure client
    connection, 191
checking for user authentication, 191
and client protocol, 193
and computers with similar names, 193
creating, 67
finding, 192
identifying, 191
replacement for PDCs and BDCs, 65
Debugging Mode, 132
Decrypting files and folders, 329
Default gateways, 91-92
Deferred printing, 381
Defrag command, 340
Defragmenting a drive, 339-340
DEL command (DOS), 240
Delay (packet delivery), 455
Desktop control (Remote Assistance), 419
DESX (Data Encryption Standard XORed), 327
Device drivers, 50, 120, 132-133, 155
Device Manager, 117-118, 132-133
Devices, 8-12
    overloaded, 500-501
    viewing details of, 252
Devices for Incoming Connections dialog
    box, 433
DFS (Distributed File System) snap-in, 537-538
DHCP Allocator (ICS), 161
DHCP (Dynamic Host Configuration
    Protocol), 83, 93, 97-98
DHCP leases, 98
DHCP snap-in, 536-537
Diagramming your network, 494
Dial-in connections, 25, 137, 139-141, 430, 432
Dial-in server connection, disabling, 443
Dial-in technologies, 26-30
Dialing Location, 139-143
Dialing Location area code rules, 141-143
Dial-up connection icon, 96
Dial-up connection to the Internet, 135-136
Dial-up Preferences, 436-438
DiffServ Code Point (DSCP), 465-468
DiffServ (Differentiated Services), 456,
    460-461, 465-470
DiffServ-based QoS performance objects, 470
DIR command (DOS), 240, 482
Directory Security (Web Site Properties),
    224-225

Discrete traffic modeling, 516
Disk Defragmenter snap-in, 339-340
Disk fragmentation, 330, 339-340
Disk Management snap-in, 340-341
Disk Queue Length, 515
Disk quotas, 323-326
Disk subsystem, monitoring, 514-515
Disk-image copying, 58
Distribution system, explained, 24, 176
DMA (direct memory access), 118
DMZ (demilitarized zone), 218
DNS (Domain Name System), 104-109
DNS hostname, setting and changing,
    105-107
DNS Proxy, 161
DNS server address, 95-96
DNS server search order, establishing, 109
DNS servers
    entering the location of, 79
    preferred and alternate, 108-109
    URL conversion to IP addresses, 78
DNS suffix, changing primary, 107
DNS tool, 538-539
DNS zone transfers, 495
Documenting your network, 494-495
Domain accounts, 194
Domain connectivity, 187-193
Domain controllers, 63
Domain flattening, 65
Domain local groups, 310
Domain model, Windows XP and, 186-187
Domain names
    connection-specific, 107-108
    issuance of, 77
Domain replication, 186
Domain resources, accessing, 194-198
Domain upgrades, 67
Domain verification process, 190
Domains (see also DCs)
    as collections of OUs, 200
    connecting Windows XP clients to, 188
    explained, 184-186
    how they work, 185-186
    identifying DCs of, 191
    joining, 187-190
    joining manually, 188-190
    logon errors prevent access to, 193
    and security, 194

unable to find domain controller, 192
unable to join, 191-192
unable to log onto, 193
verifying membership in, 190
Windows products residing in, 186
DOS commands for troubleshooting, 240
DoS (denial-of-service) attacks, 169, 295
Dotted-decimal format (IP addresses), 80-81
Downloading files for offline use, 372-374
Dr. Watson, 258-260
Drive mapping, 347-349
Drive sharing, 344-347
Drives
converting to NTFS, 337-342
defragmenting, 339-340
formatting with NTFS, 337-342
unmapping, 348
Dropped packets, 20, 169
DRR (deficit round robin) scheme, 462
Drwtsn32.exe utility, 258
Drwtsn32.log file, 258
DSCP (DiffServ Code Point), 465-468
DSCP Value of Conforming Packets (QoS), 465-467
DSCP Value of Nonconforming Packets (QoS), 467-468
DSL configuration, 128-129
DSL (digital subscriber lines), 26, 28-29, 127-129
DSL hardware, 127-129
DSL Lite, 28-29
DSL modems, 29, 128
DSSS (direct sequence spread spectrum), 23
Dual-boot installations, 51
DVD drives, 7
Dynamic content, explained, 235

❖ E

Edge device, explained, 89
EF (Expedited Forwarding) traffic class, 460
Effective Permissions, 312
EFS (Encrypting File System), 278, 327-329, 379
EHealth (Concord), 522
Electrical pulses, fluctuations in voltage of, 5
Elementary NTFS structure, 339
E-mail server, defined, 10
Enable Boot Logging, 132
Enable VGA Mode, 132

Encrypted data transmission, 294-299
Encryption, 232
of files and folders, 328
for high-speed LAN security, 172
of Offline Files, 379-380
Encryption levels for Remote Desktop, 405-406
Error Reporting, 244
ESP (Encapsulation Security Protocol), 442, 450-451
Ethernet, 17, 18-20
architecture, 19-20
vs. ATM, 23
carrier sensing and frame collisions, 19
raw bandwidth, 22
EULA (Microsoft End User License Agreement), 68
Event Properties dialog box, 250
Event Viewer tool, 247, 249, 539-540
Extended service set, 176
External modem installation, 121

❖ F

Fast Ethernet, 18
Fast User Switching, turning off, 369, 395
FAT drives, permissions on, 358-359
FAT (file allocation table) file system, 43
floppy disk use of, 338
vs. NTFS, 43-44, 318
overhead, 44
FAT to NTFS conversion, 44, 337-342
FEK (file encryption key), 327
File access levels, 345-347
File extensions, that are not synchronizable, 397
File gateway, 478-479
File permissions, 335
File and Printer Sharing for MSN, 344-345
File server, defined, 10
File share, identifying, 195
File structure, NTFS, 331
File system structure, designing, 57
File systems, 43-44
File transfers (Remote Assistance), 419
Files (see also Offline files and folders)
accessing with network disconnected, 368
automatic caching of, 373
decrypting, 329

disabling in Terminal Services, 407
encrypting, 328
marking for encryption, 327
moving to Windows Briefcase, 390-391
NTFS compression for, 319-322
NTFS permissions for, 229
pinning, 373
redirecting a browser request to, 234-235
restoring, 40-42
Files in a Briefcase, updating, 393-394
Firewalls, 46, 168, 449. *See also* ICF
FireWire drives, 497
First octet rule, 81
Flat topology (network), 495
Floppy disks, use of FAT, 338
Flows (packet streams)
and connections, 457-458
packet data elements of, 457-458
Folder access levels, 345-347
Folder compression, 319
Folder Options dialog box, 197, 369-370, 380
Folder permissions, 334-337
Folder Redirection, 64, 369
Folders (*see also* Offline files and folders)
auditing, 289
automatic caching of, 373
decrypting, 329
encrypting, 328
NTFS compression for, 319-322
NTFS permissions for, 229
pinning, 373
sharing, 344-347
Forest, defined, 200
Fortezza, 212
Fpsrvwin tool, 215
FQDN (fully qualified domain name), 106
Fractionalized T1, 31
Fragmentation, 330, 339-340
Frame header, 16
Frame relay, 31-32
Frames, 16-17, 31-32
FrontPage, 214-217
FrontPage Server Extensions, 215-217, 547-548
FrontPage Server Extensions snap-in, 215-217
FSMO (Flexible Single Master Operations), 65
FTP authentication, enabling, 230-231
FTP server, configuring, 226-227
FTP service, 208, 226

FTP sites, home directories for, 233
Full Control (FAT) permission, 359
Full Control (NTFS) permission, 360
Full synchronization, 383

❖ G

Gateway to files, activating, 478-479
Gateway for NFS (SFU 3.0), 487-488
Gateway to printers, activating, 479
Gateways, 91-92, 477
Ghost imaging, 58
Gigabit Ethernet, 18, 20
GINA (Graphical Identification and Authentication), 300
G.Lite, 28
Global Catalog, 202
Global groups, 202, 310
Globally routable addresses, 83
GRE (generic routing encapsulating) packets, 450
Group permissions, 335
Group Policy snap-in, 38, 50, 313-315
auditing from, 288
IntelliMirror and, 199
managing offline files, 376-378
managing QoS levels, 464-469
settings for Offline Files, 376-378
Terminal Services, 404-407
Groups, 202-203, 313-315, 335
GSNW (Gateway Service for NetWare), 477-479
activating a file gateway, 478-479
activating a printer gateway, 479
creating a gateway, 478
enabling, 478
setting permissions, 479
Guaranteed service type (QoS), 466, 468-469

❖ H

Hard drive compression, 319
Hard drive interfaces, 497
Hard drive requirements, 54-55
Hard drive space per user, limiting, 323-326
Hardware, 116-133
Hardware components (IIS), 218-219

Hardware connection overview, 116-120
Hardware inventory, 63
Hardware messages when trying to connect, 264
Hardware problem-solving, 130-133
Hardware Update Wizard, 133
Hashing (authentication), 213
Help Services Group, 304
Help and Support Center, 42
    Ask a friend to help, 421-422
    Fixing a Problem, 252-253
    Network Diagnostics, 253-254
High level encryption (Remote Desktop), 405
High-speed data rates (WLAN), 172
Home directories, for web or FTP sites, 233
Host computer (data sharing), 137
Hosts file, 104
Hot fixing, 43
HP OpenView, 522-523
HTTP Compression, 209
HTTP (Hypertext Transfer Protocol), 14
HTTP IIS Manager, 221-222
HTTP service, 208
Hubs (network), 11-12, 263
Hung programs, 242-244
Hz (hertz), 5

❖ I

IANA (Internet Assigned Numbers Authority), 77
ICANN (Internet Corporation for Assigned Names and Numbers), 77
ICF (Internet Connection Firewall), 37, 46, 167-168, 281
    configuring, 169-170
    incompatibilities, 168-169
    overview of, 167
    placement of, 168
    security logging, 281-284
    on a workgroup, 167-170
ICF logging, 169, 282-284
ICF security log, 169, 282-284
ICMP (Internet Control Message protocol), 266
ICMP object counter, 470
ICMP options (ICF), 169
ICMP rules, 281
ICS clients, 160-161, 163

ICS (Internet Connection Sharing), 44-45, 91, 159-167
    components of, 161
    features of, 160-161
    manual configuration, 163-165
    in Network Setup Wizard, 161-162
    with QoS, 461-462
    setting up, 161-165
    troubleshooting, 166-167
    VPN model, 165-166
ICS server, 160-161, 163-165
ICS Troubleshooter, 166-167
IEEE 802.1p standard, 463
IEEE 802.1x authentication, 179-180
IEEE 802.3 Ethernet standard, 20
IEEE 802.5 Token Ring standard, 21
IEEE 802.11 standard, 23-24, 176
IEEE 802.11a standard, 24
IEEE 802.11b standard, 23
IEEE (Institute of Electrical and Electronics Engineers), 19
IETF (Internet Engineering Task Force), 19, 80
IETF IP address classes, 80
IIS console, 220
IIS 5.1 features, 208-214
IIS 5.1 reliability and stability, 209-212
IIS (Internet Information Services/Server), 207-236
    access control, 224-226
    application environment, 213-214
    application protection, 209
    authentication, 229-231
    configuring, 221-227
    configuring web services, 222-226
    hardware and networking components, 218-219
    installing, 217-220
    intranet content management, 217
    logging, 223-225
    managing, 213, 221-222
    minimum requirements for installation, 218-219
    placement considerations, 217-218
    publishing to FTP folders, 227-228
    publishing to web folders, 227
    Remote Desktop Web Connection, 408
    security features, 224-226, 228-232
    setting default pages, 227-228

software components, 219
using, 227-236
virtual directories, 223
IIS snap-in, 213
In-building WLAN equipment, 174
Include directive, 235
Incoming Connections icon, 434
Incoming Connections Properties
  dialog box, 448
Incoming dial-up connection, 433
Indexing Service (Windows), 331-332
Infrared light, 170
Inheritance, 333
Installation ID, 69
Installation options (Windows XP), 57-61
Installation reparation, 241-242
Installing servers, 61-66
Instances (of objects), 503
Integrated Windows Authentication, 212
IntelliMirror, 199-200
Interactive logon procedure (remote
  access), 431
Interactive logon process components, 300-301
Interconnectivity with other systems,
  110-111, 473-492
Interconnectivity protocols, 110-111
Internet access policy for users, 496
Internet chat, 352
Internet connection IP address, displaying, 96
Internet Connection Wizard, 135-136
Internet connections
  creating, 134-139
  for Remote Desktop, 408-410, 413-414
  for VPN clients, 445
Internet layer (TCP/IP), 72-73
Internet Protocol (TCP/IP) Properties dialog
  box, 95, 101
InterNIC, 77
Interoperability (WLAN), 172
Interix tool, 484-485
Intranet content management (IIS 5.1), 217
Intranet web server placement, 218
IntServ (integrated services), 458
Inventory of hardware and software, 63
Invitation ticket (Remote Assistance), 424, 426
Invitations (Remote Assistance), 420-426
IP address name resolution, 104-110
IP address translation services, 90

IP addresses, 77, 83-92
  assigning, 93-96
  blocks of reserved private, 89
  checking assignment of, 99
  classes of, 80-82
  displaying for Internet connection, 96
  in dotted-decimal format, 80-81
  format of, 78-79
  ICS server, 161
  issuance of, 77
  methods to resolve names to, 104
  octet ranges, 81-82
  private, 89-91
  public, 83
  setting manually, 101
  setting up in Windows XP, 97-111
  vs. subnets, 87
  URL conversion into, 78
  viewing, 251
IP addressing, 77, 83-92
  alternate, 94, 103-104
  static, 94, 100-103
IP datagrams, 16, 73, 75-77
IP (Internet Protocol), 12, 495
IP message transport protocols, 74
IP networks, best-effort service, 454
IP version 4, 83
IP version 6, 83
Ipconfig.exe tool, 96-99, 267-268
IPSec, 192, 294-299
  how it works, 295-296
  modes, 442
  negotiation, 296
  policies, 296-298
  rule properties, 299
  security areas, 442
IPSec Monitor, 451
IPSec Policy Agent, 296
IPSec Policy Management snap-in, 297-298
IPX (Internetwork Packet Exchange)
  protocol, 474
IPX/SPX protocol, installing, 474-475
IPX/SPX/NetBIOS Compatible Transport
  Protocol), 475, 477
IrDA (Infrared Data Association), 170-171
IRQ (interrupt request), 118, 133
ISDN adapter, 126-127
ISDN BRI circuit, 28

Index **561**

ISDN channels, 27
ISDN connection, 138-139, 265
ISDN hardware, 125-127
ISDN (Integrated Services Digital Network), 26-28, 125-127, 430-431
ISO (International Standards Organization), 12
IUI (Intelligent User Interface), 34

❖ J

Jitter, 454-455

❖ K

KCC (Knowledge Consistency Checker), 186
KDC (Kerberos Key Distribution Center), 48, 301, 303
Kerberos, 47-48, 193, 212, 302-303

❖ L

LAN cabling, problems with, 260
LAN components, that should be installed, 154-155
LAN connection, for Remote Desktop, 407-408, 412-413
LAN Connection Properties dialog box, 262
LAN segmentation, 8, 16
LANs (local area networks), 8, 17-18, 152-155, 260-263
Laptop connections, 435-440
Laptop synchronization options, 386-388
Last Known Good Configuration, 132, 241
Last mile problem, 25-26, 30
Layer 2 priority value (packets), 468-469
LDAP (Lightweight Directory Access Protocol), 14
Leased lines (T1 and T3), 30-31
Legacy applications, 40-41
Links, redirecting, 233-235
Linux/UNIX connections, 483-492
Lmhosts file, 104
Local account access, 431
Local disk drives, connecting to remote computer, 414
Local Disk Properties dialog box, 325, 336-337
Local files, using with Remote Desktop, 416
Local groups, 202
Local ports, connecting to remote computer, 414
Local printer
    sharing, 349
    using with Remote Desktop, 416
Local Security Policy snap-in, 279-281, 540-541
    managing, 280-281
    viewing, 279-280
Local Security Settings dialog box, 280-281
Local Users and Groups snap-in, 306
Log events, viewing, 539
Log files (IIS), 224
Log On Locally rights, 231
Log On To Windows dialog box, 190
Log view (System Monitor), 510-511
Logging (IIS), 209, 223-225
Logical multihoming, 100
Logon, 299-302, 304
Logon attempts, auditing, 288
Logon errors preventing access to a domain, 193
Logon procedure (Kerberos), 48
LPP (Lightweight Presentation Protocol), 14
LPR/LPD protocol, 483
LSA (Local Security Authority), 48, 300, 303
L2F (Layer 2 Forwarding), 443
L2TP (Layer 2 Tunneling Protocol), 110, 165, 443
Lucent VitalSuite, 521

❖ M

MAC layer (802.11 protocol), 17, 24, 176
MAC (media access control) addresses, 16-17
Mapping a network drive, 347-349
MAU (media access unit), 21
Maximum Connections property (IIS), 222
Mbps (megabits per second), 5
McAfee VirusScan Online, 47
MDI (multiple document interface), 246
Media sense, 176
Memory counters, monitoring, 513-514
Message, sending to a user, 365-366
Message digest, 213
Message-handling protocols, 15

Microsoft, sharing error information with, 244
Microsoft .NET e-commerce initiative, 352
Microsoft .NET Passport account, 352
Microsoft .NET Passport Wizard, 352
Microsoft .NET Server, 61
Microsoft Product Compatibility list, 52
Migration (to Windows XP)
    design stages, 56-57
    logical design stage, 56-57
    preparation, 56-61
    steps, 66-68
    of workstations, 68
MMC (Microsoft Management Console), 50-51, 246-248
MMC snap-ins, 203, 246-248
Modem connection, troubleshooting, 125, 133
Modem properties, 123-124
Modems (modulator/demodulators), 26, 120-125
    configuring, 121-125
    installing, 121
    QoS with, 462
    troubleshooting, 264
Modify permission (NTFS), 361
Mounts (UNIX resource), 491
Msconfig utility, 245-246
Multihoming, 100-102
Multimaster replication, 186
Multiple-domain model, 65
Multiplexed, explained, 27
Multiprocessor systems, 55
My Network Places, 152-153, 194

❖ N

Name ping, 262-263
Name resolution, 104-110, 450. *See also* DNS
NAT (Network Address Translation), 38, 90-91, 161, 450
Native mode, going to from mixed mode, 68
Nbtstat tool, 270-271
NDS tree connections, 481-483
NDS (Novell Directory Services), 474, 481-483
.NET Administrative Tools, 203-205, 525-552
.NET e-commerce initiative, 352
.NET Framework Configuration tool, 540-542
.NET Logon Service, 301
.NET Passport account, 352

.NET Passport Wizard, 352
.NET Server, domains and, 187
Net use command
    mapping a network drive, 349
    NDS tree printer connection, 483
    NetWare server login, 481
    NetWare volume access, 480
Net view command, 481-482
.NET Wizards tool, 542-543
NetBEUI (NetBIOS Extended User Interface), 111, 156-158
NetBIOS (Network Basic Input/Output System), 14, 105-106
NetScout nGenius Capacity Planner, 519-520
NetWare
    connections, 474-483
    printers, 482-483
    resources, 480-483
    servers, 481-482
    volumes, 480
Network access control, 431
Network adapters
    enabling QoS 802.1p on, 463
    problems with, 260
    viewing details of, 252
Network administration workload distribution, 185
Network applications, explained, 14
Network bottlenecks, common sites of, 513
Network Configuration Operators, 304
Network connections
    checking, 139
    creating, 115-147
    viewing, 153-155, 194-195, 249-251
    viewing details of, 251-252
Network Connections window, 96, 153-154, 444
Network construction, 496
Network control service type (QoS), 466, 468-469
Network device addresses, spoofed, 91
Network devices, 8-12
    overloaded, 500-501
    viewing details of, 252
Network Diagnostics, 252-254
Network drive mapping, 347-349
Network failure points, 261
Network file, working on after disconnection, 368

Network Identification Wizard, 188-189
Network interface layer (TCP/IP), 72
Network layer (OSI), 14, 16-17
Network layer protocols, 17
Network Load Balancing Manager, 205, 542-543
Network Monitor, 451
Network Neighborhood, 194
Network performance monitoring, 493-524
Network performance overview, 494-501
Network printers, viewing, 196
Network probes, 517-518
Network problem-solving, 259-273
Network resources, viewing, 195
Network security, 277-315
Network segmentation, 497-501
Network segmentation via router, 498-499
Network segmentation via switch, 500-501
Network Setup Disk, 151-152
Network Setup Wizard, 150-152, 161-162
Network shares, 343-366, 373-374
Network simulation, 515-521
Network simulation tools, 519-521
Network specifications, 17
Network subsystem, monitoring, 515
Network Support help, 251
Network technologies, 16-24
Network topology, 63, 494, 516-517
Network traffic, 461, 516-518
Network troubleshooting tools and scenarios, 265-273
Networked printer, using, 352
Networking components (IIS), 218-219
Networking devices vs. PCs, 4
Networking features of Windows XP, 34-39, 42-48
Networking fundamentals, 3-32
Networking protocols, standardizing, 65-66
NetworkVantage (Compuware), 523-524
New Connection Wizard, 134-138, 433
    broadband connection, 138
    dial-in connection, 137
    information requested by, 137-138
    ISDN connection, 138-139
    Public Network, 445
    on remote access client, 435-436
    User Permissions, 434
    VPN Server Selection, 445

New Server Cluster Wizard, 532
NFS files, marked as sparse, 331-332
NFS (Network File System) protocol, 483, 485
    UNIX configuration, 491-492
    XP client configuration, 491
NFS servers, 490-492
NGenius Capacity Planner, 519-520
NIC (network interface cards), 5
Nltest.exe, 190-191
Novell NetWare. *See* CSNW; GSNW; NetWare
NTFS (New Technology File System), 43
    built-in compression, 43, 319-322
    converting drives to, 44, 337-342
    default cluster sizes, 330
    elementary structure of, 339
    vs. FAT, 43-44, 318
    features of, 318-332
    formatting drives with, 337-342
    optimization, 330-331
NTFS permissions, 228-229, 332-337, 360-361
NTFS security, 44, 317-342
NTFS version 5.0, 318-319
NTFS version 4.0, 318
NTLM protocol, 303
NWLink IPX/SPX/NetBIOS Compatible Transport Protocol, 475, 477

❖ O

Objects, System Monitor views of, 503
OC (optical carrier), 23
Octet ranges for IP addresses, 81-82
Octets, explained, 79
ODBC Data Source Administrator, 534-536
OFDM (Orthogonal Frequency Division Multiplexing), 24
Offer Remote Assistance feature, 424-426
Offline files and folders, 64, 367-397
    deleting, 374-375
    enabling encryption of, 379-380
    establishing policies for, 379
    with Fast User Switching enabled, 396
    with Folder Redirection, 369
    managing from Group Policy, 376-378
    in Offline Files folder, 372
    permissions, 376
    security and, 376-380
    settings per user/per group, 376

shortcut to, 371-372
    specifying automatically, 373
    specifying manually, 373
    synchronizing, 370, 382-386, 396-397
    troubleshooting, 394-397
Offline Files tab of Folder Options dialog box, 369-370
Offline Files Wizard, 370-371
Offline mode, printing in, 380-382
Open Files view of Computer Management, 363-364
OpenView (HP), 522-523
Orphan file (Briefcase), 393
OSI (Open Systems Interconnect) reference model, 12-16, 73
OUs (Organizational Units), 65, 314-315, 200
Out-of-process applications, 209
Outstanding packets (QoS Packet Scheduler), 465

❖ P

Packet collisions, 19, 22
Packet data elements of flows, 457-458
Packet delivery delay, 454-455
Packet marking, 461
Packet priority levels, ToS bits for, 460
Packet Scheduler (QoS), 461-462, 464-469
Packets, 8-9, 15-16
    vs. datagrams, 73
    dropped, 20, 169
    with TTL (time to live) value, 268
Paging file, explained, 513
Parent frame, 246
Partial octet subnetting, 87-88
Password authentication, in Terminal Services, 406
Password Authentication property (IIS), 223
Password management, 306-308
Password Reset Wizard, 279
Password tasks, 306-309
Passwords
    backing up to disk, 309
    changing for a user, 306-307
    restoring forgotten, 308
    stored, 308
PAT (Port Address Translation), 90
PATH message (RSVP QoS), 458-459

Pathping tool, 271-273
Payload data (message), 15
PcAnywhere, 402
PCMCIA modem installation, 121
PCs, vs. networking devices, 4
PDC (primary domain controller), 67, 184-185
Peer-to-peer network, 174
Per web site bandwidth throttling, 209
Perfmon.exe, 469-471
Performance counters, 503, 505-507, 513-515
Performance Monitor (Windows NT), 469
Performance monitoring. *See* System Monitor tool
Performance objects (System Monitor), 469-471, 504
Performance overview (network), 494-501
Performance problem areas, 496-497
Performance tool, invoking System Monitor as, 544
Per-hop behaviors, 460
Permissions, 228-229, 332-337, 358-361
    editing, 311
    inheritance of, 333
    for offline files, 376
    setting for a NetWare resource, 479
    setting for a shared resource, 359
    user or group, 332-335
    viewing for a user, 310-311
Phone and Modem Options dialog box, 122
Physical layer (802.11 protocol), 176
Physical layer (OSI), 14, 16
Pilot design, 57
Ping command, 192, 262-263, 265-266
Pinning a file or folder, explained, 373
Plug and Play devices and services, 118-119, 349-350
Port numbers, TCP and UDP, 75
Port scanning (hacking), preventing, 167
Ports, logical, 15
Power Users, 304
PPoE (PPP over Ethernet), 111
PPP (Point-to-Point Protocol), 111, 442, 449
PPTP filtering, 450
PPTP (Point-to-Point Tunneling Protocol), 39, 110-111, 441, 443, 449
PPTP for VPN across ICS, 165
Predictor (Compuware), 520-521
Preferred DNS servers, 108-109

Presentation layer, 14
PRI (Primary Rate Interface), ISDN, 27
Primary DNS suffix, changing, 107
Print job, starting manually, 381
Print server, 10, 350
Printer
    changing temporarily, 381-382
    disabling in Terminal Services, 406
    using networked, 352
Printer gateway, 479
Printer installation, 278, 381-382
Printer Properties dialog box, Sharing tab, 350-351
Printers
    auditing, 288
    sharing, 349-352
    viewing, 196
Printing
    deferred, 381
    to a NetWare printer, 482-483
    in Offline mode, 380-382
Prioritization QoS, 456-457
Private connection between devices, 11
Private (IP) addresses, 89-91
Probes (network), 517-518
Process accounting data logs, 209
Process throttling, in IIS 5.1, 209
Process tracking, 288
Processors, 6
    monitoring, 514
    and performance problems, 497
Product Compatibility list, 52
Protecting data when converting to NTFS, 338-339
Protocols
    adding, 93
    binding to services and clients, 157-158
    checking, 262
    installing, 156-158
    security, 302-303
    standardizing, 65-66
Protocols to manage connections, in OSI layers, 13
Proxy server, 168
Public (IP) addresses, 83, 90
Public telephone system, 25
Public-to-private IP address translation, 90
Publishing to FTP folders (IIS), 227-228
Publishing to web folders (IIS), 227
PVCs (permanent virtual circuits), 31
PXE (Pre-Boot Execution Environment), 59

❖ Q

QoS 802.1p, enabling on a network adapter, 463
QoS levels, managing and establishing, 464-469
QoS Packet Scheduler, 461-462, 464-469
QoS (Quality of Service), 20, 22, 453-471
    concepts, 456-458
    with ICS, 461-462
    with modems and Remote Access, 462
    monitoring, 469
    setup steps, 462
    in Windows XP, 461-471
Qualitative service type (QoS), 467-469
Quick synchronization, 383
Quota Entries window, 324-326

❖ R

RAM (random access memory)
    monitoring, 513-514
    and performance problems, 496
    requirements for Windows XP, 54
Raw bandwidth, 454-455
Rbfg.exe (Remote Boot Floppy utility), 59
RCP (Remote Call Procecure), 14
RDP (Remote Desktop Protocol), 404
Read & Execute permission (NTFS), 361
Read permission (FAT), 359
Read permission (NTFS), 361
Reconnection of a network share, 373-374
Recovery Console, 240
Redirecting a browser request, 233-235
Regedit.exe tool, 99
Registry, making changes in, 99-100, 246
Remote access, 430-440
    configuring, 431-434
    levels of, 431
    problems with, 264-265
    QoS with, 462
Remote Access Auto Connection Manager, 437-438

Remote access client, 432, 435-436
Remote access server setup, 432-434
Remote Assistance, 35, 37-38, 417-428
    accepting an invitation, 426-428
    configuring, 420
    desktop control, 419
    enabling, 421
    features of, 419
    vs. Remote Desktop, 418
    security issues of, 420
    sending invitations, 420-426
    steps to using, 37
    uses for, 424, 427-428
Remote Desktop, 35-37, 402-417, 544
    color support, 403
    connections, 403, 412-415, 545
    customized view, 416
    encryption levels for, 405-406
    features of, 403-404
    full-screen view, 415
    LAN connection, 407-408, 412-413
    options, 417-418
    vs. Remote Assistance, 418
    security issues, 404-407
    versions of, 403
Remote Desktop client, 403, 410-411, 416
Remote Desktop Connection InstallShield Wizard, 411
Remote Desktop Connection tool, 410-411
Remote Desktop server, 403
    accessing via the Internet, 408-410, 413-414
    adding a user, 408
    configuring, 407-410
Remote Desktop Users, 304
Remote Desktop Web Connection, 403, 408-410, 413-414
Remote features of Windows XP, 35-39
Remote node, 432
Remote Storage tool, 545-546
Replication (domain), 186
Replicator group, 305
Report view (System Monitor), 511-512
Reservable bandwidth (QoS Packet Scheduler), 465
Reservation state (RSVP QoS), 459
Resolve File Conflicts message, 396
Resolve File Conflicts options, 383

Resource redirection (Remote Desktop), 403-404
Resource sharing, 343-366
Restore points, 41, 255-259
Restore (System Restore), 40-42, 255-258
RESV message (RSVP QoS), 458
Rights, viewing for a user, 310-311
RIS (Remote Installation Services), 59-60
Road Warrior connections, 435-440
Roaming user profiles, 64, 194, 199
Roaming (wireless), 176-177
Rollback feature (System Restore), 40-41
Routable IP address, 441
Route aggregation, 459
Router hops, 79
Router IP address, 91
Routers, 8-9, 79, 91, 498-499
RPCs (remote procedure calls), 490
RRAS (Routing and Remote Access Service) tool, 546-547
RSVP (resource reservation) QoS, 456-460, 469-470
Run As, 301-302

❖ S

SA (security association), 295-296
SACLs (system access control lists), 311
Safe Mode, 130-131, 239
Safe Mode With Command Prompt, 131, 239-240
Safe Mode With Networking, 131, 239
SAM (Security Account Manager), 301
SAMBA, 488-490
SAS (Secure Attention Sequence), 303
Satellite connection, 30
Scheduled Synchronization Wizard, 385-386
Schema (Active Directory), 200
Scriptless ASP pages, 214
SCSI drives, 497
Secret key encryption, Kerberos, 48
Secure channel, defined, 191
Secure Server (Require Security) IPSec policy, 296
Security, 277-315. *See also* Permissions
    Active Directory, 64
    auditing, 287-290
    callback feature and, 439

Index **567**

domains and, 194
in IIS, 224-226, 228-232
IPSec, 442
Kerberos, 47-48
Local Security Policy snap-in, 279-281
NTFS, 44
of offline files, 376-380
remote access and, 431
Remote Assistance, 420
Remote Desktop, 404-407
SAMBA, 490
server, 294-315
shared access and, 356-361
virtual directory, 224
WebDAV, 212-213
Windows XP, 46-48, 278-294
wireless and, 35
Security Configuration and Analysis snap-in, 291-294
Security configuration database
analyzing, 292-294
creating, 291-292
Security descriptor (file), 44
Security groups, 309-310
Security log events, viewing, 539
Security log (ICF), 169, 281-284
Security Options local policy folder, 280
Security options (NTFS), 317-342
Security policies (IPSec), 296-299
Security policies (VPN), 443-444
Security principles, built-in, 310
Security protocols, 110, 302-303
Security tab of Local Disk Properties dialog box, 336
Security tab on New Folder Properties dialog box, 360
Security Templates snap-in, 284-287
Segmentation (network), 497-501
Selective Startup mode, 132, 246
Send Console Message window, 366
Server Extensions Administrator tool, 547-548
Server Extensions (FrontPage), 215-217
Server for NFS (SFU 3.0), 486
Server (Request Security) IPSec policy, 296
Server security mode (SAMBA), 490
Servers, 10
installing, 61-66
organization of, 63

preparation for migration, 63
problems with, 263
securing, 294-315
with specialized functions, 10
upgrading, 66-67
viewing details of, 252
Service logon, 300
Services, 528
binding protocols to, 157-158
installing, 158-159
Services snap-in, 548-549
Session layer, 14
Sessions (connections), 458
Sessions view of Computer Management, 362-363
Sets (802.11 LAN), 176
Setup Wizard, 242
Seven-layer stack, 13-14
SFU (Services for UNIX) 3.0, 484-488
Client for NFS, 486-487
Gateway for NFS, 487-488
NFS components used by, 485
Server for NFS, 486
system requirements, 484-485
SGC (Server-Gated Cryptography), 212
Share security mode (SAMBA), 490
Shares (network) and sharing, 343-366
enabling, 344-345
identifying, 195
reconnecting, 373-374
Shared access, controlling, 356-366
Shared control of a computer (Remote Assistance), 424, 427
Shared folders on a LAN, listing, 152-153
Shared resource, setting permissions for, 359
Shared-secret authentication protocol, 303
Shares view of Computer Management, 361-362
Sharing applications, 352-356
Sharing documents using WebDAV, 210
Sharing a folder with Simple File Sharing off, 358
Sharing a folder with Simple File Sharing on, 357
Sharing folders and drives, 344-347
Sharing a printer, 349-352
Sharing resources, 343-366

Sharing tab of Local Disk Properties dialog box, 337
Sharing tab of Printer Properties dialog box, 350-351
Shortcuts
    deleting, 245
    to offline files and folders, 371-372
SID (security identifier), 303, 310-311, 323
SIMMs, large-capacity, 54
Simple File Sharing, 333-334, 344
    security and, 356-358
    turning off, 312, 333-334
Simulation tools, 519-521
Simulations, 515-519
    running, 519
    testing, 518
Single points of failure, 495
Single-domain model, 65
Site, defined, 528
64-bit processors, 6
64MB SIMMs, 54
Slow link, explained, 373
SMB (Server Message Block) protocol, 371, 488, 490
Smb.conf file, 488-490
SMP (symmetric multiprocessors), 55
SMS (System Management Server), 60
SMTP (Simple Mail Transfer Protocol), 14
Snap-ins (MMC), 203, 246-248
Soft-state protocol, 459
Software inventory, 63
Software Settings (Group Policy), 313
SOHOs (small organizations and home offices), 159
SONET (Synchronous Optical Network), 23
Sparse command, 332
Sparse files, 331-332
Special Permissions (NTFS), 361
SPID (Service Profile Identifier), 265
Spoofing of network device addresses, 91
SSIs (server-side includes), 235
SSL (Secure Sockets Layer), 212, 232
Stack (OSI), 15
Star topology, 21
Startup folder, 245
Startup modes (Windows XP), 238-241
Startup programs, stopping, 245-246
Stateful firewall, explained, 167

Static IP addressing, 94, 100-104
Status command, 249-250
Status monitor (connections), 139
Storage, and performance problems, 497
Stored User Names and Passwords, 308
Subclasses (Active Directory objects), 202
Subnet broadcasts, 104
Subnet example (partial octet), 87-88
Subnet example (whole octet), 84-87
Subnet masks, 83-89, 251
Subnetting, 83-89
Switch port load balancing, 500
Switches, 8, 11
    vs. hubs, 11-12
    network segmentation via, 500-501
    problems with, 263
    splitting of bandwidth, 11
Synchronization, 382-388
    of Briefcases, 392-394
    configuring, 384-385
    of offline files, 370, 396-397
    options for laptops, 386-388
    scheduling, 385-386
    types of, 383
Synchronization Manager, 382-383
SysPrep (System Preparation tool), 58-59
System Configuration Utility, 245-246
System log events, viewing, 539
System Monitor tool, 469-471, 501-515
    Alert view, 507-510
    Chart view, 505-507
    default objects, 505
    default view, 502
    invoking as Performance tool, 544
    Log view, 510-511
    performance objects, 469-471
    Properties dialog box, 508
    Report view, 511-512
    views, 502-512
    what to monitor, 512-515
System processor, monitoring, 514
System requirements (Windows XP), 49-55
    for advanced hardware, 53-55
    for Windows XP Professional 64-Bit Edition, 49-50
System Restore, 40-42, 255-258
System-monitoring tools, third-party, 521-524
Systems, interconnectivity with other, 473-492

Index

❖ T

Task Manager, 243
TCO (Total Cost of Ownership), 313
TCP (Transmission Control Protocol), 14, 74-75, 450, 457, 462
TCP/IP Address dialog box, 102
TCP/IP addresses, managing, 96-97
TCP/IP addressing in Windows XP, 92-110
TCP/IP Autoaddressing (APIPA and DHCP), 97-100
TCP/IP connection, configuring, 94-96
TCP/IP settings, configuring, 130
TCP/IP stack, and OSI seven-layer model, 73
TCP/IP (Transmission Control Protocol/Internet Protocol), 65, 71-110
    abstract layers, 72
    installation, 92
    troubleshooting tools, 265
TDM (time-division multiplexing), 31
Telephone lines, analog, 26
Telephony tool, 549-550
Templates (security), 284-287
Temporary printer driver, installing, 381-382
10 Gigabit Ethernet, 19-20
Terminal Server Licensing tool, 550-551
Terminal Services, 402, 404-407
Terminal Services Manager, 550-551
Test system, 57
TFTP (Trivial File Transfer Protocol), 74
TGT (ticket-granting ticket), 48
32-bit processors, 6
Thresholds, for alerts, 507
Throttling, in IIS 5.1, 209
Timer resolution (QoS Packet Scheduler), 465
Timestamp (Kerberos), 193
TLS (Transport Layer Security), 212
Token Ring, 21-23
T1 and T3 leased lines, 30-31
Topology (network), 494-495, 516-517
ToS (Type of Service) field bits, 460
Tracert (Trace Route) utility, 268-269
Traffic modeling, network simulators, 516
Traffic (network), 516-518
Traffic shaping, 461
Transport layer (OSI), 14-15
Transport layer (TCP/IP), 72
Transport mode (IPSec), 442
Transport protocols (IP message), 74
Trees, defined, 200
Triple-DES (3DES) algorithm, 327
Trunk vs. dial-in technologies, 26
Trunks (WAN), 25-26
Trusted domain, defined, 190
TTL (time to live) value, packet, 268
Tunnel mode (IPSec), 442
Tunnels (VPN), 39, 111, 165, 440-441, 449
Tuple, defined, 458

❖ U

UDP flows, 457
UDP object counter, 470
UDP performance object, 471
UDP ports 137 and 138, 450
UDP (User Datagram Protocol), 14, 74
    as an unreliable protocol, 74
    vs. TCP, 74-75
Unattended installation, 58
UNC (Universal Naming Convention), 195-198
Universal groups, 202-203, 310
UNIX, Windows client access to, 488-492
UNIX configuration file for SAMBA, 488-490
UNIX configuration (NFS), 491-492
UNIX connections, 483-492
Upgrade Advisor, 53
Upgrading servers, 66-67
Upgrading from Windows NT/9X/2000, 49-70, 92
URL (Uniform Resource Locator), 77-78
User names, stored, 308
User password, changing, 306-307
User permissions. *See* Permissions
User profiles, roaming, 194
User security mode (SAMBA), 490
User switching, in Windows XP, 279
User accounts (users), 304, 306
    creating/managing/deleting, 305
    Internet access policy for, 496
    limiting hard drive space for, 323-326
    number of accessing volume/folder, 336
    sending messages to, 365-366
    switching to administrator from, 301
Username/Password property (IIS), 223

❖ V

Versions of files, synchronizing, 382-386
View Status of This Connection, 96
Virtual circuit, explained, 23
Virtual circuit orientation (ATM), 22
Virtual directories, 223-224
Virtual memory, 55, 513
Virus blocking, 47
VirusScan Online, 47
VitalSuite (Lucent), 521
Voice chat (Remote Assistance), 424, 428
VoIP (voice over IP), 419, 454
Volume permissions, 334-337
Volumes, compressing, 320-322
Volumes on a NetWare server, displaying, 482
VPN client, troubleshooting, 449-450
VPN client Internet connection, 445
VPN client Properties dialog box, 447
VPN connections, 440-451
    configuring, 447
    connecting to the Internet, 39
    creating, 39, 444-446
    dialing into an ISP, 39
    disabling, 443
    receiving, 446-448
    troubleshooting, 448-451
VPN icon, 444
VPN server, configuring, 446-447, 449
VPN server name or IP address, 445
VPN server Properties dialog box, 448
VPN tunnels, 39, 111, 165, 440-441, 449
VPNs (virtual private networks), 38-39, 111
    across ICS, 165-166
    secure tunnel through the Internet, 441
    security policies for, 443-444

❖ W

WAN technologies, 24-32
WAN trunk technologies, 30-32
WANs (wide area networks), basic kinds of, 25
Warning levels (disk quotas), 324
Web authentication, enabling, 229-230
Web authoring and management. *See* FrontPage
Web server, defined, 10
Web Server Certificate Wizard, 212
Web server placement, 218
Web services (*see also* IIS)
    configuring, 222-226
    domains and, 187
Web site authentication, setting, 230
Web site content, managing and updating, 232-236
Web Site Properties dialog box, 224-225
Web usage reports, 224
WebDAV (Web Distributed Authoring and Versioning), 209-213
WEP key, 179-180
WEP (wireless equivalent privacy), 172
Whoami, 310-311
Whole octet subnet example, 84-87
Windows Briefcase, 388-394
    Briefcase Status column, 393
    briefcase synchronization, 392-394
    copying briefcases to a laptop, 391
    moving files to, 390-391
    starting a new briefcase, 389
    updating files in, 393-394
    using briefcase files, 391-392
Windows Compatibility Mode, 40-41
Windows Indexing Service, 331-332
Windows Messenger
    Application Sharing, 352-356
    Conversation window, 353
    Sharing session window, 354
Windows .NET Administrative Tools, 203-205, 525-552
Windows NT Challenge and Response, 212
Windows NT Performance Monitor, 469
Windows NT/9X/2000, upgrading from, 49-70
Windows products residing in a domain, 186
Windows Script Commands, 214
Windows 2000, Gateway Services for NetWare, 478
Windows 2000 Server, 62
    domains and, 187
    system hardware minimums, 66
Windows XP clients
    access to UNIX, 488-492
    binding protocols to, 157-158
    connecting to a workgroup, 150-159
    connecting workstations, 136-137

Index **571**

domains and, 187-188
installing manually, 156
troubleshooting, 261-263
Windows XP Professional
activating, 68-70
adding protocols, 93
built on Windows NT/2000, 40
and the domain model, 186-187
installation glitch, 130
installation input requests, 62
installation options, 57-61
on its own partition, 51
migrating to, 56-57
networking features, 34-39, 42-48
new in, 34-42
remote features, 35-39
security features, 46-48, 278-294
security improvements, 278-279
setting up IP addresses, 97-111
startup modes, 238-241
system requirements, 49-55
TCP/IP addressing in, 92-110
30-day trial period, 69
troubleshooting, 238-259
UNC usage, 197-198
upgrading to from another Windows, 55-56
wireless features, 34-35
Windows XP Professional 64-Bit Edition
device drivers, 50
system requirements, 49-50
Win.ini file, 246
Winlogon, 300
WINS replication, 495
WINS (Windows Internet Name Service), 104-105, 109-110, 552
Winsock Proxy Client, 450
Wireless, 23-24, 35
Wireless configuration, setting up automatic, 177-178
Wireless connections, 170-181
Wireless device, connecting to a WLAN, 180-181

Wireless Ethernet (Wi-Fi or 802.11b), 34
Wireless features of Windows XP, 34-35
Wireless network adapters, 34
Wireless networking
advantages of, 171-172
configuration of, 177-181
Wireless networks, building, 173-176
WLAN adapters, 172
WLAN cells, 24
WLANs (Wireless Local Area Networks), 23, 171-176
access points, 24, 34, 172-173, 175
authentication, 179-180
connecting a device to, 180-181
installation, 172
viewing a list of available, 178
Word size (computer bits), 6
Workgroup connections, 149-181
Workgroups, ICF on, 167-170
Workstations, migrating, 68
WPA (Windows Product Activation), 68
WPAN (Wireless Personal Area Network), 170-171
Write permission (NTFS), 361

❖ X

XDR (External Data Representation), 490
Xerox Corporation, 18
XML (Extensible Markup Language), 187

❖ Z

Zero (client) configuration, 177
ZIP compression, 319
ZipMagic, 319
Zone transfers (DNS), 495

INTERNATIONAL CONTACT INFORMATION

AUSTRALIA
McGraw-Hill Book Company Australia Pty. Ltd.
TEL +61-2-9415-9899
FAX +61-2-9415-5687
http://www.mcgraw-hill.com.au
books-it_sydney@mcgraw-hill.com

CANADA
McGraw-Hill Ryerson Ltd.
TEL +905-430-5000
FAX +905-430-5020
http://www.mcgrawhill.ca

**GREECE, MIDDLE EAST,
NORTHERN AFRICA**
McGraw-Hill Hellas
TEL +30-1-656-0990-3-4
FAX +30-1-654-5525

MEXICO (Also serving Latin America)
McGraw-Hill Interamericana Editores S.A. de C.V.
TEL +525-117-1583
FAX +525-117-1589
http://www.mcgraw-hill.com.mx
fernando_castellanos@mcgraw-hill.com

SINGAPORE (Serving Asia)
McGraw-Hill Book Company
TEL +65-863-1580
FAX +65-862-3354
http://www.mcgraw-hill.com.sg
mghasia@mcgraw-hill.com

SOUTH AFRICA
McGraw-Hill South Africa
TEL +27-11-622-7512
FAX +27-11-622-9045
robyn_swanepoel@mcgraw-hill.com

**UNITED KINGDOM & EUROPE
(Excluding Southern Europe)**
McGraw-Hill Education Europe
TEL +44-1-628-502500
FAX +44-1-628-770224
http://www.mcgraw-hill.co.uk
computing_neurope@mcgraw-hill.com

ALL OTHER INQUIRIES Contact:
Osborne/McGraw-Hill
TEL +1-510-549-6600
FAX +1-510-883-7600
http://www.osborne.com
omg_international@mcgraw-hill.com